The Diversity of Normal Behavior

THE DIVERSITY OF NORMAL BEHAVIOR

Further Contributions to Normatology

EDITED BY
Daniel Offer, M.D.
AND
Melvin Sabshin, M.D.

BasicBooks
A Division of HarperCollins*Publishers*

The Diversity of normal behavior: further contributions to normatology / edited by Daniel Offer and Melvin Sabshin.
p. cm.
Includes bibliographical references and index.
ISBN 0-465-01685-5
1. Mental health. I. Offer, Daniel. II. Sabshin, Melvin. III. Title: Normatology.
RA790.D58 1991
616.89—dc20 91-70847
CIP

A division of HarperCollins Publishers
Printed in the United States of America
Designed by Ellen Levine
91 92 93 94 CC/RRD 9 8 7 6 5 4 3 2 1

Contents

PART II: CONTEXTUAL CONTRIBUTIONS

PART III: THEORETICAL AND EPISTEMOLOGICAL CONTRIBUTIONS

Contributors

Terrance Brown, M.D.
Department of Psychiatry, University of Chicago.

Sheila Cooperman, M.D.
Associate Director of Program Development, Silver Hill Hospital, New Canaan, Connecticut.

Kelly Cozza, M.D.
Captain, Medical Corps, U.S.A.; Department of Psychiatry, Walter Reed Army Medical Center.

Edward F. Foulks, M.D., Ph.D.
Sellars-Polchow Professor of Psychiatry and Neurology, Tulane University; Associate Chief of Staff, New Orleans Veterans Administration Medical Center.

Allen J. Frances, M.D.
Professor of Psychiatry, Cornell University, Payne Whitney Psychiatric Clinic.

Richard J. Frances, M.D.
Professor of Clinical Psychiatry, UMDNJ New Jersey Medical School.

Carol S. Fullerton, Ph.D.
Research Assistant Professor, Department of Psychiatry, Uniformed Services University of the Health Sciences.

Robert E. Hales, M.D.
Colonel, Medical Corps, U.S.A.; Chairman, Department of Psychiatry, Pacific Presbyterian Medical Center.

Bruce G. Link, Ph.D.
Columbia University, New York State Psychiatric Institute.

Theodore Millon, Ph.D.
Professor in Psychiatry, Harvard Medical School; Professor of Psychology, University of Miami.

Stephen J. Morse, J.D., Ph.D.
Ferdinand Wakeman Hubbell Professor and Associate Dean for Academic Affairs, University of Pennsylvania Law School.

Daniel Offer, M.D.
Professor of Psychiatry, Northwestern University Medical School; Editor-in-Chief, Journal of Youth and Adolescence.

John M. Plewes, M.D.
Lieutenant Colonel, Medical Corps, U.S.A.; Acting Consultant in Psychiatry to the Army Surgeon General.

David Reiss, M.D.
Professor of Law and Psychiatry, George Washington University Medical Center.

Robert M. Rose, M.D.
Senior Program Advisor, MacArthur Foundation.

Loren H. Roth, M.D., M.P.H.
Chief, Adult and Clinical Services, Director, Law and Psychiatry Program, Professor of Psychiatry, Western Psychiatric Institute, University of Pittsburgh School of Medicine.

Melvin Sabshin, M.D.
Medical Director, American Psychiatric Association.

Sharon Schwartz, Ph.D.
Columbia University, New York State Psychiatric Institute.

Robert J. Ursano, M.D.
Professor, Department of Psychiatry, Uniformed Services University of the Health Sciences.

Fredrick S. Wamboldt, M.D.
Assistant Professor, Department of Psychiatry, University of Colorado Health Sciences Center; Assistant Faculty Member, Department of Medicine, National Jewish Center for Immunology and Respiratory Medicine.

Robert M. Wettstein, M.D.
Western Psychiatric Institute and Clinic, University of Pittsburgh School of Medicine.

Thomas A. Widiger, Ph.D.
Professor, Department of Psychology, University of Kentucky.

Introduction

Daniel Offer
and
Melvin Sabshin

Twenty-five years ago we published our first book on a new scientific discipline that we called normatology. The book, entitled *Normality* (Offer and Sabshin 1966), was an attempt to focus attention on the profound conceptual and methodological dilemmas in clarifying what is meant by normal[1] behavior. It was a pioneering work in two ways. In it we attempted to discuss in a new, scientific manner the ancient question what normal behavior consists of. And, as few psychiatrists had studied normal behavior, we attempted to document why such studies would contribute to the field of normatology and to a better understanding of psychopathology. We revised the book some years later (Offer and Sabshin 1974) to encompass the emerging empirical literature. By the time our third volume was published as *Normality and the Life Cycle* (Offer and Sabshin 1984), interest in the field had developed significantly. This volume is part of the continuing effort to accelerate the evolution of a scientific normatology.

Several factors have contributed to these developments. Psychiatry has undergone massive changes during the past two decades. In contrast to the post–World War II period, psychiatry became more involved in objectifying its nosological base with the publication of the third edition of the

[1]We use the terms *normal* and *healthy* interchangeably throughout.

Diagnostic and Statistical Manual of Mental Disorders (DSM-III) and its revision (DSM-III-R) (American Psychiatric Association 1980, 1987). Empirically based studies of psychiatric disorders became a focus of an evolving effort to alter the nature of psychiatric diagnosis and treatment. It became evident that much work needed to be done to define the boundary between normal behavior and psychopathology. To do this more effectively, studies of subthreshold behavioral patterns and of normal adaptation throughout the life cycle must complement studies of disorders. Normatology's utility in these studies is beginning to be recognized by a number of nosologists and is having an impact on DSM-IV.

Simultaneously, policymakers have become increasingly aware of the need to define mental disorders more precisely. Decision makers concerned with limiting insurance reimbursement to those conditions that are more severe and more easily understood to be medical disorders are beginning to challenge those who employ a wider definition of psychiatric disorders. By limiting reimbursement, they also are questioning the validity of labeling less severe behavioral patterns as disorders. We predict that this attempt to circumscribe the field of psychiatric disorders will grow more powerful by the beginning of the next century and that decision makers will seek to ascertain why some individuals with high genetic loading for disorder and highly stressful environments fail to become ill. Such questions will help to galvanize greater interest in normatology for both scientific and pragmatic reasons. This volume will help to provide researchers and clinicians with concepts and methods to cope more effectively with these questions.

In previous publications we explored the dimensions of normatology. A new discipline, normatology encompasses all knowledge available from the biological, psychological, and social sciences regarding normality, normal behavior, and normal development. The integration of the multiple perspectives of normality requires empirical studies. New methods that focus on the normal will need to be developed for these new studies as well as new terminology. The field of normatology has had special appeal to some behavioral scientists, especially to psychologists. Among psychiatrists, normatology has not yet achieved wide recognition. In part, this relates to the rapid developments of neuroscience, molecular genetics, and psychopharmacology in present-day psychiatry, developments that have focused on studies of clinical syndromes. No concise knowledge of the variations of normal or healthy functioning has yet been developed. Nevertheless, there are signs that interest in normatology may soon grow. It is known that many individuals, despite their high genetic loading for psychopathology and/or highly stressful environments, do not become ill;

scientists and clinicians are becoming increasingly interested in exploring why this occurs. Those responsible for policy decisions about therapeutic interventions also are seeking answers to this question. With the simultaneous development of new technologies to study human adaptation over the life cycle, academic and clinical psychiatrists will be able to investigate the psychobiological basis for normatology. Psychologists and other behavioral scientists will, of course, be even more interested in fostering these developments.

Competing conceptions of normality, and criteria for distinguishing mental health and normality from psychological disorders, have been discussed for at least the last three centuries. In addition to conceptual and philosophical issues, the definition of normality carries with it important implications for social issues, clinical practice, and mental health policy formation. (See chapter 1.)

When we first described theoretical conceptions of normality (Offer and Sabshin 1966), we stated that there were four perspectives of normality. We have recently increased this to five separate models, which are best described by Elmen and Offer (1991). All the models are useful for addressing certain, if not all, perspectives of human behavior.

The first perspective is *normality as health,* or the absence-of-pathology model. This model defines disorder by the presence of symptomatology, physical signs, and/or laboratory abnormalities, and defines health or normality as the absence of signs and symptoms. Within this model, a healthy person is one who is reasonably free of undue pain, discomfort, disability, distress, and other features of disorder. In this perspective, health refers to a reasonable rather than an optimal state of functioning. Thus normality is equated with health, and health is seen as a nearly universal phenomenon. This is the standard bearer of medicine in general and has been most useful to physicians throughout the world.

The second perspective, *normality as utopia,* is one favored at least implicitly by most psychoanalysts; it is antithetical to the first perspective in that it tends to identify most people as suffering from psychopathology and only a minority of persons as healthy. This may be attributed to the fact that health is equated with the ideal, utopian functioning that few individuals, if any, ever achieve. According to this perspective, the typical or average individual falls considerably short of the ideal and is therefore seen as pathological. This perspective is problematic, according to Kendell (1975), because the healthy functioning it describes is almost impossible to attain. According to Freud (1937), normality is an ideal fiction and thus by definition cannot be attained. However, this model clearly describes the ideal or end point of optimal functioning. Its principle of self-actualization demonstrates what one should strive for.

The third perspective, *normality as average,* relies heavily on assessing the functioning or behavior in particular cultures and ethnic groups. Once the range of behavior is documented, this perspective defines both extremes as deviant and the mean, or the majority, as normal. As this model accepts a culture's own definition of what is normal, normality in one culture might be deviance (or pathology) in another, theoretically at least. This perspective is useful for empirical studies of normality and health because it is the least judgmental. According to its social scientific backers, it just describes what each culture defines for itself.

The fourth perspective is *normality as transactional systems.* Contrary to the first three models, which describe individuals in cross-sectional terms (like snapshots of behavior), this model emphasizes normality as the result of individuals changing and adapting as part of a social system that also fluctuates over time. Patterns of adjustment and disturbance are examined longitudinally with respect to transactions between person and social system. This perspective is the one most relevant to studying development because it deals with normality as the result of interacting systems (biological, psychological, and social) over time.

The fifth perspective, *normality as pragmatism,* appears somewhat simplistic, but some practitioners consider it useful. From this perspective mental disorders are nothing more and nothing less than the conditions clinicians treat. This model defines as normal those "conditions" and behaviors that rarely, if ever, bring people to clinicians. Proponents of this model have pointed out that defining normality is an evaluative task, and that this evaluation must be relative to the society and its citizens. There is, of course, tremendous societal variation in how these "conditions" are defined. This last perspective considers the relevance of the particular definition of normality for health delivery systems and policy implications. It is an atheoretical perspective that deals with practical clinical experiences.

Our goals in this volume are to consider the new empirical data, clinical observations, theoretical conceptualization, and general understanding of normal human behavior, or normatology. This, in turn, will help further our understanding of the complexities of psychopathology, because we will have a meaningful yardstick for comparisons and evaluation. In 1984 we stated that the field of normatology will ultimately encompass all research and theory relating to normal human behavior. We continue to hold this view on the importance of studying normal behavior. Future researchers and clinicians will require a comprehensive understanding of the vicissitudes of health and normality as well as of psychotherapy.

Over the years we have been increasingly impressed with the complexity and diversity of normal behavioral variations throughout the life cycle. Indeed, we believe that a taxonomy of normal behavior would dwarf the taxonomy of psychopathology. To highlight the broad slope of normal behavior, we have entitled the book *The Diversity of Normal Behavior* and have divided the book into parts that emphasize the diversity. Among the questions discussed are clinical, contextual, theoretical, and epidemiological ones. Within each category we have selected prototypic topics, although we recognize that our choice of chapters only scratches the surface. Many other topics, methods, settings, and philosophical issues could have demonstrated the diversity of normality. As in our previous work, however, we have emphasized the role of empirical studies in answering the many questions we have posed to our authors.

We selected the chapters in this volume to illustrate how diverse the field of normatology has become. We asked each contributor to respond to the same general questions.

1. Do you consider your field to have a major theory of psychopathology?
2. If your answer to question 1 is yes, would the same theory be applicable to normatology? Would another be applicable?
3. Are social factors, biologic factors, and psychological factors relevant at all to definitions of normality and mental health? If yes, how much and under what circumstances?
4. To what extent do the boundaries between mental health and mental illness and between normal and psychopathological behavior cause theoretical and practical dilemmas in your field?
5. What types of psychosocial indicators and/or biological markers do you believe can or could later predict emotional well-being?
6. Why do some individuals adapt well even though they have a host of factors stacked against them (that is, children of schizophrenic parents; children with chronic illness; children growing up in the ghetto)?
7. What are the two or three most important *policy implications* for the field of "mental health" that emerge from your chapter?
8. In the twenty-first century, what would be the major questions in your field pertinent to any or all of the above questions? Do you believe that increased international communications would reduce the variance of basic personality types from one culture to another (for example, will more similar life-styles or more similar dietary habits reduce differences)?

We also asked the contributors specific questions relevant to their own fields. These questions concerned how normality can be defined, assessed, studied, and understood. Each contributor was free, of course, to write the chapter from his or her own vantage point. While most authors responded to our questions, many authors developed their own and some authors went far beyond the questions.

We asked the authors of the first nine chapters specific questions. We asked the authors of chapters 10 and 11 to write their own overviews of normatology; two very different overviews emerged. Chapter 12 is our own perspective of the field. The more important questions for the first nine chapters are presented below. The chapters of this volume present the answers to these and other questions.

Chapter 1: Psychiatric Diagnosis and Normality

1. To what extent does the task of establishing the boundaries between normal behavior and psychopathology cause practical and theoretical dilemmas in the development of psychiatric nosology?
    a. Are these problems different from nosology in other fields of medicine?
    b. If there are differences, how would you explain them? (For example, do etiologically based classifications reduce the problem considerably?)
    c. What types of research might clarify the problems or dilemmas in psychiatric nosology, especially in so far as defining the boundaries discussed above?
    d. How might clarification of these problems or dilemmas contribute to a theory of normal behavior?
2. What is the underlying premise that makes one select a factor (a list of signs and symptoms) to be included in the DSM-III? Is it empirical, conceptual, or both?
3. Do you conceptualize the nonpathological population as a homogenous group? If not, how do you subdivide or classify the nonpathological (that is, normal) group?
4. Would it be useful to develop DSM-N (*N* for normatological) diagnoses or criteria?

Chapter 2: Psychotherapy: Medical Intervention and the Concept of Normality

1. Is a theory of psychopathology as relevant to the process of psychotherapy as is the use of biological treatment?
2. To what extent does the task of establishing the boundaries between normality and psychopathology cause practical and theoretical dilem-

mas in the development of criteria for the various therapeutic interventions, including the beginning, the middle, and the termination of treatment?

a. Are these problems unique to psychiatry, or are they also pertinent in other medical treatment?
b. If there are differences, how would you explain them?
c. Do nonmedical psychotherapists utilize the same distinctions between normality and psychopathology as medical therapists? If not, what boundaries do nonmedical psychotherapists use?
d. How might clarifications of these problems contribute to a theory of normal behavior?

Chapter 3: Normality and Stress: Response and Adaptation

1. Does the field of stress research have an explicit or implicit theory of psychopathology?
2. Would the theory of psychopathology described in question 1 also be applicable to coping with stress or normal behavior in general (for example, would it use more or fewer genetic hypotheses to explain coping than to explain vulnerability to psychopathology)?
3. Is there a continuum from normal to psychopathological responses to stressful stimuli or situations? Or might there be qualitative differences between psychopathological reactions and normal coping? Does the field of stress research have a theoretical problem in dealing with the boundaries between psychopathology and normality? If there is such a problem, is it currently handled in an arbitrary statistical fashion (for example, pathological responses are defined as X standard deviations from the mean response)?
4. Can the social context be the predominant variable in predicting the incidence of psychopathological reactions to stress?
5. What, if any, psychosocial indicators and/or biological markers are the best predictors of successful coping with commonly stressful stimulus or social contexts?
6. To what extent can psychosocial or biological interventions be utilized to prevent psychopathological reactions to stress?

Chapter 4: The Boundaries of Alcoholism

1. Is alcoholism best defined by a disease model? If so, is it a unitary disease concept, which includes multiple diseases, or can alcoholism be conceived of as a constellation of subdisease categories?

2. What moral, social, psychological, and biological factors are relevant to the determination of whether alcoholism should be defined as a disease? To what extent do all the above factors play a role in determining the boundaries between social drinking ("normal" drinking) and the disease alcoholism?
3. Do you believe that the concept of psychopathology is relevant to alcoholism or to various aspects of it? Are there some people who drink a great deal but do not manifest any medical or psychological diagnosable illness?
4. Is it reasonable to assume that the first stages of alcoholism are part of a psychiatric disease?
5. Do you believe that antecedent psychopathology leads to alcoholism in a significant number of cases, or do you believe that psychopathology is largely a consequence of alcoholism?

Chapter 5: Normality in the Military

1. To what extent, if any, is there a different concept of normal behavior for those individuals who serve in the four different branches of the armed forces and the general population?
2. To what extent does military life (warfare, separation and disruption of families, and so on) determine deviant behavior and/or psychopathology among the military?
3. Are there situations in the military that protect against psychopathology (for example, "finding a home in the army") or encourage more normal behavior? Also, do some people function better under conditions of military stress than others?
4. What indicators can predict failure or mental illness among recruits?

Chapter 6: Task Performance and the Social Construction of Meaning: Juxtaposing Normality with Contemporary Family Research

1. What basic theories of normal behavior are fundamental to the field of family psychiatry? To what extent do theories of normal behavior in individuals contribute or fail to contribute to the functioning of the family?
2. To what extent do the boundaries between normal and pathological behavior in a family system or in individual members of the family cause theoretical and practical dilemmas in your field?
3. Can the family be used to reduce the potential for mental illness in its

individual members? Can it, at times, cause a breakdown in members who seem to have been functioning well?

4. Why do some families adapt well despite a host of factors stacked against them?
5. What are the essential factors for a well-functioning family?
6. Should there be a separate diagnostic axis (in a multiaxial system) for family functioning?

Chapter 7: Transcultural Psychiatry and Normal Behavior

1. Does transcultural psychiatry have a major theory of psychopathology? Of normality?
2. To what extent and in what ways do the boundaries between mental illness and mental health—and/or between normal and psychopathological behavior—cause theoretical and practical dilemmas in transcultural psychiatry?
3. Are some cultures so configured that they have a significantly higher prevalence and/or incidence of mental illness? (The emphasis here is on those illnesses not induced by infectious, nutritional, or degenerative processes.)
4. Are some cultures so configured that they tend to promote a higher incidence of mental health—and/or to reduce the prevalence and incidence of mental illness?
5. Has the increasing productivity and preeminence of biological psychiatry had an impact on transcultural psychiatry?
6. Looking ahead to the twenty-first century, what would be some of the major questions in transcultural psychiatry pertinent to any or all of the above questions?

Chapter 8: Sociological Perspectives on Mental Health: An Integrative Approach

1. Do you consider that the social sciences have major explanatory theories of psychopathology or normality?
2. Many social scientists use a definition of normality and deviant behavior based on empirical studies of social systems. By and large, do social scientists consider mental illness a subclass of deviancy and perceive it to be the opposite of normality? Would some scientists have the same attitudes toward physical illness, or would they be more likely to accept

physical illness as illness? If so, would this be based on the perception that physical illness has objectifiably measurable biological abnormalities?

3. If you consider mental illness a subclass of deviancy, what criteria would you use to determine the boundaries among the subclass, other subclasses, and normality?
4. If in fact you are willing to accept the validity of psychiatric illness and normal behavior, to what extent are social factors relevant in the determination of the boundaries between them and to what extent are social factors relevant in causing psychiatric illness?

Chapter 9: The Concept of Normality in the Law

1. While we recognize that much of the recent debate on the insanity defense has centered on the *severity* of psychopathology appropriate for such a defense, questions about the boundaries between normality and psychopathology are still pertinent to the use of that defense and to many other aspects of forensic psychiatry. Furthermore, in forensic psychiatry there has been considerable confusion between and among deviant behavior, moral problems, and psychopathology. What comments do you have on these assertions?
2. Looking back on the Durham decision, do the boundary problems between normality and psychopathology contribute to difficulties in its implementation?
3. Assuming that criminal behavior is not necessarily accompanied by psychiatric illness, are there any situations in which specific types of criminal behavior are correlated significantly with mental illness?

REFERENCES

American Psychiatric Association. 1980. *Diagnostic and Statistical Manual of Mental Disorders,* 3rd ed. (DSM-III). Washington, D.C.: APA.

———. 1987. *Diagnostic and Statistical Manual of Mental Disorders,* 3rd ed., rev. (DSM-III-R). Washington, D.C.: APA.

Elmen, J., and Offer, D. 1991. "Adolescent Turmoil." In *Handbook of Clinical Intervention with Adolescents,* ed. P. Tolan and B. Cohler. New York: John Wiley & Sons.

Freud, S. [1937] 1959. "Analysis Terminable and Interminable." In *Collected Papers of S. Freud,* trans. J. Strachey, vol. 5, pp. 316–358. New York: Basic Books.

Kendell, R. 1975. *The Role of Diagnosis in Psychiatry.* Oxford: Blackwell Scientific Publications.

Offer, D., and Sabshin, M. 1966. *Normality:* New York: Basic Books.

———. 1974. *Normality,* rev. ed. New York: Basic Books.

———. 1984. *Normality and the Life Cycle.* New York: Basic Books.

PART I

CLINICAL CONTRIBUTIONS

CHAPTER 1

Psychiatric Diagnosis and Normality

Allen J. Frances, Thomas A. Widiger, and
Melvin Sabshin

The definition of mental disorder and the differentiation of normality from abnormality are obviously crucial and fundamental steps in developing a psychiatric nomenclature, in defining the domain of psychiatry, and in understanding the epistemology of psychiatric diagnosis. The conception of just what is meant by a mental disorder can have considerable impact on clinical practice, professional responsibilities, social issues, and criminal-forensic proceedings. As Kendell (1975) indicates, "there is no concept in medicine more fundamental than that of disease or illness" (p. 9). It is particularly timely now to review definitions of mental disorder as efforts are just beginning to develop the fourth edition of the American Psychiatric Association's *Diagnostic and Statistical Manual of Mental Disorders* (DSM-IV), scheduled to be published in 1992.

The purpose of this chapter is to consider prior attempts at defining illness, health, and mental disorder; to discuss various conceptual issues that impair any very satisfying attempt at arriving at a definition; to suggest research that might be helpful in demarcating the boundaries of normality and mental disorder; and to discuss some of the public health, forensic, social, clinical, and professional issues that are influenced by a definition. Past attempts to define the boundary between psychiatric illness and normality have failed to provide a definition that is without inconsistencies, contradictions, and controversies. In this chapter we hope only to illuminate, not to resolve, the various problems and issues that hinder attempts to define a boundary between psychiatric disorder and normality.

Historical Overview

Alternative definitions and criteria for health, normality, and mental disorders have been presented ever since the beginning of medicine.[1] We provide a few illustrations, loosely organized with respect to whether the definition focuses on illness or health.

Definitions of Disease and Disorder

In the seventeenth century Sydenham pioneered the systematic explication of the natural history, patterns, and course of various diseases. He believed diseases were the organism's attempt to restore its usual (healthy) functioning (Temkin 1963).

> A disease, in my opinion, how prejudicial soever its causes may be to the body, is no more than a vigorous effort of Nature to throw off the morbific matter, and thus recover the patient. For as God has been pleased so to create mankind, that they should be fitted to receive various impressions from without, they could not, upon this account, but be liable to different disorders; which arise (1) either from such particles of the air, as having a disagreement with the juices, insinuate themselves into the body, and mixing with the blood, taint the whole frame; or (2) from different kinds of fermentations and putrefactions of humours detained too long in the body, for want of its being able to digest, and discharge them, on account of their being too large bulk, or unsuitable nature. (Syndenham 1922, p. 38)

The development of morbid anatomy and histology in the nineteenth century demonstrated clearly that many physical illnesses were often accompanied by structural damage to the body (Kendell 1975). Some then considered these lesions, or the structural damage itself, to constitute the illness. This belief is represented well by the early pathologist Virchow (1981):

[1]See Caplan, Engelhardt, and McCartney 1981; Cavenar and Walker 1983; Kendell 1975; Klein 1978; Offer and Sabshin 1966; Roth and Kroll 1986; and Wing 1978.

> Ever since we recognized that diseases are neither self-subsistent, self-contained entities, nor autonomous organisms, nor entities that have invaded the body, nor parasites rooted in it, but rather that they represent only the course of corporeal appearances under changed conditions—since this time, healing has had to encompass maintaining or restoring the normal conditions of life. . . . Scientific medicine has as its object the discovery of changed conditions, characterizing the sick body or the individual suffering organ. (P. 188)

Griesinger, in his influential text entitled *Mental Pathology and Therapeutics* (originally published in 1845), similarly argued that mental disorders were ultimately morbid diseases of the brain.

> Insanity itself, an anomalous condition of the faculties of knowledge and of will, is only a symptom . . . To which organ do the indications of the disease belong? What organ must necessarily and invariably be diseased where there is madness? . . . Physiological and pathological facts show us that this organ can only be the brain; we therefore primarily, and in every case of mental disease, recognise a morbid action of that organ. (1965, p. 1)

To him, psychiatry and neuropathology were not closely related fields, but were or should be identical fields (Zilboor and Henry 1941). More current neurophysiological models of mental disorder can be found in the work of Guze (1978), Schneider (1950), and Wing (1978).

The biological/neurochemical model is attractive to many for it appears to remove subjective judgments (that is, potential biases), reducing the concept of illness to a physically verifiable, objective criterion.

> The assumption is made that some neurological defect, perhaps a very subtle one, will ultimately be found for all the disorders of thinking and behavior. . . . "Mental illnesses" are thus regarded as basically no different than all other diseases (that is, of the body). The only difference, in this view . . . is that the former, affecting the brain, manifest themselves by means of mental symptoms. (Szasz 1960, p. 113)

Others, however, have suggested that this creates a straw man, an easy target for a critique of the concept of mental disorder. If mental illness is a disease of the brain, then it is difficult to defend the argument that aberrant affective, cognitive, and interpersonal behavior patterns that are without apparent structural lesion or neurochemical dysfunction are mental illnesses.

Ausubel (1961) attempted to take a more descriptive approach that was not tied to any particular etiological model, defining disease "as including any marked deviation, physical, mental, or behavioral, from normally desirable standards of structural and functional integrity" (p. 71). Scadding (1967) combined the statistical deviancy model with the criterion of a biological disadvantage to a species, and defined disease as "the sum of the abnormal phenomena displayed by a group of living organisms in association with a specified common characteristic or set of characteristics by which they differ from the norm for their species in such a way as to place them at a biological disadvantage" (p. 877). Kraepelin (1917), in a similar fashion, suggested that "the standard we use in recognising the morbid features of a man's mental life is his departure from the average in the direction of inefficiency" (p. 295).

To Meyer (1948), who opposed Kraepelin's emphasis on diagnosis, mental disorders were "a faulty response or substitution of an insufficient or protective or evasive or mutilated attempt at adjustment" (p. 199). Meyer argued that disorders, especially mental ones, were reactions of the whole organism to its environment rather than a particular structural lesion or contagion. Engel (1960) provides a biopsychosocial adjustment model of disorder, suggesting that "disease corresponds to failures or disturbances in the growth, development, functions, and adjustments of the organism as a whole or any of its systems" (p. 459). Engel (1980) emphasizes that function and dysfunction occurs interactively across the cellular, organ, organism, person, social, and community systems, and no sharp boundary between health and sickness can be demarcated because they vary as a function of cultural, social, and psychological factors. The systems model resembles Cannon's (1932) concept of homeostasis in its emphasis on the interaction of biological, psychological, and sociological systems and Hippocrates' concept of health as involving a balance among forces.

The sociologist Talcott Parsons (1981) attempted to define the respects in which health and illness can be considered to be universal categories applying to all human beings in all societies. He believed there were common components to somatic and mental disorders, but noted that cultural and social factors increase as one progresses from the purely somatic to the purely mental. He defined health as the optimum capacity for the effective performance of valued tasks, with the primary criterion for mental health being role performance and social functioning. The attribution of illness entitled the person to occupy a particular role in society, that of the sick person (Klein 1978). The sick role would exempt people from certain normal responsibilities because they could not help being ill and could not get well on their own accord. However, they were also expected to reduce their social burden by seeking appropriate treatment.

Klein (1978) incorporated Parsons's concepts into his more complicated model.

> Disease is defined here as covert, objective, suboptimal part dysfunction, recognizing that functions are evolved and hierarchically organized. It is argued that disease is not simply an arbitrary social evaluation but is derivable from the concept of optimal biological functioning, within an evolutionary context. Illness is always secondary to disease, but also requires a social judgment that there is sufficient incapacity to warrant the assignment of the exempt sick role. Mental illness is the subset of all illness that presents evidence in the cognitive, behavioral, affective, and motivational aspects of organismal functioning. It must be believed that something has gone wrong to attribute illness. For functional disorders, involuntary impairment is a key inference, supported by a range of evidence. (P. 70)

Spitzer, the chair of the task force empowered by the American Psychiatric Association to develop the third edition of the *Diagnostic and Statistical Manual of Mental Disorders,* attempted to develop a definition of mental disorder that would guide the judgments of which conditions to include and exclude from DSM-III.

> A medical disorder is a relatively distinct condition resulting from an organismic dysfunction which in its fully developed or extreme form is directly and intrinsically associated with distress, disability, or certain other types of disadvantage. The disadvantage may be of a physical, perceptual, sexual, or interpersonal nature. Implicitly there is a call for action on the part of the person who has the condition, the medical or its allied professions, and society. A mental disorder is a medical disorder whose manifestations are primarily signs or symptoms of a psychological (behavioral) nature, or if physical, can be understood only using psychological concepts. (Spitzer and Endicott 1978, p. 18)

The definitions provided in DSM-III (American Psychiatric Association 1980) and DSM-III-R (APA 1987) were based in large part on this one. Table 1.1 presents the APA definitions. Spitzer and Endicott's criteria for identifying when a particular condition qualified as a mental disorder are presented in table 1.2.

TABLE 1.1

DSM-III and DSM-III-R Definitions of Mental Disorder

DSM-III:
In DSM-III each of the mental disorders is conceptualized as a clinically significant behavioral or psychological syndrome or pattern that occurs in an individual and that is typically associated with either a painful symptom (distress) or impairment in one or more areas of functioning (disability). In addition, there is an inference that there is a behavioral, psychological, or biological dysfunction, and that the disturbance is not only in the relationship between the individual and society. (APA 1980, p. 6)
DSM-III-R:
In DSM-III-R each of the mental disorders is conceptualized as a clinically significant behavioral or psychological syndrome or pattern that occurs in a person and that is associated with present distress (a painful symptom) or disability (impairment in one or more important areas of functioning) or with a significantly increased risk of suffering death, pain, disability, or an important loss of freedom. In addition, this syndrome or pattern must not be merely an expectable response to a particular event, e.g., the death of a loved one. Whatever its original cause, it must currently be considered a manifestation of a behavioral, psychological, or biological dysfunction in the person. Neither deviant behavior, e.g., political, religious, sexual, nor conflicts that are primarily between the individual and society are mental disorders unless the deviance or conflict is a symptom of a dysfunction in the person, as described above. (APA 1987, p. xxii)

Definitions of Health and Normality

Definitions of disease imply a definition of health, sometimes implicitly and at other times explicitly. Hippocrates, writing on the nature of man during the fourth century B.C., addressed both concepts of health and disorder: "Health is primarily that state in which these constituent substances [of blood, phlegm, yellow bile, and black bile] are in the correct proportion to each other, both in strength and quantity, and are well mixed" (1983, p. 262), for "these are the things that make up its constitution and cause its pains and health" (p. 262). Various mixtures, distributions, and imbalances of these four humors were associated not only with physical diseases and mental disorders but also with the normal variation in temperaments. Galen, writing in the second century A.D., indicated that "we naturally find yellow bile appearing in greatest quantity in ourselves at the warm periods of life, in warm countries, at warm seasons of the year, and when we are in a warm condition; similarly in people of warm temperaments, and in connection with warm occupations, modes of life, or dis-

TABLE 1.2

Spitzer and Endicott (1978) Operational Criteria for a Mental Disorder

A. The condition, in the fully developed or extreme form, in all environments (other than one especially created to compensate for the condition), is directly associated with at least one of the following:

1. Distress—acknowledged by the individual or manifested.
2. Disability—some impairment in functioning in a wide range of activities.
3. Disadvantage (not resulting from the above)—certain forms of disadvantage to the individual in interacting with aspects of the physical or social environment because of an identifiable psychological or physical factor. The following forms of disadvantage, even when not associated with distress or disability, are now considered, in our culture, as suggestive of some type of organismic dysfunction warranting the designation of medical disorder.
    a. Impaired ability to make important environmental discrimination.
    b. Lack of ability to reproduce.
    c. Cosmetically unattractive because of a deviation in kind, rather than degree, from physical structure.
    d. Atypical and inflexible sexual or other impulse-driven behavior which often has painful consequences.
    e. Impairment in the ability to experience sexual pleasure in an interpersonal context.
    f. Marked impairment in the ability to form relatively lasting and nonconflictual interpersonal relationships.

B. The controlling variables tend to be attributed to being largely within the organism with regard to either initiating or maintaining the condition. Therefore, a condition is included only if it meets both of the following criteria:

1. Simple informative or standard educational procedures do not lead to a reversal of the condition.
2. Nontechnical interventions do not bring about a quick reversal of the condition.

C. Conditions are not included if the associated distress, disability, or other disadvantage is apparently the necessary price associated with attaining some positive goal.

D. Distinctness from other conditions in one or more of the following features: clinical phenomenology, course, response to treatment, familial incidence, or etiology.

eases" (1952, p. 194). A clear distinction between normality and abnormality was difficult to achieve, except in the extreme cases seen by physicians. Complete health was considered to be a state rarely achieved. The typical person would be normal in the sense of being of average health (or of average ill health) rather than healthy in an absolute sense.

Freud (1963) likewise considered mental health to be an ideal state no one achieved. "A normal ego is, like normality in general, an ideal fiction . . . Every normal person is only approximately normal: his ego resembles that of the psychotic in one point or another, in a greater or lesser degree" (p. 253). His assertion of a psychopathology of everyday life is well known; apparently normal behavior is an expression of the same conflicts that underlie the behavior recognized as being abnormal. The average person is normal only in the statistical sense. "The statistically normal mind can be regarded only as a mind which has responded in the usual way to the moulding and deforming influence of its environment" (Jones 1942, pp. 1–2).

Menninger (1942), however, defined mental health as the adjustment of human beings to the world and to each other with a maximum of effectiveness and happiness: "Not just efficiency, or just containment—or the grace of obeying the rules of the game cheerfully. It is all of these together. It is the ability to maintain an even temper, an alert intelligence, socially considerate behavior, and a happy disposition. This, I think, is a healthy mind" (p. 2).

Shoben (1957) attempted to avoid the suggestion that normality implied being happy, free from conflict, and without problems. He proposed a model of "integrative adjustment, as characterized by self-control, personal responsibility, social responsibility, democratic social interest, and ideals" (p. 188). "Integrative adjustment does not consist in the individual's fitting a preconceived behavioral mold. It may well consist in the degree to which his efforts fulfill the symbolic and social potentialities that are distinctively human" (p. 189).

Jahoda (1958), in an influential overview of the concept of mental health, emphasized that no single criterion was sufficient or adequate. She listed six:

1. Self-acceptance, self-confidence, and/or self-reliance.
2. Self-actualization, growth, development, and/or the realization of one's potential.
3. Integration and coherence of the personality, as evidenced by a balance of psychic forces, a unified outlook on life, and resistance to stress.
4. Accurate perception of reality, as evidenced by empathy, social sensitivity, and perceptions being free from distortions by needs.
5. Autonomy, self-determination, and/or independence.
6. Environmental mastery, as evidenced by the ability to love, adequacy in work and play, adequacy in interpersonal relations, efficiency in meeting situational requirements, capacity for adaptation and adjustment, and efficiency in problem solving.

These six criteria resemble closely Maslow's eleven manifestations of psychological health and normality (adequate feelings of security, adequate self-evaluation, adequate spontaneity and emotionality, efficient contact with reality, adequate bodily desires and the ability to gratify them, adequate self-knowlege, integration and consistency of personality, adequate life goals, ability to learn from experience, ability to satisfy requirements of the group in which he lives, and adequate emancipation from the group; Maslow and Mittelmann 1951). The World Health Organization, in its 1946 constitution, put it more simply: health is "a state of complete physical, mental, and social well-being and not merely the absence of disease or infirmity" (1981, p. 83).

Five Definitional Models

It is evident from these examples that a variety of attempts have been made to distinguish health from illness. Five major perspectives on health and illness can be distinguished (Offer and Sabshin 1966).

The Absence-of-Pathology Model

The first model defines disorder by the presence of symptomatology, physical signs, and/or laboratory abnormalities, with the absence of these phenomena connoting a state of health or normality. A healthy person is one who is reasonably free of undue pain, discomfort, disability, distress, disadvantage, and other features of disorder (Romano 1950; Spitzer and Endicott 1978). Biological perspectives tend to emphasize this model. According to Barton (1959), "medicine has developed this useful way of looking at health and the normal to the extent that health as the antonym of disease has become a part of the philosophy or tradition of physicians" (p. 233). The goal of treatment in this model is to free the person from the presence of the grossly observable symptoms rather than to increase functioning to an optimal or ideal state. Health is a reasonable rather than an optimal level of functioning. This model has also guided the research assumption that there is a "normal," undifferentiated, and undefined control group. Persons who fail to meet the criteria for a mental disorder are said to be normal, and distinct from a clinical sample. It has also dominated epidemiology and nosology, wherein qualitative distinctions are made between the ill and the healthy or normal. A relative minority of persons are defined as being ill, and the large set of undifferentiated persons who remain from the residual category of the healthy or normal. Explicit inclusion criteria for healthy, normal functioning are rarely provided.

The Utopia Model

The second perspective focuses on the opposite pole, that of normality or health and, complementary to the first, tends to result in a minority of persons being identified as healthy. Health is typically defined as a kind of utopic, ideal functioning that is obtained rarely and by few persons. The normal—the typical or average—is in fact pathological in that it is considerably short of the ideal. Treatment attempts to help the patient actualize or reach his or her full potential, to optimize functioning in some ideal manner. This is evident in humanistic and psychoanalytic models of treatment (Freud 1961; Rogers 1959). However, the analytic model emphasizes pathology while the humanistic model emphasizes health. Despite all the efforts to describe adaptation, sublimation, and the ultimate therapeutic goal of the control of the id by the ego, psychoanalytic terms and concepts concern pathological functioning. Quite literally, psychoanalysis lacks the language and methodology to describe normal or healthy functioning (Sabshin 1988). The humanistic models of Rogers (1959) and Maslow and Mittelman (1951) focus on concepts of healthy functioning.

The Statistical Model

The third perspective defines normality as the average level of functioning. This model is evident primarily in the psychometric models of psychopathology in psychology. Physicians have had difficulty in applying this model because the average is relative to an arbitrary population that might itself be dysfunctional, and the boundary between normality and deviance is arbitrary as well. However, this model is evident in many medical diagnoses and classifications, such as hypertension, and it implicitly informs the interpretation of countless laboratory, biochemical tests.

The Systems Model

A fourth perspective is transactional (Offer and Sabshin 1966). Normality from this perspective is the functional interplay of interacting systems that operate and fluctuate in a relative adaptivity over time. While the prior perspectives tend to be cross-sectional, the transactional emphasizes multiple processes and multiple levels of adaptation (for example, biological, cognitive, affective, interpersonal, occupational, and familial) whose interactions need to be studied longitudinally. There is as much variation in the patterns and forms of normal adaptation as there are differences in the patterns and types of psychopathology.

The Pragmatic Model

The fifth and final model is a pragmatic one. In this model mental disorders are simply the conditions clinicians treat. Conditions for which persons do not seek treatment are not considered pathological. Mental health professionals provide a particular function or purpose within society: They provide treatment for conditions that provide pain, discomfort, or distress to those having those conditions. In any particular society, disorders are those conditions that persons find sufficiently troublesome to seek professional help for. There are obvious difficulties with this model, but it is realistic in the sense that defining a condition as a disorder is inherently evaluative, and this evaluation is necessarily relative to the society and the citizens within that society.

Each of these models, however, has proven problematic or inadequate in distinguishing normality/health from abnormality/disorder/illness.[2] For example, the evidence of a lesion, biological marker, family history, and/or neurochemical dysfunction can provide useful indicators of pathology (Robins and Guze 1970), but a biological etiology or pathology might not be present or determinable in all cases of mental disorder (Roth and Kroll 1986; Spitzer and Endicott 1978). Moreover, the standard or optimal pattern of neurochemical structure and function is itself ambiguous and arbitrary (Kendell 1975). Neurochemical functioning often varies on a continuum, with no discrete boundary between normality and abnormality.

Transactional and system models are appealing in their emphasis on function rather than structure, but they are also relative to the needs or values of a particular system and are not helpful in informing clinical, social, and forensic decisions regarding the boundaries of abnormality and normality (Moore 1978). The utopia health models have been equally troublesome, basically because the features of healthy functioning describe an ideal functioning that is unattainable. The model is not especially useful in resolving concrete, practical decisions concerning a distinction between abnormality and normality (Kendell 1975).

Defining mental disorders as those conditions treated by mental health professionals is obviously circular, possibly self-serving, and arbitrarily relative to the complaints and economics of the local patients and interests of the local clinicians. It does not attempt to define what is meant by the concept of a mental disorder (Moore 1978). Suffering and distress are useful indicators, but many people who are ill, even physically, do not complain or even suffer, because they experience no symptoms (a "silent disease," Meehl 1986), they accept their incapacity, or they find some benefit from it (Kendell 1975). Suffering, for example, is not a prominent feature of antisocial personality disorder or mania. Deviancy from a norm

[2]See Gorenstein 1984; Kendell 1975, 1986; Klein 1978; Roth and Kroll 1986; and Szasz 1987.

clearly results in many inconsistencies, as deviant behavior is at times adaptive, and it is relative to the standards and values of a particular reference group that might itself be pathological or at least functioning at a low level.

Conceptual Issues

A number of conceptual issues that are themselves difficult to resolve impedes the effort to formulate a definition of mental disorder and mental illness. These include the effort to develop operational definitions, the distinction between definitions and diagnoses, the use of a categorical versus a dimensional model of classification, and the emphasis on diagnosing maladaptive rather than adaptive behaviors. We discuss each of these issues here, without the unrealistic ambition of attempting to resolve them. However, we suggest potential pathways toward their eventual resolution or at least clarification.

Hypothetical Constructs and Operational Definitions

The exceptions, flaws, and inconsistencies of each of the definitions have suggested to some that the concept of a mental disorder is an illusory, arbitrary abstraction that mental health professionals are using to justify their interventions (Szasz 1960, 1987). "If the statistical definition, the social definition, the theory-based definition, and the subjective discomfort definition all fall short of an adequate representation of mental illness, it seems reasonable to wonder if we really know just what we are trying to define" (Gorenstein 1984, p. 52). The concept of mental disorder, however, is a hypothetical construct that cannot be defined so explicitly that no ambiguous case can occur (Meehl 1986; Widiger and Trull 1985). It would be nice if the boundaries between normality and abnormality were subject to clear criteria, but as is true for most scientific constructs, and particularly those in the life sciences, explicit (operational) definitions in which each criterion is always met are not feasible (Leahey 1980; Meehl and Golden 1982; Rorer and Widiger 1983). Scientific constructs can rarely be reduced to an explicit set of observables without losing their explanatory power and their theoretical meaning. Observable features contribute to the definition of what is meant by a concept in a probabilistic fashion, but they are often insufficient to provide an infallible definition (Leahey 1980; Hempel 1965). For example, the concept of intelligence is a valid scientific construct, but it cannot be so explicitly defined that its presence, absence, or degree can be precisely measured. Intelligence tests are helpful, indicating what is meant by the concept of intelligence, but intelligence is not equal to a score on an intellegence test nor is it equivalent to the skills, abilities, or functions measured by any particular intelligence test.

Mental disorders are associated with but are not equivalent to distress, dyscontrol, disadvantage, disability, inflexibility, irrationality, deviation from social norms, biogenetic etiology, biochemical covariates, and so forth. These features, along with statistical deviancy, inflexibility, irrationality, violation of social norms, genetic etiology, dyscontrol, and so forth, are best thought of as fallible indicators for the presence of a disorder rather than as providing an operational definition. Distress, dyscontrol, and disability are not fundamental features that are present in all instances of a mental disorder. They do not define what is meant by a mental disorder. They instead indicate with various degrees of probability the likelihood that a person is suffering from a disorder. They are useful in the determination of when a particular condition might represent a mental disorder and in assessing the validity of the concept, but they are not infallible in this assessment. Ambiguous, boundary, and controversial cases will occur. Specification, explication, and clarification of these indicators and validators of mental disorders are helpful in improving the assessment and validation of the concept of mental disorder, but they will not likely provide an infallible definition of what is meant by a mental disorder.

For example, distress (such as anxiety, depression, or anger) is a useful indicator for the presence of a mental disorder because it suggests that there is something wrong (an impairment) within the organism. Dysfunction within the organism is often accompanied or expressed by dysphoric mood. However, distress is not an infallible indicator because it is at times adaptive and/or voluntary. A person who is depressed over the loss of a loved one is experiencing and expressing dysphoria, but it is a reflection of the value he or she placed on the relationship. Bereavement is not considered pathological unless there are additional indicators of a mental disorder. An absence of distress might be more suggestive of a mental disorder than its presence. For example, normal development is said to involve "identity crises" and "separation anxiety," and the absence of dysphoria associated with these events might be more indicative of pathology than its presence. Organismic dysfunction can impair the ability of a person to experience dysphoria (for example, anhedonia in some cases of schizoid personality disorder and the high threshold for anxiety in some cases of antisocial personality disorder), and a person may respond to a dysfunctional behavior pattern by denying its importance or simply accepting its presence (as in some cases of psychosexual disorder and dysfunctions).

The absence of an explicit, operational definition leaves room for misdiagnosis, controversy, and debate. Critics can cite ambiguous cases that suggest to them that the concept is an illusory, self-serving abstraction. However, the validity of the construct does not require or rest on the presence of an explicit definition that provides a set of infallible criteria for identifying its presence. There are ambiguous, boundary cases for many valid concepts in science. The validity of mental disorder as a scientific concept depends on obtaining empirical results that are consistent with theories of psychopathology and normality and in refuting rival or alternative theories. Data relevant to the validity of the construct of a mental disorder include the indicators of psychopathology, such as distress, disability, inflexibility, disadvantage, family history, treatment response, external correlates (for example, laboratory test data), and course (Robins and Guze 1970; Spitzer and Williams 1985). Data relevant to the concept of health include its fallible indicators, such as flexibility, self-confidence, productivity, self-esteem, autonomy, efficiency, stable relationships, and so forth. These data, taken together, provide considerable support for the validity of a distinction between the concepts of mental disorder and healthy functioning. As Kety (1974) argued with respect to the hypothesis that schizophrenia is not a mental disorder, "if schizophrenia is a myth, it is a myth with a strong genetic component" (p. 961). In sum, one cannot define absolutely or unambiguously what is meant by a mental disorder, but one can define it in a manner that is sufficient for empirical hypothesis testing. Like other hypothetical constructs in physics, astronomy, psychiatry, and psychology, there are enough data, taken together, to support the construct's validity (Meehl 1986; Moore 1975; Widiger and Trull 1985).

Dimensions versus Categories

There has been a debate for some time in psychiatry regarding whether mental disorders are best conceived as qualitatively distinct conditions or as degrees along a continuum of functioning.[3] DSM-III-R disavows a commitment to either position. "There is no assumption that each mental disorder is a discrete entity with sharp boundaries (discontinuity) between it and . . . no mental disorder" (APA 1987, p. xxii). Nevertheless, the DSM-III-R follows the tradition of providing criteria for categorical diagnoses. Patients are not rated with respect to the extent to which they are

[3]See Blashfield 1986; Kendell 1975; Mezzich 1979; Millon 1981; and Strauss 1975.

schizophrenic or depressed, but as whether or not they have schizophrenia or major depression.

Traditionally, it has been medical practice to make a qualitative distinction between normality and abnormality. The Spitzer and Endicott (1978) definition for a medical disorder also specifies that a disorder involves "a relatively distinct condition" (p. 18). The preference for categorical distinctions probably results in part from the fact that most medical decisions are themselves categorical. The decision to hospitalize, to use group or marital therapy, and to use electroconvulsive therapy or antidepressants is a categorical one. There are few shades of gray in the decisions that must be made, and dimensional diagnoses may be perceived as ambiguous with respect to these decisions. However, many disorders, including physical disorders such as hypertension, diabetes, and respiratory disease, have no sharp boundaries (Roth and Kroll 1986). Even a broken leg occurs in varying degrees (for example, hairline and stress fractures).

A categorical model requires a qualitative distinction that in many cases, and especially for the mental disorders, is often arbitrary and results in residual categories that are clearly not distinct conditions (Moore 1978). For many purposes it may be preferable to acknowledge that abnormality and normality are distributed along a continuum, with no clear boundaries. Even Kraepelin (1917), who greatly contributed to the current emphasis on identifying distinct, homogeneous syndromes (Blashfield 1984; Klerman 1986), acknowledged that "wherever we try to mark out the frontier between mental health and disease, we find a neutral territory, in which the imperceptible change from the realm of normal mental life to that of obvious derangement takes place" (p. 295). Although categorical distinctions are particularly problematic in personality disorders, it also seems likely that affective disorders, anxiety disorders, and even schizophrenia might lie along a spectrum (dimension) of pathology (Cloninger 1987; Frances 1982; Mirsky and Duncan 1986; Widiger and Frances 1985*b*).

The practice of making a qualitative, categorical distinction between persons with disorders (ill, sick, or insane) and those without (healthy, normal, and sane) also exacerbates controversies regarding the definition and diagnosis of mental disorders. Categorical diagnoses encourage stereotyping, or the perception of members of the disordered category to be qualitatively distinct from "normal" persons and homogeneous with respect to (undesirable) traits that are associated with mental disorders (Cantor and Genero 1986). Psychiatric diagnoses have been notoriously problematic with respect to this labeling and stereotyping. If a person has a mental disorder, people tend to assume or attribute stereotypic features of the prototypic (extreme) cases. While some mental disorders involve distinct conditions with specific etiologies (Meehl 1977), many probably do not.

It must be recognized, however, that what appears as a continuum with respect to phenotypic variation may mask an underlying latent class taxon. Intelligence is optimally measured on a continuum, but its variation is probably the result in part of discrete genotypic events. There might then be discrete subtypes of affective and anxiety disorders and schizophrenia that remain to be defined on etiological or pathogenic grounds. It is very difficult to identify empirically when a diagnostic variable is best conceptualized categorically or dimensionally (Cloninger et al. 1985; Gangestad and Snyder 1985), but this should be a major focus of future research.

Adaptation versus Maladaption

The overlapping gray area and at times arbitrary distinction between normality and abnormality would be clarified if diagnosis was not simply a binary decision of ill versus normal/healthy but was instead a comprehensive description of adaptive and maladaptive functioning. Each patient has adaptive abilities and strengths as well as a maladaptive behavior pattern or syndrome, but classification in psychiatry has focused almost exclusively on abnormal functioning and has neglected the assessment of normal functioning. Neither the psychoanalytic nor the Kraepelinian models of psychopathology that dominate American psychiatry place much consideration on what is normal in the assessment of a patient's functioning (Sabshin 1988). Humanistic and community psychiatry models emphasize healthy and adaptive functioning, but these perspectives have not had much impact on nosology and classification. Diagnoses have been confined to identifying disorders, not strengths. However, the neglect of what is normal and adaptive in a patient's functioning not only provides an incomplete description but also can be misleading and stereotyping if it implies that the patient lacks adaptive strengths.

The multiaxial system of classification, in which patients are assessed with respect to their physical disorders, severity of psychosocial stressors, and global functioning, provides more comprehensive description (APA 1987; Williams 1985*a,b*), but the focus is still pathological. It might be informative and less stereotyping to identify patients' strengths, resources, and characteristic manner of adaptive functioning as well as their liabilities, problems, and characteristic manner of maladaptive functioning. Distinguishing normality and health is difficult and arbitrary in part because persons are healthy and normal in some respects but not in others. There is no single boundary between normality and abnormality, but rather a variety of ways in which behavior, affect, cognition, and relationships can be maladaptive and adaptive. Assessing the latter as well as the former would decrease the artifactual qualitative distinction between persons with some characteristics of illness versus those with fewer. Persons would then not be lumped into two broad, poorly differentiated classes of the mentally ill and the normal/healthy.

The DSM-III-R provides assessments of patients on five axes: Axis I is for most clinical syndromes; Axis II is for developmental disorders and personality disorders; Axis III is for physical disorders; Axis IV is for a rating of the overall severity of psychosocial stressors; and Axis V is for a rating of the global level of functioning (APA 1987). A comprehensive multiaxial system might also provide a description of the person's normal, adaptive personality traits. As personality disorders are to a large extent maladaptive variants of normal personality traits (APA 1987; Widiger and Frances 1985*a*), a classification of abnormal personality should bear some systematic relationship to a classification of normal personality. A classification confined only to the maladaptive variants provides an incomplete, inadequate description of a patient's personality. Personality disorders are important to diagnose in patients with other clinical syndromes because they can substantially affect the presentation, course, and treatment of those syndromes (Frances 1980). The same could be said for normal personality traits. In fact, normal and adaptive traits could be as important to determining the likely course, presentation, and treatment of an Axis I condition as the maladaptive traits. Knowing that a person is adaptively assertive and conscientious can be as important as knowing that he or she is maladaptively dependent.

The nature of the relationship between maladaptive personality disorders and normal personality traits would be a useful focus for future research. Some personality disorders might represent extreme variants of common traits (for example, avoidant personality disorder as an extreme form of introversion), while others could be characterologic (chronic and pervasive) variants of other mental disorders (for example, schizotypal personality disorder as a characterologic variant of schizophrenic pathology). There are also a variety of dimensional models of personality (Cloninger 1987; McCrae and Costa 1983; Frances and Widiger 1986). Future research could address which model is optimal for representing maladaptive traits and the factors that determine when and under what conditions a trait becomes maladaptive. Maladaptivity could represent intense or extreme variants of some traits, a narrow or rigid expression for others, and/or a particular pattern or combination of traits. Some personality traits might be inherently maladaptive, and others might be only under certain circumstances (for example, occupational advancement versus the maintenance of a relationship).

The severity of psychosocial stressors assessed on Axis IV and the global assessment of functioning on Axis V of DSM-III-R might also benefit from a normatologic perspective and research (Sabshin 1988). The Axes IV and V ratings address important aspects of functioning not addressed by a clinical diagnosis of a mental disorder (Williams 1985*a,* 1985*b*), but the ratings are perhaps too global and nonspecific to be particularly informative. For example, Axis IV involves a rating from 1 to 6 to indicate the overall severity of a psychosocial stressor or multiple stressors occurring in the year preceding the current evaluation that might have contributed to the development of a new mental disorder, the recurrence of a prior disorder, and/or the exacerbation of a current disorder. This rating is informative but could go further. For example, besides noting the specific psychosocial stressor(s) involved (APA 1987, p. 19), a comprehensive assessment would describe strengths, deficits, and supports in various areas of functioning (familial, social, occupational, financial, and so forth).

The global assessment of functioning on Axis V could be similarly differentiated and associated with Axis IV. There are a variety of major stressors in life (occupational, financial, legal, relational, physical health, and developmental) and a variety of ways to respond effectively and ineffectively to them (Lazarus and Folkman 1984). An effort to define the various coping strategies by which stress can be handled adaptively would clarify a distinction between normality and abnormality. Defining unhealthy, maladaptive functioning is difficult without understanding healthy, adaptive functioning (Sabshin 1988). The considerable research on the assessment and classification of adaptive coping (Allred and Smith 1989; Carver, Scheier, and Weintraub 1989; Kobasa 1982) could inform the research on maladaptivity. What is maladaptive in some contexts can be adaptive in others. Inaccurate, exaggerated, and overly positive self-evaluation, exaggerated perceptions of control or mastery, and unrealistic optimism would appear to suggest mental disorder but might in fact be characteristic of normal human thought and adaptive functioning in response to negative threats (Taylor and Brown 1988). What is stressful and what is an adaptive response could also interface with the assessment on Axis II, as stress and optimal functioning could be relative to a person's characteristic manner of functioning.

Research to identify the manner and conditions under which behavior becomes maladaptive would likely need to be multiaxial and longitudinal. Behavior that is adaptive under one condition and time (perhaps within one's family of origin) might not be adaptive at another (as within a marriage or occupation). Maladaptive personality traits reflect in part a vulnerability to future dysfunction that can be identified only longitudinally. Longitudinal studies would be helpful in identifying which traits ultimately prove maladaptive and under what conditions.

Implications

The conceptual issues just mentioned hinder any effort to provide an adequate definition of mental disorder and normality. Nevertheless, explicit or implicit definitions of normality and pathology do have substantial public health, forensic, social, clinical, and professional implications that follow from the assumptions regarding the concept of a mental disorder.

Public Health Statistics and Epidemiology

The DSM manual is not and cannot be a completely culture-free document. Its use is undoubtedly influenced by the conditions, resources, and interests of the particular society in which the diagnoses are made. As we indicated earlier, the DSM is a manual for the diagnosis of clinically significant mental disorders; clinical significance is determined not only by the interests and concerns of the persons who seek psychiatric treatment but also by the resources of the community. Countries with more resources for the treatment of mental disorders naturally tend to recognize more disorders. Fewer resources result in some possibly maladaptive behavior patterns being accepted as a "way of life" rather than being seen as a disorder.

Tolerance as well as resources also affects a definition of mental health. For example, alcohol abuse is difficult to define uniformly across cultures. In a draft of the tenth edition of the *International Classification of Diseases,* the definition of "harmful use" (comparable to the DSM concept of substance abuse) was confined to physical or mental harm and specifically excluded adverse social consequences such as job loss, arrest, and marital difficulties. This was done because of the difficulty in defining a universal social standard. Job loss and arrest are indicative of alcohol abuse in the United States, but it is hard to disentangle social consequences from cultural acceptance and enforcement standards. A businessman who was caught with one alcoholic drink in Saudi Arabia could lose his job. Is this suggestive of alcohol abuse? Even if he persisted in his drinking and lost his next job, it is still difficult to disentangle a defiance of a cultural standard from a mental disorder. At the opposite extreme is a society that tolerates substantially high levels of drug use. Fewer social consequences would transpire when there are more liberal laws regarding driving while intoxicated (DWI) and public drunkenness. Even within one country and community, standards change over time. Today there are more consequences to alcohol use than there were twenty years ago (for example, tougher DWI laws) and fewer consequences than during prohibition.

It therefore becomes difficult to determine if there is a greater prevalence of cases of, for example, alcohol abuse, simple phobia, or bulimia in the United States, or if this country simply has more resources and a lower threshold of tolerance. Thus differences in the epidemiology of disorders across countries and communities may not reflect real differences in the rate of various disorders but rather differences in the resources and values of various countries and communities. Research on the cross-cultural variation in the acceptability and adaptivity of behavior patterns would be helpful in determining whether a universal threshold or norm for abnormality is even feasible, or whether the concept of mental disorder is always and to some extent relative to a particular cultural setting.

Forensic Implications

There is an uneasy relationship between the judicial and psychiatric assessment of human behavior (Hart 1968; Liefer 1964). Criminal responsibility requires not only the conjunction of a proscribed act *(actus reus)* but also an appropriate degree of intentionality and mental capacity *(mens rea).* "Defendants who lack the ability (the capacity) to rationally control their behavior do not possess free will . . . [and] therefore, they should not be punished or handled similarly to all other criminal defendants" (Insanity Defense Work Group 1983, p. 683). The judicial system often calls upon psychiatrists and psychologists to offer expert opinions regarding the mental capacity of a defendant, as these professionals are concerned with identifying and treating persons who have diminished mental (cognitive, affective, or behavioral) capacities.

However, there is substantially less recognition of free will in psychiatry and psychology than is generally tolerable to the judicial system (Liefer 1964). Psychopathology is not thought to occur as a result of free will or choice. The psychodynamic, neurochemical, social learning, and other models of psychopathology are deterministic. Persons who suffer from schizophrenia, depression, phobias, psychosexual disorders, or personality disorders are not thought to have chosen to have these disorders.

The boundary between mental disorders and normality becomes particularly problematic and controversial when the proposed mental disorder directly or indirectly involves criminal behavior, such as kleptomania, voyeurism, pedophilia, and antisocial personality disorder. As a result, some conditions that have been labeled mental disorders (for example, antisocial personality disorder) are simply (and appropriately) not recognized by most judicial bodies as cause for reduced criminal responsibility. Paraphiliac rapism was considered but not included in DSM-III-R (even in an appendix) in part because of the legal controversies and dilemmas that might arise by identifying repeat rapists as having a mental disorder.

The forensic problem is due in part to making the categorical assumption that a presence of a mental disorder suggests complete, uniform, or a comprehensive loss of control. Impairment in self-control varies both across and within the various mental disorders. Loss of control of behavior, thoughts, feelings, and acts is not absolute or complete. Dyscontrol, like the mental disorders themselves, occurs in various forms and degrees.

The presence of a mental disorder, therefore, does not by itself render a judgment regarding the criminal responsibility a person might have for an act associated with a mental disorder. Its presence does suggest some degree of dyscontrol, but the ability to refrain from performing any particular act must be assessed in the context of the conditions and history of each particular case. How to assess the degree to which a person has control over an aspect of his or her behavior is a difficult but fundamental empirical question that would clearly inform this issue (Howard and Conway 1986).

Social Implications

A definition of mental disorder has important social implications, because the "labeling" of a person as having such a disorder has pejorative connotations and can have substantial negative social repercussions. The consequences of being labeled mentally ill at times may have been exaggerated (Gove 1982), and there are also advantages and benefits to being given a mental disorder diagnosis (Klein 1978), but clearly there is also a substantial social stigma attached. In most cases of a misdiagnosis, the costs certainly outweigh the benefits.

The concept of a mental disorder is inherently evaluative in its social context (Moore 1975). A society that did not value flexibility, freedom of choice, self-control, spontaneity, happiness, rationality, and maximization of potential probably would not have a concept of a mental disorder. A person with a mental disorder lacks abilities and capacities that most everyone in society values. The threshold for the clinical significance of a mental disorder is also relative to these values.

The concept of a physical disorder also "suffers" from the same limitation.

> All departments of nature below the level of mankind are exempt both from disease and from treatment. The blight that strikes at corn or at potatoes is a human invention, for if man wished to cultivate parasites rather than potatoes (or corn) there would be no "blight.". . . Outside the significance that man voluntarily attaches to certain conditions, there are no illnesses or diseases in nature. . . . Out of his anthropocentric self-interest, man has chosen to consider as "illnesses" or "diseases" those natural circumstances which precipitate the death (or the failure to function according to certain values) of a limited number of biological species: man himself, his pets and other cherished livestock. . . . The medical enterprise is from its inception value-loaded; it is not simply applied biology, but a biology applied in accordance with the dictates of social interest. (Sedgwick 1973, pp. 30–31)

Medicine (and society) can live with this value judgment, but it is substantially more difficult to assess optimal psychosocial functioning and particularly dysfunction at a clinically significant level warranting a psychiatric diagnosis than it is to determine optimal physical functioning (although the threshold for labeling a person physically handicapped can also be controversial). Value judgments tend to be more controversial and problematic in psychological than in physical disorders. For example, a society in which more power and authority is possessed by the male sex might be prone to impose masculine biases on the judgment of what is desirable, optimal, or healthy (Kaplan 1983*a,b*). Femininity (and females) may be inappropriately associated with a greater degree of psychopathology. Psychiatry can also be used for political repression, if it is assumed that simple opposition to social norms is a sufficient basis for diagnosing mental disorders (Spitzer and Endicott 1978). The alleged abuses of psychiatry in the Soviet Union are a case in point (Bloch 1981). The recognition of the potential costs of misdiagnosis contributed to DSM-III-R decisions to make the criteria for the diagnosis of schizophrenia more restrictive (Spitzer, Andreasen, and Endicott 1978) and to place late luteal phase dysphoric disorder and self-defeating personality disorder in an appendix as proposed diagnoses that are in need of further research (APA 1987).

Clinical Implications

Clinicians rarely concern themselves with defining what is meant by a mental, medical, or physical disorder (Kendell 1975). They are often too busy treating their patients to engage in what would appear to be a useless academic exercise. This neglect may not be problematic for physicians much of the time. People usually do not seek medical care inappropriately, and when they do it is often apparent to the physician (although other factors, such as economics, often determine who seeks treatment, when, and/or for what problems). Guze's (1978) pragmatic definition of a mental disorder as anything the public considers to be the responsibility of a physician is useful and appropriate in this practical respect. The disorders needing diagnostic criteria and treatment are the ones for which people are seeking treatment.

However, at times a more critical self-reflection is important. Clinicians rarely turn away prospective patients, and in some instances the nature of the complaint should be reviewed and the assumptions of the possible treatment reconsidered. For example, a male adolescent who today felt concerned about masturbation would more likely be treated for his anxiety and shame than for his masturbation, but in the not-so-distant past masturbation could very likely have been considered a disorder (Engelhardt 1974). Freud (1971) himself once commented that "it is the prolonged and intense action of this pernicious sexual satisfaction which is enough on its own account to provoke a neurasthenic neurosis" (p. 150). Engelhardt (1974) provides other examples, such as the disease of drapetomania that would provoke slaves to try to escape from their masters.

Professional Implications

A definition of mental disorder has implications for professional responsibilities to the extent that it suggests that one or another particular profession is more qualified than others to identify or treat the disorder. One of the most heated controversies during the construction of DSM-III was the proposal to include a definition specifying that mental disorders are a subset of medical disorders (Spitzer and Endicott 1978). The definition was proposed to refute Szasz's argument (1961) that mental illness is a myth and has nothing to do with medicine (Spitzer 1985), and it was intended to indicate how the problems mental health professionals address are appropriately conceptualized as medical disorders and not simply "problems in living." However, by indicating the appropriateness of the medical model, the proposal also served to "delineate the areas of responsibility of the medical system from those of other societal systems which also have as their purpose improving or otherwise changing human functioning" (Spitzer and Endicott 1978, p. 17). Appropriateness of a medical model suggested priority of the medical profession (Moore 1978). Schacht and Nathan (1977), members of the American Psychological Association's liaison committee to the DSM-III, suggested that insurors and legislators might interpret the proposed definition as providing quasi-official recognition of the primacy of physicians in the diagnosis and treatment of the disorders identified in DSM-III.

> Since these disorders are inclusive of virtually every psychological ill to which men and women are heir, little will be left for psychologists and other mental health professionals to work with. Even less will be left if legislators and third-party payers conclude that, since these conditions are all "medical disorders," they must first be evaluated by physicians, who will then decide whether they or ancillary mental health professionals (e.g., the psychologists) will treat the disorder. (1977, p. 1024)

Some have suggested that the concern was a tempest in a teapot (Millon 1983). Spitzer and Endicott (1978) indicated that "the listing of a condition as a mental disorder for us says nothing about whether it can also be appropriately conceptualized as a psychological disorder, or which profession can best study or treat it" (p. 36). However, they also acknowledged that "there is pressure for the medical profession, and psychiatry in particular, to define its area of prime responsibility" (p. 37). The definition of mental disorders as a subset of medical disorders would likely have the effect of assigning primary authority to the medical profession, no matter the original intent (Schacht 1985). The offending phrase was therefore not included in the final draft of the DSM-III because of its potential for fanning the fires of interprofessional rivalry (Spitzer 1985; Spitzer and Williams 1982).

Spitzer and Endicott (1978), however, also indicated that for a condition to be considered a mental disorder, "simple informative or standard educational procedures" and "nontechnical interventions" cannot bring about a reversal of the condition (p. 27, table 2). Mental disorders require the "specialized knowledge or training" of a mental health professional (p. 28). "The distinction between a nontechnical and a technical intervention here depends on whether or not some specialized knowledge or training with regard to biological functioning is required, other than that which is part of the general knowledge of all informed members of society" (p. 28). The inclusion of a need for professional intervention within the criteria for mental disorder is to some degree tautological and reminiscent of possibly self-serving definitions of mental disorder as anything seen by a mental health professional (Blashfield 1984; Kendell 1975, 1986). It suggests that mental health professionals are the only persons capable of treating mental disorders. While this may be true in some cases, it is not always true, and it may confuse professional boundary issues with the conceptual distinction between abnormality and normality. Some physical disorders are not treated by physicians and some need little to no treatment. A flu and a common cold are no less of a physical (medical) disorder because they can be successfully treated without professional interventions. They are less severe than most of the disorders treated by physicians, but they are still disorders. Disorders do not cease to be disorders when their cures are public knowledge and are easily treated.

MENTAL AND PHYSICAL DISORDERS

One of the more problematic definitional issues is the use of the term *mental* to refer to the disorders classified in the DSM, which implies that there is a distinction between physical disorders and mental disorders. In fact, there is a separate axis in DSM-III-R for the placement of "physical" disorders (Axis III) and a separate section for "organic mental" syndromes and disorders (APA 1987). Historically, there has also been a tendency for disorders to leave psychiatry for another branch of medicine (typically neurology) when a specific biogenetic or neurochemical etiology and/or treatment are determined. The implication that mental disorders do not have a biogenetic etiology is clearly inconsistent with current models of psychopathology.

Much of this problem reflects a perpetuation of an archaic mind-body dualism. Cognition, affect, and motoric functioning are ultimately expressions of the nervous system. Psychosocial events affect neurochemical functioning, and alterations in neurochemistry affect psychosocial functioning. The distinction between mind and body is not particularly meaningful, and it contributes to illusory and misleadingly reductionistic differentiations (for example, functional versus organic disorders).

Mental disorders typically have a multifactorial etiology, and comprehensive models of etiology and pathology consider an interaction of biological, psychological, and social (marital/familial) factors. The relative importance of each domain varies across disorders and across patients within disorders. "Mental" disorder is an unusually poor term to describe these biopsychosocial conditions, but we have not been able to think of a better one.

Boundary Conditions

The absence of a set of infallible criteria, the arbitrariness of a categorical distinction between normality and abnormality, and the influence of subjectivity (values and biases) in the assessment of mental health and disorder result in a number of controversial boundary conditions. The decision regarding whether a problem represents a mental disorder and whether it warrants professional interventions in many cases requires additional research and assessment of cultural and professional values. We illustrate some of the problems and issues with a discussion of caffeine dependence, late luteal phase dysphoric disorder, and two of the personality disorders (histrionic and dependent).

Caffeine Dependence

Nicotine (tobacco) dependence and caffeine intoxication were recognized for the first time as mental disorders in DSM-III (APA 1980). They were not given formal recognition earlier in part due to a lack of recognition of their presence (for example, caffeinism was confused with anxiety disorders) and to a social acceptance of their presence. If a significant proportion of a society engages in a maladaptive behavior pattern, there is a tendency to miss or to ignore its maladaptivity.

Caffeine dependence has not yet been considered a mental disorder because the public is not sufficiently distressed by this dependence. In contrast, nicotine dependence is classified as a mental disorder because the public is now sufficiently aware of the negative consequences of smoking and is sufficiently disapproving of smoking. Although caffeine dependence is less disabling and disadvantageous than nicotine dependence, it is still disabling and disadvantageous, to a degree only arbitrarily less than nicotine dependence.

Late Luteal Phase Dysphoric Disorder

Many women report at least mild emotional changes associated with specific phases of the menstrual cycle, including affective lability; feelings of irritablity, anger, tension, depression; and/or self-deprecating thoughts. These emotional changes might temporarily interfere with work, social activities, and/or relationships (Rubinow and Roy-Byrne 1984). Whether to give formal recognition in DSM-IV to a menstrual cycle–related disorder is quite controversial due to the social repercussions that might accompany such a designation. There is clearly the potential for categorical stereotyping, exaggerating the diagnosis to the point of suggesting that many females are sick or unreliable. The level of distress and impairment that does occur is minimal in most women who express distress and would not warrant professional intervention. The criteria presented in the appendix to DSM-III-R required "serious" interference with social or occupational functioning, but "serious" was not explicitly defined and is certainly subject to various interpretations. The potential for biases with respect to what constitutes a "serious" impairment is evident.

Histrionic and Dependent Personality Disorders

Organismic dysfunction can be expressed in a person's overall personality style. Personality disorders are to a large extent maladaptive (exaggerated, inflexible, narrow, or rigid) variations of common personality traits.[4] As such, it is to be expected that females will be more susceptible to disorders that involve exaggerations or extreme variants of stereotypic feminine traits (for example, the histrionic and dependent personality disorders) and males will be more susceptible to disorders that involve exaggerations or extreme variants of stereotypic masculine traits (for example, the antisocial and obsessive-compulsive personality disorders) (Widiger and Frances 1985*a;* Williams and Spitzer 1983). While these traits may be due in part to inequitable sex-role socialization (Carmen, Russo, and Miller 1981; Chesler 1972), that factor is relevant primarily to the etiology for the maladaptive behavior pattern rather than for the validity of its diagnosis (Williams and Spitzer 1983). Social-cultural factors contribute to the development of a variety of mental disorders (for example, psychosexual dysfunctions and psychophysiological disorders). Personality disorders are not alone in this influence.

Nevertheless, the diagnostic criteria for disorders that occur in one sex more than another are susceptible to sex biases.[5] The concept of a mental disorder is inherently evaluative (Moore 1975), and a society or a profession that values the traits stereotypic of one sex more than those of the other may possess a lower threshold for diagnosing a disorder in one sex than the other. For example, at what point emotionality becomes exaggerated (histrionic), devotion becomes dependency (dependent), and cooperation becomes sacrificial (self-defeating) is not explicit, and there is

[4]See APA 1987; Frances 1980; Millon 1981; and Widiger and Frances 1985*b*.
[5]See Caplan 1987; Chodoff 1982; Kaplan 1983*a;* Simons 1987; and Walker 1987.

considerable room for biases to influence the judgment. Biases with respect to the relative value of femininity versus masculinity can affect the threshold for determining impairment in social and occupational functioning. Stereotypically masculine traits have been associated with higher ratings of social desirability than stereotypically feminine traits, but it is not clear whether this association reflects the relative value of instrumental (masculine) versus expressive (feminine) traits to adaptive functioning or a masculine bias with respect to expressive (feminine) traits.[6] Kaplan (1983*a*) went so far as to suggest that "a healthy woman automatically earns the diagnosis of Histrionic Personality Disorder" (p. 789). Systematic epidemiological studies have not yet been conducted, but it is likely that the criteria for the DSM-III-R histrionic (and dependent) personality disorders are sufficiently restrictive as to result in a low prevalence in normal community samples and few (false positive) misdiagnoses. A more serious concern is whether the criteria for disorders that occur more often in women are less restrictive than the criteria for disorders that occur more often in men. Kaplan (1983*a*) suggested, for example, that the personality disorders that involve maladaptive variants of stereotypically masculine behavior (for example, antisocial and obsessive-compulsive personality disorders) include additional, sex-neutral features of psychopathology (such as perfectionism and indecisiveness) that raise the threshold for diagnosis.

Sex bias in diagnosis is difficult to assess (Widiger and Settle 1987). Differential sex prevalence in any particular disorder is inconclusive because some disorders do occur more often in one sex group than another (Kass, Spitzer, and Williams 1983; Wakefield 1987; Williams and Spitzer 1983). Differential sex prevalence across all of the disorders or all of the personality disorders may also be inconclusive because an increased prevalence of females may reflect their increased willingness to acknowledge symptomatology (Phillips and Segal 1969) or a bias in the clinicians making the diagnoses rather than in the criteria themselves (Ford and Widiger, in press). It might be more informative to determine whether the criteria and cutoff points used in DSM-III-R tend to underdiagnose psychopathology in males and overdiagnose psychopathology in females. Do "normal" males who fail to meet enough of the criteria for antisocial or obsessive-compulsive personality disorders to obtain a diagnosis display more impairment in functioning than "normal" females who meet a comparable number of items for the histrionic or dependent personality dis-

[6]See Locksley and Colten 1979; McCrae and Costa 1983; Nicholls, Licht, and Pearl 1982; and Spence 1984.

orders? If so, the criteria for the former disorders might be more restrictive than the criteria for the latter ones.

Conclusions

The concepts of mental disorder and normality are difficult and perhaps even in some ways impossible to define clearly and infallibly. Attempts at a consistent definition have been made throughout the history of medicine with only limited success. The failure of any operational definition and the lack of clear boundaries between normality and disorder belie any attempt to arrive at a conclusive and infallible definition. The definitions that are proposed and the boundary between normality and disorder shift with increasing knowledge, across time, and across cultures. Multiaxial and longitudinal research is needed to identify the interactive conditions under which behavior becomes maladaptive and the functional relationship among stress, personality, and disorder. There is no one best way to define disorders, and different definitions may be based on different perspectives (etiology, pathogenesis, physiology, psychology, and so on). Different definitions may have very different theoretical, scientific, clinical, public health, forensic, social, and professional implications. Thus what is required is a practical, flexible, and probabilistic definition of mental disorder that recognizes its own necessary imprecision and takes into account the numerous and substantial implications of whatever definition is used.

REFERENCES

Allred, K. D., and Smith, T. W. 1989. "The Hardy Personality: Cognitive and Physiological Responses to Evaluative Threat." *Journal of Personality and Social Psychology* 56:257–266.

American Psychiatric Association. 1980. *Diagnostic and Statistical Manual of Mental Disorders,* 3rd ed. Washington, D.C.: APA.

———. 1987. *Diagnostic and Statistical Manual of Mental Disorders,* 3rd ed., rev. Washington, D.C.: APA.

Ausubel, D. 1961. "Personality Disorder Is Disease." *American Psychologist* 16:69–74.

Barton, W. 1959. "Viewpoint of a Clinician." In *Current Concepts of Positive Mental Health,* ed. M. Jahoda. New York: Basic Books.

Beckham, E. E., and Leber, W., eds. 1985. *Handbook of Depression.* Homewood, IL: Dorsey.

Blaney, P. 1975. "Implications of the Medical Model and Its Alternatives." *American Journal of Psychiatry* 132:911–914.

Blashfield, R. K. 1984. *The Classification of Psychopathology.* New York: Plenum Press.

———. 1986. "Structural Approaches to Classification." In *Contemporary Directions in Psychopathology,* ed. T. Millon and G. Klerman, pp. 363–380. New York: Guilford Press.

Bloch S. 1981. "The Political Misuse of Psychiatry in the Soviet Union." In *Psychiatric Ethics,* ed. S. Block and P. Chodoff. New York: Oxford University Press.

Broverman, I.; Broverman, D.; Clarkson, F.; Rosenkrantz, P.; and Vogel, S. 1970. "Sex-role Stereotypes and Clinical Judgments of Mental Health." *Journal of Consulting and Clinical Psychology* 34:1–7.

Cannon, W. 1932. *The Wisdom of the Body.* New York: W. W. Norton.

Cantor, N., and Genero, N. 1986. "Psychiatric Diagnosis and Natural Categorization: A Close Analogy." In *Contemporary Directions in Psychopathology. Toward the DSM-IV,* ed. T. Millon and G. Klerman, pp. 233–256. New York: Guilford Press.

Caplan, A. L.; Engelhardt, H. T.; and McCartney, J. J., eds. 1981. *Concepts of Health and Disease. Interdisciplinary Perspectives.* Reading, MA: Addison-Wesley.

Caplan, P. J. 1987. "The Psychiatric Association's Failure to Meet Its Own Standards: The Dangers of Self-defeating Personality Disorder as a Category." *Journal of Personality Disorders* 1:178–182.

Carmen, E. H.; Russo, N. F.; and Miller, J. B. 1981. "Inequality and Women's Mental Health: An Overview." *American Journal of Psychiatry* 138:1319–1330.

Carver, C. S.; Scheier, M. F.; and Weintraub, J. K. 1989. "Assessing Coping Strategies: A Theoretically Based Approach." *Journal of Personality and Social Psychology* 56:267–283.

Cavenar, J., and Walker, J. I. 1983. "Normality." In *Signs and Symptoms in Psychiatry,* ed. J. Cavenar and H. Brodie, pp. 19–36. Philadelphia: J.B. Lippincott.

Chesler, P. 1972. *Women and Madness.* New York: Doubleday.

Chodoff, P. 1982. "Hysteria and Women." *American Journal of Psychiatry* 139:545–551.

Cloninger, C. 1987. "A Systematic Method for Clinical Description and Classification of Personality Variants." *Archives of General Psychiatry* 44:573–588.

Cloninger, C.; Martin, R. L.; Guze, S. B.; and Clayton, P. J. 1985. "Diagnosis and Prognosis in Schizophrenia." *Archives of General Psychiatry* 42:15–25.

Ellis, A. 1987. "The Impossibility of Achieving Consistently Good Mental Health." *American Psychologist* 42:364–375.

Engel, G. 1960. "A Unified Concept of Health and Disease." *Perspectives in Biological Medicine* 3:459–485.

———. 1980. "The Clinical Application of the Biopsychosocial Model." *American Journal of Psychiatry* 137:535–544.

Engelhardt, H. T. 1974. "The Disease of Masturbation: Values and the Concept of Disease." *Bulletin of the History of Medicine* 48:234–248.

Feigl, H. 1956. "Philosophical Embarrassments of Psychology." *American Psychologist* 14:115–128.

Fenichel, O. 1945. *The Psychoanalytic Theory of Neurosis.* New York: W. W. Norton.

Finn, S. 1982. "Base Rates, Utilities, and DSM-III: Shortcomings of Fixed-rule Systems of Psychodiagnosis." *Journal of Abnormal Psychology* 91:294–302.

Ford, M., and Widiger, T. (In press). "Sex Bias in the Diagnosis of Histrionic and Antisocial Personality Disorders." *Journal of Consulting and Clinical Psychology.*

Frances, A. 1980. "The DSM-III Personality Disorders. A Commentary." *American Journal of Psychiatry* 137:1050–1054.

———. 1982. "Categorical and Dimensional Systems of Personality Diagnosis: A Comparison." *Comprehensive Psychiatry* 23:516–527.

Frances, A., and Cooper, A. 1981. "Descriptive and Dynamic Psychiatry: A Perspective on DSM-III." *American Journal of Psychiatry* 138: 1198–1202.

Frances, A., and Widiger, T. A. 1986. "The Classification of Personality Disorders: An Overview of Problems and Solutions." In *Psychiatry Update: American Psychiatric Association Annual Review,* ed. A. Frances and R. Hales, vol. 5, pp. 240–257. Washington, D.C.: American Psychiatric Press.

Freud, S. [1901]1961. "Psychopathology of Everyday Life." In *The Standard Edition of the Complete Psychological Works of Sigmund Freud (hereafter Standard Edition),* ed. J. Strachey, vol. 6. London: Hogarth Press.

———. [1937]1963. "Analysis Terminable and Interminable." In *Therapy and Technique,* ed. P. Rieff, pp. 233–271. New York: Collier.

———. 1971*a.* "Heredity and the Aetiology of the Neuroses." In *Standard Edition,* vol. 3. London: Hogarth Press.

———. 1971*b.* "Introductory Lectures on Psychoanalysis." In *Standard Edition,* vol. 15. London: Hogarth Press.

Galen. 1952. "On the Natural Faculties," trans. A. Brock. In *Great Books of the Western World,* ed. R. M. Hutchins, vol. 10, pp. 167–215. Chicago: Encyclopaedia Britannica.

Gangestad, S., and Snyder, M. 1985. " 'To Carve Nature at Its Joints': On the Existence of Discrete Classes in Personality." *Psychological Review* 92:317–349.

Gorenstein, E. E. 1984. "Debating Mental Illness." *American Psychologist* 39:50–56.

Gove, W. R. 1982. "The Current Status of the Labelling Theory of Mental Illness." In *Deviance and Mental Illness,* ed. W. R. Gove. Beverly Hills, CA: Sage.

Griesinger, W. [1867]1965. *Mental Pathology and Therapeutics.* New York: Hafner Publishing Co.

Guze, S. B. 1978. "Nature of Psychiatric Illness: Why Psychiatry Is a Branch of Medicine." *Comprehensive Psychiatry* 19:295–307.

Guze, S. B., and Helzer, J. E. 1987. "The Medical Model and Psychiatric Disorders." In *Psychiatry,* ed. R. Michels and J. Cavenar, vol. 1. Philadelphia: J. B. Lippincott.

Hare-Mustin, R. T. 1983. "An Appraisal of the Relationship Between Women and Psychotherapy." *American Psychologist* 38:593–601.

Hart, H. L. A. 1968. *Punishment and Responsibility.* Oxford: Clarendon Press.

Hempel, C. [1959]1961. "Introduction to Problems of Taxonomy." In *Field Studies in the Mental Disorders,* ed. J. Zubin, pp. 3–22. New York: Grune & Stratton.

Hempel, C. [1954]1965. *A Logical Appraisal of Operationism. Aspects of Scientific Explanation and Other Essays in the Philosophy of Science.* New York: Free Press.

Hippocrates. 1983. "The Nature of Man," trans. J. Chadwick and W. Mann. In *Hippocratic Writings,* ed. G. Lloyd. New York: Penguin.

Howard G. S., and Conway, C. G. 1986. "Can There Be an Empirical Science of Volitional Action?" *American Psychologist* 41:1241–1251.

Insanity Defense Work Group. 1983. "American Psychiatric Association Statement on the Insanity Defense." *American Journal of Psychiatry* 140:681–688.

Jahoda, M. 1958. *Current Concepts of Positive Mental Health.* New York: Basic Books.

Jones, E. 1942. "The Concept of a Normal Mind." *International Journal of Psycho-analysis* 23:1–8.

Kaplan, M. 1983*a.* "A Woman's View of DSM-III." *American Psychologist* 38:786–792.

———. 1983*b.* "The Issue of Sex Bias in DSM-III. Comments on the Articles of Spitzer, Williams, and Kass." *American Psychologist* 38:802–803.

Kass, F.; Spitzer, R. L.; and Williams, J. B. W. 1983. "An Empirical Study of the Issue of Sex Bias in the Diagnostic Criteria of DSM-III Axis II Personality Disorders." *American Psychologist* 38:799–801.

Kendell, R. E. 1975. *The Role of Diagnosis in Psychiatry.* Oxford: Blackwell Scientific Publications.

———. 1982. "The Choice of Diagnostic Criteria for Biological Research." *Archives of General Psychiatry* 39:1334–1339.

———. 1983. "DSM-III: A Major Advance in Psychiatric Nosology." In *International Perspectives on DSM-III,* ed. R. L. Spitzer, J. B. W. Williams, and A. E. Skodol, pp. 55–68. Washington, D.C.: American Psychiatric Press.

———. 1986. "What Are Mental Disorders?" In *Issues in Psychiatric Classification,* ed. A. M. Freedman, R. Brotman, I. Silverman, and D. Hutson, pp. 23–58. New York: Human Sciences Press.

Kety, S. 1974. "From Rationalization to Reason." *American Journal of Psychiatry* 131:-957–963.

Kiesler, D. 1986. "The 1982 Interpersonal Circle: An Analysis of DSM-III Personality Disorders." In *Contemporary Issues in Psychopathology,* ed. T. Millon and G. Klerman, pp. 571–597. New York: Guilford Press.

Klein, D. F. 1978. "A Proposed Definition of Mental Illness." In *Critical Issues in Psychiatric Diagnosis,* ed. R. L. Spitzer and D. F. Klein, pp. 41–71. New York: Raven Press.

Klerman, G. L. 1986. "Historical Perspectives on Contemporary Schools of Psychopathology." In *Contemporary Directions in Psychopathology. Toward the DSM-IV,* ed. T. Millon and G. Klerman, pp. 3–28. New York: Guilford Press.

Kobasa, S. C. 1982. "The Hardy Personality: Toward a Social Psychology of Stress and Health." In *Social Psychology of Health and Illness,* ed. G. Sanders and J. Suls, pp. 3–32. Hillsdale, NJ: Lawrence Erlbaum.

Kraepelin, E. 1917. *Lectures on Clinical Psychiatry,* 3rd ed. New York: William Wood and Co.

Lazarus, R. S., and Folkman, S. 1984. *Stress, Appraisal, and Coping.* New York: Springer.

Leahey, T. H. 1980. "The Myth of Operationism." *Journal of Mind and Behavior* 1:127–143.

Liefer, R. 1964. "The Psychiatrist and Tests of Criminal Responsibility." *American Psychologist* 19:825–830.

Locksley, A., and Colten, M. 1979. "Psychological Androgyny: A Case for Mistaken Identity?" *Journal of Personality and Social Psychology* 37:1017–1031.

Maslow, A., and Mittelmann, B. 1951. "The Meaning of 'Health' ('Normal') and of 'Sick' ('Abnormal')." In *Principles of Abnormal Psychology: The Dynamics of Psychic Illness,* pp. 12–21. New York: Harper.

McCrae, R. R., and Costa, P. T. 1983. "Social Desirability Scales: More Substances than Style." *Journal of Consulting and Clinical Psychology* 51:882–888.

Meehl, P. E. 1977. "Specific Etiology and Other Forms of Strong Influence: Some Quantitative Meanings." *Journal of Medicine and Philosophy* 2:33–53.

———. 1986. "Diagnostic Taxa as Open Concepts: Metatheoretical and Statistical Questions About Reliability and Construct Validity in the Grand Strategy of Nosological Revision." In *Contemporary Directions in Psychopathology. Toward the DSM-IV,* ed. T. Millon and G. Klerman, pp. 215–231. New York: Guilford Press.

Meehl, P. E., and Golden, R. R. 1982. "Taxometric Methods." In *Handbook of Research Methods in Clinical Psychology,* ed. P. Kendall and J. Butcher, pp. 127–181. New York: John Wiley.

Menninger, K. 1942. *The Human Mind,* 2nd ed. New York: Alfred A. Knopf.

———. 1963. *The Vital Balance: The Life Process in Mental Health and Illness.* New York: Viking Press.

Meyer, A. [1908]1948. "Substitutive Activity and Reaction-Types." In *The Commonsense Psychiatry of Dr. Adolf Meyer,* ed. A. Lief, pp. 193–206. New York: McGraw-Hill.

Mezzich, J. 1979. "Patterns and Issues in Multiaxial Psychiatric Diagnosis." *Psychological Medicine* 9:125–137.

Millon, T. 1981. *Disorders of Personality. DSM-III: Axis II.* New York: John Wiley.

———. 1983. "The DSM-III. An Insider's Perspective." *American Psychologist* 38:804–814.

Mirsky, A., and Duncan, C. 1986. "Etiology and Expression of Schizophrenia: Neurobiological and Psychosocial Factors." *Annual Review of Psychology* 37:291–319.

Moore, M. S. 1975. "Some Myths About 'Mental Illness.' " *Archives of General Psychiatry* 32:1483–1497.

———. 1978. "Discussion of the Spitzer-Endicott and Klein Proposed Definitions of Mental Disorder (Illness)." In *Critical Issues in Psychiatric Diagnosis,* ed. R. Spitzer and D. Klein, pp. 85–104. New York: Raven Press.

Morey, L., and McNamara, T. 1987. "On Definitions, Diagnosis, and DSM-III." *Journal of Abnormal Psychology* 96:283–285.

Nicholls, J.; Licht, B.; and Pearl, R. 1982. "Some Dangers of Using Personality Questionnaires to Study Personality." *Psychological Bulletin* 92:572–580.

Offer, D., and Sabshin, M. 1966. *Normality. Theoretical and Clinical Concepts of Mental Health.* New York: Basic Books.

Parsons, T. [1958]1981. "Definitions of Health and Illness in the Light of American Values and Social Structures. In *Concepts of Health and Disease, Interdisciplinary Perspectives,* ed. A. Caplan, H. Engelhardt, and J. McCartney, pp. 57–82. Reading, MA: Addison-Wesley.

Phillips, D., and Segal, B. E. 1969. "Sexual Status and Psychiatric Symptoms." *American Sociological Review* 34:58–72.

Redlich, F. C. 1981. "The Concept of Health in Psychiatry." In *Concepts of Health and Disease. Interdisciplinary Perspectives,* ed. A. L. Caplan, H. T. Engelhardt, and J. J. McCartney, pp. 373–389. Reading, MA: Addison-Wesley.

Robins, E., and Guze, S. 1970. "Establishment of Diagnostic Validity in Psychiatric Illness: Its Application to Schizophrenia." *American Journal of Psychiatry* 126:983–987.

Rogers, C. 1959. "A Theory of Therapy, Personality and Interpersonal Relationships, as Developed in Client-centered Framework." In *Psychology: A Study of a Science,* ed. S. Koch, vol. 3. New York: McGraw-Hill.

Romano, J. 1950. "Basic Orientation and Education of the Medical Student." *Journal of the American Medical Association* 143:409.

Rorer, L. G., and Widiger, T. A. 1983. "Personality Structure and Assessment." *Annual Review of Psychology* 34:431–463.

Roth, M., and Kroll, M. 1986. *The Reality of Mental Illness.* New York: Cambridge University Press.

Rubinow, D. R., and Roy-Byrne, P. 1984. "Premenstrual Syndromes: Overview from a Methodologic Perspective." *American Journal of Psychiatry* 141:163–172.

Sabshin, M. August 1988. "Normality and the Boundaries of Psychopathology." Paper presented at the First International Congress on the Disorders of Personality, Copenhagen, Denmark.

Scadding, J. G. 1967. "Diagnosis: The Clinician and the Computer." *Lancet* 2:877–882.

Schacht, T. E. 1985. "DSM-III and the Politics of Truth." *American Psychologist* 40:-513–521.

Schacht, T. E., and Nathan, P. E. 1977. "But Is It Good for the Psychologists? Appraisal and Status of DSM-III." *American Psychologist* 32:1017–1025.

Schneider, K. 1950. "Systematic Psychiatry." *American Journal of Psychiatry* 107:334–335.

Sedgwick, P. 1973. "Illness—Mental and Otherwise." *Hastings Center Report* 3:19–58.

Shoben, E. J. 1957. "Toward a Concept of the Normal Personality." *American Psychologist* 12:183–189.

Simons, R. C. 1987. "Self-defeating and Sadistic Personality Disorders: Needed

Additions to the Diagnostic Nomenclature." *Journal of Personality Disorders* 1:161–167.

Spence, J. 1984. "Masculinity, Femininity, and Gender-related Traits: A Conceptual Analysis and Critique of Current Research." In *Progress in Experimental Personality Research,* ed. B. Maher and W. Maher, pp. 1–97. New York: Academic Press.

Spitzer, R. L. 1981. "The Diagnostic Status of Homosexuality in DSM-III: A Reformulation of the Issues." *American Journal of Psychiatry* 138:210–215.

———. 1985. "DSM-III and the Politics-Science Dichotomy Syndrome. A Response to Thomas E. Schacht's 'DSM-III and the politics of truth.'" *American Psychologist* 40:522–526.

Spitzer, R. L., and Endicott, J. 1978. "Medical and Mental Disorder: Proposed Definition and Criteria." In *Critical Issues in Psychiatric Diagnosis,* ed. R. L. Spitzer and D. F. Klein, pp. 15–39. New York: Raven Press.

Spitzer, R. L., and Williams, J. B. W. 1982. "The Definition and Diagnosis of Mental Disorder." In *Deviance and Mental Illness,* ed. W. R. Gove, pp. 15–31. Beverly Hills, CA: Sage.

———. 1985. "Classification in Psychiatry." In *Comprehensive Textbook of Psychiatry,* 4th ed., ed. H. Kaplan and B. Sadock, vol. 1, pp. 591–613. Baltimore: Williams & Wilkins.

Spitzer, R. L.; Andreasen, N.; and Endicott, J. 1978. "Schizophrenia and Other Psychotic Disorders in DSM-III." *Schizophrenia Bulletin* 4:489–509.

Spitzer, R. L.; Williams, J. B. W.; and Skodol, A. 1980. "DSM-III: The major achievements and an overview." *American Journal of Psychiatry* 137:151–164.

Strauss, S. 1975. "A Comprehensive Approach to Psychiatric Diagnosis." *American Journal of Psychiatry* 132:1193–1197.

Sydenham, T. [1676]1922. "Medical Observations." In *Selected Works of Thomas Sydenham, M.D.,* ed. J. D. Comrie. New York: William Wood & Co.

Szasz, T. S. 1960. "The Myth of Mental Illness." *American Psychologist* 15:113–118.

———. 1961. *The Myth of Mental Illness: Foundations of a Theory of Personal Conduct.* New York: Hoeber-Harper.

———. 1981. "The Concept of Mental Illness: Explanation or Justification?" In *Concepts of Health and Disease. Interdisciplinary Perspectives,* ed. A. L. Caplan, H. T. Engelhardt, and J. J. McCartney, pp. 459–473. Reading, MA: Addison-Wesley.

———. 1987. *Insanity. The Idea and Its Consequences.* New York: John Wiley.

Taylor S. E., and Brown, J. D. 1988. "Illusion and Well-being: A Social Psychological Perspective on Mental Health." *Psychological Bulletin* 103:193–210.

Temkin, O. 1963. "The Scientific Approach to Disease: Specific Entity and Individual Sickness." In *Scientific Change: Historical Studies in the Intellectual, Social and Technical Conditions for Scientific Discovery and Technical Invention from Antiquity to the Present,* ed. A. Crombie, pp. 629–647. New York: Basic Books.

Tuma, A. H., and Maser, J., eds. 1985. *Anxiety and the Anxiety Disorders.* Hillsdale, NJ: Lawrence Erlbaum.

Virchow, R. [1847]1981. "Concerning Standpoints in Scientific Medicine." In *Con-*

cepts of Health and Disease. Interdisciplinary Perspectives, ed. A. Caplan, H. Engelhardt, and J. McCartney, pp. 187–196. Reading, MA: Addison-Wesley.

Wakefield, J. C. 1987. "Sex Bias in the Diagnosis of Primary Orgasmic Dysfunction." *American Psychologist* 42:464–471.

Walker, L. E. A. 1987. "Inadequacies of the Masochistic Personality Disorder Diagnosis for Women." *Journal of Personality Disorders* 1:183–189.

Widiger, T. A., and Frances, A. J. 1985*a.* "Axis II Personality Disorders: Diagnostic and Treatment Issues." *Hospital and Community Psychiatry* 36:619–627.

———. 1985*b.* "The DSM-III Personality Disorders. Perspectives from Psychology." *Archives of General Psychiatry* 42:615–623.

———. 1987. "Definitions and Diagnoses: A Brief Response to Morey and McNamara." *Journal of Abnormal Psychology* 96:286–287.

Widiger, T. A., and Kelso, K. 1983. "Psychodiagnosis of Axis II." *Clinical Psychology Review* 3:491–510.

Widiger, T. A., and Settle, S. 1987. "Broverman et al. Revisited: An Artifactual Sex Bias." *Journal of Personality and Social Psychology* 53:463–469.

Widiger, T. A., and Trull, T. 1985. "The Empty Debate over the Existence of Mental Illness: Comments on Gorenstein." *American Psychologist* 40:468–470.

Wiggins, J. 1979. "A Psychological Taxonomy of Trait-descriptive Terms: The Interpersonal Domain." *Journal of Personality and Social Psychology* 37:395–412.

———. 1982. "Circumplex Models of Interpersonal Behavior in Clinical Psychology." In *Handbook of Research Methods in Clinical Psychology,* ed. P. Kendall and J. Butcher, pp. 183–221. New York: John Wiley.

Williams, J. B. W. 1985*a.* "The Multiaxial System of DSM-III: Where Did It Come From and Where Should It Go? I: Its Origins and Critiques." *Archives of General Psychiatry* 42:175–180.

———. 1985*b.* "The Multiaxial System of DSM-III: Where Did It Come From and Where Should It Go? II: Empirical Studies, Innovations, and Recommendations." *Archives of General Psychiatry* 42:181–186.

Williams, J. B. W., and Spitzer, R. L. 1983. "The Issue of Sex Bias in DSM-III. A Critique of 'A Woman's View of DSM-III' by Marcie Kaplan." *American Psychologist* 38:793–798.

Wing, J. K. 1978. *Reasoning About Madness.* New York: Oxford University Press.

Zilboor, G., and Henry, G. 1941. *A History of Medical Psychology.* New York: W. W. Norton.

CHAPTER 2

Psychotherapy: Medical Intervention and the Concept of Normality

Robert J. Ursano and
Carol S. Fullerton

The concept of normality is plagued with multiple definitions—depending on who is speaking and what sociocultural group(s) they represent. Of course this reflects the fact that normality is inevitably a value-oriented concept defined by the norms and values held by a particular group. To call some behaviors "normal" and others "abnormal" is a value judgment. Value judgments are a necessary and unavoidable part of the diagnosis and treatment of mental illness. Even if it was desirable, they cannot be eliminated. Treating clinicians hold in mind a picture of what health would be for a particular patient, and treatment is never pursued without a picture of where the boundary of "normal" is for him or her. Frequently we disguise this process by speaking of the "maximum treatment benefit." Such value judgments are attributes of both the individual and the culture in which one was raised and in which one lives. They should not be viewed as obstacles but rather as a part of the study of normality (Grinker 1967).

If the concept of normality is to have any usefulness in medical practice, it should include the "normality" of disease and death in life. Much of the rest of the world does not share the "delusion" of health that has developed in the American population. When an American prisoner of war held in Vietnam was preparing to return to the United States, he voiced concern to his guards about his health after passing several tapeworms in his stool.

The guard replied, "Oh, no, those are supposed to be there. They keep you from getting fat." Disease and illness, like health, are a part of the human condition and of the "normal."

Normality—mental health—is in many ways far more complex than pathology (Hartman 1939). Mental health is recognized by an individual's ability to identify and flexibly use multiple choices of action. The individual's ability to subordinate desires and "tendencies" is the difference between health and neurotic behavior (Hartman 1958), the ability to pursue a goal flexibly and temporarily or permanently give up certain desires for the overall goal (see p. 124). Pathology, in contrast, is a constriction of behaviors, cognitions, and affects. From this perspective, the study of normality is the study of the processes through which maximum choice and opportunity is available to the individual within a given psychosocial context and with certain biological givens.

Offer and Sabshin (1974, 1984) addressed the need for new concepts and research that would contribute to a meaningful definition and research strategy for the study of normality. They helped clarify this difficult issue by identifying four perspectives of normality: normality as health, normality as utopia, normality as average, and normality as a transactional system. Of the four definitions they proposed, three are primarily related to the medical perspective (health, average, and transactional system).

The concept of normality as utopia, which found a home in early psychoanalytic writings, is less prominent today. The ego psychology writings of Hartman (1958) and Rappaport (1942, 1967), and the work of Adolf Meyer (1952) led much psychiatric thinking to a transactional systems model, placing the individual in a social context, where adaptation and interactions between systems to maintain homeostasis were prominent. Offer and Sabshin (1984) further removed normality from the ideal by suggesting that research or discussions of normality should begin with knowing "for whom, under what circumstances, and for what purposes" (p. 170) the concept is being used. In addition, the modern cost-benefit requirements of treatment and the development of more brief and focused psychotherapeutic treatments (Ursano and Hales 1986; Ursano and Silberman 1988) have forced clinicians and researchers to reconsider treatment goals. The good side of this reorientation is a recognition that idealistic treatment goals may reflect a lack of understanding of the complexity of behavior; the down side is that regardless of the attainability of some goals, our society may not be willing or able to pay their costs.

A theory of normality is central to psychotherapeutic work. In fact, it is used daily by clinicians and is an important aspect of research and theory about psychotherapeutic change. In the current cost-sensitive environment, it is most important that we not confuse cost-benefit ratios with health (normality); they are not the same. Clinicians must stay alert to these two distinct pressures in order to best aid the health of patients and understand the biological and psychosocial underpinnings of behavior.

In this chapter we discuss psychotherapy as a medical intervention. To the extent that psychotherapeutic techniques—in particular, the effects of the doctor-patient relationship on the patient's behavior and compliance—are a part of most medical interventions, we are addressing how medical interventions in general require a knowledge of normality. However, psychotherapy per se, directed to the relief of pain and symptoms and the prevention of future illness, is very dependent on a concept of normal. In the first section of this chapter, we review the perspective of psychotherapy as a medical intervention and how it depends on a concept of normality that is most closely related to morbidity and mortality. In the next section we examine how the basic sciences of psychotherapy—those that study behavioral change itself—use and shed light on normality. Finally we review some elements of psychotherapeutic process and the stages of treatment to identify where the clinicians are making implicit, if not explicit, reference to a theory of normality in their everyday work.

Psychotherapy as a Medical Intervention

Many of the conceptual issues in the relationship between psychotherapy and normality are not unique to psychotherapeutic treatment but rather are a part of the relationship of any medical intervention to normality or health. Psychotherapy—the cure directed toward changing behavior through verbal means—aims to eliminate symptoms and increase the patient's productivity and enjoyment of life. Through talking, one provides understanding, guidance, support, and new experiences. Psychopathology usually limits the patient's ability to see and experience options and choices and to use behaviors that would be in his or her best interests. Feelings, thoughts, and behaviors are constricted, repetitive, painful, and lead to increased morbidity (biological and psychosocial) and, potentially, mortality. Through the various psychotherapies, the treating therapist attempts to increase the patient's range of behavioral options and decrease painful constricting symptoms and thus alter the risk of morbidity and mortality.

The brain is the target organ of psychotherapy. Behavior, thoughts, and emotions are basic brain functions (Kandel 1979; Reiser 1984). If psychotherapy is to change behavior, thoughts, and emotions, changes in brain functions and patterning must result. If a particular behavior is maintained by neuron *A* firing to neuron *B*, in order for this behavior to change, neuron *A* must now connect with neuron *C*. This analogy underscores the powerful and basic biological alterations caused by psychotherapeutic interventions and the rich model necessary to understand behavioral change through psychotherapy.

Health and disease (medical and psychiatric) exist within a complex (sociocultural)-behavioral-psychological system that is biological-historical (developmental)-context sensitive. Medical treatments, including psychotherapy, aim to alter morbidity or mortality through intervention in multiple areas within this complex system. Medical interventions are many and diverse. Some are directed toward prevention, others toward the early detection and treatment of disease, and still others to minimizing the crippling and limiting effects of illness. Inoculation against rubella, education about smoking, and the surgical removal of a tumor are each a form of medical intervention; all are directed at maintaining or reestablishing health.

The focus of psychotherapeutic treatment on psychological and behavioral rather than biological variables does not, therefore, distinguish it from other medical treatments. Nor does the glib assumption that psychotherapy deals with normal and healthy individuals while other medical interventions do not. The complexity of our model of health, however, is more evident from this perspective on medical treatment. In fact, all medical interventions—even biological treatments—require a broad conceptualization, a multivariant view, of health and of treatment. A simplistic view of biology will not explain our interventions. For example, it is important to remember that a strep throat is not a penicillin deficiency. In fact, the strep throat is not even the major medical concern and reason for treatment. The type of medical intervention used is not necessarily directly related to the most obvious disease process. Rather disease and medical treatment are a part of the complex relationship between health and illness in a given patient with a particular disease.

Is what is treated by psychotherapy intrinsically different from what is treated in other areas of medicine? We think not. What is treated is disease. Society has always played a large role in defining what is a medical disease in all parts of medicine. Only in modern times has medical science on its own attempted to define disease. Medical science now has the ability to identify pathologic agents that affect health—that is, morbidity and mortality—in conditions that society may not have defined as abnormal or aberrant, or conditions where society is not willing to pay the cost necessary to eradicate the illness.

For example, until recently blood cholesterol levels between 200 to 240 milligrams per deciliter (mg/dL) were considered "normal" in the United States. The average blood cholesterol level for adult Americans is 215 to 220 mg/dL; 50 percent of American adults have blood cholesterol levels over 200 mg/dL. However, in the last ten years, studies have indicated that compared to other countries, such as Japan, this is an elevated cholesterol level. Although previously modern medicine treated cholesterol levels above 240 mg/dL vigorously and, with new medications, met with some success, the new perspective is that blood cholesterol should be below 200 mg/dL. Thus what is "normal" as defined by statistical normality in an American population is not what is healthy. A large percentage of the current population of the United States is at increased risk of heart disease due to elevated blood cholesterol. An educational campaign has begun to alert the American population to this dilemma; attempts are being made to change patterns of diet and exercise in order to lower blood cholesterol. What we used to call "normal" is now "abnormal."

Changes in the diagnosis of homosexuality and personality disorders over the past fifteen years reflect similar effects of social context. The impact of society on the definition of disease is not only seen in psychiatric illness but throughout medicine.

At times the psychotherapies have been criticized because they are used—or said to be used, although the research literature is nonexistent—to "treat" healthy individuals, to make them happier or give them a richer life. This gross oversimplification focuses our attention to an important aspect of medical intervention and the concept of health or normality. Are medical "treatments" ever used for other than disease prevention and treatment?

When the gynecologist prescribes birth control pills to a young newly married woman wishing to postpone childbirth, is he treating a disease or preventing morbidity or mortality? The same prescription given for endometriosis is clearly a treatment to relieve pain and alter symptoms and morbidity. Is rhinoplasty for cosmetic reasons a treatment for a disease? Rhinoplastic surgery in response to trauma or burns certainly is. In addition, there are certainly some severe psychiatric illnesses in which patients may experience decreased self-concern and heightened self-esteem as a result of rhinoplasty. However, in the vast majority of cases, rhinoplasty is not sought for any disease process. What of the athlete who comes to a physician and describes himself as abnormally built because he lacks sufficient muscular bulk? We know that the provision of anabolic steroids will increase his muscular bulk but at some risk to health. However, is the absence of muscular bulk a disease process? For some of these conditions, society is willing to pay the cost. Birth control pills are frequently included as a part of health insurance; cosmetic surgery rarely is. Still other treatments (prescriptions of steroids to increase muscular bulk of an athlete) are illegal. A wide array of medical procedures are used outside the realm of the treatment of disease.

Therefore, we should distinguish the question: Is a medical treatment being used to treat a disease? from: "Does a medical treatment have an effect in nondisease states?" These two questions are frequently confused. Many medical treatments have impacts seen as desirable when they are not being used for the treatment of disease. That psychotherapies may have a "positive" effect on some nondisease (that is, healthy, normal) conditions should not be confused with whether a psychotherapy is being used for the treatment of a disease. The relationship between therapeutic intervention and normality is, therefore, not whether the psychotherapies may have beneficial effects with "normal" (healthy) individuals but rather when and how the psychotherapies are used to treat psychiatric disease and how a theory of normality influences this process.

The health or normality of patients clearly enters into the selection of medical treatments, including the psychotherapies. Psychoanalysis perhaps is most criticized for treating very healthy individuals. However, consider the following example. If a patient has had numerous myocardial infarctions and is in the final stages of congestive heart failure, is he or she recommended for triple bypass coronary surgery? Or rather is the patient who has not yet had an infarction and who has a single left main descending artery occlusion the candidate for this treatment? Obviously the latter. The selection of medical intervention is always dependent on the patient's ability to undergo the procedure. Similarly, different psychotherapies make different demands on the patient and therefore have different selection criteria.

The concept of health as the absence of morbidity and mortality is a central part of all medical interventions, including psychotherapy. Although the immediate target of a psychotherapy is not a biological variable, its strategic goals are to change biology. The confusion over whether psychotherapy is a medical intervention has generally been based on an incomplete definition of medical disease and intervention that has been fostered by a narrow view of high-technology and tertiary care medicine. When psychotherapy is used in the treatment or prevention of disease, it is a medical procedure, and its needs for a theory of normality are similar to those of other medical interventions.

The Basic Sciences of Behavioral Change

Human behavior in its broadest sense—as it is used in this chapter—includes affects, cognitions, and actions (behavior). Behavioral change is the result of biological changes at the brain level caused by direct biological effects (for example, toxins, tumor), maturation (unfolding of biological history), or the effects of life experience, past and present, as it interacts with one's biology. One life experience may be psychotherapy. If normality is important to psychotherapy, it should show up as an operational if not clearly defined variable in attempts to understand the mechanisms of action of this medical intervention as well as in clinical practice. The basic sciences of psychotherapy that study the mechanisms of psychotherapeutic action have not been clearly defined, although they are evident and rapidly advancing. Is normality important to those sciences attempting to understand behavioral change and how events in the outside world effect behavior and therefore the biology of individuals?

Behavioral Change

Behavioral change is part of the natural course of child and adult development.[1] The sciences we now use to describe the effects of life experience—of the "outside" world—sometimes more directly experienced while other times mediated by feelings, thoughts, fantasies, and actions—on the inside (human biology)—are frequently far from the biological paradigm. The systems that determine and maintain behavior are highly interactive. Included in this interactive matrix are the biological givens upon which learning and experience take place, the structures and schemata both innate and acquired through the individual's developmental history of life experience, and the socioenvironmental context in which a behavior occurs (Haggard 1974). The study of normality—normal functioning—is part of the study of the interaction of these systems that organize, mediate, regulate, constrain, and direct behavior and, ultimately, psychological health. Although we lack much data to help us understand the interface between the various elements of this system (Mohl 1986; Ursano 1986), an outline has emerged.

Basic to understanding how psychotherapy works is our need to understand how words cause a change in behavior. Many examples are obvious

[1]See Colarusso and Nemiroff 1981; Erikson 1950, 1980; Levinson et al. 1978, 1986; and Lidz 1968.

but consider the following example. Everyone is familiar with Gestalt diagrams, ambiguous figures in which a picture can appear to be a beautiful woman or an ugly witch depending on how it is seen. An individual may look and look and not see the "other figure" in the picture until someone says, "If you look at this beautiful woman and instead of seeing a feather there, you see that that's a nose . . ." and it becomes an ugly witch. One wonders whether the witch was there before! The amount of information that was reaching the brain was exactly the same with the beautiful woman as with the witch; the same amount of visual information was reaching the occipital cortex. What occurred was a reorganization. A new way of organizing the same information resulting in a new meaning. Change occurred following the friend's intervention, which resulted in the reorganization of information in the brain. The individual then experienced a somewhat fuller range of meanings and therefore possible behaviors.

Contextual Regulators of Biology

Our behavior is always in a delicate balance with the world around us. We are extremely dependent on our social environment for our day-to-day biopsychosocial functioning. Animal studies have shown that a wide array of infant systems (activity level, sucking, central nervous system neurochemistry, arousal, sleep) are regulated by the mother-infant interaction. These "maternal regulators" range from body warmth and tactile sensation to olfactory stimulation (Hofer 1984). Hofer explored the health consequences of maternal separation in humans and several animal species. He demonstrated that bereavement produced biologic changes and discussed bereavement in terms of withdrawal of an important regulator "that served to entrain and synchronize the biologic clocks of the survivor" (p. 190). Environmental regulators have also been described in studies of sensory deprivation as well as studies of biologic rhythms that are regulated by environmental events (Hofer 1984; Kandel 1979). Both social and sensory deprivation can result in profound and enduring alterations in neurological connections. Social interactions are extremely important to the synchrony of biologic rhythms in humans, and their disruption can result in disturbances that affect health.

Thus social relationships function as biologic regulators. Relationships with others have profound effects on physical and psychological health. In empirical studies of both humans and animals, high levels of social relatedness are related to mental and physical health.[2] Conclusions drawn by Spitz (1946) and Cassel (1976) and Cobb (1976) thirty years later indicated the role of social relationships in buffering the potentially negative effects of psychosocial stress on health. Social supports appear to decrease vulnerability to mental as well as physical disorders and also to enhance recovery from existing disorders. Social networks appear to also directly effect morbidity and mortality (Berkman and Syme 1979; House, Robins, and Metzner 1982). Berkman and Syme (1979) looked at a large probability sample of adults in Alameda County, California. They identified social networks (the extent of social ties measured by marriage, contact with friends and family, church membership, and other group memberships) as a significant predictor of mortality. House, Robins, and Metzner (1982) replicated these findings using a range of biomedical assessments as well as self-reports. Their data indicated that social networks predicted mortality eleven to thirteen years later. Subsequently these studies have been replicated in different countries with remarkable consistency to the findings.

Clearly, the presence of another person alters the biobehavioral interactions in a manner that allows new behavior to occur. Yet despite the long history of the observation, we have little explanation for the common clinical observation that the presence of a supportive other allows a phobic individual to approach the phobic object (Zajonc 1965). For many years it has been known that the death of a spouse greatly increases risk for physical illness (Singer 1974; Lynch 1979). The study of bereavement is, in fact, the study of the loss of a social/interpersonal regulator of the biopsychosocial system.

In general, the goal of many psychotherapies—and perhaps one of the central curative elements in all types of psychotherapeutic work—is the alteration of withdrawal, social detachment, and the increased availability of both internal experiences of social relatedness and actual interpersonal behaviors. Such alterations change the probability of disease. The world of mental and symbolic and representational events where individuals hold the image of another in their mind, including memories, hopes, expectations, and fantasies, is at least as important as the actual interpersonal interactions (Hofer 1984) and is the target of psychodynamic interventions. These internal representations also serve as biologic regulators, although research in this area is more difficult (Loftus 1979). The regulatory action of important human relationships upon biologic systems—both by

[2]See Harlow and Harlow 1965; House, Robins, and Metzner 1982; House, Landis, and Umberson 1988; and Suomi and Harlow 1975.

actual interactions and also by the internal, symbolic experiences of the relationship—are important aspects of normal functioning (Schwartz 1983).

Individual History

Past context is alive in the present through biology and memory (Cohler 1980; Cohler and Boxer 1984; Loewald 1980). One's culture, society, group, and family provide a present context. Whether the context is the family, the larger social system, or the normally abnormal immediate situation created by a trauma or disaster, the definition of what is normal and, therefore, what is pathological depends on this context.

The concepts of adaptation and coping are frequently used to understand the relationship of individuals to their socioenvironmental context. Hartman (1939, 1958) highlighted the importance of adaptation and the ego's role in organizing and controlling various "normal" (nonconflicted) functions of motility, perception, reality testing, action, and cognition directed to mastery and competence (White 1963).

Both adaptation and coping, however, tend to emphasize a static albeit homeostatic balance. Frequently this is at the cost of viewing how context interacts with an individual and vice versa. In addition, both adaptation and coping focus away from what the individual is adapting to or coping with. Any organism is prepared only for an "average expectable environment" (Hartman 1958). To consider an individual without a context does not allow us to assess an individual's capacity or the presence of normal or pathological processes. Adaptation might better be thought of as the ability or flexibility to learn through experience and to change behaviors in the face of new and challenging situations (Kubie 1974).

Renee Spitz (1965) originally identified elements of the mother-child relationship that served as elicitors and organizers of specific behaviors. Similarly, the psychodynamic psychotherapist listens for the metaphoric use of language to identify the expression of a particular organization (cluster of feelings, thoughts, and behaviors) formed in the past that influences current behavior and feelings. Traumatic events also appear to be able to create new organizers of cognitions, affects, and behaviors in the adult (Ursano 1987). By exploring the past and present meaning of events and their contextual and factual components, the therapist joins the patient in creating an experience that is aimed at altering the organizers of behavior—restructuring how information is organized at the biological, affective, and cognitive levels (Michels 1984).

An individual's expectations, anticipated present and future, also organize our perceptions and expectations (Cohler and Boxer 1984; Elder 1974). Thus the effects of being part of a particular cohort—a group traveling through time together although possibly separated geographically—is part of normal functioning. Individuals carry with them their place in time. Neugarten (Neugarten 1966; Neugarten and Hagestad 1976) examined the effect of the anticipated time of important life events on individuals' experience of themselves. When the expected time of a particular life event—birth of children, death, marriage, financial loss—comes and goes without any change, individuals' perceptions of themselves are altered. Such expectations of the timing of life events develop primarily through life experiences in the family as a cohort in a particular time (for example, during an economic depression in the country or a parent's loss of educational and job opportunities). Such life events lead to a particular picture of what constitutes "normality." At various phases of life, such schemata serve to organize and direct behavior and one's experience of the present and anticipated future. Lieberman (1961) felt it was the disruption of such patterned expectations that led to increased mortality when the elderly were moved to nursing homes.

Individual Context

Cohler (1980) and others have emphasized that an individual's view of the past and the future is influenced both by early memory and by the individuals present context. Memories are continually being revived at different periods of life. Past experience also provides symbolic vehicles through which an individual can express cognitions, affects, and behaviors to make them known to those about them (Holloway and Ursano (1984). The current social context and the individual's view of the past and present greatly influence his or her "normal" language, metaphors, and symbols used to communicate experiences and recall the past.

Zbrowski (1952), in his now-classic study, examined the expression of pain from a cultural context. For example, an individual of Irish or Jewish descent is unlikely to let a physician know he or she is experiencing pain. However, individuals of Mediterranean descent may be much more likely to express their pain and discomfort vocally. Medical students on obstetrical floors commonly observe this. Yet no one would suggest that the function of pain-receiving neurons of these individuals is necessarily any different. The context and the symbols available to express the meaning of an event affect both its experience and its expression.

The family is a unique unit with a shared system of established norms. Emde and Sorce (1984) cite the example of the colicky child in a family with a mother who sees this behavior as a major problem compared with a mother who has seen this behavior before and knows that her child will outgrow it. Recent findings concerning schizophrenia, high expressed emotions in the family, and the increased probability of relapse and hospitalization similarly emphasize the contextual risk factors of the family's microsocial system for an individual with schizophrenia (Leff and Vaughn 1981). The distinction between the normal individual in an abnormal environment and the abnormal individual in a normal environment is less clear than in years past. Anthony (1980) has described diseases due to "environmental deficiency" as a new focus in understanding health and illness.

Responses to trauma and disaster—the normal person in an abnormal environment—provide an additional perspective on normality and context. The resiliency of the personality is the most common finding in the face of trauma, yet we know little about this area (Rutter 1985; Singer 1981; Ursano 1987). Many individuals experience some transitory symptoms. The "normal" response includes the appearance of these symptoms and their "metabolism" and then a return to baseline. The same symptoms in a different context or if persistent indicate pathology (Rundell et al. 1989; Ursano 1987). In situations of trauma that include extreme and intense stress and chaos, it is impossible to ascribe meaning in the usual way to such extraordinary events. In the absence of meaning, individuals and groups attempt to construct meaning through the use of language, symbols, and rituals.

Behavioral change—including changes in cognitions, affects, and behavior—is the goal of psychotherapy. The basic sciences of this clinical treatment are only beginning to become clear and allow us to formulate testable hypotheses. These sciences include the study of biological regulators, the effects of social supports, interpersonal relations, past experience on brain organization and the influence of present and past context on symbolic expression. Knowledge in these areas will further our understanding of how "what is outside" (a therapist and words) affect "what is inside," and is central to clarifying the mechanisms of action of psychotherapy.

Psychotherapy and Normality

The psychotherapies include the psychoanalytic psychotherapies (psychoanalysis, intensive long-term psychoanalytically oriented psychotherapy, brief psychodynamic psychotherapy), cognitive psychotherapy, supportive psychotherapy, the behavior therapies, and the group therapies (group, family, couples). Although the different psychotherapies overlap substantially in their definitions as to what constitutes a symptom or pathology, their understanding of the cause of pathology varies greatly.

The different psychotherapies target various aspects of psychological functioning for change. The psychoanalytic psychotherapies focus primarily on the effects of past experience on molding patterns of behavior through particular cognitions (defenses) and interpersonal styles of interaction and perception (transference) that have become repetitive and interfere with health. Cognitive psychotherapy focuses mainly on dysfunctional cognitions and attempts to demonstrate their unreality and malfunction. Interpersonal therapy looks at interpersonal behaviors and focuses on maintaining and strengthening interpersonal supports. Supportive psychotherapy makes use of a broad range of techniques—psychoanalytic, behavioral, cognitive, and interpersonal—to stabilize the patient's self-esteem and interpersonal behaviors. Behavior therapy is based on conditioning theory and concepts of how rewards and punishments sustain or alter behaviors. Group therapies range from psychoanalytic perspectives to the interpersonal and systems models. They focus on transactions within couples, families, and groups from a systems perspective rather than an individual pathology model (Ursano and Hales 1986; Ursano and Silberman 1988).

Psychotherapy depends on what the patient is able to bring into focus in treatment and make comprehensible and discussable (Coleman 1968). In all cases, the patient should feel meaningfully engaged and involved with the therapist who must be able to hear what the patient has to say. Reactions in and to the treatment setting itself are frequently the bread and butter of the therapeutic experience and form a central part of the psychoanalytic perspective in particular.

All psychotherapists struggle to establish the conditions under which their interventions can be heard and be effective. Issues of continuity, the activity of the therapist, degree of support for the patient, and the recognition of reality constraints on behavioral change are themes confronting all psychotherapies. The prescription of psychotherapy is as important as the prescription of a psychopharmacologic agent (Frances and Clarkin 1981). In psychotherapy as in all other medical practices, the understanding of which patient, for which treatment, at which time remains a difficult medical judgment.

In psychotherapy, it is as important to identify areas of health within the patient as it is to identify the areas of pathology. Substantial therapeutic errors are created, particularly among young trainees, when they "pathologize" all the patient presents. This is usually the result of an insufficient evaluation of the patient and, in particular, an insufficient assessment of the longitudinal and contextual development of symptoms in a life. For each patient, the clinician holds in trust a picture of what "health" for this individual in this social context may be (Loewald 1980). For example, the treatment of a phobia through desensitization is done with an understanding of what constitutes normal behavior in the face of a bridge, an airplane, or a snake. One's interventions are made with, as Loewald says, a picture of what the patient can become.

The concepts of health and pathology and, therefore, normality pose different questions in the various stages of psychotherapeutic treatment.

The Evaluation Phase

Normality and pathology are assessed during the evaluation sessions prior to commencing psychotherapy. The evaluation is essential to the identification of the signs and symptoms of illness as well as interpersonal, intrapsychic, and cognitive/defensive targets for change. Only after a thorough evaluation can an appropriate prescription of psychotherapy be made, including duration, focus, and intensity, with a plan similar to the pharmacologic management of a patient. Similarly, only by thoroughly evaluating the patient can the therapist undertake a psychotherapy, recognizing the potential detrimental effects and hopeful outcomes.

The patient who describes feeling furious at his or her spouse cannot be accurately evaluated unless information is obtained about whether the spouse is threatening, demeaning, controlling, or even absent. Such contextual issues substantially affect the assessment of whether the patient's anger represents a healthy expression of independence and drive for autonomy or an expression of unmet dependency needs.

The effect of the patient's psychosocial context on psychotherapeutic success is not well understood. Although psychotherapeutic treatment takes place in an office, the patient brings to the treatment a real life full of experiences that may or may not facilitate the technical procedure of psychotherapeutic treatment. Attempting to treat a broken ankle in a jogger requires more than a cast. Similarly, a marital partner's support can be critical to the success or failure of a psychotherapeutic undertaking. One might also ask whether it is fruitful for a narcissistic patient to begin psychotherapy when there are continual rewards coming from the outside environment and the patient has not yet experienced a confrontation with "reality"—a social context that includes limitations on the grandiose wishes and ideas. Perhaps in such a case psychotherapy should be deferred. At a minimum, such a psychotherapy would be a long and arduous task in which the patient would have to become aware of the grandiose wishes and how they are being used defensively to protect against feared wishes, anxieties, and sadness.

The evaluation process is distinct from the psychotherapy per se, although they have much in common. Interventions and technical procedures during the evaluation phase are different from the technical conduct of the psychotherapy. During the evaluation phase the treater is responsible for diagnosis, treatment recommendations, and evaluation of the interaction between the patient's ego strength, physical health, and selection variables as well as different treatment options (including "no treatment indicated") (Frances and Clarkin 1981; Ursano and Silberman 1988). In establishing the therapeutic alliance (the working relationship with the healthy portion of the patient's functioning), the normality—health—of the patient is most important. An inaccurate assessment of the patient's ability to form a working relationship either due to the patient's pathology, the current social context, or the particular doctor-patient match can lead to either a very brief or a long but unproductive treatment.

The Middle Phase

In the middle phase of nearly all psychotherapies concerns about "normal" and "abnormal" are suspended. One rarely considers what is "abnormal" in the patient while engaged in the working process. All psychotherapies require establishing a nonjudgmental doctor-patient relationship. With the patient, the therapist identifies those areas of functioning causing difficulties and intervenes as appropriate, whether by interpretation, identification of schema, or development of new relaxation strategies and a hierarchy of anxiety states. In all cases, it is done in a collaborative spirit with the patient and as problem solving rather than eliminating pathology or creating normality. This is a technical aspect of psychotherapeutic work and the doctor-patient working relationship. If the therapist or the patient remains focused on what is normal (or abnormal), a therapeutic impasse frequently ensues.

This therapeutic orientation does not mean that issues of normality and pathology are forgotten. Psychoanalysis in particular has been criticized as being directed toward "understanding" and not to changing "pathology." This critique, however, represents a misunderstanding of the analyst's technical orientation versus the goals of treatment. The statement that the psychoanalyst must be goalless throughout treatment is a technical aspect of the treatment focusing attention away from seeing the patient as "abnormal." The strategic goal of psychoanalysis as a medical treatment is the alleviation of the signs and symptoms of illness, the patient's pain and distress, and rehabilitation to minimize impairment. These are the *sine qua non* of all medical treatments. However, the technical interventions (the tactical, minute-to-minute goals) involved in a psychoanalytically oriented treatment mandate a suspension of judgment. This does not mean that the overall goal of the treatment is not relief from a disease, nor does it mean that the psychoanalyst is not interested in the patient's becoming "healthy." Rather, in the context of administering the treatment, this goal is suspended and is not used to orient the technical interventions. This is similar to saying that surgeons want to stop bleeding. However, in the technical procedure of removing an appendix or doing a heart transplant, the surgeon is not always focused on halting bleeding. Other technical procedures supercede this goal in order to accomplish the long-term objective of removal of a diseased appendix or successful heart transplant. Treatment goals are always prioritized. In any medical treatment, preoccupation with one particular goal to the exclusion of a flexible approach oriented to the technical accomplishment of the needed procedure always interferes with medical treatment (Michels 1984).

In the middle phase of treatment, the therapist's neutrality does not indicate a lack of hope; rather the therapist holds in mind an awareness of what the patient can become in the hoped-for future (Loewald 1980). In the technical maintenance of a neutral stance, the therapist is equidistant from the patient's wishes, feelings, internal rules and goals of behavior, and reality. The therapist has an implicit vision, usually unarticulated, of what constitutes health and growth for each patient. Only with such a view does the therapist have a strategic as well as tactical approach to the psychotherapeutic undertaking. Interventions are always constructed with a long-term view of increasing the patient's health and growth. The interventions reflect the therapist's understanding of what constitutes health and normality.

Termination Phase

The termination phase of psychotherapy is intimately connected to the therapist's formulation of what constitutes normality and health. Usually, "normal" includes increased behavioral flexibility and the patient's experience of a broader range of possible actions. The patient's ability to attain "life goals" rather than an idealized concept of "cure" (Ticho 1972) is an indicator of termination being near. Rarely does the patient or the therapist experience that "everything is fixed." In part this is because different problems and conflicts are available to be worked on at different times of one's life. Within these problem areas, the therapist makes decisions concerning the resolution of symptoms, the return of health, and the establishment of normal behavior—feelings, thoughts, and actions.

In a psychoanalytic treatment, the therapist also looks for a change in the patient's understanding of the past. The patient's understanding of his or her past and its relationship to the present becomes another gauge of normality. The therapist assesses to what extent the past is intruding into the present and distorting the patient's perceptions and behaviors. At termination the patient also has developed a more "normal" (less fixed and related to the past) perception of the therapist. The working relationship seems to expand and occupy more of the treatment.

In all treatment modalities the therapist assesses the return of "normal" functioning by the removal of symptoms and the accompanying morbidity. But when is a phobia gone? When is detachment resolved? When is the anxiety or the sadness the patient experiences normal? These are the bread and butter of the termination, both for the therapist and the patient.

Conclusion

All medical treatments use the concepts of average, health, and interacting systems to define their focus and their mechanisms of action. Psychotherapy does likewise. When used to alter morbidity and mortality, psychotherapy is a medical treatment in the best traditions of medical intervention. Health and disease (illness), rather than "normal" per se, are the usual concerns of medicine. The use of words such as *normal* and *abnormal* contribute to the medical perspective as a shorthand to indicate health and illness. However, they are now so value laden that they can obscure important clinical and research questions.

Frequently medicine in general overlooks its dependency on understanding health. This has in part been a result of the focus on high technology and medical centers as the paradigm of medical care. The preventive medicine perspective returns health and prevention to the language and focus of medicine and medical interventions and clarifies the importance of "normality" to medical intervention.

The emerging basic sciences of behavioral change and the clinical practice of psychotherapy constantly confront the need to understand "normal" functioning and to define health. The interplay of social context, past and present, on the biology and behavior of the individual highlights the systems interactions central to understanding behavioral change and the effects of psychotherapy. The clinician practicing psychotherapy makes constant use of concepts of what is "normal" to guide the selection of patients, the interventions of treatment, and the timing of termination. The basic sciences of psychotherapy must address the biological, historical (developmental), social context (sociocultural), behavioral, and psychological variables that explain behavioral change in its broadest sense. Our ability to better understand the interacting systems that define, regulate, and organize behavior will aid the clinical care of our patients and their psychotherapeutic treatment.

REFERENCES

Anthony, E. J. 1980. "Psychoanalysis and Environment." In *The Course of Life: Psychoanalytic Contributions Toward Understanding Personality Development,* ed. S. I. Greenspan and G. H. Pollock, vol. 3, pp. 201–240. Bethesda, MD: National Institute of Mental Health.

Berkman, L. F., and Syme, S. I. 1979. "Social Networks, Host Resistance and Mortality: A Nine-Year Study of Alameda County Residents." *American Journal of Epidemiology* 109:186–204.

Cassel, J. 1976. "The Contribution of the Social Environment to Host Resistance." *American Journal of Epidemiology* 104:107–123.

Cobb, S. 1976. "Social Support as a Moderator of Life Stress." *Psychosomatic Medicine* 38:300–314.

Cohler, B. J. 1980. "Adult Developmental Psychology and Reconstruction in Psychoanalysis. In *The Course of Life: Psychoanalytic Contributions Toward Understanding Personality Development,* ed. S. I. Greenspan and G. H. Pollock, vol. 3, pp. 149–200. Bethesda, MD: National Institute of Mental Health.

Cohler, B. J., and Boxer, A. M. 1984. "Middle Adulthood: Settling into the World—Person, Time and Context." In *Normality and the Life Cycle,* ed. D. Offer and M. Sabshin, pp. 145–203. New York: Basic Books.

Colarusso, C. A., and Nemiroff, R. A. 1981. *Adult Development.* New York: Plenum Press.

Coleman, J. 1968. "Aims and Conduct of Psychotherapy." *Archives of General Psychiatry* 18:1–6.

Elder, G. 1974. *Children of the Great Depression.* Chicago: University of Chicago Press.

Emde, R. N., and Sorce, J. F. 1984. Infancy: Perspectives on Normality. In *Normality and the Life Cycle,* ed. D. Offer and M. Sabshin, pp. 3–29. New York: Basic Books.

Erikson, E. 1950. *Childhood and Society.* New York: W. W. Norton.

———. 1980. *Identity and the Life Cycle.* New York: W. W. Norton.

Frances A. J., and Clarkin, J. F. 1981. "No Treatment as the Prescription of Choice." *Archives of General Psychiatry* 3:542–545.

Grinker, R. R. 1967. "Normality Viewed as a System." *Archives of General Psychiatry* 17:320–324.

Haggard, E. A. 1974. "A Theory of Adaptation and the Risk of Trauma." In *A Child and His Family: Children at Psychiatric Risk,* ed. J. E. Anthony and C. Koupernick, vol. 3, pp. 47–61. New York: John Wiley.

Harlow, H., and Harlow, M. K. 1965. "The Affectional System." In *Behavior of Nonhuman Primates,* ed. A. Schrier, H. Harlow, and I. Stollnitz, vol. 2, pp. 289–334. New York: Academic Press.

Hartman, H. 1939. "Psychoanalysis and the Concept of Health." *International Journal of Psychoanalysis* 20:308–321.

——— 1958. *Ego Psychology and the Problem of Adaptation.* New York: International Universities Press.

Hofer, M. A. 1984. "Relationships as Regulators: Psychobiologic Perspective on Bereavement." *Psychosomatic Medicine* 46: 183–197.

Holloway, H. C., and Ursano R. J. 1984. "The Viet Nam Veteran: Memory, Social Context and Metaphor." *Psychiatry* 47:103–108.

House, J. S.; Robins, C.; and Metzner, H. M. 1982. "The Association of Social Relationships and Activities with Mortality: Prospective Evidence from Tecumseh Community Health Study." *American Journal of Epidemiology* 116:123–140.

House, J. S.; Landis, K. R.; and Umberson, D. 1988. "Social Relationships and Health." *Science* 241:540–545.

Kandel, E. R. 1979. "Psychotherapy in the Single Synapse: The Impact of Psychiatric Thought on Neurobiologic Research." *New England Journal of Medicine* 301:1028–1037.

Kubie, L. S. 1974. "The Essential Difference Between Health and Neuroses." In *Normality,* ed. D. Offer and M. Sabshin, pp. 201–206. New York: Basic Books.

Leff, J. P., and Vaughn, C. E. 1981. "The Role of Maintenance Therapy and Relatives' Expressed Emotion in Relapse of Schizophrenia: A Two-year Follow-up." *British Journal of Psychiatry* 139:102–104.

Levinson, D. J. 1986. *"A Conception of Adult Development." American Psychologist* 41(1):3–13.

Levinson, D. J.; Darrow, C. N.; Klein, E. B.; Levinson, M. H.; and McKee, B. 1978. *The Seasons of a Man's Life.* New York: Knopf.

Lidz, T. 1968. *The Person.* New York: Basic Books.

Lieberman, M. 1961. "Relationship of Mortality Rates to Entrance into a Home for the Aged." *Geriatrics* 16:515–519.

Loewald, H. 1980. *Papers on Psychoanalysis.* New Haven: Yale University Press.

Loftus, E. F. 1979. "The Malleability of Human Memory." *American Scientist* 67:312–320.

Lynch, J. J. 1979. *The Broken Heart.* New York: Basic Books.

Meyer, A. 1952. *Collected Papers of Adolf Meyer,* vols. 1–4. Baltimore, MD: Johns Hopkins University Press.

Michels, R. 1984. "Psychoanalytic Perspectives on Normality." In *Normality and the Life Cycle,* ed. D. Offer and M. Sabshin, pp. 289–301. New York: Basic Books.

Mohl, P. C. 1986. "Is Psychotherapy a Biological Treatment?" Paper presented at the annual meeting of the American Psychiatric Association, Washington, D.C.

Neugarten, B. L. 1966. "Adult Personality: A Developmental View." *Human Development* 9:61–73.

Neugarten, B. L., and Hagestad, G. O. 1976. "Age and the Life Course." In *Handbook of Aging and Social Sciences,* ed. H. Binstock and E. Shanas, pp. 35–55. New York: Van Nostrand Reinhold.

Offer, D., and Sabshin, M. 1974. *Normality.* New York: Basic Books.

———. 1984. *Normality and the Life Cycle.* New York: Basic Books.

Rappaport, D. 1942. *Emotions and Memory.* New York: Science Books.

———. 1967. *The Collected Papers of David Rappaport.* New York: Basic Books.

Reiser, M. F. 1984. *Mind, Brain, Body.* New York: Basic Books.

Rundell, J. R.; Ursano R. J.; Holloway, H. C.; and Silberman, E. K. 1989. "Psychiatric Responses to Trauma." *Hospital and Community Psychiatry* 40:68–74.

Rutter, M. 1985. "Resilience in the Face of Adversity." *British Journal of Psychiatry* 147:598–611.

Schwartz, G. L. 1983. "Psychobiology of Health: A New Synthesis. In *Psychology and Health,* ed. R. Lazarus, J. D. Matarazzo, B. G. Melamed, and G. E. Schwartz, pp. 149–193. Washington, D.C.: American Psychological Association.

Singer, M. T. 1974. "Engagement-Involvement: A Central Phenomenon in Psychophysiological Research." *Psychosomatic Medicine* 36:1–17.

———. 1981. "Vietnam Prisoners of War, Stress and Personal Resiliency." *American Journal of Psychiatry* 138:345–346.

Spitz, R. 1946. "Anaclitic Depression: An Inquiry into the Genesis of Psychiatric Conditions in Early Childhood. *Psychoanalytic Study of the Child* 2:313–342.

———. 1965. *The First Year of Life.* New York: International Universities Press.

Suomi, S. J., and Harlow, H. F. 1975. "The Role and Reason of Peer Relationships in Rhesus Monkeys." In *Friendship and Peer Relations,* ed. M. Lewis and L. A. Rosenblum. New York: John Wiley.

Ticho, E. 1972. "Termination of Psychoanalysis: Treatment Goals, Life Goals." *Psychoanalytic Quarterly* 41:315–333.

Ursano, R. J. 1986. *"Discussion: The Interface of Psychodynamics in Psychopharmacology."* Paper presented at the annual meeting of the American Psychiatric Association, Washington, D.C.

———. 1987. "Comments on Post-Traumatic Stress Disorder: The Stressor Criterion." *Journal of Nervous and Mental Disease* 75:273–275.

Ursano, R. J., and Hales R. 1986. "A Review of Brief Individual Psychotherapies." *American Journal of Psychiatry* 143:1507–1517.

Ursano, R.J., and Silberman, E. K. 1988. "Individual Psychotherapies." In *Textbook of Psychiatry,* ed. J. Talbot, R. Hales, and S. Yudofsky, pp. 855–890. Washington, D.C.: American Psychiatric Press.

White, R. W. 1963. "Ego and Reality in Psychoanalytic Theory." *Psychological Issues,* 3(3), Monograph 11. New York: International Universities Press.

Zajonc, R. B. 1965. "Social Facilitation." *Science* 145:269–274.

Zbrowski, M. 1952. "Cultural Components in Response to Pain." *Journal of Social Issues* 8: 16–30.

CHAPTER 3

Normality and Stress: Response and Adaptation from an Endocrine Perspective

Robert M. Rose

Stress and the problems in the adaptation to stressful stimuli have become a topic commanding much interest recently. Individuals increasingly speak of how stressed they are, as in being "stressed out," and much popular writing claims that many of our ills, both psychological and physical, derive from the impact of excessive stress in our lives and poor adaptation to or coping with stressful events. The public's concern about the negative impact of stress, and the emerging belief that it is necessary to control stress to maintain health, has led to the establishment of many groups offering to assist individuals in stress management.

A major motivation to cope better with stress is the wish to diminish the dysphoric feelings of anxiety and excessive worry or sadness that often constitutes the emotional responses to stressful events. An additional impetus relates to the belief that excessive stress has major, deleterious effects on physical health, both in causing or precipitating new illness or in serving to prolong or intensify existing illness.

This potential negative impact of stress on health was a crucial component of Selye's original concept of the General Adaptation Syndrome, or GAS (Selye 1950). He argued that individuals who were subjected to repeated or prolonged stress eventually could no longer adapt, became exhausted, and then became ill. Thus he postulated three stages of alarm, adaptation, and exhaustion. The model was based primarily on studies of rats exposed to high levels of noxious, uncontrolled stress, with the final stage of exhaustion characterized by failure of the adrenal cortex to secrete glucocorticoid hormones, following a period of excessive secretion of these hormones.

This model became extended to humans, and theorists such as Levi (1971) and others argued that some of our more prevalent illnesses, such as hypertension, coronary heart disease, and others, could be viewed as "diseases of civilization." This model argued that individuals became ill because of excessive stress, characterized by high levels of adrenal hormones, with their significant negative effects on bodily function. In addition, after a variable, prolonged period of excessive secretion, there possibly ensued a period of exhaustion, in which the glands could no longer secrete even adequate levels of hormones.

Selye's model of the GAS was combined with Cannon's concept of response to environmental challenges—the "flight-or-fight" response. The endocrine response to fearful or provocative stimuli is well worked out, characterized by brief and often intense elevations of catecholamines—epinephrine (also called adrenaline) from the adrenal medulla and norepinephrine (noradrenaline) primarily from the autonomic sympathetic nerves throughout the body. This response, occurring within seconds of a challenging event, calls forth many physiological changes—elevation of blood sugar, increased cardiac output, shunting of blood to the brain and musculature, and other changes, designed to enhance the organism's ability to flee or engage in fight.

This argument claims that despite the appropriateness of such a response from a historical or evolutionary perspective when flight or fight meant survival, it is not so useful or adaptive for modern humans. Thus if individuals repeatedly experience such endocrine changes but are not involved in *utilizing* the increased level of blood sugar or the other physiological changes—if, for example, they must sit in the car blocked in traffic or walk away instead of punching the boss in the nose—they are placed at a greater risk of becoming ill.

Thus the concept that prolonged or excessive stress leads to illness is based on an extension of both Selye's and Cannon's observations. Simplified, it argues that excessive stress leads to too frequent or prolonged endocrine secretion, which is physiologically damaging itself and may lead to an inability, following chronic stress, to secrete adequate levels of hormones.

Despite the interest in the possible negative health consequences of prolonged stress and the increasingly common belief in this model, there are major problems in the data documenting the presence of inappropriate and excessive hormonal secretion accompanying chronic stress.

A very powerful system appears to facilitate habituation of the endocrine changes to stressful stimuli. As reviewed by Rose (1980, 1984), most studies show a rapid return to baseline levels in these endocrine responses in response to repeated stressful stimuli. Given the very profound physiological actions of the cortisol in humans (cortisol is our primary adrenal glucocorticoid), it is not surprising that the natural propensity is for it to return to baseline levels rapidly.

These observations pose two problems. A very large literature demonstrates that cortisol is a sensitive and reliable index of the state of arousal in stress (Mason 1968, 1975*a*). Based on many observations that cortisol levels reflect the degree to which individuals are under stress, does the return to baseline indicate that such individuals have adapted? Have they adapted even though they might continue to report feeling stressed or continue to experience the same dysphoric feelings that they associate with continued stress, even though their cortisol is no longer elevated?

The other problem is related to the pathophysiology of chronic stress. What evidence is there that under certain circumstances or with particular individuals, chronic or repeated stress is associated with continued elevations of catecholamines, cortisol, or other hormones, in the face of the powerful force toward habituation of the endocrine responses to stress?

Thus, even if the psychological and physiological responses to stress do dissociate—and there appears to be much evidence that this is the case—one cannot posit that it is the prolonged and inappropriate continued elevations in cortisol that predisposes to future illness.

Given the increased interest in the potential negative effects of stress and the possible role of excessive hormonal secretion, it is useful to review the information we have about responses to stress, including what we know about adaptation and habituation.

As has been pointed out most cogently by Folkman (1984) and Folkman and associates (1985), what we experience as stressful depends on our appraisal of the specific events or challenges we confront in our environment. This in turn depends intimately on our past experiences, our successes or failures in dealing with these occurrences, and other idiosyncratic strategies. Thus a large literature has emerged that speaks to the issues of psychological evaluation, appraisal, adaptation, and coping with stressful life events. Although this literature is clearly relevant to a discussion of responses to stress, we focus on it only in the context of the endocrine responses to stress.

Psychological factors underlying the response and adaptation to stress clearly are crucial determinants of the outcome. Yet here we explore the *consequence* of these individual differences in responses to stress. While other physiological systems change significantly with stress, this chapter considers only relevant endocrine changes. This limitation is based on the centrality of endocrine responses in the risk for illness following stress and the abundant literature over the past thirty years describing an increasing number of hormonal systems as responsive to stressful stimuli.

The chapter summarizes information relating to *adaptation to repeated or chronic stress,* primarily with studies of humans in their natural environment, such as at work, preparing for examinations, responses to acute events including training in the military, as well as laboratory studies. We focus, where possible, on the relevance of individual differences, when they have been assessed and when more than group values are reported, which is usually the case. We also review some studies attempting to understand how endocrine responses to stress may change across the life span, from neonates to old age.

Individual Differences

The importance of individual differences in endocrine responses to stress cannot be overestimated. Almost all published reports of groups of individuals exposed to a wide variety of stressful conditions find significant variability in the observed endocrine responses. Some authors have concluded that this variability merely reflects the unpredictability of the response to stress. Furthermore, it is now clear that there are major dissociations between what individuals claim to be stressful and their physiological responses to stress.

In any attempt to explain this variability, or to predict who will show an endocrine response, it is usually not sufficient just to ask individuals how stressful they feel a given experience is and expect that answer to relate closely to the observed magnitude of their endocrine response.

This is not to say that individual differences in response to stressful psychological events cannot be predicted. Rather, we must emphasize that these differences in response are a reflection of the variety of psychological factors involved in the appraisal and interpretation of the challenging events, and that these issues usually cannot be captured by asking individuals if they are experiencing stress.

Another reason for the variability in the human stress response is that in human studies, the stressful stimuli usually studied are nowhere near as severe as those studied with animals. In animal studies most stresses are uncontrollable, offering little opportunity for escape, and are highly salient in that they have great consequences for the animal. This is not the case for most human studies. Yet even with studies that do not employ the most severe stressors, many reports have shown considerable variability in individual response.

Despite these problems, numerous studies have successfully predicted individual differences in response to stress, by attempting to estimate how effectively the subjects have minimized or isolated themselves from the potential impact of these events. One of the earliest of these studies involved the parents of children dying of leukemia (Wolff 1964*a*), which employed interviews and intensive observations of these parents living on a special floor in the hospital, while their children were being treated. Another early study involved young men during the first month of army basic combat training, which, similar to the parent study, also employed interviews combined with close observation of the individuals (Rose et al. 1968). Two other early studies involved men in combat situations in Vietnam (Bourne et al. 1967*a,* 1967*b*).

All these studies attempted to assess how successful individuals were in protecting or isolating themselves from what they felt was most challenging or threatening for them in their current situation. In general, when the individuals were observed or judged to be successful, their hormonal responses were observed or predicted to be lower than those of individuals who were seen as less successful in their attempts to cope.

Consistent with the conceptual models developed by Lazarus and Folkmann (1984), the impact of the stressful life events was critically contingent upon the individuals' appraisal of the situation as novel, threatening, or challenging to them. The study by Wolff and colleagues (1964) demonstrates that one way individuals cope with potentially overwhelming life events is to distance themselves or even to deny the danger or consequences that face them or their loved ones. What also was impressive in this study was that when individuals had to confront the true nature of these events in an interview, or in the face of significant deterioration in their child, there were very significant increases in cortisol excretion along with evidence of significantly increased psychological distress.

In the study of young recruits in basic combat training, verbal reports of distress or denying such distress were not necessarily good predictors of endocrine response (Rose, Poe, and Mason 1968). Observations revealed behavior inconsistent with what men said, and the authors correctly concluded that some individuals' claims of being unconcerned with their status in training was more wishful than actual.

A study by Katz and collaborators (1970) of patients going to the hospital for diagnostic breast biopsies emphasized the importance of attitudes or perceptions that serve to distance individuals from the potential impact of the stressful event. They were able to predict the cortisol levels in these patients prior to surgery. Those women who minimized or denied the possibility that they might have cancer were the ones who had the lowest cortisol secretion compared to individuals who admitted to being significantly worried about the outcome and significance of the biopsy.

The more stressed group were quite worried and dysphoric, which, of course, can be viewed as reasonable and appropriate in this situation. However, they were not successful in isolating themselves from the procedure and had higher cortisol levels. The other women, who were not so concerned, had significantly lower cortisol levels, often waited for a longer time before seeking medical attention, and thus in some ways endangered their lives. They could be considered as having successfully coped with the stressfulness of anticipating the biopsy, but with potentially negative consequences.

What often appears to be more important from a physiological perspective is not so much the degree to which the psychological strategies employed may provide a healthier, more adaptive long-term outcome but rather the degree to which they are effective in diminishing the potential distress of the current life event. In other words, there appears to be some priority attached to turning off the psychological system that activates endocrine arousal associated with exposure to stress.

Novelty

One theme that has emerged from many studies investigating endocrine responses to a variety of stressful stimuli is the importance of novelty. The degree to which a particular stimulus or event is novel to the individual often determines how stressful it is. When no longer novel, it loses it capacity to induce endocrine changes. What also has emerged from these studies is the ubiquity with which novel stimuli, given some degree of challenge or threat, are capable of eliciting a variety of endocrine responses.

This is such a common occurrence that Mason (1975*b*) concluded that it is precisely the novelty and/or degree of unexpectedness that constitutes the stressful nature of the stimulus. He found this to be true even for physical stressors. He exposed rhesus monkeys to a significant reduction in calories, to hypoxic environments, or even to significant heat or cold, in such a way that the animals were unaware of the changes—by providing the animals with nonnutritive food or making the change very gradually. Under these circumstances the animals had no opportunity to apprise these changes as novel and threatening, and significant endocrine response was absent. This was true even in the face of significant environmental changes that by themselves would be thought to be stressful and/or demanding of adaptation.

Mason concluded that it was precisely the psychologically stressful qualities of the event—its novelty, threat, or uncertainty—that are most important in activation of the endocrine response. This contrasts with what Selye referred to as the ubiquity of stressors in the environment, combining together many types of physical and psychological stimuli.

Anticipation

A major component in the importance of novelty in endocrine responses to stress is influence of expectation. Arthur (1987), in a review on stress and anticipatory vigilance, summarized much of the literature and suggested that it is during the period of anticipation of stressful events, not during the actual confrontation, that individuals have the greatest degree of endocrine response. The importance of anticipatory vigilance is also consistent with the observation of how individuals respond when threatened, a characteristic of Cannon's fight model. However, in a number of the studies Arthur reviews, what he interprets as a lack of evidence of endocrine changes during confrontations with the stimulus may in part be explained by the development of adaptation to repeated stress rather than the absence of an endocrine response to any initial confrontation.

Perhaps one of the most interesting studies involving exposure to a situation that was almost entirely anticipatory in nature was that reported by Czeisler and associates (1976). In this study repeated blood samples were drawn for cortisol analysis around the clock from patients scheduled for cardiac surgery studies the following morning. Late in the evening, when approaching the time of lowest cortisol levels during the diurnal cycle, technicians came in and prepped the patients' chests with antiseptics for the surgery the next morning.

Rather than having low cortisol levels, the individuals had a very large increase in cortisol at this time of night. This study is a most impressive example of the psychological determinants of stress, emphasizing the importance of anticipation of a threatening, novel event. No physical distress was experienced, just the worry and concern triggered by the stimulus of the preparation for the next morning's surgery.

One of the first reports of the importance of habituation in repeated exposure to stress was reported by Mason (1968), studying rhesus monkeys undergoing a continuous three-day session of avoidance of electric shock. The animals were quickly trained to push a lever when a stimulus light appeared to avoid an upcoming electric shock. Despite the presence of very large, dramatic increases in cortisol during the first experience of this continuous avoidance task, along with significant changes in other hormones, such as catecholamines, the animals adapted rapidly to this experience. By their third or fourth exposure to this avoidance task, no hormone rates were elevated. Interestingly, in many animals not only was there no elevation in cortisol, but there was evidence of active suppression of adrenal cortical secretion during the seventy-two-hour session.

In subsequent research a variety of investigators have replicated this finding. It is now reasonable to conclude that repeated stress leads to habituation of the endocrine secretory response. Bourne, Rose, and Mason (1967*a*, 1967*b*) measured the urinary cortisol metabolites in helicopter medics in Vietnam who were involved in medical evacuation flights. Strikingly, not only were the levels low compared with those of other individuals, but there were no differences in cortisol excretion on days in which the medics were flying compared to days when they remained in base and not exposed to danger. Parallel with the absence of any endocrine arousal associated with flying days was the observation that men employed a variety of psychological strategies that seemed to help them minimize or deemphasize the dangers they felt they were exposed to while flying.

Although these observations and interpretations were made after the data was collected, it is reasonable to conclude that these individuals were not only habituating with respect to their endocrine responses, but similar to the study of patients with breast cancer, they were minimizing the degree to which they would permit themselves to feel the dysphoria or the risk of exposing themselves to being shot down while on the medical evacuation flights.

It is, of course, possible to argue that both the helicopter medics and many of the patients awaiting breast biopsy continued to experience significant psychological distress, despite the absence of any continued elevations in cortisol. What mitigates against this interpretation was the absence of elevated cortisol levels in any of the medics, despite the observation that an entirely different kind of stressor—sustaining an injury to the scalp—did lead to an acute elevation in cortisol. Thus it was presumed that these men were turning off the stressful response specific to repeated flying.

The cortisol levels of the women were predicted based on the interpretation of how effective they were in denying or isolating themselves from the worry or fear of the significance of the biopsy. Thus there appears to be some considerable, active change in the psychological perception of potentially stressful events that leads both to habituation of the endocrine response and a parallel diminution of psychological distress.

Endocrine Responses to Repeated Stress

Perhaps the most surprising finding in individuals who have been studied following exposure to repeated stress has been the rapidity with which various endocrine systems adapt to repeated exposure to the stressful stimulus. In 1978 Ursin, Baade, and Levine reported the catecholamine, cortisol, and other endocrine responses following repeated jumping during parachute training. What was most impressive was the fact that there was a very significant increase in epinephrine and norepinephrine on the first day of the jump. These catecholamine responses were somewhat diminished on the second day, but by the fifth day they were not elevated over a baseline. For cortisol, there was an elevation before jumping on day 1, which probably reflects an anticipatory response, as well as the slight elevation on the same day following the jump. However, by the second day there were no significant cortisol elevations either before or after the jump, and evidence of habituation was observed through day 11 of training.

The ratings of how fearful the men were during the repeated jumps appears to have paralleled the endocrine responses. It is of note that by the second day, their fear score had dropped dramatically from the first day. Thus in this particular study the psychological estimates of stress could not be dissociated from the physiological ones; both diminished rapidly by the second jump.

This is in contrast to a study by Curtis and associates (1976) in which phobic individuals were studied when they were confronted numerous times with a phobic object (a flooding in vivo). Despite very large increases in anxiety, measured by self ratings and investigator observations, the plasma cortisol levels failed to rise when the individuals were exposed to the phobic object. Since the therapy used to treat the phobias involved the exposure to the dreaded object, this represents a study of repeated stress. It is interesting that despite the behavioral changes and intensity of symptoms in those exposed to the phobic object, the endocrine responses appeared to have been completely habituated.

Dutton and associates (1978) compared catecholamine and cortisol levels from ambulance paramedics and fire fighters on the days they worked compared to days off. There were no differences in the fire fighters in catecholamines or cortisol on working days; there was a slight increase in cortisol on the days off. However, for the paramedics who reported their jobs to be more exhaustive and less satisfying, requiring too much responsibility, there was a significant increase in levels of epinephrine and norepinephrine on days they worked. There were no significant differences in cortisol levels on work days and days off.

In a study of the dissociation between cortisol and catecholamines, Frankenhauser (1975) found that norepinephrine secretion appears to be related to whether or not the situation demands increased attention or vigilance, independent of the degree of challenge or threat, which provokes epinephrine and cortisol secretion. This might explain some of these findings, but the fact that epinephrine was also elevated suggests the paramedics experienced some novelty and increased anticipation on work days compared to days off.

In a similar study, Cullen, Fuller, and Dolphin (1979) compared the levels of cortisol in truck drivers driving eleven hours a day for four consecutive days with levels on nondriving days. They failed to find any significant elevations in cortisol on the days when the drivers were driving long hours.

Similarly, experienced pilots also fail to show any elevations in either of these hormone systems associated with the stress of strenuous flying. In contrast, novice pilots do show significant endocrine response on flying days (Pinter et al. 1979).

Rose and associates (1982) followed a group of over four hundred air traffic controllers for several years and collected plasma samples for cortisol every twenty minutes for five hours while they were working. The study subjects were all journeymen air traffic controllers on the job at least for four to five years. They had worked in the same position with the same responsibilities for at least one or two years. On at least two separate occasions, 201 individuals were studied, with researchers contrasting the days when the cortisol levels were higher versus lower. On the high-cortisol day, the workload was increased only slightly. However, on that day there was a small increase in the individuals' estimates of the subjective difficulty of work that day.

These results suggested that in experienced controllers, cortisol is not closely associated with the amount of work done or the behavioral response to work. Individuals must remain attentive to possible problems emerging, but most of the time the work was of routine nature and without significant novelty. Some men did show a very large increase in cortisol with significant increases in workload. Notably, this subsample of men who showed this large increase were not found to be more stressed, less competent, or more dissatisfied at work. In general, not only did their peers judge these cortisol responders to be competent, but they also described themselves as more satisfied with their work and reported that they were provided more freedom at work.

The authors concluded that these findings may reflect an interaction between life events and endocrine arousal described by Singer (1974) when she spoke about increased engagement or involvement, not only distress leading to increased endocrine secretion. Many of these air traffic controllers who showed increased cortisol in response to rising workload possibly might be seen as more highly invested in what they were doing, which in turn could account for their high level of satisfaction, reported competence, and higher support from supervisors.

In other words, elevations in tonic levels of cortisol in a work situation may not necessarily be reflective of increased stress but rather of increased involvement. It is difficult to dissociate these two, as most studies have not made measurements in both these domains.

In more recent studies, Berger and associates (1987) and Bossert and coworkers (1988) reported cortisol responses in twelve normal young men exposed to five different stress situations: a quiz, mental arithmetic, stress film, cold pressor test, and a physical exercise test. They found there was a high degree of individual variability. Those who responded to one test did not necessarily respond to other tests. On average, all the subjects showed significant increases in cortisol in all five test situations. However, the authors were unable to generalize which individuals tended to be responders and which were nonresponders. In addition, they found that subjective judgments of stress did not predict cortisol secretion.

The studies by Berger, Bossert, and associates are in contrast to a report by Lundberg and Forsman (1980), who did find a consistency in catecholamine and cortisol excretion patterns in various experimental conditions for twenty-four male and twenty-four female university students. The experimental stresses took place at different times of the day but included a monotonous vigilance task, a time estimation task, a reaction time task, a word conflict color test, and a nonengaging movie. What is most impressive about the study is not the fact that there were major increases in cortisol or catecholamines, as the changes were small compared to baseline, but rather that the individuals who responded to one experimental task tended to respond to others.

Unfortunately not enough studies are reported in the literature to determine whether or not there are stable differences among individuals, such that some respond much more readily to any potentially stressful event, while others are much more resistive to the impact of novelty or threat in their endocrine responsivity.

In general, the available studies do support the importance of habituation and also its relative rapidity of onset. In a study with animals Kant and associates (1985) documented that habituation to repeated stress is stressor specific. In this study they repeatedly exposed animals to a variety of stresses (restraint, running stress, and shock) and found that animals that had multiple exposures over ten days showed habituation in each of the three conditions. However, on the eleventh day, if a new stress different from the one the animals had been chronically exposed to was administered, they showed an increased response again.

A study by Wittersheim, Brandenberger, and Follenius (1985) documents the ability of individuals to respond to repeated stress. They studied individuals who were involved over the course of several hours in a short-term memory task. This was a novel stimulus associated with mental strain and was associated with an increase in cortisol levels. Several hours later, while still performing the short-term memory tasks, individuals were required to complete a multiple-choice task. This second, additional stimulus showed an increase in cortisol levels even though the subjects had begun to adapt with declining cortisol levels during the second hour of the short-term memory task.

In summary, these studies suggest that it is not the exposure to stress that quickly habituates in some generic way but that it is the specific stress that is adapted to. Although no human study replicates Kant and associates' design of many days of repeated stress with the imposition later of an acute stressor, the available literature suggests their results may also be applicable to humans. Thus the individual remains potentially able to respond to a novel stressor. These studies emphasize the importance of appraisal and evaluation in adaptation. They also raise questions as to how often chronic stress, at least when there is little change in the nature of the stressor, leads to prolonged elevations in endocrine secretion, which could form the basis of a maladaptive pathophysiological state.

Laboratory Studies

Exposure of normal subjects to various tasks in the laboratory permits a more precise manipulation of the experimental conditions in an attempt to tease apart the factors underlying the stress response. In a series of interesting studies by Breier (1989) and Breier and associates (1987), individuals were exposed to controllable and uncontrollable noise stress. They were led to believe that they could control the noise if they discovered the correct responses in the computer. However, there was no way to turn off the noise in the uncontrollable phase, thus a certain degree of deception was involved. Researchers found that there were much greater increases in adrenal cortical activity with the uncontrollable noise as compared to controllable noise, as estimated by measuring the plasma adrenocorticotropic hormone (ACTH) levels, the hormone from the pituitary responsible for stimulating the adrenal gland to secrete cortisol. This increase in ACTH was paralleled by a significant increase in self-ratings of helplessness and sense of loss of control. In another study (Brier 1989) where they used the same paradigm but studied depressed individuals, these researchers found that the magnitude of the increase of cortisol among the depressed patients was greater in those who reported increases in helplessness. The correlation between plasma ACTH levels and reported helplessness during uncontrollable noise stress was $r = 0.80$.

In another recent report using the psychological stress to exposure to uncontrollable noise, Sanders, Freilicher, and Lightman (1990) reported increases in plasma oxytocin following this stimulus. This is a novel study as oxytocin has not been studied previously in response to psychological stress in human subjects. Interestingly, the women who exhibited the greater oxytocin response also were found to be more emotional on a self-report questionnaire, as measured by visual analog scales, contrasting happy/unhappy, fearful/calm, and so on. In addition, these authors replicated the finding that the stressful response in oxytocin occurred primarily in high but nonlow emotional women in over three different studies with three different subject groups.

Blumenthal and coworkers (1990) assessed the responses to mental arithmetic in individuals before and after an aerobic exercise training, contrasting them with others engaged in Nautilus training without a significant aerobic training component. They found that during the mental arithmetic task, the post-training aerobic group experienced a greater reduction in epinephrine secretion and had a faster recovery time compared to those who were in the Nautilus program. These changes in endocrine responsivity were paralleled by a similar reduction in the magnitude of cardiovascular measures associated with the mental arithmetic task in the aerobic exercise group.

In another study by Bullinger and associates (1984), in an attempt to study how endocrine responses might be related to the perception of pain, blood was drawn from volunteers before and immediately after a one-minute immersion of the nondominant hand in ice water, the cold pressure test. Although serum levels of beta-endorphin (related to pain perception), cortisol, and prolactin only were measured, cortisol showed a significant increase as a function of the test. There was, interestingly enough, only a small change in beta-endorphin levels with the cold pressure test, and most of the psychological measures did not correlate with cortisol or beta-endorphin.

A study by Arnetz and Fjellner (1986) also found the general difficulty investigators have in relating psychological variables to the magnitude of endocrine response. Their two psychological stressors involved the Stroop color test and a timed mental arithmetic task. They measured urinary catecholamines and cortisol. They did find a significant change in epinephrine, which was predicted by the degree of extroversion by Eysenck's personality inventory (multiple $R = 0.50$, $R_2 = 0.25$), but the battery of psychological measures did not predict changes in norepinephrine or cortisol.

The predictive utility of various tests of psychological attributes varies in studies. In general, there tends to be little that is replicable from study to study, when one uses standard assessment of personality attributes to predict endocrine responses. What does appear to have greater utility is when the psychological characteristic being measured relates more specifically to the specific impact of the stressor. For example, the relationship between feelings of helplessness and the sense of failure, and hence stressfulness, of being unable to turn off an uncontrollable noise. This is especially intense in depressed individuals who carry with them more intense feelings of helplessness into all experiences.

Stressful Life Activities

Perhaps one of the most commonly studied areas of normative life activity is that of examination stress. Over forty years ago George Thorn and associates (1953) evaluated changes in blood eosinophil, an early measure of adrenal cortical activity, in response to examinations in medical students.

In general, individuals who are to take examinations show elevations in a variety of hormone systems. It is perhaps appropriate here to mention that in addition to cortisol and catecholamines, there is now significant evidence documenting that other hormonal systems are stress responsive (Mason, Brady, and Tolliver 1968; Rose 1980, 1984). These include a growth hormone, prolactin, testosterone, and estrogens. In general, a somewhat elevated or more intense level of stress is required before these other hormones show significant changes. Growth hormone and prolactin tend to increase under more intensely stressful conditions, while testosterone and estrogens tend to be suppressed, although this effect takes place over a much longer time frame than the more rapid elevations seen in cortisol, catecholamines, growth hormone, and prolactin.

It is not surprising, therefore, that although numerous authors continue to report changes in catecholamines or cortisol with examination stress, more authors fail to find changes in prolactin with examination stress. Semple and associates (1988) did find changes in catecholamine excretion at the time of examination but failed to find significant changes in urinary cortisol or prolactin.

This is in contrast to a report by Vassend, Halvorsen, and Norman (1987), who studied individual responses to examinations and found a significant increase in reported anxiety, global stress, high blood pressure, and serum prolactin. Their finding of small changes in cortisol appears to be an exception to the usual observation of cortisol elevations as a precursor to increased prolactin. Lovalo and coworkers (1986) followed fifty-eight male medical students before and during a final-exam week. They reported that plasma cortisol levels did increase significantly, by approximately 20 percent, during the examinations. They also measured Type A and Type B personality traits among these individuals and found no significant differences for the A's and B's; both showed the rise in cortisol during exam week.

Some of the conflicting findings might be explained by the nature of the sample collection relative to the examination period. Perhaps the most sensitive means of assessing the impact of an exam is to collect multiple plasma samples immediately before, during, and after the exam. Urinary values tend to average out the more short-lived responses that may occur when the examinations last for only a few hours during the day. In the study measuring prolactin levels, only one value a day was obtained for several months before, during, and after the examination rather than multiple samples on the day of the examination.

Chronic Stress and Daily Living

Studies of individuals followed longitudinally and their responses of exposure to repeated life stresses may provide a better way to assess the relationship between endocrine secretion and chronic stress. Unfortunately, very few studies of this sort are available to let us evaluate when individuals do *not* habituate to chronic stress, and especially when the chronic, repeated stress relates to usual life events. The few studies relating to this topic are most interesting.

Payne and associates (1984) reported on eight members of a cardiac thoracic surgery team ranging in rank from house officer to consultant. Samples were taken for hormonal measurements on twelve twenty-four-hour periods on different days during the work week, over three months. The authors not only obtained recordings of the electrocardiogram during the day when the team was operating but also collected questionnaire data. The urine samples for each twenty-four-hour period were assayed from VMA (the major end product of catecholamine metabolism) along with cortisol.

The researchers found that 72 percent of the time, the team members had endocrine values greater than the normal range, as indicated from the literature (control subjects were not evaluated in this study). These findings suggest that performing surgery with its complex physiological and psychological requirements is associated with some degree of continued elevations in cortisol.

More interesting and difficult to interpret was the observation that the cortisol levels were significantly higher in the more experienced surgeons. Thus the rank-order correlation for length of experience and mean cortisol calculated over the entire study period for seven surgeons was $r\tilde{s} = 0.96$. This finding—that those who were the most experienced had the highest cortisol level—is at variance with other studies, which generally find that novice status is associated with higher cortisol levels. The researchers also found that when individuals reported having more stress, their cortisol level for those days was above average, even though no overall relationship between individuals' rating of the magnitude of stress on a given day and the corresponding endocrine responses was shown. Thus, even though those with more experience showed higher cortisol levels chronically, they did not necessarily report higher levels of distress associated with their work compared to the more inexperienced surgeons.

In recent years investigators have focused more on the potential impact of minor stresses rather than major life changes, such as a death in the family, moving, or taking a new job. These include everyday irritants or inconveniences that have been referred to as "hassles" of everyday life. It has been argued (Brown 1974) that these are much more commonplace than the major life events that have usually been studied, and may have a greater impact on health.

Brantley and associates (1988) developed a Daily Stress Inventory (DSI) as a measure of minor stressful life events, designed to be filled out on a daily basis. They studied twenty normal adult male subjects, volunteers from a local teaching hospital. The subjects were asked to fill out the Daily Stress Inventory, for ten days concurrent with the collections of twenty-four-hour urine to measure cortisol levels. The authors selected the two days in which the subjects had the most frequent events and contrasted those with the two days out of the ten in which they scored the lowest.

The authors found a significant increase in cortisol contrasting the two days of high and low stress ($F_{(1, 17)} = 9.36, P < .01, R_2 = .32$). They also found a significant increase in VMA (the catecholamine metabolite) comparing high- and low-stress days. Using a time series analysis, they also attempted to evaluate the relationship across all ten days between stress scores and the endocrine measures, and found this to be significant for some of the men they followed. This is one of the few studies to attempt to assess the relationship between the accumulated hassles of daily living and the changes in urinary cortisol excretion.

Another study by Lambert and associates (1987) also measured stress hormone excretion chronically in a larger sample of young adults to evaluate the relationship between Type A behavior and endocrine activity. They measured both urinary cortisol and catecholamines. Interestingly, and perhaps counterintuitively, they found that those individuals with higher Type A scores had lower levels of both hormones compared to Type B's. It is not clear whether or not this study evaluated real differences in the response to stress among Type A and B subjects. The data were collected in the context of the subjects' entry into a longitudinal prospective study of human, biological, and social growth. There is insufficient information on whether the individuals involved experienced much novelty or distress during the days of their initial interviews and testing.

In an unusual study, only briefly reported, Nanji, Greenway, and Bigdeli (1985) found a relationship between levels of growth hormones and chronic stress. The study involved soldiers who spent varying periods of time in an active war zone, the Iran-Iraq war. The individuals studied, however, had been admitted to the hospital for battle fatigue and thus had significant behavioral manifestations of chronic distress.

Interestingly, the authors found a correlation between the time the soldiers spent in the war zone and their serum levels of growth hormone. Approximately forty males age eighteen to thirty-three were studied, and most spent either one or two months in the war zone or nine to twenty-four months in the war zone with few between two and nine months. This was an interesting and provocative study, as the growth hormone is secreted very episodically and plasma levels are usually highly variable. A single determination is not generally a reliable index of the magnitude of growth hormone secretion.

Even though the population was obviously clinically distressed, the study is provocative. The possibility of growth hormone being elevated following prolonged but not short times in a war zone is of interest. The absence of a parallel difference in cortisol levels also is of interest but is not discussed extensively.

In order to evaluate the possibility that chronic stress has a significant impact or predisposes an individual for illness by a long-term excess cortisol secretion, one might ask if there are any studies in which the cortisol level is elevated associated with chronic stress. In the few available studies that show some relationship between chronic stress and cortisol level, only a slight, although statistically significant, increase in cortisol level over baseline levels is seen, an increase that is physiologically not very impressive.

Posttraumatic Stress Disorder (PTSD)

In an attempt to correlate endocrine changes with the presence of chronic distress, a number of endocrine studies have been done in patients with posttraumatic stress disorder (PTSD).

Clinically, these individuals experience significant, intrusive thinking, flashbacks, and in general as a group are chronically maladapted. There are some problems in the definition and epidemiology of posttraumatic stress disorder (Breslau and Davis 1987), but nevertheless a group can be identified that continues to reexperience past traumatic events, even though this occurs internally and not externally in their environment.

Mason and associates (1986) reported that mean cortisol levels in hospitalized patients with PTSD were significantly lower than in controls and patients with other psychiatric disorders, in contrast to PTSD patients' overt signs of anxiety or depression and in contrast to elevations in their urinary catecholamines. In a follow-up report, this same group of investigators (Yeheda et al. 1990) extended their findings of low urinary cortisol in an additional sample of PTSD patients. They found the lower cortisol levels were independent of the presence of symptoms of major depression, which if present would tend to elevate the cortisol values. The authors argued that similar to many studies, the lower cortisol levels reflect a physiological adaptation to the chronic stress associated with PTSD.

In another study of individuals diagnosed as PTSD, Hoffman and coworkers (1989) measured serum cortisol, ACTH, and plasma endorphin in twenty-one patients and twenty controls. They found some elevation in cortisol levels in the morning among the PTSD patients, but overall lower levels compared to controls. Smith and associates (1989) attempted to evaluate the hypothalamic pituitary adrenal axis in patients with PTSD by measuring ACTH and cortisol following administration of corticotropin-releasing hormone, the hypothalamic hormone that stimulates the pituitary to secrete ACTH. They found the PTSD patients had significantly lower ACTH responses compared to normal volunteers. They also noted that cortisol levels tended to be somewhat reduced.

These studies argue that PTSD, although clearly involving chronic psychological distress, is not necessarily associated with elevated levels of cortisol despite the fact that there is some indication that catecholamines may be increased. Thus the studies parallel the other studies showing a dissociation of psychological distress and physiological arousal as measured by continued elevations of cortisol activity.

Despite the absence of studies showing such endocrine changes in chronic psychological distress, there is information indicating that chronic illness is associated with increased adrenocortical activity. Parker, Levin, and Lifrak (1985) evaluated adrenocortical adaptation in patients with medical illness. The twenty men who were studied were aged twenty-six to eighty-six with an average age of 58.9. These patients suffered from a variety of illnesses, including chronic infections, carcinoma, pneumonia, and neurological syndromes. They were compared to the control group of twenty-five men, with the same average age, who worked at the hospital.

The researchers found a significant shift in the adrenal activity toward an increased production of cortisol, away from the pathway leading to other adrenal hormones, favoring increased production of cortisol. Thus there was a three- to fourfold increased ratio of cortisol secretion over that of the other adrenal steroids.

The authors interpret these results as indicating that the stress of a variety of chronic physical illnesses causes a profound increase in cortisol secretion, which may reflect an attempt to adapt to the physiological burdens associated with chronic illness. As we will see, long-term excess cortisol production is unusual and carries with it a significant physiological risk of its own. This is probably why it is unusual and much physiological adaptation leads away from excess corticoid activity.

Studies over the Age Span

It appears that the capability for adrenal responses as well as habituation of this response occurs very early in life. Anders and associates (1970) showed that in normal human infants, cortisol increased markedly after crying compared to when the infants were lying quietly. These results were found in children as young as one week of age. Cathro and coworkers (1969) studied infants who were born with Rh incompatibility or asphyxia; they found that those infants with the more difficult postpartum course in the hospital showed higher levels of cortisol.

Gunner and associates (1985) studied eighty healthy, full-term male newborns two to three days old who were scheduled to be circumcised. Blood was sampled by a heel stick and individual infants were followed before, during, and after circumcision. The infants had a brisk increase in cortisol during circumcision followed by a return to baseline by 240 minutes. Behavioral distress during the circumcision was related to elevations in cortisol.

In a study documenting the early habituation that occurs in adrenocortical activity, Gunner (1991) followed forty-nine healthy newborns who were examined twice during discharge examinations performed on two consecutive days prior to leaving the hospital. The results showed that there were significant elevations in cortisol only in response to the first discharge examination. No elevated cortisol was noted in the second examination despite the fact that the newborns continued to exhibit behavioral distress on both examinations. This study documents not only that rapid habituation occurs in very young humans but also that this habituation occurs in the face of continuing behavioral distress.

Various authors also studied the responses of young children following separation from their mother. This has been studied extensively in different species of monkeys. Young rhesus monkeys show a vigorous adrenocortical response to separation, which does diminish as the separation progresses. In addition, the changes in adrenocortical activity do not directly parallel changes in attitude or behavior (Gunner 1991). These same results have been found in New World squirrel monkeys.

Tennes, Downey, and Vernadakis (1977) studied urinary cortisol excretion rates and anxiety in normal one-year-old infants. They found no clear evidence of an endocrine response to separation in these human infants, despite their observations that infants who were more anxious or agitated had higher cortisol rates compared to less anxious infants.

Gunner (1990) attempted to replicate Tennes's findings, using salivary cortisol determinations and studying separation of babies from their mothers at nine months and again at thirteen months. At nine months the babies experienced a total of forty-nine minutes of separation; at thirteen months this experience lasted only nine minutes. The researchers found no significant elevations of salivary cortisol following the separation experience, unlike that observed among nonhuman primates.

The explanation for these observations is unclear and may represent the fact that short separations from their mothers were a common occurrence, a rather minor stressor to which the babies had already habituated. Separations for a much longer period of time, such as days or weeks, which have been employed with nonhuman primates, might indeed provoke very significant cortisol responses, but clearly in most circumstances would be unethical.

There is now increasing evidence about the possible relationship between variables assessing temperament in developing children and adrenocortical activity. Kagan, Reznick, and Snidman (1987) reported a longitudinal study on two cohorts of children selected in the second and third year of life to be extremely cautious and shy contrasted with children who are seen to be fearless, outgoing, and uninhibited. The stressor was exposure to unfamiliar events. In the unfamiliar environment the inhibited children tend to show adrenal activation as measured by salivary cortisol, and some showed increased levels of norepinephrine. These studies were expanded and replicated in a report in 1988 by the same authors (Kagan, Reznick, and Snidman) in which the children were reevaluated at seven years of age. Cortisol levels continued to be elevated in the shy children, but in a follow-up study by Kagan and associates (1988), the absolute levels at age seven were not as discriminating of the two groups as they had been when the same children were four or five.

Gunnar, Connors, and Isensee (1989) have also studied the relationship between temperament and adrenocortical reactivity in infancy. These workers found that although adrenocortical activity was not associated with measures of differences in attachment behavior, there was evidence that infants who were prone to experience greater distress in various laboratory situations at approximately one year also had higher cortisol levels.

No other studies of later periods of development have attempted to assess the interaction among exposure to stressful events, differences in temperament, and adrenocortical activity. However, Nottelmann and associates (1987) studied the relationship between developmental processes in early adolescence and levels of various gonadal sex hormones. This involved fifty-six normal boys and fifty-two normal girls ages nine to fourteen. The adolescents' psychosocial adjustment was assessed by various self-questionnaires including the Offer Self Image Questionnaire for Adolescence, and parent ratings of adolescent behavioral problems. The relationship between these measures of adjustment and various hormones were stronger and more consistent for the boys than for the girls.

Overall, the authors found that individuals with more psychological problems, including negative emotional tone, diminished body and self-image, and difficult social relationships, had lower levels of various gonadal hormones compared to those with a more positive self-image. Thus those boys with lower levels of testosterone were found to have more problems in social relationships. Unfortunately, this was not a longitudinal but a cross-sectional study, and it is not yet clear the degree to which the psychological distress or relative maladaptation preceded the slowing of maturation as reflected by a lower stage of male physical development and lower levels of male sex hormones.

Studies with rhesus monkeys (Rose et al. 1978) showed that in male monkeys about to enter adolescence, the onset of their increase in testosterone can be delayed for a year. This rise in testosterone usually occurs in the third year and is associated with marked behavioral changes, such as the onset of sexual copulation and the loss of earlier play behavior. This delay occurs when significantly stressful events occur just prior to when these normal maturation changes occur.

There is recent evidence that the adrenocortical response to stress alters significantly in normal aging. These findings were originally worked out in rodents, but later found to occur, albeit less dramatically, in nonhuman primates and man (Sapolsky et al. 1987). It appears as if, in aging, there is a significant change in the sensitivity of glucocorticoid receptors in the brain. As these receptors grow less sensitive to rising cortisol levels, aging animals have a defect attenuating the stress response—cortisol levels remain high for a significantly longer period of time. Sapolsky also reported that aged individuals are also delayed in habituating to mild stressors and show prolonged responses to stressors compared to younger animals.

The defect appears to be a change in the corticosteroid receptors in the hippocampus in aging animals. This defect may be caused by excessive levels of cortisol in response to the impact of prolonged stress, which has been demonstrated experimentally in rodents. Unlike the rat, the receptor dysfunction in aging humans appears to be more a vulnerability than an obligatory defect.

There are several examples of the physiological consequences of prolonged high levels of glucocorticoids that occur naturally in the life of animals. These are very dramatic and appear to reflect a programmed senescence that is associated with intense periods of reproductive activity. The studies are worth reviewing as they exemplify the consequences of naturally occurring prolonged elevations of glucocorticoids, which in turn raises questions about the frequency of such an occurrence in animals without such a dramatic, terminal course in their lives.

Sapolsky and associates (1987) reviewed two relatively unusual events related to excessive glucocorticoid secretion as triggers of programmed aging in animals. In a certain shrewlike marsupial *(Antechinus stuartii, Antechinus swainsonii)*, all the males die immediately after a very intense mating season. The endocrinological underpinnings of this have been studied. Apparently there is a combination of hypercortisolism associated with markedly elevated androgen levels. In this state there is a decreased sensitivity to feedback inhibition of cortisol, which leads to the very high levels of glucocorticoids. These males develop a wide range of steroid-induced pathologies, including gastric ulceration, hemorrhage, anemia, and manifestations of marked suppression of the immune system (Lee and Donald 1985). A similar phenomena may occur in the Pacific salmon in their final return to spawn in the same fresh water where they were born. During the final stage of their lives, they experience hyperactivity of gonadal secretion along with very high levels of glucocorticoid.

These examples are of interest not because of a direct parallel with humans but rather as exemplars of excessive adrenocortical activity in the context of a very specific life event, which may well provide the species with an evolutionary advantage. It may well be that some individuals, who have been exposed to excessive stress with an associated chronic elevation in cortisol, are unable to moderate appropriately their adrenal responses in old age, secondary to changes in steroid receptors in the brain. The degree to which this occurs in humans is as yet unclear. The animal findings provide us with a model of the consequences of chronic stress, but to date no studies in humans have shown very dramatic and prolonged increases in adrenal activity, which, as the examples show, can have the most profound consequences.

Summary

Judged by endocrine criteria, most humans show relatively quick adaptation to a variety of stressful stimuli or exposure to novel environments. The adrenocortical response of individuals is a product of their assessment of the stimulus as novel along with their judgment of it being potentially challenging or threatening. In most studies the response to repeated situations shows adaptation by the second or third exposure.

It is also clear that individuals may continue to experience psychological distress to the repeated stress, even in the face of return of endocrine secretion to baseline, prestress levels.

In most studies significant individual differences are observed. These can be predicted, usually not just by asking the individual if he or she is "being stressed" but rather by assessing the degree to which the individual is successful in isolating him- or herself from the sense of threat or potential distress involved.

No studies document the possibility of prolonged, detrimental endocrine secretion provoked by the continuation of the stressful situation in humans. In part this may relate to the fact that, unlike many animal studies, the stressors employed are almost always much milder and permit adaptation. It is also probable that even with more severe stimuli, there is a very great propensity for endocrine responses to habituate, given their powerful physiological activity.

However, recent data do suggest that the endocrine responses to stress in the elderly may not habituate as rapidly. This may have pathophysiological consequences yet to be demonstrated in humans.

REFERENCES

Anders, T. F.; Sachar, E. J.; Kream, J.; et al. 1970. "Behavioral State and Plasma Cortisol Response in the Human Newborn." *Pediatrics* 46(4):532–537.

Arnetz, B. B., and Fjellner, B. 1986. "Psychological Predictors of Neuroendocrine Responses to Mental Stress." *Journal of Psychosomatic Research* 30(3):297–305.

Arthur, A. Z. 1987. "Stress as a State of Anticipatory Vigilance." *Perceptual and Motor Skills* 64:75–85.

Baumgartner, A.; Graf, K. J.; and Kurten, I. 1988. "Prolactin in Patients with Major Depressive Disorder and in Healthy Subjects." *Society of Biological Psychiatry* 24:286–298.

Berger, M.; Bossert, S.; Krieg, J. C.; Dirlich, G.; Ettmeier, W.; Schreiber, W.; and von Zerssen, D. 1987. *Society of Biological Psychiatry* 22:1327–1339.

Blumenthal, J. A.; Fredrikson, M.; Kuhn, C. M.; Ulmer, R. L.; Walsh-Riddle, M.; and Appelbaum, M. 1990. "Aerobic Exercise Reduces Levels of Cardiovascular and Sympathoadrenal Responses to Mental Stress in Subjects Without Prior Evidence of Myocardial Ischemia." *American Journal of Cardiology* 65:93–98.

Bohlin, G.; Eliasson, K.; Hjemdahl, P.; Klein, K.; and Frankenhaeuser, M. 1986. "Pace Variation and Control of Work Pace as Related to Cardiovascular, Neuroendocrine, and Subjective Responses." *Biological Psychology* 23:247–263.

Bossert, S.; Berger, M.; Krieg, J. C.; Schreibert, W.; Junker, M.; and von Zerssen, D. 1988. "Cortisol Response to Various Stressful Situations: Relationship to Personality Variables and Coping Styles." *Neuropsychobiology* 20(1):36–42.

Bourne, P. G.; Rose, R. M.; and Mason, J. W. 1967*a*. "Urinary 17-OHCS Levels.

Data on Seven Helicopter Ambulance Medics in Combat." *Archives of General Psychology* 17:104–110.

———. 1967*b*. "Urinary 17-OHCS Levels. Special Forces "A" Team Under Threat of Attack." *Archives of General Psychology* 19:135–140.

Brantley, P. J.; Dietz, L. S.; McKnight, G. T.; Jones, G. N.; and Tulley, R. 1988. "Convergence Between the Daily Stress Inventory and Endocrine Measures of Stress." *Journal of Consulting and Clinical Psychology* 56(4):549–551.

Breier, A. 1989. "Experimental Approaches to Human Stress Research: Assessment of Neurobiological Mechanisms of Stress in Volunteers and Psychiatric Patients." *Biological Psychiatry* 26:438–462.

Breier, A.; Albus, M.; Pickar, D.; Zahn, T. P.; Wolkowitz, O. M.; and Paul, S. M. 1987. "Controllable and Uncontrollable Stress in Humans: Alterations in Mood and Neuroendocrine and Psychophysiological Function." *American Journal of Psychiatry* 144:1419–1425.

Breslau, N., and Davis, G. C. 1987. "Posttraumatic Stress Disorder. The Stressor Criterion." *Journal of Nervous and Mental Disorders* 175(5):255–264.

Brown, G. W. 1974. "Meaning, Measurement, and Stress of Life Events." In *Stressful Life Events: Their Nature and Effects,* ed. B. S. Dohrenwend and B. P. Dohrenwend. New York: John Wiley.

Bullinger, M.; Naber, D.; Pickar, D.; Cohen, R. M.; Kalin, N. H.; Pert, A.; and Bunney, W. E., Jr. 1984. "Endocrine Effects of the Cold Pressor Test: Relationships to Subjective Pain Appraisal and Coping." *Psychiatry Research* 12:227–233.

Cathro, D. M.; Forsyth, C. C.; and Cameron, J. 1969. "Adrenocortical Responses to Stress in Newborn Infants." *Archives of Diseases of Childhood* 44:88–95.

Cullen, J.; Fuller, R.; and Dolphin, C. 1979. "Endocrine Stress Responses of Drivers in a 'Real-life' Heavy-goods Vehicle Driving Task." *Psychoneuroendocrinology* 4:107–115.

Curtis, G.; Buxton, M.; Lippman, D.; et al. 1976. " 'Flooding in vivo' During the Circadian Phase of Minimal Cortisol Secretion: Anxiety and Therapeutic Success Without Adrenal Cortical Activation." *Biological Psychology* 11(1):101–107.

Czeisler, C. A.; Moore Ede, M. C.; Regestein, Q. R.; et al. 1976. "Episodic 24-hour Cortisol Secretory Patterns in Patients Awaiting Elective Cardiac Surgery." *Journal of Clinical Endocrinology Metabolism* 42(2):273–283.

Dutton, L. M.; Smolensky, M. H.; Leach, C. S.; et al. 1978. "Stress Levels of Ambulance Paramedics and Fire Fighters." *Journal of Occupational Medicine* 20(2):111–115.

Folkman, S. 1984. "Personal Control and Stress and Coping Processes: A Theoretical Analysis." *Journal of Personality and Social Psychology* 46:839–852.

Folkman, S.; Lazarus, R. S.; Gruen, R. J.; and DeLongis, A. 1985. "Appraisal, Coping, Health Status, and Psychological Symptoms." *Journal of Personality and Social Psychology* 50:571–579.

Frankenhaeuser, M. 1975. "Experimental Approaches to the Study of Catecholamines and Emotion." In *Emotions—Their Parameters and Measurement,* ed. L. Levi. New York: Raven Press.

Gunnar, M. R. 1991. "Maternal Separation and Activation of the Adrenocortical System in Human Infants: Comparisons with Other Primate Species. In *Stress and Coping,* vol. 4, ed. T. Field et al.

Gunnar, M. R.; Connors, J.; and Isensee, J. 1989. "Lack of Stability in Neonatal Adrenocortical Reactivity Because of Rapid Habituation of the Adrenocortical Response." *Developmental Psychobiology* 22(3):221–233.

Gunnar, M. R.; Malone, S.; Vance, G.; and Fisch, R. O. 1985. "Coping with Aversive Stimulation in the Neonatal Period: Quit Sleep and Plasma Cortisol Levels During Recovery from Circumcision." *Child Development* 56:824–834.

Gunnar, M. R.; Mangelsdorf, S.; Larson, M.; and Hertsgaard, L. 1989. "Attachment, Temperament, and Adrenocortical Activity in Infancy: A Study of Psychoendocrine Regulation." *Developmental Psychology* 25(3):355–363.

Hoffman, L.; Watson, R. B.; Wilson G.; and Montgomery, J. 1989. "Low Plasma Beta-endorphin in Post-traumatic Stress Disorder." *Australian and New Zealand Journal of Psychiatry* 23:269–273.

Kagan, J.; Reznick, J. S.; and Snidman, N. 1987. "The Physiology and Psychology of Behavioral Inhibition in Children." *Child Development* 58(6):1459–1473.

———. 1988. "Biological Bases of Childhood Shyness." *Science* 240(4849):167–171.

Kagan, J.; Reznick, J. S.; Snidman, N.; Gibbons, J.; and Johnson, M. O. 1988. "Childhood Derivatives of Inhibition and Lack of Inhibition to the Unfamiliar." *Child Development* 59(6):1580–1589.

Kant, G. J.; Eggleston, T.; Landman-Roberts, L.; Kenion, C. C.; Driver, G. C.; and Meyerhoff, J. L. 1985. "Habituation to Repeated Stress Is Stressor Specific." *Pharmacology Biochemistry & Behavior* 22:631–634.

Katz, J. L.; Weiner, H.; Gallagher, T. F.; et al. 1970. "Stress, Distress, and Ego Defenses." *Archives of General Psychology* 23:131–142.

Lambert, W. W.; MacEvoy, B.; Klackenberg-Larsson, I.; Karlberg, P.; and Karlberg, J. 1987. "The Relation of Stress Hormone Excretion to Type A Behavior and to Health." *Journal of Human Stress Research and Management* 13(3):128–135.

Lee, A. K., and McDonald, I. R. 1985. "Stress and Population Regulation in Small Mammals." *Oxford Reviews of Reproductive Biology* 7:261–304.

Levi, L., ed. 1971. *Society, Stress, and Disease,* vol. 1, *The Psychosocial Environment and Psychosomatic Diseases.* New York: Oxford University Press.

Lovallo, W. R.; Pincomb, G. A.; Edwards, G. L.; Brackett, D. J.; and Wilson, M. F. 1986. "Work Pressure and the Type A Behavior Pattern Exam Stress in Male Medical Students." *Psychosomatic Medicine* 48 (½):125–133.

Luger, A.; Deuster, P. A.; Kyle, S. G.; Gallucci, W. T.; Montgomery, L. C.; Gold, P. W.; Loriaux, D. L.; and Chrousos, G. P. 1987. "Acute Hypothalamic-Pituitary-Adrenal Responses to the Stress of Treadmill Exercise: Physiologic Adaptations to Physical Training." *New England Journal of Medicine* 316(21):1309–1315.

Lundberg, U., and Forsman, L. 1980. "Consistency in Catecholamine and Cortisol Excretion Patterns over Experimental Conditions." *Pharmacology Biochemistry and Behavior* 12:449–452.

Mason, J. W. 1968. "A Review of Psychoendocrine Research on the Pituitary-Adrenal Cortical System." *Psychosomatic Medicine* 30:576–607.

———. 1975. "A Historical View of the Stress Field: Part One." *Journal of Human Stress* 1(1):6–12.

———. 1975*b*. "Psychologic Stress and Endocrine Function." In *Topics in Psychoendocrinology,* ed. E. J. Sachar. New York: Grune & Stratton.

Mason, J. W.; Brady, J. V.; and Tolliver, G. A. 1968. "Plasma and Urinary 17-hydroxycorticosteroid Responses to 72-hour Avoidance Sessions in the Monkey." *Psychosomatic Medicine* 30:608–630.

Mason, J. W.; Giller, E. L.; Kosten, T. R.; Ostroff, R. B.; and Podd, L. 1986. "Urinary Free-cortisol Levels in Posttraumatic Stress Disorder Patients." *Journal of Nervous and Mental Disease* 174(3):145–149.

Meyerhoff, J. L.; Oleshansky, M. A.; and Mougey, E. H. 1988. "Psychologic Stress Increases Plasma Levels of Prolactin, Cortisol, and POMC-derived Peptides in Man." *Psychosomatic Medicine* 50:295–303.

Nanji, A. A.; Greenway, D. C.; and Bigdeli, M. 1985. "Relationship Between Growth Hormone Levels and Time Spent by Soldiers in an Active War Zone." *Hormones and Behavior* 10:348–350.

Nottelmann, E. D.; Susman, E. J.; Inoff-Germain, G.; Cutler, G. B.; Loriaux, D. L.; and Chrousos, G. P. 1987. "Developmental Processes in Early Adolescence: Relationships Between Adolescent Adjustment Problems and Chronologic Age, Pubertal Stage, and Puberty-related Serum Hormone Levels." *Journal of Pediatrics* 110(3):473–480.

Parker, L. N.; Levin, E. R.; and Lifrak, E. T. 1985. "Evidence for Adrenocortical Adaptation to Severe Illness." *Journal of Clinical Endocrinology and Metabolism* 60(5):947–952.

Payne, R. L.; Rick, J. T.; Smith, G. H.; and Cooper, R. G. 1984. "Multiple Indicators of Stress in an 'Active' Job—Cardiothoracic Surgery." *Journal of Occupational Medicine* 26(11):805–808.

Pinter, E. J.; Tolis, G.; Guyda, H.; et al. 1979. "Hormonal and Free Fatty Acid Changes During Strenuous Flight in Novices and Trained Personnel." *Psychoneuroendocrinology* 4:79–82.

Rose, R. M. 1980. "Endocrine Responses to Stressful Psychological Events." *Psychiatric Clinics of North America* 3(2):251–276.

———. 1984. "Overview of Endocrinology of Stress." In *Neuroendocrinology and Psychiatric Disorder,* ed. G. M. Brown. New York: Raven Press.

———. 1987. "Neuroendocrine Effects of Work Stress." In *Work Stress: Health Care Systems in the Workplace,* ed. J. C. Quick, R. S. Bhagat, J. E. Dalton, and J. D. Quick. New York: Praeger.

Rose, R. M.; Poe, R. O.; and Mason, J. W. 1968. "Psychological State and Body Size as Determinants of 17-OHCS Excretion." *Archives of Internal Medicine* 121:406–413.

Rose, R. M.; Bernstein, I. S.; Gordon, T. P.; and Lindsley, J. G. 1978. "Changes in Testosterone and Behavior During Adolescence in the Male Rhesus Monkey." *Psychosomatic Medicine* 40(1):60–70.

Rose, R. M.; Jenkins, C. D.; Hurst, M.; Herds, J. A.; and Hall, R. P. 1982. "Endocrine Activity in Air Traffic Controllers at Work. II. Biological, Psychological and Work Correlates." *Psychoneuroendocrinology* 7(2/3):113–123.

Sanders, G.; Freilicher, J.; and Lightman, S. L. 1990. "Psychological Stress of Exposure to Uncontrollable Noise Increases Plasma Oxytocin in High Emotionality Women." *Psychoneuroendocrinology* 15(1):47–58.

Sapolsky, R.; Armanini, M.; Packan, D.; and Tombaugh, G. 1987. "Stress and Glucocorticoids in Aging." *Endocrinology and Metabolism Clinics* 16(4):965–980.

Selye, H. 1950. *Stress: The Physiology and Pathology of Exposure to Stress.* New York: MD Publications.

Semple, C. G.; Gray, C. E.; Borland, W.; Espie, C. A.; and Beastall, G. H. 1988. "Endocrine Effects of Examination Stress." *Clinical Sciences* 74:255–259.

Singer, M. T. 1974. "Engagement-involvement: A Central Phenomenon in Psychophysiological Research." *Psychosomatic Medicine* 36:1–17.

Smith, M. A.; Davidson, J.; Ritchie, J. C.; Kudler, H.; Lipper, S.; Chappell, P.; and Nemeroff, C. B. 1989. "The Corticotropin-releasing Hormone Test in Patients with Posttraumatic Stress Disorder." *Society of Biological Psychiatry* 26:349–355.

Susman, E. J.; Nottelmann, E. D.; Dorn, L. D.; Inoff-Germain, G.; and Chrousos, G. P. 1988. "Physiological and Behavioral Aspects of Stress in Adolescence." *Advances in Experimental Medicine and Biology* 245:341–352.

Tennes, K.; Downey, K.; and Vernadakis, A. 1977. "Urinary Cortisol Excretion Rates and Anxiety in Normal One-year-old Infants." *Psychosomatic Medicine* 39: 178–187.

Thorn, G. W.; Jenkins, O.; and Laidlaw, J. C. 1953. "The Adrenal Response to Stress in Man." *Recent Progress in Hormone Research* 8:171.

Ursin, H.; Baade, E.; and Levine, S., eds. 1978. *Psychobiology of Stress: A Study of Coping Men.* New York: Academic Press.

Vassend, O.; Halvorsen, R.; and Norman, N. 1987. "Hormonal and Psychological Effects of Examination Stress." *Scandinavian Journal of Psychology* 28:75–82.

Warren, M. P., and Brooks-Gunn, J. 1989. "Mood and Behavior at Adolescence: Evidence for Hormonal Factors." *Journal of Endocrinology and Metabolism Clinics* 69(1):77–83.

Wittershein, G.; Brandenberger, G.; and Follenius, M. 1985. "Mental Task-induced Strain and Its After-effect Assessed Through Variations in Plasma Cortisol Levels." *Biological Psychology* 21:123–132.

Wolff, C. T.; Hofer, M. A.; and Mason, J. W. 1964. "Relationship Between Psychological Defenses and Mean Urinary 17-OHCS Excretion Rates: II. Methodological and Theoretical Considerations." *Psychosomatic Medicine* 26:592.

Wolff, C. T.; Friedman, S. B.; Hofer, M. A.; et al. 1964. "Relationship Between Psychological Defenses and Mean Urinary 17-OHCS Excretion Rates: I. A Predictive Study of Parents of Fatally Ill Children." *Psychosomatic Medicine* 26:576.

Yehuda, R.; Southwick, S. M.; Nussbaum, G.; Wahby, V.; Giller, E. L.; and Mason, J. W. 1990. "Low Urinary Cortisol Excretion in Patients with Posttraumatic Stress Disorder." *Journal of Nervous and Mental Disease* 178(6):366–369.

CHAPTER 4

The Boundaries of Alcoholism

Richard J. Frances
and Sheila Cooperman

Though more has been written about the chemical ethanol than any other substance, there has been considerable controversy about whether alcoholism (usually equated with alcohol dependence) is an illness and how to define its boundaries. Deciding on set points in what is a continuum of problems has been difficult and the definitions have shifted, influenced by empirical evidence, clinical judgment, and social, economic, and political forces. In the revised third edition of the *Diagnostic and Statistical Manual of Mental Disorders* (DSM-III-R; American Psychiatric Association 1987), the definition of dependence was significantly expanded to include psychosocial criteria in addition to criteria of tolerance and withdrawal symptoms, and severity criteria of mild, moderate, and severe were introduced (see table 4.1). The diagnosis of abuse was narrowed to a residual group that had significant problems with alcohol not sufficient to warrant the label of dependence (see table 4.2).

The definition of when alcohol use becomes a problem and how to define it in the DSM-III-R relates to issues of medical morbidity, mortality, development of tolerance, withdrawal symptoms, and a variety of psychosocial problems including alcohol use that interferes with important social, work, and legal obligations. Though amount of alcohol used, tolerance, and withdrawal phenomena may be objectively measured, often the more subtle and early signs of a problem are psychosocial, including alcohol use that interferes with important social, work, and legal obligations and depend in part on a culture's tolerance of patterns of substance use. Maladaptive behavioral changes that accompany the substance use are most frequently targeted as symptoms that cross the line from use to abuse. Impaired control, persistence of symptoms that co-occur with cognitive changes, and physiological disturbances are more likely to be seen as undesirable across cultures (APA 1987). The question of where to distinguish alcohol use from hazardous, harmful, abuse and dependence may vary with age and with individual characteristics. For example, the same amount of alcohol may have greater effects on the nervous system as one ages; loss of tolerance is seen in the elderly. Alcohol use may be hazardous, harmful, or abusive in populations with certain medical problems, such as liver disease and ulcers.

The boundaries between alcohol use, abuse, dependence, and normality are complicated and involve a number of paradoxes. Though most Americans drink, only a small percentage drink alcoholically. In American culture the mean and median person is a mild to moderate user of alcohol. Alcohol is the most widely used psychoactive substance in the United States, even more than nicotine. The national average consumption rate is somewhere around two ounces of alcohol per day; 10 percent of the population consumes about half of the alcohol produced (APA 1987). Per person over the age of fourteen, in 1987 the average annual consumption of absolute alcohol was 2.54 gallons. Although that amount is declining slightly and at the lowest level since 1970, alcohol still has a vast negative impact on public health (Seventh Special Report to the U.S. Congress on Alcohol and Health 1990). More than 70 percent of the population will report having used alcohol in the past month. Though this percentage is likely to vary across subculture and gender, most Americans drink regularly from high school on, even though the legal drinking age has been moved to twenty-one in most states. Of high school seniors, 92 percent have tried alcohol and nearly two-thirds are current drinkers (Johnson et al. 1988). This pattern may be contrasted with other cultures, such as Islam, where alcohol use is proscribed by the Koran and only a minority drink, or China, where a minority drinks alcohol. Alcohol use can be related to its cost and other cultural and biological factors.

Another paradox in the relationship between alcohol problems and normality is that those who tend to be relatively allergic to alcohol effects are most likely to be protected against developing an alcohol problem and may use alcohol in safe quantities. Goodwin (1985) has suggested that the alcoholic may be biologically predisposed to tolerate large quantities of alcohol with few ill effects and is not allergic to the effects of alcohol, whereas those who are made sick by relatively smaller quantities of alcohol may have a built-in protection. Schuckit (1987) has found that sons of alcoholics have greater tolerance to alcohol's effects. The Oriental flush is an example of low tolerance leading to a protective effect. Chinese people have a variant of alcohol dehydrogenase enzyme. It leads to a toxic buildup of acetaldehyde that is not metabolized to acetic acid. The flush syndrome includes headaches, bright red faces, gastrointestinal discomfort, rapid pulse, increased blood pressure, and resembles a small disulfiram alcohol reaction (Seventh Special Report 1990).

Also paradoxical is that in the same families where there is a high density of and high risk for alcoholism, there are greater numbers of abstainers from alcohol, perhaps in reaction to their fear of developing a problem. Moderate alcohol use may be an unreasonable goal for those with a high family density of alcoholism, and prevention for this group should include strategies that would promote abstinence.

An interesting question is whether or not it is more normal to drink mildly or moderately than not to drink at all. Many people who do not drink at all do so because they fear developing a problem, they have had a problem and later stopped, and/or they have a medical problem that may be worsened by drinking or that may reduce desire for drinking, such as depression, gastric ulcers, pancreatitis, or cardiac problems. Whether or not moderate intake of alcohol is protective against heart disease is controversial. Those who do not use alcohol might have higher additional risk factors, such as disease, which would mitigate the reported benefit of moderate drinking. Most studies have not adequately controlled for the possibility of these additional risk factors. With proper controls, it may be discovered that alcohol does not have any positive effect on cardiac function (Shaper, Wannamether, and Walker 1988).

As so many people drink alcohol and have been doing so for many years, it is of teleologic interest to ask what the beneficial effects of drinking are and how drinking benefits society and health. Though long debated by poets, philosophers, and theologians, benefits and risks of alcohol use are not fully understood scientifically. Alcohol is used as a social lubricant, an aid in disinhibiting people, a form of recreation and relaxation, and it can be used as a means of obtaining an altered state of consciousness. Alcohol use has also been thought of as a means of controlling feeling states, as an aid in denial and removal of painful affects, as enabling risk-taking behavior, and as a rationale for antisocial behavior (the so-called devil-made-me-do-it defense). Individuals may attribute independently desired behavior to the effects of drinking and attempt to avoid responsibility for it.

Alcohol has also played important economic, ritualistic, and social roles that have contributed to widespread use.

In this chapter we begin with models of alcoholism, a term first used by the Swedish physician Magnes Huss in 1849, then concentrate on the illness model; discuss recent definitions and examples of dangerous use; describe how culture, sex, and age differences affect the boundaries; detail techniques used for diagnostic screening; describe alcoholism's impact on families, its effects of psychiatric comorbidity, and what the public policy implications are of an illness model.

Models for the Development of Alcoholism

A variety of definitions and models of alcohol use, abuse, and dependence tend to either emphasize moral or illness aspects of the problem.

1. For centuries moralists have viewed alcohol use as a form of gluttony. In this view the alcoholic is seen as a self-indulgent, spineless person, unable to exert self-control or willed self-discipline. Movements such as the Women's Christian Temperance Union and the Anti-Saloon League in the nineteenth century promulgated the view that alcoholism was immoral.
2. Alcoholics Anonymous emphasizes a disease model. This model has for the most part been accepted by the American Medical Association and the American Psychiatric Association. It reduces the stigma of addiction and will be the major focus of this chapter. This model overlaps with some of the models to be described.
3. In the sociocultural model, alcohol use is seen in a broader social context in which sociocultural expectations are considered. Alcohol use may have different meanings in different cultures, may be used for ritual religious purposes, and may have culture-specific patterns (Jellinek 1960).
4. Alcoholism may be seen as a result of purely hereditary and biological factors. This relates closely to a medical model.
5. Alcohol use and addiction may be viewed as either a form of self-medication for other psychiatric problems or as a result of certain temperaments, such as sensation seeking or antisocial (Khantzian 1985).
6. Conversely, alcohol dependence may be seen as contributing to a variety of psychiatric problems. A broader view takes into account a complex interaction in which alcohol contributes to, is the primary

etiology of, coexists with, or interacts with a variety of psychiatric disorders (Meyer 1986).

9. The most widely accepted modern disease model sees alcoholism as a biopsychosocial illness that takes into account genetic vulnerability interacting with complex psychosocial and cultural factors and covers most of the issues just mentioned except for the moral model (Kissin 1983).

Alcoholism as an Illness

The Alcoholics Anonymous (AA) model views alcoholism as a disease in which a person cannot stop drinking despite the urgings of others or in the face of varying life crises. It is thought that vulnerability exists when the drinking starts and may be biological. This vulnerability is seen as an "allergy to alcohol," and the alcoholic reacts to alcohol in a different way from the nonalcoholic (this is the inverse of the Goodwin model mentioned earlier). In the AA view, the only way to stop the disease's progress is by total abstinence, and though alcoholism can be arrested it cannot be cured (Heather and Robertson 1983).

Jellinek (1960) has divided alcoholics into five categories based on the assumption that alcoholism is a disease. The Alpha alcoholic has psychological dependence without becoming physically addicted. Drinking does not get out of control, and the drinking pattern does not appear to worsen progressively. Beta alcoholics are those who experience physical consequences as a result of their drinking but do not become psychologically or physically dependent on alcohol. Gamma alcoholics do experience physical dependence, loss of control, and increased tolerance to the effects of alcohol, and constitute the most common American pattern of drinking. Delta alcoholics, a pattern commonly found in continental Europe, have physical dependence without loss of control and are unable to remain abstinent without experiencing withdrawal symptoms. The final category, Epsilon alcoholics, are those who drink periodically in binges. Alpha and Beta are close to modern definitions of abuse and Gamma and Delta fit with dependence or alcoholism.

Bean-Bayog (1986) sees alcoholism as a traumatic event that in and of itself can produce psychopathology. She views the development of alcoholism as a painful experience that begins gradually and leads to out-of-control drinking patterns in which individuals have little awareness of what has happened to them. Their repeated efforts to control their behavior without getting treatment for the underlying issues which lead to their drinking produce traumatic disruptions in their lives and have placed them in numerous potentially dangerous situations, such as driving motor vehicles while intoxicated. They may be stigmatized, subject to blows to their self-esteem, and experience numerous personal and financial losses as a result of their alcoholism. In order to prevent future recurrence, their underlying vulnerability needs to be treated. Treatment should focus on dealing with the consequences of their behavior and on teaching them how to protect themselves from reexperiencing future trauma if pathological drinking continues.

In Khantzian's (1985) self-medication hypothesis, individuals have a predisposition to develop addiction by virtue of their vulnerability to painful affect and psychological conflicts. He postulates that addicts use drugs to medicate their symptoms despite the risks and consequences secondary to the drug use. According to Khantzian (1986), addicts use drugs to modulate their feeling states and to adapt to life. He indicates that this is consistent with some of the newer neurochemical studies regarding transmitters as well as genetic studies on the inheritance of substance abuse disorders.

Vaillant (1983) conceives of alcoholism as both a disease and a behavior disorder. He likens alcoholism to essential hypertension; both have no one specific known etiology but are due to a pathologic process. Both are multifactorially determined and have no universally accepted definition upon which all clinicians agree. Vaillant argues that alcoholism should be understood and studied as a behavior disorder. To treat the disorder, the disease concept is the more useful framework.

Genetic studies of alcoholism indicate that alcoholism runs in families. Some of the most compelling data comes from Danish adoption studies and twin studies (Goodwin 1983). Children of biological parents who are alcoholic and have been raised in nonalcoholic homes and have no knowledge of their parents have higher rates of alcoholism. Children who are adopted by alcoholics and who have no family history of alcoholism do not show higher rates of alcoholism as adults. These data led Goodwin to discuss familial versus nonfamilial alcoholism and have led to other typologies, such as Cloninger, Dunwiddie, and Reich's (1989) type 1 and type 2 alcoholics. Type 1 alcoholics have a later onset, are often anxious and inhibited, are more affected by environmental issues, and are less likely to have antisocial problems. Type 2 alcoholics are more likely to be male, have early onset of problems, more antisocial problems, drink for stimulation, show more risk-taking behavior, and have a greater biological predisposition to the development of alcoholism.

DSM and Other Modern Definitions of Alcoholism

The modern concept of alcoholism as an illness has evolved over two hundred years and fits the DSM-III-R definition of a mental disorder. It is "a clinically significant behavioral psychological syndrome or pattern that occurs in a person and that is associated with present distress (a painful symptom) or disability (impairment in one or more important areas of functioning) or with a significantly increased risk of suffering death, pain, disability, or an important loss of freedom" (APA 1987, *xxii*). Alcoholism causes morbidity, mortality, and has a discrete symptom complex, a clinical course and outcome, and though its etiology involves a complex interplay of genetic with environmental, cultural and psychological factors, there are important biological vulnerabilities as in the case of many other psychiatric and medical disorders (such as major depression, hypertension, diabetes, and coronary artery disease).

The effects of alcohol misuse can cause a spectrum of problems that form a continuum which makes placing set points for defining levels of the problem difficult. The criteria used to set boundaries of inclusion or exclusion for diagnosis of abuse and dependence (the term *dependence* is often equated with alcoholism) are being considered in planning the DSM-IV. Every attempt is being made to review carefully the literature for empirical data that can aid in setting the points properly and analyzing each criterion involved in making the diagnosis. In a study of 215 outpatients in Germany, Hiller, Mombour, and Mittelhammer (1989) found a high diagnostic efficiency for DSM-III-R criteria of dependence. All the DSM-III-R criteria were supported compared to additional alcoholism characteristics; the most clearly distinguishing features were those that referred to impaired control over use and to physical dependence. In this study, presence of two criteria was sufficient to diagnose alcohol dependence reliably, although the DSM-III-R requires three criteria.

At one end of the spectrum of alcohol problems is severe dependence with tolerance (both pharmacodynamic and metabolic) and withdrawal (Edwards 1986). These patients have severe physical withdrawal effects from abstinence including craving, compulsion to drink, loss of control over drinking, and requiring increased quantities of alcohol to achieve the same effect. Here we have a stronger data base and an empirical underpinning for a diagnosis, and the agreement about diagnosis is generally easier. More controversial are the set points of what constitutes abuse, and where abuse differs from mild dependence, and where mild dependence ends. Here distinctions are ultimately likely to be influenced by public acceptance, cultural factors, economic realities, and clinical considerations. It becomes very difficult to determine at what point harmful or hazardous use of alcohol becomes severe enough to be labeled abuse. At the less severe end of the scale, biological testing is less precise and less able to provide a clear diagnosis, and clinical signs and symptoms become more subjective.

Edwards and Gross (1976) first proposed the alcohol dependence syndrome (ADS), a dimensional phenomena with varying severity and a psychophysiologic basis, and eliminated the term *alcoholism.* ADS served as a model for the World Health Organization's (WHO) *International Classification of Diseases* (ICD-9) and the DSM-III definitions. The ICD-9 did not include alcohol-related disabilities as criteria whereas they are included in DSM-III and DSM-III-R. Evident in the DSM-III-R is a trend that broadens the concept of dependence. In part this trend is based on a greater public awareness of alcohol and drug abuse problems and less public acceptance of heavy substance use and the consequent psychosocial problems that result (see table 4.1) (APA 1987). Cultural acceptance of use of illegal substances has declined since the 1970s. Awareness of the high danger of cocaine use, for example, is reflected in the development of the diagnosis of cocaine dependence.

During the creation of the psychoactive substance section of the DSM-III-R, controversy arose as to whether expansion of the concept of dependence should lead to elimination of the concept of abuse, which was kept as a residual category (see table 4.2) (APA 1987). The controversy stems from the concern that when the concept dependence is broadened to include mild dependence and abuse is added, a large segment of the population can be identified as having an alcohol problem. The boundary between subthreshold and alcohol disorders forms a continuum that is hard to quantify. On the one hand, a broad concept of dependence contributes to earlier screening, evaluation, prevention, and treatment; however, it also leads to a higher percentage of the population being labeled with a mental illness. The use of the terms *mild, moderate,* and *severe* is a way to indicate and label the continuum of severity (see table 4.1) (APA 1987).

Currently efforts are underway to develop DSM-IV and ICD-10 criteria for worldwide use by 1994. Likely they will include many features from their predecessors, including a dimensional model of dependence with severity criteria. It is hoped that they will synthesize most valid items. Though worded differently, the currently proposed ICD-10 alcohol dependence criteria overlaps with DSM-III criteria in areas of compulsion, loss of control, relief drinking, withdrawal, tolerance, progressive neglect of other activities, and harmful consequences. Whereas the proposed ICD-10 includes a criteria for narrowing of personal repertoire, the DSM-III-R does not but adds items related to time spent involved with alcohol and

TABLE 4.1

DSM-III-R Criteria for Psychoactive Substance Dependence

A. At least three of the following:

(1) substance often taken in larger amounts or over a longer period than the person intended

(2) persistent desire or one or more unsuccessful efforts to cut down or control substance use

(3) a great deal of time spent in activities necessary to get the substance (e.g., theft), taking the substance (e.g., chain smoking), or recovering from its effects

(4) frequent intoxication or withdrawal symptoms when expected to fulfill major role obligations at work, school, or home (e.g., does not go to work because hung over, goes to school or work "high," intoxicated while taking care of his or her children), or when substance use is physically hazardous (e.g., drives when intoxicated)

(5) important social, occupational, or recreational activities given up or reduced because of substance use

(6) continued substance use despite knowledge of having a persistent or recurrent social, psychological, or physical problem that is caused or exacerbated by the use of the substance (e.g., keeps using heroin despite family arguments about it, cocaine-induced depression, or having an ulcer made worse by drinking)

(7) marked tolerance: need for markedly increased amounts of the substance (i.e., at least a 50% increase) to achieve intoxication or desired effect, or markedly diminished effect with continued use of the same amount

(8) characteristic withdrawal symptoms . . .

(9) substance often taken to relieve or avoid withdrawal symptoms

B. Some symptoms of the disturbance have persisted for at least one month, or have occurred repeatedly over a longer period of time.

Criteria for Severity of Psychoactive Substance Dependence:

Mild: Few, if any, symptoms in excess of those required to make the diagnosis, and the symptoms result in no more than mild impairment in occupational functioning or in usual social activities or relationships with others.

Moderate: Symptoms or functional impairment between "mild" and "severe."

Severe: Many symptoms in excess of those required to make the diagnosis, and the symptoms markedly interfere with occupational functioning or with usual social activities or relationships with others.[1]

In Partial Remission: During the past six months, some use of the substance and some symptoms of dependence.

In Full Remission: During the past six months, either no use of the substance, or use of the substance and no symptoms of dependence.

[1]Because of the availability of cigarettes and other nicotine-containing substances and the absence of a clinically significant nicotine intoxication syndrome, impairment in occupational or social functioning is not necessary for a rating of severe Nicotine Dependence.

TABLE 4.2

DSM-III-R Criteria for Psychoactive Substance Abuse

A. A maladaptive pattern of psychoactive substance use indicated by at least one of the following:
  (1) continued use despite knowledge of having a persistent or recurrent social, occupational, psychological, or physical problem that is caused or exacerbated by use of the psychoactive substance
  (2) recurrent use in situations in which use is physically hazardous (e.g., driving while intoxicated)

B. Some symptoms of the disturbance have persisted for at least one month, or have occurred repeatedly over a longer period of time.

C. Never met the criteria for Psychoactive Substance Dependence for this substance.

interference with role obligations. Both systems keep alcohol abuse as a residual category. If the DSM-IV can closely approximate ICD-10, there will be less confusion in interpreting cross-cultural diagnostic studies and a clearer international diagnostic dialogue on alcohol dependence (Seventh Special Report 1990).

In ICD-10 substance use disorders have specified clinical states that include acute intoxication, harmful use, dependence syndrome, withdrawal state, withdrawal state with delirium, psychotic disorder, late-onset psychotic disorder, and amnesic syndrome. The term *abuse* is not used, but harmful use, hazardous use, and misuse are defined. *Harmful use* is a clinical diagnostic term denoting a pattern of psychoactive substance use that damages physical or mental health and that may be accompanied by social consequences. This category is similar to the DSM-III-R concept of substance abuse, which usually includes social consequences. *Hazardous use* is defined as risk that a pattern of substance use will probably lead to harmful consequences with future damage to physical or mental health, but does not include risk of social consequences. In contrast to harmful use, it has public health significance even though there is no current clinical disorder. *Misuse* denotes use of a psychoactive substance not consistent with legal or medical guidelines, such as nonmedical use of prescription medications. The term was used instead of abuse in order to denote a less judgmental attitude. The development of alcohol problems, therefore, fits into a continuum that is more dimensional than categorical, though the categories are developed for definitional purposes.

According to a recent redefinition of alcoholism by the National Council on Alcoholism and Drug Dependence and the American Society of Addiction Medicine (1990), "alcoholism is a primary chronic disease with genetic, psychosocial, and environmental factors influencing its development and manifestations. The disease is often progressive and fatal. It is characterized by continuous or periodic impaired control over drinking, preoccupation with the drug alcohol, use of alcohol despite adverse consequences and distortions in thinking, most notably denial" (p. 1). This definition, which is similar to the DSM-III-R dependence category, emphasizes that alcoholism is separate from other disorders and is not a symptom of an underlying disease state. The emphasis on disease involves voluntary disability, and the inclusion of the term *denial* underlines that trend. This definition remains broad, is more difficult to put into operational terms than the more specific DSM-III-R criteria, and may not adequately include those who have alcoholism secondary to other psychiatric causes.

This definition also raises the question of whether alcoholism is one or several disorders. Data must be analyzed to see whether they can be further categorized. A number of overlapping categories have been suggested, such as Alpha-Beta-Gamma-Delta-Epsilon, primary versus secondary, familial versus nonfamilial, continuous versus episodic, those with or without loss of control, and type I versus type II, and measures of severity have also been introduced. The complexity of alcoholism in regard to other psychiatric disorders that may coexist, result from, cause or interact with it is discussed later in this chapter. The high incidence of alcoholism and its tendency to lead to a greater chance of hospitalization when combined with other disorders may contribute to the high incidence of comorbidity in hospitalized populations. Alcoholism can mimic or be concealed by a number of psychiatric disorders, and intoxication, withdrawal, and chronic effects may be hard to separate. Though the data tend to support a discrete inheritance of alcoholism as a separate illness (Schuckit 1986), the concept of a possible more nonspecific psychiatric vulnerability (Winokur et al. 1974) has not been fully disproven.

We feel that alcohol dependence more often is a primary problem, although it can be a secondary problem, and it occurs in those with greater or lesser biological and cultural contributions. Though currently none of the subtypes has been adequately tested, we expect that the concept of alcoholism includes multiple paths. Eventually some of the newer subtypes may become established by the data.

Areas of Potentially Dangerous Alcohol Use

It is very easy to diagnose and treat a chronic illness like alcoholism late in its course; early in its course it may be easier to treat or prevent and yet harder to detect. Diagnosis is more difficult because of denial. Denial may be part of the patient's character. It is heightened by alcohol's toxic effects; is shared by the family, employer, the health care system; and is increased by the wish to avoid social stigma. Developing criteria that clearly separate the gradations from use of alcohol to harmful, hazardous use, abuse, and dependence has been difficult. Drinking and driving just once may be hazardous, for example. Any drinking during pregnancy may be harmful. An individual may appear to be functioning quite well in many spheres or compared to others and still have significant impairment. For example, it was reputed that the actor Richard Burton could perform *Hamlet* after drinking a quart of vodka. Very often the alcoholism is not noted until significant work or health problems appear.

An area of controversy is the use of alcohol during pregnancy; no safe level of use has been found in pregnant women. One of the extreme consequences of alcohol use is fetal alcohol syndrome (FAS). FAS is one of the most prevalent causes of mental deficiency in the United States (Fisher and Karl 1988). Alcohol has long been known to cause high rates of fetal and infant mortality, morbidity, and physical and mental retardation even when taken in moderate quantities during pregnancy (Seventh Special Report 1990).

The incidence of FAS is between 0.4 and 3.1 per thousand (Sokol, Miller, and Reed 1980) in the United States. Partial expression of the syndrome is thought to be higher (Fisher and Karl 1988). The diagnosis is made when an infant shows a combination of central nervous system dysfunction (mental retardation, microcephaly, or irritability), growth retardation and facial dysmorphia consisting of short palpebral fissures, hypoplastic philtrum, thin upper vermillion border, and small chin (Fisher and Karl 1988). Nearly all FAS babies have been born to heavy drinkers or to those who drink heavily on a frequent basis. A major risk to the fetus is thought to occur when the mother consumes the equivalent of six drinks of hard liquor per day (National Institute on Alcohol Abuse and Alcoholism 1977). Some babies may be predisposed genetically to the damage of alcohol, and some risk factors in addition to the use of alcohol may act in combination to produce alcohol-related birth defects (Martin et al. 1979).

FAS may be at the outer limit of damage caused to the fetus by alcohol use during pregnancy. There are more subtle neurological and behavioral effects observed in children whose mothers drank lightly, moderately, or fairly heavily (0.1 ounce or less per day, 0.1 to 0.9 ounces per day, and 1 ounce or more per day, respectively). These effects include delayed ability to stop responding to extraneous stimuli (Streissguth, Martin, and Barr 1983), weak suck, increased body tremors, and less intense body activity

(Martin et al. 1979). Evaluation of current data suggest that for pregnant women, no level of alcohol consumption may be safe (Seventh Special Report 1990). This controversy has led to public health warnings and labeling on bottles about the effects of alcohol during pregnancy.

Another area in which the use of alcohol has been considered dangerous by treatment experts in the past has been in the recovery from alcoholism. Helzer and associates (1985) reviewed 1,289 cases of diagnosed alcoholics at five and seven years after treatment; they found that 1.6 percent of the patients were able to maintain a moderate drinking pattern, defined as daily consumption of up to six drinks over a two-year period. When they included patients who occasionally drank but were mostly abstinent, the percentage rose to 6 percent. According to this study, only rarely can an alcoholic return to moderate drinking. This is particularly notable as alcoholism is first among thirty psychiatric diagnoses in men under sixty-five and fourth for women between the ages of eighteen and twenty-four (Myers et al. 1984; Regier et al. 1984), and between 19 and 30 percent of men met DSM-III criteria for alcohol abuse or dependence some time during their life (Robins et al. 1984).

Alcohol use may be abusive in subpopulations that have medical problems in which the use of alcohol is contraindicated, such as those with liver disease, ulcers, and gastrointestinal disease. In some cases the self-medication of a medical diagnosis may lead to the development of alcoholism. An example is benign familial tremor, which is characterized by worsening with writing, eating, drinking and when there is an emotionally stressful situation. It appears to be slowly progressive, annoying, and potentially embarrassing. There appears to be no specific pathology or neurochemical deficit, and two substances appear to alleviate the symptoms, alcohol and propranolol. While alcohol has a long history of being effective in decreasing the severity of the tremor, using a potentially addictive substance for a chronic disease can be hazardous and lead to dependence (Wells and Duncan 1980).

Cultural and Sex Differences

Though amount of alcohol used, tolerance, and withdrawal phenomena can be objectively measured, the more subtle and early signs of a problem may be more heavily psychosocial and depend in part on the tolerance of a culture for use of a particular substance. Maladaptive behavior changes that accompany the use of substances are what become targeted most frequently as symptoms that cross the line from use to abuse. Impaired control, persistence of symptoms that co-occur with cognitive changes, and physiologic disturbances are seen as undesirable across cultures (APA 1987).

Helzer and associates (1990) did the best international cross-cultural epidemiologic alcohol study building on the national epidemiologic catchment area study using DSM-III and the Diagnostic Interview Scale (DIS). In the five countries they studied, there was wide variation in lifetime prevalence but similarity in onset, symptomatic expression, and risk factors, such as male sex and age cohort effects. As opposed to schizophrenia, there is greater variation of incidence for alcoholism. This indicates the importance of the cultural context when definitions are held constant. The clinicians doing the study felt the items in the DSM-III and the DIS were appropriate to their various settings. In summary, phenotypic expression of alcohol problems is therefore similar across cultures, though numbers of those with different severity vary with cultural context. Acceptance of a threshold for calling alcoholism a problem is likely to vary in each culture, though the need for internationally accepted standards is great especially if comparisons such as this study are done.

For example, in French culture mild social lapses due to drinking are viewed very differently from in Chinese culture, where behavior associated with the use of alcohol may lead to loss of face or be considered shameful. In Islamic culture prohibitions against drinking are due to social and religious sanctions with consequent reduced use. What appears to be abnormal behavior may be considered quite usual within some subcultures. For example, homeless minority men in Newark who face stressful and hopeless life situations may consider it fairly normal to spend a high percentage of their welfare checks on alcohol. It may be viewed as one of the few available escapes from a very painful life situation. Though objectively in this instance alcohol may lead to major morbidity and mortality and is clearly seen as abusive by medical and psychiatric observers, within the subculture many have accepted and view this behavior as a normal part of life and one of life's few remaining pleasures.

Another example of a subculture effect was the widespread acceptance of heavy drinking in the U.S. Navy until the early 1970s in officers' and enlisted men's clubs. This followed a tradition dating back to the British navy issuing daily rum rations to sailors. Drinking together was a way to socialize and find acceptance as well as support. Change occurred when the costs of such acceptance in terms of impaired performance of duties and excessive health costs attributable to alcoholism were recognized.

In the United States blacks are more likely to abstain from alcohol than whites, and black men are more likely to drink less heavily than white men. In contrast, white women are more likely to drink less heavily than black women. There is a higher rate of alcohol use and abuse among Hispanic men than in the general population, and Hispanics born in the United States drink more heavily than those born in their native countries. Nearly half of Hispanic women do not drink alcohol (Sixth Special Report to the U.S. Congress on Alcohol and Health, 1987).

Asian Americans, especially women of all Asian groups, have high rates of abstaining from alcohol. Overall there are low rates of alcoholism and alcohol abuse in Asian Americans (Sixth Special Report 1987). In contrast, American Indians have high rates of alcoholism and alcohol abuse. Injury and illness due to alcohol is three times greater in American Indians than in the general population. Cirrhosis is the fourth leading cause of death in this population (Sixth Special Report 1987).

Alcohol affects women in slightly different ways than it does men. The same volume of alcohol has greater effects on women, possibly related to the fact that more alcohol is metabolized in men's gastrointestinal tracts. Women's perhaps greater sensitivity to alcohol's effects may contribute to their lower tolerance for alcohol and their lower tendency to develop abuse and dependence problems (Frezza et al. 1990). It is still not clear how much lower rates of alcoholism in women relate to these biological protective factors versus cultural factors in the use of alcohol.

In studies that look at the development of alcoholism in women, there appears to be some evidence of genetic transmission. Significant differences exist between men and women; women begin their abuse at a later age but present for treatment at the same time, which may indicate that their disease process accelerates more rapidly. Women appear to be as vulnerable to the physical consequences of excessive alcohol consumption as men, but their alcohol-related diseases are evident after only 14.2 years of excessive drinking compared to 20.2 years in men. In addition, when compared to men, women had been drinking heavily for a shorter period of time before their first diagnosed alcohol-related disease, such as gastrointestinal bleeding, malnutrition, anemia, or hypertension (Ashley et al. 1977; Blume 1986). Women are more likely to indicate that their alcohol abuse began in response to stress and to come to treatment complaining of family conflicts and health problems, whereas men are more likely to be experiencing legal difficulties or occupational conflicts (Blume 1986).

Age Differences

Recent efforts have been made to control alcohol use in youth. Some of the more common questions that have been raised are whether it is best to proscribe alcohol use in youth, ritualize it, or teach responsible drinking. It may also be that there are subgroups of adolescents for whom any alcohol use may be risky, such as children in high-density alcoholic families. The development of alcohol abuse and dependency tends to occur in late adolescence or early adulthood. The age of onset of alcohol problems is later for women than men. Alcohol use in teenagers may be a stepping-stone to other substance use and may also be correlated with increased risk-taking behavior and sexual activity.

The behavior of drug-free adolescents is significantly different from that of those who are abusing substances. The nonabusers are more cautious and careful in the kinds of behavior they engage in and are seen as more mature. They appear to have more secure childhoods, optimistic personalities, confront their life problems without avoidance, and do not like the effects of alcohol. They have realistic views of their problems and do not feel driven to use drugs or alcohol. They have long-term goals and do not come from families that use drugs and alcohol to handle their life problems (Hendricks 1989).

In the geriatric population, the lower prevalence of alcohol abuse may be secondary to a change in the body's response to alcohol. The elderly have decreased volume of body water, hormonal changes, differences in tissue sensitivity, and differing rates of metabolism and elimination that contribute a reduced tolerance to the effects of alcohol (Straus 1984). The two groups over the age of sixty-five who do abuse alcohol are those who began drinking abusively earlier in life and who have continued into their later years and those who had started drinking heavily late. Approximately two-thirds of the elderly who abuse alcohol fall into the first category and may have the physical concomitants of alcoholism, such as liver disease, pancreatitis, and gastrointestinal disease. The other third are people who usually began drinking in response to life events, such as change in living situation, loss of friends and loved ones, or loss of a job (Holzer et al. 1984; Sixth Special Report 1987; Williams 1984).

Screening for Alcoholism

Blood alcohol levels have been used to indicate tolerance and dependence on alcohol. If the person does not show the usual picture of intoxication at blood levels of 150 mg%, it is highly likely that he or she is dependent on and tolerant to the effects of alcohol (Gallant 1988). Other indications of alcoholism include increased levels of liver enzymes, such as gamma-glutamyl transpeptidase (GGTP) and serum glutamic oxalacetic transaminase (SGOT), alkaline phosphatase, uric acid, triglycerides, bilirubin, and macrocytosis on the hemogram (Gallant 1988; Morse and Heest 1979).

Carbohydrate-deficient transferrin appears to be a sensitive and specific marker for alcohol abuse. Kapur, Wild, and Triger (1989) detected carbohydrate-deficient transferrin in nineteen out of twenty-two alcoholics who used 80 grams or more of alcohol for three weeks prior to testing. There appear to be few false positives for this laboratory measure. At this time the use of the screen is experimental, but it may prove helpful in future diagnostics of alcoholism.

Nonlaboratory tests can be useful as well. One indirect method is the MacAndrew's Alcoholism Scale, which is derived from forty-nine items on the Minnesota Multiphasic Personality Inventory (Babor and Kadden 1983). It does not directly assess drinking behavior but rather the impulsive, acting-out behaviors observed in substance abusers (Gallant 1988).

Questionnaires such as the Michigan Alcohol Screening Test (MAST, see table 4.3) assess an alcoholic's history by the responses to a twenty-five-item true/false instrument. A commonly used, simple assessment can be done by asking four questions with the beginning letters CAGE. *C*—Have you ever thought of *c*utting back on your drinking? *A*—Do you get *a*nnoyed by others complaining about your alcohol use? *G*—Do you ever feel *g*uilty about your drinking? *E*—Do you ever need a morning *e*yeopener? (Ewing 1984).

Alcoholic Families

In some families alcoholism is a norm for generations. The impact of this raises the question of whether there is a specific syndrome of adult children of alcoholics, or if the problems that arise from growing up in an alcoholic family are generically related to any dysfunctional family. There has been a recent rapid growth in support groups and psychoeducational literature for adult children of alcoholics. Scientific research available about adult children of alcoholics is limited and has not demonstrated specific effects. However, the kinds of behaviors noted have also been observed in families where there has been chronic parental illness due to mental or physical reasons. Commonalities are the lack of opportunity to learn what is normal as opposed to abnormal (Miller and Tuchfeld 1986), an inconsistent model of healthy adult relationships (O'Brien, Woody, and McLellan 1983), and neglect that causes wounds to self-esteem (Wegscheider-Cruse 1985). Adult children of alcoholics have had to survive the pathology within the family and have learned to remain aloof and cut off from the experience

TABLE 4.3

Michigan Alcoholism Screening Test (MAST)

Directions: If a statement says something true about you, put a check in the nearby space under YES. If a statement says something not true about you, put a check in the nearby space under NO. Please answer all questions.	Yes	No
1. Do you feel you are a normal drinker?		
2. Have you ever awakened the morning after some drinking the night before and found that you could not remember a part of the evening?		
3. Does your wife/husband (or parents) ever worry or complain about your drinking?		
4. Can you stop drinking without a struggle after one or two drinks?		
5. Do you ever feel bad about your drinking?		
6. Do friends or relatives think you are a normal drinker?		
7. Do you ever try to limit your drinking to certain times of the day or to certain places?		
8. Are you always able to stop drinking when you want to?		
9. Have you ever attended a meeting of Alcoholics Anonymous (AA)?		
10. Have you gotten into fights when drinking?		
11. Has drinking ever created problems with you and your wife/husband?		
12. Has your wife/husband (or other family member) ever gone to anyone for help about your drinking?		
13. Have you ever lost friends (girlfriends or boyfriends) because of your drinking?		
14. Have you ever gotten into trouble at work because of your drinking?		
15. Have you ever lost a job because of your drinking?		
16. Have you ever neglected your obligations, your family or your work for two or more days in a row because you were drinking?		
17. Do you ever drink before noon?		
18. Have you ever been told you have liver trouble?		
19. Have you ever had delirium tremens (DTs), severe shaking, heard voices or seen things that were not there after heavy drinking?		
20. Have you ever gone to anyone for help about your drinking?		
21. Have you ever been in a hospital because of your drinking?		
22. Have you ever been a patient in a psychiatric hospital or on a psychiatric ward of a general hospital where drinking was part of the problem?		
23. Have you ever been seen at a psychiatric or mental health clinic, or gone to a doctor, social worker, or clergyman for help with an emotional problem in which drinking played a part?		
24. Have you ever been arrested, even for a few hours, because of drunk behavior?		
25. Have you ever been arrested for drunk driving or driving after drinking?		

of affect. This can contribute to distortions and misperceptions in order to deny a parent's alcoholism. They may have learned this from observing the nondrinking parent. Mental health professionals may misdiagnose these types of denial, viewing them as borderline symptoms rather than as a void of normal experiences in the area of relationships (Miller and Tuchfeld 1986).

Adult children of alcoholics may appear more sensitive to changes in their environments as they have had to wonder repeatedly whether their parent will be drunk or sober upon return home and have had to continually face an unpredictable home life. Adaptation to this chaos can contribute to the children fitting into the environment rather than to developing a strong sense of self and independence or separateness from what is going on around them. Instead they have achieved a pseudoindependence early in life by having to take on the responsibilities forfeited by their alcoholic parent. As with the alcoholic, the children are at risk for acting impulsively. This may be a sign of an immature personality rather than due to a psychiatric disorder. Education and clarification of issues can improve the functioning of adult children of alcoholics (Miller and Tuchfeld 1986).

Comorbidity

Any discussion of alcohol and normality would not be complete without a focus on the interaction between alcohol and the development of psychiatric symptomatology. In this section we discuss how alcoholism may be mistaken for other psychiatric disorders as well as the interaction or relationship between alcohol and other psychiatric disorders.

Alcohol is a central nervous system depressant and is a "great mimicker" of psychiatric symptoms (Schuckit 1983). The most common symptoms are consistent with anxiety, depression, mania, memory impairment, and psychoses. These may become apparent during intoxication, withdrawal, or longer-term abstinence. Semlitz and Gold (1986) recommend a two- to three-week drug-free interval prior to making a definitive psychiatric diagnosis and instituting a trial of medication if the symptoms appear to warrant this intervention.

During withdrawal from alcohol, one can observe increased agitation, tension, diaphoresis, increased blood pressure, and rapid heart rate as well as increased temperature. There may be confusion diagnostically as to whether this is due to an anxiety disorder or a manifestation of the alcohol withdrawal syndrome. High levels of anxiety may be prominent at the end of the withdrawal phase and when there is a prolonged period of abstinence (Bukstein, Brent, and Kaminer 1989). Again, this may be confused with an anxiety disorder as opposed to a time-limited concomitant of recovery from alcoholism.

Crowe and associates' (1980) family study of anxiety neuroses, later termed *panic disorder,* observed that there appears to be a fourfold greater frequency of alcoholism in male relatives of those diagnosed with a panic disorder. This supports a possible genetic vulnerability to both alcoholism and anxiety disorders within the same family.

The pharmacologic action of alcohol can cause sadness (Schuckit 1979*a*) that can feel like desperation and dependency and may last from two to four weeks (Schuckit 1986) and can be confused with symptoms of a major depression. This drug-induced effect will resolve over a relatively short period of time, usually five to seven days, in contrast to primary affective disorders, which have symptoms that generally last for longer time. Schuckit (1979*a*) suggests that an alcoholic may have a deteriorating life situation that combines with the drug-induced sadness and can add to the difficulty in differentiating an affective disorder.

As people experience impaired judgment when they are depressed or manic, they may attempt to medicate themselves to induce an alcohol euphoria or to alleviate their tensions and worsen their original symptoms. Alcohol can precipitate symptoms that can appear to be mania. Genetic studies (Schuckit 1986) have shown few consistent reports that those with a primary affective disorder are at higher risk for developing alcoholism. This adds to the problem of diagnosing true affective disorders when alcoholism also presents. However, while depressive symptomotology is frequent in alcoholism, especially during withdrawal, it is most often transitory.

Alcohol has a direct effect on neurons and can lead to memory dysfunction. While this can be a short, time-limited event, prolonged alcohol use may lead to significant irreversible memory deficits. Alcohol intoxication can cause slurring of speech, impaired short-term memory, and lead to disorientation, which can be confused with a permanent organic brain syndrome. The impairment from acute intoxication is usually of a temporary nature, but delirium tremens may develop during withdrawal and can cause memory dysfunction (Schuckit 1983). Delirium tremens can be confused with a psychotic process, as delusions and hallucinations can be observed during the autonomic hyperactivity of withdrawal. Again, these symptoms may clear within a week. Caution should be taken when considering the mode of treatment and final diagnosis.

Long-standing memory impairment from alcohol use may be consistent with Wernicke-Korsakoff (ataxia and sixth-nerve paralysis or global deterioration with recent memory dysfunction being significantly worse) or alcoholic dementia, but it is important to distinguish between the transitory, reversible changes due to alcohol use from the irreversible ones (Schuckit 1983).

Alcohol is associated with psychotic symptoms, which can occur when one is withdrawing from alcohol, as in alcoholic hallucinosis, or in delirium tremens. Visual and auditory hallucinations can occur as well as paranoid delusions (Schuckit 1983, 1982). As with other psychiatric symptoms that co-occur with alcohol use, these psychoses usually clear within a short period of time without the use of a neuroleptic. Only rarely do delusions or hallucinations remain for longer than a week. The etiology of these psychotic symptoms has not been identified, and it is unclear whether they are an indirect or direct effect of alcohol. There does not appear to be a connection between these psychotic processes and schizophrenia. No studies have shown an increased rate of alcoholism in families of schizophrenics (Schuckit 1983).

It is also important to point out the high rates at which alcoholism does occur in addition to other psychiatric diagnoses. Helzer and Pryzbeck (1988) reviewed previous studies of clinical populations that indicated there was a high co-occurrence of alcoholism and psychiatric disorders. They were interested in determining whether there were similar findings in the general population of those who were not in treatment. They used data from the Epidemiologic Catchment Area survey (Regier et al. 1984) of approximately 20,000 persons located in five areas of the United States. Alcoholism was found to be the most common diagnosis, 13 percent of the total sample. Approximately 34 percent of the total sample met DSM-III criteria for a psychiatric disorder in their lifetime. Of the 13 percent of the total sample that met criteria for alcoholism, 47 percent of them had another psychiatric diagnosis.

Alcoholics had a greater degree of drug dependence diagnoses, 18 percent, and 9 percent of the alcoholics were addicted to opiates, sedatives, or stimulants. The most frequent associations between alcoholism and other diagnoses were in order of strongest to weakest: antisocial personality disorder, drug abuse/dependence, and mania. The other affective disorders of depression and dysthymia were not markedly overrepresented. The authors hypothesize that those rates may be lower in a nonclinical sample.

Alcoholism was five times more common in men than women, but 65 percent of the women alcoholics had a second diagnosis compared to 44 percent of men. It seems that women had a higher prevalence of all diagnoses except antisocial personality disorder. Alcoholism precedes depression in 78 percent of men; and depression precedes alcoholism in 66 percent of women. In men, antisocial personality disorder is about four times more common in alcoholics; it is twelve times more common in women alcoholics than in the general population.

Hesselbrock, Meyer, and Keener (1985) used the National Institutes of Mental Health Diagnostic Interview Schedule and DSM-III criteria to evaluate psychopathology in hospitalized alcoholics. Their group consisted of 231 men and 90 women, 17 percent blacks and 83 percent whites, from a broad range of socioeconomic backgrounds. In their study, approximately 4 percent of the men were abusers and 96 percent were dependent on alcohol. The most common diagnosis, antisocial personality disorder, was diagnosed in 49 percent of the male alcoholics. Forty-five percent of the men were substance abusers and 32 percent suffered from major depression. In men, psychopathology was subsequent to the development of alcoholism except for antisocial personality disorder and panic disorder.

A different pattern of dual diagnosis emerged in women. Major depression was the most frequent second diagnosis in 52 percent of the women; phobias, in 44 percent; and substance abuse, in 38 percent. Antisocial personality disorder was diagnosed in 20 percent of the women. In contrast to men, women demonstrate psychopathology prior to the onset of alcoholism.

Only 3 percent of alcoholic men and women are diagnosed with bipolar disorder. Other conclusions were that alcoholics with a major depression, substance abuse, or phobias experienced more psychological problems than those without these diagnoses. Those with alcoholism, antisocial personality disorder, and a substance abuse disorder began drinking at an earlier age and had a more rapid progression to problematic drinking.

A follow-up study on this same population performed one year later (Rounsaville et al. 1987) assessed the relationship between the dual diagnosis of alcoholism and other psychiatric disorders. Those men who had a major depression had a worse outcome when compared to men who were not depressed. Women had a worse drinking outcome if they carried no additional diagnosis. Those women with a major depression had approximately the same outcome as those with other diagnoses except if they had elevations on the Minnesota Multiphasic Inventory (MMPI).

Men with antisocial personality disorder and with other disorders had poorer outcomes than the group with no other diagnosis. Women diagnosed with antisocial personality disorder had a poorer prognosis or outcome than those with major depression.

The best prognosis in men was seen in those who were diagnosed with alcoholism alone. Major depression and antisocial personality disorder were associated with a poorer prognosis. The best prognosis in women was in the group with major depression. In summary, alcoholism frequently is comorbid with other psychiatric and medical problems and can cause, result from, interact with, or coexist in complicated ways that are hard to sort out.

Public Policy Implications

An illness model of alcoholism can reduce the stigma of addiction and emphasize treatment and public health policy measures, rather than placing most efforts on legal restrictions and law enforcement. The more data and facts we have about epidemiology, course, etiology, and complications, the better our public policy will be.

The moral stigma of alcoholism has been reduced in the United States by the increasing public acceptance of an illness model. This acceptance has been fueled partly by an increasing scientific base supporting it, partly by the massive growth of twelve step self-help programs such as AA, and partly by important public figures openly discussing their own problems. However, recent efforts to criminalize adolescent alcohol use, to prosecute mothers abusing substances during pregnancy, and to link Social Security or disability benefits to willful misconduct may damage the trend to a more enlightened public attitude. For example, the Veterans Administration may disallow education benefits if they determine that a delay in applying for benefits was due to willful misconduct.

The drinking age has risen to twenty-one in most states. The question of where public policy should focus—on targeting those at high risk, on prevention, on early detection, on treatment or law enforcement or both—is important. Not enough research has been done on the effects of focusing on each of these areas. Though reducing the number of adolescent traffic fatalities may alone justify raising the legal drinking age, the full impact of the law has not been well studied. It has not yet been well researched whether tough laws that reduce the risk of alcohol abuse in teenagers are worth the negative consequences of stigmatizing adolescents who do experiment with drinking and who obtain or distribute alcohol to peers. It is also not clear whether such policies have more devastating effects in urban inner-city, poor areas with high crime rates and a population already stigmatized by drug abuse, AIDS, racial problems, unemployment, poverty, and lack of decent housing. Moral approaches that stigmatize the alcoholic have also had negative effects on those needing medical treatments, including organ transplants, and have made it more difficult for alcoholics to obtain adequate insurance coverage and employment.

The prosecution of mothers for harming fetuses during pregnancy has concentrated on young mostly poor, mostly black or Hispanic, and mostly crack cocaine addicts, and may further frighten those most in need of prenatal care from using those services. Women who are more heavily addicted to alcohol or other substances are less likely to heed public health messages and are in greater need of alcohol treatment services, which are mostly not available in urban poor areas. Active assessment, case finding, and care is needed for these women, not a prison record and an additional burden of blame.

The question of "willful misconduct" or "willful neglect" was raised in a Supreme Court case in which a veteran sued for an extension of time for educational benefits. He claimed his alcoholism-related disability prevented him from taking advantage of them. According to Veterans Administration (VA) regulations, if the alcoholism was secondary to another psychiatric illness the benefits would be given, but if the alcoholism was primary, then the VA would view it as willful neglect. The Supreme Court decided that the VA could write its own regulations, but specifically stated that it was not commenting on the question of the illness model. Subsequent public response led Congress to rewrite the VA regulations to include alcoholism as a primary illness.

The question of whether Social Security or other benefits should be used to force treatment has also been raised. Some argue that discontinuance of welfare checks, housing, and disability benefits should be threatened if treatment recommendations are not followed. On the other hand, treatment is not available, adequate, or effective for most disadvantaged patients; by withdrawing benefits, they would face greater risk of homelessness and additional suffering. The illness model supports developing public policy that fosters increasing general public health measures with greatest efforts at prevention, early detection, treatment, and addressing social problems that contribute to the most devastating effects of addictions.

The scientific advances that may lead to good biological markers for alcoholism and possibly to the discovery of specific genes for vulnerability to alcoholism can provide new means of prevention and early detection but may also raise policy and ethical problems. If screening tests are available for an alcoholism gene, could they be used to screen out vulnerable job applicants, further stigmatizing those at risk for alcoholism? Would insurance companies refuse to insure those with chemical markers? Would parents select among fetuses those without the alcohol gene? Alcoholism occurs only in those at risk who also drink; that could lead to unnecessary stigmatization for those who have the genetic potential but do not drink. The public will need to ponder the implications of these developments. The fact that alcoholism often has a biologic component reduces stigma in the sense that a person should not be held responsible for his or her genes.

Though alcoholism is frequently used in defense arguments for reducing court sentencing due to diminished capacity, with crime frequently related to alcohol use, our society does not accept drinking as reducing responsibility for actions. "The devil made me do it" excuse is used to justify many an alcoholic's actions; but in most instances this has not held up in the courts. Intoxication effects on judgment have been used to plead for a reduction of charges from intended murder to reckless endangerment, and blackouts or partial seizures have also been used as an argument for diminished capacity. Increasingly the public has grown intolerant of driving while intoxicated, especially as groups such as Mothers Against Drunk Drivers have launched major campaigns to keep up public awareness.

Though most alcoholics are not sociopathic, 20 to 30 percent of males who are hospitalized for alcoholism meet criteria for antisocial personality, and a high percentage of antisocial patients are alcoholic. Alcohol affects relationships for most individuals and negatively affects moral behavior. Is alcohol use a willful phenomenon for which those who choose to use it should be held fully responsible and accountable for their behavior, or is an addict driven to continue a cycle of addiction, once the addiction has begun, based on very deep brain neurochemistry that may not be totally under higher levels of control? The issue remains quite controversial. Perhaps some allowance should be made for the difference between judging a person's behavior before he or she is aware of a diagnosis and has a treatment plan versus an individual who has the disease and has been confronted with it, but continues to refuse treatment and to commit antisocial acts. Having treatment as an alternative form of sentencing raises problems including its limited availability and effectiveness, society's need to hold everyone accountable, and the ubiquitous use of alcohol. However, some first offenders (especially for minor crimes) who had not been aware of their diagnoses benefited more from a mandated treatment program than from prison sentences.

The question of casual use versus hazardous or harmful use of substances has important medical and legal implications. For example, probably no safe level of tobacco use has been established. Therefore, all public health programs tend to aim for prevention of smoking rather than its control, though the substance is legal and widely used. A high percentage of tobacco smokers are dependent. Even those who are not dependent have an increased measurable risk of medical problems on relatively low doses of tobacco. The terms used in defining the continuum of problems also have implications regarding whether early detection and prevention programs take on more of a moral and social function or a medical one.

An example of how a moral approach can be reinforced is that *casual use* is the term chosen by the federal government for occasional use of cocaine that does not lead to physical dependence and major psychosocial problems. In choosing the word *casual* to describe this pattern of cocaine use, the president's drug control strategy team aimed at differentiating "casual use," which is thought to be volitional, planned, and possibly dangerous to other people, as willful and therefore subject to criminal punishment, as opposed to being a medical problem. An alternative term, such as hazardous use, might have actually been better in that it would describe the reality that any use of cocaine is hazardous to the user and possibly to others. However, this would have implied that cocaine use may be a medical as well as a moral problem in those who do not become dependent; a public health rather than a police strategy to deal with the problem might result.

Conclusion

This chapter has discussed the definition and boundaries of alcoholism from a number of perspectives, emphasizing an illness model that takes into account biological and psychosocial roots and criteria that are descriptive and supported by empirical data. New diagnostic formulations such as the DSM-IV should try to refine these criteria on the basis of data and attempt to avoid, where possible, the complicated political and economic considerations that are bound to affect where the set points are drawn.

REFERENCES

American Psychiatric Association. 1987. Diagnostic and Statistical Manual of Mental Disorders, 3rd ed., rev. Washington, D.C.: American Psychiatric Association.

American Society of Addiction Medicine. 1990. Newsletter, Summer.

Ashley, M. J.; Olin, J. S.; le Riche, W. H.; et al. 1977. "Morbidity in Alcoholics:

Evidence for Accelerated Development of Physical Disease in Women." *Archives of Internal Medicine* 137:883–887.

Babor, T. F., and Kadden, R. 1983. "Screening for Alcohol Problems: Conceptual Issues and Practical Considerations." In *Early Identification of Alcohol Abuse,* ed. N. C. Chang and H. M. Chao, pp. 1–30. Washington, D.C.; Department of Health and Human Services.

Blume, S. 1986. "Women and Alcohol." *Journal of the American Medical Association* 256; 1467–1470.

Bean-Bayog, M. 1986. "Psychopathology Produced by Alcoholism." In *Psychopathology and Addictive Disorders,* ed. R. Meyer, pp. 334–345. New York: Guilford Press.

Bukstein, O. G.; Brent, D. A.; and Kaminer, Y. 1989. "Comorbidity of Substance Abuse and Other Psychiatric Disorders in Adolescents." *American Journal of Psychiatry* 146; 1131–1141.

Cloninger, C. R.; Dunwiddie, S. H.; and Reich, T. 1989. *Epidemiology and Genetics of Alcoholism in Review of Psychiatry,* ed. A. Tasman, R. F. Hales, and A. J. Frances, vol. 8, pp. 293–309. Washington, D.C.: American Psychiatric Press.

Crowe, R. R.; Pauls, D. L.; Slymen, D. J.; and Noyes, R. 1980. "A Family Study of Anxiety Neurosis." *Archives of General Psychiatry* 37: 77–79.

Edwards, G. 1986. "The Alcohol Dependence Syndrome. A Concept as Stimulus to Enquiry." *British Journal of Addiction* 81:171–183.

Edwards, G., and Gross, M. M. 1976. "Alcohol Dependence: Provisional Description of a Clinical Syndrome." *British Medical Journal* 1:1058–1061.

Ewing, J. A. 1984. "Detecting Alcoholism, the CAGE Questionnaire." *Journal of the American Medical Association* 252:1905–1907.

Fisher, S. E., and Karl, P. I. 1988. "Maternal Ethanol Use and Selective Fetal Malnutrition." In *Recent Developments in Alcoholism,* ed. M. Galanter, pp. 277–289. New York: Plenum Press.

Frezza, M.; DiPadova, C.; Pozzato, G., Terpin, M.; Baraona, E.; and Lieber, C. S. 1990. "High Blood Alcohol Levels in Women." *New England Journal of Medicine* 322:95–99.

Gallant, D. M. 1988. *Alcoholism: A Guide to Diagnosis, Intervention, and Treatment.* New York: W. W. Norton.

Goodwin, D. W. 1983. "The Genetics of Alcoholism." *Hospital and Community Psychiatry* 34:1031–1034.

———. 1985. "Alcoholism and Genetics." *Archives of General Psychiatry* 42:171–174.

Heather, N., and Robertson, I. 1983. *Controlled Drinking.* New York: Methuen.

Helzer, J. E., and Pryzbeck, T. R. 1988. "The Co-occurrence of Alcoholism with Other Psychiatric Disorders in the General Population and Its Impact on Treatment." *Journal of Studies on Alcohol* 49:219–224.

Helzer, J. E.; Canino, G. J.; Yeh, E. K.; Bland, R. C.; Lee, C. K.; Hwa, H. G.; and Newman, S. 1990. "Alcoholism—North America and Asia: A Comparison of Population Surveys with the Diagnostic Schedule." *Archives of General Psychiatry* 47:313–319.

Helzer, J. E.; Robins, L. N.; Taylor, J. R.; Carey, K.; Miller, R. H.; Combs-Orme, T.; and Farmer, A. 1985. "The Extent of Long Term Moderate Drinking Among Alcoholics Discharged from Medical and Psychiatric Treatment Facilities." *New England Journal of Medicine* 312:1678–1682.

Hendricks, L. 1989. *Kids Who Do/Kids Who Don't.* Summit, NJ: PIA Press.

Hesselbrock, M.; Meyer, R. E.; and Keener, J. J. 1985. "Psychopathology in Hospitalized Alcoholics." *Archives of General Psychiatry* 42:1050–1055.

Hiller, W.; Mombour, W.; and Mittelhammer, O. 1989. "A Systematic Evaluation of DSMIIIR Criteria for Alcohol Dependence." *Comprehensive Psychiatry* 30:403–418.

Holzer, C. III; Robins, L. N.; Meyers, J. K.; Weissman, M. M.; Tischler, G. L.; Leaf, P. J.; Anthony, J.; and Bednarski, P. B. 1984. "Antecedents and Correlates of Alcohol Abuse and Dependence in the Elderly." In *Nature and Extent of Alcohol Problems Among the Elderly,* ed. G. Maddox, L. N. Robins, and N. Rosenberg, pp. 217–244. Washington, D.C.: United States Government Printing Office, National Institute on Alcohol Abuse and Alcoholism.

Jellinek, E. M. 1960. *The Disease Concept of Alcoholism.* New Haven, CT: College and University Press.

Johnson, E. M.; Amatetti, S.; Funkhouser, J. E.; and Johnson, S. 1988. "Theories and Models Supporting Prevention Approaches to Alcohol Problems Among Youth." *Public Health Reporter* 103(6):578–585.

Kapur, A.; Wild, G.; and Triger, D. R. 1989. "Carbohydrate Deficient Transferrin: A Marker for Alcohol Abuse." *British Medical Journal* 299:427–431.

Khantzian, E. J. 1985. "The Self Medication Hypothesis of Addictive Disorders: Focus on Heroin and Cocaine Dependence." *American Journal of Psychiatry* 142:-1259–1264.

———. 1986. "A Contemporary Psychodynamic Approach to Drug Abuse Treatment." *American Journal of Drug and Alcohol Abuse,* 12:213–222.

Kissin, B. 1983. "The Disease Concept of Alcoholism." In *Research Advances in Alcohol and Drug Problems,* ed. R. G. Smart, F. B. Glaser, and Y. Irail, pp. 243–297. New York: Plenum Press.

Martin, D. C.; Martin, J. C.; Streissguth, A. P.; and Lund, C. A. 1979. "Sucking Frequency and Amplitude in Newborns as a Function of Maternal Drinking and Smoking." In *Currents in Alcoholism,* ed. M. Galanter, vol. 5. New York: Grune & Stratton.

Meyer, R. E. 1986. "How to Understand the Relationship Between Psychopathology and Addictive Disorders: Another Example of the Chicken and the Egg. In *Psychopathology and Addictive Disorders,* ed. R. G. Meyer, pp. 3–16. New York: Guilford Press.

Miller, S. I., and Tuchfeld, B. S. 1986. "Adult Children of Alcoholics." *Hospital and Community Psychiatry* 37:235–236.

Morse, R. M., and Heest, R. D. 1979. "Screening for Alcoholism." *Journal of the American Medical Association* 242:2628–2690.

Myers, J. K.; Weissman, M. M.; Tischler, G. L.; Holzer, C. E.; Leaf, P. J.; Ovaschel,

H.; Anthony, J. C.; Boyd, J. H.; Burke, J. D. Jr.; Kramer, M.; and Staltzeman, R. 1984. "Six Month Prevalence of Psychiatric Disorders in Three Communities: 1980–1982." *Archives of General Psychiatry* 41:959–967.

National Institute on Alcohol Abuse and Alcoholism. 1977. *Critical Review of the Fetal Alcohol Syndrome.* Rockville, MD: Alcohol, Drug Abuse, and Mental Health Administration.

O'Brien, C. P.; Woody, G. E.; and McLellan, A. T. 1983. "Modern Treatment of Substance Abuse." *Drug and Alcohol Dependence* 11:95–97.

Ouelette, E. M.; Rosette, H. L.; Rosman, P.; and Weiner, L. 1977. "Adverse Effects on Offspring of Maternal Alcohol During Pregnancy." *New England Journal of Medicine* 297:528–530.

Regier, D. A.; Myers, J. K.; Kramer, M.; Robins, L. N.; Blazer, D. G.; Hough, R. L.; Eaton, W. W.; and Locke, B. A. 1984. "The NIMH Epidemiologic Catchment Area Program." *Archives of General Psychiatry* 41:934–941.

Robins, L. N.; Helzer, J. E.; Weissman, M. M.; Orvaschel, H.; Burke, J. D. Jr.; and Regier, D. A. 1984. "Lifetime Prevalence of Specific Psychiatric Disorders in Three Sites." *Archives of General Psychiatry* 41:949–958.

Rounsaville, B. J.; Dalinsky, Z. S.; Babor, T. F.; and Meyer, R. E. 1987. "Psychopathology as a Predictor of Treatment Outcome in Alcoholics." *Archives of General Psychiatry* 44:505–513.

Schuckit, M. A. 1979*a.* "Alcoholism and Affective Disorder: Diagnostic Confusion." In *Alcoholism and Affective Disorders,* ed. D. W. Goodwin and C. K. Erickson, pp. 9–19. New York: Spectrum.

———. 1979*b. Drug and Alcohol Abuse.* New York: Plenum Press.

———. 1982. "The History of Psychiatric Symptoms in Alcoholics." *Journal of Clinical Psychiatry* 43:53–57.

———. 1983. "Alcoholism and Other Psychiatric Disorders." *Hospital and Community Psychiatry* 34:1022–1026.

———. 1986. "Genetic and Clinician Implications of Alcoholism and Affective Disorder." *American Journal of Psychiatry* 143:140–147.

———. 1987. "Biological Vulnerability to Alcoholism." *Journal Consulting Clinical Psychology* 55:301–309.

Semlitz, L., and Gold, M. S. 1986. "Adolescent Drug Abuse, Diagnosis, Treatment, and Prevention." *Psychiatric Clinics of North America* 9:455–473.

Seventh Special Report of the U.S. Congress on Alcohol and Health. 1990. Rockville, MD: National Institute on Alcohol Abuse and Alcoholism.

Shaper, A. G.; Wannamether, G.; and Walker, M. 1988. "Alcohol and Mortality in British Men: Explaining the U-Shaped Curve." *Lancet* 2:1267–1273.

Sixth Special Report to the U.S. Congress on Alcohol and Health. 1987. Rockville, MD: National Institute on Alcohol Abuse and Alcoholism.

Sokol, R. J.; Miller, S. I.; and Reed, G. 1980. "Alcohol Abuse During Pregnancy: An Epidemiologic Study." *Alcoholism: Clinical and Experimental Research* 4:135–145.

Straus, R. 1984. "Alcohol Problems Among the Elderly: The Need for a Biobehavioral Perspective." In *Nature and Extent of Alcohol Problems Among the Elderly,* ed. G.

Maddox, L. N. Robins, and N. Rosenberg, pp. 9–28. Washington, D.C.: National Institute on Alcohol Abuse and Alcoholism, U.S. Government Printing Office.

Streissguth, A. P.; Martin, D. C.; and Barr, H. M. 1983. "Maternal Alcohol Use and Neonatal Habituation Assessed with the Brazelton Scale." *Child Development* 54:-1109–1118.

Vaillant, G. 1983. *The Natural History of Alcoholism.* Cambridge, MA: Harvard University Press.

Wegscheider-Cruse, S. 1985. *Choice-Making (for Co-dependents, Adult Children and Spirituality Seekers).* Pompano Beach, FL: Health Communications.

Wells, C. E., and Duncan, G. W. 1980. *Neurology for Psychiatrists.* Philadelphia: F. A. Davis Company.

Williams, M. 1984. "Alcohol and the Elderly: An Overview." *Alcohol Health and Research World* 8:3–9.

Winokur, G. A.; Cadoret, R.; Dorzab, J. A.; et al. 1974. The Division of Depressive Illness into Depression Spectrum Disease and Pure Depressive Illness. *International Pharmacopsychiatry* 9:5–13.

PART II

CONTEXTUAL CONTRIBUTIONS

CHAPTER 5

Normality in the Military

Robert E. Hales, Kelly Cozza, and John M. Plewes

According to Offer and Sabshin (1974), normality can be defined in four operational ways: normality as health, normality as average, normality as a system, and normality as utopia. As we discuss, each of these concepts receives varying emphasis in the military depending on what component of normality is being studied. Here we examine normality in the military by studying soldiers—their development in the military and performance in selected situations—and the military family.

In formulating concepts concerning normality, the military presents some unique opportunities. First, one of the basic reasons for having a strong federal government is the defense of the country. The amount of money spent on defense is the largest portion of the federal budget, and the military is the largest employer in the United States. Also, no other issue generates more controversy than conscription of citizens into the military during wartime, as occurred most recently during the Vietnam war. Finally, many of the current leaders of American psychiatry have had combat experience, have served in the military, or have been trained in a military psychiatry residency program. Consequently, the military has had a unique impact on the development of psychiatry in the United States and on the development of the concepts of normality.

The Soldier

Selection and Nonselection

In selecting citizens for military service, the military clearly uses the normality as health model. Using the army as an example, Army Regulation 40-501, *Standards of Medical Fitness* (1987), specifically excludes individuals who have a previous history of psychosis, personality disorder, or psychoneurotic "reaction" that required hospitalization or prolonged care by a physician. However, Stevens and Werheim (1970), in a study that investigated the diligence in applying these criteria, noted a number of limitations. The psychiatrist who examines possible inductees bases his or her assessment on an adequate history. No formal mental status examination or thorough personal and psychiatric history is obtained. However, sometimes inductees falsely deny a previous history of psychiatric illness. The Armed Forces annually accepts an average of 20,000 men who should have been rejected for medical defects that existed prior to entry into military service; 12.3 percent of these prior medical conditions were psychiatric illnesses (Stevens and Wearheim 1970). Although their article was published over twenty years ago, the standards of AR 40-501 have changed little, even while a newer nomenclature system for classifying psychiatric disorders has been developed.

Prediction of Normality

A related question concerns how to predict who will successfully complete basic training or a tour of military service, or, in other words, who will be a "normal" or "good" soldier. Though failure to adapt in a military setting has been seen as a multidimensional problem, Mirin (1974), in a review of the literature, concluded that examining physicians were surprisingly unanimous in the way that they had characterized the young, low-ranking enlisted man who is most at risk for failure.

> Their backgrounds include broken homes, poverty and emotional . . . deprivation, there are usually gross signs of poor adjustment prior to entry into the military. . . . the work history . . . usually consists of sporadic employment at marginal, menial tasks. . . . they approach life as very limited; they have no interest or constructive activities. . . . low tolerance for frustration and poor ability to tolerate anger. (Friedman 1972, p. 119)

Friedman's conclusion was documented by Roness (1976), who studied the civilian background of Norwegian soldiers who performed well in the military and those who did not. In this well-designed study, Roness found that a lower level of education, poor adjustment at school and work, problems with social contacts, a lack of social activities, treatment for psychiatric disorders, marriage, children, or engagement predicted a poorer outcome than soldiers without these characteristics. Specific psychiatric factors found to predict poor outcome were: disharmony during childhood, poor emotional relationships with parents, authoritative upbringing, "nervousness" in childhood, unwanted pregnancies, and psychiatric disorders in parents and close relatives. It is significant that these variables were never incorporated into the rejection criteria for Norwegian civilians to serve in the military.

Roff (1960) conducted a study in which 110 men, who were seen in the Child Guidance Clinic during their grade school or high school years and who saw service in World War II, were evaluated to determine which preservice factors may have predisposed them to develop psychiatric difficulties. It was found that those youngsters who antagonized or were disliked by their classmates to an unusual degree developed psychiatric difficulties while on military service some years later. Unfortunately no specific exclusion criteria were developed from this study. A related work by Georgoulakis (1980) found that those basic combat trainees who sought counseling during basic training did not differ from their colleagues in any other significant factors. In fact, those who sought counseling tended to reenlist at a higher rate, enjoyed their time in the army, would recommend the military to their friends, and viewed basic training in the same manner as those who completed their basic training without counseling.

Work by U.S. Navy investigators has been particularly effective in predicting those sailors who will subsequently develop psychiatric illness and those who will be unable to complete their tour of duty. Booth and colleagues (1978) used a recruitment temperament survey designed specifically for identifying navy enlistees who are most likely to experience either psychiatric or administrative difficulties. By applying this instrument to over 1,000 navy medical corpsman, they found that twenty-six items discriminated significantly between those corpsman who became psychiatric casualties and those who did not. The instrument is reported to be 21 percent sensitive and 7 percent specific (Coche and Steer 1974). In another study, Plag and Goffman (1966) studied a variety of background characteristics and demographic variables to predict who would successfully complete a four-year tour of duty. The authors found that a combination of five recruit characteristics (education, family stability, expulsions from school, arithmetic test scores, and mechanical test scores) were found to give the best prediction of who would be effective for a tour of duty. Of all the variables, education had the highest correlation for success. This work has not been replicated and has not been used in the development of exclusion criteria for military members.

In contrast to those studies that found good predictors of success, Manning and Ingraham, in a more recent paper (1981), attempted to identify characteristics of soldiers who completed basic training but were unable to succeed in their first unit. They studied soldiers who were separated for administrative reasons, including such areas as being nonproductive; having a personality disorder; separation for hardship, marriage, or pregnancy; alcohol or drug abuse; or misconduct. In analyzing many demographic characteristics, including education, they found that those who were separated before their tour tended to be slightly younger, less well educated, and received more disciplinary actions but were otherwise undistinguished from the successful group. The authors concluded that the most distinguishing feature of the soldiers that they studied (those who did not complete a tour) was the *absence* of distinguishing features. They found that the lack of a high school diploma was the best demographic variable in distinguishing the dischargees from the tour completers. Manning and Ingraham concluded that the characteristics of the military organization itself may have contributed to a high attrition rate. For instance, it is only in the military that young high school graduates or dropouts from a low or lower middle-class socioeconomic group take their first jobs in a city 500 to 5,000 miles away from family, friends, and home. Such a situation removes many integral support systems. In basic training soldiers find others in the same predicament and are able to build a new reward system to assist them in the assimilation process. However, the same process is repeated with a different group of individuals during advanced individual training (AIT). Following AIT, soldiers are then reassigned to their first duty unit, with a different cohort of friends and often in an overseas location. Consequently the military may be blamed for creating a series of circumstances where soldiers may sometimes not succeed.

Although those individuals with lower educational levels and a history of psychiatric disorders usually do not succeed in the military as well as those with more education and no psychiatric history, other investigators have indicated that the military may provide a stabilizing influence for its recruits. For instance, a Norwegian group (Sund 1971) found that conscriptees felt to have neurotic characteristics (based on a personality inventory given at the time of conscription) were not different from a normal control group in their fitness for service, amount of psychiatric treatment, or frequency of alcohol problems, legal offenses, or adverse administrative action. The authors hypothesized that motivation and the military unit were more important factors than neurotic personality elements. For instance, many patients with borderline personality disorders successfully complete their military tour of duty, and the military's ability to accept projections and survive splitting may be an important factor for this successful outcome (Bird 1980).

The all-volunteer force, which began in fiscal year 1973, presented unique challenges for the military. Just prior to the initiation of the all-volunteer force, the percentage of soldiers who failed to complete their first tour of duty nearly doubled, from 8 percent in 1963 to 15 percent in 1973, and the psychiatric hospitalization rate increased from 10 to 18 per 1,000 persons per year (Rothberg and Datel 1978). In comparing the mental aptitude of individuals entering the military prior to the all-volunteer force (1972) and seven years later (1979), Lockman and Quester (1983) found that the soldiers' performance on the Armed Forces Qualification Test (AFQT), a measure of a recruit's trainability, had changed little. In fact, the real change was a compression of AFQT scores into a narrower range (Marlow 1983). Although it has been stated that the better educated men with the highest AFQT scores get the better performance ratings (Stouffer et al. 1949) and that the more intelligent, healthier, and socially mature soldiers make better combat fighters (Egbert et al. 1957), studies performed during World War II demonstrated that unit performance is governed more by the soldier's perception of the unit and its members than intelligence or other factors (Stouffer et al. 1949). The most important variables identified for individuals to succeed in combat were confidence in combat, skill, stamina, and willingness for combat. All these factors were reinforced by pride in the company and a sense of mutual trust among officers, noncommissioned officers, and lower enlisted men. As a result, one might conclude that although individual intelligence scores, past educational accomplishments, or the lack of a previous psychiatric diagnosis may predict success in accomplishing a tour of duty, other factors outside the individual may predict individual success in combat.

In summary, the advent of the all-volunteer force has not resulted in a decrease in the quality of soldiers recruited. In fact, although there have been year-to-year variations, there is no significant change in the percentage of high school graduates or AFQT scores. Although the all-volunteer force has been fairly representative of society, except for the disproportional representation of blacks (19 percent of FY 1982 recruits) (Lochman and Quester 1985), the real problem has been the decreasing size of the male youth cohort to be drawn on for the all-volunteer military. Using the concept of normality as average, the military is still attracting individuals within an average intelligence range.

Basic Training

The impact of basic training on young adolescents, usually between the ages of seventeen and twenty-two, may be quite traumatic. The form and content of basic training varies among the services. The army and marines, where combat with the enemy is a principal mission, have a more intense training experience than the navy and air force, where support roles are usually assumed (Arkin and Dobrofsky 1978). In spite of these differences, basic training in all four services is directed toward learning basic combat skills. Embodied in this "combat" training is a basic right of passage, which intentionally disrupts individual, civilian patterns of adjustment and replaces it with achievement of group goals, unquestioning acceptance of authority, and development of conformity of official attitudes. Military discipline (appearance, cleanliness, respect for rank, and attention to detail) is of essential importance in the basic training process and serves to emphasize individual conformity and to socialize the individual into his role in the military process.

In spite of the increasing percentage of women entering the military, basic training remains male-oriented (Eisenhart 1975). Much of the training is physically demanding and challenging. The exercises and tasks are designed to build tough, combat-ready men. We use the term *men* purposely in that women are prevented by law in assuming combat roles yet they still participate in basic (combat) training. Long grueling marches, in addition to developing physical stamina, cause recruits to function under high-stress conditions. Many of the verbal commands placed on the recruits by drill instructors are intended to teach them to function under stress. These activities and inspections and drills are rooted in the belief that obedience and training is a prerequisite to discipline during combat (Hauser 1973).

Another major purpose of basic training is to develop identity with a group. Emphasis on teamwork seeks to build high morale, identity with, and loyalty to the group's goals; individual needs and goals are of secondary importance. The military promotes teamwork by emphasizing how combined skills of a unit will increase their chances for survival during combat. Although individual competition is fostered and supported, such efforts are subordinated to the unit's mission and role. Also, an entire unit may be punished for one individual's improper behavior or performance.

Basic training also conditions a soldier for his later relationships with his family (Arkin and Dobrofsky 1978). The soldier is separated from his family during this period. No leaves are permitted, and family relations are denied. The intent is to increase the recruit's self-reliance and help him learn not to depend on family members for assistance. Basic training also seeks to socialize the recruit as not being integral to his family's functioning and attempts to guide the family into an appropriate support role for him. Arkin and Dobrofsky (1978) contend that basic training seeks to sever contacts between the soldier and his family in order to develop a fully socialized, military-oriented soldier.

As previously indicated, many authors have undertaken work to identify who will successfully complete basic training and who will fail. Some used highly sophisticated statistical analyses (Georgoulakis 1979), self-report personality inventory items (Lachar et al. 1974), the Minnesota Multiphasic Personality Inventory (MMPI) (Callan 1972), the Health Opinion Survey (McCarroll et al. 1981), and an Air Force Medical Evaluation Test (Bloom 1977). Others found that such surveys are not necessary and indicated that those individuals most likely to fail basic training were married men (Shively 1979) or only children (Taintor 1970). What is interesting about reviewing these studies is that commonsense indicators of successful completion of basic training are similar to what one would expect in being a good employee in a civilian setting. For instance, those soldiers who had a previous history of substance abuse or psychiatric disability were at high risk to fail basic training. Additionally, an instructor's concern about a recruit's emotional stability or lack of a positive attitude also foreshadowed an unsuccessful outcome. One would expect that such variables would also predict failure at completing training in the civilian community. On the other hand, previous successful adjustment to high school, to authority figures, no arrests, and motivation for success in military training all tend to predict a successful outcome in basic training. In other words, although basic training as a socialization process is quite stressful, soldiers who successfully complete this experience probably represent those who will be successful in other endeavors after they leave the military.

Barracks and Garrison Life

Military members usually live either on the military installation or close to it. The military tends to provide a total environment for its service members, including schools, recreational facilities, youth groups, officer and noncommissioned officer clubs, and various wives' clubs. Officers and enlisted personnel are separated from each other by both well-defined and informal social systems. The community on post is organized according to rank, military specialty, unit, and place of residence, whether you live in the barracks, in on-post housing, or off post. When assigned overseas, service members are more likely to center on on-post activities. Additionally, fluctuations in the value of the dollar greatly affect their ability to travel and purchase goods.

Usually surrounding the military base are nightclubs, stores, bars, cleaners, motels, pawnshops, and other services, catering especially to lower-ranking enlisted men. The immediate community usually provides a substantial portion of the community support for those military service members and their families who do not live on post. It also becomes a part of the experience for family members.

Life in the barracks is summarized in a classic work by Ingraham entitled *The Boys in the Barracks* (1984). It is an extensive discussion of life in the barracks for army soldiers and is generally applicable to service members in the navy, marines, and air force. The information on structure, after hours, and affiliation that follows is summarized from this book.

STRUCTURE

Most army posts are located in rural areas far removed from major population centers because of their need for large tracts of land for training. As a result, soldiers in the barracks are usually isolated geographically from the civilian community. Although the post may contain thousands of acres, only a small portion is in regular use. An army post may be much like an American small town with industrial sections and sections containing recreational facilities and residential communities. Army posts usually have grown in spurts during periods of war and have no identified business district. The barracks are usually located near the industrial section, where training occurs. The post facilities that soldiers may wish to use may be located many blocks to several miles from the barracks. Consequently, soldiers without cars usually are isolated from the rest of the post.

Soldiers who live in the barracks also have little information about events or recreational opportunities outside the post. Few soldiers read local newspapers, and post newspapers usually emphasize operating hours of various facilities used principally by married soldiers and their families. Posts are usually divided into married and unmarried sections. Many of the recreational activities are oriented toward families.

The primary allegiance of most first-term soldiers remains the family and longtime friends and relatives. They assume that their siblings do not respect soldiers. These same individuals have mixed feelings about "lifers," those committed to an army career.

Garrison duty is not particularly demanding and provides considerable free time. The usual duty day begins at 7:00 A.M. and ends at 4:00 or 4:30 P.M. Most activities during the duty day are accomplished in small work groups where the chief activities serve to establish and maintain status relationships. Social interactions on the weekends and evenings focus on groups of two or three soldiers who get together for specific activities, such as going to a baseball game, to a nightclub, to town, or to a nearby larger city. Soldiers usually always associate with their barracks mates and rarely identify with individuals outside this structure.

AFTER HOURS

After duty hours, officers and noncommissioned officers (NCOs) usually leave the barracks areas to join their families. Barracks dwellers remain in the vicinity, and military rank becomes less important. The company representative is called the CQ, usually a junior sergeant, who rarely enters the barracks. At the battalion level there is usually a staff duty officer and an NCO, both of whom rarely visit the barracks area.

Most barracks areas are more like dorm rooms with approximately twelve feet square for two individuals. Each room usually contains a bed, desk, chair, and wall locker. There is a lot of flexibility for decorating the rooms.

AFFILIATIONS

Soldiers in the barracks have been characterized by many different names. This has been summarized quite well by Rustad (1982). Barracks "rats" are a social type of single GIs whose major interests during off-duty time are listening to high-power stereos, drinking, taking drugs, and fighting. The "goons" are those soldiers who are in the process of being administratively or judicially separated from the military for poor work performance. They usually spend the day performing menial duties and spend their free time causing problems for command. "Heads" are those soldiers who are preoccupied with substance abuse and sell drugs to other soldiers living in the barracks. "Lifers" wear hair shorter than specified by military parameters. Often they spend time at the Rod and Gun Club and the NCO Club. The "juicers" are those soldiers who abuse alcohol and prefer country music. "Trained killers" are those who identify themselves strictly in terms of aggressiveness and combat readiness. "Turkeys" are illiterate, incompetent, or poorly motivated to perform their duties. "Students" define themselves in terms of future professional roles rather than their current military duties. Finally, the "rednecks" are those social types who listen to country music and participate in the rodeo and stock car circuits. They can easily be identified by their cowboy boots, Stetson hats, and pickups or vans. Rednecks often characterize themselves as "lifers." Although these stereotypes may be somewhat humorous, they do describe some of the varying social stratifications within the barracks structure.

The relative frequency of these stereotypes varies over time. For instance, in the late 1970s drug use or nonuse divided the barracks into two separate groupings, with more elaborate subtypings within this framework. Also, any "normal" unit would be made up of selected numbers of individuals falling within each of these catagories. Not to have a mix of these categories would probably mark a unit as not entirely "normal." For each individual, the degree to which he fits one of these stereotypes determines in part his degree of normality.

Aerospace Operations

Military flyers are a relatively homogenous population that is largely male. They are usually between twenty-one and thirty years of age, well above average in intelligence, and manifest a great deal of courage, energy, and control. They have high achievement needs and a low tolerance for personal imperfection. They are usually in excellent physical health and tend to avoid dealing with feelings. They vigorously avoid contact with mental health professionals because of their fear that such contact would endanger their careers. Consequently, they ignore marital difficulties, emotional distress, substance abuse, and other problems.

Pilots and air crews are required to take long flights across time zones and frequently can have around-the-clock work/rest schedules. Often they will develop psychological or physical performance decrements after such travel due to jet lag. Fatigue, psychosomatic complaints, sleep disturbances, and mood changes are frequently noted. Other problems for pilots and crews relate to the physiologic stress of high gravitational forces, cold temperatures, and required attachment to physiologic support equipment, such as special suits, oxygen, and communication equipment.

Although flyers are a special group and usually have few psychiatric or physical disabilities, they are not immune to such symptoms. In fact, of air crew members referred to the USAF School of Aerospace Medicine Evaluation Team between 1975 and 1979, 13 percent were disqualified from flying for psychiatric reasons. Approximately 50 percent of those psychiatrically grounded flyers later returned to flying duties. The most common symptoms were adjustment disorders, anxiety, affective or psychophysiologic disorders (Ursano and Holloway 1985).

Operations at Sea

Sailors at sea also experience unique stresses. Living conditions are usually quite cramped, and sailors must be on constant alert for special missions. Whether in a submarine or on a ship, sailors face extensive climactic changes, strange noises, heat, humidity, and seasickness. Often significant decreases in workload present problems with boredom. The periodic shifts from no requirement for performing duties to maximal work are extremely disruptive. The need to rescue casualties at sea, battle conditions, and training exercises are examples of stressful situations encountered by sailors.

As will be discussed in the section on combat operations, the demands of living aboard a ship vary according to the captain, crew, and ship. Larger ships, such as carriers, often have extensive facilities and more room for social activities. On smaller vessels, especially submarines, the space available for the crew is quite limited. Immediately prior to going out to sea for extended periods of time which can last anywhere from ninety days to six months, sailors frequently will exhibit psychiatric problems or present to physicians with psychosomatic difficulties. The secondary gain of being relieved from going out to sea is usually an important factor.

A lower percentage of sailors in nuclear submarines manifest psychiatric disturbances than in surface ships (Gunderson 1976). Part of this reason may be related to the stringent criteria that sailors must meet for serving on a submarine. In one study (Satloff 1967), 3.8 percent of all submariners were referred for psychiatric assessment. Forty-eight percent were returned to duty; however, 52 percent were either disqualified from submarine duty or discharged from naval service. The principal psychiatric diagnosis was a personality disorder. One might expect that in such cramped conditions, sailors with character disorders would certainly interfere with the productive functioning of the submarine.

Similar to sailors, the submariner has a cycle of training reflected in the refitting of the ship, the training of crews, and return to home base. The refit period is characterized by intense physical activity and high stress. It is during this period that the sailors are at highest stress and when separation issues with spouses and children must be handled effectively. The cruises are usually three to twelve months in duration, depending on the type of submarine. Upon return to home base, the submariner may often face hostility and depression from his spouse.

Combat Operations

In examining combat operations, one may look at three phases of the soldier's response to this challenging situation: the precombat period, combat itself, and postcombat adjustment.

PRECOMBAT

In anticipation of battle, soldiers frequently develop anxiety-related symptoms: nausea, tremulousness, tachycardia, incontinence, sleep disturbance, and multiple psychosomatic symptoms. At this time, soldiers may be referred to psychiatrists for behavioral problems, claimed homosexual activity, and conscientious objector declarations (Jones 1967). Soldiers also become at higher risk for becoming casualties through self-inflicted wounds or by not taking malaria tablets in a malaria-endemic area. Also at this time soldiers present with many minor physical complaints and seek treatment. The desired secondary gain is to avoid combat. Only extreme cases may disable a soldier and prevent him from functioning in the unit.

COMBAT

The intensity and length of exposure to combat are the most important factors in determining who will become a combat psychiatric casualty. It was well established during World War II that the percentage of psychiatric casualties increased directly with increasing numbers of wounded in action (Glass 1961). The risk of becoming a casualty is much lower in units with high cohesion and high morale. For instance, during World War II, neuropsychiatric casualties in all the airborne units never exceeded 5.6 percent of all casualties, although, on the average, 23 percent of all cases evacuated medically were for psychiatric reasons (Tiffany 1967). Units with good discipline and leadership usually have lower casualty rates (Belenky et al. 1983). Also, units that operate in a combat support role, with a fluctuation from intense combat to boredom, are at high risk. Finally, units that are rapidly advancing, retreating, or surrounded have low psychiatric casualty rates.

It is difficult to anticipate who will become a psychiatric casualty in combat. However, individuals from stable homes, with a good educational background, and from middle-class socioeconomic groups usually recover more rapidly. On the other hand, soldiers with character and behavioral disorders have a poor prognosis for recovery once they become a psychiatric casualty.

The type of psychiatric symptoms manifested by combat casualties is quite variable. Some may exhibit paralysis, significant anxiety, or dissociative disorders. Psychosis is rare. Similar to precombat symptoms, soldiers may present with physical symptoms that may mimic more serious disorders: numb feet similar to frostbite, bizarre behavior related to heat stroke, or hyperventilationlike symptoms. The desire of such soldiers is to remove themselves from combat. Once evacuated, symptoms intensify and become fixed to justify their deserting their buddies.

Psychiatrists have managed combat casualties by using the principles of immediacy, proximity, centrality, simplicity, and brevity. Soldiers are treated quickly (immediacy), as close to the front as possible (proximity), using a centralized psychiatric screening service (centrality), using simple treatment such as rest and food (simplicity), and for only one or two days (brevity) before being returned to duty. The employment of such principles reduced the incidence of psychiatric disorders from as high as 101 per 1,000 troops per year during World War II to 12 per 1,000 troops per year during 1965 and 1966 in Vietnam (Jones 1980). Israeli military psychiatrists have found that 80 to 90 percent of soldiers who develop psychiatric symptoms could be returned to duty within seventy-two hours after providing rest and rehabilitation. Their follow-up studies found that psychiatric combat casualties who returned to their units had little or no risk at becoming psychiatric casualties again. Such soldiers who have been returned to units have been readily accepted back (Belenky et al. 1983).

Some soldiers who engage in combat commit atrocities. In Vietnam a special problem was that of "fragging," whereby men used explosives in assaults on superior officers. The predominant characteristics of this group included brutality in their family backgrounds, poor self-image, lack of critical observation, and feelings of insecurity and vulnerability. Many of these soldiers had evidence of antisocial personalities and were often intoxicated on drugs and alcohol during the incidents (Bond 1976). Also, many soldiers with combat exposure who were followed by psychiatrists reported acts of personal "violence" (acts against a person at close range judged to be unnecessary from a military point of view) (Yager 1975). A teenager who was sent to Vietnam and who committed atrocities reported feeling insecure, frightened, frustrated, and angry at being separated from his family in a distant land with a bad climate, experiencing daily fears of death, fighting an illusive enemy and in an unpopular war (Langner 1971). Commitment of atrocities was not unique to Vietnam; it has occurred in other wars. It is difficult to predict who will be involved in such activities, but those who abuse substances and who have an antisocial personality disorder are at greater risk.

POST COMBAT

A number of studies have been undertaken to learn more about soldiers who have been exposed to combat and who later develop psychiatric difficulties. One comprehensive study analyzed Swedish soldiers who served in the United Nation Forces from 1961 to 1962 in the Congo (Kettner 1972). Those Swedish soldiers who served in combat, in contrast to those who did not, had a greater accident proneness and lower income. Those soldiers who developed combat exhaustion (psychiatric disturbances) were not different in background or in psychologic testing from those who did not. Follow-up analyses further indicated that those soldiers who experienced combat exhaustion did not have a worse social or medical outcome. The author did find that younger soldiers had a higher rate of combat exhaustion than older men (Kettner 1972).

With regard to American forces, posttraumatic stress reactions were first described in flight personnel who returned to the United States from Europe at the end of World War II (Grinker and Spiegel 1945). More recently many reports have been published concerning Vietnam veterans. In one study (Strange and Brown 1970) Vietnam returnees who later developed psychiatric problems were noted to have increased disciplinary problems and alcohol abuse, more problems with intimate relations, and a higher incidence of depression. These same individuals did not have an increased incidence in aggressive behaviors or suicidal attempts. Other studies found an increased prevalence of depressive disorders in Vietnam veterans one year (Helzer et al. 1976) and two years (Nace et al. 1977) after their tours of duty. Others (Borus 1973*a* and 1973*b*) have documented the significant military, family, social, and emotional adjustment that Vietnam veterans had to make when assigned to garrison units in the United States. Many of these soldiers felt used or bored in garrison, felt that they had no meaningful mission, and did not spend much time with their new group since they identified most closely with their Vietnam buddies. With regard to family adjustments, they had to reenter a restructured family (if they were married) that had learned to live without them. About half of the group felt that they had learned from their Vietnam experience; the other half felt worse. Of those who felt worse, 25 percent had serious emotional difficulties.

Early studies found differences between those soldiers who had experienced combat in Vietnam and those who had not (DeFazio et al. 1975). These findings were later replicated by others (Scruggs et al. 1980; Stretch and Figley 1984). Soldiers who had seen combat experienced more frequent diarrhea, disturbed sleep patterns, depressive symptoms, inability to relax, and difficulty in relating to others. Approximately twice as many of the combat group experienced nightmares and smoked marijuana as the noncombat veterans. The responses of the Vietnam veterans to the war were as diverse as the individuals who served. Vietnam veterans who organized against the war felt significant guilt feelings, self-punishment, feelings of being scapegoated, rage, and violent impulses (Shatan 1973), whereas many others were able to adjust successfully, despite the fact that the military did not provide much institutional support upon their return home (Borus 1973*b*). Of the symptoms experienced by the Vietnam veterans, a number of investigators reported about their anger, aggression, and rage.[1]

In trying to generalize about how soldiers will respond to future combat, one must keep in mind that Vietnam was a highly unpopular war, similar to Korea. Feelings of alienation and betrayal pervaded Vietnam veterans after their return to the United States (Egandorf 1982). Scenarios of future conflicts emphasize intense combat sustained over several days, not allowing soldiers any time for respite or sleep. The number of casualties from combat will be quite high, and the expected rates of psychiatric casualties will also be high. Consequently, in contrast to the Vietnam experience where there was a period of boredom interrupted by brief periods of intense combat, future wars are expected to see major units engaged in sustained, fierce fighting.

In reviewing the literature pertaining to emotional difficulties and adjustment problems experienced by Vietnam veterans, one is struck by the diversity of responses of the veterans, independent of the degree of trauma experienced in Vietnam. In a review of nearly thirty-three studies, Figley (1978) concluded that personality, family life, and psychosocial variables correlate statistically with the veteran's current functioning and that the war experience was not the most important factor to consider. Additionally, although much attention has been given to those soldiers who experienced psychiatric difficulties, much less has been written about those who successfully adjusted and who have not required psychiatric intervention.

Alcoholism

Alcohol has been a problem for military soldiers since biblical times. For instance, Roman soldiers frequently attacked barbarian forces late on a feast night to take advantage of their excessive drinking. The use of alcohol

[1]See Fox (1974), Renner (1973), VanPutten et al. (1973), and Yager (1976).

in the British Royal Navy of the eighteenth and nineteenth centuries was also well documented (Dunbar-Miller 1984). All sailors consumed grog twice a day. Grog was actually eight ounces of rum diluted by four ounces of water. Since World War II, alcohol and substance abuse has been a problem for United States forces. In a recent survey of alcohol and drug abuse among American military personnel, it was estimated that 84 percent of all military personnel—officers and enlisted—drink alcohol. Approximately 12 percent drink more than 3.5 ounces a day, and 34 percent of those surveyed felt that alcohol had decreased their work performance in the past year (Allen and Mazzuchi 1985). In comparison with a similar study conducted in 1980 (Burt 1982), it was noted that alcohol usage is resulting in a greater percentage of personnel reporting work impairment than in the past (34 percent versus 27 percent). Of note also is a significant increase in heavy daily alcohol consumption among senior army officers, increasing from 1 percent in 1980 (Burt 1982) to 7 percent in 1982 (Allen and Mazzuchi 1985). With regard to general trends, it should be noted that alcohol use varies significantly according to an individual's rank. The highest prevalence of alcohol use is among senior officers (91 percent), but heavy drinking is confined almost exclusively to enlisted personnel, with rare reports of heavy usage in officers. Additionally, the risk for medical problems secondary to alcohol use decreases with rank. The most likely individuals to develop alcohol dependence are junior and senior enlisted individuals. Finally, as the rank of the individual increases, the probability of work impairment decreases.

Soldiers in front-line combat units tend to drink more than those in support units (Allen et al. 1981). Furthermore, those soldiers who consume a large amount of alcohol daily (five or more drinks) not only were of lower rank but also were younger, less educated, less experienced in the service, had received more judicial punishment, were more often single, and were less committed to an army career. There were no differences in race, religion, or sex. In a study of navy enlisted men who recently reenlisted for another tour of duty, Shuckit (1976) found that 9 percent of the sailors surveyed met the criteria for alcoholism. Of the remaining 91 percent who were nonalcoholics, those with family histories of alcohol problems resembled alcoholics on a number of factors, including high rates of minor alcohol-related problems, such as arguments with wife or girlfriend, physical fights, blackouts, or drunken driving arrests.

Substance Abuse

A high incidence of polydrug abuse and heroin addiction was a significant problem for the military in Vietnam, after 1970, when the intensity of combat operations decreased. Once heroin was marketed in the country in 1970, the army psychiatric evacuation rates out of the country increased from 4.4 per 1,000 troops in the second quarter of 1971 to 95.8 per 1,000 in the last quarter of 1972 (Holloway 1974). A study conducted in 1971 revealed that 43 percent of lower-ranking enlisted men had used heroin and that approximately 20 percent of this group considered themselves addicted (Holloway 1974). Heroin use in Vietnam was a transient phenomenon, not associated with criminal behavior, and most of the users felt that they could still function at their jobs (Ingraham 1974). Additionally, many soldiers indicated that they used marijuana to control anxiety and aggression, as an antidepressant, and to increase their acceptability with other members of the unit (Mirin and McKenna 1975). These substance abuse problems increased as exposure to combat and combat casualties decreased. Such a trend suggested that boredom and loss of group cohesion were generating an evacuation syndrome, manifested in part by substance abuse.

A number of studies examined drug abuse in Vietnam returnees. There was no difference between drug use in Vietnam returnees and the army as a whole (Rohrbaugh et al. 1974). In the early 1970s the percentage of soldiers using drugs was nearly 50 percent (Cook et al. 1975). Through use of random drug testing, prevention, and due to a general decrease in drug use in society at large, the percentage of military in 1982 reporting illicit drug use dropped to only 5 percent of E-1s (privates) to E-5s (sergeants) (Allen and Mazzuchi 1985). This figure represents a 34 percent decline since 1980 (Burt 1982). The problem of substance abuse for the military is that, similar to civilian life, substance abusers use more psychiatric and social care than nonabusers (Benson 1984). For instance, in the Scandinavian military, although 4 percent of all military conscripts required inpatient psychiatric care, 18 percent of high-frequency drug users receive such care (Benson 1984). Consequently, increasing the percentage of psychiatric casualties is a significant negative effect of substance abuse.

Gender Issues

With the creation of the all-volunteer force and the cessation of American involvement in Vietnam, the percentage of women entering the military has increased dramatically. For instance, prior to 1971 women represented 1.3 percent of the total enlisted force, while in 1976 the percentage increased to approximately 6 percent (Hoiberg 1978). Additionally, beginning in 1976, women entered the military academies, with the first classes graduating in 1980. In a study of new women volunteers to the air force, it was found that their ability to adjust to military life was quite similar to that of men. Women experienced similar job satisfaction and peer acceptance as men and reported better social adjustment (Kirstein 1978). Furthermore, when those women who required psychiatric hospitalization were compared with men, there were no significant differences in diagnosis, treatment, or outcome. The only difference between the two groups was in the increase in the chief complaint of depression in women in a ratio of approximately two to one, similar to the civilian population (Kirstein 1978; Weissman and Klerman 1977). With regard to job satisfaction, a navy study revealed that women felt that their supervisors were not as approachable as men thought they were and that women felt less positive about peer interactions and support. At the same time, women had the same satisfaction with their job as men (Durning 1982).

Women may now serve in any position in the military except where precluded by law or policy (Landrum 1978). Women may not serve in jobs directly related to combat. For instance, women are generally excluded from navy shipboard positions whereas the army does assign women to units where they may be exposed to combat. Women in the military tend to cluster in the lower enlisted ranks, with close to 90 percent in the lowest four grades (Landrum 1978).

The military must wrestle with many problems in having women in the military. Among the ones that generate the most discussion is their direct participation in combat (Andrews 1979; Feld 1978). Other issues relate to pregnancy, single-parent mothers, and lack of female role models in officer and upper enlisted ranks. Additionally, many men in the military still maintain paternalistic views toward women and view them as sexual objects rather than as coworkers. An increasing percentage of enlisted and officer women are marrying other members of the armed forces. Consequently, more administrative decisions concerning joint assignments, especially with children involved, must be made.

An interesting issue raised by the inclusion of women in the armed forces is how it places in jeopardy some established military traditions: namely, that women and children remain at home while the soldier fights for them during war. The implication is that the soldier dedicates his life for his country and in return, his family provides social support. The inclusion of women in the armed forces changes this traditional perception. Additionally, selected military groups, such as airborne units, define their existence as an elite fighting force willing to assume dangerous tasks. The assignment of significant numbers of women in such units has changed these fundamental premises.

Probably the most significant discriminator that will be nearly impossible to overcome relates to the differences in women's physical abilities. The difficulties women have encountered have been summarized quite well by Priest and associates (1978) at West Point and by Durning (1978) at the U.S. Naval Academy. These physiologic differences, especially in upper body strength, cannot be corrected by policy decisions. Additionally, the cultural upbringing of women in the United States fosters certain beliefs, attitudes, and ideals that military service cannot change.

In a survey of first-term enlisted individuals at major army bases, Hicks (1978) found that most enlisted men felt that women can make a valid contribution to the army but that nearly 20 percent felt that the "Army is a man's world and women can't really belong to it." The use of women for combat-related or other nontraditional job roles also received minimal support from the enlisted men. Most women agreed that women should stay out of combat, but there was less agreement between sexes in women participating in combat-related, nontraditional activities. One of the reasons for this discrepancy was that women seemed to feel that their opportunities for advancement in an army career would be less if they did not assume such roles. On the other hand, women enter the military for slightly different reasons from men—for education, training, and job opportunities; whereas men note patriotism and job opportunities as reasons for enlisting (Rustad 1982). As the percentage of women in the military increases, and the acceptance of women as an equal economic force in society at large improves, resistances to women in the military should generally subside.

Military Psychiatrists

As the military psychiatrist may determine the normality or abnormality of service members, the differences between military psychiatrists and their civilian counterparts deserve discussion. An important area of emphasis for military psychiatry is that of consultation to other mental health professionals, commanders, and other physicians, whereas in civilian practice, the emphasis is on individual psychotherapy. Psychotherapy is practiced in the military; however, because of a shortage of psychiatrists, military psychiatrists must often supervise other mental health workers who actually deliver the care. This situation is especially true for smaller community hospitals. Another type of consultation is "command consultation." As emphasized previously, during combat one of the most significant factors determining who will become a psychiatric casualty relates to the degree of unit cohesion, esprit de corps, and the view of individual service members concerning the effectiveness of the unit. Military psychiatrists often provide consultation to commanders to help identify problems that may be interfering with the development of good unit cohesion. This type of consultation seeks to establish conditions that may reduce the incidence of subsequent psychiatric casualties or behavioral problems (Glass 1961; Hales and Jones 1983). Finally, military psychiatrists provide extensive consultation to other medical specialists. As many posts have only one or two psychiatrists, it is important for them to be able to provide guidance, especially to family practice and general internal medicine specialists, concerning the management of common psychiatric disorders: depression, adjustment disorders, and family/marital problems.

Another emphasis in military psychiatry is upon community psychiatry and prevention (Hausman and Rioch 1967). Through the application of primary, secondary, and tertiary preventive psychiatric services, military psychiatrists attempt to minimize psychiatric casualties in garrison or training environments. Primary prevention seeks to establish in military environments conditions that are likely to reduce the incidence of behavioral problems. One important method, as previously emphasized, is the use of command consultation. Secondary prevention relates to the early identification and prompt treatment of psychiatric disorders. The establishment of Community Mental Health Centers in the vicinity of troop populations, seeing referrals in unit areas, and the assignment of a psychiatrist to all active army divisions reinforces the ability of military psychiatrists to conduct effectively secondary preventive measures. Tertiary prevention, similar to the civilian community, seeks to minimize the adverse consequences of having a psychiatric disorder and to return soldiers to duty or civilian life as quickly as possible so that they may continue with their careers and personal life.

Another principal difference between military psychiatry and civilian psychiatry concerns the limits of confidentiality for patients. An important goal of military psychiatry rests on restoration rather than alteration of personality and its use of effectiveness, not happiness, as a criterion for successful intervention (Jones 1980). To accomplish this goal, a commander needs to have knowledge of the mental and physical health of the troops. As a result, absolute confidentiality is not afforded the military psychiatrist; however, unit commanders do not have unrestricted access to such material, and soldiers are made quite aware of the purpose of psychiatric interviews when they are referred. Because of the importance of a therapeutic relationship, command grants military psychiatrists sufficient latitude to maintain this confidentiality (Talbott 1969). At the same time they are required to recommend administrative discharges for those service members who have a personality disorder and to recommend medical separation for those with psychosis or serious neurotic disorders (depression, anxiety disorders, and others). As emphasized by several authors, the conflicting responsibility of the military psychiatrist—to the patient and to command—may precipitate ethical dilemmas (Clausen and Daniels 1966; Scott-Brown 1973).

Another difference between military and civilian psychiatrists is that military psychiatrists' organizational goals must take precedence over individual goals (Bey and Chapman 1974). Such a situation is essential because the purpose of the military is to defend the country and to protect the national interests. Military psychiatrists have important roles in preserving the ability of the military to accomplish these goals. Additionally, the population served by military psychiatrists is medically screened prior to entry into the service; civilian psychiatrists may see a wider range of patients with various medical and psychiatric disorders. As previously indicated, however, the screening procedures are not always effective in excluding from service those individuals with severe psychiatric or medical disorders.

There are differences, too, with regard to how ineffective soldiers in units are handled. Traditional views hold that when individuals have problems functioning effectively in an organization, it represents a conflict in shared responsibility between the individual and the organization. However, in the military, investigations of problems are usually directed to the individual's difficulty in adapting to the unit, with little responsibility for the system to change (Atkinson 1971). Psychiatrists become involved in this process by evaluating such soldiers for a possible personality disorder diagnosis and recommendation to command for subsequent administrative separation. Some have argued that psychiatrists' involvement in administrative evaluations places them in the center of conflict between their responsibilities as physicians to "do no harm" and the institutional needs of the military services (Nicholson et al. 1974); still others argue that such involvement helps educate command about how to improve its soldiers' welfare and is one of the basic ways psychiatrists serve command needs (Jeffer 1979).

As in the civilian community, in the military a great amount of stigma is placed on seeking psychiatric care. Here a psychiatric diagnosis could result in the loss of security clearance, medical discharge, or administrative separation. Other reasons that military personnel fear being identified as psychiatric patients concern their belief that it will limit their career and future promotions. One study documented that higher-ranking military persons used psychiatric services less than predicted, supporting the hypothesis that the higher one advances in rank in the military the more stigma there is with seeking psychiatric care (Schmidt and Hancey 1979).

Additionally, a survey of the effect of rank on inpatient psychiatric treatment revealed that younger patients and those with lower education showed significantly more rank consciousness, while ward personnel, regardless of rank, with the greatest involvement in the therapeutic community showed the least rank consciousness (Raybin and Flickinger 1972).

The Military Family

The military community is comprised of approximately 2.1 million children having a median age of 5.3 years. Ninety percent of these children are under thirteen years of age (Shaw 1979). Prior to World War II the military family operated in a relatively closed social system and spent a great amount of their time on post. However, more recently, the military has been viewed more as a "job," and service members and their families have increasingly lived off post and associated more with nonmilitary people.

As indicated previously, the military installation is a highly structured, observant community. The behavior of family members is closely scrutinized by other families. The wife of a military service member, depending on rank, is expected to participate in various unit functions and other social groups. Rank permeates the social environment. Enlisted and officer personnel are assigned housing based on rank. The housing of officers and enlisted is almost always separated. A post attempts to provide every conceivable facility for the service member's family: youth clubs, teenage clubs, officers' and noncommissioned officers' clubs, schools, recreational facilities, garages, and so on. Additionally, free medical care and limited dental care is provided for the service member's family. Such an environment has been characterized as living in a fish bowl (Frances and Gale 1973).

All military families must face other unique stressors: frequent separations of the father (or mother) from the family unit for either unaccompanied overseas tours or unaccompanied shorter assignments; assignment to combat; frequent moves of which the family has no or little control; and early retirement (Creel 1981). Each of these issues is discussed in more depth later. How military families adapt to these unique stresses usually depends on whether or not the military mother and father have identified positively with the military community and are sensitive to the unique stresses that this places on themselves and their children (Shaw and Pangman 1975). Furthermore, the military community, even though it provides many of the essentials for its family members, does not provide for many of its needs. Rather than creating dependent and passive people, the military community creates an environment whereby military families operate quite independently in developing their options and demonstrating their independence from the military (Rodriguez 1984). Such a situation is expected from a large bureaucracy that provides basic needs to all but that does not consider individual aspirations. Finally, other unique characteristics of the military family include: living in an environment where the mission must come first; the need to adapt the family to the regimentation and conformity required of the military; the prospect of early retirement for spouses; feelings of detachment from the mainstream of nonmilitary life; the knowledge that any assignment is of limited duration; and the lack of personal control over pay, promotion, or benefits (Ridenour 1984).

Psychosocial Problems

Do children and spouses in the military family have higher rates of psychopathology, and are there higher rates of divorce or child abuse? The answer to all these questions seems to be no. With regard to the presence of psychopathology in children, some (Cantwell 1974; Lagrone 1978; White 1976) suggest that conduct and behavioral problems in military children are much higher than in the civilian community and suggest that such symptoms are manifestations of a "military family syndrome." Others (Morrison 1981) have reported lower incidences of both conduct disorder and drug and alcohol abuse. The lack of controls for rank and socioeconomic data, the availability of free psychiatric services, and the lack of agreement of diagnostic categories make many of these studies suspect (Jensen, Lewis, and Xenakis 1986). In summary, no definitive conclusions can be made as to whether the incidence of various psychiatric disorders is higher in military children than in the civilian population.

Divorce

The incidence of divorce is lower in the military than in civilian populations. In a study of air force officers (Williams 1976), it was reported that the number of divorced men per 1,000 married men ranged from 1 to 1.5 per year compared to 3.0 to 3.5 for the entire U.S. married male population. When examining children evaluated in a psychiatric clinic, Morrison (1981) found 36 percent of the military children had divorced parents in contrast to 59 percent of the civilian children. At the same time, within the military, the likelihood of divorce is two and one-half times greater in enlisted than officer families (Kenny 1967). Many factors in the military discourage divorce: pay rates favor married families, especially for housing; married status is often viewed as important for promotion, especially among officers; and fewer accommodations are made for single parents.

Child Abuse

The relative incidence of child abuse in the military, compared to civilian populations, is unclear because of the lack of reliable civilian estimates (Cohen and Sussman 1976). Some authors argue that the incidence of child abuse is five times higher in the military (Lagrone 1978; Ward 1975), while others maintain the incidence is lower (Myers 1979). It has been stated that the reporting system for child abuse in the military is far superior than for civilian communities, thus leading to increased rates (Lanier 1978; Miller 1976). In a prospective study of child abuse sponsored by the National Center on Child Abuse and Neglect, it was reported that military families comprised only 40 percent of the reported cases of child abuse, although they account for over 60 percent of the population (Wallace and Dycus 1978). Usually the child abuser is the father (Schnall 1978). Junior enlisted personnel constitute approximately three-fourths of reported cases (Acord 1977). The majority of the abused victims are male and under five years of age (Lanier 1978).

Although child neglect is reported to be six to ten times higher than child abuse in civilian populations (Shafii and Shafii 1982), studies of military populations show that physical abuse is twice as common as neglect (Brewster and Postel 1976). The relative lack of neglect may be attributed to the steady employment of military personnel, readily available free medical care, and the closer scrutiny of military families, especially for those who live on post.

In summary, then, military families are probably quite similar to their civilian counterparts in terms of frequency of psychiatric disorders and child abuse and neglect. With regard to divorce, the percentage is probably slightly lower.

Geographic Mobility

Military families experience many moves during a service member's career. For instance, one author noted that military adolescents ages sixteen to eighteen had experienced an average of 5.8 family moves (Darnauer 1976). It is not uncommon for senior military officers and enlisted men with approximately twenty years service to report fifteen to twenty moves in their career. Studies have failed to reveal a consistent relationship between emotional and behavior problems in military children due to geographic mobility (Gabower 1960; Pederson and Sullivan 1964; Shaw and Pangman 1975). More important than geographic mobility appears to be the parental attitudes toward moving and the military way of life (McKain 1973). One reason that may mitigate against a negative effect upon children in the military is the shared value system of military members. All expect to move after a three- or four-year tour of duty, and the ready acceptance of these moves by families as a part of the military way of life reduces their significant adverse effects on the family. Additionally, most military installations are relatively similar in the types of on-post facilities. Housing varies from post to post and the size and quality of quarters is rank dependent. Jobs are usually quite similar, regardless of location, if the service member is serving in his occupational specialty.

Military children readily accept newly arriving children and provide opportunities for them to fit in. Rather than adverse effects, O'Connell (1981) found that mobility in children from ninth to twelfth grades was an adaptive experience and may have been a positive growth factor, leading to increased self-confidence and interpersonal skills.

Many children live overseas. It is estimated that there are over 130,000 school-age children being educated in U.S.–supported schools in the European area alone (Bower 1967). The impact of these foreign cultures on children has not been well studied. The special problems of children living in foreign cultures relates to their difficulty in making friends in the host country, their lack of knowledge with the language, the feeling of uninvolvement with the rest of the host country, physical separation from the rest of the culture, and a loss of stability as a result of the transient living circumstances. For adolescents, in particular, such a move may foster a regressive shift toward more dependent behavior (Bower 1967). Finally, the moral norms of the host society, its standards of conduct, and its shared values may create undo stress for children, especially adolescents. For instance, the use of beer and other alcoholic beverages by younger children in Germany may be an accepted part of development but may conflict with the American parent's values. Additionally, younger children whose mothers work may be cared for by women from the host country, with a possible effect on the child's later development.

In summary, those military families possessing sound inner strength and reasonable communication skills usually adjust more readily than those families with preexisting pathology and poor communication systems. Wives who had poor identification with the army community and limited integration into the informal social life around them have more difficulties adjusting to the moves (McKain 1973).

Father Separation

In the military, children and spouses frequently experience sustained periods of father absence, either because of unaccompanied overseas tours (usually of one-year duration) or because of operational duties, especially on board navy ships where tours range from three to twelve months. Wives more likely to experience psychiatric symptoms because of separation from their husbands are younger (without established coping mechanisms), less educated, and usually married to enlisted service members (Macintosh 1968). The child's reaction to father absence is determined by the child's gender, developmental stage, length of the father absence, mother's capacity to expand her parental role, and prior quality of the father-child relationship (Shaw 1979). In examining doll play behavior of twenty children during periods of prolonged father absence because of World War II, Bach (1946) found decreased aggressive fantasies and increased feminine doll-playing patterns in boys. With regard to the family's adjustment to the returning father, Hill (1949) and Boulding (1950) found that good marital adjustment prior to separation predicted good reunion adjustment and that families that only partially "closed ranks" suffered more during his absence but did better at reunion than those families that "closed ranks" completely at the time of father separation. These studies suggest that separation and reunion have differential effects.

Good response to separation may foreshadow a poor response to reunion and vice versa. Other families may cope poorly or well with both processes. Disturbances surrounding the separation from father cannot be separated from the crisis of reunion. As Crumley and Blumenthal (1973) emphasize, "absence and reunion represents a continuum that the child faces at critical times in his development regardless of his ego capacity to deal with the situation" (p. 776). Those psychological processes particularly affected by separation and reunion are superego formation, the capacity to tolerate depressive feelings, and the degree of object relations (Crumley and Blumenthal 1973).

With regard to the effect of the father's absence on the development of later psychopathology or behavioral problems, Pedersen (1966) found that by the age of fifteen, 85 percent of the children referred to an army psychiatric clinic had experienced long-term separations from their fathers. Furthermore, the severity of the boys' psychiatric disturbances was related to the length of the previous father absence. On the other hand, Nice (1978) studied the adjustment of children immediately prior to their fathers' deployment to sea and upon their return. On various subscales of the California Test Personality, the children demonstrated significant gains. Such findings have been supported by others (Garmezy 1974; Hillenbrand 1976). It is interesting that most studies tend to show fewer problems with girls, although no studies have focused specifically on the effects of military father absence on girls' development.

With regard to cognitive development, father absence in military children has been shown to result in higher verbal and math scores on college entrance examinations (Carlsmith 1964; Funkenstein 1963). Additionally, it is reported that female students who experienced military father absence in the first five years of life scored higher on both verbal and total aptitude scores than those women whose fathers were present (Oshman 1975). In general, it should be noted that military children, compared to their civilian counterparts, tend to have higher median IQs. Forty thousand American children assigned to Europe scored above the seventy-fifth percentile on the Iowa Achievement Test as compared to a cultural norm of 50 percent (Kenny 1967).

War and Combat Stress

The Israeli wars have resulted in a number of contributions to the literature on the effects of war on families and children. Similar to earlier work completed during World War II (MacDonald 1943), Milgram and Milgram (1975) found a twofold increase in anxiety in fourth- and fifth-grade students from the beginning to the end of the Yom Kippur War. The degree of anxiety was greatest in boys and families of higher socioeconomic status. Those children and families with the lowest prewar anxiety subsequently developed the highest postwar anxiety symptoms. Another study found that wartime stress resulted in increased mother-child conversations and time spent together (Cohen and Dotan 1976). This report, published following the 1973 Arab-Israeli war, supports work completed during World War II that found increased anxiety and depression in children (Rosenbaum 1944; Zitello 1942). No studies have attempted to separate the differential effects between separation from the father who might have been assigned to an overseas, noncombat zone and a father assigned to combat.

A child's response to father absence is often related to the mother's reaction to his absence. In studying children of navy service members, Trunnell (1968) reported that the greater the mother's psychopathology, the more likely there would be a more severe disturbance in the child's response to the father's absence. Another significant factor is how the mother talked about the father in his absence (Bach 1946). Additionally, psychologically healthy mothers were more able to counteract the effect of the father absence (Pedersen 1966). In summary, recurrent father/husband absence may contribute to marital discord, marital strictness toward the children, and the mother assuming more of the traditional father roles in the family (Marsella et al. 1974; Rienerth 1978).

Frequent separations of the husband have been reported to cause an increased number of medical visits by the wife (Nice 1981; Snyder 1978) and higher depression scores (Beckman et al. 1979). Also, as mothers assume increasing responsibilities and management of the families, many are not willing to give up their new responsibilities and competencies when the husband returns. Adjustment in the family's female-centeredness (Rienerth 1978) have to be made. This sometimes results in marital discord and additional adjustment problems for the children.

Studies have been published concerning the reunion of families to fathers who were prisoners of war (POWs). Psychological issues experienced by POW wives when their husbands returned centered on themes of desertion, role ambiguity, repressed anger, sexuality, censure, and social isolation. Children experienced separation anxiety, role distortion, and sleep disturbances, with boys more significantly affected than girls (Hall and Simmons 1973). It should be emphasized that the traumatic experience of prolonged captivity markedly affects the service member/father/husband and frequently results in later psychiatric illness. As Ursano (1981) reported, nearly 25 percent of POWs had diagnosable psychopathology at five-year follow-up. This high rate was neither necessary nor sufficient to explain postcaptivity responses.

During the soldier's imprisonment, families experienced a significant amount of problems: an increase in alcohol use, signs of marital dissatisfaction, and pronounced concerns with physical health (McCubbin and Dahl 1976). Additionally, 37 percent of wives were in psychiatric treatment and 75 percent stated a need for psychiatric treatment. Approximately 12 percent of the POW children had been in psychiatric treatment with another 20 percent judged to require treatment. On reunion, 30 percent of marriages ended in divorce (Hunter 1980).

Though some contend that the effect of the reunion, especially between father and son, may have a significant disruptive influence on the family, Dahl and colleagues (1976) studied this question by comparing a group of children whose fathers were missing in action and did not return with a group of children whose fathers were POWs and were eventually reunited with the family. They found that the reunited children did better than the nonreunited group on two subscales of the California Test of Personality: freedom from nervous symptoms and community relations. Similar to the findings from families who were separated from fathers/husbands, those who had a better marital relationship prior to the POW experience and whose wife was more able to handle the increased burdens of being a single parent prior to the spouse's prolonged imprisonment tended to cope better with the reunion (McCubbin and Dahl 1976). Again, it is difficult to distinguish differential effects of the captivity or war trauma itself and the separation.

As previously emphasized, POW and combat experiences have a significant impact on the service member. How he responded to the stresses depended on the presence or absence of preexisting psychopathology and the level of adaptation prior to combat. Other studies have revealed that up to two to three years are required to reestablish a homeostatic balance within the family if the father was separated more than five years because of his being a prisoner of war (Hunter 1980, 1984).

Cross-Cultural Marriages

Compared to civilian families, in the military there is a higher percentage of cross-cultural families. It has been estimated that 21 percent of army spouses speak English as a second language (Jensen, Lewis, and Xenakis 1986) and that one-third of military children living in the Pacific originate from cross-cultural families (Cottrell 1978). Although the families function relatively well while living in the wife's native country, upon returning to the mainland United States families later develop more problems. Husbands, initially attracted by the unique cross-cultural characteristics of their spouses, report feeling ignored by neighbors after their return to the United States. Foreign-born wives who sought psychiatric treatment describe such difficulties as homesickness, lack of friends and social supports, and problems learning new language (Druss 1965). Others (Orthner and Bowen 1982) reported that the wives of cross-cultural marriages reported more regrets about the marriage, more sexual dissatisfaction, and poorer marital communication than other military wives. Children of cross-cultural families report more difficulties during the father's absences and raise additional questions about their own identity (Cottrell 1978). The work in these areas is quite limited and would benefit from more systematic studies.

Military Retirement

Retirement from the military produces potentially stressful changes for the service member, his children, and spouse. With over 1 million retired service members, the possible adverse effects are significant. Retired military service members often have to start second careers in their mid-forties to early fifties. How they and their families adjust usually correlates with the perceived direction of the social mobility of this change. Downwardly mobile retirees and spouses report lower psychological well-being and upwardly mobile individuals report improved self-image (Platte 1976). It has been found, however, that the majority of retirees report a loss of occupational prestige as a result of their retirement. This is especially true for officers. Those retirees who are able to identify with their civilian colleagues report greater psychological well-being than those who are not (Garber 1971). The geographic relocation and change in status affects the entire family (Biderman and Sharp 1968), with the retirement process characterized as a disruption of "emotional equilibrium." The retiree frequently experiences psychosomatic symptoms; the wives, gynecologic problems; and the children, conduct disorders (Griffen and McNeil 1967).

Military retirement is a process of shifting away from a relatively closed social system with well-defined roles for the service member to one in which there is less role specificity, as rank and identified status are less well defined. Adolescent children whose father is encountering uncertainty about his social, economic, and occupational identity will experience similar problems. For instance, Shaw (1979) describes an adolescent boy seen for psychiatric evaluation for symptoms of depression experienced when his father retired. The child described that in the military community he was a colonel's son but this identity was no longer applicable in the civilian world. The son had to develop a new civilian peer group on the basis of his own achievement and not his father's.

Military retirement has been described by some authors as a retirement syndrome, with three distinct phases: a preretirement phase, which occurs two to three years prior to the actual retirement; a period of role confusion, immediately prior to the retirement; and the early postretirement phase where the service member must successfully transition to a new role (McNeil and Griffen 1967). During each phase of the retirement syndrome, service members often experience irritability, apprehension, increased alcohol use, depression, and somatic complaints.

What is unique about military retirement is that service members must go on to lead productive lives and that they retire at a much earlier age than the civilian community. In the civilian community individuals seldom have to wrestle with new roles, as they frequently retire at age sixty-five to seventy and look forward to a life of leisure and relaxation. Additionally, the service member often has job difficulties and is irritable with family members. Officers may experience increased symptoms because of their perceived failure to achieve career goals (Berrey and Stoebner 1968). Additionally, senior NCOs who remain in the military thirty years or more may exhibit increased symptoms of anxiety, tension, insomnia, and concentration, characterized as the "old soldiers' syndrome" (Greenberg 1965; Milowe 1964). Service members who have skills readily transferrable to the civilian community experience a less severe retirement syndrome. It has been estimated that approximately 25 percent of military specialties are combat related and nontransferrable to the civilian community (McNeil and Griffen 1967). For service members with these types of skills, the transition to retirement would be expected to be more difficult. It should be emphasized that because of the increased similarity between military and civilian occupational specialties in the 1980s, most military retirees are able to obtain satisfactory civilian employment (Biderman and Sharp 1968).

Military wives also experience similar symptoms and loss of status. In the military the wife shares her husband's position in the social system. She becomes accustomed to expecting special treatment because of her husband's rank and experience, which is at the highest level just prior to retirement. This is especially true for officers whose spouses perform a number of "mandatory" social functions for other wives in the unit. When wives no longer experience special treatment after retirement, this may cause increased difficulties for their normal adjustment. Additionally, wives are frequently disappointed because their expectations of retirement are not fulfilled. For instance, they might believe that their husbands will spend more time with them. When this does not materialize, they may manifest depressive symptoms (Cretekos 1973). Individual case histories are well described by Greenburg (1966).

In summary, military retirement is part of an overall midlife adjustment for service members, wives, and children. Similar to other circumstances in the military, those emotionally healthy adults usually are able to adapt most effectively to this transition. Correspondingly, those who have a strong marital relationship and healthy families also usually make a successful adjustment (Strange 1984).

Conclusion

Military service members and their families are a reflection of society. Civilians who desire to enter the military are largely a healthy group, both physically and psychiatrically, because of screening guidelines that exclude many with physical defects or mental disorders. Also, most enlistees have at least a high school education. The basic and advanced training to become a soldier, sailor, or airman with an occupational specialty is intense and demanding, and those who finish this training frequently complete their tours of duty honorably and without incident. The military way of life places unique demands on service members and their families. Those service members, spouses, and children who were better adjusted prior to military-associated stresses—combat, overseas assignments, family separations, and others—usually are able to adapt with minimal emotional disequilibrium. What distinguishes military service members and their families from their civilian counterparts is their ability to adjust to so many stresses in a generally healthy and constructive manner. Such a capacity, in turn, is reflective of the generally healthy societal cohort from which these people are drawn.

Appendix

Psychiatric Support to Operation Desert Storm

Between August 1990 and April 1991, the United States Army participated in the liberation of Kuwait from the occupation of the armed forces of Iraq. The Persian Gulf War, or Operation Desert Storm (ODS), saw an unprecedented level of psychiatric support provided to Army soldiers. As noted in the preceding chapter, the concepts for preventing and treating battle fatigue casualties and posttraumatic stress disorder (PTSD) had been developed in previous wars. The principles were employed in an effective fashion in this conflict.

Mental health care was provided by psychiatrists, social workers, psychologists, psychiatric nurses, occupational health officers, and behavioral science, psychological, and occupational health specialists assigned to civilian mental health sections, large and small hospitals of all types, and combat stress control (CSC) teams. A mental health team, composed of a psychiatrist, psychologist, social worker, and behavioral science specialists, was assigned to each combat division. They worked as an organic part of their unit before and after deployment and conducted much of the combat stress control management. Mental health professionals assigned to the hospitals were in charge of psychiatric wards and conducted limited outpatient care. The CSC teams functioned as education and treatment teams, provided directed unit liaison and support to division units having organic psychiatric support, and provided area support to divisions that were otherwise unsupported.

The conflict chronology can be divided into five phases: preparation and predeployment, deployment and buildup to the theater of operations, the air war, the ground war, and cease-fire and redeployment. The first phase included preparation for duty while in garrison, training, and evaluation and included the period up to the time in early August 1990 that U.S. forces became involved in the Gulf War. The initial part of this phase is a continuing one, with army units always training to fulfill various changing mission requirements.

The second phase, deployment and buildup, saw the army participate in the largest medical logistical operation ever seen in the armed forces. In just over five months (August 9, 1990 to January 16, 1991), 198 medical units ranging in size from small surgical and preventative medicine teams to 1,000 bed hospitals were deployed in the theater and moved into place for battle. The inherent mental health support of combat divisions and hospitals also deployed, as did three of the Army's seven CSC teams. Prior to the initiation of the air war on January 16, 1991, a CSC team was assigned to each of the two corps (the seventh and eighteenth), and one was held in reserve. Some personnel from the third team were reassigned to one of the two forward teams to enhance forward treatment capability, and the remainder set up a reconditioning unit in the rear of the two corps areas.

Phase three, the air war, was the allied bombing campaign over Kuwait and Iraq. Most medical units remained at their prebattle locations and continued to evaluate and treat patients. This phase lasted from January 16 to February 24, 1991, when the fourth phase, the ground war started. It ended remarkably quickly on February 28, 1991, with a unilateral cessation of hostilities initiated by the U.S.-led coalition of forces.

The final phase, cease-fire and redeployment, began on February 28 and is ongoing at this writing. During this phase, the various mental health elements began assisting in the debriefing of units in the theater, with special attention paid to those units which took casualties (soldiers killed in action, missing in action, wounded, or prisoners of war). Debriefing should ideally be accomplished in theater and should continue for a month or more after the units return home.

This war was different from previous wars and exercise deployments for several reasons. An important contrast to the Vietnam War experience was the tremendous popular support shown to the troops by the public at home. Other factors—a short war leading to victory, extremely low numbers of physical casualties, the absence of alcohol or drug use in the theater, the higher average age and educational level of the soldiers, the all-volunteer nature of the troops, and the presence of a clear no-rotation policy—significantly contributed to a low number of battle fatigue and PTSD casualties.

Several statistics help in understanding the positive effect of these facts in reducing the rate of psychiatric casualties (see table 5.1). Before the

TABLE 5.1

Dates	Phase	Rate per 1,000 per Year
07 Aug. 1990–01 Dec. 1990	Buildup	2.8
01 Dec. 1990–17 Jan. 1991	Buildup	2.0*
17 Jan. 1991–24 Feb. 1991	Air War	2.4
25 Feb. 1991–31 Mar. 1991	Ground War and Cease Fire	3.3
07 Aug. 1990–31 Mar. 1991	Overall	2.7

*CSC teams arrived in theater, November 1990

arrival of the CSC teams, psychiatric casualties were not being screened by mental health workers prior to evacuation from the theater. After the teams arrived, the rate dropped dramatically, and the evacuation diagnoses shifted from being predominately adjustment disorders and personality disorders to being major psychiatric disorders, such as mood disorders and psychoses. Such a diagnostic trend reflected the increased effectiveness of the CSC teams in minimizing unnecessary evacuations. For instance, there were only 240 psychiatric evacuations from the theater during the entire operation. Approximately 95 percent of the over 2,000 soldiers seen by the CSC teams were returned to duty within a week.

The overall rate of psychiatric evacuations was 2.7 per 1,000 per year, the lowest figure yet achieved in wartime. It is significant to examine this rate as compared with the active phases of the conflict, and the arrival of the CSC teams. The CSC teams reduced evacuation rates during the buildup phase and after the air war and ground operations began.

The hard work and dedication of all components of the U.S. Forces, whether training at summer camp, deployed in combat, or providing vital services in the local community, paid real dividends. The lessons learned during this conflict will assist military psychiatrists in providing support to soldiers who must fight in future wars.

REFERENCES

Acord, L. D. 1977. "Child Abuse and Neglect in the Navy." *Military Medicine* 142:862–864.

Allen, J., and Mazzvohi, J. 1985. "Alcohol and Drug Abuse Among American

Military Personnel: Prevalence and Policy Implications." *Military Medicine* 150: 250–255.

Allen, J., et al. 1981. "Symptom Clusters Among Heavy Alcohol Consuming Military Personnel." *Substance and Alcohol Actions/Misuse* 2:161–176.

Andrews, M. A. 1979. "Women in Combat?" *Military Review* 59(7):28–34.

Arkin, W., and Dobrofsky, L. R. 1978. "Military Socialization and Masculinity." *Journal of Social Issues* 34:151–168.

Army Regulation 40-501. *Standards of Medical Fitness, Change #35."* 9 March 1987. Washington, D.C.: Department of the Army.

Atkinson, R. M. 1971. "Ineffective Personnel in Military Service: A Critique of Concepts and Rehabilitation Practices from a Psychiatric Viewpoint." *American Journal of Psychiatry* 127:1612–18.

Bach, G. R. 1946. "Father-Fantasies and Father-Typing in Father-Separated Children." *Child Development* 17:63–80.

Beckman, K., et al. 1979. "Depression in the Wives of Nuclear Submarine Personnel." *American Journal of Psychiatry* 136:524–526.

Belenky, G. W., et al. 1983. *Israeli Battleshock Casualties: 1973 and 1982.* WRAIR Report No. NP-83-4. Washington, D.C.: Walter Reed Army Institute of Research.

Bellino, R. 1969. "Psychosomatic Problems of Military Retirement." *Psychosomatics* 10:318–321.

Benson, G. 1984. "Drug-Related Medical and Social Conditions in Military Conscripts." *ACTA Psychiatrica Scandinavia* 70:550–558.

Berrey, B. R., and Stoebner, J. B. 1968. "The Retirement Syndrome: A Previously Unreported Variant." *Military Medicine* 133:5–8.

Bey, D. R., and Chapman, R. E. 1974. "Psychiatry—The Right Way, The Wrong Way and the Military Way." *Bulletin of the Menninger Clinic* 38:343–354.

Biderman, A. D., and Sharp, L. M. 1968. "The Convergence of Military and Civilian Occupational Structures: Evidence from Studies of Military Retired Employment." *American Journal of Sociology* 73:381–399.

Bird, J. R. 1980. "The Borderline Patient and Military Life." *British Journal of Medical Psychology* 53:85–90.

Bloom, W. 1977. "Air Force Medical Evaluation Test." *Medical Service Digest, United States Air Force* 28:17–20.

Bond, T. C. 1976. "The Why of Fragging." *American Journal of Psychiatry* 133:1328–1331.

Booth, R. F., et al. 1978. "Predictors of Psychiatric Illness Among Navy Hospital Corpsmen." *Journal of Clinical Psychology* 34:305–308.

Borus, J. F. 1973*a*. "Reentry, I. Adjustment Issues Facing the Vietnam Returnee." *Archives of General Psychiatry* 28:501–506.

———. 1973*b*. "Reentry, II. Making It Back in the States." *American Journal of Psychiatry* 130:850–854.

Boulding, E. 1950. "Family Adjustments to War Separations and Reunions." *Annals of the American Academy of Political and Social Sciences* 272:59–67.

Bower, E. M. 1967. "American Children and Families in Overseas Communities." *American Journal of Orthopsychiatry* 37:787–796.

Brewster, T., and Postel, K. L. 1976. "Managing Child Abuse: A Multidisciplinary Approach for Naval Hospitals." *U.S. Navy Medicine* 67:8–10.

Burt, M. D. 1982. "Prevalence and Consequences of Alcohol Use Among U.S. Military Personnel, 1980." *Journal of Studies on Alcohol* 43:1097–1107.

Callan, J. P. 1972. "An Attempt to Use the MMPI as a Predictor of Failure in Military Training." *British Journal of Psychiatry* 121:553–557.

Cantwell, D. P. 1974. "Prevalence of Psychiatric Disorders in a Pediatric Clinic for Military Dependent Children." *Journal of Pediatrics* 85:711–714.

Carlsmith, L. 1964. "Effect of Early Father Absence on Scholastic Aptitude." *Harvard Education Review* 34:3–21.

Clausen, R. E., and Daniels, A. K. 1966. "Role Conflicts and Their Ideological Resolution in Military Psychiatric Practice." *American Journal of Psychiatry* 123:280–287.

Coche, E., and Steer, R. A. 1974. "The MMPI Response Consistencies of Normal, Neurotic and Psychotic Women." *Journal of Clinical Psychology* 30:194–195.

Cohen, A. A., and Dotan, J. 1976. "Communication in the Family as a Function of Stress During War and Peace." *Journal of Marriage and Family* 38:141–148.

Cohen, S. J., and Sussman, A. 1975. "The Incidence of Child Abuse in the United States." *Child Welfare* 54:432–433.

Cook, R. F., et al. 1975. "Patterns of Illicit Drug Use in the Army." *American Journal of Psychiatry* 132:1013–1017.

Cottrell, A. B. 1978. "Mixed Children: Some Observations and Speculations." In *Children of Military Families: A Part and Yet Apart,* ed. E. J. Hunter and D. S. Nice, pp. 61–81. Washington, D.C.: U.S. Government Printing Office.

Creel, S. M. 1981. "Patient Appraisal of Current Life and Social Stressors in a Military Community." *Military Medicine* 146:797–801.

Cretekos, C. 1973. "Common Psychological Syndromes of the Army Wife." *Military Medicine* 138:36–37.

Crumley, F. E., and Blumenthal, R. S. 1973. "Children's Reactions to Temporary Loss of the Father." *American Journal of Psychiatry* 130:775–782.

Dahl, B. B., et al. 1976. "War-Induced Father Absence: Comparing the Adjustment of Children in Reunited, Non-Reunited and Reconstituted Families." *International Journal of Sociology and the Family* 6:99–108.

Darnauer, P. 1976. "The Adolescent Experience in Career Army Families." In *Families in the Military System,* ed. H. I. McCubbin, B. B. Dahl, and E. J. Hunter, pp. 42–46. Beverly Hills, CA: Sage Publications.

DeFazio, V. J., et al. 1975. "Symptom Development in Vietnam Era Veterans." *American Journal of Orthopsychiatry* 45:158–163.

Druss, R. G. 1965. "Foreign Marriages in the Military." *Psychiatric Quarterly* 39:220–226.

Dunbar-Miller, R. A. 1984. "Alcohol and the Fighting Man—An Historical Review." *Journal of the Royal Army Medical Corps* 130:12–15.

Durning, K. P. 1978. "Women at the Naval Academy." *Armed Forces and Society* 4:569–588.

———. 1982. "Attitudes of Enlisted Women and Men Toward the Navy." *Armed Forces and Society* 9:20–32.

Egbert, R. L., et al. 1957. "Fighter 1: An Analysis of Combat Fighters and Non-Fighters." In *HumRRO Technical Report 44.* Washington, D.C.: George Washington University.

Egendorf, A. 1982. "The Postwar Healing of Vietnam Veterans: Recent Research." *Hospital and Community Psychiatry* 33:901–908.

Eisenhart, R. W. 1975. "You Can't Hack It Little Girl: A Discussion of the Covert Psychological Agenda of Modern Combat Training." *Journal of Social Issues* 31:13–23.

Feld, M. D. 1978. "Arms and the Woman." *Armed Forces and Society* 4:557–568.

Figley, C. R. 1978. *Stress Disorders Among Vietnam Veterans: Theory, Research and Treatment.* New York: Brunner-Mazel.

Fox, R. P. 1974. "Narcissistic Rage and the Problem of Combat Aggression." *Archives of General Psychiatry* 31:801–811.

Frances, A., and Gale, L. 1973. "Family Structure and Treatment in the Military." *Family Process* 12:171–178.

Friedman, H. J. 1972. "Military Psychiatry." *Archives of General Psychiatry* 26:118–122.

Funkenstein, D. H. 1963. "Mathematics, Quantitative Aptitudes, and the Masculine Role." *Disease of the Nervous System* 24:140–146.

Gabower, G. 1960. "Behavior Problems of Children in Navy Officers' Families." *Social Casework* 41:177–184.

Garber, D. L. 1971. "Retired Soldiers in Second Careers: Self-Assessed Change, Reference Group Salience, and Psychological War-Being." *Dissertation Abstracts International* 32:3430A.

Garmezy, N. 1974. "Children at Risk: The Search for the Antecedents of Schizophrenia. Part II: Ongoing Research Programs, Issues and Intervention." *Schizophrenia Bulletin* 9:55–125.

Georgoulakis, J. M. 1979. "Social Factors and Perceived Problems as Indicators of Success in Basic Combat Training: Part One." *Military Medicine* 144:592–596.

———. 1980. "Basic Combat Trainees who Adjusted to the Military: A Three-Year Follow-up Study." *Military Medicine* 145:789–790.

Glass, A. J. 1961. "The Current Status of Army Psychiatry." *American Journal of Psychiatry* 117:673–683.

Greenberg, H. R. 1965. "Depressive Equivalents in the Pre-Retirement Years: The Old Soldier Syndrome." *Military Medicine* 130:251–255.

———. 1966. "Psychiatric Symptomatology in Wives and Military Retirees." *American Journal of Psychiatry* 123:487–490.

Griffen, M. B., and McNeil, J. S. 1967. "Effect of Military Retirement on Dependents." *Archives of General Psychiatry* 17:717–722.

Grinker, R. R., and Spiegel, J. P. 1945. *Men Under Stress.* Philadelphia: Blakiston.

Gunderson, E. K. 1976. "Health and Adjustment of Men at Sea." In *The Social*

Psychology of Military Service, ed. N. Goldman and D. Semal, pp. 67–80. Beverly Hills, CA: Sage Publications.

Hales, R. E., and Jones, F. D. 1983. "Teaching the Principles of Combat Psychiatry to Army Psychiatry Residents." *Military Medicine* 148:24–27.

Hall, R. C., and Simmons, W. C. 1973. "The POW Wife." *Archives of General Psychiatry* 29:690–694.

Hauser, W. L. 1973. *America's Army in Crisis.* Baltimore: Johns Hopkins University Press.

Hausman, W., and Rioch, D. 1967. "Military Psychiatry: A Prototype of Social and Preventive Psychiatry in the United States." *Archives of General Psychiatry* 16:727–739.

Helzer, J. E., et al. 1976. "Depressive Disorders in Vietnam Returnees." *Journal of Nervous and Mental Disorders* 163:177–185.

Hicks, J. M. 1978. "Women in the U.S. Army." *Armed Forces and Society* 4:647–657.

Hill, R. 1949. *Families Under Stress: Adjustment to the Crises of War Separation and Reunion.* Westport, CT: Greenwood Press.

Hillenbrand, E. D. 1976. "Father Absence in Military Families." *Family Coordinator* 25:451–458.

Hoiberg, A. 1978. "Women as New 'Manpower.' " *Armed Forces and Society* 4:555–556.

Holloway, H. C. 1974. "Epidemiology of Heroin Dependency Among Soldiers in Vietnam." *Military Medicine* 139:108–113.

Hunter, E. J. 1980. "Combat Casualties who Remain at Home." *Military Review* 60:28–36.

———. 1984. "Treating the Military Captive's Family." In *The Military Family,* ed. F. Kaslow and R. Ridenour, pp. 167–196. London: Guilford Press.

Ingraham, L. H. 1974. " 'The Nam' and 'The World' Heroin Use by U.S. Army Enlisted Men Serving in Vietnam." *Psychiatry* 37:114–126.

———. 1984. *The Boys in the Barracks.* Philadelphia: Institute for the Study of Human Issues.

Jeffer, E. K. 1979. "Psychiatric Evaluations for Administrative Purposes." *Military Medicine* 144:526–528.

Jensen, P. S.; Lewis, R. L.; and Xenakis, S. N. 1986. "The Military Family in Review: Context, Risk, and Prevention." *Journal of the American Academy of Child Psychiatry* 25:225–234.

Jones, F. D. 1967. "Experiences of a Division Psychiatrist in Vietnam." *Military Medicine* 132:1003–1008.

———. March 31–April 4, 1980. "Current Status of Military Psychiatric Principles and Procedures." Paper presented at the Army Medical Department Military Psychiatry Conference, El Paso, Texas.

Kenny, J. 1967. "The Child in the Military Community." *Journal of the American Academy of Child Psychiatry* 6:51–63.

Kettner, B. 1972. "Combat Strain and Subsequent Mental Health. A Follow-up Study of Swedish Soldiers Serving in the United Nations Forces 1961–62." *ACTA Psychiatrica Scandinavica* (Suppl.) 230:1–112.

Kirstein, L. 1978. "Female Soldiers Special Adjustment." *Military Medicine* 143:695–697.

Lachar, D., et al. 1974. "Psychometric Prediction of Behavioral Criteria of Adaption for USAF Basic Trainees." *Journal of Community Psychiatry* 2:268–277.

Lagrone, D. 1978. "The Military Family Syndrome." *American Journal of Psychiatry* 135:1040–1043.

Landrum, C. 1978. "Policy Dimensions of an Integrated Force." *Armed Forces and Society* 4:689–694.

Langner, H. O. 1971. "The Making of a Murderer." *American Journal of Psychiatry* 127:950–953.

Lanier, D. 1978. "Child Abuse and Neglect Among Military Families." In *Children of Military Families: A Part and Yet Apart,* ed. E. J. Hunter and D. S. Nice, pp. 101–119. Washington, D.C.: U.S. Government Printing Office.

Lockman, R. F., and Quester, A. O. 1985. "The AVF: Outlook for the Eighties and Nineties." *Armed Forces and Society* 11:169–182.

McCarroll, J. E., et al. 1981. "The Health Opinions Survey: Predicting Illness in Military Trainees." *Military Medicine* 146:463–465.

McCubbin, H. I., and Dahl, B. B. 1976. "Prolonged Family Separation in the Military: A Longitudinal Study." In *Families in the Military System,* ed. H. I. McCubbin, B. B. Dahl, and E. J. Hunter, pp. 112–144. Beverly Hills, CA: Sage.

MacDonald, M. W. 1943. "Impact of War on Children and Youths: Intensification of Emotional Problems." *American Journal of Public Health* 33:336–338.

Macintosh, J. 1968. "Separation Problems in Military Wives." *American Journal of Psychiatry* 125:260–265.

McKain, J. L. 1973. "Relocation in the Military: Alienation and Family Problems." *Journal of Marriage and the Family* 35:205–209.

McNeil, J. S., and Griffen, M. B. 1967. "Military Retirement: The Retirement Syndrome." *American Journal of Psychiatry* 123:848–854.

Manning, F. J., and Ingraham, L. H. 1981. "Personnel Attrition in the U.S. Army in Europe." *Armed Forces and Society* 7:256–270.

Marlow, D. H. 1983. "The Manning of the Force: The AVF and the Draft." In *Conscripts and Volunteers: Military Requirements, Social Justice and the All-Volunteer Force,* ed. R. K. Fullinwider, pp. 189–199. Totowa, NJ: Rowman and Allanheld.

Marsella, A. J., et al. 1974. "The Effects of Father Presence and Absence Upon Maternal Attitudes." *Journal of Genetic Psychiatry* 125:257–263.

Miligram, R., and Miligram, N. 1975. "The Effects of the Yom Kippur War on Anxiety Level in Israeli Children." Paper presented at the International Conference on Psychological Stress and Adjustment in Time of War and Peace, Tel Aviv, Israel.

Miller, J. K. 1976. "Perspectives on Child Maltreatment in the Military." In *Child Abuse and Neglect,* ed. R. E. Helper and C. H. Kempe, pp. 267–291. Cambridge: Ballinger.

Milowe, I. D. 1964. "A Study in Role Diffusion: The Chief and Sergeant Face Retirement." *Mental Hygiene* 48:101–107.

Mirin, S. M. 1974. "Ineffective Military Personnel." *Archives of General Psychiatry* 30:398–402.

Mirin, S. M., and McKenna, G. J. 1975. "Combat Zone Adjustment: The Role of Marihuana Use." *Military Medicine* 140:482–483.

Morrison, J. 1981. "Rethinking the Military Family Syndrome." *American Journal of Psychiatry* 138:354–357.

Myers, S. 1979. "Child Abuse and the Military Community." *Military Medicine* 144:23–25.

Nace, E. P., et al. 1977. "Depression in Veterans Two Years After Vietnam." *American Journal of Psychiatry* 134:167–170.

Nice, D. S. 1978. "The Androgynous Wife and the Military Child." In *Children of Military Families: A Part and Yet Apart,* ed. E. J. Hunter and D. S. Nice, pp. 25–37. Washington, D.C.: U.S. Government Printing Office.

———. 1981. "The Course of Depressive Affect in Navy Wives During Family Separation." *Military Medicine* 148:341–343.

Nicholson, P. T., et al. 1974. "Ineffective Military Personnel. II. An Ethical Dilemma for Psychiatry." *Archives of General Psychiatry* 30:406–410.

O'Connell, P. V. 1981. "The Effect of Mobility on Selected Personality Characteristics of Ninth and Twelfth Grade Military Dependents." Ph.D. diss., University of Wisconsin-Milwaukee.

Offer, D., and Sabshin, M. 1974. *Normality: Theoretical and Clinical Concepts of Mental Health,* 2nd ed. New York: Basic Books.

Orthner, D. K., and Bowen, G. L. 1982. *Families in Blue: Phase II.* Air Force Contract #F33600-81-R-0290, Office of the Chief of Chaplains, U.S.A.F., Bolling Air Force Base, Washington, D.C.

Oshman, H. P. 1975. "Some Effects of Father Absence Upon the Psychological Development of Male and Female Late Adolescents: Theoretical and Empirical Considerations." Ph.D diss., University of Texas-Austin.

Pederson, F. A. 1966. "Relationship Between Father-Absence and Emotional Disturbance in Male Military Dependents." *Merrill-Palmer Quarterly* 12:321–331.

Pederson, F. A., and Sullivan E. J. 1964. "Relationships Among Geographic Mobility, Parental Attitudes, and Emotional Disturbance in Children." *American Journal of Orthopsychiatry* 34:575–580.

Plag, J. A., and Goffman, J. M. 1966. "The Prediction of Four-Year Military Effectiveness from Characteristics of Naval Recruits." *Military Medicine* 131:729–735.

Platte, R. J. 1976. "The Second Career: Perceived Social Mobility and Adjustment Among Recent Army Retirees and Wives of Army Retirees." In *Families in the Military System,* ed. H. I. McCubbin, B. B. Dahl, and E. J. Hunter, pp. 258–287. Beverly Hills, CA: Sage.

Priest, R. F., et al. 1978. "Coeducation at West Point." *Armed Forces and Society* 4:589–606.

Raybin, J. B., and Flickinger, W. C. 1972. "Rank and the Military Therapeutic Community." *Comprehensive Psychiatry* 13:335–346.

Renner, J. A. 1973. "The Changing Patterns of Psychiatric Problems in Vietnam." *Comprehensive Psychiatry* 14:169–81.

Ridenour, R. I. 1984. "The Military Service Families and the Therapist." In *The Military Family,* ed. F. Kaslow and R. Ridenour, pp. 1–17. London: Guilford Press.

Rienerth, J. G. 1978. "Separation and Female Centeredness in the Military Family." In *Military Families: Adaptation and Change,* ed. E. J. Hunter and D. S. Nice, pp. 169–184. New York: Praeger.

Rodriguez, A. R. 1984. "Special Treatment Needs of Children of Military Families." In *The Military Family,* ed. F. Kaslow and R. Ridenour, pp. 46–72. London: Guilford Press.

Roff, M. 1960. "Relation Between Certain Preservice Factors and Psychoneurosis During Military Duty." *United States Armed Forces Medical Journal* 11:152–160.

Rohrbaugh, M., et al. 1974. "Effects of the Vietnam Experience on Subsequent Drug Use Among Servicemen." *International Journal of the Addictions* 9:25–40.

Roness, A. 1976. "Civil Background Variables Significant to the Development of Psychiatric Disorders During Military Service." *Behavioral Neuropsychiatry* 8:19–26.

Rosenbaum, M. 1944. "Emotional Aspects of Wartime Separations." *The Family* 24:337–341.

Rothberg, J. M., and Datel, W. E. 1978. "Military Outcome of Trainees: A Partial Replication." *Military Medicine* 143:111.

Rustad, M. 1982. *Women in Khaki: The American Enlisted Woman.* New York: Praeger.

Satloff, A. 1967. "Psychiatry and the Nuclear Submarine." *American Journal of Psychiatry* 124:547–551.

Schmidt, J. P., and Hancey, R. 1979. "Social Class and Psychiatric Treatment: Application of a Decision-Making Model to Use Patterns in a Cost-Free Clinic." *Journal of Consulting and Clinical Psychology* 47:771–772.

Schnall, S. N. 1978. "Characteristics in Management of Child Abuse and Neglect Among Military Families." In *Children of Military Families: A Part and Yet Apart,* ed. E. J. Hunter and D. S. Nice, pp. 141–162. Washington, D.C.: U.S. Government Printing Office.

Scott-Brown, A. W. 1973. "Service Psychotherapy. Special Aspects of the Therapeutic Relationship." *Journal of the Royal Navy Medical Service* 59:122–125.

Scruggs, J. C., et al. 1980. "The Vietnam Veteran: A Preliminary Analysis of Psychosocial Status." *Military Medicine* 145:267–269.

Shafii, M., and Shafii, S. L. 1982. "Physical and Sexual Abuse." In *Pathways of Human Development,* ed. M. Shafii and S. L. Shafii, pp. 181–191. New York: Grune & Stratton.

Shatan, C. F. 1973. "The Grief of Soldiers: Vietnam Combat Veterans' Self-Help Movement." *American Journal of Orthopsychiatry* 43:640–653.

Shaw, J. 1979. "The Child in the Military Community." In *Basic Handbook of Child Psychiatry,* ed. J. Noshpitz, vol. 1, pp. 310–316. New York: Basic Books.

Shaw, J., and Pangman, J. 1975. "Geographic Mobility and the Military Child." *Military Medicine* 140:413–416.

Shively, S. L. 1979. "Effects of Marital Status on Outcome of Basic Training." *Military Medicine* 144:750–751.

Shuckit, M. A. 1976. "Family History as a Predictor of Alcoholism in U.S. Navy Personnel." *Journal of Studies on Alcohol* 37:1678–1685.

Snyder, A. I. 1978. "Periodic Marital Separation and Physical Illness." *American Journal of Orthopsychiatry* 48:637–643.

Stevens, A., and Werheim, K. 1970. "Psychiatric Problems in Evaluating Fitness for Military Service." *Behavioral Neuropsychiatry* 2:6–12.

Stouffer, S., et al. 1949. *The American Soldier: Combat and Its Aftermath,* vol. 2. Princeton: Princeton University Press.

Strange, R. 1984. "Retirement From the Service: The Individual and His Family." In *The Military Family,* ed. F. Kaslow and R. Ridenour, pp. 217–225. London: Guilford Press.

Strange, R. E., and Brown, D. E. 1970. "Home From the War: A Study of Psychiatric Problems in Vietnam Returnees." *American Journal of Psychiatry* 127:488–492.

Stretch, R. H., and Figley, C. R. 1984. "Combat and the Vietnam Veteran: Assessment of Psychosocial Adjustment." *Armed Forces and Society* 10:311–319.

Sund, A. 1971. "Personality Inventories as Selective and Prognostic Criteria." *Military Medicine* 136:97–104.

Taintor, Z. 1970. "Birth Order and Psychiatric Problems in Boot Camp." *American Journal of Psychiatry* 126:80–86.

Talbott, J. A. 1969. "Community Psychiatry in the Army. History, Practice, and Applications to Civilian Psychiatry." *Journal of the American Medical Association* 210: 1233–1237.

Tiffany, W. J. 1967. "The Mental Health of Army Troops in Vietnam." *American Journal of Psychiatry* 123:1585–1586.

Trunnell, T. L. 1968. "The Absent Father's Children's Emotional Disturbances." *Archives of General Psychiatry* 19:180–188.

Ursano, R. J. 1981. "The Vietnam Era Prisoner of War: Precaptivity Personality and the Development of Psychiatric Illness." *American Journal of Psychiatry* 138: 315–318.

Ursano, R. J., and Holloway, H. 1985. "Operational Military Psychiatry." In *Comprehensive Textbook of Psychiatry,* 4th ed., ed. H. I. Kaplan and B. J. Saddock, pp. 1900–1909. Baltimore: Williams & Wilkins.

VanPutten, T., et al. 1973. "Traumatic Neuroses in Vietnam Returnees." *Archives of General Psychiatry* 29:695–698.

Wallace, A., and Dycus, J. 1978. "Group Treatment: An Auxiliary to Emergency Foster Care Service in a Military Community." In *Children of Military Families: A Part and Yet Apart,* ed. E. J. Hunter and D. S. Nice, pp. 45–49. Washington, D.C.: U.S. Government Printing Office.

Ward, S. 1975. "Suffer the Little Children—And Their Family." *Medical Service Digest* 26:4–17.

Weissman, M. M., and Klerman, G. 1977. "Sex Differences and the Epidemiology of Depression." *Archives of General Psychiatry* 34:98–112.

White, J. W. 1976. "An Analysis of First Year Referrals to a New Military Child Psychiatry Clinic." *United States Navy Medicine* 67:18–21.

Williams, J. 1976. "Divorce and Dissolution of the Military Family." In *Families in the Military System,* ed. H. I. McCubbin, B. B. Dahl, and E. J. Hunter, pp. 209–236. Beverly Hills, CA: Sage.

Yager, J. 1975. "Personal Violence in Infantry Combat." *Archives of General Psychiatry* 32:257–261.

———. 1976. "Postcombat Violent Behavior in Psychiatrically Maladjustive Soldiers." *Archives of General Psychiatry* 33:1332–1335.

Zitello, A. K. 1942. "The Impact of War on Family Life, II. Mother-Son Relationships." *The Family* 23:257–263.

CHAPTER 6

Task Performance and the Social Construction of Meaning: Juxtaposing Normality with Contemporary Family Research

Frederick S. Wamboldt and David Reiss

In prior works, Offer and Sabshin (1974, 1984) have spoken with knowledge on the subject of normality in individuals by specifying what is and is not known. The primary vehicle driving their discussions has been the *four perspectives on normality:* normality as health, normality as utopia, normality as average, and normality as transactional systems. The challenge of this chapter is to remain as forthright in dealing with the question of normality, yet simultaneously add another level of complexity—specifically, the certitudes and uncertainties that surround the concept of "family." All of us have had extensive experience in family life—so the "family" seems at first both intuitive and transparent. Yet to illustrate the complexity, consider the following questions.

First, can families themselves be normal, or does normality as a construct apply only to individuals within families? Second, can a family be said to have normal processes if one member of the family has a psychiatric illness? What about those "resilient" or "invulnerable" individuals, who enter adult life looking quite good, if not exceptional, despite growing up in severely dysfunctional families? Are they normal? And what if their

The writing of this paper was done at the George Washington University Medical Center and supported in part by NIMH Physician Scientist Award, #K11-MH00607, on which Dr. Wamboldt is the principal investigator and Dr. Reiss is the sponsor.

dysfunctional families actively have contributed to these individuals' resiliency? Finally, what relevance do our considerations of family life have for the current psychiatric diagnostic system, with its traditional focus on disorders in individual persons?

This chapter is divided into five sections. In each, we use examples from contemporary family research to explore what is known and unknown about the questions just asked. In the first section we present three common views on what comprises a family and use recent trends in family life to argue that two of these definitions can profitably be used to discuss the relationship of normality to family life. The next two sections contain this discussion, first by examining research evaluating the "normality" or "competence" of family task performance and then by describing research parsing out how families, as interpersonal groups in intimate transaction, actively construct and become organized around shared meaning systems. In the final two sections we illustrate the clinical importance of these two research fronts, arguing that knowledge of family task performance and family meaning systems can help explain why some individuals exhibit such good coping despite being reared in adverse environments, and finally suggesting that this same knowledge could improve our current psychiatric diagnostic system.

Defining the Family

Where should we draw the line separating family from nonfamily? To explore this question, ask yourself which of the following social groups should be considered to be families.

1. A young dual-career couple who have voluntarily remained childless.
2. The teenage mother, her infant daughter, the thirty-two-year-old grandmother, and the grandmother's male friend who all live under the same roof and as a group have created a warm and supportive home life.
3. The recently naturalized Asian nurse, his wife and two children, whose dutifully mailed monthly checks remain the sole source of support for his parents and handicapped sister still living abroad.
4. The man, estranged from his origin family and stricken with AIDS, whose gay partner has provided with love and devotion nearly all practical and emotional care during his life-draining illness.
5. A young father with a serious drinking problem, the son of deceased alcoholic parents, who at best only dimly perceives any connections

between the abuse he directs at his wife and toddler and the abuse he both witnessed and experienced growing up.

6. The seven-year-old girl and her divorced parents whose dual custody agreement requires the child to live alternately in two homes: the first, with father, his new wife, and her three children; the second, with mother, her new husband, and their two-year-old son.

As these questions illustrate, it is much more difficult to define the "family" than an individual. Individuals are physical realities, palpably bounded at the very least by layers of skin. Yet families are collections of individuals, bounded more complexly by an amalgam of legal conventions, social customs, and interpersonal meanings. Depending on the viewpoint one uses to define the family, the preceding social groups might be viewed as normal families, peculiar families, or nonfamilies.

Viewpoints on What Comprises a Family

Three overlapping viewpoints on the family can be identified in contemporary usage. The first is based on *family structure.* For example, an extended family is any group of individuals related by blood, marriage, or adoption; a nuclear family also lives together in one household. The emphasis here is on the biological or sociolegal legitimacy of connection among family members. A second viewpoint focuses on whether or not certain *tasks of family life* are met: The family is a psychosocial system consisting of an adult and one or more individuals that works toward mutual need fulfillment, nurturance, and development. Finally, there is the *transactional* viewpoint: The family is a group of intimates, related by strong reciprocal affection and loyalties, with a history and a future, who share a sense of home. The central element of this latter class of definitions is the representational and emotional bonds (that is, sense of group identity and existential meaning) that arise out of recurrent transaction.[1]

[1]The term *transaction* has two related uses in the family research field. The first usage describes transactional models of individual development (for example, Sameroff and Chandler 1975) in which what classical research theory calls "independent variables" (such as the level of intellectual stimulation provided by the environment and the verbal intelligence of a child) not only influence a "dependent variable" (child academic performance) but also over time change themselves in an interdependent fashion (children with high verbal abilities may actively seek out stimulating environments through library visits, requests to parents, and so on, and thereby improve not only their academic performance but also the supposedly "independent" stimulatory potential of their environment).

In the second usage, this notion of interdependent change over time is restricted to a more experiential, interpersonal phenomenon. An exemplar here is Dewey and Bentley's (1949) discussion of how two persons' behavioral interaction, if occurring in the proper context, becomes a transaction in which the participants undergo internal change and become increasingly interdependent as each other's beliefs, values, behaviors, and emotions are recursively modified over time.

Which view is correct? That answer depends on one's purpose. In clinical practice it seems prudent to retain the option of using any or all of these definitions. For example, all the social groups described at the beginning of this section can be considered "families" under at least one of these definitions. As clinicians we can readily imagine any of these groups appearing for psychiatric consultation with a complaint reflecting a relationship or family problem. In family research the operational definition most commonly used is a structural one—a family is a household. This equation is primarily a choice of convenience; who lives with whom is much easier to assess and measure than the tasks being performed and/or the subjective experience of shared meaning.

Having said this, the task for this chapter is to examine how the family when viewed under any of these definitions relates to the concept of normality. We begin this task with a selective overview of the historical trends in family life over the past century. The trends seen suggest that one of these definitions, the one based on family structure, although easily measured and therefore useful for research purposes, is much less well suited for exploring the concept of normality, whereas the other two, concerning family task performance and meaning construction, warrant greater scrutiny.

Historical Trends in Family Life

It is widely assumed that, at the minimum, the American family has undergone major changes during the past century. At times one even hears declarations that the American family is moribund. Typically, the industrial revolution is fingered as the agent of the family's downfall—the purported mechanism being an erosion of the presumed stronger antediluvian ties between nuclear and extended family. Interestingly, current evidence suggests that much more of family life has stayed the same than has changed (see Hareven 1984; Keniston 1977; Reiss and Hoffman 1979 for more detailed discussions). Particularly stable has been the structure of the American family.

Indeed, there is little evidence to suggest that the industrial revolution or any other recent historical change has altered the ties between nuclear and extended families. In fact, there have been very few changes in the patterns of family structure over the past century. Then as now, few individuals live alone (fewer than 5 percent), most live with relatives (more than 90 percent), the vast majority marry at least once (more than 95 percent), and most people whose marriages are ended through death or divorce remarry (more than 75 percent). Moreover, across this time the household has been peopled primarily with parents and their young children, that is, nuclear family members; the rate of extended family members living with child-rearing relatives has remained at around 15 percent.

Still, changes underlie this prevalent illusion of massive family breakdown. For example, the geographic mobility of families has increased. Yet sociological studies suggest that the degree of affectional and psychological ties between nuclear and extended families remains very strong (reviewed by Troll and Bengston 1982). There are, however, three other ways that the industrial revolution has changed family life. The first has resulted in changes in family structure, the next has affected the tasks families face, while the third has influenced the systems of social meaning used by families. Each will be discussed in more detail.

FROM FAMILY AS PRODUCER TO FAMILY AS CONSUMER

The family has changed from being the locus of economic production to the site of economic consumption, with a resulting decrease in the financial independence of families from the broader community. Two important trends can be linked to this loosening of financial independence. In sheer economic terms, children, as another set of hands, used to be a major boon to the family economy; in contemporary times they are a significant liability costing tens of thousands of dollars each for a middle-class family to raise from birth through high school. This burden may be not insignificant; contemporary couples are having fewer and fewer children, and more and more couples are choosing to remain childless (currently about 10 percent).

Perhaps the most important change tied to this severing of family economic interdependence has been the steady rise in divorce rates throughout this century (now seemingly leveled off at 40 percent of new marriages). Cherlin (1981) convincingly has argued that while increasing opportunities for greater financial independence for women have preceded rises in the divorce rate, the other major explanation for the rising divorce rate, changes in public attitudes, appears to occur after the fact. The possibility of work outside the home has allowed women to base their decision concerning whether or not to suffer through a noxious marriage on factors other than economic survival. But to harken back to the stability of family structure, despite the rising divorce rate, essentially the same percentage of children (about 40 percent) spend part of their childhood years in a single-parent home as they did years ago due to a corresponding decrease in the death rate over the past century.

FROM PRACTICAL TO EMOTIONAL FAMILY RELATIONSHIPS

As the practical tasks of maintaining the family economy have lessened, family life has evolved to be more concerned with the function of creating and nurturing the emotional bonds between family members. Sentiment has moved to eclipse finances as the functional hub of family life. Certainly in terms of husband-wife relationships the industrial revolution began the process of moving the modal family structure from one in which the husband was more dominant and autocratic to a more companionate marital relationship (Fitzpatrick 1988; Hareven 1984). For married couples the bulk of life's emotional fulfillment now is expected to come from family relationships. (It is important to underscore that this shift from practical to emotional family relationships more aptly describes middle-class, white families than a variety of other minority groups including blacks, recent immigrants, and poor people [Hareven 1984; Harrison, Serafica and McAdoo 1984].)

Additionally, the functions of parents vis-à-vis their children have changed. Keniston (1977) has described the job of postindustrial parents as that of the "weakened executive." When children were a junior contributor to the family industry, parents had direct and rather universal control over them. Over the past century a number of technically specialized institutions have taken over many traditional family child-raising functions, such as secular education, religious instruction, and health care. Given these important and powerful community influences, modern parents' executive and managerial powers have been diminished in three important ways. First, by and large, our culture paradoxically does not acknowledge the power of these extrafamily influences. Thus, if a child develops problems it is his or her parents who get much of the blame. Yet research has found many social influences not fully under the control of a family, such as socioeconomic status, occupational status, and the availability of quality health care, to be major, potentially reversible factors in child outcome.[2] Second, to the degree that the production of income is valued, child rearing as a job without pay is devalued by American society. As the 1980s close in the United States maternity benefits remain meager, paternity benefits are essentially nonexistent, and the demand for high-quality day-care resources far exceeds the supply. Finally, parents usually have received less training than the more expert teachers, health care professionals, and others who provide services for their children and hence in many ways enter their interactions with these professionals from a one-down position.

In summary, the tasks facing families have changed over time. Indeed, the financial independence of families from the broader community has decreased over the past century, while the expectations that family life is the center of life's emotional satisfaction has increased. Yet despite the

[2]See Elder (1974); Kohn (1977); Kohn and Schooler (1983); Komarovsky (1940); Pearlin et al. (1981); and Werner and Smith (1982).

changes in functions of family life, the question still remains, "Can families be said to exhibit normal functioning?"

FROM COMMUNITYWIDE TO FAMILY-BASED SOCIAL MEANING SYSTEMS

A final trend relates more closely to our own research—through the years of American history, families have become more active originators of the explanatory systems used to organize their own behavior and to understand the world they find themselves in. One of us (Reiss 1981) has compared two different models of family life from American history that differ greatly in the latitude the family had to actively and independently construe the meaning of important events in their social world.

On one hand was the Puritan family, described by Demos (1970) as the "little commonwealth." Within this extremely homogeneous society, the meaning and explanatory systems that arose within Puritan families deeply reflected the values and conceptions of the larger community. In practice, social and legal codes structured and organized virtually all of a family's life, down to rather fundamental choices. For example, Puritan families were bound by law to build their houses within a half-mile radius of the town's meeting house and church. Additionally, fathers were charged with supervising their children's studies of Scripture and faced public penalties and censure for dereliction of duty.

A clear contrast is provided by the pioneer families who settled the Great Plains during the mid-nineteenth century. Isolated from a larger community and confronted with the danger and desolation of the prairies, these families by necessity became to a great extent the active creators of their own civilization. They had great latitude in deciding how to structure the relationships within their families, what of their pasts to hold onto, and how to give meaning to the world they lived within.

Our own research has proceeded from the assumption that contemporary American families are more similar to their pioneer than their Puritan counterparts in terms of their ability to actively and independently develop out of their ongoing transactions a shared understanding of their social world. As such, our work has focused on measuring the meaning systems used by families and exploring how the variability in such systems empirically relates to the intra- and extrafamily relationships formed by families. Later we explore how this variability in family meaning systems relates to the concept of normality.

VIEWS OF THE FAMILY, HISTORICAL TRENDS, AND NORMALITY

Three important conclusions can be gleaned from our overview of the recent history of the American family. First, although clearly the least common denominator, the stability of the household as the dominant family unit throughout this century offers considerable support for the central place of structural definitions in the family research field. Yet who is present within these households shows so much variability that it seems imprudent to label the nuclear family household, or any other, as the "normal" family structure. For example, throughout recent history nearly 40 percent of children do not enter their adult years in a two-parent family. Further, research has shown quite clearly that nonnuclear families can function as well as more traditional nuclear families provided they have access to the material and interpersonal resources required to master the various tasks of family life.[3] Hence, searching for a "normal" or "healthy" family structure is a wasted effort.

Second, the tasks of family life have expanded and become more complex over time. Families still are expected to provide for the bulk of their own basic practical needs, yet their economic livelihood is more entwined with that of the community in which they reside. Additionally, families have increasingly begun to seek the vast majority of the emotional satisfaction expected out of life from their relationships with family members. Finally, we have argued that the task of raising and socializing children has become more complex as more nonfamily members have come to play key roles. A family's ability to perform any or all of these tasks may indeed be measurable, and thereby provide an index of a family's normality or health.

Third, contemporary families have significant latitude to actively and independently organize their ongoing transactions in a manner that both builds and reinforces their own system of social meaning. Hence, knowledge of family meaning systems may be important to our consideration of normality and health in family life; yet it is less clear whether the normality and/or health refers to the family or the individuals within the family. The following sections explore the connections between the concept of normality and research exploring how families perform key tasks and develop systems of shared meaning.

Normality and Family Task Performance

In their day-to-day activities families face a variety of functional demands that are thoroughly entwined across biological, environmental, temporal, relational, and developmental lines.

[3]See Eiduson and Alexander (1978); Hetherington, Cox, and Cox (1982); Kellam, Ensminger, and Turner (1977); and Kellam et al. (1982).

The Many Tasks of Family Life

A number of tasks confront the nuclear family over its life span. These include (1) generating and maintaining an intimate and mutually supportive marital relationship; (2) providing instrumental and affectional nurturance to children; (3) adequately socializing and launching these children into the community; (4) fostering the individual development of the family's parents as adults; and (5) managing the nuclear family's relationship with kin and the community at large.[4]

The first point to be made regarding these tasks is that none seems to depend solely on the behavior of any one family member. Even for the nurturance of infants, there is now little doubt that the infant is a very active participant in the quality of his or her care. For example, temperamentally "easy" babies elicit better care from their parents than do more "difficult" babies (Korner 1971; Thomas et al. 1963), presumably because they provide their parents with more "readable" clues and respond more clearly and unambiguously to their parents' care (Goldberg 1977). Also, good nurturance of infants appears to be much more than a dyadic task—fathers (Parke 1979) and/or grandmothers (Furstenburg, Brooks-Gunn, and Morgan 1987; Kellam, Ensminger, and Turner 1977, 1982) are increasingly being recognized as critical players in early infant development. The point to be stressed is that the successful accomplishment of these tasks is more properly seen as a family-level achievement, rather than the sole responsibility of one or more individuals within the family. In other words, all involved family members likely have contributed to any observed outcome. This "systemic" or interactional viewpoint has become increasingly prominent in modern theories of family functioning.

Second, the successful performance of many family tasks can impede or disrupt the performance of others. For example, researchers have found that a couple's level of marital satisfaction consistently drops as they go across the transition to parenthood, with this effect lasting for at least two

[4]A number of family *life cycle* models have been proposed that attempt to link these tasks in sequential form (Carter and McGoldrick 1980; Duvall 1957; Hill 1964). While conceptually appealing, the simple sequence central to these life cycle models has been criticized by family *life course* researchers in two regards (Elder 1978; Nock 1982). First, the stages within these cycles are almost universally linked to the phases of child rearing. Yet giving such high status to what is merely one of many demands of family life seems a troublesome, value-based assumption. Second, while some evidence exists that the proposed life cycle sequence represents the modal sequence for American families, it does not hold for the majority due to the frequency of such events as childlessness, divorce, and death, which "personalize" the life course of any specific family. For these reasons, our discussion of family task performance borrows much more heavily from the life course perspective and therefore makes no assumption that family development follows any set sequence.

years after the birth of their first child (Belsky, Spanier, and Rovine 1983; Cowan et al. 1978; LaRossa and LaRossa 1981). Additionally, difficulty handling one task can frequently lead to problems in the management of other tasks. For example, depressed women have been shown to have deficits in both their child-rearing and marital functioning (Keitner et al. 1985; Merikangas et al. 1985; Weissman and Paykel 1974). Similarly, marital conflict is reliably related to child-rearing problems (for reviews see Bloom, Asher, and White 1978; Emery 1982; Hetherington, Cox, and Cox 1982). The important point is that one is simultaneously involved in a variety of entwined relationships within the nuclear family. This interdependence allows changes in any single person or relationship to reverberate throughout other relationships inside the family.

Many researchers view this tension between different family demands as resulting from the reciprocal connections between the life courses of the individuals within the family (for example, Burton and Bengston 1985; Elder 1984; Hagestad and Burton 1986). For example, *ready or not,* when one's children become parents the original parents ascend to the role of grandparents. Indeed research has shown that while normative family transitions such as becoming a parent or a grandparent appear less stressful than commonly supposed (Kessler, Price, and Wortman 1985; Pearlin et al. 1981), one of the strongest mediating variables determining the level of stress of such events is the degree to which life changes are perceived by the participants as occurring "on-time" (Neugarten 1979). In Burton's study (Burton and Bengston 1985; Hagestad and Burton 1986), women in their thirties who have just become grandmothers as a result of their teenage daughters having a baby and who also *experience themselves as at an acceptable age* to be a grandparent provide more competent help to the young mother-infant dyad than do those women who see the transition to grandparenthood as happening "too early." Due to this interdependence of family relationships, successful development within families requires the presence of some means for handling competing, potentially conflicting interests.

It is equally clear that relationships outside of the household are also entwined with relationships inside the family. Although families may differ in the degree to which they are responsive to extrafamily events, no family has a shell impervious to the community in which it resides. Consider several examples of important links. The first is between the individual and the community at large: Parents' occupational experience causally influences the values and practices they use in raising their children (Kohn 1977; Kohn and Schooler 1983). The second is between family members and their extrahousehold social ties: Bott (1971) demonstrated the potential cost of relationships outside the home. Individuals entering marriage with close-knit yet *independent* social networks tend to form marriages with less shared experience; the marital relationship assumes secondary status to these other extranuclear family relationships. Additionally, compelling clinical evidence also points to the potential conflicts of loyalty that arise from the fact that most individuals are for a major portion of their lives simultaneously members of at least three families: their origin family, their family of procreation, and their spouse's family of origin.[5]

In summary, the functioning of any family depends on the performance of all involved members and represents multiple compromises within a complexly interrelated and entwined web of relationships both inside and outside the family.

Competent Family Task Performance

Given this panoply of diverse and potentially discordant tasks that a family must manage, the possibility of identifying "healthy" or "normal" family functioning at first glance seems an imposing if not star-crossed task. However, given that science never has shown great respect for astrological admonitions, it is not surprising that several lines of contemporary research are actively exploring the determinants of competent family task performance. The first set of research has attempted to measure global self-reports of family functioning from the individual members of a family. The second has investigated in precise detail the specific interpersonal behaviors required successfully to handle discrete salient family tasks, such as the resolution of relationship conflict.

GLOBAL APPRAISALS OF FAMILY TASK PERFORMANCE

Several research groups have developed global measures of the health/competence of a family's task performance. Typically, these models of family functioning and their associated research instruments have arisen out of clinical pragmatics. The central driving question usually is "What areas of family functioning are most crucial for the healthy development of family members?"

Two general assumptions about families tend to be inherent in these models. First, healthier, more competent families form and maintain *coherent relationship organization.* That is, in healthy families the boundaries of membership and the allocation of roles is clear. Given the complexity of

[5]See Boszormenyi-Nagy and Spark (1973); Bowen (1978); Selvini-Palazzoli et al. (1978); Wamboldt and Reiss (1989); and Wamboldt and Wolin (1988).

modern family life, the family whose relational boundaries are ambiguously drawn is likely to flounder in perpetual change—chaos. On the other hand, the family with more coherent organization gains the stability and self-directedness to adapt (choose to change) rather than being merely buffeted by internal and external events. Erikson's (1964) words regarding an individual's identity echo this sentiment: "Identity connotes the resiliency of maintaining essential patterns in the process of change. Thus, strange as it may seem, it takes a well-established identity to tolerate radical change" (p. 96).

The second general characteristic of healthier, more competent families is that they assume a *proactive adaptive posture* concerning their intra- and extrafamily relationships. Hence in these models adaptation is viewed not as reflexive responses to external or internal events but rather as purposive deliberate actions. To genuinely adapt, families need to monitor the important relationships in their lives, anticipate changes that need to be made, and actively take steps to make the necessary adjustments (Lee 1988; Melito 1985; Steinglass et al. 1987). (Much has been written about homeostatic mechanisms as important regulatory processes in families. Yet such reflexive, rapid responses to the contingencies of the immediate situation have little to do with adaptation. They are merely interpersonal habits that allow for more habitual relationships during the smooth-sailing plateaus of family development. If used during periods of developmental transition and crisis, they typically lead to fixation, not adaptation [Reiss 1981; Steinglass et al. 1987].) While these are indeed complex functions of family life, a handful of research groups have published provisional evidence that a family's global performance along these two more general dimensions of family functioning can be measured reliably.

Perhaps the most successful exemplar of this line of work is the McMaster Model of Family Functioning (Epstein, Bishop, and Baldwin 1982; Epstein, Bishop, and Levin 1978). In this model six areas of family functioning (problem solving, communication, roles, affective responsiveness, affective involvement, and behavior control) are seen as most critical to managing three major domains of tasks (providing for basic instrumental needs [food, money, shelter]; facilitating emotional development; and managing crises and hazards). Family normality, health, or competence explicitly is seen as a linear function. Families better able to successfully perform the tasks in each of these domains are viewed as more healthy or competent. In their clinical reports describing the model, Epstein, Bishop, and Baldwin (1982) have stressed a sequential hierarchy concerning the instrumental and emotional task domains. In their words, "Families whose functioning is disrupted by instrumental problems rarely, if ever, deal effectively with affective problems. However, families whose functioning is disrupted by affective problems may deal adequately with instrumental problems" (p. 119). To paraphrase, some families can be sufficiently organized so that basic practical family life task needs can be handled, yet a higher level of competence is required to monitor over time the emotional needs of family members and adapt appropriately.[6]

A research instrument, the *Family Assessment Device* (FAD), has been developed to reflect the McMaster Model. In its present form the FAD is a sixty-item self-report questionnaire with seven subscales. Six of these subscales correspond to the six areas of family functioning in the McMaster Model; the final subscale, General Functioning (GF), is viewed as an overall measure of the health/pathology of the family. The items comprising the GF subscale are listed in table 6.1.

Preliminary reports concerning the FAD are encouraging. Reliability is good and the subscales appear relatively independent once the level of the GF subscale is controlled (Epstein, Baldwin, and Bishop 1983; Miller et al. 1985). The instrument's validity has received provisional support—the FAD can discriminate nonclinical families from families with at least one member receiving psychiatric treatment (Miller et al. 1985); and a large-scale epidemiological study found the GF subscale to be strongly associated with a number of relevant markers of family dysfunction, including the presence of marital violence or current alcohol-related family tensions, history of parental psychiatric hospitalization, or police record

[6]Another very similarly conceived model of family functioning exists. This model, the Beavers System Model, has two component constructs. The first has been labeled family adaptability, health, or overall competence. Again, as in the McMaster Model, this family competence construct is conceived of as a linear, continuous dimension, that in this case can be divided into a number of ordinal categories identifying disturbed, midrange, adequate, and optimal families. The second construct is a stylistic one that describes two types of organizational patterns of relationships identified in disturbed families: Centripetal families exhibit enmeshed relationships; centrifugal families have isolated and distant relationships. Interestingly, the clinical correlates associated with their ordinal competence categories echo those from the McMaster Model: Optimal families handle both emotional and practical needs within all family relationships; adequate families differ in that significant emotional tension is present in at least some important family relationships, often the marital relationship; midrange families adequately have established stable organization and can handle basic practical needs but do so via rigid and harsh control of family members at the expense of emotional development; while dysfunctional families cannot manage either stable organization or adapt to promote emotional development (Beavers 1982). Additionally, scores generated from the research instrument associated with the Beavers model have been shown to be highly correlated with scores from the McMaster Model's research questionnaire (Hampson, Beavers, and Hulgus 1988).

A third prominent model of family functioning, the Circumplex Model (Olson, Sprenkle, and Russell 1979), relates family health to curvilinear, rather than linear, functions. This model has met with less success, at least partly due to its confounding of chaotic change (lack of organization) and ability to change (adaptability) (Hampson, Beavers, and Hulgus 1988; Lee 1988).

TABLE 6.1

Items Comprising the General Functioning Subscale, McMaster Family Assessment Device (Epstein, Baldwin, and Bishop 1983)[a]

Planning family activities is difficult because we misunderstand each other.
In times of crisis we can turn to each other for support.
We cannot talk to each other about the sadness we feel.
Individuals are accepted for what they are.
We avoid discussing our fears and concerns.
We can express feelings to each other.
There are lots of bad feelings in the family.
We feel accepted for what we are.
Making decisions is a problem for our family.
We are able to make decisions about how to solve problems.
We don't get along well together.
We confide in each other.

[a]Responses are strongly agree, agree, disagree, strongly disagree.

(Byles et al. 1988). Taken together, these tests of this instrument support the hypothesis that family health/competence can be operationalized as at least an ordinal, if not a continuous linear, variable.

Nonetheless, this line of work still faces two major challenges. First, a family-level construct, the health/competence of a family's functioning, is being assessed through the self-reports of individual family members. Yet such reports are really individual perceptions and hence could quite conceivably reflect more about the individual making them than the family itself. The McMaster group has dealt with this measurement problem by using averages of responding family members' answers as a family-level measure—a far from satisfactory solution. Indeed, another research group using an analogous questionnaire has reported clear male-female and family role differences in individuals' perceptions of their family (Hampson and Beavers 1987). At this time it seems wise, therefore, to see these measures of family health/competence as individual perceptions, subject to a vast range of potential biases and distortions, rather than as indices of inherent qualities of the family itself.

Second, the validity studies of these global family health models have reported associations between a family health scale score and some discrete adjustment or outcome measure, such as family psychiatric history, adjustment to chronic illness, and so on. What remains for these research groups to demonstrate is that their measures of family health/competence truly reflect variations in the actual interactional process of families. That is, what specifically is it that healthier, more competent families do differently from less healthy, less competent families? While the clinical models that these research instruments have been derived from do make statements about family processes, the reported research has not yet shown that it is in fact the quality of family process that determines the reports given on these instruments. At this point the reported validity correlations could be confounded. For example, common method variance may account for the findings: Individuals happy in their current life circumstances for whatever reason may give positive reports across a variety of questionnaires, including a family health scale, regardless of the actual interactional patterns within their family.

DETAILED STUDIES OF FAMILY INTERACTIONAL PROCESS

A second line of research has taken a very different approach to the study of family task performance, focusing on the behavioral details of what families do together rather than what they say about their functioning. As a rule, the research in this area draws heavily on the perspective of behavioral psychology and has led to the development of many successful and innovative approaches to marital and family therapy. (Further discussion of these approaches to therapy appears in Wamboldt, Wamboldt, and Gurman 1985.) In general terms, the central research questions asked have been of the form, "What specific behaviors make families with problem X different from families without problem X?" Generally speaking, these researchers have paid close attention to relevant methodological issues and have used careful, finely honed observations of the sequences of interactional behavior within family dyads to explore their research questions.

As an example of this line of research, we will discuss the work of Gottman and colleagues (see Gottman 1979 for more details concerning this work). The question pursued by this group has been "Why do some marriages succeed while others fail?" The three phases of their research map quite nicely onto the three-step process followed within mainstream medical epidemiology: First, cross-sectional studies are used to identify potential risk factors; second, the causal nature of the observed risk factor-outcome associations are tested in prospective, longitudinal studies; and finally, the research findings inform prevention/intervention strategies that are subsequently empirically tested.

The initial studies of this research group were designed to identify potentially changeable factors that discriminated marriages at high risk of marital failure from those at low risk. After a careful review of prior research in this area, the researchers decided to focus their attention on the ability of couples to resolve salient conflicts in their relationship. They reasoned that without this ability, the inevitable conflicts of intimate life would remain unresolved and generate a toxic burden that over time could erode the couple's satisfaction with, and hence their commitment to, the marriage. The genius in their work was the degree to which they carefully dissected the process of resolving conflict. Their work has uncovered the following differences between very satisfied (nondistressed) and very dissatisfied (distressed) couples as potential risk factors (reviewed in Gottman 1979; Notarius and Pellegrini 1987):

1. Distressed couples experience their conflict discussions as less rewarding and indeed do exhibit more negative behavior in their interaction than do nondistressed couples.
2. The negative behavior in distressed couples is more reciprocal; that is, a negative comment from one spouse has a high probability of being followed by a negative response from the partner; spouses in nondistressed couples often respond with neutral or even positive affect after negative comments.
3. In large part due to the former difference, the conflict discussions of nondistressed couples show an orderly sequential progression through three stages (agenda-building, exploration, resolution) while distressed couples engage in long loops of negative interaction (descriptively labeled "cross-complaining") that keeps them stuck in the agenda-building phase.
4. A key behavior missing in distressed couples is acknowledgment and validation of the partner's position: "You are saying . . ."
5. This acknowledgment/validation deficit is particularly prominent in the behavior of women in distressed marriages as compared to that of women in nondistressed relationships. Men in both types of marriages tend not to be particularly good at acknowledging and validating their partner's position.

The second phase of this research has attempted to use cohort studies to evaluate the ability of the identified risk factors to predict future relationship problems—that is, to identify the risk factors as potential causal agents. In two separate studies Markman, a former graduate student of Gottman, has reported that the perceived positiveness of conflict discussion in premarital couples was strongly associated with level of marital satisfaction at follow-ups ranging from two to five and one-half years (Markman 1979, 1981; Markman et al. 1987). Similarly, Levenson and Gottman (1985) have reported that the degree to which a woman reciprocates her husband's negative behaviors in a conflict discussion is strongly predictive of declines in the couple's marital satisfaction three years later. Poor conflict resolution does appear to precede marital distress.

The final phase of this work has involved the creation and implementation of prevention strategies based on the research findings. An initial report of the effectiveness of a premarital risk-reduction program incorporating these research findings has been recently published (Markman et al. 1987). Unfortunately, the program's effect was less clear cut than had been hoped, in part because those couples judged to be most in need of the program tended to decline to participate—certainly a common occurrence even in more traditional medical prevention programs.

Viewed as a whole, this entire line of work is one of the best in contemporary family research. The ability to resolve relationship conflict does appear to be causally related to subsequent marital success/failure. Furthermore, given the unequivocal association between marital difficulties and other personal and family problems (Bloom, Asher, and White 1978; Emery 1982; Hetherington, Cox, and Cox 1982), the ability of a couple to resolve the conflict within their relationship is also likely to be predictive of many other important aspects of family life.

Can we conclude, therefore, that normal, healthy, or competent families must be able to resolve marital conflicts? The answer to this question is not an easy one. On one hand, the research just discussed suggests that conflict resolution is a toxin-clearing function as vital to maintaining healthy family relationships as adequate hepatic and renal function is to maintaining an individual's health. Indeed, it seems quite likely to us that the research of Gottman and colleagues will produce important new strategies for promoting healthier marriages. Yet the regulation of family relationships in some ways is more complex than the toxin-clearance metaphor suggests. While poor hepatic or renal function is incompatible with individual health or normality, there is some research evidence that suggests that the presence of marital conflict is not an unconditional sign of relationship dysfunction. Indeed, Fitzpatrick (1988) presents a compelling, data-based argument that many couples (consistently comprising up to one-third of large research samples) not only agree to disagree, but actually look to their conflict as an important indication that their individual identities have not been subsumed in their relationship. Borrowing Fitzpatrick's terms, the difference between such conflict-tolerant Independent couples and the more Traditional couples for whom conflict is toxic is one of meaning. The Independent couples have established a shared understanding that within their relationship conflict equals success, or at minimum, conflict is not a disaster.

This move from the behavioral specifics of family interaction to the more symbolic level of shared meanings—what does the specific interactional pattern mean to the family?—reflects movement from one class of definitions of "normality" to another. Using the Offer and Sabshin (1974, 1984) definitions, the interactional research just discussed fits family task performance into the normality as health, normality as average, or normality as optimal classes. Similar to a measure of renal function, say creatinine clearance, the level of a couple's conflict resolution skills could be labeled using such evaluative, scaled descriptors as good or bad; low, adequate, or high. Yet we have just suggested that even if one knows that a couple experiences chronically high levels of conflict, that couple cannot unconditionally be labeled dysfunctional, abnormal, or unhealthy. Also needed is an understanding of the specific shared meaning that the couple has of their interactional behavior. This formulation seems in line with Offer and Sabshin's (1974, 1984) transactional definition of normality—in this case what is important is the "goodness of fit" between the interaction that occurs within the family and the type of relational group that family understands themselves to be. In the next section we discuss research exploring such family-level understanding.

Family Transaction, Representation, and Normality

There is a longstanding tradition in psychiatry, as well as throughout much of social science, to regard the "understanding" a person has of both self and others as arising out of the transactions that person has with his or her significant others.[7] Out of this clinical and scholarly tradition has grown a line of family research that has explored the family's construction of social reality, broadly defined as their sense of history, current belonging, and future that arises out of the family's recurrent transaction, orchestrates their roles and behavior, and generates bonds of affection and loyalty. Such a family-based meaning system involves two related sets of assertions: one concerning group identity, "Who are we as a family?"; the second concerning the world at large, "How does the world work? What is the place of our family within that world?" As an example of this research we discuss the work of Reiss and colleagues, who have developed a pioneering method for measuring such family meaning systems (Reiss 1981; Reiss and Klein 1987).

Family Paradigm Theory

Twenty years ago, while using a standardized laboratory task to study the association between family interaction and thought disorder in schizophrenic patients, Reiss (1971, 1981) observed that despite having received exactly the same instructions, different families "misunderstood" these instructions in characteristic manners. Indeed, these "misunderstandings" seemed to vary across two definable dimensions. First, some families per-

[7]See Berger and Luckman (1966); Bowlby (1969); Cooley (1909); Gustafson (1986); Mead (1934); and Sullivan (1953).

ceived the task to be potentially masterable; they never appeared to doubt that a solution could in fact be found. Others experienced the ambiguity in the instructions as a potential threat or trick; their goal was to minimize their losses in what they saw as a no-win situation. Second, some families "heard" that this was a task in which they were all to work together, even though no such instruction was given. Conversely, others had little to no verbal communication throughout the task. Still other families did talk about the task among themselves but nonetheless solved the task in independent, highly individualistic ways. As this laboratory task, the Card Sort Procedure (CSP), was refined to explore these observations, an additional dimension of variation in the response of families was noted: Some families allowed their solutions to the task to change as new information was presented to them; others "solved" the task quite early on after having received very little information and afterward selectively inattended to any contradictory data that came their way.

In an attempt to explain these observations, Reiss (1981) proposed that his laboratory task by virtue of its inherent ambiguity and novelty may function like a projective test and tap into the family's latent tendencies for dealing with novel and ambiguous settings that arise in their day-to-day life. In other words, the family's response might not be explained solely by the specific characteristics of the laboratory setting; it may generalize to the family's usual relational experience. Reiss has conceptualized these latent tendencies as the family's shared views of their interpersonal world. To accentuate the objective quality of this family-level "reality" as experienced by families, Reiss has termed this system of meaning the *family's paradigm.* To date, without doubt, the Family Paradigm Model as operationalized via the Card Sort Procedure is the most thoroughly researched measure of family-based systems of meaning.

The Card Sort Procedure currently used is an observer-scored, laboratory-based task consisting of two phases—an individual phase and a family phase. During each phase a word puzzle is solved by sorting a deck of sixteen cards into logical groupings. The patterns of these solutions can be either simple/superficial or detailed/complex. Family members are visually isolated in booths for the tasks but can discuss the task with each other via intercom during the family phase. Based on the behavior shown as family members jointly solve a series of logical puzzles, a series of measures have been derived to index the three orthogonal dimensions of the family's paradigm (consult Reiss 1981 for details concerning the development and evolution of these dimensions): The first refers to the degree to which the family perceives their environment as complex yet masterable *(configuration);* the second, to the degree to which family members believe that they are expected to act as a group *(coordination);* and the third, to the degree to which the family expects the world to provide them with potentially useful, novel information *(closure).*

The Card Sort Procedure has demonstrated sound psychometric properties. Test-retest reliability over a six-month period ranged from 0.43 (closure) to 0.86 (coordination) across the three dimensions (Oliveri and Reiss 1984). In addition, the three-factor solution, representing the dimensions of configuration, closure, and coordination, has been repeatedly replicated in Reiss's laboratory (Oliveri and Reiss 1981*a;* Reiss 1981; Reiss and Klein 1987) as well as abroad (Shulman and Klein 1982, 1983).

This procedure has demonstrated significant construct validity by predicting families' responses to major life problems arising in a variety of medical settings including psychiatric hospitalization (Costell and Reiss 1982; Costell et al. 1981; and Reiss et al. 1980) and chronic illness and death of a family member (Reiss, Gonzalez, and Kramer 1986). Additionally, the Card Sort Procedure appears to relate to families' experience of the relationships within their household (Oliveri and Reiss 1982) as well as to characteristics of their relationships with friends and kin (Oliveri and Reiss 1981*b;* Reiss and Oliveri 1983*a*).[8]

Studies of psychopathology within families have also supported the validity of the procedure. Different behavior on both the Card Sort Proce-

[8]Despite this impressive collection of results using the Card Sort Procedure, the family's problem-solving behavior, and hence their paradigm, could still be attributable to the skills and/or characteristics of the individuals (or subgroup of individuals) comprising the family, and therefore not be a true family-level phenomenon. Three studies have explored this possibility. First, the families' behavior during the Card Sort Procedure has been found to be independent of such variables as the social class, educational level, and intellectual, perceptual, and personality attributes of the individual family members (Oliveri and Reiss 1981*a;* Reiss and Oliveri 1983*b*). Second, a double-blind, placebo-controlled experimental design was used to explore the impact on Card Sort Procedure behavior of pharmacologically impairing one family member, the adolescent, one hour prior to testing (via a 175 mg dose of secobarbital). The results of this experiment showed that while the performance of the drugged individuals did deteriorate, the families maintained their characteristic form of problem-solving behavior. Secondary analyses strongly suggest that this preservation of family problem-solving style was accomplished through the rapid, compensating verbal behaviors of the nondrugged parents (Reiss and Salzman 1973). Finally, in a second experiment, matched groups of environment-sensitive and consensus-sensitive families were observed during a more tightly controlled problem-solving task. By using computer terminals as the sole means of communication between family members, two aspects of the families' communication were separately manipulated: information concerning the problem and information concerning the source (that is, which family member was communicating). As predicted, the individuals in consensus-sensitive families performed as well as the members of environment-sensitive families when little or no source communication was allowed. However, in the public mode, when both problem and source communication was permitted, deficits analogous to those seen during the Card Sort Procedure appeared in the consensus-sensitive families. Apparently, individual skills were inhibited by a family-level process once the individuals' behavior was under family scrutiny (Reiss 1971). Taken together, these studies allow an extremely important and unique conclusion to be drawn: the Card Sort Procedure measures a property of the *family as a group* that is not reflective of the socioeconomic, attentional, perceptual, cognitive, or representational attributes of its component members.

dure and other similar laboratory tasks has been demonstrated for families in which one member has a conduct disorder, schizophrenia, or no history of psychiatric illness (summarized in Reiss 1981; Reiss and Klein 1987). Indeed, these results have been discussed as indicating differing types of families: Environment-sensitive families contained individuals with no history of psychiatric illness; individuals with diagnoses of schizophrenia came from consensus-sensitive families; and individuals with conduct disorders had distance-sensitive families. Table 6.2 summarizes the Card Sort Procedure behavior of these three family types. Behaviorally, environment-sensitive families (no psychiatric illness) could effectively communicate and transmit information among themselves and could seek out and process incoming information; consensus-sensitive families (schizophrenic members) also communicated effectively but showed deficits in the ability to process incoming information; distance-sensitive families (conduct-disordered members) showed very individualistic and impulsive behavior corresponding to deficits in both domains (Reiss 1981). Families containing individuals with alcoholism, again an impulsive, undercontrolled disorder, have shown Card Sort Procedure behavior similar to the conduct-disordered families (Davis et al. 1980; Steinglass 1979).

Subsequent studies have demonstrated that "normal" families (no history of psychiatric illness in any family member) have scores evenly distributed across the three paradigm dimensions; that is, normal families can be found in all of the family types (Davis et al 1980; Oliveri and Reiss 1981*a*). There are at least three potential explanations for this discrepancy. First, there is the issue of sensitivity and specificity of the psychiatric diagnosis. The families in the earlier studies underwent a much more rigorous psychiatric screening and hence had more reliable diagnoses. With more fully elaborated family pedigrees of psychiatric disturbance, a

TABLE 6.2

Card Sort Procedure Classification of Three Family Types

Psychiatric Diagnosis (Family Type)	Card Sort Procedure Dimensions		
	Configuration	Coordination	Closure
No Psychiatric Illness (Environment-sensitive)	High	High	High
Schizophrenia (Consensus-sensitive)	Low	High	Low
Conduct Disorder/Alcohol Abuse (Distance-sensitive)	Low	Low	Low

clearer relationship between family paradigm type and psychopathology may be found as the "contaminating" effects of false negative and false positive cases are lessened. Second, the family paradigm types may identify families at risk for specific types of psychiatric problems. As prior studies of psychopathology by the Reiss group have all used either case-control or cross-sectional designs, they could assess only family history and current presence of psychopathology. Still, some of these "normal" families, if faced with sufficient stress, might develop not only psychopathology but a particular, potentially predictable type of disturbance. The longitudinal, cohort studies required to test this possibility remain to be done. Third, most contemporary models of pathogenesis are multifactorial. Accordingly, while research has identified seemingly toxic patterns of family interaction that precede the development of psychiatric symptoms in high-risk populations (for example, communication deviance and negative affective style; Doanne et al. 1981; Goldstein 1985), there is no evidence to suggest that family interaction acting alone can cause major psychiatric illness. Current models of pathogenesis typically include at least three components, all of which are integrally related to outcome: (1) the hereditary and constitutional vulnerability of the individuals at risk; (2) the quality and quantity of environmental stress; and (3) the available coping capacity within the environment (Rosenthal 1970; Zubin and Spring 1977). The finding of nonclinical families across the three family types empirically defined by the Card Sort Procedure is consistent with these models. The type of family paradigm, as a reflection of salient aspects of family environment, could affect any of these three factors (formative, precipitating, and supportive roles of environment), yet still be only one part of the etiological picture. In the next section we explore further the interrelationships between family meaning systems and normality.

Family Meaning Systems and Normality

Early writings concerning family paradigm theory stressed the "normality" and health-promoting characteristics of the environment-sensitive family type. Indeed, a family who views the world as an understandable, potentially masterable place (high configuration), as expecting the family to function as a unified group (high coordination), and as containing potentially valuable new experiences (high, or delayed, closure) appears on face to be quite well equipped for meeting life's challenges. Yet in contrast to the task performance models of family functioning, which are integrally grounded in a "more equals better" conception of health and normality, the family meaning systems perspective generally takes a different view—

normal or healthy family functioning depends on the "goodness of fit" between the family's view of their social world and the challenges that confront that particular family. In this latter "transactional" perspective, some families may be particularly well equipped to handle certain challenges, while other equally competent or normal families may be better suited to navigate successfully through different difficult situations. Indeed, Reiss, Gonzalez, and Kramer (1986) found in a study of patients with end-stage renal disease that three family characteristics usually viewed as strengths (the family's intellectual and socioeconomic resources, their intactness as a group, and their joint ability to solve problems) powerfully, yet "paradoxically," predicted early death. The "paradox" here, we argue, is only surprising when family health is viewed from the linear task performance perspective. From the family meaning system perspective, we have simply found an interesting result in need of further explanation—why do these specific family characteristics lead to the observed outcome in this particular circumstance? It is from this stance that Reiss and Klein (1987) have recently stated, "Intrinsically, no paradigm is more adaptive or more health-promoting than another" (p. 221). In summary, just as there is little reason to believe that any one individual personality style is more or less normal across all settings, there currently is no evidence that any one type of family meaning system is uniformly better, even though knowledge of a family's meaning system may prove useful in predicting the healthiness or competence of that family's performance in a specific situation.[9]

Families and Resilience to Bad Environments

From the clinical point of view, an extremely important consideration is those individuals who, despite having grown up in what to all appearance were quite toxic and unsupportive environments, manage to reach their adult years looking quite unscathed. In this section we examine the concept of resilience, highlighting ways that knowledge of family task performance and family meaning construction can add to the understanding of resiliency in individuals.

[9]Accordingly a typology based on families' paradigms may not map directly onto a typology derived from a task performance model, such as the ordinal family types proposed within the McMaster Model, even though associations might be predicted based on published descriptions of these differing types of families. Indeed, attempts to relate Card Sort Procedure behavior to seemingly analogous subscales of widely used self-report measures of family culture (the Family Environment Scale—Moos and Moos 1986) and orientation (Family Adaptability and Cohesion Scales—Olson, Sprenkle, and Russell 1979) have been singularly unsuccessful (Oliveri and Reiss 1984; Sigafoos et al. 1985).

Individual Contributions to Resilient Outcomes

Considerable excitement has been generated across the past two decades by a series of investigations that have explored the "invulnerable," "resilient," or "stress-resistant" child.[10] As a comprehensive review of this literature is well beyond the scope of this chapter, we will limit our discussion to several summary points.

Antecedent to any discussion of resilience is the concept of risk. Resilient children have escaped an anticipated outcome. To date the best marker of risk for mental illness remains a crude one, namely having a parent with a major psychiatric disorder. The expectations for psychiatric illness in an individual given psychiatric illness in a parent are revealing (for a brief review and references, see Richters 1987). While the risk of being diagnosed as having schizophrenia is 1 percent for an individual in the general population, having one parent with schizophrenia raises the risk to 10 to 15 percent for schizophrenia, and 35 to 50 percent for having some psychiatric diagnosis. If both parents are ill with schizophrenia, the risk of schizophrenia rises to about 45 percent. Although these risk figures do represent an order-of-magnitude change from the general population's risk, they are by no means figures of doom. The vast majority of children with one schizophrenic parent will not become schizophrenic themselves; in fact, most will evidence no major psychiatric disturbance. Furthermore, an intriguing finding from several studies is that a percentage of children equal to those who succumb to the disorder (approximately 10 percent) evidence "superior" outcomes (Heston 1966; Kaufman et al. 1979; Rutter 1981).

Prior research suggests two different individual-based paths toward resilience—both involve distancing oneself from the "risky" environment. The first path involves keeping considerable interpersonal distance between oneself and *all* other people. Resilient children are described as having greater capacity for self-soothing (Kagan 1966), which can connote a greater ability to manage without others. Other descriptions accentuate self-centered, narcissistic qualities combined with a lack of concern for others, if not frank, active exclusion or rejection.[11] Indeed, the costs of this "individualistic" mode of resilience may be high—these children may be the ones who most clearly manifest the "checkerboard of strengths and weaknesses" described so well by Murphy and Moriarty (1976).

The second path involves a more sophisticated, psychologically compe-

[10]See Anthony and Cohler (1987); Anthony and Koupernik (1974); Garmezy (1971); Murphy and Moriarty (1976); Rutter (1985); and Werner and Smith (1982).

[11]See Anthony (1987); Fisher et al. (1987); Grunebaum et al. (1982); and Rutter (1981).

tent, *selective* form of distance. The key issue here is the child's "representational competence." This term was coined by Anthony (1984) to refer to the child's ability to process, interpret, and ultimately make some sense out of environmental trauma. As Erikson (1964) noted, life events can have an "actuality" based on the facts and a "reality" based on the meaning given these facts. Some children may be better able to construct these health-promoting "realities." Such ability is certainly predicated on intelligence (Rutter 1981; Worland, Weeks, and Janes 1987) but is also shaped by a specific mode of psychological processing—these children do not seem free of traumatic past memories but rather have shown the ability to place such memories into a more forward-looking perspective (Felsman and Vaillant 1987; Main and Goldwyn 1984). Behaviorally, this ability is reflected by a combination of objectivity, curiosity, and self-directedness that together provide the resistance to the toxic elements of the environment (Anthony 1984, 1987; Bennett et al. 1987; Steinglass et al. 1987). Presumably it is this latter group of children who in adulthood would look like the "achieved normals" described clinically by Broderick and Pulliam-Krager (1979) and in several recent research programs (Main and Goldwyn 1984; Steinglass et al. 1987). Anticipating the discussion of the next section, it may be the presence of good interpersonal skills in these children (Felsman and Vaillant 1987) that permits them to seek out the social transactions with a "supportive other" that ultimately becomes manifest as "representational competence."

Family Contributions: I. Maintaining Task Performance Despite Illness

Major illness threatens the successful performance of many family tasks. Families can do better or worse in maintaining their performance during such times. For example, consider parental support for the growth and development of young children, a vital set of tasks that cannot be placed on hold for long. Contemporary family research has clearly shown that one important contribution families can make to the resiliency of their children is the degree to which well family members can mobilize themselves to provide for the basic practical and emotional needs of their children, despite the presence of other family problems (Anthony 1984; Musick et al. 1987; Werner and Smith 1982). Such "deficits" in parenting can be filled three ways.

First, in the case of medical or psychiatric impairment of a parent, the more the afflicted parent can continue to function in their child-rearing role, especially if the mother is the ill parent, the better the child outcome. The best evidence here comes from studies of children at risk for emotional disorder by virtue of having mothers possessing a psychiatric diagnosis. Across a growing number of studies, dimensions of maternal illness, such as chronicity, severity, and age of children at onset,[12] are consistently found to be much better predictors of child outcome than is the diagnosis—that is, whether mother has schizophrenia or affective illness. Indeed, in some studies the outcomes of children with parental schizophrenia are indistinguishable from those children who have a parent with affective illness (Lewine 1984; Richters 1987). In those studies in which differences are found for various parental psychiatric diagnoses, the effect is due to the better outcome of those children whose mothers have bipolar affective disorder (Fisher et al. 1987; Hammen et al. 1987; Wynne 1987). It seems very likely that these dimensions of illness provide at least a crude window on the ability of some mothers to meet their children's needs despite being afflicted with a serious illness.

Second, other family members, typically fathers or grandmothers, can compensate for the child-rearing deficit. In the landmark Woodlawn study of children at risk due to severe poverty, Kellam and associates (1977) found that father absence was a much less important risk factor than was *mother aloneness.* The presence of certain other adults, especially one of the children's grandmothers, had clear ameliorative effects. In fact, the psychological health and social adjustment of children in mother-grandmother families was equivalent to that of children within mother-father families, while the outcome of children in both these two family types was much better than that shown by children in mother-alone families. Analogous findings have been reported by other studies of mothers raising children in poverty (Werner and Smith 1982) as well as studies of children born to teenage mothers (Furstenburg, Brooks-Gunn, and Morgan 1987) and mothers with psychiatric illness (Fisher et al. 1987; Rutter 1985).

Finally, other nonfamily members can play this compensatory role. Yet even here it seems that the family has the interesting role of constructing a system of meaning within the family that allows outside influence. Musick and colleagues (1987) noted in the process of running a comprehensive intervention program for high-risk children that those children who did well in the program appeared to be "enabled" by their mothers to do so. In their words: "The children who improved were those whose mothers enabled them to turn to significant others within the therapeutic nursery environment, and to 'use' positively what was offered to enhance

[12]See Fisher et al. (1987); Hammen et al. (1987); Lewine (1984); Richters (1987); Sameroff, Seifer, and Zax (1982); Seifer and Sameroff (1987); and Wynne (1987).

their development" (p. 240). They further characterized these mothers in four ways: (1) their own psychosocial functioning improved as a result of the treatment program; (2) they had social resources outside of the treatment program; (3) they at least episodically showed positive affect and emotional availability toward their children; and (4) they appeared to differentiate between their own and their child's needs—at the minimum, they showed no overt projection of "badness" onto their infants.

Interestingly, in their descriptive comments of two case examples, one of a mother-infant pair that did well in treatment and another of a dyad that did not do well, we were impressed not only by the traits of these mothers but also by aspects of their extended families that appeared linked to this enabling process. While neither mother would be considered as having an optimal origin family or current marriage, their families did differ greatly in the qualities of their interpersonal relationships. Cindy, the mother of an infant who gained little from involvement in the program, had a relational environment filled mostly with emotional deprivation yet peppered with ad hominem attacks from both Cindy's mother and husband. This rejecting and critical behavior from mother and husband seemed linked to their interpreting her illness as a moral weakness or a personal flaw, not as a disease process. With such a construction it is not surprising that they offered Cindy little to no support. Carol, on the other hand, had a family that despite weakness appeared "good enough." On the down side the conflicting values of her immigrant parents led to inconsistent messages from them during her childhood. Not surprisingly, she exhibited some acting out. However, both of Carol's parents seemingly cared enough to be in conflict about her upbringing. Similarly, her husband is described as being "capable of genuine caring and concern for his family" (p. 242). Most important, Carol's difficulties were viewed by her family as an illness causing a problem for them all to help solve, a challenge that required a group effort. As a family, they became actively involved with the treatment program, albeit gingerly at first. Carol was someone who needed their help, not a "bad" person. Reading this account, we argue that this family-level act of assigning meaning to a member's symptomatic behavior was an integral determinant of the very different styles of relating that were established by these young mothers, their infants, and a treatment agency outside of their families. (Hooley [1987] has recently advanced a similar argument to propose that families' construction of the meaning of psychiatric illness may be the phenomenon that underlies the research construct of expressed emotion, which has proven to be a powerful family influence on the course of several major psychiatric illnesses.)

Family Contributions: II. Preserving Shared Family Experience Despite Illness

The shared meaning system of any family can be viewed as a dynamic, evolving entity that is in part both constructed and conserved through the family's ritual activities.[13] Major illness can corrupt or disrupt the family's shared view of their world by threatening the conduct of the family's cherished rituals. In this section we use the research of Wolin and colleagues to argue that families that can protect crucial aspects of their shared family experience in the face of serious illness contribute to the resiliency of their offspring.

Wolin's group has used an innovative series of studies to explore psychosocial factors that influence the transmission of alcoholism across generations. In doing so they have uncovered an intriguing pathway whereby families' conduct of their ritual practices influences the resiliency of their children at risk. Results from two of their studies are especially relevant.

In the first, they investigated the ritual practices, especially dinnertimes and holidays, of twenty-five families containing at least one adolescent or young adult (mean age = 24.5 years). At least one parent met standard research criteria for either problem drinker or alcoholic (Goodwin et al. 1974). Families were classified as transmitters and nontransmitters based on whether or not at least one of their children met the criteria for either problem drinker or alcoholic *or* had married a person who met these criteria. Using a semistructured interview, the families' reports of their ritual practices were obtained for the period of heaviest drinking and a period of time before heaviest drinking. Based on whether or not the family's rituals had remained unaltered during the period of heaviest drinking, families were classified as distinctive (rituals preserved) and subsumptive (rituals invaded/destroyed). As predicted, subsumptive families were found to have a significantly higher rate of transmission of alcohol problems into the next generation than were families that protected their rituals despite the alcoholism of at least one family member (Wolin, Bennett, and Noonan 1979; Wolin et al. 1980).

In a second study, their research model was expanded to include the mate selection decisions made by the young adult with the alcoholic parent. The researchers reasoned that by choosing a spouse with or without a family history of alcoholism, the young adult was making a statement accepting or rejecting the alcohol-related aspects of his or her own origin family. Their sample consisted of sixty-eight married couples, for whom

[13]See Reiss (1981); Steinglass et al. (1987); Wamboldt and Wolin (1988); and Wolin and Bennett (1984).

at least one of their parents met criteria for alcoholic or problem drinker. Members of the couple were interviewed separately concerning the ritual practices of their origin families and conjointly about their current family. As predicted, the following three factors were found to protect young adults at risk for the intergenerational transmission of alcoholism: (1) protection of rituals by the origin family with the history of alcoholism; (2) choice of a spouse from a nonalcoholic family; and (3) greater "deliberateness" on the part of the new couple as they established their own rituals and traditions (Bennett et al. 1987). The last two factors bespeak a resilience on the part of the individual at risk, reminiscent of Anthony's (1984) notion of representational competence. However, their replicated finding that protection of family rituals enhances the offspring's resilience suggests an important family-level contribution. Despite the presence of a chronic medical problem that clinical experience has found to be quite corrosive of family relationships, some families are able to protect important aspects of their shared experience from the threat posed by parental alcoholism. This action by the family appears to counteract the tendency of familial psychopathology to repeat in the succeeding generation.

Summary

This section has raised several important concepts about those individuals who enter adulthood looking quite good despite having experienced bad environments. First, resiliency is not a one-way street; factors from both the individual as well as the family can influence the ultimate outcome. Indeed, we have presented data that even families with parental psychiatric illness can nonetheless add to the resiliency of their offspring. Furthermore, these family contributions relate to the two family processes that we have discussed—the ability to perform adequately the many tasks of family life and the ability to preserve key aspects of the family's shared experience as a transacting group.

Conclusion: Family, Normality, and Psychiatric Diagnosis

At this moment the findings of contemporary family research exist in a form that could be readily assimilated within our current system of psychiatric diagnosis.

Diagnosis and the Practice of Scientific Medicine

The diagnosis of a disease is given to a person by a physician with the primary goal of alleviating the patient's suffering. This occurs because establishing the correct diagnosis increases the likelihood that effective treatment will be directed at the patient's disease. Most frequently, medical disease is defined roughly in the following manner: "Any condition associated with discomfort, pain, disability, death, or an increased liability to these states, regarded by physicians and the public as properly the responsibility of the medical profession, may be considered a disease" (Goodwin and Guze 1979, p. 215). It is important to stress that this definition allows a number of differing types of clinical and research information to be used in establishing that a disease exists. As medical knowledge about any disease grows, the specific criteria for the diagnosis of that disease evolve from being descriptions of clustered symptoms (for example, headache), to descriptions of consistent signs and anatomic alterations (for example, squamous cell carcinoma), to statements concerning the etiologic agent (for example, pneumococcal pneumonia). When the criteria for diagnosis are in the early symptom-based stages, as is the case of most diseases in psychiatry, these criteria must be carefully validated based on their ability to predict clinical course, outcome, and treatment response. The tragedy of not paying attention to such validation is that patients may bear avoidable additional suffering because the potential efficiency of treatment is lessened.

With the publication of the third edition of the *Diagnostic and Statistical Manual of Mental Disorders* (DSM-III, American Psychiatric Association 1980), the field of psychiatry took a great stride as the diagnosis of psychiatric problems was firmly planted within the realm of standard scientific method. Whenever possible, diagnostic criteria were operationally defined, theoretical and philosophical biases were avoided, prior research was considered, and future research of the initial set of diagnostic criteria was encouraged. Indeed, the manual has recently been revised to incorporate subsequent research findings that have challenged positions taken by the original system (DSM-III-R, APA 1987).

Given this incorporation of scientific method into the process of establishing psychiatric diagnoses, those findings of contemporary family research that can stand up to rigorous scientific scrutiny *and* that are relevant to the process of psychiatric diagnosis can logically be assimilated, even though they may challenge positions currently held. The key condition for assimilation is that either the precision or the validity of the diagnostic system is improved in a way that advances the cause of treating persons in distress.

Psychiatric Diagnosis and the Individual Level

From the perspective of family researchers, despite the careful and diligent effort that went into making the DSM-III system free of theoretical or philosophical bias, one important bias still seems to remain. Specifically, within the DSM-III system, psychiatric diagnosis is concerned solely with individuals:

> In DSM-III-R each of the mental disorders is conceptualized as a clinically significant behavioral or psychological syndrome or pattern that occurs *in a person* and that is associated with present distress (a painful symptom) or disability (impairment in one or more important areas of functioning) or with significantly increased risk of suffering, death, pain, disability, or an important loss of freedom. . . . Whatever its original cause, it must currently be considered a manifestation of a behavioral, psychological, or biological dysfunction *in the person.* (APA 1987, p. xxii; italics added)

This choice certainly has its merits; it is common sense that *mental* disorders should be located within the individual. Yet the findings of contemporary family research do underscore that individuals exist within a complex and entwined web of relationships. If one broadens the province of diagnosis to include all *psychiatric* disorders, there is at least one important way in which this assumption concerning the location of disorder limits the ability of psychiatry to alleviate suffering most effectively. Specifically, the possibility that *relationships* themselves may be disordered is not considered.

Marital Distress as a Relationship Disorder

Let us for the moment raise the status of the current "V-code" diagnosis, Marital Problem, and see whether or not this relationship disorder meets the common criteria used to define a medical disease.

First, marital distress is a very prevalent problem in psychiatric settings. Indeed, marital distress has been reported as the single most common chief complaint presented to mental health professionals (Veroff, Kulka, and Douvan 1981).

Second, marital distress is a cohesive syndrome that can be operationally defined. Available research findings, such as that of Gottman and associates (Gottman 1979) described earlier, suggest relevant observable diagnostic criteria from which there is every reason to believe that clinicians could make reliable diagnoses. Indeed, if diagnostic criteria were defined, they could be validated by comparing clinician diagnoses with well-established research instruments (for example, Snyder 1979; Spanier 1976).

Third, without doubt marital distress is associated with considerable suffering, pain, disability, and increased risk for death. As mentioned earlier, research has firmly established that this suffering and risk extends not only to the married couple themselves but also to their children (see reviews by Bloom, Asher, and White 1978; Emery 1982; Hetherington, Cox, and Cox 1982). Other studies have established links between marital distress and important physiological processes within individuals, including autonomic arousal (Levenson and Gottman 1985) and immune functioning (Kiecolt-Glaser et al. 1987). These latter studies underscore the breadth of the potential interconnections between relationship and biomedical factors within the "web of causality" (MacMahon and Pugh 1970) determining psychiatric as well as other medical problems.

Fourth, marital distress is not a simple correlate of individual disorders. Evidence exists that serious marital problems can occur in the absence of major psychopathology in either partner. For example, Bentler and Newcomb (1978) reported that a history of prior divorce did not predict failure of new marriages at four-year follow-up. This suggests that many people can find a better match for themselves the second time around. Accordingly, characteristics of the relationship, such as "goodness of fit," may be more important for marital outcome than presence or absence of individual psychopathology. Hence, we propose that individual psychopathology need not be either a necessary or a sufficient cause of marital failure.

Fifth, marital distress tends to be transmitted across generations. In other words, like many other medical and psychiatric disorders, it exhibits a discrete family history (Glenn and Kramer 1987; Greenberg and Nay 1982; Mueller and Pope 1977).

Sixth, specific treatments with documented effectiveness are available for marital distress (see review by Wamboldt, Wamboldt, and Gurman 1985). Many of these treatments target problems in the relationship itself, not in the individual partners. Furthermore, successful treatment of a relationship disorder, such as marital distress, may prevent the development of subsequent medical and psychiatric problems *within the individuals* comprising the family. Given the prevalence of marital distress, such a finding would have far-reaching public health ramifications. Future family research would be well advised to explore this possibility.

Finally, if marital problems are not recognized, the treatment of other psychiatric disorders can be impaired. For example, Rounsaville and associates (1979) reported that in a study of depressed women successfully treated with antidepressant medication, the presence of a distressed marriage at the end of the initial course of medication predicted which women would relapse during maintenance therapy. This study again suggests that individual-level disorders may overlap but need not be equivalent to relationship disorders.

Accordingly, we conclude that except for the DSM-III convention that the disorder occur inside the individual, marital distress meets widely accepted medical and psychiatric criteria for considering a set of signs and symptoms to be a clinical disorder. Based on these data, marital distress and a variety of analogous relationship disorders—for example, parent-child attachment disorders (Bretherton and Waters 1985), coercive disorders (Patterson 1982) and family violence disorders—appear ready and conceptually appropriate for inclusion in a future diagnostic system.

Relationship Disorders and Psychiatric Diagnosis: Closer than First Meets the Eye

How could a set of relationship disorders be assimilated into the DSM classification system? While a full discussion of this question could easily fill another book, it seems that the formal characteristics of the schema established in DSM-III hold up surprisingly well for relationships disorders. Specifically, Axis I and Axis II define two distinct classes of individual disorders. Axis I contains ego-dystonic disorders related to problems with the *performance of some key mental task.* Organic mental syndromes and disorders require "a psychological or behavioral abnormality associated with transient or permanent dysfunction of the brain (APA 1987, p. 98). For schizophrenia there invariably are "characteristics disturbances in several of the following areas: content and form of thought, perception, affect, sense of self, volition, relationship to the outside world, and psychomotor behavior" (APA 1987, p. 188). In dissociative disorders there "is a disturbance or alteration in the normal integrative functions of identity, memory, or consciousness" (APA 1987, p. 269). Throughout Axis I the diagnostic categories refer to inadequate or abnormal performance of at least one task of mental functioning.

Axis II defines ego-syntonic disorders related to the individual's characteristic *system of understanding social relationships.* For example, the individual with Avoidant Personality Disorder expects to be rejected by others: "the essential feature of this disorder is a pervasive pattern of social discomfort, fear of negative evaluation, and timidity, beginning by early adulthood and present in a variety of contexts" (APA 1987, p. 351), while "the essential feature" of an individual with Paranoid Personality Disorder "is a pervasive and unwarranted tendency, beginning by early adulthood and present in a variety of contexts, to interpret the actions of people as deliberately demeaning or threatening" (APA 1987, p. 337).

Using the constructs advanced throughout this chapter, Axis I is concerned with disorders of task performance; Axis II, with disorders of meaning construction. A potential revision of the DSM could argue based on available research data that disorders of task performance and meaning construction can occur on the *relationship level* as well as on the *individual level.*

This reformulation of psychiatric disorders into the parallel, equivalent tracks of mental disorder and relationship disorder opens two exciting possibilities for the field. First, a very important practical change occurs in that very common presenting complaints involving disordered relationships become publicly validated as full-fledged diagnoses worthy of third-party reimbursement. This would eliminate the current subterfuges used to give at least one family member a diagnosis of adjustment disorder or dysthymic disorder so that insurance payments can be received when marital or family therapies of established effectiveness are used to treat what the clinician conceives as a primary relationship disorder.

Second, a more theoretically consistent and clinically useful biopsychosocial model would be created. While the multiaxial system of DSM-III is an important first attempt at operationalizing a biopsychosocial model of diagnosis, it heavily emphasizes the "bio" and "mental" parts of the model. The bulk of the "interpersonal" and "social" information is carried by the "optional" Axes IV and V—axes that have not been engaging enough to claim widespread use. As originally articulated by Engel (1977, 1980), the biopsychosocial model places all levels comprising the systems hierarchy on equal footing. There is no a priori assumption that some levels are "more equal" than others. Dysfunction within relationships is as important within the pathogenesis of medical and psychiatric illness as are cellular or mental dysfunction. Given the commitment to an a posteriori method of establishing diagnostic criteria launched with DSM-III, the slant toward mental disorders within individuals can be justified only on the quality of available research findings. We will concede that to date research into mental disorders within individuals does surpass that exploring relationship disorders. But this gap is narrowing with surprising rapidity. Indeed, we have argued that the gap is now narrow enough to justify a reconsideration of the individual-level bias present in the DSM-III formulation. The challenge for the family research field is to continue to provide the empirical data that will drive this change.

The past decade of family research has been filled with important advances. Yet much of this family research has gone relatively unnoticed within psychiatric circles. Offer and Sabshin's (1974, 1984) prior works have done much to increase the visual field of psychiatry by focusing attention on the many parameters that influence our assumptions of normality within individuals. In this chapter we have attempted to follow their lead by highlighting a number of important themes in contemporary family research that relate to the concept of normality. By examining the changes in family life over the past century, we have concluded that while the demands on families for task performance and social interpretation have grown more complex over recent history, the structure of the American family has stayed surprisingly stable. We have suggested that there seems little profit to be made in searching for the normal family structure. The concept of normality fits better with research concerning family task performance and family meaning construction. Promising research efforts suggest that both the global competence of families as well as their ability to successfully manage certain specific tasks, such as resolving relationship conflict, represent measurable dimensions of the normality or health of a family. Equally exciting research has suggested that the system of meanings constructed by families is an important determinant of what families themselves take to be normal or healthy social behavior. Finally, the clinical relevance of contemporary family research has been underscored by demonstrating that knowledge of family task performance and meaning construction adds to the understanding of resilience in individuals at risk for mental disorder as well as to the current system of psychiatric diagnosis.

While much is now known in the family research field, this is a time of exciting growth in the accumulated knowledge base, measurement strategies, and conceptual models that serve as the foundation of family research. Without doubt, much more will be learned in the near future. We hope that this chapter helps direct the eyes of psychiatry toward these promising efforts.

REFERENCES

American Psychiatric Association. 1980. *Diagnostic and Statistical Manual of Mental Disorders,* 3rd ed. Washington, D.C.: APA.

———. 1987. *Diagnostic and Statistical Manual of Mental Disorders,* 3rd ed., rev. Washington, D.C.: APA.

Anthony, E. J. 1984. "The Saint Louis Risk Research Project." In *Children at Risk for*

Schizophrenia: A Longitudinal Perspective, ed. N. F. Watt, E. J. Anthony, L. C. Wynne, and J. Roth. Cambridge: Cambridge University Press.

———. 1987. "Risk, Vulnerability, and Resilience: An Overview." In *The Invulnerable Child,* ed. E. J. Anthony and B. J. Cohler. New York: Guilford Press.

Anthony, E. J., and Cohler, B. J., eds. 1974. *The Invulnerable Child.* New York: Guilford Press.

Anthony, E. J., and Koupernik, C., eds. 1974. *The Child in His Family: Children at Psychiatric Risk.* New York: John Wiley.

Beavers, W. R. 1982. "Healthy, Mid-range and Severely Dysfunctional Families." In *Normal Family Processes,* ed. F. Walsh. New York: Guilford Press.

Belsky, J.; Spanier, G. B.; and Rovine, M. 1983. "Stability and Change in Marriage Across the Transition to Parenthood." *Journal of Marriage and the Family* 45:567–577.

Bennett, L. A.; Wolin, S. J.; Reiss, D.; and Teitelbaum, M. 1987. Couples at Risk for the Transmission of Alcoholism: Protective Influences. *Family Process* 26:111–129.

Bentler, P. M., and Newcomb, M. D. 1978. "Longitudinal Study of Marital Success and Failure." *Journal of Consulting and Clinical Psychology* 46:1053–1070.

Berger, P. L., and Luckman, T. 1966. *The Social Construction of Reality.* New York: Doubleday.

Bloom, B. L.; Asher, S. J.; and White, S. W. 1978. "Marital Disruption as a Stressor: A Review and Analysis." *Psychological Bulletin* 85:867–894.

Bott, E. [1957] 1971. *Families and Social Network: Roles, Norms, and External Relationships in Ordinary Urban Families,* 2nd ed. New York: Free Press.

Boszormenyi-Nagy, I., and Spark, G. 1973. *Invisible Loyalties: Reciprocity in Intergenerational Family Therapy.* New York: Harper & Row.

Bowen, M. 1978. *Family Therapy in Clinical Practice.* New York: Jason Aronson.

Bowlby, J. 1969. *Attachment and Loss. Vol. 1, Attachment.* New York: Basic Books.

Bretherton I., and Waters, E., eds. 1985. *Growing Points in Attachment Theory and Research.* Monographs of the Society for Research in Child Development. Chicago: University of Chicago Press.

Broderick, C. B., and Pulliam-Krager, H. 1979. "Family Process and Child Outcomes." In *Contemporary Theories About the Family,* ed. W. R. Burr, R. Hill, F. I. Nye, and I. L. Reiss. vol. 1. New York: Free Press.

Burton, L. M., and Bengston, V. L. 1985. "Black Grandmothers: Issues of Timing and Continuity of Roles." In *Grandparenthood: Research and Policy Perspectives,* ed. V. L. Bengston and J. Robertson. Beverly Hills, CA: Sage.

Byles, J.; Byrne, C.; Boyle, M. H.; and Offord, D. R. 1988. "Ontario Child Health Study: Reliability and Validity of the General Functioning Subscale of the McMaster Family Assessment Device." *Family Process* 27: 97–104.

Carter, E. A., and McGoldrick, M., eds. 1980. *The Family Life Cycle: A Framework for Family Therapy.* New York: Gardner Press.

Cherlin, A. J. 1981. *Marriage, Divorce, Remarriage.* Cambridge, MA: Harvard University Press.

Cooley, C. H. 1909. *Social Organization.* New York: Charles Scribner's Sons.

Costell, R., and Reiss, D. 1982. "The Family Meets the Hospital: Clinical Presentations of a Laboratory-based Family Typology." *Archives of General Psychiatry* 39: 443–48.

Costell, R.; Reiss, D.; Berkman, H.; and Jones, C. 1981. "The Family Meets the Hospital: Predicting the Family's Perception of the Treatment Program from Its Problem Solving Style." *Archives of General Psychiatry* 38:569–577.

Cowan, C. P.; Cowan, P. A.; Coie, L.; and Coie, J. D. 1978. "Becoming a Family: The Impact of a First Child's Birth on the Couple's Relationship." In *The First Child and Family Formation,* ed. W. Miller and L. Newman. Chapel Hill: University of North Carolina Press.

Davis, P.; Stern, D.; Jorgenson, J.; and Steier, F. 1980. *Typologies of the Alcoholic Family: An Integrated Systems Approach.* University of Pennsylvania: Wharton Applied Research Center.

Demos, J. 1970. *The Little Commonwealth.* New York: Oxford University Press.

Dewey, J., and Bentley, A. 1949. *Knowing and the Known.* Boston: Beacon Press.

Doanne, J. A.; West, K. L.; Goldstein, M. J.; Rodnick, E. H.; and Jones, J. E. 1981. "Parental Communication Deviance and Affective Style: Predictors of Subsequent Schizophrenia Spectrum Disorders in Vulnerable Adolescents." *Archives of General Psychiatry* 38:679–685.

Duvall, E. M. 1957. *Family Development.* Philadelphia: Lippincott.

Eiduson, B. T., and Alexander, M. W. 1978. "The Role of Children in Alternative Family Styles." *Journal of Social Issues* 34:149–160.

Elder, G. H., Jr. 1974. *Children of the Great Depression.* Chicago: University of Chicago Press.

———. 1978. "Family History and the Life Course. In *Transitions: The Family and the Life Course in Historical Perspective,* ed. T. K. Hareven. New York: Academic Press.

———. 1984. "Families, Kin, and the Life Course: A Sociological Perspective." In *Review of Child Development Research.* vol. 7; *The Family,* ed. R. D. Parke. Chicago: University of Chicago Press.

Emery, R. 1982. "Interparental Conflict and the Children of Discord and Divorce." *Psychological Bulletin* 92:310–330.

Engel, G. L. 1977. "The Need for a New Medical Model: A Challenge for Biomedicine." *Science* 196:129–136.

———. 1980. "The Clinical Application of the Biopsychosocial Model." *American Journal of Psychiatry* 137:535–544.

Epstein, N. B.; Baldwin, L. M.; and Bishop, D. S. 1983. "The McMaster Family Assessment Device." *Journal of Marital and Family Therapy* 9:171–180.

Epstein, N. B.; Bishop, D. S.; and Baldwin, L. M. 1982. "McMaster Model of Family Functioning: A View of the Normal Family." In *Normal Family Processes,* ed. F. Walsh. New York: Guilford Press.

Epstein, N. B.; Bishop, D. S.; and Levin, S. 1978. "The McMaster Model of Family Functioning." *Journal of Marital and Family Counseling* 4:19–31.

Erikson, E. H. 1964. *Insight and Responsibility.* New York: W. W. Norton.

Felsman, J. K., and Vaillant, G. E. 1987. "Resilient Children as Adults: A 40-year

Study." In *The Invulnerable Child,* ed. E. J. Anthony and B. J. Cohler. New York: Guilford Press.

Fisher, L.; Kokes, R. F.; Cole, R. E.; Perkins, P. M.; and Wynne, L. C. 1987. Competent Children at Risk: A Study of Well-functioning Offspring of Disturbed Parents." In *The Invulnerable Child,* ed. E. J. Anthony and B. J. Cohler. New York: Guilford Press.

Fitzpatrick, M. A. 1988. *Between Husbands and Wives: Communication in Marriage.* Beverly Hills, CA: Sage Press.

Furstenburg, F. F. Jr.; Brooks-Gunn, J.; and Morgan, S. P. 1987. *Adolescent Mothers in Later Life.* New York: Cambridge University Press.

Garmezy, N. 1971. "Vulnerability Research and the Issue of Primary Prevention." *American Journal of Orthopsychiatry,* 41:101–116.

Glenn, N. D., and Kramer, K. B. 1987. "The Marriages and Divorces of the Children of Divorce." *Journal of Marriage and the Family* 49:811–825.

Goldberg, S. 1977. "Social Competence in Infancy: A Model of Parent-Child Interaction." *Merrill-Palmer Quarterly* 23:163–177.

Goldstein, M. J. 1985. "Family Factors that Antedate the Onset of Schizophrenia and Related Disorders: The Results of a Fifteen-year Prospective Longitudinal Study." *Acta Psychiatrica Scandinavica* 71:7–18.

Goodwin, D. W., and Guze, S. B. 1979. *Psychiatric Diagnosis,* 2nd ed. New York: Oxford University Press.

Goodwin, D. W.; Schulsinger, F.; Hermansen, L.; Guze, S. B.; and Winokur, G. 1974. "Alcohol Problems in Adoptees Raised Apart from Alcoholic Biological Parents." *Archives of General Psychiatry* 28:238–243.

Gottman, J. M. 1979. *Marital Interaction: Experimental Investigations.* New York: Academic Press.

Greenberg, E. F., and Nay, W. R. 1982. "The Intergenerational Transmission of Marital Instability Reconsidered." *Journal of Marriage and the Family,* 44:335–347.

Grunebaum, H.; Weiss, J.; Cohler, B.; Hartman, C.; and Gallant, D. 1982. *Mentally Ill Mothers and Their Children.* Chicago: University of Chicago Press.

Gustafson, J. P. 1986. *The Complex Secret of Brief Psychotherapy.* New York: W. W. Norton.

Hagestad, G. O., and Burton, L. M. 1986. "Grandparenthood, Life Context, and Family Development." *American Behavioral Scientist* 29:471–484.

Hammen, C.; Gordon, D.; Burge, D.; Adrain, C.; Jaenicke, C.; and Hiroto, D. 1987. "Communication Patterns of Mothers with Affective Disorders and Their Relationship to Children's Status and Social Functioning." In *Understanding Major Mental Disorder: The Contribution of Family Interaction Research,* ed. K. Hahlweg and M. J. Goldstein. New York: Family Process Press.

Hampson, R. B., and Beavers W. R. 1987. "Comparing Males' and Females' Perspectives Through Family Self-report." *Psychiatry* 50:24–30.

Hampson, R. B.; Beavers, W. R.; and Hulgus, Y. F. 1988. "Commentary: Comparing the Beavers and Circumplex Models of Family Functioning." *Family Process* 27:85–92.

Hareven, T. K. 1984. "Themes in the Historical Development of the Family. In *Review of Child Development Research,* vol. 7; *The Family,* ed. R. D. Parke. Chicago: University of Chicago Press.

Harrison, A.; Serafica, F.; and McAdoo, H. 1984. "Ethnic Families of Color." In *Review of Child Development Research,* vol. 7; *The Family,* ed. R. D. Parke. Chicago: University of Chicago Press.

Heston, L. 1966. "Psychiatric Disorders in Foster Home Reared Children of Schizophrenic Mothers." *British Journal of Psychiatry* 112:819–825.

Hetherington, M.; Cox, M.; and Cox, R. 1982. "Effects of Divorce on Parents and Children." In *Nontraditional Families,* ed. M. Lamb. Hillsdale, N.J.: Erlbaum.

Hill, R. 1964. "Methodological Issues in Family Development Research." *Family Process* 3:186–206.

Hooley, J. M. 1987. "The Nature and Origins of Expressed Emotion." In *Understanding Major Mental Disorder: The Contribution of Family Interaction Research,* ed. K. Hahlweg and M. J. Goldstein. New York: Family Process Press.

Kagan, J. 1966. "Reflection and Impulsivity: The Generality and Dynamics of Conceptual Tempo." *Journal of Abnormal Psychology* 71:17–24.

Kaufman, C.; Grunebaum, H.; Cohler, B.; and Gamer, E. 1979. "Superkids: Competent Children of Schizophrenic Mothers." *American Journal of Psychiatry* 136:1398–1402.

Keitner, G. I.; Baldwin, L.; Epstein, N. B.; et al. 1985. "Family Functioning in Patients with Affective Disorders: A Review." *International Journal Family Psychiatry.* 6:405–437.

Kellam, S. G.; Adams, R. G.; Brown, C. H.; and Ensminger, M. E. 1982. "The Long-term Evolution of the Family Structure of Teenage and Older Mothers." *Journal of Marriage and the Family* 44:539–554.

Kellam, S. G.; Ensminger, M. E.; and Turner, R. J. 1977. "Family Structure and the Mental Health of Children." *Archives of General Psychiatry* 34:1012–1022.

Keniston, K. 1977. *All Our Children.* New York: Harcourt Brace Jovanovich.

Kessler, R. C.; Price, R.; and Wortman, C. 1985. "Social Factors in Psychopathology: Stress, Social Support, and Coping Processes." *Annual Review of Psychology* 36:531–572.

Kiecolt-Glaser, J. K.; Fisher, L. D.; Ogrocki, P.; Stout, J. C.; Speicher, C. E.; and Glaser, R. 1987. "Marital Quality, Marital Disruption, and Immune Function." *Psychosomatic Medicine* 49:13–34.

Kohn, M. L. 1977. *Class and Conformity: A Study in Values.* Chicago: University of Chicago Press.

Kohn, M. L., and Schooler, C. 1983. *Work and Personality: An Inquiry into Social Stratification.* Norwood, NJ: Ablex.

Komarovsky, M. 1940. *The Unemployed Man and His Family.* New York: Columbia University Press.

Korner, A. 1971. "Individual Differences at Birth." *American Journal of Orthopsychiatry* 41:608–619.

LaRossa, R., and LaRossa, M. M. 1981. *Transition to Parenthood: How Infants Change Families.* Beverly Hills, CA: Sage.

Lee, C. 1988. "Theories of Family Adaptability: Towards a Synthesis of Olson's Circumplex and the Beavers Systems Model." *Family Process* 27:73–85.

Levenson, R. W., and Gottman, J. M. 1985. "Physiological and Affective Predictors of Change in Relationship Satisfaction." *Journal of Personality and Social Psychology* 49:85–94.

Lewine, R. R. J. 1984. "Stalking the Schizophrenia Marker: Evidence for a General Vulnerability Model of Psychopathology." In *Children at Risk for Schizophrenia: A Longitudinal Perspective,* ed. N. F. Watt, E. J. Anthony, L. C. Wynne, and J. Roth. Cambridge: Cambridge University Press.

MacMahon, B., and Pugh, T. F. 1970. *Epidemiology: Principles and Methods.* Boston: Little, Brown.

Main, M., and Goldwyn, R. 1984. "Predicting Rejection of Her Infant from Mother's Representation of Her Own Experience: Implications for the Abused-abusing Cycle." *Child Abuse and Neglect* 8:203–217.

Markman, H. J. 1979. "The Application of a Behavioral Model of Marriage in Predicting Relationship Satisfaction of Couples Planning Marriage." *Journal of Consulting and Clinical Psychology* 47:743–749.

———. 1981. "Prediction of Marital Distress: A 5-year Follow-up." *Journal of Consulting and Clinical Psychology* 49:760–762.

Markman, H. J.; Duncan, S. W.; Storaasli, R. D.; and Howes, P. W. 1987. "The Prediction and Prevention of Marital Distress: A Longitudinal Investigation." In *Understanding Major Mental Disorder: The Contribution of Family Interaction Research,* ed. K. Hahlweg and M. J. Goldstein. New York: Family Process Press.

Mead, G. H. 1934. *Mind, Self and Society.* Chicago: University of Chicago Press.

Melito, R. 1985. "Adaptation in Family Systems: A Developmental Perspective." *Family Process* 24:89–100.

Merikangas, K. R.; Prusoff, B. A.; Kupper, A. J.; et al. 1985. "Marital Adjustment in Major Depression." *Journal of Affective Disorder* 9:5–11.

Miller, I. W.; Epstein, N. B.; Bishop, D. S.; and Keitner, G. I. 1985. "The McMaster Family Assessment Device: Reliability and Validity." *Journal of Marital and Family Therapy* 11:345–356.

Moos, R., and Moos, B. 1986. *Family Environment Scale Manual,* 2nd ed. Palo Alto: Consulting Psychologists Press.

Mueller, C. W., and Pope, H. 1977. "Marital Instability: A Study of Its Transmission Between Generations." *Journal of Marriage and the Family* 39:83–93.

Murphy, L. B., and Moriarty, A. 1976. *Vulnerability, Coping and Growth: From Infancy to Adolescence.* New Haven: Yale University Press.

Musick, J. S.; Scott, F. M.; Spencer, K. K.; Goldman, J.; and Cohler, B. J. 1987. "Maternal Factors Related to Vulnerability and Resiliency in Young Children at Risk." In *The Invulnerable Child,* ed. E. J. Anthony and B. J. Cohler. New York: Guilford Press.

Neugarten, B. 1979. "Time, Age and the Life-Cycle." *American Journal of Psychiatry* 136:887–894.

Nock, S. L. 1982. "The Life-Course Approach to Family Analysis." In *Handbook of Developmental Psychology,* ed. B. B. Wolman. Englewood Cliffs, NJ: Prentice-Hall.

Notarius, C., and Pellegrini, D. 1987. "Differences Between Husbands and Wives: Implications for Understanding Marital Discord." In *Understanding Major Mental Disorder: The Contribution of Family Interaction Research,* ed. K. Hahlweg and M. J. Goldstein. New York: Family Process Press.

Offer, D., and Sabshin, M. 1974. *Normality,* 2nd ed. New York: Basic Books.

———. 1984. *Normality and the Life Cycle: A Critical Integration.* New York: Basic Books.

Oliveri, M. E., and Reiss, D. 1981*a.* "A Theory-based Empirical Classification of Family Problem-solving Behavior." *Family Process* 20:409–418.

———. 1981*b.* "The Structure of Families' Ties to Their Kin: The Shaping Role of Social Construction." *Journal of Marriage and the Family* 43:391–407.

———. 1982. "Families' Schemata of Social Relationships." *Family Process* 21:295–311.

———. 1984. "Family Concepts and Their Measurement: Things Are Seldom What They Seem." *Family Process* 23:33–48.

Olson, D. H.; Sprenkle, D. H.; and Russell, C. S. 1979. "Circumplex Model of Family and Marital Systems I: Cohesion and Adaptability Dimensions, Family Types and Clinical Applications." *Family Process* 18:3–28.

Parke, R. D. 1979. "Perspectives on Father-Infant Interaction." In *Handbook of Infant Development,* ed. J. Osofsky, pp. 549–591. New York: John Wiley.

Patterson, G. R. 1982. *Coercive Family Process.* Eugene, OR: Castalia Publishing Co.

Pearlin, L. I.; Lieberman, M. A.; Menaghan, E. G.; and Mullan, J. T. 1981. "The Stress Process." *Journal of Health and Social Behavior* 22:337–356.

Reiss, D. 1971. "Intimacy and Problem Solving: An Automated Procedure for Testing a Theory of Consensual Experience in Families." *Archives of General Psychiatry* 25:442–445.

———. 1981. *The Family's Construction of Reality.* Cambridge, MA: Harvard University Press.

Reiss, D., and Hoffman, H., eds. 1979. *The American Family: Dying or Developing.* New York: Plenum Press.

Reiss, D., and Klein, D. 1987. "Paradigm and Pathogenesis: A Family-centered Approach to Problems of Etiology and Treatment of Psychiatric Disorders." In *Family Interaction and Psychopathology. Theories, Methods and Findings,* ed. T. Jacob. New York: Plenum Press.

Reiss, D., and Oliveri, M. E. 1983*a.* "The Family's Construction of Social Reality and Its Ties to Its Kin Network: An Exploration of Causal Direction." *Journal of Marriage and the Family* 45:81–92.

———. 1983*b.* "Sensory Experience and the Family Process: Perceptual Styles Tend to Run in but Not Necessarily Run Families." *Family Process* 22:289–308.

Reiss, D., and Salzman, C. 1973. "The Resilience of Family Process: Effect of Secobarbital." *Archives of General Psychiatry* 28:425–433.

Reiss, D.; Costell, R.; Jones, C.; and Berkman, H. 1980. "The Family Meets the Hospital: A Laboratory Forecast of the Encounter." *Archives of General Psychiatry* 37:141–154.

Reiss, D.; Gonzalez, S.; and Kramer, N. 1986. "Family Process, Chronic Illness, and

Death: On the Weakness of Strong Bonds." *Archives of General Psychiatry* 43:795–804.

Richters, J. E. 1987. "Chronic Versus Episodic Stress and the Adjustment of High-risk Offspring." In *Understanding Major Mental Disorder: The Contribution of Family Interaction Research,* ed. K. Hahlweg and M. J. Goldstein. New York: Family Process Press.

Rosenthal, D. 1970. *Genetic Theory and Abnormal Behavior.* New York: McGraw-Hill.

Rounsaville, B. J.; Weissman, M. M.; Prusoff, B. A.; and Herceg-Baron, R. L. 1979. "Marital Disputes and Treatment Outcome in Depressed Women." *Comprehensive Psychiatry* 20:483–490.

Rutter, M. 1981. "Stress, Coping and Development: Some Issues and Some Questions. In *Stress, Coping and Development in Children,* ed. N. Garmezy and M. Rutter. New York: McGraw-Hill.

———. 1985. "Resilience in the Face of Adversity: Protective Factors and Resistance to Psychiatric Disorder." *British Journal of Psychiatry* 147:598–611.

Sameroff, A. J., and Chandler, M. 1987. "Reproductive Risk and the Continuum of Caretaking Causality." In *The Invulnerable Child,* ed. E. J. Anthony and B. J. Cohler. New York: Guilford Press.

Sameroff, A. J.; Seifer, R.; and Zax, M. 1982. "Early Development of Children at Risk for Emotional Disorder." *Monographs of the Society for Research in Child Development* 47:1982.

Seifer, R., and Sameroff, A. J. 1975. "Multiple Determinants of Risk and Invulnerability." In *Review of Child Development Research,* vol. 4., ed. F. D. Horowitz, M. Hetherington, S. Scarr-Salapatek, and G. Siegel. Chicago: University of Chicago Press.

Selvini-Palazzoli, M.; Boscolo, L.; Cecchin, G.; and Prata, G. 1978. *Paradox and Counterparadox.* New York: Jason Aronson.

Shulman, S., and Klein, M. M. 1982. "The Family and Adolescence: A Conceptual and Experimental Approach." *Journal of Adolescence,* 5:219–234.

———. 1983. "Distance-sensitive and Consensus-sensitive Families: The Effect of Adolescent Referral for Psychotherapy." *American Journal of Family Therapy* 11:45–58.

Sigafoos, A.; Reiss, D.; Rich, J.; and Douglas, E. 1985. "Pragmatics in the Measurement of Family Functioning: An Interpretive Framework for Methodology." *Family Process* 24:189–203.

Snyder, D. K. 1979. "Multidimensional Assessment of Marital Satisfaction." *Journal of Marriage and the Family* 41:813–823.

Spanier, G. B. 1976. Measuring Dyadic Adjustment: New Scales for Assessing the Quality of Marriage and Similar Dyads." *Journal of Marriage and the Family* 38:15–28.

Steinglass, P. 1979. "The Alcoholic Family at Home: Patterns of Interaction in Dry, Wet and Transitional Stages of Alcoholism." *Archives of General Psychiatry* 38:578–584.

Steinglass, P.; Bennett, L. A.; Wolin, S. J.; and Reiss, D. 1987. *The Alcoholic Family.* New York: Basic Books.

Sullivan, H. S. 1953. *The Interpersonal Theory of Psychiatry.* New York: W. W. Norton.

Thomas, A.; Chess, S.; Birch, H.; and Korn, S. 1963. *Behavioral Individuality in Early Childhood.* New York: New York University Press.

Troll, L. E., and Bengston, V. L. 1982. "Intergenerational Relations Throughout the Life Span." In *Handbook of Developmental Psychology,* ed. B. B. Wolman. Englewood Cliffs, NJ: Prentice-Hall.

Veroff, J.; Kulka, R. A.; and Douvan, E. 1981. *Mental Health in America: Patterns of Help Seeking from 1957 to 1976.* New York: Basic Books.

Wamboldt, F. S., and Reiss, D. 1989. "Defining a Family Heritage and a New Relationship Identity: Two Central Tasks in the Making of a Marriage." *Family Process* 28:317–335.

Wamboldt, F. S.; Wamboldt, M. Z.; and Gurman A. 1985. "Marital and Family Therapy Research: The Meaning for the Clinician." In *The Meaning of Family Therapy Research,* ed. L. L. Andreozzi and R. F. Levant, pp. 10–26. Family Therapy Collection, vol. 15. Rockville, MD: Aspen Systems Press.

Wamboldt, F. S., and Wolin, S. J. 1988. "Reality and Myth in Family Life: Changes Across Generations." *Journal of Psychotherapy and the Family* 4:141–165.

Weissman, M. M.; and Paykel, E. W. 1974. *The Depressed Woman: A Study of Social Relationships.* Chicago: University of Chicago Press.

Werner, E. E., and Smith, R. S. 1982. *Vulnerable but Invincible: A Longitudinal Study of Resilient Children and Youth.* New York: McGraw-Hill.

Wolin, S. J., and Bennett, L. A. 1984. "Family Rituals." *Family Process* 23:401–420.

Wolin, S. J.; Bennett, L. A.; and Noonan, D. L. 1979. "Family Rituals and the Recurrence of Alcoholism over Generations." *American Journal of Psychiatry* 136: 589–593.

Wolin, S. J.; Bennett, L. A.; Noonan, D. L.; and Teitelbaum, M. 1980. "Disrupted Family Rituals: A Factor in the Intergenerational Transmission of Alcoholism." *Journal of Studies in Alcoholism* 41:199–214.

Worland, J.; Weeks, D. G.; and Janes, C. L. 1987. "Predicting Mental Health in Children at Risk." In *The Invulnerable Child,* ed. E. J. Anthony and B. J. Cohler. New York: Guilford Press.

Wynne, L. C. 1987. "Parental Psychopathology and Family System Variables as Predictors of Child Competence." In *Understanding Major Mental Disorder: The Contribution of Family Interaction Research,* ed. K. Hahlweg and M. J. Goldstein. New York: Family Process Press.

Zubin, J., and Spring, B. 1977. "Vulnerability: A New View of Schizophrenia." *Journal of Abnormal Psychology* 86:103–126.

CHAPTER 7

Transcultural Psychiatry and Normal Behavior

Edward F. Foulks

Transcultural psychiatry attempts to extend the principal understandings of biomedical psychiatry of North America and apply them to other cultures and societies. When psychiatric diagnostic categories are applied to studies in other societies, the endeavor is always unavoidably comparative. North American psychiatry has recently developed more precision in defining the categories of mental illness in the third edition of the *Diagnostic and Statistical Manual III,* revised (DSM-III-R; American Psychiatric Association 1987) and is extending this quest in its planned future revisions. Diagnostic criteria in DSM-III-R reveal the potential for high interrater reliability. DSM-III-R has also been translated into languages other than English and is being evaluated for use in other societies.

Although DSM-III-R was developed from the experience of psychiatrists in the United States, its influence has become international (Spitzer, Williams, and Skodol 1983). The DSMs are in fact part of a larger system of classification, the *International Classification of Diseases* (ICD), used by the World Health Organization (WHO). The next ICD (ICD-10) is to be published in 1992 and will change psychiatric nomenclature considerably.

The author wishes to acknowledge gratitude to James Donovan, doctoral candidate in anthropology, Tulane University, for his valuable discussions and contributions to this chapter and to the construction of figure 7.1.

Thompson (1988) has prepared a "crosswalk" that translates DSM-III-R categories into ICD-9-CM (clinical modification) categories. WHO currently views "mental health problems as strikingly similar across cultures, and there is now sufficient evidence to show that their management along similar lines helps patients regardless of culture" (WHO 1981, p. 19). This view also advocates using modern mental health techniques to change communities' traditional beliefs, values, child-rearing practices, and so on, where they are recognized to be psychopathogenic.

The basic premise of the DSM-III-R is that the psychiatric disorders described therein as well as their required diagnostic criteria are "real entities," potentially discoverable in certain proportions in all human groups worldwide. This assumption is supported by increasing evidence that some psychiatric disorders have a genetic predisposition and by large-scale epidemiological surveys that have reported that similar symptom clusters are found in patients from widely divergent cultural and societal areas (WHO 1973).

Recent psychiatric research has focused on the discovery of the biological basis of behavior and emotion. The quest supposes that ultimately psychiatric disorders will not only be defined with phenomenological precision, but by measurable deviations from normal neurophysiology as well. The sciences of psychiatry have not yet realized this goal, but promises and expectations currently abound.

Aiding American psychiatry in its quest for universals in behavior and emotions and their deviations are a number of kindred sciences, including psychoanalysis, psychology, sociology, and linguistics. Researchers in each of these disciplines have reported explicit evidence supporting developmental, perceptual-cognitive, social structural, and grammatical universals found in all human groups. In a general sense, such evidence has become by now not only convincing to most psychiatrists but also an implicit assumption in their practice. They apply the same judgmental yardsticks regarding the vicissitudes of childhood and family life, defense mechanisms, degrees of environmental stress, moral behavior, and so on to all patients, no matter what their race, ethnic group, socioeconomic status, or castastrophic experience. With such assumptions, the concept of "normality/abnormality" is also taken for granted as a human universal.

The Concept of "Normality"

When we attempt to define the concept of normality/abnormality, however, the subject becomes more elusive. Offer and Sabshin (1984) have discussed this concept from several different perspectives: the statistical normal; normality as health; normality as a utopian goal; normality as pragmatism; and normality as a progressively developing transactional system of adaptation. The concept of normality/abnormality, however, becomes muddled when considered from a transcultural perspective. While there is no denying that behavioral and mental deviations are recognized as such by people in diverse cultures (see Westermeyer and Wintrob 1979), the conceptual dichotomy posed by categories of "normal" and "abnormal" themselves are foreign ideas in most non-Western societies.

The idea of normality versus abnormality would appear to be relatively unique to Western European historical scientific tradition. Within this tradition, there has been a distinct tendency to categorize observed phenomena in terms of dichotomous traits. While this way of thinking has usually yielded pragmatic and measurable solutions to understanding our world, it has at times resulted in major conceptual dilemmas with inappropriate forced dualistic conclusions.

Such tendencies are revealed, for example, in our unending struggles with the mind-brain dichotomy in English language psychiatric theory.[1] Despite attempts to be holistic, the schisms created by the great biological psychiatry versus psychoanalysis debate still leave us to ponder where the superego is located on neurological substratum or how a tricyclic-antidepressant can help resolve depression related to oedipal guilt, for example. The *currently espoused* biopsychosocial model of George Engel (1980) attempts to render a more synthetic framework from which to understand human behavior by demonstrating the formal interrelationships between these different disciplinary spheres of investigation. Dichotomization within psychiatric practice and politics goes on nevertheless, often to the dismay of the psychiatric clinician.

Ironically, when we "really" think about the mind and the brain, it is of course inconceivable that one could exist independently of the other. It is likewise inconceivable that "normal" can exist without the presence or possibility of "abnormal." Humans in all societies tend to become accustomed to a predictable physical and social environment. Each society obtains conventions in speaking, dressing, interacting, and relating that are socially prescribed and expected. Most societies have idealized rules of etiquette as well as pragmatic readjustments of these general rules that can occur under special circumstances. During mass in Catholic societies, for example, individuals who in daily life would not likely subscribe to notions of material transformations or to the act of cannibalism believe they

[1]For a further discussion of this linguistic problem see Wierzbicka (1989).

consume the flesh and blood of their God transformed from bread and wine. While inconsistent in many respects with other aspects of life, such behavior is still expected behavior in its unique context and thereby considered "normal." But such social judgments remain complex and are affected by a network of interacting variables and social values. Abnormal in the preceding context might be considered going to the altar for second servings, or not praying, or believing in another religion or diety. The subtleties of recognizing the abnormal in this case would depend on the observer's familiarity with the society's adaptations of Roman Catholic ritual and belief.

The Concept of "Deviancy"

While perhaps subtle and difficult for outsiders to define, the abnormal or deviant seems to be ubiquitously found across human societies. Robert Edgerton, a leading scholar of psychological anthropology, wrote that "deviance [the abnormal] occurs in the small as well as the large, the simple as well as the complex. [It] may take different forms and frequencies from one society to another, but [it] is ubiquitous. . . . [the abnormal] are common and natural—they are . . . an inevitable part of social life, as is their denunciation, regulation, and prohibition" (1978, p. 465). Paradoxically, then, abnormal people are a "normal" part of all human societies and cultures. Is their presence in all societies an unlikely, serendipitous coincidence, or do they serve an essential evolutionary or social structural function?

Normal people in a society are at least implicitly defined by traditional traits that are ideal as well as those that are not. The ideal, normal Inuit (Eskimo), for example, would be reasonable, humorous, generous, and cooperative. He or she should not be aggressive, assertive, stingy, or covetous. Individuals manifesting the latter traits are recognized as deviant or *nuthkavihak* (crazy), and pressures are brought to bear to bring them to conformity with the rest of the group.

In small societies, such as those found among the Inuit, however, the nonconforming individual is actually less likely to be labeled as deviant than he or she is in larger-scale societies (Raybeck 1988). Personally well-integrated values characterize smaller societies and stabilize their definitions of social life. In contrast, larger societies often contain multiple competing values that in themselves can contribute to conflict in the members' personal integration. The interdependence and equality among members of small-scale societies inhibits the labeling of individuals as deviant, and when it does occur, it is less likely to result in loss of power or status as it does in larger societies. A nonconforming person is often still able to be a contributor to a small community and is often linked to other people through a variety of interpersonal and kinship ties. The nonconforming person in a larger community is less likely to be an essential contributor and often has weakened family and social network ties to others. In such cases, labeling such a person as deviant costs others in the community very little in terms of social contributors and in terms of risk to social cohesiveness. Indeed, the labeling of deviants in large-scale societies may actually enhance social integration of others by weeding out the misfits.

Raybeck (1988) has discussed other differences in labeling deviancy. He points out that labeling in smaller societies adds very little new cognitive information to others in the community because everyone already knows a great deal about the offending individuals' past history and current behavior. The behavior may be subjected to gossip and other mechanisms of social control, but labeling for purposes of exclusion is unlikely. Members of smaller communities know one another in a multidimensional fashion that renders comparatively simple, stereotypic labels less useful than they might be in larger societies where they are used to categorize people quickly. Some of the socially integrative factors of smaller societies as well as their tendency not to utilize deviant labels in public may contribute to the fact that first-break schizophrenics have a better prognosis for avoiding rehospitalization in such societies. The evidence that schizophrenics in less industrially developed nations have a better prognosis is discussed later in this chapter. It should be noted, however, that while smaller societies may tend to use deviant labels in public less frequently, they nevertheless recognize deviances of mental disorder, attempt to differentiate them categorically from mystical status, and have developed nomenclatures for behavioral and mental aberrations (Murphy 1976; Westermeyer and Wintrob 1979).

It has been argued that the deviant or abnormal person in social evolution is equivalent to the mutated gene in biological evolution. Most mutations appear to have no adaptive value and drift or are selected out of breeding populations. The rare one provides for the development of a new trait of adaptive value that becomes perpetuated as an advancement in biological evolution. The abnormal by definition departs from the socially conservative normal, and like a mutation it provides an unlikely possibility for adaptive change when such change becomes necessary or desirable. On the other hand, the abnormal person does not usually seem to be adaptive as an individual, nor does he seem to possess traits that are adaptive to his society.

Deviancy and Human Adaptation

In Senegal, deviant people are felt to be possessed and thus closer to the revered ancestor spirits.[2] Despite the practical disadvantages of having such people in their midst, their existence reassures fellow villagers that the community is in closer touch with important supernatural forces. Another example of adaptation is to be found among the Cargo cults of Melanesia. Throughout this area of the South Pacific, the distress that followed initial contact with outside colonial nations and especially the forced invasions of foreign cultures during World War II resulted in the spontaneous formation of religious cults. These cults were organized around the common belief that the ghosts of dead ancestors will return to the living on earth and bring with them a "cargo" consisting of goods and wealth displayed by colonials in the area. Some groups misidentified white-skinned visitors in their communities as ghosts of their dead relatives. Cargo cults were started by a prophet—often a misanthropic individual who professed to see, hear, and be possessed by ancestor spirits. In his book, *Stone Age Crisis* (1975), Burton-Bradley vividly describes several Cargo-cult prophets whom he was asked to examine for forensic-psychiatric reasons. Sensitive to New Guinea societies, Burton-Bradley was still able to discern symptoms that included auditory and visual hallucinations, delusions, loose associations, catatonic behavior, and inappropriate affect in many of these cult leaders. In order to do so, he asked the appropriate questions regarding their roles in the context of their community culture.

In most cases there did not appear to be any community consensus as to whether the cult leader was a supernaturally possessed, legitimate prophet or was insane by local standards. The cult's followers professed his inspiration; his detractors (and there were always some) proclaimed him a fake, a criminal, or mentally ill. Here stigmatizing deviance versus extolling it seemed to be a matter of factional cultural choices, not unlike those expediently proclaimed by conservatives versus liberals in all societies.

The political utility of establishing normality and defining deviance thus becomes a salient issue. In their study of witchcraft in Puritan times, Erikson (1966) suggests that deviant behavior and its accompanying sanctions served the important functions of maintaining the boundaries of

[2]R. Franklin, 1989, personal communication. Tulane University School of Tropical Medicine and Public Health.

normal social behaviors. The assumption here is that there is a cultural centrifugal force, a separation-individuation tendency in all members that requires sanctioning if society is to remain cohesive. Society requires those individuals who become deviant as examples to all others of the behaviors that are not allowed. The sanctions likewise demonstrate what would happen to others if they behaved in the same way. From this perspective, the deviant individual is a scapegoat required by society to embody the sinful tendencies of all its members and to expiate the accompanying collective guilt through the institution of stigmatizing sanctions.

Other than "those who uphold the conservative social order," what then remains of the concept of normality across cultural groups? Are there norms of personality specific to ethnic groups, and by connotation is departure from these norms identified from within as abnormal? Kardiner (1945), Mead (1961), Benedict (1934*a*), Sapir (1963), and others wrote of the "basic personality" of each culture. They reasoned that individuals in any given society subscribe to a certain set of beliefs, values, and attitudes that are for the most part historically derived. This set of values in turn determines attitudes and behaviors regarding the raising of children. This results in unique and fairly consistent child-rearing practices for a given culture. According to developmental theories of personality formation, such uniformities in child rearing will result in uniformities in the basic personality of individuals so raised. The basic personality of individuals in a society would collectively require and fashion cultural institutions in order to meet their common emotional needs. Such cultural institutions are termed projective systems and are considered to be a reflection of the basic needs of individuals in a particular society. Projective systems might include but are not confined to myths, dramatic expression, material arts, poetry, literature, games, and other endeavors with affective content. According to this formulation, "basic personality" is seen as normal and deeply engrained.

"Normality" in a Foreign Society

An example of the replication of the uniformity of the basic personality is found in the recent work of Briggs (1970) among the Inuit of Canada. In her book entitled *Never in Anger,* Briggs collected and translated into English Utku-Inuit emotional terms and outlined the real-life contexts in which they were manifest. Briggs's work as well as my own observations of Inuit socialization practices reveals an implicit theory of Inuit ideal emotional development from childhood to adulthood, as well as a theory of psychopathology based on developmental deviations.

According to the Inuit, *naklik* is one of the most valued emotional human qualities. *Naklik* means to take care of others, such as a mother caring for her child; being alert to the needs of others and acting to fulfill them. Inuit say that "Jesus" *nakliks* his people. Not only do mothers *naklik* their children, but all adults are expected to assume a *naklik*ing attitude toward others in general, including strangers.

With increasing reason, shyness develops out of respect. Shyness refers to an apparent dignified humility highly valued by adult Inuit. A man or a woman with appropriate shyness would not aspire to seek a leadership position, for example. In a cross-cultural context, the quality of shyness often renders taking an assertive position in the classroom socially inappropriate. Thus ideal Inuit shyness is abnormal behavior in the context of the American classroom.

Inuit believe that cleverness develops with further development of reason; cleverness is a most highly valued quality in Inuit adults. Cleverness in this case refers to a person's ability to turn a misfortune into humor. The ideal Inuit personality combines the ability to nurture, shyness, cleverness, and a goodly amount of reason.

Of course, most people in Inuit societies exhibit deviations from these highly valued traits. When deviations occur, such as not caring for others or being somewhat boastful, or not smiling or joking, the person is noticed and remarked upon by others, usually in an appropriate, joking fashion. More severe deviations from the valued ideals also occur, however. For example, Inuit believe that some mothers and parents *naklik* (or spoil) their children too much. This results in children persisting with fussy *(urulu)* behavior beyond the age when it is appropriately manifested. *Urulu* means to be obviously annoyed and showing an "unsmiling" attitude.

Children are expected to overcome *urulu* feelings and manifestations. In North Alaska, Inuit are taunted in childhood by a process termed affectionate teasing. Affectionate teasing is done in order to test the degree to which the child has emotional control over fussiness and to teach the child to develop control when it's lacking. Inuit children, for example, are sometimes taught to use the chamber pot by the mother's holding them naked at arm's length and letting their urine or feces drop to the floor. Often there is an audience of relatives of friends looking on, who usually find the scene amusing. On other occasions, children are poked in the ribs, or candy or toys are withheld from them until they throw a temper tantrum. At these times, onlookers usually laugh and joke about the child. Mothers who seem to be overprotective of such children are felt to inhibit the child's ability to develop control of fussiness. Inuit believe that this results in fussiness being a persistent, unfortunate quality of personality.

Anger, whether openly displayed or repressed, is considered frightening by Inuit. People who clog up emotions, who become unsmiling, and who are obviously under stress are considered by others as prone to potentially explosive behavior. Explosive behavior can take one of two forms. The moody person can explode into angry rage and is feared by others. Others are more prone to dissociative states that in traditional times would be manifest in a brief cathartic outburst of ritualized emotional display often accompanied by amnesia for the episode. Violence to others or to property rarely occurred during such states. While these outbursts were well recognized as a result of obsessions plus stress, they were usually not as feared as overt hostility.

Psychopathology is thus socially identified among Inuit as conforming to four categories:

1. Too little *ihuma:* that is, lacking reason and being unable to control anger or depression.
2. Too much *ihuma:* that is, brooding, moody, perhaps dangerous compulsive behavior.
3. Clogged up emotion, entailing the belief that whenever emotions such as anger are clogged up, they will eventually burst forth in a dangerous way or result in soul loss.
4. *Naklik*ing too much, which results in painful longing or loneliness.

Inuit cosmology includes the notion that all animate and many inanimate things possess *inua,* or spirits, that have active relationships with human beings. The *inua* of seals is believed to represent humanlike qualities and physical manifestations in the seal which can be loosened from the animal and dealt with as an external entity. Angry *inua,* for example, can become tormenting spirits to human beings. Appeased and pleased *inua* can become friends of human beings. Some humans can become possessed by *inua* spirits of animals or objects. These become introjects and their characteristics become identified with the concept of the self. "Normality" among the Inuit is thus of different dimensions from that found by those who use the yardstick of DSM-III-R to contrast with the normal.

A major issue in conceptualizing normality from the standpoint of the cultural anthropologist is the requirement of differentiating the ideal-personality type, the typical personality, and the atypical personality, all contained within a circle of cultural functionality (see figure 7.1). When questioning people in a society about what they are like and how one should raise children and conduct life, ideal personality types are most often revealed. Briggs's work reveals much about Inuit concepts of ideal

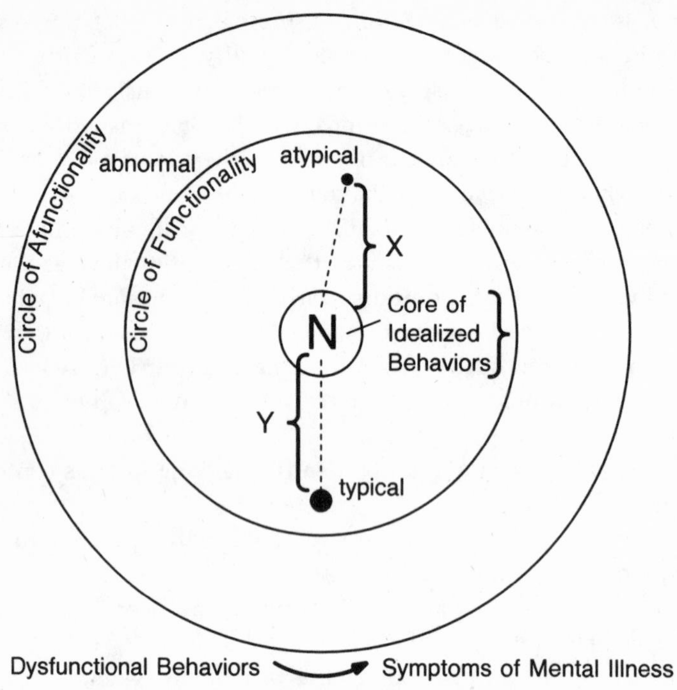

FIGURE 7.1
THE DISTRIBUTION OF BEHAVIOR VALUE
JUDGMENTS IN SOCIAL SPACE

[= lines of normalcy. Here, x = y, so the typical behavior is as normal as the atypical behavior. All points within the circle of functionality are normal. All points within the circle of afunctionality are abnormal. The radius of the circle of functionality is proportional to the degree of structure framing a behavior; the radius of the circle of afunctionality is proportional to the amount of inefficiency the culture can tolerate having attached to the behavior.]

normal personality. Her observations include many individuals who did not conform to these ideals, who nevertheless were still considered bona-fide group members. Some ethnographers of the Inuit have described uncooperative sullen attitudes and feuds among the same people who value so highly the cooperative humble characteristics mentioned earlier. Typical behaviors in these groups differed from ideal personality types as construed from within, but both ideal and typical behaviors were recognized as part of the normal Inuit life.

In Inuit and in many other societies including our own, there are also individuals who manifest atypical behavior and aberrant personality differences that are neither ideal nor average. The *angakok* or shaman in Inuit society is an example of such an atypical person. *Angakok* are capable of intense trance states and ritualized soul loss; are often bisexual and fearsome; and lead lives that are considered ecstatic by the standards of their societies. However, such individuals are not considered abnormal, but rather are an essential element and play important roles in their cultures. Actors, artists, and others who transcend social rules but who are considered to make major contributions to our society are likewise atypical personalities who are considered within the circle of functionalities of our society, and therefore normal. Kleinman (1988) has argued recently that within the circle of cultural functionality in our own society are many individuals with atypical personality problems, such as eating disorders, a myriad of character disorders, and neurotics. He argues that such individuals manifest culturally defined psychiatric disorders relative only to their own society and that the only potential universal disorders that transcend cultural definitions are psychiatric diseases, such as schizophrenia, major affective disorders, and organic brain syndromes.

The Typical and Average Across Cultures

"The traditional anthropological method of describing culture traits [is] in terms of the typical, average, or preferred behavior" (DeVos and Miner 1959, p. 333). Typical and average have a conceptual basis in statistics. "Typical" behaviors are modal behaviors, those that are most frequently observed. "Average" behaviors, on the other hand, refer to actions that constitute the probabilistic "best guess," or the behavioral mean. By definition, typical behaviors are most frequent. It is important that these be contrasted with average behaviors, which no given individual may in fact practice.

The conjunction of two or more typical behaviors yields another typical behavior—albeit at a more general level of analysis—only when the modal instances of these behaviors are co-occuring. Imagine that for culture X the methods of food preparation have been carefully dissected. For each step of the process, the modal or typical behavior can be identified. The idealized depiction of the entire process, which would detail sequentially the typical behaviors for each step, is itself typical only if most food preparers display modal behaviors for most steps. If they do not, as is likely, the idealization is an average of the process, links in this chain being composed of a sequence of modalities. Despite the accuracy of this depiction, no single individual may in reality perform the sequence of tasks in the described manner.

The relationship between typical and average behaviors is more intimate, however. If one steps back in perspective from an average chain, it becomes a new typical category. Hence, continuing our illustration, the averaged depiction of the method of performing each step of food preparation becomes the typical behavior in which food preparation is accomplished by performing the steps without reference to the method of each step. This process of magnification or, inversely, of microscopic scrutiny, can be carried on theoretically ad infinitum. Ethnographers reveal much about their chosen vantage point when they choose to describe behaviors as being typical, instead of reducing such a typicality into an averaged chain itself composed of typical modes (Donovan 1988).

Identification of normal behaviors as opposed to typical ones entails a qualitatively different kind of analysis. Whereas any alert observer can count behavioral acts and thus correctly label typicalities, identification of normal behavior seems to require knowledge less about the act and its frequency than about the meanings and significances attached to it.

Normal behaviors are most often not equivalent to typical ones. Typical behaviors especially need not be judged normal. To take one example, male homosexuality is not in our culture considered entirely normal, despite the typicality that "almost 50 per cent [of males unmarried until the age of 35] have homosexual experience" (Kinsey, Pomeroy, and Martin 1949, p. 623). Even further, atypical behaviors can be deemed even more normal than are typical ones, as evidenced in the psychoanalytic construct of the mature (but rare) genital character.

The assertion that judgments of normality are cultural must take into account the competing claims that normal standards are defined relative to conditions incumbent upon a universal standard of disease and health, or in our case, of mental disorder versus mental health. For instance, Devereux (1980) claims that "from a psychiatric point of view the valid criteria for normality are absolute, that is, they are independent of the norms of any given culture or society but are identical with the criteria for Culture as a universal human phenomenon" (p. 5).

Mialet (1980, p. 1082) proposes that "normal" is most usefully equated with a state of being "not ill" *(l'état de non-maladie).* He suggests that this way of defining what constitutes normalcy requires an intensifying need to articulate the meanings of "disease" and "illness." A universal standard of what behaviors constitute mental disorder becomes the most elusive and difficult pursuit for psychiatrists working cross-culturally. A universal standard of human normality, however, raises the possibility of instances arising when behaviors are typical and normal autoculturally (emically) but typical and abnormal when viewed heteroculturally (etically). It should not go unremarked that these etic evaluations are almost always "us" looking at "them," where "us" is twentieth-century, Western industrial society and "them" is everyone else. The question can often be reduced to one of "How do they measure up to our standards?"

The "Sick Society"

A finding of cultural patterns that are both typical and abnormal necessitates, by their definitions, the introduction of the controversial concept of the "sick society." Explicitly, typicalities are modal behaviors, and these behaviors are transmitted by cultural traditions. If modal behaviors in a culture are also abnormal, then not only are the presenting individuals abnormal, but so too is the culture that acts as the transmitter of the abnormal behavior infecting its constituent members. Thus the culture is "sick" in terms of both a group of diseased individuals and also in the metaphysical sense in which culture is a transcendent quality independent of its populace. Depending on the precise impairment, such as epidemic alcoholism, suicide, and so on, the society may or may not be able to present a façade of normal living. But the implications of a concept such as "sick society" entails the idea that some societies might become so disabled that they were incapable of meeting the needs of their members and would thus become dysfunctional.

Examples abound in the ethnological literature of child-rearing practices that seem from a Western standpoint to be psychopathogenic. In many societies, such as Inuit, Vietnamese, and so on, children are allowed to suckle on their mothers' breasts and sleep with mother and father until around age five. In others, mothers and other caregivers masturbate the genitalia of their infants in order to soothe and calm fussiness. In many parts of the Muslim world boys are circumcised in public ritual ceremony at age six to eight. Stoller and Herdt (1985) have vividly described universal, obligatory, exclusive homosexuality from puberty to heterosexual marriage when in the early twenties among a New Guinea people.

These socialization practices are at variance with those advocated in the United States, and no doubt they have an effect in shaping personality structures. In most of these cultures, socialization practices are of course a reflection of fundamental values and life ways, and their effects on personality are considered to be in the service of producing culturally adjusted individuals. Herein lies the dilemma of constructing a culture-free universal nosology of Axis II personality disorders. Passive-dependent personality, for example, may be adaptive in some societies while it is not in others, including our own.

Other examples of the pathogenicity of culture are those minorities and/or migratory groups experiencing acculturation pressures from an imposing majority culture. Berry et al. have developed a model from which to understand the nature of acculturation pressure and the psychopathology that often results. They have proposed that societies which reject both the values of the dominant culture as well as their own traditional ones obtain a marginal status that creates identity confusion and associated psychopathologies of despair, suicide, and substance abuse. Examples of marginal societies experiencing those acculturation difficulties are ubiquitous in today's industrializing world.

It should be noted, however, that major schools of anthropological thought have reacted to apparent ethnocentric biases regarding the idea of a "dysfunctional" society. The structional-functionalist school, for example, maintains that social systems promote themselves for significant "intervals in time in a steady state during which a high degree of cohesion and solidarity characterizes the relationships among its members" (Harris 1968, p. 515). So closely interrelated are the facets of a culture that dysfunction in one must reverberate throughout the whole, hobbling the entire system. It is furthermore argued, however, that a society capable of maintaining equilibrium in its environment over an extended period of time can hardly be called dysfunctional. If being nonnormal is to be diseased, yet being diseased does not impair functioning, then one is left to wonder about the salience of the concept "disease." But if a diseased condition does impair functioning, then how can any successful society—that is, one that has propagated itself through time—be termed "sick"?

One way around this conundrum is to propose that "sick societies" can be functional, but only minimally so. Without the alleged abnormality, they would somehow be "more" successful than they are already. All things considered, a heterocultural pronouncement of another's abnormality, where autoculturally nothing is seen but normality, communicates more about the observer than about the observed. Normality does not seem to be a universal category whose standards are ubiquitous to all humans, save perhaps in the most extreme of mental disorders. Recognition of an abnormality is usually a cultural perogative. According to Murphy (1959):

> the antithetical concepts of health and disease are value judgments. Hence, merely to describe certain behavioral characteristics in a people

> is meaningless for mental health until either the writer or the reader assesses these characteristics in terms of some definition, saying, although perhaps not explicitly, that he regards certain traits as unhealthy, etc. Such judgment implies a standard, and for any sociopsychiatric study to be meaningful that standard needs to be quite clear to the reader. . . . (P. 291)

The Health/Disease Model and DSM-III-R

Axes I and II of the DSM-III-R include many mental disorders whose occurrences and presentations may be strongly influenced by cultural factors. Given our current state of knowledge regarding the neurological substrate of these disorders, it is difficult to support a strict disease versus health model of psychological normality and illness. Even in the example of schizophrenic disorders, these issues are not at all clear. The schizophrenias are no myth; they are a very real and often tragic phenomenon in many different societies. Cross-cultural workers have looked upon the manifestations of psychosis in other societies as products of the social, cultural, moral, and legal contexts. However, most have been struck by the similarities in symptomatology seen between their cases and those in Western mental hospitals. Dunham (1965) summarized epidemiological reports from abroad and concluded that prevalence rates for schizophrenia "are quite comparable" worldwide, ranging from 2 to 9 per 1,000. In another summary in 1976, Murphy cited rates of nonhospitalized schizophrenics in Sweden (5.7 per 1,000), Eskimo (4.4 per 1,000), Canadian (5.6 per 1,000), and Yoruba (6.8 per 1,000). Observing that the rates of mental illness patterns were more striking for their similarity from culture to culture than for their differences, he suggested that the causes of schizophrenia, whether genetic or experimental, are ubiquitous across human groups. The WHO's International Pilot Study of Schizophrenia (IPPS) attempted systematically to verify these findings by utilizing the Present State Examination (PSE) on hospitalized psychotic patients in seven different nations across the world. Research psychiatrists from India, Nigeria, Colombia, Denmark, the United Kingdom, the Soviet Union, and the United States were trained to use this instrument in their own languages and were able to obtain high levels of interrater reliability at home and abroad. In each national research center a group was found that manifested core symptoms of the schizophrenic syndrome. As Kleinman (1988) has recently pointed out, however, most significant was the fact that most of the psychotic patients in each of these research centers failed to meet the diagnostic inclusion criteria for the study. One might conclude, therefore, that the study demonstrated that schizophrenia does exist across cultures, but other types of psychosis, perhaps more culturally specific, also exist. The study did not examine the prevalence or incidence of either the classical schizophrenia syndromes or the other types of psychosis.

Evolution and the Biological Basis of Mental Disorders

The finding that schizophrenia can be identified in such widely geographically separated populations raises further questions regarding the transmission of the genetic traits involved. If schizophrenia were entirely a biological impairment in the human brain, it would be selected against and would presumably have disappeared in at least some populations. If it were an adaptively neutral trait, some genetic drifting would have no doubt occurred rendering the condition more common in some populations than in others. The ubiquitous nature of schizophrenia indicates that at least some of its traits are linked to biologically adaptive qualities.

One possibility is that schizophrenia has provided a selective advantage in triggering necessary social changes in conservative populations. Over the span of human history and prehistory, the process of culture change has been relatively slow until the recent era. From time to time, however, societies have departed from the usual incipient process of oscillation and change in culture patterns. Such processes have been documented in previous studies of innovation, acculturation, and nativistic and revitalization movements. Revitalization movements are deliberate, organized attempts by some members of a society to construct a more satisfying culture by rapidly accepting multiple innovations. Such rapid structural changes are often the result of an initial severe disorganization of the sociocultural system caused by environmental stresses that have pushed the system beyond the usual limits of its equilibrium.

Cultures evolve over time as do species, with incipient change being easily recognizable over hundreds or thousands of years, but not apparent from one generation to the next. Mead (1954) has emphasized that societies throughout history have generally tended to be traditional and conservative with an orientation toward the past, turning first to the tried and tested methods in attempting to solve problems. This tendency toward conservation of prevailing social structures is basic to human nature and finds expression on the psychologic level in ethnocentrism and various adverse emotional responses to change or the anticipation of change.

Rapid shifts in social and biologic milieu, however, occur frequently enough to necessitate a mechanism by which individuals and societies can rapidly restructure their ways of living in order to meet new environmental challenges. With sudden climatic change, changes in flora or fauna, or disease epidemics, cultural responses may not be adequate to maintain human biological requirements. Disease, famine, subsequent loss of pride and values, and social disorganization of corporate institutions and of family life may occur. Under conditions of disorganization, the system—at least from the standpoint of some of its members—is unable to ensure the reliable satisfaction of certain values that are held to be essential to continue well-being and self-respect. Under such circumstances, individuals tend to become internally disorganized and to manifest symptoms of their distress in anxiety, depression, shame, guilt, and apathy to various degrees. Some individuals, because of constitutional proclivity, are prone to develop behaviors and modes of thinking that have high affective impact on others and that often provide a nidus for social resynthesis.

This process has been best exemplified in Wallace's (1970) work on the Seneca Indians of New York and the rise of the religion of Handsome Lake. Among the Seneca, the stereotypes of the good hunter, the brave warrior, and the forest statesman were the images of success and value; but because of political changes in the United States during the mid-eighteenth century, the Seneca people had become confined to tiny isolated reservations, a situation that made achievement of their ideals virtually impossible. The hunter could no longer hunt; the warrior could no longer fight; and perhaps more shattering, the forest statesman was an object of contempt and ridicule.

Many Senecas became personally disorganized. Fear of witches increased, clans and families squabbled, and many turned to drink and neglected their family responsibilities. Handsome Lake was such a person who, from 1799 to 1801, in states of exhaustion and distress, hallucinated angel messengers from the Creator who brought him the "New Way of Handsome Lake." Handsome Lake's brother, Corn-Planter, announced these visions to his people. The messages contained the prescription to put away such vices as abortion, infertility magic, and drinking. In addition, a new code of socialization was instituted that emphasized the nuclear family over clan and lineage, and sanctioned men's working in the fields—formerly a woman's occupation. Handsome Lake's psychological aberrances apparently provided a mechanism for cultural restructuralization that was adopted by the Seneca people. The Seneca who accepted the way of the Great Spirit no longer drank, nor could the whites convince them to do so. Once they saw that the women would not jeer at them, the men took up the plow and began to raise pigs and cattle. While reading and speaking English never did become widespread, the Seneca did accept the local Quakers' advice to live in log cabins, and gradually the face of the communities brightened. The grim, poverty-stricken villages, plagued with drunkenness and despair, became comfortable and even prosperous. As a successful revitalization movement, Handsome Lake's religion acquired a set of formalized rituals and a text and became a lasting institution that still exists today.

Similar patterns of response to social disequilibrium have been documented in diverse societies in other areas of the world. Cargo cults in Melanesia have already been mentioned. While most of these cult movements were abortive, some gave rise to social change. Mead (1961) has given a detailed account of Paliau's movement on Manus that brought modernization, town planning, sumptuary laws, and an economic design for building a centralized treasury. This political and cultural advancement was seemingly made possible by the integrative catalyst of a mystic—Wapi on Rambutjon—who hallucinated voices instructing him to tell his people to destroy all their old possessions in expectation of the millennium.

In this regard, similarities in the life histories of schizophrenics and of prophets are also worth noting. Prophetic powers, whether they are acquired by heredity or by spontaneous possession, usually begin to be manifest early in life. Most commonly a future prophet is marked during adolescence by psychologic characteristics, experiences, and behavior that set him or her apart from other people. Adolescents destined to become seers have been described as tending toward introversion or solitude, as absentminded, as having antisocial attitudes with a propensity toward dreams and visionary experiences, and as having nervous and highly excitable temperaments. Both the prophet and the schizophrenic evidence a family history of the behavior. Both exhibit a preepisode personality characterized as sensitive and socially withdrawn. Both experience special states of consciousness under conditions of sociocultural disintegration. In premodern societies, the experience of hearing voices and being influenced by spirits is held to be valid—most people believe in spirits and spirit possession. People may have learned from childhood that such experiences can occur. Interestingly, these beliefs are universal in human groups, although actually experiencing voices is not. Thus in such societies prophet's pronouncements are often not cognitively dissonant. Their experience, in fact, may be institutionalized and given the structure of ritual and lore within the prevailing social system. In today's society, these traits seem to confer no adaptive advantage to society or to the afflicted individual. Even in the premodern situation, prophets themselves often suffer and dread the calling.

The presence of individuals with such psychological characteristics may have had adaptive advantage in premodern populations facing disintegration. Social disintegration itself has been found to affect certain predisposed individuals to experience internal disequilibrium and auditory hallucinations, which often relate an idiosyncratic explanation or plan of action. The ideas of these individuals may not always offer a coherent new order. Instead, they often merely provide a mystical, affective focus, bringing people together in ritual and communal behavior that in turn provides the social ordering necessary for more mundane, concrete group adaptations to the prevailing problems of the society.

While not directly investigating incidence rates of schizophrenia per se, Leighton et al. (1963) proposed that social disintegration generates disintegration of personality. They used ten indices of disintegration.

1. Instability and low level of income.
2. Cultural confusion—in this case weak, confused, conflicting values (e.g., French versus English).
3. Secularization—that is, the absence of religious values.
4. Frequency of broken homes.
5. Few and weak associations in groups, both formal and informal.
6. Few and weak leaders.
7. Few patterns of recreation and leisure-time activity.
8. High frequency of hostile acts and expressions.
9. High frequency of crime and delinquency.
10. Weak and fragmented network of communications.

In so-called disintegrated areas of the country (as gauged by communities with high scores on the ten indices of disintegration), the prevalence rate of psychiatric disorders was high for both sexes and significantly higher than in other areas rated lower in disintegration. These findings indicate that while mental disorder is found worldwide, its prevalence in localized communities is dependent on the degree of social cohesion. In other studies, Holmes and Rahe (1967) have shown that the stress produced on individuals as a result of change and breakdown in their social networks produces a significantly higher risk of mental disorder. Indices used as parameters of social network breakdown include death of spouse, divorce, marital separation, death of close family member, personal injury or illness, retirement, changes in business or financial state, change to a different line of work, change of responsibilities at work, and so on. They concluded that those individuals who had a high life crisis score—indicating a large number of life changes in a short period of time—would be more likely to develop a major health change than those who had a low score during the same time, indicating a relatively homeostatic period with few demands on the coping mechanisms of the physiologic systems. It has also been observed in many studies of the military that units in which there is high morale based on confidence in one's leaders, in the abilities of one's comrades, and in the effectiveness of one's weapons have lower incidences of psychologic breakdown than in units where there is no confidence in leadership and a lack of trust among the men.

Social instability and schizophrenia have been linked in other ways as well. Migration and social mobility with accompanying disruption of social and family ties have also been implicated in the increased risk for schizophrenia, as has disenfranchisement of lower socioeconomic classes in stratified societies. Individuals without affinal or sanguine familial ties are also at higher risk.

Zubin, Magaziner, and Steinhauer (1983) have recently proposed that a person with a certain degree of genetic loading for schizophrenia may or may not experience cardinal symptoms depending on the occurrence of triggering stressful life events versus moderating influences, such as social supports, ecological factors, and premorbid personality. Reich, Cloniger, and Guze (1975) attribute the variance in expression of genetic predisposition to the presence of multifactorial developmental and environmental factors.

Inherited Traits—Axis I and Axis II Spectrum Disorders

The persistence of the genetic factors in schizophrenia in all human populations may also be related to the fact that this disorder represents the maladaptive end of a spectrum of adaptive temperamental traits. Newborn babies have been observed to possess temperamental qualities that are only gradually modified during maturation. Freud remarked in 1937 that "each ego is endowed from the first with individual predispositions and trends, though it is true that we cannot specify their nature nor what determines them." Only recently have neuroscience and personality assessment methods revealed the potential nature of underlying human temperamental qualities.

Cloniger (1987) has discussed these basic personality traits from the perspective of required adaptive capabilities that all humans possess to varying degrees. He believes it is the innate variation in the relative quantity of each trait in interaction with environmental demands that results in those enduring qualities that define personality. He proposes that personality disorders such as those listed in DSM-III-R represent the outcomes of extreme strength or extreme weakness of one or more traits interacting with the strength and weakness of others. Evidence based on the relatively fixed nature of certain trait categories on test-retest reliability indices indicates the presence of three basic interacting predispositions in reacting to environmental stimuli. The first trait, harm avoidance, is revealed by the observation that some individuals are predisposed to react to changes in their environment with apprehensive cautiousness; others, in a fearless, uninhibited way; and most, somewhere in between. The second basic trait, reward dependence, is evidenced in the tendency of some people to be detached and emotionally tough-minded in evaluating situations and other people; others, sentimental and moody; and most, somewhere in between. The third fundamental trait dimension is novelty seeking, with some individuals impulsively driven toward novelty to the point of risk taking and personal pain; others are more cautious, reflective, and conservative; and most lie somewhere in between. There is evidence that the harm-avoidance axis derives its regulation from the sevitonergic system of the brain; the novelty-seeking axis by the dopaminergic system; and the reward-dependence axis by the norepinephrine system. It is the relative strength and weakness of each of these systems interacting with each other vis-à-vis the environment that determines personality. Figure 7.2 clarifies this interactive concept and postulates that the extremes of these axes possibly predetermine personality disorders. Thus the schizoid personality, for example, is reflective, detached interpersonally, and uninhibited. Cloninger (1987) and Siever et al. (1990) postulate further that genetic factors may be related to the expression of these three neurotemperamental systems, and the exaggeration of any of them may relate the Axis II personality disorders to Axis I disorders. Thus schizophrenia would represent a further exaggeration of the traits that determined the schizotypal personality, and these disorders would be seen in genetically related individuals, which is in fact the case.

Spectrum disorders based on primary disturbance in enduring personality traits have also been proposed for borderline-affective disorders, impulse-antisocial disorders, and anxiety disorders. Basic, inborn psychological traits along the fundamental dimensions of mood/affect, impulse/action, attention/cognition, and anticipated adversity/anxiety may represent the manner in which any organism reacts specifically to given stimuli or generally to a variety of stimuli. As Post, Rubinow, and Ballenger (1986) have demonstrated, patients can become more vulnerable to potentiating stimuli as the neurophysiological processes involved become more easily initiated through "kindling," an observation of how the social environment may foster the development of a particular personality trait. Therefore live events and social learning can condition basic temperamental

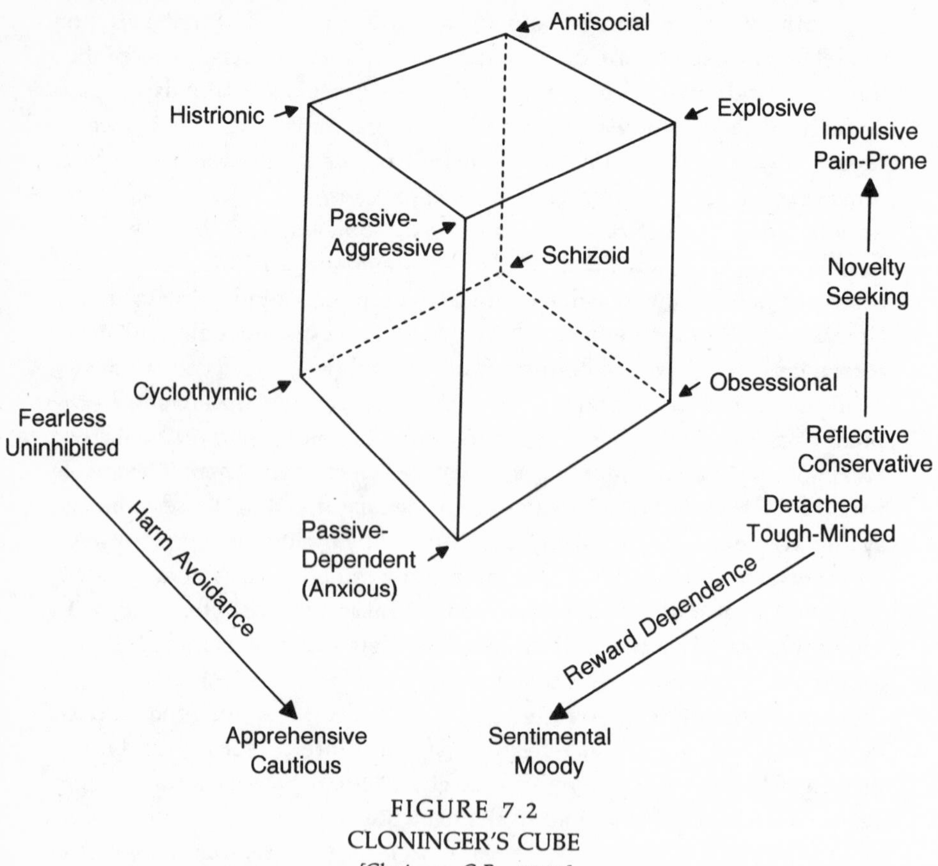

FIGURE 7.2
CLONINGER'S CUBE
[Cloninger, C.R., 1987]

proclivities, facilitating their release and in some cases enhancing responses to a pathological degree. Ambelas (1987) has found, for example, that while first admissions for bipolar disorder may be precipitated by a threatening event, subsequent episodes may require less provocation and eventually become autonomous.

Social and cultural factors may therefore be of paramount significance in preventing and potentiating the occurrence of disturbances in the basic temperamental regulation biologically present in a population. Studies of the nature of childhood socialization experiences, the degree of social support, and the frequency and severity of the occurrence of traumatic life events have indicated that these sociocultural factors are implicated in the incidence of mental disorders in a population. Many studies have shown that the death of a parent in early childhood or separation from a parent for a year or more before age seventeen are risk factors for later depression.[3] Psychoanalytic approaches are similarly predicated on understanding that early trauma in life may influence the vulnerability of self in later life in forms in which the self creates others as equivalent victims or in the forms in which the self seeks to master, over and over again, what was overwhelming. According to ego psychology, life trauma, early and/or later, "overloads the psychic apparatus with information and affect leading to strange affect" effects on perception, thinking, memory, and affect (Horowitz 1989, p. 186). The biological basis for such observations is only recently becoming better understood.

Cultures vary tremendously in terms of child-rearing practices and the extent that they provide stress-buffering social environments. Social network cohesiveness and imbeddedness seem to provide one with supportive others and with values and rationale in the face of stresses. Such networks may by their nature render environments less stressful. The recent research of Brown and Harris (1986) indicates that the lack of social support, especially in the context of stressful life events, causes depression.

Stressful life events themselves are a social-cultural variable that has been found to be associated with producing psychopathology. Brown, Bifulco, and Harris (1987) have developed methods of assessing life's traumatic events, which they call the Life Event and Difficulty Schedule. Their studies have revealed that depressed patients experienced an excess of severe threatening events one year prior to the onset of their illness. In their earlier work, Holmes and Rahe (1967) discovered similar relationships between changes in the status quo of one's life and the onset of illness.

That culture can affect the genesis of psychopathology is therefore well established. Culture determines the values and techniques of childrearing. Culture affects the constellation and structure of family life. Cultural norms establish the degree of appropriate familial-expressed emotion. Culture establishes the nature of labeling of disorder, of hierarchies of resort to care, of the degree of scapegoating. Culture factors are involved in determining social support networks. Culture change, migration, war, socioeconomic status, and social inequalities are also important factors in shaping and stressing populations. As cultures vary on these dimensions, so should the prevalance and manifestation of psychopathology.

Culture may also affect the biological selection of personality traits; for

[3]See Bowlby (1980); Brown and Harris (1978); Freud (1953); Lloyd (1980); Paykel (1982); and Roy (1987).

example, if basic human temperaments are genetically determined, could they not become factors selected for or against by the implicit social and environmental requirements of especially isolated breeding populations? Would some societies, such as the Inuit, genetically select for the traits of cautious apprehension, reflective, stoical, and sentimental in their breeding preferences and practices? This of course introduces the difficult and as yet unfounded notion of a racial or innate cultural personality.

The foregoing discussion also has relevance for the concept of normality/abnormality. A universalist might argue that the extremes of neurotemperamental traits represent inborn patterns of neurotransmitter disregulation. Such states would be abnormal from a physiological perspective. Normality in this case would be defined by moderate regulation of transmitter systems and would be represented within and below the surfaces and edges of the cube depicted in figure 7.2. Within the parameters of the cube, there still exists a myriad of points of trait confluence that could define cultural ideals and culturally "normal" types. Cloninger (1987) argues that "normal" adjustment to society (presumably American) can be obtained when only one axis is functioning within the mean. Deviations of three axis traits, however, will result in at least personality disorder. One might speculate whether, even in these extreme cases, culture could provide alternatives to the maladjusted or sick role. For example, traits resulting on the one hand in antisocial personality might on the other be channeled into becoming a professional daredevil, SWAT team police officer, or combat-ready soldier. Evidence for such cultural accommodation and adaptation of temperamental traits is found in recent epidemiological studies of affective disorders. Weissman and Myers (1978) found that the bipolar disorders are uncommonly prevalent in professionals in the higher social classes. An association between social achievement and manic-depressive disorder had been reported earlier by Woodruff and Associates (1971), leading to the assumption that the convergence of a cyclothymic temperament and certain cognitive strengths could lead to economic and social success in some people. Andreason (1987) has also found increased prevalence of affective disorders among successful writers and their first-degree relations.

A Culturally Relative Model of Normality/Abnormality

A pictorial representation of the relative polar coordinates and sundry evaluative categories of behavior was offered in figure 7.1. The point of reference for cultural acts is a set of ideal behaviors. By "ideal" is meant those behaviors that are consensually deemed as appropriate to the specific circumstances and morally correct in the eyes of the group's value system. Behaviors in this set are what the culture member "ought" to do, whether or not he or she in fact actually behaves accordingly. Although it is a question of inherent interest, how a behavior attains this particular cultural status need not concern us.

Ethnographic observation locates modal behaviors that, depending on the particular foci of interest, fall off from the idealized set by varying degrees. Culture members may or may not be aware that their actual behaviors are not equivalent to their idealized ones; as Harris (1979) notes, persons can act in one way while sincerely believing that they behave in another. Data solicited verbally, then, are qualitatively different from those directly observed.

As discussed, these modal behaviors are equivalent to ethnographically typical ones. Observations of atypical behaviors for the same observational focus would lie elsewhere within the second circle of the illustration and are differentiated from the typical by their smaller size. Were finer resolution to be applied, the large dot marking the typical behavior would be seen to be the average of a set of typicalities. Here, though, the dot is solid, and hence it is typical. In other words, when a group of typical behaviors are viewed as a set, the cluster is average; when one interprets the same group as a single case of the next level of integration, the cluster is typical.

Knowing that a behavior is typical or atypical does not determine its relative normality. As depicted graphically, normality is not a coordinate in social space but is instead a functional relationship of the perceived distance of the behavior from idealized behavior epicenter. In our hypothetical case, although the typical and atypical behaviors are widely separated, they are equally "normal" because they lie the same distance from the middle.

This reading of normality as being less an adherence to a prescribed behavior and more a relationship between real and ideal allows for many of the intuitive insights displayed by culture members. Specifically, there does seem to be a continuum of normality. Behaviors are not simply normal or abnormal; they can also be "fairly normal," "almost abnormal," or "quite abnormal." Linear distance accurately captures this continuum of determination, with short distances separating real and ideal being deemed "more normal" than are larger ones.

Quite likely, no moral significance is attached to normality in a culture save in the extremes; little social articulation would occur for the middle range. A very short distance implies that actual behaviors are very close approximations to the idealized behaviors. The moral imperative of the latter can therefore partially attach itself to the former. This transference can occur with any atypical behaviors. Where the tie is to atypical behavior, the ethnographer should see behavior used to signify the morally (religiously) superior individuals; when it is typical, one expects relatively minor increases in distance (increases in the line of normality) to be the object of strong opprobrium by the group.

At the other extreme, strong importance is attached to the fact that the line of normality is not so great that it crosses over into the abnormal. The circumference of the second circle demarcating this transition has been termed the "circle of functionality." Social behaviors and the institutions in which they operate occur within the context of cognitive expectations for that exchange. Social actors cannot continually be negotiating the rules of each encounter; instead, the culture articulates a set of roles from which an individual chooses depending on the context. Once roles have been assumed, and after mutual recognition has been achieved between parties as to what those roles are, the interacting individuals are expected to behave accordingly. Consequently, the immediate needs of the social setting can be addressed without renegotiation.

To the extent that actual behaviors fall within the range of expectation for an assumed role, those behaviors are deemed normal. Benedict (1934b) reached much the same conclusion: "A normal action is one which falls well within the limits of expected behavior for a particular society" (p. 73).

This claim forces the assertion that standards of normality are not simply culturally relative as opposed to human universals. If the speculations presented here are valid, then it will be found to be simplistic if not meaningless to say that behavior X is considered normal in culture A but not in culture B. Rather, the claim must be framed in terms of appropriate roles: Behavior X, never considered normal in culture B, is emically normal in culture A for actors in the roles S and T, but not R.

A second conclusion from this construction is that the distance of the circle of functionality from the idealized center is directly proportional to the degree to which the roles framing the behaviors are articulated. In highly structured exchanges, seemingly trivial deviations from expectation can be regarded as intolerably abnormal (for example, court etiquette). On the other hand, where relationships are relatively formless, as among friends, behaviors can be expected to stray far indeed before they are judged abnormal (for example, alcohol abuse, eating disorders).

A final speculative step must be taken. How does abnormality relate to conceptions of mental illness? At the outset, there appears to be no requirement that these categories do in fact relate in any systematic way.

Abnormality and mental illness are frequently operational in separate social spheres. In a very real sense we could recapitulate the discussion for normality, instead using mental illness as the focus. One major difference between the two texts would be that, in a nontrivial way, some categories of mental illness are probably organically based human universals while others are entirely culture-bound (see Simons and Hughes 1985). Intermediate cases would be where the disease category is cross-culturally represented but the presenting symptoms are culturally specific. Consequently, any discussion of mental illness requires a great deal of specificity about what type is meant. Although not all abnormal behaviors are indicative of mental illness, all symptoms of mental illness are considered abnormal, either in degree or in kind. As criteria of abnormality are culturally relative, so too must be symptom constellations.

The identification of culturally represented symptoms is a knotty problem. According to this model, abnormal behaviors are outside the circle of functionality and are "unexpected" responses to socially structured exchanges. Crossing this perimeter, however, places the behavior in the zone of afunctionality. This means that while the behaviors evinced are sufficiently deviant to fail to further the goals of the social exchange, they are not so severe as to impede them. These acts would be surprising but inconsequential to the extent that the system can tolerate inefficiency.

The tying of definitions of abnormality to measures of social efficiency is not without precedence. Note the following:

> A universal standard of normality and abnormality has been the goal of many researchers. A possible approach within this context is the "efficiency" concept developed by Wishner. Briefly, *efficiency* is the ratio of focused to diffuse energy expended by an individual in meeting a task demand. Wishner's research indicated that more inefficiency is associated with psychopathology. (Marsella 1979, p. 243)

Beyond the buffer zone of afunctionality lies the social wasteland of dysfunctional behaviors, those that are actively counterproductive first to the establishment of cooperative relationships with other culture members and second to the fulfillment of the purely personal needs of the individual. These behaviors are the raw material for symptom formation.

Although the rubric of "mental illness" is recognized by many if not most cultures, especially when it is defined in terms of being "nonphysical," the recognized diseases vary widely. Signifiers for each of these diseases will vary even more so. The placement of behaviors in the area of dysfunctionality is principally a function of the contents of the idealized core, the degree of structure of social roles framing the behaviors, and the capacity of the culture to tolerate nonproductive or inefficient behaviors. All vary from culture to culture and even from context within a given culture. For instance, the same behaviors that are normal or expected for males can be abnormal when performed by a female.

By virtue of the preceding, it should be clear that, just as heterocultural (etic) determinations of abnormality are neither anthropologically useful nor logically defensible, etic diagnoses of mental illnesses are even less so. The farther from the core of idealized behaviors one moves, the more cultural relativity one must allow for and the less valid is the transitivity of social intuitions from one culture to another. As the behaviors subject for organization into symptoms for mental illnesses are the farthest removed from the core, transitivity should be assumed to be negligible.

A Brief Application of the Model

Homosexuality is a useful example to examine from the standpoint of our model. According to the model, homosexuality would parse as follows: Instances of at least single encounters are very nearly typical of the life histories of individuals, and especially so when one considers males only. Primary homosexuals are, however, comparatively rare, with exclusive ones falling off no lower than 4 percent who are "exclusively homosexual throughout their lives" (Kinsey, Pomeroy, and Martin 1949, p. 651).

Within the idealized core are strong proscriptions against engaging in the behavior. Commission is illegal in most states (Boggan et al. 1983), and the Supreme Court has recently upheld the right of the states to promulgate such laws (Bowers v. Hardwick, 1986). A homosexual proposition has been used in our society as an acceptable defense in murder cases (Freiberg 1988). These facts place homosexuality far into the area of cultural dysfunctionality as defined by this model.

Given our cultural ideology, homosexuality is a behavior suitable for classification as a mental illness, and indeed our mental health professions have for quite some time viewed it as such. It must be immediately noted that this particular perspective on homosexuality is very American. Latin cultures and the city-states of ancient Greece have equally clear reactions to homosexual activity. In many ways they directly parallel that of the United States, save for one very important feature: Only the passive partner can expect social denigration. "Homosexuality" as we understand it is unknown to these cultures (compare Fry 1985); neither the Greeks nor the Latins have a word directly comparable. Instead, their vocabulary singles out the passive partner almost exclusively. The critical difference between our culture and these is that here masculinity is defined by with whom you have sex, while in Latin America it is by what you do when you have sex. Indeed, the most common derogatory term in Mexico is *puto,* which translates as "male whore." Here we see different behaviors being thrust out into the area of dysfunctionality; behaviors we might have assumed to be structured similarly are not.

Mental deviations are clearly real; what are arbitrary, however, and culturally specific are the cluster of symptoms and the relative weight assigned to each item within a cluster. Recognizing that human behaviors must be understood in cultural context to in fact be understood at all is the first step toward seeing things through the eyes of the actor instead of those of a judge.

REFERENCES

Ambelas, A. 1987. "Life Events: A Special Relationship?" *British Journal of Psychiatry* 150:235–240.

American Psychiatric Association. 1987. *Diagnostic and Statistical Manual of Mental Disorders,* 3rd ed., rev. Washington, D.C.: American Psychiatric Association.

Andreasen, N. 1987. "Creativity and Mental Illness: Prevalence Rates in Writers and Their First-degree Relatives." *American Journal of Psychiatry* 144:1288–1292.

Benedict, R. 1934*a*. *Patterns of Culture.* Boston: Houghton Mifflin.

———. 1934*b*. "Anthropology and the Abnormal." *Journal of General Psychology* 10(1):59–82.

Berry, J.; Kim, U.; Minde, T.; and Mok, D. 1987. "Comparative Studies of Acculturative Stress." *International Journal of Migration Research* 21:491–511.

Boggan, E.; Carrington-Haft, M.; Lister, C.; Rupp, J.; and Stoddard, T. 1983. *The Rights of Gay People.* New York: Bantam Books.

Bowers, Attorney General of Georgia, v. Hardwick et al. 1986, June 30. *Supreme Court Reporter* 106:2841.

Bowlby, J. 1980. *Attachment and Loss,* vol. 3. *Loss: Sadness and Depression.* New York: Basic Books.

Briggs, J. 1970. *Never in Anger: Portrait of an Eskimo Family.* Cambridge, MA: Harvard University Press.

Brown, G. W., and Harris, T. 1978. *The Social Origins of Depression.* London: Tavestock.

———. "Stressor, Vulnerability, and Depression: A Question of Replication." *Psychological Medicine* 16:739–744.

Brown, G. W.; Bifulco, A.; and Harris, T. 1987. "Life Events, Vulnerability, and Onset of Depression: Some Refinements." *British Journal of Psychiatry* 150:30–42.

Burton-Bradley-B.G. 1975. *Stone Age Crisis: A Psychiatric Appraisal.* Nashville: Vanderbilt Univ. Press.

Cloninger, C. R. 1987. "A Systematic Method for Clinical Description and Classification of Personality Variants." *Archives of General Psychiatry* 44:573–588.

Devereux, G. [1956] 1980. "Normal and Abnormal." In *Basic Problems of Ethnopsychiatry,* trans. B. Miller Gulati and G. Devereux, pp. 3–71. Chicago: University of Chicago Press.

DeVos, G., and Miner, M. 1959. "Oasis and Casbah—A Study in Acculturative Stress." In *Culture and Mental Health,* ed. Marvin K. Opler, pp. 333–350. New York: Macmillan.

Dunham, H. 1965. *Community and Schizophrenia: An Epidemiological Analysis.* Detroit: Wayne State University Press.

Edgerton, R. 1978. "The Study of Deviance—Marginal Man or Everyman?" In *The Making of Psychological Anthropology,* ed. G. Spindler, pp. 442–476. Berkeley: University of California Press.

Engel, G. 1980. "The Clinical Application of the Biopsychological Model." *American Journal of Psychiatry* 137:535–544.

Erikson, K. 1966. *Wayward Puritans. A Study in The Sociology of Deviance.* New York: John Wiley.

Freiberg, P. 1988. "New Life for the 'Gay Panic' Defense." *The Advocate* 499:10–13.

Freud, S. 1953. "Mourning and Melancholia." In *Sigmund Freud: Collected Papers,* ed. E. Jones, vol. 4, pp. 152–170. New York: Basic Books.

Freud, S. 1953. "Analysis, Terminable and Interminable." In *Sigmund Freud: Collected Papers,* ed. E. Jones, vol. 5, p. 343. New York: Basic Books.

Fry, P. 1985. "Male Homosexuality and Spirit Possession in Brazil." *Journal of Homosexuality* 11(3/4):137–153.

Harris, M. 1968. *The Rise of Anthropological Theory.* New York: Harper & Row.

Harris, M. 1979. *Cultural Materialism: The Struggle for a Science of Culture.* New York: Vintage Books.

Holmes T., and Rahe R. 1967. "The Social Readjustment Rating Scale." *Journal of Psychosomatic Research* 11:213–218.

Horowitz, M. 1989. "Inferring Earlier Traumas." *Contemporary Psychology* 34(2):185–186.

Jamison, K. 1989. "Mood Disorders Not Uncommon Among Writers, Artists, Composers." *U.S. Medicine* 4–5.

Kardiner, A. 1945. *The Psychological Frontiers of Society.* New York: Columbia University Press.

Kinsey, A. D.; Pomeroy, W.; and Martin, C. 1949. *Sexual Behavior in the Human Male.* Philadelphia: W. B. Saunders.

Kleinman, A. 1988. *Rethinking Psychiatry.* New York: Macmillan.

Leighton, D.; Harding, C.; Macklin, D.; MacMillan, A.; and Leighton, A. 1963. *The Character of Danger,* vol. 3, *The Sterling County Study of Psychiatric Disorder and Sociocultural Environment.* New York: Basic Books.

Lloyd, C. 1980. "Life Events and Depressive Disorder Reviewed, I: Events as Predisposing Factors. *Archives of General Psychiatry* 37:529–535.

Marsella, A. 1979. "Cross-cultural Studies of Mental Disorders." In *Perspectives on Cross-Cultural Psychology,* ed. A. Marsella, R. Tharp, and T. J. Ciborowski, pp. 233–262. New York: Academic Press.

Mead, M. 1954. "Cultural Discontinuities and Personality Transformation." *Journal of Social Issues* (Suppl.) 8:3–6.

———. 1961. *New Lives for Old: Cultural Transformation—Manus 1928–1953.* New York: Mentor.

Mialet, J. P. 1980. "Normalite, normativite et marginalite." *Annales Medico Psychologiques* 138(9):1079–1093.

Murphy, H. B. M. 1959. "Culture and Mental Disorder in Singapore." In *Culture and Mental Health,* ed. M. K. Opler, pp. 291–316. New York: Macmillan.

Murphy, J. 1976. "Psychiatric Labeling in Cross-Cultural Perspective." *Science* 191: 1019–1028.

Offer, D., and Sabshin, M. 1984. *Normality and the Life Cycle.* New York: Basic Books.

Paykel, E. S. 1982. "Life Events and Early Environment." In *Handbook of Affective Disorder,* ed. E. S. Paykel. New York: Guilford Press.

Post, R.; Rubinow, D.; and Ballenger, J. 1986. "Conditioning and Sensitization in the Longitudinal Course of Affective Illness." *British Journal of Psychiatry* 149:191–201.

Raybeck, D. 1988. "Anthropology and Labeling Theory: A Constructive Critique." *Ethos* 16:371–397.

Reich, T.; Cloninger, C. R.; and Guze, S. B. 1975. "The Multifactoral Model of Disease Transmission, I: Description of the Model and Its Use in Psychiatry." *British Journal of Psychiatry* 127:1–10.

Roy, A. 1987. "Five Risk Factors for Depression." *British Journal of Psychiatry* 150:536–541.

Sapir, E. 1949. *Language.* New York: Harcourt, Brace and World, Inc.

Siever, L.; Keefe, R.; Bernstein, D.; Coccaro, E.; Klar, H.; Zemishlany, Z.; Peterson, A.; Davidson, M.; Mahon, T.; Horvath, T.; and Mohs, R. 1990. "Eye Tracking Impairment in Clinically Identified Patients with Schizotypal Personality Disorder." *American Journal of Psychiatry* 147:740–745.

Simons, R., and Hughes, C. C. 1985. *The Culture Bound Syndromes: Folk Illnesses of Psychiatric and Anthropological Interest.* Boston: Reidel Press.

Spitzer, R.; Williams, J.; and Skodol, A. 1983. *International Perspectives on DSM-III.* Washington, D.C.: American Psychiatric Association Press.

Stoller, R., and Herdt, G. H. 1985. "Theories of Origins of Male Homosexuality." *Archives of General Psychiatry* 42:399–404.

Thompson, J. 1988. "Crosswalk Available." *Psychiatric News.* July 1.

Wallace, A. F. C. 1970. *The Death and Rebirth of the Seneca.* New York: Knopf.

Weissman, M., and Myers, J. 1978. "Rates and Risks of Depressive Symptoms in a United States Urban Community." *Acta Psychiatrica Scandinavica* 57:219–231.

Westermeyer, J., and Wintrob, R. 1979. "Folk Criteria for the Diagnosis of Mental Illness in Rural Laos." *American Journal of Psychiatry* 136:755–761.

World Health Organization. 1973. *The International Pilot Study of Schizophrenia.* Geneva: WHO.

———. 1981. *Social Demensions of Mental Health.* Geneva: WHO.

Wierzbicka, A. 1989. "Soul and Mind: Linguistic Evidence for Ethnopsychology and Cultural History." *American Anthropologist* 91(1):41–58.

Woodruff, R.; Robbins, L; Winokur, G.; et al. 1971. "Manic Depressive Illness and Social Achievement." *Acta Psychiatrica Scandinavica* 47:237–249.

Zubin, J.; Magaziner, J.; and Steinhauer, S. 1983. "The Metamorphosis of Schizophrenia from Chronicity to Vulnerability." *Psychological Medicine* 13:551–557.

CHAPTER 8

Sociological Perspectives on Mental Health: An Integrative Approach

Sharon Schwartz
and
Bruce G. Link

Sociology makes a unique contribution to understanding behaviors designated as mental illness through focusing on the level of analysis peculiar to this discipline—the social. Sociology is the analysis of human relations, an examination of how individuals form groups, come to a shared understanding of the world, and devise rules and roles to orchestrate human interactions. An interest in deviant behaviors, and mental illness as a subcategory thereof, derives from this concern with social order. Understanding deviance, defined as behaviors that break social rules, enlightens us about the nature and limits of those rules and adds to our store of knowledge about conformity, social order, and conflict (Rubington and Weinberg 1968). This perspective highlights the intimate relationship between the normal and the abnormal.

In Offer and Sabshin's (1984) formulation of the concepts and meaning of normalcy, the sociological approach usually considers the normal, at least in regard to mental health, to be the absence of disorder. Much more emphasis is placed on examining mental illness than mental health. Even when mental health or well-being is explicitly considered, it is usually measured by scales of anxiety, depression, and demoralization with the low end of the scales, the absence of symptoms, designated as well-being.[1] The focus on

[1]See, for example, Hayes and Ross 1986; Hughes and Gove 1981; Liker 1982; Thoits 1983; Turner 1981.

the abnormal, however, does not imply a lack of concern for the normal. Indeed, abnormality is often examined to gain clues about normality. The rules, roles, and expectations regarding normal, mentally healthy behaviors are often inexplicit and subtle. They become obvious only in the breach, when the rules are broken and sanctions are applied. The application of sanctions helps to clarify the boundaries between the normal and the abnormal.

Offer and Sabshin's consideration of normalcy as utopia, or something more than the absence of disorder, is nearly absent in sociological studies of mental health. This is due, in part, to the focus on the social rather than the individual and the consequent tendency toward relativism and viewing the normal itself as problematic. What is considered superior functioning for an individual may lead to negative consequences for society. Good mental health in a particular context may be dysfunctional in another context. What is viewed as good and functional is often dependent on who is doing the viewing and what value hierarchy is being applied. While these issues arise in the examination of mental illness as well, they become even more problematic in the examination of what is superior mental health. Sociological studies have therefore focused mainly on the relationship between social factors and mental illness or psychological problems.

Within this framework, two distinct sociological approaches can be identified—the social epidemiological and the societal reaction. While sharing a concern about the influence of social factors, these perspectives differ significantly in the questions asked, the sharpness of the boundaries between the normal and the abnormal, and even in the way mental illness is defined. Although individual researchers are likely to accept concepts from both these perspectives, we emphasize their distinct aspects in order to bring into focus both the special contributions and particular blind spots of each. We therefore begin our discussion of these perspectives in distilled form. Later we point out how these perspectives can be modified and adapted to form a unified sociological perspective on mental disorder.

In the social epidemiological perspective, the starting point for analysis is the effect of the social context on the individual who deviates. Mental illnesses are defined as either discrete disease entities, psychiatric analogues to physical disorders, or psychological entities, such as demoralization, where disorder is conceptualized on a continuum of distress and well-being. In either case, mental disorder is viewed as "a defect or an illness . . . located somewhere in the makeup of the individual" that is influenced by social factors (Spitzer and Denzin 1968). The norm-breaking behaviors are considered either as consequences of an underlying mental disorder or as indications of an individual's psychological problems. The social factors affecting the distribution of these disorders or symptoms in the population are the focus of analysis. The salient issues are: Who are the mentally ill? How did they become mentally ill? What sociocultural conditions are most likely to produce mental illness?

In the second perspective, the focus of inquiry is shifted away from the individual who commits the deviant act to the social context that defines the act and the performer as "deviant." Here "mental disorder" is not viewed as an entity residing within the individual or a problem with the individual's psyche but rather as a label and role conferred upon the individual. This approach attends to the social definitions of deviance. Here the salient questions become: What are the circumstances under which a person gets set apart as a deviant? What action do others take on the basis of this redefinition? What are the consequences of the adoption of this role? The boundaries between mental illness and other forms of deviant behavior are viewed as necessarily indistinct, for the label applied is not inherent in the nature of the act but is the result of interactions between the individual's characteristics and actions and society's definitions and judgments. Mental illness is seen as a social construct that is subjectively problematic rather than objectively given. Thus whereas the social epidemiological perspective examines how social factors cause mental disorders or psychological problems, the social reaction perspective examines how social factors shape conceptions of "mental illness" and the "mentally ill."

We examine sociological explanations of mental disorders from both these perspectives and attempt to show that although these two approaches have different views on the basic issues of normalcy, and can even be juxtaposed as in fundamental conflict, they can also be viewed as complementary perspectives allowing a more complete appreciation of the role of the social world in understanding mental disorders.

Social Epidemiological Perspective

The focus of the social epidemiological perspective is on how social factors cause mental disorders. Of central concern are the detection and measurement of the boundaries between the normal and the abnormal and between the different types of abnormal. The construct of mental illness is usually conceptualized as the province of other disciplines, such as psychology or psychiatry, and their definitions are accepted. However, the application of the nomenclature of these disciplines to epidemiological research necessitated considerable reevaluation, adjustment, and alteration. For example, in moving from studies of clinical populations, the province of psychiatrists, to community populations, the province of epidemiology, the nomenclature had to be expanded (Committee on Nomenclature and Statistics 1952). Additionally, methods of case identification and measurement in the community had to be devised. Indeed, the measurement issues are so central that Dohrenwend (1983) delineated three generations of psychiatric epidemiological studies on this basis.

In the first generation of studies, those conducted before World War II, key informants and agency records supplied the information necessary to identify cases (Dohrenwend and Dohrenwend 1974*a*). Such procedures are, of course, likely to underestimate untreated cases of disorders that are characterized mainly by subjective distress. In contrast, the second-generation studies relied on direct interviews usually without supplementation by data from key informants and official records. These studies utilized three basic types of interviews: (1) a single psychiatrist or a small team headed by a psychiatrist personally interviewed community residents and recorded diagnostic judgments on the basis of these interviews without explicit procedures (see, for example, Hagnell 1966; Kato 1969; Lin 1953); (2) standard and explicit data-collection procedures were used where identification depended on psychiatrists' evaluations of protocols compiled from the interview responses (see, for example, Leighton et al. 1963; Srole et al. 1962); or (3) respondents were presented with a standardized set of questions that have fixed alternative response categories with preassigned weights associated with them (see, for example, Meile 1972; Phillips 1966). This methodology was much more likely to include cases of distress. The third generation of studies have just begun to appear with data based on DSM-III criteria.

Differences in nomenclature and method of case identification has become a critical issue. For example, the median rate for all types of disorders in the first-generation interview studies was 3.6 percent, compared to a median of close to 20 percent in second-generation interview studies conducted after World War II. The difference dramatically illustrates the effect of the change in nomenclatures following World War II on the rates of mental disorders counted in communities.

Even among the second-generation studies, the different types of case identification methods have led to great variations in the prevalence they report, with some studies finding overall rates of 50 percent and more while others report rates of under 1 percent (Dohrenwend and Dohrenwend 1974*a*). These problems have led to new methodologies in the third-generation studies.

Nevertheless, most investigators present their findings in terms of similar broad nosological distinctions. Thus many provide data on at least some of the following major types of mental disorders: schizophrenia involving behaviors that come closest to the layperson's stereotype of what is insane or crazy; affective psychoses including unipolar and bipolar or manic-depressive psychosis; neuroses, whose hallmark is extreme anxiety and the panic, rituals, and phobias that can accompany it; and personality disorders, especially those that manifest themselves in antisocial behavior and that include problems in the abuse of alcohol and drugs. Moreover, there appears to be considerable agreement among the epidemiological investigators as to the nature of these vividly contrasting symptom complexes or syndromes despite sharp differences in where the investigators draw the boundaries among the different types and between all types and "normality." The reason for inferring such agreement is that, despite the differences in concepts and methods, there are, as we will see, strong consistencies from study to study in relationships between various types of mental disorder and such variables as gender and social class (Dohrenwend and Dohrenwend 1974*a,* 1974*b*). The social epidemiological approach to mental disorders is to examine these consistent associations, explain why they occur, and analyze the implications that can be derived from them for the role of social factors in the development and course of mental disorders.

We begin our exposition of this approach by briefly recounting the results of the epidemiological studies. In doing so we draw on a review of these studies by Link and associates (in press) and report their summary of some of the main findings. Their report updates a series of reviews by the Dohrenwends (Dohrenwend 1983; Dohrenwend and Dohrenwend 1969, 1974*a,* 1974*b,* 1976, 1981). Following this review of basic findings we illustrate how those working in social epidemiology approach these issues in their research. Finally we end with a conclusion about the success of this approach in terms of elucidating the causes of major mental disorders.

The True Prevalence Studies

The epidemiological studies of mental disorders that we review concern prevalence rates for adults in community populations. These rates usually refer to the presence of disorders regardless of their time of onset and duration. Additionally they refer to current cases of disorder whether or not the individuals involved have been in treatment with members of the mental health professions. It is for this reason that they have come to be known as "true prevalence" studies as opposed to studies of treated prevalence.

There are sixteen first-generation studies, more than sixty second-generation studies (Dohrenwend and Dohrenwend 1974*a,* p. 425; Dohrenwend et al. 1980). The third-generation studies now available come in the form of a descriptive epidemiology of major disorders with diagnoses made via DSM-III criteria in what are called the Epidemiological Catchment Area (ECA) studies (Myers et al. 1984; Robins et al. 1984). There are surprising consistencies in the distribution of the mental disorders in these studies according to such important social characteristics as gender and social class. Most consistencies are evident in the relatively low-rate, narrow-definition first-generation studies, the relatively high-rate, more inclusive second-generation studies (Dohrenwend and Dohrenwend 1969, 1974*a,* 1974*b,* 1976, 1981), and the first reports of the third-generation ECA studies. In what follows we review these consistent relationships by drawing on three main sources: the Dohrenwend and Dohrenwend review (1974*a*) of first- and second-generation true prevalence studies, the Neugebauer, Dohrenwend, and Dohrenwend (1980) review of studies conducted from 1950 to the late 1970s in the United States and Western Europe, and the published results of the ECA studies (Myers et al. 1984; Robins et al. 1984).

SOCIAL CLASS/SOCIOECONOMIC STATUS

The association of mental disorders with social class has proved remarkably persistent in the true prevalence studies conducted since the turn of the century and holds for most of the important subtypes of mental disorder. The findings to date as summarized by Link and Dohrenwend (with some minor revisions) are as follows:

> The highest overall rates of mental disorder were in the lowest social class in twenty-eight out of the thirty-three studies. This relationship was strongest in the studies conducted in urban settings or mixed urban and rural settings (nineteen out of twenty studies, Dohrenwend and Dohrenwend 1974*a*).
>
> When attention is restricted to studies conducted in the United States and northern Europe since 1950, Neugebauer, Dohrenwend, and Dohrenwend's (1980) review shows seventeen of twenty studies with a higher rate in the lowest as opposed to the highest class. The average low- to high-class ratio across these studies is 2.59. The ECA study found consistently higher lifetime prevalence rates of all disorders combined among those with less than a college education than among college graduates (the breakdown used in published accounts to date). This finding held across all three reporting sites (Baltimore, New Haven, St. Louis) (Robins et al. 1984). The published report of six-month prevalence did not report rates by a social class indicator (Myers et al. 1984).

The inverse relationship with class was consistent for schizophrenia (five out of seven studies) in the Dohrenwend and Dohrenwend review (1974*a*). Further support for this finding is present in Eaton's (1985) review of incidence studies (fifteen out of seventeen studies showed higher incidence rates in the lowest social class). Moreover, the lifetime prevalence figures reported by the ECA study show that schizophrenia and schizophrenoform disorders are from two to five times more prevalent among noncollege graduates as opposed to graduates.

The inverse class relationship holds as well for personality disorders characterized mainly by antisocial behavior and substance abuse (eleven out of fourteen studies, Dohrenwend and Dohrenwend 1974*a*); five out of six, Neugebauer, Dohrenwend, and Dohrenwend 1980). The ECA reports consistently higher lifetime prevalence rates for lower-status persons across diagnoses of antisocial personality, alcohol abuse/dependence, and drug abuse dependence (eight out of nine comparisons). The only exception is for drug abuse/dependence in the Baltimore site.

Two studies that provide relevant data (Brown and Harris 1978; Weissman and Myers 1978) indicate that the current prevalence of major depression as defined by Feighner criteria (Feighner et al. 1972) and Research Diagnostic Criteria (Spitzer, Endicott, and Robins 1978) is inversely related to social class, though perhaps only for women, who show higher rates of depression than males (Weissman and Klerman 1977). In addition Dohrenwend and colleagues' (in press) recent study in Israel shows the same inverse relationship for major depression as the previously mentioned studies. Note that these studies use criteria for affective disorder that are similar to those contained in the DSM-III.

Finally, rates of the severe, nonspecific psychological distress or demoralization are consistently highest in the lowest social class as measured by screening scales such as the Langner twenty-two-item index (eight out of eight studies, Link and Dohrenwend 1980).

In summary, then, all of the major types of functional mental disorders and nonspecific psychological distress that have been investigated in epidemiological field studies, possibly excepting bipolar affective disorder (but not unipolar affective disorder or major depression), appear to show an inverse relationship with social class in either males or females or in both sexes.

GENDER

Most true prevalence studies provided data on mental disorders according to gender, though often not for the various types of disorder. The findings can be summarized as follows:

There are no consistent gender differences in rates of functional psychoses in general (thirty-four studies, Dohrenwend and Dohrenwend 1974*a*; nineteen studies, Neugebauer, Dohrenwend, and Dohrenwend 1980) or in relation to one of the two major subtypes, schizophrenia (twenty-six studies, Dohrenwend and Dohrenwend 1974*a*; eleven studies, Neugebauer, Dohrenwend, and Dohrenwend 1980). Here the ECA departs from the pattern. Each ECA site found females to have higher lifetime rates of schizophrenia/schizophrenoform disorder (Robins et al. 1984), and two of three show the same result for six-month prevalence (Myers et al. 1984). Rates of the other main subtype, manic-depressive psychosis (as defined prior to DSM-III), are generally higher among women (eighteen out of twenty-four studies, Dohrenwend and Dohrenwend 1974*a*). Neugebauer, Dohrenwend, and Dohrenwend's (1980) review of post–World War II studies reported rates of affective psychosis and found women to have higher rates in six, men in two, and no difference in three. The average female-to-male ratio was 2.96 in this category. The ECA shows no clear pattern for the DSM-III diagnosis of a manic episode, which resembles but is by no means the same as the pre–DSM-III manic depressive disorder (Myers et al. 1984; Robins et al. 1984).

Rates of neurosis are consistently higher for women regardless of time or place (twenty-eight out of thirty-two studies, Dohrenwend and Dohrenwend 1974*a*). The Neugebauer, Dohrenwend, and Dohrenwend review (1980) of recent U.S. and Northern European studies found the relationship to hold for all eighteen studies, with an average female to male ratio of 2.86. The ECA studies used more recent DSM-III classification, which does not make the neurotic psychotic distinction. However, for such disorders as dysthymia, panic, obsessive compulsive, social phobia, simple phobia, and agoraphobia, women had consistently higher rates across all sites for both six-month and lifetime diagnoses.

ECA rates of Major Depression deserve separate mention since they may have been diagnosed as either psychotic or neurotic depression in the pre–DSM-III era. Women were more likely than men to have this disorder across all three sites and for both lifetime and six-month prevalence.

By contrast, rates of personality disorder are consistently higher for men regardless of time or place (twenty-two out of twenty-six studies, Dohrenwend and Dohrenwend 1974*a*; ten out of fourteen, Neugebauer, Dohrenwend, and Dohrenwend 1980). Neugebauer, Dohrenwend, and Dohrenwend report a female-to-male ratio of 0.66 for this category. The ECA studies are entirely consistent with these earlier studies in showing that men predominate at each site in both lifetime and six-month prevalence for drug abuse/dependence, alcohol abuse/dependence, and antisocial personality.

Rates of nonspecific distress or demoralization were higher in women in seven out of seven studies reviewed by Link and Dohrenwend (1980).

The gender ratio therefore appears to vary based on the type of disorder under investigation. The clearest results are found for demoralization and depression, where women predominate, and antisocial personality disorder and substance abuse, where males are in the majority.

Examples of Useful Strategies for Investigating the Role of Social Factors in Etiology

The consistent findings from the true prevalence studies on social class and gender, coupled with the fact that social scientists have documented vast differences in the social experiences of people differentially located according to these variables, suggest the importance and the possible yield of studies that try to explain these findings. Still, these studies do little more than allow the possibility of an effect of social position on mental disorder. Equally compatible with the facts on social class and mental disorder are explanations that claim the relationship arises because those persons who develop such disorders do not fare well in the attainment of social positions that confer high status. This "social selection" position contrasts with a "social causation" perspective, which attributes the social class association to socioenvironmental exposures that are more prevalent in lower-class environments. Similarly, the descriptive epidemiology according to gender can be attributed either to biological differences between the sexes or to differences in gender roles. Because of these ambiguities, investigators using the social epidemiology approach have gravitated toward two strategies that allow the unraveling of these controversies.

STUDIES SEEKING STRATEGIC CONTRASTS

The first kind of study is one which locates strategic circumstances that allow a relatively clear-cut interpretation with respect to the importance of social factors as potential causes. Some recent examples illustrate the type of study we have in mind.

In order to study the impact of different cultural situations on the patterning of psychopathology in women, Schwartz (1985) studied married women in the right as opposed to the left wing of the orthodox Jewish community. The design held many factors constant (for example, sex, work status, immigration status) but built in a sharp contrast in the adherence to culturally prescribed feminine sex roles. The right wing strictly adhered to traditional feminine sex roles explicitly codified in writing. The left wing, while accepting the same rules, allowed far more adaptation to newer secular values emphasizing the equality of women. As she expected, Schwartz found depression considerably more prevalent among the right-wing women she studied. Antisocial or acting-out behavior was not extensive in either group, but left-wing women were much more likely to have engaged in drug and alcohol use than those from the right wing. The key to the significance of this study lies in its location of a culturally determined variation on sex-role expectations among otherwise quite similar women. This fact renders the results more interpretable concerning the impact of social factors on psychopathology.

Kessler, House, and Turner (1987) conducted a second study exemplifying this approach. They wished to determine the impact of unemployment on mental health but recognized that impaired persons might become unemployed partly because of their psychological difficulties. As a result they included in their study of unemployed Michigan workers a series of questions investigating the circumstances that led to the unemployment. They were able to distinguish between persons who may have played a part in bringing on their unemployment and those who were victimized by such factors as plant closings. Those effects found among the "victimized" group were due to social experiences associated with unemployment, the researchers felt. That unemployment that was the result of circumstances beyond an individual's control can cause psychopathology and that unemployment is more prevalent among lower-class workers strongly suggests that at least part of the social class/psychopathology association is due to social causation.

STUDIES SEEKING TO IDENTIFY MECHANISMS

A second kind of study that can help elucidate the role of social factors in the etiology of mental disorders is the type that proposes to "explain" the social class and gender findings by identifying the intervening variables that account for these associations. These variables can be consistent with either social selection or social causation explanations. Key is the fact that those who would explain class and gender differences without invoking social factors would propose different intervening processes than those who believe these differences reflect social causation. The success or failure of hypotheses about the mechanisms each group identifies will reflect on the plausibility of the more global issues involved. If intervening variables consistent with one explanation are more successful than those associated with the other, we would tend to interpret the observed class and gender associations in terms of that explanation.

Consider by way of illustration a recent research project on the relationship between social class and schizophrenia that attempted to identify a mechanism consistent with a social causation explanation. Studies of the social mobility of schizophrenic patients show that social selection processes play a role in producing the consistent finding of the highest rate of this disorder in the lowest social class.[2] The studies are convincing in this regard because the occupations of first-admission schizophrenic patients are lower in social standing than one would expect given their class origins. These results leave room for argument, however, as to whether the social selection processes are strong enough to rule out an important role for environmental factors associated with social class.[3] In this regard Link, Dohrenwend, and Skodol (1986) presented evidence that suggested a possible role for class-linked stress despite the clear findings of downward mobility presented in earlier studies. First, they noted that people who develop schizophrenia attain a level of education that is comparable to similar people who do not develop it. This means that the downward mobility occurs between the time a person completes education and the time of the occupation held at first admission—a period of several years for many who develop the disorder. Link, Dohrenwend, and Skodol then examined an important event that occurs during this period, the acquisition of a first full-time occupation held for six months or more. In a study of schizophrenic episode cases and community well controls they found no evidence to suggest that the schizophrenic cases were downwardly mobile into these first jobs. This finding tends to rule out selection explanations that might attribute occupational exposures in these jobs to downward movement in socioeconomic status. Given this, it was of particular interest that they found that schizophrenic cases were more likely than well controls to hold blue-collar jobs that entailed noisome conditions: noise, hazards, extreme heat, extreme cold, fumes, and excessive humidity. Such jobs, it should be noted, indicate exposure to intense stimulation, and research has shown that individuals who develop schizophrenia are susceptible to overstimulation of various kinds (Leff and Vaughn 1985, pp. 195–208). It is possible, therefore, that vulnerable individuals find jobs with noisome features particularly stressful in such a way as to contribute to the onset of the disorder and to a downward trajectory in the occupational sphere.

[2]See Eaton (1980); Eaton and Lasry (1978); Goldberg and Morrison (1963); and Turner (1968).
[3]See Dohrenwend and Dohrenwend (1969, pp. 41–48); Eaton (1980); Kohn (1972); Mechanic (1972); and Turner (1968).

The strategy of investigating explanatory links can be applied to the gender issue as well. Rosenfield (1989), for example, has investigated women's exposure to role-related "demands" and their access to control over these demands in attempting to explain their higher rates of depressive symptoms. Lennon's (1987) recent work provides another example. She notes that powerful sociocultural forces sift and sort men and women into very different occupations. Once located in these occupational destinations, people are exposed to very different daily conditions of work. Lennon asks whether these differing conditions explain why women experience more psychological distress whereas men drink alcohol excessively. Tests of social mechanisms can also challenge their plausibility. Thoits (1987) investigated women's exposure and reaction to various types of life events. She found that neither perceptions of control nor exposure to events could explain gender differences in distress. In this case a test of a possible mechanism was not supported; other explanatory mechanisms must be sought. Together tests such as these will reflect on the plausibility of social factors as potential causes of mental disorder.

Evidence on Social Factors in Etiology

Any discussion of the usefulness of the social epidemiology perspective must consider the powerful pendulum swing toward genetic and biological approaches that has occurred over the past two decades. Consider the comments made by Leonard Heston in his award-winning lecture to the prestigious American Psychopathological Association: "the facts make it clear that searches for specific environmental factors external to the body juices are likely to prove dead ends. Such research has been done too long and too intensely with no result." Moreover, the best solution to the failure of the environmental agenda in Heston's view is to achieve a major reorientation, shifting significant "human and material resources in the direction of hard ball biology . . ." (Heston 1988, p. 212). Has the investigation of social factors been such a wrong-headed dead end?

This chapter exposes the reader to a considerable body of research challenging Heston's view. But the case against his view can be made stronger by explicitly considering just two examples of research on the social environment. The first addresses life events and depression, the second family education and schizophrenia. George Brown and colleagues working in England and Bruce Dohrenwend and colleagues working in New York City have been the two main champions of stressful life events as possible environmental risk factors for major mental disorders. In the mid-1970s Rabkin and Struening (1976) reviewed stressful life events research and drew a conclusion that Heston and other skeptics of the social epidemiology approach would find confirming. Associations between life events and health indicators were at best moderate—correlations of 0.3 were among the strongest found. Moreover, the measures of life events, most typically the Holmes and Rahe Social Readjustment Scale, included occurrences that could easily be caused by psychopathology or by personal dispositions that would make one prone to developing psychopathology. Clear causal inferences were not possible even for the modest correlations that were found in this research.

Brown would not be surprised by this "failure"—the measures of life events were so poor that one could hardly expect otherwise. Specifically, Brown noted the following flaws in the Holmes and Rahe life event measure and how it has been used: (1) the vagueness of some items (such as "revision of personal habits;") (2) empirical evidence of low reliability and validity; (3) the insensitivity of the list method's "dictionary" nature, which equates all events that occur within a life event category, such as birth of a child or divorce, irrespective of the context in which they occur; and (4) the practice of adding events that are very different qualitatively (such as divorce and personal injury) into a summative score.

Brown and his colleagues set about developing a new method of assessing stressful life events designed to overcome these drawbacks. In this approach thirty-eight types of events are defined and illustrated with examples. After establishing the occurrence of an event, a respondent is queried about the details of his or her life at the time of the event, thus providing contextual information. Based on this information objective raters determine the likely "threat" that the event poses. The resulting measure is called "contextual threat."

Dohrenwend and associates recognized the vast improvement that Brown's approach represented in its ability to capture variability within event categories. However, they took issue with his method because "contextual threat" incorporates many socioenvironmental factors (for example, the availability of social support, housing conditions) in ratings of how much "threat" an event posed. How was one to know whether life events per se or other contextual factors were responsible for an association with depression? As a result this group developed a method of rating life events that kept events and other socioenvironmental factors as separate as possible. Moreover, they paid close attention to the possibility that events might be caused by psychopathology or by dispositions thereto. They developed a list of twelve event categories that were rated as fateful—that is, outside of the individual's ability to influence their occurrence—and as involving loss (for example, death of a loved one, laid off). Moreover, descriptions of these "fateful loss" events were rated; any that were likely to have been under the individual's control—for example, a report of being "laid off" that was a euphemism for being fired—were removed from measure.

Clearly Brown's "contextual threat" and Dohrenwend's "fateful loss" measures have different theoretical underpinnings and consequently different operationalizations. In addition their studies used different diagnostic criteria and different ways of sampling cases. These facts make their reports of strong associations between life events and depression all the more striking. For example, Brown and Harris (1978, p. 177) find that the odds of developing depression are over twelve times greater for those exposed to an event involving contextual threat than for those unexposed. Dohrenwend and associates' more constricted yet more interpretable measure yields, as expected, a smaller odds ratio. In their study those exposed to fateful loss have nearly three times greater odds of developing depression as someone without such an event (Shrout et al. 1987).

Given the strength of these associations, their location in a network of theoretical propositions (see especially Brown and Harris 1978), and the considerable care that was taken to rule out alternative explanations (see especially Dohrenwend et al. 1987; Shrout et al. 1987), a strong environmental contribution to this disorder is suggested.

A second successful area of investigation concerns the program of research on "expressed emotion" and psychoeducational family interventions. This research started with a broad epidemiological finding about the nature of the "living arrangement" schizophrenic patients experience when discharged from a hospital (Brown 1959; Brown, Carstairs, and Topping 1958). Patients who returned to parents or wives did not fare as well as those who returned to lodgings or to brothers and sisters. Brown and his colleagues set upon a course of studies to determine why this might be so. As a result of careful observation of families, they developed the notion of "expressed emotion" and developed ratings for it (Brown, Birley, and Wing 1972). Subsequent studies isolated the two most important aspects of expressed emotion, criticism and overinvolvement, and showed that schizophrenic cases who returned to families rated high on these measures were far more likely to relapse than those who returned to families low on these dimensions (Leff and Vaughn 1985). Finally, as a consequence of these intriguing results, intervention programs were developed that sought to modify the family context through education and support. Experiments evaluating these interventions have shown remarkable success in reducing the probability of relapse in schizophrenia (Falloon et al. 1982; Leff et al. 1982). Compared to an expected relapse rate of

40 to 45 percent for patients receiving standard treatment (including drugs), these studies show rates of 0 to 20 percent over nine months to one year with various psychoeducation and family intervention (as reported in Anderson, Reiss, and Hogarty 1986). While there is controversy about the "expressed emotion" concept and about just what it is about the social interventions that is effective, these studies indicate that purely social interventions can make a substantial difference in relapse rates of people diagnosed with schizophrenia.

Let us return now to Heston's dismissal of the social epidemiology approach. Certainly his remarks reflect the fact that the pendulum has swung in recent years toward genetic and biological factors. But has the force behind the pendulum swing been what he supposes it to be—the failure of environmentally oriented research? Even if we only consider the two examples just discussed the answer must be an emphatic no. The progression in life events research from the dismal picture in the mid-1970s (Rabkin and Struening 1976) to the much stronger outlook one can derive from the progression represented by Brown's and Dohrenwend's work groups in the late 1980s is too dramatic to evoke "dead-end" imagery. The research on family education and support has shown similar progress. Indeed, if we had the will to implement it broadly, this type of social intervention could dramatically reduce the burden of schizophrenia. The pendulum has swung, and may yet swing farther, but whatever the source of its movement, one would be hard-pressed to claim that the cause rested with stagnation in, or the failure of, environmentally oriented research.

The Societal Reaction Perspective

Theoretical Formulation

The labeling perspective contrasts sharply with the social epidemiological perspective just described. While the epidemiological perspective examines the social causes of mental illness, the labeling perspective examines its social construction. Whereas the social epidemiologists are concerned with the detection and measurement of the boundaries between the normal and the abnormal, the labeling perspective is concerned with how these boundaries are devised.

We discuss this perspective's theoretical formulation of deviant behavior in general and its application to mental disorder in particular. As we will see, this perspective is controversial and has stimulated considerable debate. As a result, we review this debate and consider its implications for the sociological understanding of deviant behavior.

The labeling perspective is grounded on the premise that there is no act which is universally defined as deviant under all circumstances. What constitutes a deviant act, what makes it deviant, is that it breaks certain rules about how people should behave or be in a particular society and in a particular context. As Kai Erikson (1966) notes:

> Deviance is not a property inherent in certain forms of behavior; it is a property conferred upon these forms by audiences which directly or indirectly observe them. Sociologically, then, the critical variable in the study of deviance is the social audience which eventually decides whether or not any given action or actions will become a visible case of deviance. (P. 6)

The social audience is critical not only in determining what constitutes a deviant act but also in determining who of those who commit such acts come to be labeled deviant. Rule-breaking behavior is common and usually transient. Persons may break rules for a variety of reasons, without significant consequence. This initial rule breaking is not of central interest to labeling theorists. However, such rule-breaking behavior becomes significant when it is accompanied by labeling—when the rule breaker is noticed and his or her identity is redefined in terms of this deviant act. The application of this label, particularly when it is applied by official labelers, such as police and psychiatrists, has significant consequences leading to a reformulation of society's definition of the rule breaker and the actor's own redefinition of him - herself. Deviant behaviors and social roles based on them resulting from responses to this label constitute what Edwin Lemert (1951) called "secondary deviance."

The application of the deviant label is powerful because deviance can become a "master status." For example, a fence who is labeled "a criminal" is not simply viewed as having a particular illegal occupation, rather he or she is set aside as a different type of person. The label "criminal" leads to assumptions about the actor's roles in all other areas of life (Becker 1963).

Thomas Scheff (1966) has applied this societal reaction approach to mental disorders most comprehensively. He raises the problematic issue of precisely what norms are being broken when the label "mental illness" is applied. Many specific rules exist that, when broken, have explicit corresponding social sanctions. For example, burglary, prostitution, and treason involve specific kinds of rule breaking and have specific sanctions codified in law. Mental illness labeling does not fall in this category. There are no clearly defined codified rules the trespass of which constitute mental illness. Rather, Scheff argues, mental illness is applied when residual rules, rules left over when the explicit categories of regulations are exhausted, are broken. These residual rules are the innumerable norms where consensus is so complete that members of the group take them for granted. Psychotic behaviors, such as talking to invisible creatures or claiming that one is Napoleon, are examples. Because the breaking of these rules is unthinkable, no explicit way of handling violation of expectations in these areas is formulated. A person who regularly violated these expectations would be thought strange, bizarre, and frightening because such behaviors violate the assumptive world of the group, the world that is to be construed to be the only one that is natural, decent, and possible.

Violation of these norms, acts of primary deviance, are extremely common, arise from diverse sources, and are not of central interest to Scheff's formulation. What is of interest is the secondary deviance in response to the label of mental illness. In particular, the two central issues for labeling theorists in studying mental disorders are: (1) How does public recognition and labeling lead to stabilized mental illness? and (2) If only a small proportion of persons who commit acts of residual deviance are labeled, what determines who is and who isn't so designated? Each of these issues will be dealt with in turn.

THE LABELING PROCESS

According to Scheff's formulation, the most important consequence of labeling someone "mentally ill" is the stabilization of residual deviance and the adoption of the role of a mentally ill person. Scheff hypothesized that the process begins with the stereotyped image of mental disorder learned in childhood and continuously reinforced in everyday interaction. When the label of mental illness is applied, this image becomes activated and has new salience for the deviant. As Scheff describes it:

> In a crisis, when the deviance of an individual becomes a public issue, the traditional stereotype of insanity becomes the guiding imagery for action, both for those reacting to the deviant and at times the deviant himself. When societal agents and people around the deviant react to him uniformly in terms of the traditional stereotypes of insanity, his amorphous and unstructured rule breaking tends to crystallize in conformity to those expectations, thus becoming similar to the behavior of other deviants classified as mentally ill, and stable over time. The process of becoming uniform and stable is completed when the traditional imag-

> ery becomes a part of the deviant's orientation for guiding his own behavior. (1966, p. 82)

However, as this label entails devaluation and the acquisition of a denigrated status, the process through which the label is accepted must be explained. First, as Scheff notes, when a deviant act becomes a public issue, confusion, anxiety, and embarrassment ensue for both the deviant and the audience. There is a state of crisis in which the players are vulnerable to cues regarding how to act in this incomprehensible situation. The stereotyped image of mental illness provides a shared basis for understanding and action. The deviant is sensitive to these cues and begins to act in accordance with them.

Once this process begins, there are impediments to returning to one's original identity. When the label is applied, the actor is set aside as a different type of person and, especially if hospitalized, cut off from all other roles and usual social interactions. Reentry to these roles is difficult. The ex-mental patient faces social stigma, discrimination, and wariness on the part of others. The label "mental illness" becomes a master status, and all the actor's current behaviors and expectations for future behaviors are redefined in terms of the stereotyped meaning of this role. Employment and social opportunities may be limited by fears that although the "mental disorder" is dormant at the moment, it may reappear at any time. This inhibits the ability to shed the mental illness label.

Further impetus to continue in this role is provided by the rewards that those who are publicly labeled may receive for continuing in the stereotyped deviant role. For example, patients who act in conformity with physicians' and staff's expectations, who display "insight" by "recognizing" symptoms and evidence of their "mental disorder," are given emotional rewards and, in a hospital system, concrete benefits. These rewards may be particularly important when other means of gratification are closed off by the stigma of the mental illness label.

DETERMINANTS OF HOW AND WHEN RESIDUAL DEVIANCE IS LABELED

According to the societal reaction perspective, acts of residual deviance become publicly recognized only under certain circumstances. Scheff (1966) organized the contingencies determining labeling into three categories: those involved in the nature of the norm-breaking behavior, the characteristics of the deviant, and the characteristics of the community.

> Other things being equal, the severity of the societal reaction to deviance is a function of first, the degree, amount and visibility of the deviant

behavior, second, the power of the deviant and the social distance between the deviant and the agents of social control, and finally, the tolerance level of the community and the availability in the culture of the community of alternative nondeviant roles." (P. 62)

Thus social factors heavily influence who, among the many who commit primary deviance, will be labeled mentally ill.

Evidence Regarding the Main Tenets of Labeling Perspective

During the 1960s the labeling perspective was the predominant sociological approach to the analysis of deviant behaviors. By the 1970s, however, this perspective came under attack. The argument revolves around determining which elements are central to defining behaviors as mental illness. Walter Gove (1970, 1975, 1980, 1982), Scheff's most persistent critic, argues that the focus should be on the deviant and his or her actions. He suggests that the crucial element in determining the persistence of mental disorder is the pathogenesis of the disease, not societal response. Striking at the essential premise of the labeling perspective, he contends that the mentally ill are not significantly stigmatized and to whatever extent they do experience rejection, it is caused by their disturbed behaviors, not their stigmatized status. The evidence regarding these two tenets of the labeling perspective, the consequences of labeling for secondary deviance and the determinants of labeling, are examined below. In reviewing this evidence in the next two sections, we draw on an earlier paper by Link and Cullen (1990).

EVIDENCE ABOUT THE LABELING PROCESS

The hypothesized process through which labeling leads to secondary deviance is built on three basic elements: mental illness is a stigmatized role, barriers exist to the resumption of normal roles once labeling occurs, and there is positive reinforcement for maintaining the role of being mentally ill once the label is applied. Each of these elements is examined in turn.

Is mental illness stigmatized? Critics of the labeling perspective have argued that the evidence suggests the mentally ill are not stigmatized. For example, according to Crocetti, Spiro, and Siassi (1971), little stigmatization of former mental patients was evident in a sample of automobile factory workers. Most workers expressed willingness to engage in social relations with ex-patients, including work, residential, and romantic relations. Similarly, Weinstein's (1979, 1983) review of the literature suggests that patients themselves do not feel uniformly stigmatized. Additionally, after concluding that stigma or negative attitudes toward the mentally ill is rare, critics of the labeling perspective argue that to whatever extent the patients do experience rejection, it derives from their behaviors, not the label.[4] A seemingly convincing approach along these lines has involved asking respondents to react to vignettes in which the conditions of "labeling" (former patient) and behavior (normal versus deviant) have been experimentally manipulated. In twelve of the fifteen studies we were able to locate, behavior was found to be a more potent determinant of people's reactions than labeling (see Link et al. 1987).

These findings have led critics to reject labeling theory notions concerning the negative consequences of labels. Gove (1982), for example, claims that "most mental patients experience some stigma, however, in the vast majority of cases the stigma appears to be transitory and does not appear to pose a severe problem" (p. 280). Crocetti and associates (1974) add that former patients "enjoy nearly total acceptance in all but the most intimate relationships" (1974, p. 88).

However, this interpretation of the evidence is not unchallenged.[5] With respect to Crocetti, Spiro, and Siassi's claim that attitudes are benign, Link and Cullen (1983) have questioned the notion that respondent reports can be taken at face value as indicators of the rejection patients encounter. Their study randomly assigned respondents to different ways of asking social distance questions about a person described in a vignette. Some were asked whether they thought an "ideal person" would allow contact with a former patient, whereas others were asked whether they themselves would allow such contact; still others were asked whether most people would. The results showed that when a vignette was "labeled" by including a reference to a history of hospitalization, the "ideal person" way of asking questions produced the most acceptance, followed by the "self" mode, with the "most people" way of asking questions producing the most rejecting responses. When the vignette was unlabeled, the "self" mode was the most rejecting. This evidence suggests that people respond in a socially desirable way when reporting their own attitudes about a group they have learned they "should" accept—the mentally ill. Such findings call into question conclusions about favorable attitudes based on the frequency of accepting responses to straightforward social distance items.

The second argument, that behavior not labeling causes rejection, has

[4]See Clausen (1981); Huffine and Clausen (1979); Kirk (1974); Lehman et al. (1976); and Schwartz, Myers, and Astrachan (1974).

[5]See Link (1982, 1987); Link and Cullen (1983); Link et al. (1987); Link et al. (1989); Nieradzik and Cochrane (1985); Palamara, Cullen, and Gersten (1986); Sibicky and Dovidio (1986).

also been challenged (Link et al. 1987; Page 1977; Sibicky and Dovidio 1986). In a review of vignette experiments on the effects of labeling, Link and associates (1987) noted that none of the studies made an attempt to assess what the label "former mental patient" meant to respondents. As a result, they conducted a study incorporating a measure of the extent to which people believe that mental patients are dangerous. The experiment varied labeling (past mental hospitalization) and objectionable behavior. A social distance measure was used as an outcome measure.

The researchers found that when the vignette described a subject who was unlabeled, beliefs about the dangerousness of the mentally ill played no part in determining social distancing responses to subject; when the vignette described a labeled subject, however, these beliefs became a potent determinant of responses. This pattern of results held regardless of the degree of objectionable behavior. In fact, Link and associates were able to show that labeling-activated beliefs about dangerousness were just as strong predictors of social distance responses as variations in behavior. Apparently a label activates beliefs about the dangerousness of mental patients, making such beliefs important for determining how much social distance a person desires from a "former mental patient."

Are there barriers to the resumption of normal roles once the label of mental illness has been applied? Estroff (1981) supplies evidence that even the meager economic benefits that patient status confers can trap patients in the mental patient role. For example, rather than easing patients' entry or reentry into conventional roles, programs such as Supplemental Social Security (SSI) cut them off from conventional society. They are marked by their use of SSI in such a way as to immediately identify them to employers as "undesirable workers." Moreover, reliance on SSI precludes patients from the social connections that employment can bring. And because SSI payments carry a social stigma, these payments make patients different in still another way, leading to further strain in interactions with others.

Link (1982) also supplies evidence that labeling can impede the resumption of nonpatient roles. He used a true prevalence study of mental disorder to define two groups: officially labeled cases and unlabeled cases that, on examination by a psychiatrist, were determined to be as impaired as the labeled cases. Holding constant the degree of psychiatric impairment, he showed that labeled cases had less income and were less likely to be fully employed than unlabeled cases.

This evidence for the negative consequences of labeling and treatment are consistent with, although not proof of, the theorized effects of labeling on secondary deviance. The effects of stigma on employment and social interactions surely make the adoption of normative adult roles difficult to achieve. However, this evidence for the continuation of the mentally ill role due to these difficulties is indirect.

Is there positive reinforcement for maintaining the role of mental illness? According to one of the core principles of social psychiatry, remaining in the mental patient role can involve "secondary gain" or unintended "benefits." This notion of secondary gain is implicit in Rosenblatt and Mayer's (1974) explanation for the tendency of some patients to be readmitted to the hospital time and again. They observe:

> Modern-day hospitals offer a wide range of amenities: palatable food; pleasant living quarters and surroundings; sports, recreation and entertainment; opportunities to interact and socialize with members of the hospital community; freedom from community violence; and so forth. For many patients, the hospital, when compared to their home environment, holds greater promise of fulfilling their needs. This becomes readily understandable when one considers that many mental patients, especially those in the state institutions, live in squalid ghettos with all the attendant deprivations. (P. 704)

Here the benefits of the hospital can be seen as generating a dependence on the institution and a concomitant investment in remaining a mental patient.

In a less direct way, Robbins and Greenly (1983) suggest that labeling in the form of treatment may provide reinforcement for a cognitive representation of experiences that make future problems more likely. They found that those with a previous history of seeking treatment were far more likely to seek treatment for an emotional problem than those without such a history. Moreover, previous treatment seekers were more likely to accept responsibility for their problems and expect them to last longer. Thus treatment, and the concomitant desire to please the providers of this treatment, may become training in the identification of problems as symptoms of mental disorders.

EVIDENCE REGARDING WHO GETS LABELED

Does the evidence support Scheff's basic hypotheses regarding who gets labeled?

Do a significant proportion of residual rule breakers go unlabeled? In a review of eleven true prevalence studies, Link and Dohrenwend (1980) found the median proportion of "true" cases ever in treatment to be 26.7 percent when all types of psychopathology were considered. For the seven studies that reported results for psychotic disorders, the median proportion in treatment was 59.7 percent; across six studies, the proportion for schizophrenia was 83.3 percent. The ECA study reporting figures on recent treatment (past six months) as opposed to lifetime treatment also found large proportions of "true" cases were not receiving treatment (Shapiro et al. 1984). There is no diagnostic category for which a majority has seen a mental health professional in the last six months. Schizophrenia, the most severe diagnosis, has the highest proportion currently in treatment, but still the highest figure across the three sites reaches only 48.1 percent (Shapiro et al. 1984).

This evidence supports Gove's notions about deviant behavior leading to labeling in that the severity of symptoms seems to be related to the probability of labeling, with schizophrenia having a higher treatment rate than less severe disorders. However, it is also clear that all those with the most severe symptomatology are treated. This allows for the effects of actor and community characteristics on labeling. Of course a large number of untreated cases could be explained by factors that have little to do with societal response hypotheses. Barriers to treatment such as distance to a treatment facility (Jarvis 1966), language differences, inconvenient hours, lack of financial resources, requirements of caring for children, and so forth could all play a part. It should also be noted that this evidence relates only to those who are formally labeled. It does not supply evidence about informal labeling in family, work, or community groups. Nor do such studies give evidence about the fate of people with one-time residual rule breaking that goes unlabeled—they are not counted as true prevalence cases unless they happen to have symptoms within the time frame the study considers. Still, evidence showing large proportions of untreated and unlabeled cases highlights a basic proposition of labeling theory—that much residual deviance goes unlabeled. And while labeling theory processes may not be the only possible explanations, they are certainly consistent with these facts and thus viable until disproven by more focused inquiry.

Do the nonsymptom characteristics of the actor affect the likelihood of labeling? In Horwitz's 1982 review of the literature, he maintains that mental illness labeling is more likely among persons who are relationally distant from the rule breaker. Husbands (Sampson, Messinger, and Towne 1964) and wives (Yarrow et al. 1955) are often reluctant to label their spouse mentally ill and delay doing so even in the face of severely disturbed behavior (see also Perrucci and Targ 1982). Friends and employers are somewhat more likely to label than spouses, as evidenced by the large role such persons often play in the labeling process (Horwitz 1977; Kadushin 1969). Finally, while they are less likely to respond to rule breakers (they can often safely ignore them), strangers are perhaps the most likely to label the behavior of others "mental illness." A good example of this is the apparent public perception that most of the homeless are deinstitutionalized mental patients when the facts suggest otherwise (Snow et al. 1986).

There is also some evidence that social class status may affect labeling. Horwitz indicates that higher social class persons are more likely to label themselves and others than lower-class persons. Epidemiological studies of the true prevalence of psychiatric disorder support his assertion. The classic Midtown Manhattan study, for example, showed that 52 percent of the upper class who were designated as impaired by the staff psychiatrists had been in treatment with a mental health professional, whereas only 23 percent of the middle-status and 21 percent of the lower-status impaired respondents had been (Srole et al. 1975). Link and Dohrenwend (1980) show the same result in their review of three other true prevalence studies, noting that the highest proportion of true cases in treatment is always in the highest social class while the lowest rate is always in the lowest social class. Of course, these results can also be explained by the fact that higher-status persons are more able to afford treatment and that identification or labeling of mental illness is just as common in the lower classes. As Horwitz points out, however, this explanation is not consistent with evidence from vignette studies that ask people whether fictitious cases "have some kind of mental illness" (see also Dohrenwend and Chin-Shong 1967). Higher-status respondents are more likely to indicate that the fictitious cases have a mental disorder. Summarizing this and other research, Horwitz concludes that "an individual's location in social space predicts the probability that he or she will recognize and label mental illness" (p. 83).

While generally supportive of the labeling orientation in showing the importance of reactor characteristics, findings like those just reported can also be used to challenge certain aspects of labeling theory. In particular, Gove has used evidence of spouses' reluctance to label their partners to counteract assertions that labels are applied capriciously and without evidence of symtomatology. Strong statements by Scheff (1966, p. 129) that mental patient status is determined more by factors external to the individual than by psychiatric condition—mental illness is an "ascribed" rather than an "achieved" status—are called into question. At the same time, however, the reluctance of the family to label could be indicative of a strong fear that negative societal reaction will follow an admission that a family member is mentally ill, an interpretation consistent with other aspects of the labeling orientation.

The findings concerning social class and labeling also seem to contradict some of Scheff's specific predictions. In particular he suggests that less powerful individuals are more likely to be labeled (Scheff 1966, p. 100), and yet the results show that higher-status persons—those with more resources and presumably more power—are labeled more frequently. In its crudest form, these results challenge the attempt to attribute labeling to a lack of power. However, Scheff also contended that the community's tolerance for this type of deviant behavior may influence who gets labeled. If higher-status people are more likely to label themselves and others, this may be due to less tolerance for these types of deviant behaviors, providing support for Scheff's predictions. One as-yet unexplored possibility is that people may tend to label the more or less powerful within the context of each status group. It is clear, however, that power relations alone do not determine who gets labeled mentally ill.

Broadly conceived, then, the evidence concerning public recognition is supportive of the labeling orientation in showing that social factors predict labeling. Characteristics of the actor, the observer, and the nature of the relationship between the two influence the probability of labeling. In terms of more specific predictions, the evidence is less clear and in some cases contradicts some of Scheff's predictions.

Implications of the Labeling Perspective

The unique contribution of the labeling perspective is its emphasis on the role of the social realm in the act of defining mental illness and designating who is labeled "mentally ill." Consequently a concept of the "normal" has fluid boundaries. The standards of what is defined as mental illness are relative because the social context in which a particular behavior occurs affects whether such behavior is judged normal or abnormal, and if abnormal, what type of abnormal (Gallagher 1980). Consider, for example, the recent history of the "diagnosis" of homosexuality in the DSM. Alternatively considered a sin, an inborn disability, or an act of rebellion, homosexuality entered the DSM as a psychiatric disorder, a syndrome signifying a mental illness. Later it was voted out of that category. What changed was not the nature of the behavior but rather public attitudes toward it and the power and visibility of persons behaving this way. The very same behavior went from being a "mental illness" to an alternative life-style for some or sinful behavior for others due to changes in the norms defining proper sexual behavior.

Although some people, such as Thomas Szasz, who are often inappropriately associated with the labeling position would make a clear and definitive distinction between physical and mental disorders in terms of this etiological perspective, most labeling theorists would not make this distinction. In fact, the earliest formulations of the labeling perspective focused on physical conditions, including deafness, blindness, and paralysis. As Lemert (1951) describes it:

> At first thought such things as strength, agility and energy seem to be largely internal limits growing out of age, sex differences and damage to the organism. However, closer inspection reveals that they are originally external limits in the sense that the real debilities are overlaid or obscured by the putative limitations which the culture ascribed to age, sex and physical defect. This is most easily seen in the isolating reactions toward handicapped persons—the deaf, epileptic, crippled, physically ill and speech defectives. [For example] many of the blind are surprised and irritated to find others reacting to them as if they were deaf as well as visually disabled. (P. 14)

This is not to say that there is no internal physical "cause" of blindness or that the blind person's eyes are neurologically and/or physically normal. Rather labeling theory shifts focus and asks what makes a person who cannot see into a "blind person." The significance of blindness from this viewpoint has to do with the role and status of "the blind" that are societally defined and created (Friedson 1968; Scheff 1966). The very same physical condition can cause significant problems for the afflicted person or not, depending on social context, the power of the deviant, community attitudes, availability of services, and so on. An extreme example illustrating this point is the case of a person with a deforming facial scar who has no physical limitations but who is nonetheless assigned the role of the "physically disabled" only through societal reaction and definition. Similarly, whether or not a blind person faces problems in functioning may be more a result of financial and educational limitations than physical limitations. Just think of our notion of mental retardation and its different meaning in a context where society's rewards are based on physical versus intellectual prowess. The labeling perspective therefore would not make a definitive distinction between mental and physical disorders.

This analysis also speaks to a general critique of labeling theory found even in sociological texts on mental disorders. For example, "The central proposition raised by labeling theorists is that mental illness does not exist. Has this been proven? No and it never will be because there are many disorders stemming from biogenic factors or deeply ingrained pathological influences that are very real and far from mythical" (Gallagher 1980, p. 332). Or ". . . labeling theory has difficulty assimilating recent persuasive studies which indicate that a proportion of individuals designated as schizophrenic have a genetically transmitted disposition toward the disorder" (Grusky and Pollner 1981, p. v). In our view, such a critique is based on too expansive an interpretation of labeling theory and perhaps too narrow an interpretation of the meaning of genetic and psychological effects.

First, as is evident in its applicability to physical disorders, labeling theory contends that mental illness is a "myth" only in the sense that it is a social construction. To say this is not to deny that there is a physical "reality" behind that myth but rather that the particular aspects of the physical world that are attended, the boundaries seen between similar physical phenomena, the label given to it, and the rules and regulations defining reaction to it are all social constructions. Labeling theory does not deny the potential physical reality of schizophrenia any more than it does blindness. Rather it denies that the physical "reality" is the whole or even the most significant part of the story. As an example, the thing that has arguably contributed most in terms of "curing" blindness and physical handicap has been the translation of these roles to visually impaired and differentially labeled—that is, changes not in the physical conditions per se but in social definitions and expectations of the roles and statuses adhering to these physical conditions and social responses to them.

Second, regarding the too-narrow definition of genetic effects, we turn to Jencks's (1980, 1987) analysis, which parallels the preceding argument regarding labeling theory and physical disorders. He contends that "since there is no practical method for separating the physical and social effects of genes, heritability estimates include both. This means that heritability estimates set a lower bound on the explanatory power of the environment, not an upper bound. If genetic variation explains 60% of the variation in IQ scores, environmental variation must explain the remaining 40% but it may explain as much as 100%" (1987, p. 37). This is so because the genes may not and indeed are not likely to directly determine IQ scores but rather to influence behavior and appearance to which people in the child's environment—parents and teachers—react. A more concrete example is that of PKU, a genetic disorder that may lead to mental retardation. Genetics determine 100 percent of the variance in PKU. However, the method by which the genes have an effect is by making the body unable to process phenylalanines. By eating a diet with no phenylalanines, mental retardation is avoided. From this perspective, 100 percent of the variance of the disease is environmental, for it is the interaction between the physiological effects of the gene with the environment that produces the disease. Without either element, the disease does not appear. Similarly, one need not deny a genetic component in the development of schizophrenia for labeling theory to be of use. These genes are likely to cause physiological and neurological changes that interact with environmental stimuli and societal response.

The labeling perspective therefore does not necessarily deny genetic, neurological, or psychological causes for mental disorders. However, it contributes to our understanding of the etiology of mental disorders by radically shifting focus to societal reaction as the creator and assignor of the role known as mental illness while leaving unanalysed the internal processes and social effects on them.

Possibilities for Integration

Within the sociological framework, there are two major approaches to explaining mental disorders. While both deal with the social as the level of analysis, they have very different views about what mental illness is. The societal reaction perspective views mental illness as a social role acquired by people who break certain rules of behavior under certain conditions. From the social epidemiological perspective, mental illness is a disorder residing within the individual regardless of society's reactions to it. While a controversy has continued in sociology as to which approach is correct, we feel that an integration of both perspectives provides the best chance for illuminating the role of the social in the etiology and course of "mental disorders." Indeed, each perspective complements the strengths and weaknesses of the other. Using the analogy of blindness presented in the labeling section, the strength of the labeling perspective is to examine the social construction of the role of being a blind person in a particular society. It does not explain the causes of being unable to see. In contrast, the social epidemiological perspective examines the social causes of being unable to see, the social factors that affect internal individual processes. It leaves unexamined the social construction of the blindness role.

Each perspective directs our attention to certain aspects of the situation and away from others. For example, the medical model may make it easier to examine the benefits of drugs and psychotherapy in alleviating people's distress. The labeling perspective, from the questions it makes salient, may make it easier to examine the unintended consequences of treatment that may lead to distress and poor functioning. We agree with Mechanic's (1981) conclusion that the question should be framed in terms of which perspective is more useful for one's purposes. In each case "it is necessary to balance the gains achieved from using such a perspective against its various disadvantages" (p. 32).

An example of the fruitfulness of an integrative approach can be seen in the literature on the influences of social factors in clinicians' assessments. The basic approach in these studies is to define mental illness in terms of the disease model—an entity residing within the individual. But the questions asked derive from the labeling perspective—how characteristics of the actor, other than the symptoms of the disorder, influence how he or she is treated. This line of research has proved useful in indicating that once the actor has passed through the informal labelers to the formal labelers, societal factors matter in determining the type of label and concomitantly the type of treatment received. This literature has documented that higher-status persons receive the preferred treatment over disadvantaged clients even when diagnosis and ability to pay are held constant.[6] The potency of this effect has even been linked to the social class origins of the professional, with those from higher-status origins showing a stronger tendency to deny the favored treatment to the lower-class patients (Kandel 1966). In addition, it has been observed that Schofield's (1964) YAVIS patient—youthful, attractive, verbal, intelligent, and successful—is treated preferentially by professionals (Link and Milcarek 1980; see also Link 1983). Moreover, with respect to especially pejorative types of labeling experiences such as involuntary commitment, a number of studies have suggested that "social resources" are crucial determinants of such untoward exposures. For example, Rushing (1978) showed that holding constant the type of mental disorder and the degree of impairment, more highly educated persons were less likely to be involuntarily committed than less well educated persons. Greenley (1972) investigated the family as a social resource influencing a patient's labeling experience. His study shows that independent of the patient's clinical condition, families exert a strong influence on the length of hospitalization. Similarly in vignette experiments the interaction of the race and sex of the actor with the race and sex of the psychiatrist affected the severity of the diagnosis given (Craig, Goodman, and Haugland 1982; Loring and Powell 1988).

Another example of useful integration of these two perspectives examines labeling effects as social factors influencing symptoms of mental disorders. Link (1987) found that the degree to which a person expects to be rejected for being a mental patient is associated with demoralization, income loss, and unemployment in treated but not untreated cases of major depression and schizophrenialike disorders. Thus labeling-activated expectations of rejection were associated with conditions identified by social epidemiologists as risk factors for psychiatric disorders.

[6]See, for example, Albronda, Dean, and Starkweather (1964); Cole, Branch, and Allison (1962); Gallagher, Levinson, and Erlich (1957); Hollingshead and Redlich (1958); Link and Milcarek (1980); and Myers and Schaffer (1954).

Sociology has explanatory theories of mental disorders that enhance our understanding of their etiology, course, and consequences. These theories not only examine social factors that cause and affect mental disorders but also analyze the effects of our decisions about definition, diagnosis, and focus of attention on the creation of the mental illness role and its unintended consequences. We concur with Eaton (1980) that sociology can contribute most to understanding mental disorders through continuing efforts to clarify their meaning by examining them from many different perspectives.

REFERENCES

Albonda, H. F.; Dean, R. L.; and Starkweather, J. A. 1964. "Social Class and Psychotherapy." *Archives of General Psychiatry* 10:276–283.

American Psychiatric Association. 1980. *Diagnostic and Statistical Manual of Mental Disorders,* 3rd ed. Washington, D. C.:APA.

Anderson, C.; Reiss, D.; and Hogarty, G. 1986. *Schizophrenia and the Family: A Practitioner's Guide to Psychoeducation and Management.* New York: Guilford Press.

Becker, H. 1963. *Outsiders: Studies in the Sociology of Deviance.* Glencoe: Free Press.

Brown, G. 1959. "Experiences of Discharged Chronic Mental Hospital Patients in Various Types of Living Groups." *Millbank Memorial Fund Quarterly* 37:105–131.

Brown, G., and Harris, T. 1978. *Social Origins of Depression.* New York: Free Press.

Brown, G.; Birley, J. L.; and Wing, J. K. 1972. "Influence of Family Life on the Course of Schizophrenic Disorders: A Replication." *British Journal of Psychiatry* 121:241–258.

Brown, G.; Carstairs, G. M.; and Topping, G. 1958. "Post Hospital Adjustment of Chronic Mental Patients." *Lancet* 2:685–689.

Clausen, J. S. 1981. "Stigma and Mental Disorder: Phenomena and Terminology." *Psychiatry* 44:287–296.

Cole, N. J.; Branch, C. H.; and Allison, R. B. 1962. "Some Relationships Between Social Class and the Practice of Dynamic Psychotherapy." *American Journal of Psychiatry* 118:1004–1012.

Committee on Nomenclature and Statistics. 1952. *Diagnostic and Statistical Manual of Mental Disorders.* Washington, D. C.: American Psychiatric Association.

Craig, T.; Goodman, A.; and Haugland, G. 1982. "Impact of DSM III on Clinical Practice. *American Journal of Psychiatry* 139:922–925.

Crocetti, B.; Spiro, H.; and Siassi, I. 1971. "Are the Ranks Closed?: Attitudinal Social Distance and Mental Illness." *American Journal of Psychiatry* 127:1121–1127.

———. 1974. *Contemporary Attitudes Towards Mental Illness.* Pittsburgh: University of Pittsburgh Press.

Dohrenwend, B. P. 1983. "The Epidemiology of Mental Disorder." In *Handbook of Health, Health Care, and the Health Professions,* ed. D. Mechanic, pp. 157–194. New York: Free Press.

Dohrenwend, B. P., and Chin-Shong, E. 1967. "Social Status and Attitudes Towards Psychological Disorder: The Problem of Tolerance of Deviance." *American Sociological Review* 32:417–433.

Dohrenwend, B. P., and Dohrenwend, B. S. 1969. *Social Status and Psychological Disorder: A Causal Inquiry.* New York: John Wiley.

———. 1974*a.* "Social and Cultural Influences on Psychopathology." *Annual Review of Psychology* 25:417–452.

———. 1974*b.* "Psychiatric Disorders in Urban Settings." In *American Handbook of Psychiatry, 2nd ed., vol. 2., Child and Adolescent Psychiatry Sociocultural and Community Psychiatry,* ed. S. Arieti and G. Caplan, pp. 424–447. New York: Basic Books.

———. 1976. "Sex Differences and Psychiatric Disorders." *American Journal of Sociology* 81:1447–1454.

———. 1981. "Socio-environmental Factors, Stress, and Psychopathology—Part I: Quasi-experimental Evidence on the Social Causation-Social Selection Issue Posed by Class Differences." *American Journal of Community Psychology* 9:146–159.

Dohrenwend, B. P.; Dohrenwend, B. S.; Schwartz-Gould, M.; Link, B. G.; Neugebauer, R.; and Wunsch-Hitzig, R. 1980. *Mental Illness in the United States: Epidemiologic Estimates.* New York: Praeger.

Dohrenwend, B. P.; Levav, I.; Shrout, P. E.; Link, B. G.; Skodol, A. E.; and Martin, J. L. 1987. "Life Stress and Psychopathology: Progress on Research Begun with B. S. Dohrenwend." *American Journal of Community Psychology* 15:677–715.

Eaton, W. 1980. "A Formal Theory of Selection for Schizophrenia." *American Journal of Sociology* 86:149–158.

———. 1985. "Epidemiology of Schizophrenia." *Epidemiologic Reviews* 7:105–126.

Eaton, W., and Lasry, J. C. 1978. "Mental Health and Occupational Mobility in a Group of Immigrants." *Social Science and Medicine* 12:53–58.

Erikson, K. 1966. *Wayward Puritans: A Study in the Sociology of Deviance.* New York: John Wiley.

Estroff, S. E. 1981. *Making It Crazy: An Ethnography of Psychiatric Clients in an American Community.* Berkeley: University of California Press.

Falloon, I.; Boyd, J. L.; McGill, C. W.; Razani, J.; Moss, H. B.; and Gilderman, A. 1982. "Family Management in the Prevention of Exacerbations of Schizophrenia: A Controlled Study." *New England Journal of Medicine* 306:1437–1440.

Feighner, J. P.; Robins, E.; Guze, S. B.; Woodruff, R. A.; Winokur, G.; and Munoz, R. 1972. "Diagnostic Criteria for Use in Psychiatric Research." *Archives of General Psychiatry* 26:57–63.

Friedson, E. 1968. "Disability as Social Deviance." In *Deviance: The Interactionist Perspective,* ed. E. Rubington and M. Weinberg, pp. 117–120. New York: Macmillan.

Gallagher, B. 1980. *The Sociology of Mental Illness.* Englewood Cliffs, NJ: Prentice-Hall.

Gallagher, E. B.; Levinson, D. J.; and Erlich, I. 1957. "Some Sociopsychological Characteristics of Patients and Their Relevance for Psychiatric Treatment." In

The Patient and the Mental Hospital, ed. M. Greenblatt, D. Levinson, and R. H. Williams, pp. 357–379. Glencoe, Il: Free Press.

Goldberg, E. M., and Morrison, S. L. 1963. "Schizophrenia and Social Class." *British Journal of Psychiatry* 109:785–802.

Gove, W. 1970. "Societal Reaction as an Explanation of Mental Illness: An Evaluation." *American Sociological Review* 35:873–884.

———. 1975. *The Labelling of Deviance: Evaluating a Perspective.* New York: Sage.

———. 1980. "Labeling and Mental Illness; A Critique." In *Labeling Deviant Behavior,* ed. W. R. Gove, pp. 53–109. Beverly Hills, Calif.: Sage.

———. 1982. "Current Status of the Labeling Theory of Mental Illness." In *Deviance and Mental Illness,* ed. W. Gove, pp. 273–300. Beverly Hills, Calif.: Sage.

Greenley, J. 1972. "The Psychiatric Patient's Family and Length of Hospitalization." *Journal of Health and Social Behavior* 13:25–37.

Grusky, O., and Pollner, M. 1981. *The Sociology of Mental Illness.* New York: Holt, Rinehart, and Winston.

Hagnell, O. 1966. *A Prospective Study of the Incidence of Mental Disorder.* Stockholm: Svenska Bokforlaget Norstedts-Bonniers.

Hayes, D., and Ross, C. E. 1986. "The Effect of Exercise, Overweight and Physical Health on Psychological Well-Being." *Journal of Health and Social Behavior* 27:387–400.

Heston, L. 1988. "What About Environment." In *Relatives at Risk for Mental Disorder,* ed. E. Dunner, E. Gershon, and J. Barret, pp. 205–213. New York: Raven Press.

Hollingshead, A. B., and Redlich, F. C. 1958. *Social Class and Mental Illness: A Community Survey.* New York: John Wiley.

Horwitz, A. 1977. "The Pathways into Psychiatric Treatment: Some Difference Between Men and Women." *Journal of Health and Social Behavior* 18:169–178.

———. 1982. *The Social Control of Mental Illness.* New York: Academic Press.

Huffine, C., and Clausen, J. 1979. "Madness and Work: Short-and Long-Term Effects of Mental Illness on Occupational Careers." *Social Forces,* 57:1049–1062.

Hughes, M., and Gove, W. 1981. "Living Alone, Social Integration and Mental Health." *American Journal of Sociology* 87:48–74.

Jarvis, E. 1966. "Influence of Distance from and Nearness to an Insane Hospital on Its Use by the People." *American Journal for Insanity.* 22:361–406.

Jencks, C. 1980. "Heredity, Environment and Public Policy Reconsidered." *American Sociological Review.* 45:723–736.

———. 1987. "Genes and Crime." *New York Review of Books.* 12 February, 1987, pp. 33–41.

Kadushin, C. 1969. *Why People Go to Psychiatrists.* New York: Atherton.

Kandel, D. 1966. "Status Homophily, Social Context, and Participation in Psychotherapy." *American Journal of Sociology.* 71:640–650.

Kato, M. 1969. "Psychiatric Epidemiological Surveys in Japan: The Problem of Case Finding." In *Mental Health Research in Asia and the Pacific,* ed. W. Caudill and T. Lin, pp. 92–104. Honolulu: East-West Center Press.

Kessler, R. C.; House, J. S.; and Turner, J. B. 1987. "Unemployment and Health in a Community Sample." *Journal of Health and Social Behavior* 28:51–59.

Kirk, S. 1974. "The Impact of Labeling on the Rejection of the Mentally Ill: An Experimental Study." *Journal of Health and Social Behavior* 15:108–117.

Kohn, M. L. 1972. "Class, Family and Schizophrenia: A Reformulation." *Social Forces* 50:295–304.

Leff, J., and Vaughn, C. 1985. *Expressed Emotion in Families.* New York: Guilford Press.

Leff, J. P.; Kuipers, L.; Berkowitz, R.; Eberlein-Vries, R.; and Sturgeon, D. 1982. "A Controlled Trial of Social Intervention in the Families of Schizophrenic Patients." *British Journal of Psychiatry* 141:121–134.

Lehman, S.; Joy, V.; Kreisman, D.; and Simmens, S. 1976. "Responses to Viewing Symptomatic Behaviors and Labeling of Prior Mental Illness." *Journal of Community Psychology* 4:327–334.

Leighton, D. C.; Harding, J. S.; Macklin, D. B.; Macmillan, A. M.; and Leighton, A. H. 1963. *The Character of Danger.* New York: Basic Books.

Lemert, E. 1951. *Social Pathology.* New York: McGraw-Hill.

Lennon, M. C. 1987. "Sex Differences in Distress: The Impact of Gender and Work Roles." *Journal of Health and Social Behavior* 28:290–305.

Liker, J. 1982. "Wage and Status Effects of Employment in Affective Well-Being Among Ex-Felons." *American Sociological Review* 47:264–283.

Lin, T. 1953. "A Study of the Incidence of Mental Disorder in Chinese and Other Cultures." *Psychiatry* 16:313–336.

Link, B. G. 1982. "Mental Patient Status, Work and Income: An Examination of the Effects of a Psychiatric Label." *American Sociological Review* 47:202–215.

———. 1983. "The Reward System of Psychotherapy: Implications for Inequities in Service Delivery." *Journal of Health and Social Behavior* 24:61–69.

———. 1987. "Understanding Labeling Effects in the Area of Mental Disorders: An Assessment of the Effects of Expectations of Rejection." *American Sociological Review* 52:96–112.

Link, B. G., and Cullen, F. T. 1983. "Reconsidering the Social Rejection of Ex-Mental Patients: Levels of Attitudinal Response." *American Journal of Community Psychology* 11:261–273.

———. 1990. "The Labeling Theory of Mental Disorders: A Review of the Evidence." *Research in Community and Mental Health* 6:75–105.

Link, B. G., and Dohrenwend, B. P. 1980. "Formulation of Hypotheses About the Ratio of Untreated Cases in the True Prevalence Studies of Functional Psychiatric Disorders in Adults in the United States." In *Mental Illness in the United States: Epidemiological Estimates,* ed. B. P. Dohrenwend et al., pp. 114–32. New York: Praeger.

Link, B. G.; Cullen, F. T.; Frank, J.; and Wozniak, J. F. 1987. "The Social Rejection of Former Mental Patients: Understanding Why Labels Matter." *American Journal of Sociology* 92:1461–1500.

Link, B. G.; Cullen, F. T.; Struening, E.; Shrout, P.; and Dohrenwend, B. P. 1989. "A Modified Labeling Theory Approach in the Area of the Mental Disorders: An Empirical Assessment." *American Sociological Review* 54:400–423.

Link, B. G.; Dohrenwend, B. P.; and Skodol, A. E. 1986. "Socio-Economic Status and Schizophrenia: Noisome Occupational Characteristics as a Risk Factor." *American Sociological Review* 51:242–258.

Link, B. G., and Milcarek, B. 1980. "Selection Factors in the Dispensation of Therapy: The Matthew Effect in the Allocation of Mental Health Resources." *Journal of Health and Social Behavior* 21:279–290.

Loring, M., and Powell, B. 1988. "Gender, Race and DSMIII: A Study of the Objectivity of Psychiatric Behavior." *Journal of Health and Social Behavior* 29:1–22.

Mechanic, D. 1972. "Social Class and Schizophrenia: Some Requirements for a Plausible Theory of Social Influence." *Social Forces* 50:305–309.

———. 1981. "What Are Mental Health and Mental Illness?" In *The Sociology of Mental Illness,* ed. O. Grusky and M. Pollner, pp. 28–33. New York: Holt Rinehart and Winston.

Meile, R. L. 1972. "The Twenty-two Item Index of Psychophysiological Disorder: Psychological or Organic Symptoms?" *Social Science Medicine* 6:125–135.

Myers, J. K., and Schaffer, L. 1954. "Social Stratification and Psychiatric Practice: A Study of an Outpatient Clinic." *American Sociological Review* 19:307–310.

Myers, J. K.; Weissman, M. M.; Tischler, G. L.; Holzer, C. E.; Leaf, P. J.; Orvaschel, H.; Anthony, J. C.; Boyd, J. H.; Burke, J. D.; Kramer, M.; and Stoltzman, R. 1984. "Six-Month Prevalence of Psychiatric Disorders in Three Communities." *Archives of General Psychiatry* 41:959–976.

Neugebauer, R.; Dohrenwend, B. P.; and Dohrenwend, B. S. 1980. "Formulation of Hypotheses about the True Prevalence of Functional Psychiatric Disorders among Adults in the United States." In *Mental Illness in the United States: Epidemiological Estimates,* ed. B. Dohrenwend et al., p. 45–94. New York: Praeger.

Nieradzik, K., and Cochrane, R. 1985. "Public Attitudes Towards Mental Illness: The Effects of Behavior, Roles and Psychiatric Labels." *International Journal of Social Psychiatry* 31:23–37.

Offer, D., and Sabshin, M. 1984. *Normality and the Life Cycle.* New York: Basic Books.

Page, S. 1977. "Effects of the Mental Illness Label in Attempts to Obtain Accommodation." *Canadian Journal of Behavioral Science* 9:85–90.

Palamara, F.; Cullen, F. T.; and Gersten, J. 1986. "The Effect of Police and Mental Health Intervention on Juvenile Deviance: Specifying Contingencies in the Impact of Formal Reaction." *Journal of Health and Social Behavior* 29:90–105.

Perrucci, R., and Targ, D. B. 1982. "Network Structure and Reactions to Primary Deviance of Mental Patients." *Journal of Health and Social Behavior* 23:2–17.

Phillips, D. L. 1966. "The 'True Prevalence' of Mental Illness in a New England State." *Community Mental Health Journal* 2:35–40.

Rabkin, J. G., and Struening, E. L. 1976. "Life Events, Stress, and Illness." *Science* 194:1013–1020.

Robins, L. N.; Helzer, J. E.; Weissmen, M. M.; Orvaschel, H.; Gruenberg, E.; Burke, J.; and Regier, D. 1984. "Life Prevalence of Specific Psychiatric Disorders in Three Sites." *Archives of General Psychiatry* 41:949–958.

Robbins, J., and Greenly, J. 1983. "Thinking About What's Wrong: Attributions of Severity, Cause, and Duration in the Problem Definition Stage of Psychiatric

Helpseeking." In *Research in Community and Mental Health,* vol. 3, ed. J. Greenley, pp. 209–232. Greenwich, CT: JAI Press.

Rosenblatt, A., and Mayer, J. E. 1974. "The Recidivism of Mental Patients: A Review of Past Studies." *American Journal of Orthopsychiatry* 44:697–706.

Rosenfield, S. 1989. "The Effects of Women's Employment: Personal Control and Sex Differences in Mental Health." *Social Forces* 30:77–91.

Rubington, E., and Weinberg, M. 1968. *Deviance: The Interactionist Perspective.* New York: Macmillan.

Rushing, W. 1978. "Status Resources, Societal Reactions, and Type of Mental Hospital Admission." *American Sociological Review* 43:521–533.

Sampson, H.; Messinger, S.; and Towne, R. 1964. *Schizophrenic Women: Studies in Marital Crisis.* New York: Atherton.

Scheff, T. 1966. *Being Mentally Ill: A Sociological Theory.* Chicago: Aldine.

Schofield, W. 1964. *The Purchase of Friendship.* Englewood Cliffs, N.J.: Prentice-Hall.

Schwartz, C.; Myers, J. K.; and Astrachan, B. M. 1974. "Psychiatric Labeling and the Rehabilitation of Mental Patients." *Archives of General Psychiatry* 31:329–343.

Schwartz, S. 1985. "A Society Unto Themselves: A Theoretical and Empirical Examination of Women's Proclivity for Depressive Disorders." Ph.D. diss., Columbia University.

Shapiro, S.; Skinner, E.; Kessler, L.; Von Korff, M.; German, P.; Tischler, G.; Leaf, P.; Benham, L.; Cottler, L.; and Regier, D. 1984. "Utilization of Health and Mental Health Services: Three Epidemiologic Catchment Area Sites." *Archives of General Psychiatry* 41:971–978.

Shrout, P.; Link, B. G.; Dohrenwend, B. P.; and Skodol, A. E. 1987. "Characterizing Life Events as Risk Factors for Depression." Paper presented at the annual meeting of the American Psychological Association. New York, August 1987.

Sibicky, M., and Dovidio, J. F. 1986. "Stigma of Psychological Therapy: Stereotypes, Interpersonal Reactions, and the Self-Fulfilling Prophecy." *Journal of Consulting and Clinical Psychology* 33:148–154.

Snow, D.; Baker, S.; Anderson, L.; and Martin, M. 1986. "The Myth of Pervasive Mental Illness Among the Homeless." *Social Problems* 33:407–423.

Spitzer, R. L.; Endicott, J.; and Robins, E. 1978. "Research Diagnostic Criteria: Rationale and Reliability." *Archives of General Psychiatry* 23:41–55.

Spitzer, S., and Denzin, N. 1968. *The Mental Patient: Studies in the Sociology of Deviance.* New York: McGraw-Hill.

Srole, L.; Langner, T. S.; Michael, S. T.; Opler, M. K.; and Rennie, T. A. 1962. *Mental Health in the Metropolis.* New York: McGraw-Hill.

Srole, L.; Langner, T. S.; Michael, S. T.; Kirkpatrick, P.; Opler, M. K.; and Rennie, T. A. 1975. *Mental Health in the Metropolis: The Midtown Manhattan Study.* New York: Harper & Row.

Thoits, P. 1983. "Multiple Identities and Psychological Well Being: A Reformulation and Test of the Social Isolation Hypothesis." *American Sociological Review* 48: 174–187.

———. 1987. "Gender and Marital Status Differences in Control and Distress:

Common Stress versus Unique Stress Explanations." *Journal of Health and Social Behavior* 28:7–22.

Turner, R. J. 1968. "Social Mobility and Schizophrenia." *Journal of Health and Social Behavior* 9:194–203.

———. 1981. "Social Support as a Contingency on Psychological Well-Being." *Journal of Health and Social Behavior* 22:357–367.

Vanfossen, B. E. 1981. "Sex Differences in the Mental Health Effects of Spouse Support and Equity." *Journal of Health and Social Behavior* 22:130–143.

Weinstein, R. 1979. "Patient Attitudes Toward Mental Hospitalization: A Review of Quantitative Research." *Journal of Health and Social Behavior* 20:237–258.

———. 1983. "Labeling Theory and the Attitudes of Mental Patients: A Review." *Journal of Health and Social Behavior* 24:70–84.

Weissman, M. M., and Klerman, G. L. 1977. "Sex Differences and the Epidemiology of Depression." *Archives of General Psychiatry* 34:98–111.

Weissman, M. M., and Myers, J. K. 1978. "Affective Disorders in a U.S. Urban Community: The Use of Research Diagnostic Criteria in an Epidemiological Survey." *Archives of General Psychiatry* 35:1304–1311.

Williams, A. W.; Ware, J. E.; and Donald, C. 1981. "A Model of Mental Health, Life Events and Social Supports Applicable to General Populations." *Journal of Health and Social Behavior* 22:324–336.

Yarrow, M. C.; Schwartz, G.; Murphy, H. S.; and Deasy, L. 1955. "The Psychological Meaning of Mental Illness in the Family." *Journal of Social Issues* 11:12–24.

CHAPTER 9

The Concept of Normality in the Law

Stephen J. Morse, Loren H. Roth, and Robert M. Wettstein

Unlike medicine and psychiatry, which self-consciously consider and adopt explicit standards for normality, the law does not directly and self-consciously define such standards. The revised third edition of the *Diagnostic and Statistical Manual of Mental Disorders* (DSM-III-R) (American Psychiatric Association 1987) has no jurisprudential analog that contains a generic legal definition of normality and explicit criteria for abnormality. Nevertheless, Anglo-American law and legal institutions incorporate and reinforce an implicit concept of normality.

This chapter infers from legal rules and institutions Anglo-American law's concept of and criteria for normality. We begin by noting that the concept of "legal normality" is derived from the law's theory of the person as a practical reasoning being. The chapter then turns to the definition and application of the legal concept of normality, with special attention to mental health law as an exemplar, and to the relationships between normality and responsibility, normality and causation, and normality, volition, and diagnosis. Last, we examine the role of mental health professionals in legal decisionmaking concerning normality.

The authors would like to thank Richard Craswell for his thoughtful suggestions.

The Legal Concept of the Person

Anglo-American law's concept of normality is rooted in its theory of the person and the person's relationship to the state. The theory of the person must in turn be largely a theory of action because it is the concept of action that primarily distinguishes human beings from infrahuman species and inanimate objects.

Human action, unlike other natural phenomena, can be explained by reasons for action as well by "natural" causes (see Rosenberg 1988, chap. 2). When one asks about the behavior of a person, "Why did she do that?" two distinct types of answers may be given. The first explains human behavior as a product of intentions arising from the desires and beliefs of the agent. For example, suppose we wish to explain why Mary decided to attend medical school. The pertinent reason-giving explanation might be that she wishes to emulate her mother, whom she greatly admires and who is a physician, and Mary believes that the best way to do so is to become a doctor herself. This type of explanation defines human action in terms of reasons, intentions, and choices. The second type of explanation treats conduct as simply one more bit of the phenomena of the universe, subject to the same natural laws, waiting to be discovered by science, that explain all phenomena. Naturalistic explanations employ laws and causal variables at all levels of explanation, from the molecular to the sociological, that allow us best to predict and control behavior. For example, those who believe that mind can ultimately be "reduced" to brain also believe that in principle Mary's "decision" can be explained as the natural, law-governed effect of biophysical causes and that her intentions and choices are simply epiphenomenal, rather than genuine causes of her behavior. In this mode of explanation, human actions are indistinguishable from any other caused phenomena, including reflex movements, the behavior of infrahuman species, or the movements of subatomic particles.

Reason-giving explanation, currently called "folk psychology" by philosophers of social science, action, and mind, is one of the two dominant modes of explanation in the social sciences and the most common method we use to explain and predict the conduct of our fellow humans (see Flanagan 1984; Searle 1984; Stich 1983). Naturalistic explanation is the standard tool of the physical sciences and the other dominant mode in the social sciences. As clinical and experimental sciences of behavior, psychiatry and psychology are caught uncomfortably between the reason-giving and naturalist accounts of human conduct (Trusted 1987). Sometimes they treat actions as physical phenomena, sometimes as literary texts, and sometimes as a combination of the two. Reason-giving can be assimilated to naturalistic explanation by suggesting that desires and beliefs causally explain rather than simply define human action (most famously, Davidson 1963), and most social science proceeds on the assumption that reasons for action are causal as well as justificatory. But the assimilationist position is controversial; it is not clear that the two types of accounts can be so easily merged. Indeed, some claim that a fully naturalistic account of human action is conceptually impossible (Rosenberg 1988). These controversies will not be solved until the mind-body problem is "solved,"—an event unlikely to occur anytime soon—so the study of human behavior will continue to be vexed by the alternative accounts.

Law, in contrast to the naturalistic mode of explanation, is premised almost entirely on reason-giving accounts. The law's concept of a person is thus of a practical reasoning, rule-following being whose actions must be understood in terms of beliefs and desires. As a system of rules, the law presupposes a being that reasons practically, using the rules as premises in the practical syllogisms that issue in human action. To be a legal person is just to be a practical reasoner (for the best account of the law's view of person as a practical reasoner, see Moore 1984). The legal view of the person as a practical reasoner does not require that "legal persons" consistently reason and behave rationally according to any particular normative conception of rationality. It simply means that people are creatures who act for and consistently with their reasons for action and are generally capable of minimal rationality judged by conventional standards. As far as we know, only human beings reflect self-consciously on their own beliefs and desires and revise their reasons for action intentionally. Legal concepts of normality and responsibility are therefore grounded in the view of persons as practical reasoners. Although other and perhaps richer conceptions of the person and different premises for law are conceivable, Anglo-American and other Western systems of law are so based.

On occasion, the law does seem concerned with a causal account of conduct. For example, criminal law cases of legal insanity are usually supported and explained by using mental disorder as a causal variable. Even in such cases, however, the search for a causal account is triggered by the untoward, "crazy" *reasons* that seem to have motivated the defendant's behavior. Furthermore, the legal rule employed, the insanity defense, primarily addresses reasoning rather than naturalistic causes (Morse 1985). Acquittal by reason of insanity requires that the defendant was not only mentally disordered, but also, as a result, that she was unable to appreciate the wrongfulness or the nature of her act. The law excuses a legally insane defendant because her practical reasoning is impaired, not because her otherwise criminal conduct was caused. As we shall see, even cases of "volitional" problems, which are often viewed naturalistically, are best understood in terms of diminished rationality.

Anglo-American law's concept of the person is also largely individualistic and liberal (see, for example, Raz 1986). Although virtually all modern theorists reject extreme versions of individualism and libertarianism, our jurisprudence treats people as distinguishable from the larger community that constitutes our society and as capable of pursuing their own projects without undue interference. Some social theorists believe that it is impossible to conceive of persons separate from the community that provides them with a sense of personhood and identity (see, for example, Sandel 1982; Taylor 1979). For such "communitarians," the community rather than the individual is the basic moral unit because "individuals" are too enmeshed in their culture to be considered morally prior. What defines the self and gives life meaning and value, according to this view, is interaction with, membership in, and adherence to the norms of the community. In contrast, individualists agree that personhood and identity are formed in interaction with one's community and that the community surely has moral claims on the individual, but that physically and psychologically discrete persons are the basic unit. Interaction and shared culture are important precisely because they enrich individual lives (Sher 1989). In the individual view, what gives life meaning and value is that intentions and actions express individual selves (see, for example, Lomasky 1987). Consequently it is crucial that, within reasonable limits, society should facilitate and should not impede through law the pursuit of private preferences that create value for individuals.

The conflict between individualistic and communitarian theories of personhood and value is as unresolvable as the dispute about the proper mode of explaining human action (compare, for example, Rawls 1971 with Sandel 1982). Both ultimately reflect normative preferences rather than indisputable or even discoverable empirical facts. Although both theories are conceivable and attract adherents, Anglo-American law is clearly premised on the moderate individualist account. The law is addressed to people as individuals, and its concepts of normality and responsibility must be understood in terms of its individualistic grounding.

Defining and Applying Legal Normality

Legal rules are guides to conduct proclaimed by legislatures, courts, and administrative agencies that will be enforced by recourse to the power of the state, if necessary. They inform citizens in a vast array of contexts what they may or may not do, what they must or must not do, and what they are and are not entitled to. Every legal context has different rules that reflect the differing requirements for social interaction in the various contexts. These rules implicitly assume that the rule followers are usually sufficiently rational to be able to cope with the demands of the context in which the rule applies. "Legal normality" is therefore the minimal rationality or practical reasoning ability that the law believes a person must possess to perform adequately and to be accountable in the context in question. For example, in a case that addressed the rights of developmentally disabled people, and by extention the rights of all those with mental abnormalities, the United States Supreme Court wrote that abnormal people are undeniably different because they have "reduced ability to cope with and function in the everyday world" (City of Cleburne v. Cleburne Living Center 1985, p. 422). The legally normal person is "reason-able," able to reason. Although the capacity to respond rationally to the demands of a situation is a continuum concept, legal standards are generally binary, albeit without precise criteria.

The definition and degree of rationality the law requires in a given context are not self-defining according to psychological or social "facts." The concept of legal normality, like its counterparts in medicine and psychiatry, is normative; that is, it is based on shared, conventional conceptions of what we ought to expect or require compared to culturally determined baselines. The law is explicitly concerned with prescribing how people *should* act and live together, and social, moral, and political norms that are shaped by historical processes infuse legal rules and institutions. Neither legal nor medical phenomena and concepts "reveal" themselves to investigators with a label of "normality" affixed to them. Scientific and social "facts" concerning normality or any other topic do not dictate what the rules "ought" to be. Moreover, the "facts" that we can know are inevitably contingent because they are affected by their interaction with the legal rules, which are themselves part of the "facts." For example, the preferences of autonomous individuals are shaped by legal requirements that in turn reflect our understanding of those preferences (Sunstein 1986). Even in medicine, where physical findings and functionalism strongly influence notions of health and disease, cultural conventions and the evolving understanding of biophysical processes render the concepts of health and normality contingent (see, for example, Payer 1988). The norms of law and psychiatry, disciplines that deal with human behavior, can be studied objectively, but they are nonetheless irreducibly normative. The "facts" as we perceive them surely affect our conceptions of justice, but they are not dispositive.

Scientific and clinical understanding of impaired rationality and its consequences entails no necessary legal conclusions about whether irrationality ought to be the touchstone of legal normality, how irrational one must be, and what qualifies as minimally competent performance in a particular context. These questions do not have scientific answers. They are fundamentally social, moral, political, and ultimately legal judgments that must be made by the legal institutions—legislatures, courts, and administrative bodies—that our society empowers to define and apply the rules (see Roth, Meisel, and Lidz 1977 for differing approaches to the definition of competence). Indeed, the social goal the law seeks to promote in various contexts will unavoidably shape the varying, implicit definitions of normality. For example, if our society wishes to maximize both individual responsibility for harmdoing and general deterrence of future criminal behavior, insanity defense rules will be drawn to define normality broadly so as to excuse few people, and vice versa. Or, if we wish to maximize individual liberty and the reliability of contracts, competence to contract doctrines will be shaped to define few people as incompetent, and vice versa. The considerations of equity and efficiency that order our conception of a just society inevitably define legal "normality."

Finally, normality is not simply a function of "objective" *intra*personal variables. When dealing with the apparently incompetent behavior of mentally disordered people, for example, we often assume that disorder produces the incompetence, but this is an oversimplification (Morse 1987-88). Competence to perform any task is a function of the interaction between the person's cognitive and physical abilities and training, the inherent difficulties of the task, and situational variables that may affect either the person's abilities or the difficulty of the task. Virtually anyone, no matter how generally capable, can be rendered incompetent if placed under sufficient kinds of the appropriate stressors. Conversely, even extremely "incompetent" people can be made more competent to perform particular tasks by a combination of personal supports and by redesigning or redefining the necessary tasks. Provision of appropriate advice, social supports, and the like can increase the rationality of disordered people, enabling them to cope effectively in various situations they could not have coped with unaided. Note here that the definition of the conditions in which one must be able to behave competently, to be normal, is once again normatively defined. Baseline expectations are not dictated by "nature."

The inevitably normative nature of legal definitions means that they will change in response to shifting political and scientific conceptions and theories. For example, during the last three decades, changing conclusions about the proper tradeoffs among liberty, paternalism, social safety, costs, and other political issues—and not primarily new scientific or clinical theories and findings—altered the legal definition of abnormality and produced enormous modifications in the laws governing involuntary commitment of the mentally disordered. For example, in O'Connor v. Donaldson (1975) the United States Supreme Court held for the first time that continued involuntary commitment was unconstitutional if a nondangerous disordered person could live safely in the community *with the help of willing family members or friends.* The Court granted substantial weight to a citizen's substantive due process right to physical liberty and, in the context of involuntary commitment, implicitly defined normality to include the help of others. As in this instance, implicit legal definitions of normality are unlikely to satisfy everyone because they are the normative products of historical and political processes. Definitions of legal normality are not empirical and cannot be assessed by consensually validated canons of scientific procedure or even by uncontroversial notions of "what works." What succeeds according to people of one political stripe may be an abject failure to their political opponents. For some, *O'Connor* heralded a new, desirable era of autonomy and dignity for disordered people, while for others the same case marked the unfortunate further erosion of appropriate medical authority.

Legal decisions about normality in individual cases also require normative judgment. Because legal rules express normative preferences and are expressed in language, they are not precise, objectively identifiable quantitative standards. Consequently, their application must be somewhat indeterminate and shaped by social, moral, and political judgment. Indeed, they aim to provide decision makers with guided discretion to express the community's moral, political, and social judgment about the case. How much a contracting party must fail to understand a deal and its consequences to be found incompetent to contract or how much a criminal defendant must fail to appreciate the wrongfulness of her conduct to be found legally insane are once again questions that do not have purely empirical answers.

Consider, for example, the federal insanity defense applicable in all insanity defense cases in United States federal courts:

> It is an affirmative defense to a prosecution under any Federal statute that, at the time of the commission of the acts constituting the offense, the defendant, as a result of a severe mental disease or defect, was unable to appreciate the nature and quality or the wrongfulness of his acts. . . . (18 U.S.C. Sec. 20[a], 1988)

What is the definition of "severe"? Precisely how mentally disordered or developmentally disabled must the defendant be? How much lack of appreciation qualifies? Brief reflection discloses that only extreme cases will have an obvious answer and that most cases will be subject to shifting normative judgments. In conservative times or in conservative jurisdictions, judges and juries will apply this test narrowly, producing few acquittals, and in liberal times or places, they will apply it more expansively, producing larger numbers of acquittals. At the decisional level too, judgments of legal normality are inevitably normative. Facts about the person's behavior are central to the ultimate decision in individual cases, but the outcome is equally shaped by the legal decision maker's normative evaluation.

Normality and Context

Although one may infer the law's generic definition of normality—minimal rationality in the context in question—note that, like psychological normality and abnormality, legal normality and abnormality are not necessarily global. Different moral and political concerns as well as different behavioral requirements motivate the rules in different contexts. Thus the specific definition of normality also differs across contexts. One may be normal for some legal purposes and not normal for others. For example, the reasons for depriving people of physical liberty are different from those for treating them involuntarily. Further, the liberty intrusion of commitment is different from the liberty intrusion of involuntary treatment. The behavioral requirements of the two contexts differ. Consequently, the type and degree of irrationality for finding the person involuntarily committable and involuntarily treatable may also differ. Although a person may be properly subject to commitment, she may also be competent to refuse the psychotropic medications with which the hospital staff propose to treat her (Rogers v. Commissioner 1983; see also Mills v. Rogers 1982): The delusion that renders her potentially violent may not interfere with her ability to make a rational treatment decision. Similarly, an insanity acquittee who killed her infant in response to a delusional belief may retain the ability rationally to conduct her financial affairs.

Normality as Capacity

Although most legal rules refer to actual behavior, the underlying minimal rationality legal normality requires is a "capacity" rather than a behavioral performance. That is, the law considers normal a person whose behavior seems to fall below the threshold of minimal rationality and fails to meet the standard of normality as long as the person was *capable* of behaving sufficiently rationally and meeting the standard. For example, a criminal defendant who did not know what she was doing because she failed to pay attention is not legally insane. Indeed, all mental health laws employ the mental disorder criterion as a marker for the requirement that a finding of legal abnormality be premised on "unavoidable" irrationality. Because the majority of alcohol and other drug use is not considered unavoidably irrational or involuntary, in most instances we hold criminal defendants responsible if their irrational behavior is produced by ingestion of these substances. Similarly, a businessperson who made a disastrously irrational deal will not be able to avoid the contract if terrible business judgment rather than unavoidable irrationality produced it.

Some legal rules that require a judgment about abnormality appear to premise application of the rule on the person's functional incapacity or performance. For example, the application of guardianship and other disability rules seems to be based on whether the person is able to live independently, perform adequately at work, or the like. By their focus on performance, these rules do not seem to require irrationality, but irrationality or some similar incapacity is nonetheless foundational for their legitimacy. After all, the reason a person with no physical disability is unable to live independently or to perform adequately in the workplace is precisely some form of irrationality that compromises his or her ability to cope with the ordinary demands of life. Once again, if the law concludes that the person is capable of independence or holding a job, special guardianship or disability rules designed for abnormal people will not apply. Inadequate performance is a proxy and not a substitute for the lack of capacity to behave rationally in a particular context.

We rarely have direct measures of the capacity for rationality and must infer this capacity from behavioral evidence. Sufficiently irrational behavior in a given context may seem inexorably to produce the judgment that the person was incapable of rationality in that context (Green 1944). Nevertheless, the judgment of incapacity must be made to defeat the presumption of legal normality that otherwise obtains. In order to promote liberty, a liberal society such as ours will generally respect the preferences of individuals, no matter how unwise or irrational they may be, as long as the actor is capable of rationality.

The Reasonable Person

Many areas of civil and criminal law employ "reasonable person" criteria to mark the limits of liability. For example, the justificatory defense of self-defense is available to a criminal defendant only if she *reasonably* believed that she was in imminent danger of wrongful attack. Negligence liability in tort is premised on the actor's failure to act according to the standard of care expected of the ordinary reasonable person. What is the relationship between the legal conception of normality and such reasonable person standards?

Reasonable person standards are general objective, moral standards of conduct, not empirical criteria about individuals. The reasonable person standard is not simply a reflection of what the statistically normal person is capable of doing. Although the standard is informed by our understanding of the cognitive and physical capabilities of people generally, it is a normative standard that all but the most disabled are deemed capable of achieving. People who fail to meet these standards in a particular context may be fully legally normal because they do not suffer from a sufficient and unavoidable rationality defect. Indeed, most people who behave unreasonably according to these standards are legally normal. And, once again, the law presumes that all adult and most near-adult persons are legally normal; that is, that all such persons are capable of meeting the law's commands. Failure to meet the standards is a moral infirmity rather than a failure resulting from an unavoidable psychological or other type of incapacity. Thus the "abnormality" of the legally unreasonable person is "moral abnormality" under the circumstances. Unreasonable conduct demonstrates culpable indifference to the well-being of others.

All people do not have equal endowments to help them conform to reasonable person standards. For people with lesser abilities, meeting the standards will be harder than for more fortunately endowed persons. Nevertheless, the law deems it fair to impose liability in such cases even if a person had lesser cognitive and physical endowments than the statistically "normal" person, *if* he or she was capable of meeting the reasonable person standard (Hart 1968). The law is extremely stringent about its willingness to qualify objective standards, and virtually all parties will be deemed capable of meeting these standards. "Subjective" physical or psychological abnormality usually has little force in "reasonable person" cases. On occasion, however, the law recognizes that a purely objective reasonable person standard may be unfair to some legally normal people. For example, in deference to cultural socialization and other variables affecting reactions to possible violence, the law of self-defense in many jurisdictions now treats differently the standard of reasonableness expected of women and men (for example, State v. Wanrow 1977). Consequently, a female defendant claiming self-defense is entitled in these jurisdictions to be judged according to whether a reasonable woman would have believed that she was in imminent danger of wrongful attack. Note that in this case our empirical understanding of behavior has led to modification of the moral standard of expected conduct, but the standard is still moral. A woman who is unusually fearful for a woman may still fail to meet the standard and her claim of self-defense will not succeed, even though she honestly (but unreasonably) believed she was in danger.

If a person is genuinely incapable of meeting a socially just reasonable person standard in a given context, it will probably be true that the person will meet the criteria for "legal abnormality" in that context and the applicable special rule will apply. For example, a defendant who was so irrationally fearful that he or she was truly incapable of making a reasonable judgment about imminent violence—a person suffering from delusional disorder, for example—might well be legally insane.

Reasonable person standards have always been the object of criticism for creating a normatively unrealistic standard and, more recently, for reflecting the values of elites rather than reflecting social norms accurately (see, for example, Ehrenreich 1990). In our increasingly pluralistic society, one can expect critics to expose the ideological assumptions of many reasonable person standards and to suggest alternatives. For now, however, probably a substantial majority of lawyers and scholars believe that such standards properly permit individualized decision making concerning appropriate behavior in various contexts.

Normality and Responsibility

Legal normality as defined in this chapter entails legal responsibility. People capable of minimal rationality in a particular context will be held legally responsible for their behavior in that context, unless they are able successfully to claim other accepted excusing reasons unrelated to legal normality. For example, a normal and responsible businessperson may be able to avoid a contract because it was made under the influence of fraud, mistake, or duress. Similarly, a normal and responsible criminal defendant may be preventively detained without bail because he or she is dangerous or likely to flee the jurisdiction. In such cases, normality and responsibility are presumed as usual: The legal outcome is unrelated to the issue of normality and responsibility. In contrast, legal abnormality as defined in this chapter usually entails *non*responsibility. People incapable of minimal rationality will not be held legally responsible for their conduct, and nonresponsibility will be the primary determinant of the legal outcome in such cases. For example, incompetence to contract, incompetence to stand trial, involuntary civil commitment, and the insanity defense are all exceptional legal responses premised on the need for special rules to deal with nonresponsible conduct.

With few exceptions, to be discussed next, legal normality and legal responsibility are in fact synonymous. Their criteria are the same. By definition, people who are unable to behave minimally adequately are not legally normal or responsible. The moral, social, political, and legal rationales for distinguishing the normal from the abnormal and the responsible from the nonresponsible are the same. We believe that it is simply not fair or likely to be efficient to apply the usual rules to people incapable of minimal rationality. Furthermore, unavoidably irrational choices do not create the same value or meaning for a person as "responsible" choices (whether or not they are rational).

The law's treatment of children, particularly adolescents, is an apparent exception to the claim that legal normality and legal responsibility are synonymous. After all, physically and psychologically normal minors, to whom the usual juvenile laws apply, are generally not fully legally responsible. Virtually all the standard presumptions and rules that apply to adults do not apply to most minors in most instances. But no exception really exists. Physically and psychologically normal minors are *not* normally self-governing legal persons because they lack the requisite minimal rationality. As the United States Supreme Court explicitly recognized, they lack the experience and rational judgment the law usually deems necessary for full responsibility (Schall v. Martin 1984). "Normal" minors are in some relevant respects like "normal" mentally disordered or developmentally disabled people and juvenile law is analogous to mental disability law (see Garvey 1981). The "normal" laws that apply to these classes of people are thus responses to the abnormality and nonresponsibility of the members of the class. The equation of legal normality and legal responsibility with each other and with minimal rationality holds.

There are cases, of course, in which minors are treated as "normal," as adults. As children mature through adolescence, they achieve the increasing rationality that betokens adult status. Many middle to late adolescents have the cognitive and emotional maturity of many adults, and the law treats them as adults for some purposes. For example, some juveniles who commit acts that would be crimes if committed by adults may in fact be processed in the adult criminal justice system rather than in the juvenile justice system because the law deems these minors sufficiently criminally responsible. Indeed, the United States Supreme Court held that executing sixteen- and seventeen-year-old people is constitutionally permissible (Stanford v. Kentucky 1989; but see Thompson v. Oklahoma 1988, which constitutionally prohibited the execution of a defendant who was fifteen years old when he committed a capital crime). For another example, mature minors can often make fully independent decisions about procreative matters. But the law ultimately draws "bright lines," and for most purposes, minors below a certain age, usually eighteen, are treated as less than fully responsible.

The Presumption of Normality

A liberal polity's preference for permitting citizens to pursue their lives with minimal state interference entails a legal presumption of normality in virtually all contexts. That is, the law assumes that all adults are sufficiently rational to exercise their full freedoms and to assume full responsibility for their conduct. But not all people in all contexts are so rational, and the presumption of normality may be rebutted if adhering to it would undermine other important policies. In the criminal law, for example, the prosecution is entitled to rely on a presumption of legal sanity. Consequently, virtually every domain of civil and criminal law has special rules that apply to abnormal and nonresponsible people—those believed incapable of the minimal rationality necessary to perform adequately and to be held accountable in that domain. A criminal defendant, for example, may overcome the presumption of sanity by presenting evidence that satisfies the test for legal insanity.

The consequences to the individual and to society of applying special rules to those deemed abnormal are morally, politically, and fiscally weighty. Application inevitably entails some stigmatization of the affected person, even if, as in the case of the insanity defense, the person wishes to be the subject of the rule (Morse 1978). In many contexts, such as involuntary hospitalization, involuntary treatment, and guardianship, the affected person usually resists application of the rule but is nevertheless deprived of substantial liberty. Some of these laws, such as hospital commitment and transfer payments to the mentally disabled, also require enormous public expenditures. Furthermore, adjudication or administrative decision making to apply these special rules is costly. On the other hand, failure to differentiate genuinely abnormal people would also impose moral, political, and economic costs on them and on society at large. Consider, for example, the injustice of abolishing the insanity defense, or the indignity to the individual and to society of executing the insane (a practice the United States Supreme Court held unconstitutional in Ford v. Wainwright 1986), or the financial costs to an incompetent individual and his or her dependents, and potentially to society, of enforcing a financially ruinous contract. The social policies and rules may vary across contexts and producing just results includes consideration of inevitable externalities and other costs. The law's task is therefore to define abnormality in each context to achieve maximum individual and social justice. So, for example, in *O'Connor* the Supreme Court did not hold that the citizen's liberty interest compelled the *state* to expend resources to permit a nondangerous disordered person to live safely in the community.

Mental Health Law and Legal Normality

Mental health laws that treat some disordered people specially are the best specific exemplars of rules that permit rebuttal of the law's presumption of normality. All such laws have the same structure despite differing content (Morse 1978). Each requires a finding that the person under consideration is mentally disordered, that the person fails to meet a social standard for behavior in the context in question, and that the social failure is produced by the irrationality mental disorder produces. If all three criteria are met, then the person is deemed legally abnormal in that context and the special rule may apply. Otherwise, the law considers the person normal and is held accountable for her conduct. Note that mental disorder alone does not trigger special treatment, nor does failure to meet a social standard alone rebut the presumption of normality. Thus it is possible for a person to be psychologically or psychiatrically abnormal but legally normal if the mental abnormality does not produce sufficient failure to meet the legally requisite social standard. A person's abnormality will have legal consequences only if nonrectifiable irrationality produces the problematic social behavior.

Let us explore some examples of how mental health law defines legal normality and abnormality. Consider first the rules for "competence to contract." Contracting allows citizens to pursue the projects that give value and meaning to their lives and tends to create wealth. The desirability of facilitating free contractual relations is a cornerstone of liberal society and protected by the Constitution. The law will therefore enforce contracts. But most of the values promoted by contracting will not be satisfied if one or both parties to a contract was not able adequately to engage in rational contracting. (The values contracting promotes will also not be satisfied if a party contracts involuntarily, but in such instances the problem results from the constraints of the situation rather than from the actor's abnormality.) Although contracts in such cases may be efficient, they are not likely to be so. More important, the law does not wish to encourage the projects of irrational persons because they are not considered the products of their "true," autonomous selves and thus they fail to have full value. Moreover, an irrational person may lack the ability to bargain reasonably well in his or her own behalf; enforcing the bargain may therefore be unfair. Consequently, subject to some limitations, the law will not enforce the contracts of persons who are incompetent to contract (see, for example, *California Civil Code* 1989, secs. 38-39). The law defines the "legal abnormality" in question in such cases as the person's inability to understand the nature and consequences of the bargain she is making. For example, a businessperson in the throes of a manic episode may be unable to appreciate his or her true financial position and may make an irrational, disastrous deal. Or a depressed person making a choice among pension plan payout options may be unable accurately to assess her future needs and may choose an irrational option that will impoverish her in the future (Ortolere v. Teachers' Retirement Board 1964). The law's limited willingness to enforce contracts made with minors is another example, although in this instance the law applies the rule to an entire class of people rather than to individuals. Although the law generally presumes "legal normality"—that is, competence to contract—and will not find incompetence simply because a contract was a bad deal for one party (but see Green 1944), contracts may be avoided if a contracting party can demonstrate that she lacked the relevant rationality when she contracted.

Another example is competence to stand trial in the criminal justice system. The punishment and stigma consequent to a criminal conviction are perhaps the most undesirable and, indeed, terrible actions that government may impose on an individual. Therefore, the government must provide a criminal defendant a reasonable opportunity to defeat the prosecution, and the criminal justice process should not unreasonably compromise the defendant's dignity. If a criminal defendant does not understand the charges and the nature of the process and cannot assist his or her lawyer in the defense, the risk of an inaccurate and unjust conviction increases and the dignity of both the defendant and the criminal process is compromised. The United States Supreme Court has therefore held that the trial of a defendant who is incompetent to stand trial violates the Fifth and Fourteenth Amendments' requirement of due process of law (Drope v. Missouri 1975; Dusky v. U.S. 1960). The law generally defines the "legal abnormality" in this context as the defendant's inability to understand the nature of the charges and proceedings and inability to assist his or her lawyer. For example, a defendant might be so delusional or disoriented that he or she is not really aware of the nature of the proceeding. In such a case the criminal process must be halted and the defendant must be treated in an attempt to restore competence so that the criminal process may proceed. As in all other contexts, the law presumes normality. Unless the legal abnormality of incompetence to stand trial is demonstrated, the criminal justice process will proceed.

A third example is the law of involuntary civil commitment. Our liberal society largely allows people to act as they choose, subject to the nonlegal and legal consequences that may flow from their actions. For the most part, the law does not permit the state preventively to intervene in the lives of its citizens to avoid unwise and even disastrous conduct (see O'Connor v. Donaldson 1975). Once again, our society believes that the exercise of free action, with all that this implies, gives meaning and value to life. People must be allowed the liberty to pursue their goals, even if most of us believe these goals are not worth pursuing. But the law is not constrained from preventing the irrational actions of those who are unable to behave rationally. Unavoidably irrational action that does not flow from one's true, autonomous self arguably lacks fundamental value and is especially problematic if it creates substantial danger to oneself or others. The deprivation of "negative liberty"—the right to be free of unwanted external constraint on action (Berlin 1969)—is allegedly justified to the extent that unavoidable irrationality has already deprived the person of "effective" liberty (see Garvey 1981). Consequently, if a person's mental disorder and resultant irrationality renders him or her dangerous to self or others or gravely disabled, the law authorizes involuntary commitment to prevent the possible untoward consequences and, in most cases, to provide treatment. The law requires persons to possess minimal rationality to live one's life at liberty. Legal abnormality in this context is sufficient irrationality to deprive a person of accountability for danger to self or others or for grave disability (see *California Welfare & Institutions Code* 1989, secs. 5150 et seq.). State intervention is constitutional and arguably desirable in such cases.

Finally, consider the question of criminal responsibility. Almost all nonconsequential and consequential theories of punishment, including the dominant mixed-model combining retributivism, deterrence, and incapacitation currently favored in Anglo-American jurisprudence, require rationality among the people to whom the criminal laws are addressed and applied. For example, it is unjust for the state retributively to punish nonrational people. In modern jurisprudence, only rational and therefore responsible actors deserve punishment for their wrongdoing (Morse 1985). Furthermore, irrational actors are less likely to be deterred efficiently. (Successful incapacitation does not require rationality, but few would accept a purely incapacitative rationale for criminal punishment.) As a consequence, all insanity defense tests are essentially irrationality tests that seek to identify those defendants whose criminal acts were motivated by unavoidable irrationality. A defendant who did not know the nature and quality of her act, or who did not know that what she was doing was wrong, or who was unable to control herself because her irrationality produced a hard choice (a more controversial case) is excused (see, for example, M'Naghten's Case 1843; *Model Penal Code* 1962, sec. 4.01). Legal abnormality in this context is thus unavoidable irrationality in the motivational reasons for one's harmdoing.

Volition, Diagnosis, and Legal Abnormality

Mental health professionals and others may be surprised to discover the law's focus on irrationality and the general absence of so-called volitional problems from the law's implicit criteria for normality. Indeed, except for some insanity defense rules and workers' disability practice, volitional disability is generally not a separate ground for legal abnormality. Where volitional problems arise, they must be encompassed within the domain of irrationality to qualify for special legal response. Because many cases of seeming volitional difficulties are marked by or better understood as instances of irrationality, the absence of volitional criteria is not problematic in such cases. Pure volitional disability is largely ignored, however.

The law is perhaps not so wrong-headed about volition as it first seems to some mental health professionals and others. Although mental health professionals routinely conceive of some types of behavioral problems as volitional in nature, critical reflection discloses that such difficulties are far less well understood, both conceptually and empirically, than rationality problems. Most often, there is confusion between volitional problems defined empirically, on the one hand, as analogous to physical compulsion, and defined normatively, on the other hand, as the product of a threat that leaves a nonculpable actor with no reasonable alternative (Fingarette 1985; Wertheimer 1988). Crazy reasons are no more compelling than rational reasons: A crazy reason for action is not per se like a gun at one's head, and it is even less like an irresistible force that moves one's body. A person who acts for crazy reasons does not act unintentionally and without choice. He or she chooses and intentionally engages in a course of action for irrational reasons. The problem is irrationality, not compulsion or lack of choice or intent. Even affective or compulsive disorders, which appear to leave a sufferer without a will of his or her own, are always accompanied by various forms of irrationality that cannot be cleanly distinguished from the person's other psychopathology as reasons for the sufferer's behavior. Full analysis of the nature of so-called volitional difficulties is beyond the scope of this chapter, but allegedly volitional problems should almost always be properly characterized as instances of irrationality (Fingarette and Hasse 1979; Wertheimer 1988).

Some critics of the law's emphasis on rationality have claimed that reliable and valid criteria for volitional problems exist (for example, Rogers 1987), but inspection of such criteria reveals that they are firmly in the camp of folk psychology. Most describe failures of rationality in the face of strong desires, emotions, impulses, and the like. Other critics complain that the understanding of rationality defects is as primitive as the understanding of volition, but this complaint rests on a confusion about the law's implicit criteria for normality. The wellsprings of human behavior are not well understood: Behavioral scientists do not know in most cases why cognitive or so-called volitional glitches occur, even assuming that the latter exist and can be defined. But the law's concern is not why glitches occur. Rather, the law's concern is primarily whether and to what degree a problem exists, and there seems little doubt that we can identify and assess rationality defects far more easily than volitional defects. Indeed, in the wake of the unpopular Hinckley verdict, the questionable understanding and measurement of volition in part led legislatures, courts, and the American Psychiatric Association to support abolition of the volitional branch of the insanity defense (American Psychiatric Association 1984; 18 U.S.C. sec. 20[a], 1988; United States v. Lyons 1984). The law's omission may not be so misguided after all.

The role of diagnosis in definitions of legal abnormality also deserves comment. Most special legal "abnormality" rules, with the primary exceptions of the insanity defense, involuntary commitment, and guardianship laws, do not make reference to mental disorder in general or to diagnoses specifically. Even those laws that include a "mental disorder" criterion almost always simply refer generally to mental disorder, without specifying required diagnoses, signs, or symptoms. In such instances, the threshold criterion of "mental disorder" is uniformly satisfied by proof that a diagnosis is warranted. On occasion, a court will interpret a general "mental disorder" criterion to require a specific disorder or level of psychopathology, such as psychosis, but the law's usual failure to specify psychopathology or to include mental disorder at all is consistent with its approach to normality. The touchstone is sufficient practical rationality in a particular context, and no specific diagnosis or mental disorder in general indicates with the necessary specificity whether the normative, legal criterion of sufficient irrationality is present. Indeed, DSM-III-R explicitly recognizes this point by including a warning that the manual was not developed for the purpose of legal assessment. What the law requires is sufficiently detailed behavioral information to make that normative judgment. Although the law often permits a diagnosis to suffice as a proxy for abnormality, a diagnosis should be accompanied by the further data that proper application of the law in question implicitly requires.

Normality and Causation

A persistent confusion that has bedeviled theory and judgments of normality is the erroneous but tenacious belief that normality and causation are incompatible. This confusion arises from many sources, and it is common among lawyers, mental health professionals, and others concerned with legal normality and responsibility. The most obvious source is the alleged philosophical incompatibility between determinism and "free will." This chapter is not the appropriate forum to rehearse the debate about determinism and responsibility (see Moore 1985; Morse 1986), but a few observations are necessary. If determinism or universal causation is true—an unverifiable hypothesis in any case—then *all* behavior is determined or universally caused, and the presence of a determining cause for behavior, including mental abnormality, cannot distinguish the normal from the abnormal or the responsible from the nonresponsible. In contrast, if determinism or universal causation is not true and human behavior, unlike other physical phenomena of the universe, is *not* caused, then the absence of determining causes cannot distinguish the normal from the abnormal or the responsible from the nonresponsible. Some try to escape the logic of these arguments by claiming that only some behavior is caused—a position aptly termed *selective determinism* (Hollander 1973). Unfortunately, the aptness of the term is not matched by the aptness of the arguments used to support the position. Selective determinism in any of its various guises is metaphysically implausible. Even if it is somehow an accurate account of causation, its relation to normative conceptions of normality and responsibility is unpersuasive at best (see Grunbaum 1972 and Morse 1986 for a full analysis of this conclusion).

What the law requires of people for full legal normality and responsibility in a particular context is rationality, not the presence or absence of partial or complete causation. For example, the law will treat as *normal* a person with a brain tumor that has a causal effect on behavior who nonetheless behaves rationally. Conversely, the law will treat as *abnormal* a person with no identifiable lesion whom we believe is incapable of behaving rationally. We tend to assume, probably correctly in most cases, that an "abnormal" cause must be operative when a person behaves abnormally. But the touchstone of legal abnormality is unavoidably irrational behavior, even in the absence of evidence of abnormal causation or in the presence of normal causation.

A further example will help clarify this important point. Considerable reform of the insanity defense in the legislatures and courts followed John W. Hinckley, Jr.'s, acquittal by reason of insanity for the attempted assassination of President Reagan and three others. Some, including the American Medical Association (AMA), argued that the insanity defense ought to be abolished, a position that in essence would force the criminal justice system to treat all defendants, no matter how mentally disordered at the time of the crime, as legally normal for the purpose of assessing criminal responsibility (American Medical Association 1984). In response to the criticism that it would be morally unjust to convict and punish at least some defendants who were crazy at the time of the offense, the AMA made the following counterargument that demonstrated its misunderstanding of the role of causation in ascriptions of legal normality and responsibility. The AMA noted that although poverty is a "stronger" cause of crime than mental disorder, our society does not consider it unfair to convict and punish poor defendants. Therefore, the AMA concluded, it is not unfair to convict and punish crazy people (see also Morris 1982).

Contrary to the AMA's implicit assumption that punishment is somehow related to causation, the reason that we punish poor defendants has nothing to do with the causation of their behavior or the comparative "strength" of that causation. We consider defendants normal and justifiably punish them if they are minimally rational, whether they are rich or poor and without regard to the causes that may have led to the criminal behavior. And the reason that we do and should excuse at least some disordered defendants is not that their behavior is caused *simpliciter* or caused by a mental disorder, but that they are unavoidably irrational. The AMA confused the naturalistic mode of explanation, which has no necessary legal consequences, with the reason-giving mode, which does have legal consequences and which focuses on the rationality of a person's practical reasoning. To say that poverty is a stronger cause of crime than mental disorder is to assert nothing more than that poverty is more statistically predisposing—an assertion that entails no consequences for legal and moral ascriptions of normality and responsibility (but see Klein 1990).

Understanding legal normality requires comprehension of human action in terms of the rationality of practical reasoning. Understanding natural causation may facilitate controlling, changing, and predicting behavior, but it entails no inevitable legal consequences.

Normality and the Experts

Legislatures, administrative agencies, and courts routinely seek the advice of mental health experts and social scientists when they define and judge legal normality. They especially favor psychiatrists and psychologists because mental disorder and developmental disability are primary causes of legal abnormality. Unsurprisingly, the role of the expert varies in these contexts according to the law's various needs.

The primary problem the experts consistently face in all contexts is to distinguish between scientific evidence and moral, social, and political preferences. For example, the probability that a proper dose of a neuroleptic will reduce a psychotic person's delusional thinking and help him or her to regain general cognitive control and adequate functioning is a factual question about which a knowledgeable psychiatrist can give a somewhat precise statistical answer. Whether and which psychotic people the law should force to take such medication are ultimately moral, political, and social questions, however, about which knowledgeable psychiatrists can contribute relevant factual information and often have preferences based on their background and experience. Nevertheless, mental health professionals do not have scientific expertise about such ultimately legal questions. A libertarian psychiatrist may bemoan an undeniably psychotic person's unwillingness to accept treatment, but would be opposed both to forcing it on an individual person and to legislation authorizing involuntary treatment in general. A more paternalistic colleague would surely consider involuntary treatment justified (see Washington v. Harper 1990, in which the United States Supreme Court upheld a mentally disordered prisoner's liberty interest in avoiding the unwanted administration of psychotropic medication, but granted substantial deference to professional review when deciding to override the prisoner's refusal). Because law and psychiatry both partake of reason-giving accounts of behavior and both are concerned with how people live together, it is easy for experts to confuse factual and normative claims and to merge scientific descriptions with social and moral prescriptions when they judge normality.

The expert's moral, social, and political preferences affect his or her legal contributions in two primary ways. First, the expert may unwittingly or even wittingly "shape" his or her scientific or clinical opinions to promote the legal result he or she prefers for nonscientific reasons. Psychiatry and psychology do not constrain unjustified shaping because they are relatively "soft" disciplines that often require highly inferential judgments in the absence of reliable and valid measures. Consider again, for example, the criterion of "severe mental disease" in the federal criminal code's definition of legal insanity, quoted earlier. There is no precise, reliable criterion in DSM-III-R for "severity," and furthermore, "severity" in a legal definition is, at least in part, a nonscientific, moral norm. Thus a mental health professional has ample room wittingly or unwittingly to shape an opinion about severity, or even about the presence of disorder itself, in order to achieve the outcome—conviction or acquittal by reason of insanity—that he or she may think is appropriate. Indeed, some misguided mental health professionals openly admit that they alter their judgments to achieve preferred results because they disdain the law's approach to criminal responsibility (Diamond 1961). Most mental health professionals probably do not intentionally shape their opinions, but social, moral, and political preferences profoundly affect all our judgments and the criteria of mental health science do not put substantial brakes on the subjective shaping of opinions.

An expert's moral, social, and political preferences will also affect his or her testimony on the question for resolution in a case—the "ultimate legal issue." For example, in addition to testifying about a person's mental state, diagnosis, and the like, mental health experts have also traditionally opined about ultimate legal issues, such as whether a person is dangerous to others, legally insane, or incompetent to contract. As we have seen, however, dangerousness, legal insanity, and competence to contract are social, moral, and ultimately legal issues about which mental health experts have no scientific or clinical expertise because the issues are not fundamentally scientific or clinical. Nevertheless, expert testimony on these questions is usually held to assist the legal decision maker—judge or jury—because the expert allegedly is able coherently to explain the relevance of the expert testimony to the ultimate legal issue, and such ultimate issue testimony is held not to invade the province of the finder of fact. But experts can wittingly or unwittingly shape their ultimate legal issue testimony as much or more than their scientific or clinical testimony. Deciding ultimate legal issues requires no scientific or clinical expertise, and it explicitly requires a normative judgment. To return to the example of the insanity defense, liberal mental health professionals are more likely to conclude and opine that a defendant is legally insane than more conservative colleagues (Homant and Kennedy 1986). In fact, experienced criminal attorneys are quite familiar with the proclivities of local mental health experts and will rely on those known to be favorable to the client's position. To respond to problems with ultimate issue testimony, in limited areas the law does prevent experts from testifying about the ultimate issue. For example, in 1984 Congress revised the Federal Code of Evidence to prohibit experts from opining in insanity defense cases on the ultimate issue of legal insanity (Fed. Rules Evidence, sec. 704[b]), a reform supported by the American Psychiatric Association and the American Bar Association (see also *California Penal Code,* 1990, sec. 1027[c], which states that it does not presume that a psychiatrist or psychologist can determine whether a defendant was sane or insane at the time of the offense). In most contexts involving legal normality, however, experts may still offer an opinion on the ultimate legal issue, and once again, only an expert's ethics and humility can prevent the abuse that occurs when he or she offers a social, moral, and legal opinion as if it were a scientific or clinical opinion.

The law's traditional remedy for evidentiary deficiencies is the adversary model of truth-finding. The adversary system relies on presentation of one's own case and cross-examination of opposing witnesses to expose witnesses' weaknesses. For example, in Barefoot v. Estelle (1983), the United States Supreme Court was asked to reverse a death sentence based in part on expert testimony about the defendant's predicted future dangerousness if he were not executed. Petitioner Barefoot, supported by the American Psychiatric Association and the American Psychological Association, claimed that the admission of this expert testimony violated the Due Process clause of the Fourteenth Amendment because clinical predictions of future dangerousness were too inaccurate to support the imposition of capital punishment. A majority of the Justices disagreed, however, arguing that the alleged inaccuracies of such testimony were matters of weight rather than admissibility, and that the proper weight to be given such testimony could be demonstrated by cross-examination of the prosecution's witnesses and presentation of defense witnesses.

The adequacy of adversarial methods for attaining truth is controversial, of course, especially among scientists, who do not usually employ such methodology. But the law has few other tools. In appropriate individual cases, a judge may exclude particular expert testimony because it lacks sufficient scientific reliability to qualify as "expert" or because it threatens to confuse the jury or to cause prejudice. Otherwise, however, the experts' scientific and clinical caution and ethics and the rigors of cross-examination and the adversary system generally are the only general protections against the manipulation of clinical and scientific opinions. This is especially true if, as is common in involuntary commitment, guardianship, and incompetence-to-stand-trial cases, the proceeding is not truly adversarial and only one side is able to present expert testimony. In such instances, the legal decision maker will often simply defer to the sole expert (see Steadman 1979), decreasing any incentive for expert caution.

Focus on the nature of legal normality quickly discloses the appropriate scope of expert assistance in legal decision making. In each case, the issue is the allegedly abnormal person's capability rationally to perform the tasks required by the context in question. Thus, to decide if the person is legally normal, the legal decision maker requires the fullest possible understanding of the person's mental functioning and abilities in that context, and useful testimony will be tailored for its relevance to these questions. Although there is much controversy about which types of data, such as diagnoses or casual hypotheses, are useful to the law, this chapter need not attempt to resolve these disputes. It is sufficient to note that the resolution follows from understanding that a question of legal normality is inevitably normative, context-dependent, and socially, politically, and morally weighty. Experts must remember that legal normality is not for them to decide because it is not a scientific or clinical question.

Conclusion

The law has no explicit definition of or criteria for normality and abnormality, but implicit in all legal rules and institutions is the assumption that practical rationality is the foundation of the normal legal person. This is not to suggest that there is an uncontroversial definition of rationality embedded in legal discourse. Rather, the claim is the more modest assertion that the law cannot be understood except as addressed to and practiced by rational beings and that all legal rules that treat people as abnormal are fundamentally about rationality.

REFERENCES

American Medical Association (Board of Trustees). 1984. "Insanity Defense in Criminal Trials and Limitations of Psychiatric Testimony." *Journal of the American Medical Association* 251:2967–2981.

American Psychiatric Association. 1987. *Diagnostic and Statistical Manual of Mental Disorders,* 3rd ed., rev. (DSM-III-R). Washington, D.C.: APA.

Barefoot v. Estelle, 463 U.S. 880 (1983).

Berlin, I. 1969. "Two Concepts of Liberty." In *Four Essays on Liberty,* by I. Berlin, pp. xxxvii–lxiii, 118–172. London: Oxford University Press.

California Civil Code (West, 1989).

California Penal Code (West, 1990).

California Welfare & Institutions Code (West, 1989).

City of Cleburne v. Cleburne Living Center, 473 U.S. 432 (1985).

Davidson, D. 1963. "Actions, Reasons and Causes." In *Essays on Actions and Events,* by D. Davidson, pp. 3–19. Oxford: Clarendon Press, 1980.

Diamond, B. 1961. "Criminal Responsibility of the Mentally Ill." *Stanford Law Review* 14:59–86.

Drope v. Missouri, 420 U.S. 162 (1975).

Dusky v. United States, 362 U.S. 402 (1960).

Ehrenreich, N. S. 1990. "Pluralist Myths and Powerless Men: The Ideology of Reasonableness in Sexual Harassment Law." *Yale Law Journal* 99:1177–1234.

Federal Rules of Evidence.

Fingarette, H. 1985. "Victimization: A Legalist Analysis of Coercion, Deception, Undue Influence, and Excusable Prison Escape." *Washington & Lee Law Review* 42:65–118.

Fingarette, H., and Hasse, A. 1979. *Mental Disabilities and Criminal Responsibility.* Berkeley: University of California Press.

Flanagan, O. J., Jr. 1984. *The Science of the Mind.* Cambridge, MA: MIT Press.

Ford v. Wainwright, 477 U.S. 399 (1986).

Garvey, J. 1981. "Freedom and Choice in Constitutional Law." *Harvard Law Review* 94:1756–1794.

Green, M. 1944. "Proof of Mental Incompetency and the Unexpressed Major Premise." *Yale Law Journal* 53:271–311.

Grunbaum, A. 1972. "Free Will and Laws of Human Behavior." In *New Readings in Philosophical Analysis,* ed. H. Feigel, W. Sellars, and K. Lehrer, pp. 605–627. New York: Appleton-Century-Crofts.

Hart, H. L. A. 1968. *Punishment and Responsibility: Essays in the Philosophy of Law.* New York: Oxford University Press.

Hollander, P. 1973. "Sociology, Selective Determinism, and the Rise of Expectations." *American Sociologist* 8:147–153.

Homant, R., and Kennedy, B. 1986. "Judgment of Legal Insanity as a Function of

Attitude Toward the Insanity Defense." *International Journal of Law & Psychiatry* 8:67–82.

Klein, M. 1990. *Determinism, Blameworthiness, and Deprivation.* Oxford: Clarendon Press.

Lomasky, L. 1987. *Persons, Rights, and the Moral Community.* New York: Oxford University Press.

Mills v. Rogers, 457 U.S. 291 (1982).

M'Naghten's Case, 8 English Reports 718 (1843).

Model Penal Code (Proposed Official Draft) 1962. Philadelphia: American Law Institute.

Moore, M. 1984. *Law and Psychiatry: Rethinking the Relationship.* Cambridge: Cambridge University Press.

———. 1985. "Causation and the Excuses." *California Law Review* 73:1091–1149.

Morris, N. 1982. *Madness and the Criminal Law.* Chicago: University of Chicago Press.

Morse, S. J. 1978. "Crazy Behavior, Morals, and Science: An Analysis of Mental Health Law." *Southern California Law Review* 51:527–654.

———. 1985. "Excusing the Crazy: The Insanity Defense Reconsidered." *Southern California Law Review* 58:777–837.

———. 1986. "Psychology, Determinism, and Legal Responsibility." In *The Law as a Behavioral Instrument,* ed. G. Melton, pp. 35–85. Nebraska Symposium on Motivation, vol. 33, 1985. Lincoln: University of Nebraska Press.

———. 1987–88. "Treating Crazy People Less Specially." *West Virginia Law Review* 90:353–385.

Payer, L. 1988. *Medicine & Culture: Varieties of Treatment in the United States, England, West Germany, and France.* New York: Henry Holt.

O'Connor v. Donaldson, 422 U.S. 563 (1975).

Ortolere v. Teachers' Retirement Board, 25 N.Y. 2d 976 (1964).

Rawls, J. 1971. *A Theory of Justice.* Cambridge, MA: Harvard University Press.

Raz, J. 1986. *The Morality of Freedom.* Oxford: Clarendon Press.

Rogers, R. 1987. "APA's Position on the Insanity Defense: Empiricism Versus Emotionalism." *American Psychologist* 42:840–848.

Rogers v. Commissioner of the Department of Mental Health, 390 Mass. 489 (1983).

Rosenberg, A. 1988. *Philosophy of Social Science.* Boulder, CO: Westview Press.

Roth, L.; Meisel, A.; and Lidz, C. 1977. "Tests of Competency to Consent to Treatment." *American Journal of Psychiatry* 134:279–284.

Sandel, M. 1982. *Liberalism and the Limits of Justice.* Cambridge: Cambridge University Press.

Schall v. Martin, 467 U.S. 253 (1984).

Searle, J. 1984. *Minds, Brains and Science.* Cambridge, MA: Harvard University Press.

Sher, G. 1989. "Three Grades of Social Involvement." *Philosophy & Public Affairs* 18: 133–157.

Stanford v. Kentucky, 109 S. Ct. 2969 (1989).

State v. Wanrow, 88 Wash. 2d 221 (1977).

Steadman, H. 1979. *Beating a Rap? Defendants Found Incompetent to Stand Trial.* Chicago: University of Chicago Press.

Stich, S. 1983. *From Folk Psychology to Cognitive Science.* Cambridge, MA: MIT Press.

Sunstein, C. 1986. "Legal Interference with Private Preferences." *University of Chicago Law Review* 53:1129–1174.

Taylor, C. 1985. "Atomism." In *Philosophy and the Human Sciences: Philosophical Papers 2,* pp. 187–210. Cambridge: Cambridge University Press.

Thompson v. Oklahoma, 108 S. Ct. 2687 (1988).

Trusted, J. 1987. *Inquiry and Understanding: An Introduction to Explanation in the Physical and Human Sciences.* Atlantic Highlands, NJ: Humanities Press International.

United States Code (1988).

United States v. Lyons, 739 F. 2d 994 (5th Cir. 1984).

Washington v. Harper, 110 S. Ct. 1028 (1990).

Wertheimer, A. 1988. *Coercion.* Princeton: Princeton University Press.

PART III

THEORETICAL AND EPISTEMOLOGICAL CONTRIBUTIONS

CHAPTER 10

Psychiatry's Unholy Marriage: Psychoanalysis and Neuroscience

Terrance Brown

Scholars asked to treat normality from any point of view have placed upon them the burden of deciding the conceptual parameters of their analysis. Insofar as there is general agreement as to the central concepts of a field, they may proceed to consider whether normal means average, ideal, or something else, and to discuss the empirical means by which normality and deviation from it can be measured. For example, in studies of hypertension, no searching reflection on the concept of blood pressure is required. The concept is universally accepted, several measures are available, and one proceeds immediately to examining in what populations and under what conditions a certain range of measurements may be considered normal.

In psychiatry, by contrast, the study of normality takes on quite different meaning for the simple reason that psychiatrists are sharply divided on what the central concepts of the field should be. Is the discipline concerned with mind, with brain, or both? What concepts are relevant to each of these decisions? If mind is chosen, does one seek to measure intelligence, representations, behavior, existential *angst,* or ego strength? If brain is chosen, how are physical measures to be given mental meaning, or should psychiatry itself be redefined? And if both are chosen, how does one handle the difficulties inherent in the previous positions as well as the fundamental problems arising from their interaction?

In order to find answers to such questions, my analysis begins with an examination of propositions set forth in the *American Psychiatric Press Textbook of Psychiatry* (Talbott, Hales, and Yudofsky 1988). My aim is to identify the concepts in which contemporary psychiatric discourse is framed. The problems I have uncovered are so grave and numerous that discussion of normality is precluded. Until psychiatry can say coherently what things such as mind and personality are, it makes little sense to speculate about what the reaction norms of such entities might be.

Obviously, using a single text to identify psychiatric concepts carries the risk of being unrepresentative. Yet, doing so seems justified by considerations going beyond efficiency of exposition and spatial limitations. Melvin Sabshin, who introduces the book, is president and chair of the Board of American Psychiatric Press and is also medical director of the American Psychiatric Association. In his introduction, Sabshin states that "In concert with the American Psychiatric Association, the Press attempts to improve the public's understanding of psychiatry as well as to serve as an educational vehicle for professionals working in psychiatry and related fields" (1988, p. xix). In addition, many of the authors are key figures in American psychiatry. I reason, therefore, that the book represents mainstream psychiatric thought in a fairly comprehensive way.

Three excerpts from the *Textbook of Psychiatry* illustrate well the central paradox that besets psychiatry. In the first, Sabshin describes what he believes is happening to the field:

> Psychiatry is in one of the most exciting, creative, and productive phases of its long history. Fueled by the rapid acquisition of new scientific knowledge and catalyzed by external pressures requiring empirically documented objectification, the field is undergoing significant transformation. Scientific data has replaced ideology as the dominant source for understanding psychopathology; blurring of the scope and boundaries of psychiatry is being altered toward greater clarity in defining the core and the periphery of the profession. Empiricism, relevant quantification, and reaffirmation of our medical roots have become central foci of psychiatry's emergence from a period of identity diffusion. A new generation of researchers, educators, and clinicians, reflective of these changes, has moved into professional leadership in American psychiatry. (Sabshin 1988, p. xix.)

Given this introduction and the fact that the first section of the book is devoted to "Theoretical Foundations," it becomes particularly significant that the opening chapter is entitled "Neuroscience and Psychiatry." In his dramatic opening paragraph Joseph Coyle announces:

> Advances in research on the brain have occurred with a rapidly increasing pace over the last 15 years and have reached the point that neuroscience can justifiably be considered the biomedical foundation for psychiatry. Logarithmic growth in our understanding of the organization and function of the brain has made it feasible to begin to analyze behavior at the molecular level. These advances have permitted the meaningful exploitation of diagnostic and experimental methodologies directed at the brain such as nuclear magnetic resonance spectroscopy, positron emission tomography and brain electrical activity mapping to characterize structural, metabolic, and electrophysiologic abnormalities in the brains of living psychiatric patients. In addition, parallel advances in human genetics and molecular biology will permit us to define the genetic basis for heritable disorders of behavior and ultimately to determine the molecular and cellular mechanisms responsible for these disorders. These developments are progressively narrowing the Cartesian separation between mind and the brain by improving our ability to correlate mental experience with brain processes. (Coyle 1988, p. 3)

Apparently Coyle intends to keep Sabshin's promises in a particular way. Psychiatry is changing: It will be based on neuroscience. Psychiatry is becoming better defined, its identity less diffused: Psychiatrists may now view themselves as neuroscientists who study and treat disorders of behavior. Psychiatry's medical roots are reemerging: Neuroscience provides the biomedical foundation for psychiatry. Scientific data is replacing ideology: Biomedical approaches to brain anatomy and function, new diagnostic and research technologies, and genetic and molecular studies promise correlation of mental experience with brain physiology.

If the paucity of Coyle's psychological allusions causes some uneasiness, the reader may still hope that succeeding chapters entitled "Epidemiology of Mental Disorders," "Normal Growth and Development," and "Theories of Mind and Psychopathology" will indicate how psychological psychiatry intends to keep Sabshin's promises on its own terms. Unfortunately, that hope will prove illusory. The chapter on epidemiology discusses and applies epidemiological techniques to the ruling nosological system, accepting uncritically the psychological and epistemological assumptions contained therein. Readers, themselves must evaluate that system and those assumptions. More positively, the chapter on development sets out to present an evenhanded account of progress in several approaches to development. Although Coyle's psychological categories and neuronal systems are not dealt with specifically, the authors do attempt to coordinate neurodevelopmental and cognitive organization and to relate psychological changes observed during adolescence to physical changes at puberty. Regretfully, the chapter is realized only partially, contains significant errors, and fails in the end to bridge the brain-mind gap. And finally, the chapter entitled "Theories of Mind and Psychopathology" abandons Sabshin's thesis of psychiatric progress altogether, throwing up relativist defenses against neuroscience's assault:

> Each era produces communities of thinkers who invent hermeneutically useful theories that reflect underlying world views. These paradigms determine ways to think about the topic in question. In our era, theories are regarded as useful if they are confirmed by data, if they aid in our understanding of the subject being studied, or if they stimulate helpful questions, experiments, or observations. In this sense, theories are neither true nor false; instead they are more or less useful in interpreting available data, or leading to new information.

And, continues its author, Stephen Marmer:

> The theories under discussion represent the ways ingenious investigators have made sense out of human behavior. They emphasize various data, assume different notions of what constitutes proof or verification, reckon development of the personality and psychopathology according to different factors and timetables, and therefore lead to different schools of treatment. A theory of the mind and its psychopathology in fact has several components, including concepts of development, of normality, of how the mind works, even of what constitutes the mind, and a theory of treatment technique. (Marmer 1988, p. 123)

In short, rather than facing head-on the fact that psychiatry is shifting from a psychoanalytic to a neuroscience framework and analyzing the significance of that shift, rather than answering Sabshin's implicit charge that psychiatry's increasingly-abandoned psychodynamic approach lacks empirical support, rather than demonstrating either the ability or inability of neuroscience's psychological allusions to deal with human personality whole, or rather than pointing out that alongside those disorders for which neuroscience has proved helpful there are many others on which it has little bearing, Marmer chooses to treat psychology—considered only in its psychoanalytic incarnation—as an incommensurable paradigm, a different world view in the sense of Thomas Kuhn. The chasm between Coyle's neuroscience chapter and Marmer's psychoanalytic one is so large that it is difficult to find a single psychological bridge except the word *anxiety* that connects the precipices on either side. One is not even sure whether Coyle and Marmer intend their chapters to deal with the same psychopathological conditions. When Coyle speaks of "major mental disorder," he no doubt means schizophrenia and bipolar illness, and he also mentions brain disorders, anxiety disorders, and depression. By contrast, Marmer presents the psychoanalytic theory of personality with little mention of psychopathology and only weak attempts to link it to current concepts of nosology. For example, the only mention of schizophrenia or affective disorder is in a table (p. 143) relating stages of personality development to psychopathology in terms of developmental trauma or arrest. At best, then, Marmer provides a psychology applicable to personality and anxiety disorders.

The upshot of all this is that the theoretical foundations section of the *Textbook of Psychiatry* leaves the reader somewhat in a quandary. On the one hand, Sabshin claims that science replaces ideology in psychiatry and Coyle claims that neuroscience provides psychiatry with a scientific basis; on the other, Marmer claims that science is *in principle* ideological and suggests that his preferred psychoanalytic framework is as "useful" as any other. Further, Sabshin commits himself to no particular psychological theory, Coyle contends that psychiatry is the "medical specialty primarily involved in the diagnosis and management of *behavioral* disorders" (1988, p. 29), and Marmer exposits psychoanalytic personality theory while admitting that implications for psychopathology are its "weakest part" (1988, p. 147). Finally, Sabshin is concerned about biological reductionism while Coyle acknowledges quite frankly that advances in neuroscience are "increasingly reductionistic" and Marmer ignores biology, neuroscience, and reductionism altogether. Where, then, is psychiatry's new unity to be found? Merely juxtaposing viewpoints does not reconcile them. Catholicity, by itself, cannot integrate Coyle's neurophysiological exuberance with Marmer's Freudian nostalgia.

In trying to reconcile the two approaches, one must recognize that Coyle's assertion that psychiatry is undergoing a shift from psychodynamic to neuroscience paradigms draws support from many sources, both pro and con.[1] One must also recognize that there seems to be rather general agreement that the change is motivated intellectually by two considera-

[1]See Bailey (1960); Brown (1986); Engel (1977); Frazier (1987); Goode (1988); Grossman (1987); Hart (1988); Holzman (1985); Kandel (1979, 1983); Kelly (1975); Kramer (1988); Meyersburg and Post (1979); Mohl (1987); Mora (1980); Nemiah (1980); Nicholi (1988); Slavney and McHugh (1987); and Snyder (1984).

tions. On the one hand, the psychoanalytic approach that dominated American psychiatry during the fourth, fifth, and sixth decades of the century failed to provide useful answers to the problems of psychotic illness; on the other, certain drugs were discovered that have proved helpful in treating illnesses of this sort. But there is also reason to be cautious: The fact that certain mental disorders may not have yielded to psychological approaches in no way ensures that no mental disorder will; the fact that some mental disorders have proved partially amenable to a neuroscientific approach in no way guarantees that that approach will be successful for disorders overall. It is necessary, therefore, to examine Coyle's and Marmer's chapters carefully.

The Case for Neuroscience

In reading Coyle's chapter, one is struck by the considerable distance between what is claimed and what is demonstrated. At best, its wealth of information concerning neuronal chemistry and physiology, neurotransmitters, receptors, neuroanatomy, molecular neurobiology, and molecular psychopharmacology tenuously links unsystematized psychological concepts with brain biology. At worst, it employs psychological categories inadequate to frame theories either of mind or behavior and biological categories that do not encompass the cybernetic functioning of the brain. While acceptable to persons narrowly trained in biomedical technology, there is real question whether it provides an adequate conceptual basis for biologists, psychologists, sociologists, and philosophers with broader points of view. To assess that proposition, I shall examine Coyle's theses from four perspectives:

1. Can or should psychiatry be biomedical?
2. Can behavior be analyzed molecularly?
3. Is behaviorism, folk psychology, phenomenology, or information processing an adequate conception of the mind?
4. Does narrowing the Cartesian separation between mind and brain mean biological reduction?

Can or Should Psychiatry Be Biomedical?

Coyle asserts that "advances in research on the brain have occurred with a rapidly increasing pace over the last 15 years and have reached the point that neuroscience can justifiably be considered the biomedical foundation for psychiatry" (1988, p. 3). This assumes that psychiatry should have a biomedical foundation. Whether that is true depends critically on what is meant by biomedical, but on that issue Coyle is silent. The reader is forced to look elsewhere for instruction.

In one of the more thoughtful articles written on this topic in the last decade or two, George Engel (1977) identifies the biomedical model as the cause of the schism between those who would exclude psychiatry from medicine on the grounds that mental disorders are not "diseases" and those who would limit psychiatrists to dealing only with biological illnesses and treatments. In Engel's view, such a model is not only inadequate for psychiatry but is also inadequate for medicine as a whole, and he fears that, just at the moment when the rest of medicine appears ready to move beyond the biomedical model and deal with the psychosocial components of all illness, psychiatry seems poised to advance in the opposite direction. Engel's concern is shared by others (Fink 1982; Schwartz and Wiggins 1985; Zelm 1986). What then are the details of the situation?

Engel (1977) describes the biomedical model in the following way:

> The dominant model of disease today is biomedical, with molecular biology its basic scientific discipline. It assumes disease to be fully accounted for by deviations from the norm of measurable biological (somatic) variables. It leaves no room within its framework for the social, psychological, and behavioral dimensions of illness. The biomedical model not only requires that disease be dealt with as an entity independent of social behavior, it also demands that behavioral aberrations be explained on the basis of disordered somatic (biochemical or neurophysiological) processes. Thus the biomedical model embraces both reductionism, the philosophic view that complex phenomena are ultimately derived from a single primary principle, and mind-body dualism, the doctrine that separates the mental from the somatic. Here the reductionistic primary principle is physicalistic; that is, it assumes that the language of chemistry and physics will ultimately suffice to explain biological phenomena. From the reductionistic viewpoint, the only conceptual tools available to characterize and experimental tools to study biological systems are physical in nature. (P. 196)

Thus conceived, there is no escaping that the biomedical label applies to Coyle's vision of psychiatry in important ways: Behavior is to be analyzed molecularly; disorder or disease is to be understood in terms of deviations from biological norms and will eventually be diagnosed by chemical, imaging, genetic, or other "biological" examinations; psychology and psychopathology are to be reduced to the functioning and dysfunctioning of neuronal systems; treatments will be pharmacological or somatic; and so on. Moreover, when Coyle refers to biology and neuroscience as scientific and to psychology and social factors as humanistic, he is clearly guilty of the biomedical hubris Engel deplores. But Coyle's conception of psychiatry also deviates from Engel's biomedical criteria in certain ways. For example, Coyle does leave room, albeit cramped, for social, psychological, and behavioral dimensions of illness: Psychiatrists will still screen patients psychologically in order to determine who should have biological diagnostic tests; psychological and social experience may be found to play a role in "the phenotypic expression of genes and [to] ultimately affect brain neuronal systems that are involved in drives, affects, and cognitive functions" (1988, p. 30); doctors will still have to convince patients to take their medicines, and so on. More important, however, when Coyle speaks of *correlating* neurophysiological events with mental experience and thus reducing the Cartesian separation of mind and brain, he appears in some way to go against the mind-body dualism that Engel holds to be central to the biomedical approach.

When Engel says that mind-body dualism is "the doctrine that separates the mental from the somatic," he appears to imply that he himself would not separate these domains. Yet in his prescription of a biopsychosocial model for all of medicine, he does not argue that biological, psychological, and social phenomena are indistinct. He argues only that factors of all three sorts must be integrated in our conceptions of normality, disease, and treatment. It is, therefore, not the duality inherent in the biomedical approach with which Engel is concerned, but rather the principles of coordination that that approach employs. It is the reductionistic dogma which holds that psychological and social phenomena are epiphenomena to be dispensed with once adequate biological knowledge is available. In effect, Engel's concern is with the idea of a linear reductive relationship of the sciences to one another, an intellectual monster spawned by nineteenth-century mechanistic thought and living still in certain scientific backwaters.

The problem, therefore, appears as follows. On the one hand, Coyle's admission, however grudging, of the need to coordinate biological mechanisms with psychological functions signals a move toward Engel's way of thinking. On the other hand, his references to biology and neurophysiology as *science* and to psychology and sociology as *humanism*[2] make one fear

[2]For a more explicit statement of this thesis, see Slavney and McHugh 1987, p. 6: ". . . even if the humanities bring greater appreciation of the phenomenal world than is possible from the viewpoint of science alone. . . ."

that he is only paying lip service to psychology while continuing to see scientific psychiatry as biological.

Rather than try to settle the issue here, I shall for the moment simply relate it to the ancient conflict that underlay the vitalist-mechanist debate (Brown 1986; Cellérier 1983; Mayr 1982). At one extreme of that polemic, biological mechanists concerned with empirical methods and scientific certainty held that all biological theories would eventually be reduced to physical theories. In attempting to carry out their program, they oversimplified the phenomena they wanted to explain. For example, Jacques Loeb argued early in this century that "the nature of the will [is] rapidly coming within the scope of physicochemical explanation. Man's wishes and hopes, disappointments and sufferings, [find] their basis in instincts 'comparable to the life instinct of the heliotropic animals'; and for many of these instincts the chemical base [is] so clearly understood as to make it 'only a question of time' before they [are] to be fully accounted for on mechanistic lines" (Goodfield 1974, p. 74). In psychiatry, many neuroscientists appear to hold a similar point of view; Eric Kandel (1979, 1983) provides a case in point. At the other extreme, biological vitalists worried about comprehending living phenomena in all of their complexity have argued against the possibility of mechanistic explanation and have sometimes invoked entities outside the purview of scientific study. This, for example, was the case with Driesch's concept of "entelechy" in embryology. In psychiatry, Habermas's (1971; Grünbaum 1984) "movement of self-reflection" adopted by George Klein and other psychoanalysts provides a psychological analogy. But as Mayr (1982, p. 59) points out, these extremes are not the only alternatives available. In fact, in biology essentially all recent theorists who have stood against mechanistic reductionism have opposed vitalism equally. To such theorists, full understanding requires elucidating the physicochemical mechanisms that accomplish biological functions and organization, but it in no way dissolves the autonomy and distinctness of biology's concepts and theories and does not place them within the domain of physics. In fact, such thinkers argue, unless interpreted within the context of the special characteristics of living systems, the mechanisms identified have no biological meaning whatsoever. In parallel with this, I argue that neuroscientific reductionism and psychological "vitalism" are not the only theoretical alternatives available to psychiatrists. (By vitalism I mean psychological approaches that place their concepts and principles beyond the purview of scientific study or, conversely, that redefine science in order to escape the burden of justifying their beliefs.) With superior reason, psychiatrists may also insist on the uniqueness and autonomy of mental concepts and advance the view that neuroscientific mechanisms have no psychological significance outside the context of a unique, autonomous, and irreducible science of the mind. (In fact, this is Engel's position, I believe.) To do this, however, requires an adequate psychological education, which at present the majority of psychiatrists do not enjoy.

Can Behavior Be Analyzed Molecularly?

The second question I wish to raise concerning Coyle's thesis is whether behavior can be analyzed molecularly. When Coyle states that it is now "feasible to begin to analyze behavior at the molecular level" (1988, p. 3), the reader expects that somewhere in the chapter he will illustrate that contention with examples. However, the first three sections demonstrate nothing relative to the molecular analysis proposition. "Functional Anatomy of the Neuron" makes only a single reference to any psychological category: "the neuron is a cell that is highly specialized . . . to carry out the function of processing information" (1988, pp. 3–4). It does not include (nor, for that matter, does the book) any discussion of information processing or any consideration of the voluminous literature questioning whether mind can be represented in terms of information processing models. Similarly, the section entitled "Neurotransmitters" makes but a single reference to anything even remotely psychological: "It is not often appreciated . . . that psychiatry, the medical specialty most concerned with issues of communication, fostered much of the early research on the mechanisms of chemical communication among neurons in the brain" (1988, p. 5). Since, however, this idea is not elaborated, the reader must search elsewhere for a discussion that might give scientific substance to its implied analogy between psychological and neural "communication" (if such discussion is even conceivable). And the section entitled "Receptors" proves no different—there is only tangential reference to psychology. That reference, however, is significant in that it provides a faint suggestion as to how the biological-psychological linkage will be made: "A major advance in neuroscience that has had considerable impact on the understanding of information processing in the brain and the sites of action of neuroactive substances, including psychotropic medications, has been the development of strategies to characterize brain receptors" (1988, p. 10). Apparently, the inferential chain psychotropic action → transmitter-receptor → neural pathway or something similar is developing.

The following section, "Neuroanatomy," bears this suspicion out. There one learns that the best evidence implicating neuronal systems in major mental disorders has to do with "the serendipitous discovery of several classes of effective pharmacologic agents whose mechanisms of action ultimately have been defined in terms of altering synaptic neurotransmission of specific components of the reticular core" (1988, p. 16). One is further apprised that the function of the reticular core appears to be to regulate neuronal function in large areas of the brain and that disruption of its function does not produce hard neurological signs, but rather creates disturbances in drives, affects, arousal, and cognitive function—psychological categories all. Through implicative linkages of this sort, noradrenergic neurons can be correlated with reduction of anxiety and some effects of withdrawal from narcotics, alcohol, and nicotine, as well as with the effects of antidepressant drugs. Similarly, this strategy correlates serotonergic neurons with the effects of hallucinogens and buspirone, with rapid eye movements during sleep, and with aggression; it correlates dopaminergic neurons with Parkinson's disease, the extrapyramidal side effects of neuroleptic drugs, and positive feeling; it correlates cholinergic neurons with cognitive defects seen in Alzheimer's disease and with depressed mood; it correlates gamma-aminobutyric acid (GABA) neuronal systems with tardive dyskinesia; it correlates glutaminergic neurons with sensory perception, with the psychomimetic effects of certain drugs, and, perhaps, with several neurodegenerative disorders and their accompanying psychological disturbances; and it may correlate endorphin neuronal systems with stress-related analgesia and depression. While this hardly can be called analyzing behavior at the molecular level, it does tentatively link neurophysiological mechanisms to fragmentary psychological conceptions.

The section entitled "Molecular Neurobiology" takes another tack in its discussion of the techniques by which genes have been linked to familial Alzheimer's disease, Huntington's chorea, and a form of bipolar disorder. The psychological import of such findings stems, by implication, from the psychological symptoms observed in these disorders. However, Coyle does not discuss those symptoms and makes no attempt to link them to information processing or behavior, two of his implied models of the mind. Although he states that "as genes responsible for psychiatric disorders become amenable to studies with this strategy, the cellular and metabolic consequences of their expression should be uncovered, thereby leading to a better understanding of the pathophysiology of the disorder and the development of more effective therapeutic interventions" (1988, p. 25), he also realizes that such knowledge may have limited therapeutic implications. He cites, as an example, Lesch-Nyhan syndrome, for which the enzymatic defect has been known for twenty years without increasing our understanding of how it causes self-injurious behavior, dystonia, and mental retardation. All of this provides little progress in the molecular analysis of behavior.

In the final section of the chapter, entitled "Molecular Psychopharmacology," Coyle returns to the psychotropic action → transmitter-receptor → neural pathway line of reasoning. Anesthesiological studies aimed at discovering calming agents uncovered a class of drugs (chlorpromazine and its congeners) that dramatically reduced agitation, hallucinations, and delusions in acute schizophrenia; this therapeutic action was linked to dopamine receptor blockage in forebrain dopaminergic neurons; the discovery of the equally potent butyrophenone neuroleptics undermined the "dopamine hypothesis;" and the theory of DA-1 and DA-2 receptors resulted. Further, it was found that the high-affinity transport system for norephinephrine found in noradrenergic neurons was strongly inhibited by drugs found to have antidepressant properties (the tricyclic antidepressants); inhibition of similar processes of serotonin transport were subsequently discovered; such drugs have been shown to slowly desensitize cortical-limbic beta-receptors; this effect has been linked to all classes of antidepressant drugs and electroconvulsive therapy; and such drugs have also been linked to alterations in alpha-2 adrenergic receptors. All of this has led to two opposing interpretations: It is argued both that depression is due to excessive stimulation of beta-receptors and that depression is due to understimulation of such receptors. In addition, evidence of the same sort links anxiolytic agents to GABA neuronal systems. While Coyle correctly concludes that these and other findings have led to a molecular model for the actions of barbiturates, benzodiazepines, and certain other anticonvulsants and, therefore, illustrates again that certain drugs can be linked to neuronal systems and to psychological effects, he falls far short of demonstrating that behavior can be analyzed molecularly.

Taken all together, what Coyle demonstrates in his neuroscience chapter is that several psychiatric syndromes diagnosed in terms of abnormal movement, abnormal intentional structure of behavior, abnormal mood, abnormal thought, and certain other lay or folk-psychological concepts have been linked to neuronal systems whose molecular mechanisms are partially understood. What he does not demonstrate is the nature of the linkages. He does not show how any neuronal system or any combination thereof produces movement, intention, mood, or thought, let alone mental experience as a whole, nor does he provide any inkling of what the functions of such psychological entities might be. For all of these reasons, while in no way denying that the neurophysiological findings are of theoretical and therapeutic importance to psychiatry, one must reject Coyle's overenthusiastic claim that behavior can now be analyzed molecularly. Indeed, one must question whether, stated as Coyle states it, the idea of analyzing behavior molecularly has any meaning.

Is Behaviorism, Folk Psychology, Phenomenology, or Information Processing an Adequate Conception of the Mind?

The third question I ask relative to Coyle's chapter is whether behaviorism, folk psychology, phenomenology, or information processing can provide an adequate conception of mind. Coyle alludes to these entities as distinct ways in which mental phenomena might be conceived but apparently does not realize that they are more or less incompatible with one another. Moreover, he does nothing to make them relevant to the psychological conception favored in the chapters on development and psychology or to solve the formidable theoretical difficulties that they entail. A brief analysis of each is therefore warranted.

BEHAVIOR

In the paragraph from Coyle quoted on page 307, the following chain of propositions is discovered: Neuroscience is the biomedical foundation for psychiatry; neuroscience will make it possible to analyze behavior at the molecular level; neuroscience will permit diagnostic methodologies to be directed toward the brain; neuroscience will allow the molecular and cellular mechanisms responsible for heritable disorders of behavior to be defined; thus neuroscience narrows the separation between mind and brain. In light of this argument, it is not unfair to conclude that Coyle equates the behavioral and the mental. In this, of course, Coyle is not alone. It is an idea that once ruled American psychology and that is still prevalent in many American institutions. For example, American universities often include departments of behavioral rather than psychological science; American medical schools not infrequently have divisions of behavioral rather than psychological medicine; and the revised third edition of the *Diagnostic and Statistical Manual of Mental Disorders* of the American Psychiatric Association (1987) defines mental disorder as being either a behavioral or psychological syndrome, as if those adjectives were interchangeable.[3] But how justified is this equation?

If, in order to understand the relationships among the terms in question, one turns to the "Excerpts from the American Psychiatric Glossary" included in the *Textbook of Psychiatry,* one finds no entry under "mind" or

[3]To be fair, I must point out that DSM-III-R does not give this impression consistently. Later in the same paragraph one reads that mental disorders must be considered to be manifestations of behavioral, psychological, or biological dysfunctions rather than expectable responses to particular events, as if distinct categories were involved. Sometimes, then, the concepts "behavioral" and "psychological" are identical and define the "mental," and sometimes, alongside the biological, they are distinct sources of mental dysfunction.

"mental," none under "psychology" or "psychological," and none under "behavior." There is, however, an entry under "behaviorism" that bears examination:

> behaviorism: An approach to *psychology* first developed by *John B. Watson* which rejected the notion of mental states and reduced all psychologic phenomena to neural, muscular, and glandular responses. Contemporary behaviorism emphasizes the study of observable responses but is directed toward general behavior rather than discrete acts. It includes private events such as feelings and fantasies to the extent that these can be directly observed and measured. (1988, p. 1243)

This definition raises two questions. First, if behaviorism is only one approach to psychology, how justified is Coyle in granting it a privileged position? Second, if Coyle were to advance the behaviorist point of view consistently, would he prove Watsonian or contemporary in his orientation?

With regard to the first question and somewhat in anticipation of a topic to follow, I note that "information processing," a second psychological approach Coyle mentions, arose in reaction to behaviorist psychology, and that accounts of the history of information processing always include accounts of how and why behaviorism has been rejected (Gardner 1985; Johnson-Laird 1988). It is also interesting to note that there is widespread agreement among psychologists, philosophers, linguists, anthropologists, and other scholars that behaviorism is misguided in its epistemologic assumptions and empirically barren in relation to the human mind.[4] Sarvin (1980, p. 13), for example, concludes that all behaviorist notions stem from a yen for science and from the mistaken belief that the behaviorist point of view, rather than representing an arbitrary choice, represents the only possible basis for a science of psychology. Or, as Wallace (1988) comments, behaviorism stems from the quest for certainty, "a Holy Grail that requires more from science and knowing than they can possibly return and that spawns the twin demons of reductionistic dogmatism and skeptical nihilism" (p. 146). It seems, therefore, that Coyle's linking of behavioral disorders to the information-processing function of neurons as well as his equation of the behavioral and the mental is untenable.

With regard to the question of what sort of behaviorist Coyle might be, his heavy emphasis on neurochemical "explanations" appears to place him

[4]See Chomsky (1980); Grèco (1967); Haugeland (1981); Piaget (1967, 1972); Piaget and Inhelder (1969); and Putnam (1980).

in the Watsonian camp while his passing mention of mental experience, drives, affects, and cognitive functions suggest that he may be contemporary in his point of view. The problem with Watsonian behaviorism is that it makes the mental disappear altogether, which is inconsistent with Coyle's invocation of such mental categories as mood and cognition. The problem with contemporary behaviorism is that its provision for the mental in terms of *directly observable private events* is internally contradictory (compare Fodor 1981, p. 6). So whatever brand of behaviorism Coyle endorses, it proves extremely problematic for psychiatry's task of understanding and treating disorders that are mental.

FOLK PSYCHOLOGY

The second approach to mind that Coyle hints at is "folk psychology." Block (1980) comments on the term in the following way:

> The frontiers of knowledge in [psychology] are so close to the heartland of folk psychology that the conceptual issues about the mind that philosophers have long discussed are very nearly the same as the issues that impede theoretical progress in psychology. Indeed, the majority of topics of concern to contemporary philosophers of psychology would have been intelligible and, in many cases, even familiar to philosophers who lived long before the rise of modern psychology. (P. 1)

Folk psychology, then, refers to ordinary, unsystematic, intuitive, commonsense ways of conceiving psychological events. It enters Coyle's thinking through his adoption of the DSM-III-R. In a concerted effort to remain "atheoretical"[5] and "descriptive," the DSM-III-R employs popular psychological terms that it does not define or that it defines in highly inconsistent ways. For example, when one seeks a deeper understanding of the concepts in terms of which mood disorders are conceived, the glossary of DSM-III-R leads to confusion. It defines mood in terms of emotion, and gives depression, elation, anger, and anxiety[6] as examples. Emotion, depression, elation, and anger are not treated in the glossary, anxiety is defined without reference to mood, and a class of anxiety dis-

[5]"Pretheoretical" and, therefore, unscientific would more accurately label DSM-III-R's approach (compare Lyons 1977).

[6]Note that in the "Excerpts from the American Psychiatric Glossary" in the *Textbook of Psychiatry* anxiety is not included as an example of mood, affect is defined in a totally different way, and euphoria is defined as an exaggerated feeling of physical and emotional well-being. This does not seem to alleviate the degeneracy of the terms under discussion and, in fact, only provides further evidence of psychiatry's conceptual confusion.

orders is posited. This, taken together with entries concerning affect and euphoric mood, leads the reader to somewhat startling conclusions:

1. Moods are sustained, subjectively experienced feeling states or emotions, examples of which are depression, elation, anger, and anxiety.
2. Affects are behavioral expressions of emotions, sustained or not, examples of which are euphoria, anger, and sadness.
3. Anger is both a mood and an affect. In the first case, it is a sustained emotion; in the second, it is not an emotion at all but rather a behavior either momentary or, perhaps, repeated.
4. There are euphoric moods even though euphoria is an affect that is not a mood and is not like a mood, as affects are behaviors and moods are emotions.
5. Anxiety disorders are not mood disorders, although anxiety is a mood.
6. Mood disorders are inferred using an implicit and somewhat incoherent theory of relationships between concepts of emotion, mood, affects, and behavior; they are neither atheoretical nor descriptive.

If one agrees with Quine (1960) that in less advanced sciences terminology tends to uncritically assume mutual understanding and that as a science progresses it corrects that assumption by introducing definitions, this example indicates how primitive psychiatry remains. If, moreover, one is familiar with Piaget's theory of contradiction, psychiatry's terminological improvements seem to belie its claim to science, as "logical contradiction [an essential ingredient of scientific knowledge] presupposes a minimum of formalization at least in the sense of an interplay of definitions" (Piaget 1974*a*, p. 10).[7]

In sum, then, the psychological approach taken in DSM-III-R is often no more definite, no more consistent, and no more scientific than the approach taken in the streets. By substituting common-language conceptions for more elaborated ones stemming from developed psychological theories, it moves backward rather than ahead. Moreover, its positivist presupposition of pure facts or descriptions has been repeatedly refuted.[8] Like behaviorism, this approach leads nowhere and must be avoided even at the cost of terminological disputes.

PHENOMENOLOGY

The third psychological approach to which Coyle alludes is phenomenology. Perhaps it is unfair to suggest that when, in a single passage, Coyle

[7]Passages quoted from French texts have been translated by the author.
[8]See Faust and Miner (1986); Lakatos (1978); Piaget and Garcia (1983); and Suppe (1977*a*, *b*).

speaks of correlating mental experience with brain processes, he is referring to "clinical phenomenology." Caution advises, however, that the possibility be considered for two interrelated reasons. To begin with, both phenomenological philosophy and phenomenological psychiatry deal with *mental experience,* and, in a very special sense, both are descriptive, as DSM-III-R requires. Second, the term *clinical phenomenology,* as American psychiatrists employ it, is closely associated with the nosologic revolution in psychiatry and with contemporary behaviorist philosophy. For these reasons, Coyle's reference needs to be examined.

Edmund Husserl, the father of modern phenomenology, was interested in how nontemporal truths are apprehended. His solution to the problem lay in invoking methods (the transcendental-phenomenological reduction) that would free consciousness from the spatiotemporal world so that *essences* might be intuited directly. Husserl's ideas on how knowledge arrived at in this way relates to empirical scientific knowledge changed throughout his lifetime. Originally, phenomenologically derived knowledge was knowledge of a previously unsuspected realm of being to which empirical methods were not applicable. (See discussion of vitalism above.) Toward the end of his life, Husserl believed such knowledge differed from scientific knowledge only in that it approached a single realm of being in a different way: The phenomenological approach was reflective and aimed at understanding the lived world *(Lebenswelt)* rather than the world known to science (Harré and Lamb 1983; Piaget 1971; Schmitt 1967).

Phenomenological ideas entered the field of psychopathology through the work of Jaspers, Schneider, Binswanger, Boss, Minkowski, and others (de Koning 1982). In Jasper's and Schneider's hands, phenomenological psychopathology aimed at describing precisely what a patient feels with as little classification as possible, and although other orientations have developed, it remains committed to trying to capture patients' experience (Lanteri-Laura 1982, p. 53). The term *clinical phenomenology* entered American psychiatry because of renewed interest in diagnostic practice occasioned by differences in the prevalence of schizophrenia and mania in Britain and the United States. Structured interviews were developed to ensure that different diagnosticians investigated the same issues in the same way and, by using a standard system of definitions and diagnostic categories, arrived at reliable diagnoses. In the case of schizophrenia, Bleuler's defining symptoms of loosened fabric of thought, affective blunting, autism, avolition, and ambivalence were too broad and imprecise for this approach, necessitating a search for phenomena that were more definite and more clearly discontinuous with what is considered normal. As a result, Wing introduced Schneider's phenomenological descriptions, the "first-rank" symptoms of schizophrenia, into his structured interview, the Present State Examination. Thus clinicians totally innocent of any knowledge of phenomenological philosophy were introduced to phenomenologically derived criteria and began to speak of clinical phenomenology (Black, Yates, and Andreasen 1988, p. 359).

Even from these brief comments, it is obvious that the phenomenology of "clinical phenomenology" is not the same as the phenomenology of philosophy. Clinical phenomenology imports a method for apprehending the *Lebenswelt* into the world of empirical science to which it does not apply. In fact, to describe a patient's experience phenomenologically in the philosophical sense requires that psychiatric knowledge be rejected. To "describe" hallucinatory experiences, for example, requires that psychiatric concepts be "bracketed." The moment that is done, however, the concept of hallucination disappears, and it is no longer possible to distinguish hallucinatory experience from any other. If the bracketing is not carried out, phenomenological description becomes only a subtle sort of empiricism at odds with the goals and methods of the mother theory (Lanteri-Laura 1982, p. 55).

With regard to clinical phenomenology, the nosologic enterprise with which it is associated has been criticized severely. For example, Heaton (1982), in a perceptive analysis of the notion of mental health, argues that contemporary psychiatry confuses diagnosis with scientific classification. Diagnosis consists in the ability to tell that something is wrong. In psychiatry, it involves judgments of oddity, strangeness, inappropriateness, and so on. But, argues Heaton, such judgments are not objective. Rather, they depend on the history, personality, and situation of the diagnostician. For this reason, they cannot provide a basis for the scientific classification of mental illnesses. Psychiatry's attempt to solve the problem by defining mental disorders in terms of value-laden diagnostic criteria—for example, *inappropriate* affect, *bizarre* delusions, *deficient* sexual fantasies, *maladaptive* behavioral changes, *impaired* judgment—fails because formal definitions do not, themselves, furnish strict recognition rules. (See examples in Winokur, Zimmerman, and Cadoret 1988.) Diagnosticians must therefore either move outside the diagnostic system, in which case they are faced with the very problems the system was supposed to solve, or they must try to find better definitions. Heaton (1982) concludes:

> The nominal definition of disease puts the method of investigation over the subject matter, a sure sign of theoretical poverty and technical thinking. It delimits a category by attaching numerical value to questions found within the context of the investigation itself. It thus sets out to

> investigate an object with an instrument which through its own construction decides in advance just what that object is—a simple case of circularity. With an arrogance born of ignorance, the objections of classical philosophy . . . to the practice of definition without the theoretical labour of producing the concept of the object are consigned to oblivion. What that philosophy banished as a remnant of scholasticism is still flourishing under the name of scientific psychiatry. (P. 19)

So, if in his reference to experience Coyle means to suggest a phenomenological approach to mental illness, he stumbles upon two great conceptual obstacles: If "phenomenological" is taken in its philosophical sense, it is opposed to his diagnostic system and is itself internally contradictory in its present form; if "phenomenological" is taken in the sense of clinical phenomenology, it becomes empiricist description and confronts the objections to behaviorism and empiricism just outlined. In the first case, the phenomenological approach is unsuited to Coyle's neuroscience program; in the second, it is limited to subjectively distorted *description without explanation* of the conscious mind.

INFORMATION PROCESSING

Information processing is the fourth psychological approach that Coyle mentions. In the opening sentence of the section entitled "Functional Anatomy of the Neuron," he says that "the *neuron* is a cell that is highly specialized, both anatomically as well as biochemically, to carry out the function of processing information" (1988, pp. 3–4). This refers to yet another possible psychology for psychiatry. In fact, information processing is an older term for what is now known as cognitive science, the most widely practiced "academic psychology" in the United States. In a fascinating history of the development of cognitive science, Howard Gardner (1985) has identified five key features of the cognitive science approach:

1. Human cognitive activities are understood in terms of mental representations and require a level of analysis that is distinct from biology or neurophysiology, on the one hand, and separate from sociology and culture, on the other.
2. The electronic computer constitutes the most viable model of how the human mind functions.
3. In order to reduce problems to manageable proportions, certain factors such as the influence of affectivity or emotions, the contributions of history and culture, and the role of the background context in which particular actions or thoughts occur may be deemphasized or excluded.

4. Currently, philosophy, psychology, artificial intelligence, linguistics, anthropology, and neuroscience constitute the cognitive sciences and interdisciplinarity is central.
5. Cognitive science is concerned with issues that have long preoccupied epistemologists in the Western philosophical tradition.

Whether a science meeting this description might provide an appropriate framework for psychiatry depends critically on how psychiatry is conceived. If its task is to classify, explain, and treat *mental* disorders, as the title of DSM-III-R suggests, then cognitive science as a science of the mental would appear to be particularly appropriate. Within such a framework, however, it would be impossible to define mental disorders as either "behavioral or psychological" as DSM-III-R does now, as cognitive science opposes the view that a science of mind can be framed solely in terms of overt, observable behaviors. Equally, a cognitive science framework would preclude a purely neuroscientific approach because it resists the view that a science of mind can be framed solely in terms of neurophysiological events and at times even argues that the physical substrate of the mind is irrelevant to its understanding. What cognitive science would allow is a nosological system of disorders psychologically defined and further qualified along etiological lines according to whether and what sorts of biological, historical, social, or psychological factors lie at their root. Interestingly enough, despite the confusion of its rhetoric, psychiatry appears to be headed in this direction. I shall, therefore, look at the issues in some detail.

The representational point of view requires that normal mental functioning be conceived in terms of schemes, frames, scripts, images, structures, or representations of some other sort and that psychopathology be described in terms of abnormalities of representations and/or their functional issue. In that the construction and use of representations requires both an adequately functioning neurophysiological system and experience of several sorts, it would be possible to attribute neurophysiological and social-developmental etiologies to psychological disorders, but the psychological nature of syndromes would remain intact. Recent revisions of psychiatry's official nosological system illustrate these principles in several ways.

Recall in this respect that the third edition of the *Diagnostic and Statistical Manual of Mental Disorders* (DSM-III) (APA 1980) distinguished between "organic mental disorders" and "organic brain syndromes" on the basis of whether etiology was known. While the first of these categories was consistent with the implications of cognitive science, the second constituted paralogical slippage from one framework to another that was not only inconsistent with cognitive science but was also inconsistent from other points of view. Since the brain is an organ, the adjectival sequence organic-brain was redundant, because all brain syndromes are organic. At the same time, as the brain is an organ, no brain syndrome could be a mental disorder without assuming "mind" to equal "brain." Happily, this particular confusion has been removed in DSM-III-R by changing "organic brain syndromes" to "organic mental syndromes associated with Axis III physical disorders or conditions, or whose etiology is unknown." While wordy, this acknowledges the fact that either what were once called brain syndromes are disorders of orientation, memory, calculating ability, and other representational activities (which, in fact, they are) and are therefore mental, or they are disorders of decreased gray matter, multiple infarction, and so on, in which case they are neural and no longer mental.

DSM-III-R does not, however, maintain a consistent representational point of view. For example, it still includes the category "tic disorders" in which the representational dimension is difficult to specify when only involuntary movements are involved. "Functional encopresis" is also formulated in terms of involuntary defecation secondary to constipation associated with febrile illness or medication. While it may be possible to link such behavior to problems with a child's motives, the representational dimension is questionable and obscure. A different sort of example comes from the category "disruptive behavior disorders." In this case, subclasses are defined in terms of attention, inappropriate aggression, and social opposition, the first of which is an instance of and the second and third of which require representational constructs for their explanation. One wonders, therefore, why these conditions are not simply called "disruptive disorders," as they are no more behavioral than any others. In the same vein, DSM-III-R retains the concept of "personality disorders" and defines personality as "deeply ingrained patterns of behavior, which include the way one relates to, perceives, and thinks about the environment and oneself" (1987, p. 403). As Watsonian behaviorism excluded thinking from the realm of scientifically meaningful phenomena and as contemporary behaviorism, if the glossary of the *Textbook of Psychiatry* (Talbott, Hales, and Yudofsky 1988) can be believed, admits thinking only when it—impossibly—constitutes directly observable private events, the definition of these syndromes is severely flawed. From the representational point of view, all behavior above the reflex level is the end product of representations and their functioning. This means that personality, too, is a matter of representations and is mental; the observable behaviors from which it is inferred are inexplicable on any other basis. In consequence, personality should be defined in terms of "deeply ingrained patterns of relating to, perceiving, and thinking about," and so on. And, in fact, this is what is done in the text, although not in the DSM-III-R's glossary.

In sum, cognitive science's insistence on the autonomy and uniqueness of representational analysis, its assignation of explanatory but not defining roles to biology and sociology, and its identification of behavior with surface manifestations of representational activity offer a rationale for consistently naming psychiatric conditions that avoids certain pitfalls into which psychiatry has fallen. Although psychiatry currently wishes to remain descriptive and atheoretical and to that end employs an uncoordinated mixture of neurophysiological, behavioral, psychoanalytic, and folk-psychological conceptions, it converges unwittingly on the representational point of view. Whether such convergence will continue depends both on the continued focus of psychiatry on the mental and on cognitive science's increasing ability to provide an adequate theory of the mind.

The importance of electronic computers, Gardner's second defining characteristic of cognitive science, stems from the enormous difficulties involved in studying representations. Precisely those difficulties led to the behavioral revolution in the early part of the century; precisely those difficulties stand in the way of granting mentalist psychologies scientific status. If, as Alan Turing believed (Hodges 1983, p. 291), mind is specified only by its logical patterns and not by its physics or its chemistry, then *any* method of studying such patterns—including electronic simulation—will lead to understanding. Because computer simulation requires that computational procedures be specified completely, it offers, to those who accept Turing's thesis,[9] a means of studying mental processes in a way that makes them explicit and available for inspection.

The importance of computers for psychiatry is that, broadly conceived, the computer metaphor offers a plausible approach to psychiatric syndromes. Because effective computation requires both a "bug-free" program and a machine capable of executing it in a concrete way, problems can arise either at the programming level or at the physical level of the machine, or both. Moreover, because within the cognitive science framework the human mind is conceived as a self-programming program, malfunctions at either level interfere with the ongoing development of the program, which introduces a developmental dimension. By analogy, then, it is possible within this framework to model mental disorders of wholly or partially organic etiology—"hardware" disorders such as mental retardation, bipolar disorder, schizophrenia, and the like—as well as disorders

[9]Many workers, for various reasons, do not (Campbell and Bickhard 1986; Fodor 1980; Gardner 1985, pp. 40–41; Putnam 1981; responses in Pylyshyn 1980).

of a purely representational kind—"software" disorders such as personality disorders and other syndromes thought to be psychologically acquired. The computer metaphor would not allow hardware and, by extension, neurophysiological considerations to be the sole basis of psychiatry. Syndromes would, of necessity, have to do with functional patterns, and disorders due to neurophysiological causes would only constitute subsets grouped according to etiologic factors. (This discussion does not take into account certain recent developments in cognitive science, namely distributed parallel processing and connectionism, because currently the relationships of connectivist concepts with the representations central to cognitive science and with neuronal function are too obscure to say anything very definite [Gardner 1985, pp. 318–322; Smolensky 1988].)

Gardner's third key feature of cognitive science—deemphasis of affectivity, emotion, history, culture, and context—is a good deal more problematic than the first two features because it lays aside conceptual categories central to psychiatric thought. In fact, it is inconceivable that a psychology that ignores such issues would be adopted by a discipline that deals with mood, anxiety, interpersonal relationships, development, and motivational explanation. At the same time, there seems no necessary reason to view such categories as "humanistic" and opposed to science, as many psychiatrists as well as many critics of cognitive science do (Coyle 1988, p. 30; Gardner 1985, p. 42; Slavney and McHugh 1987, p. 6ff). Although cognitive science may not succeed in modeling phenomena of these sorts (Haugeland 1981), that does not mean it should not try; in fact, attempts are already being made in this direction. For example, Cellérier (1979*a,b*) has argued that in order to bring cognitive science and Piagetian psychology together, it is necessary to invoke knowledge of values ("axiological knowledge"); Blanchet (1986) and Brown and Weiss (1987) have pointed out that evaluation is a specifically affective function and that Cellérier's assertion, therefore, inserts affectivity into the cognitive realm; and Brown and Weiss (1987; Brown 1990) have integrated Piaget's, Cellérier's, and Pugh's (1977) work into a model of cognition where affectivity functions as a developing system of heuristics that is indispensable for evolving both procedures and the knowledge structures they employ. As cognitive simulations move beyond the problem-solving paradigm, or what Cellérier calls the "pragmatic transformation," and concentrate more on self-programming programs that restructure and motivate themselves, it seems certain that affective, motivational, and developmental aspects, deemphasized at present, will have to be included. And there is no a priori reason to believe that this cannot be done.

Interdisciplinarity and rootedness in classical philosophical problems,

Gardner's fourth and fifth characteristics of cognitive science, are interrelated in the following way. Epistemology as the philosophy of knowledge and, as one of the three great divisions of Western metaphysics, has been a major philosophic focus throughout history. As one of three ultimate processes or functions of consciousness, cognition, defined as knowing in the widest sense, has been a major focus of psychology since its inception. Until very recently, the difference between epistemology and cognition was held to be that the first was philosophical and the second scientific—that is, the first was concerned with the nature, truth value, and justification of beliefs while the second was concerned with their causal explanation in terms of biological constraints, education, personal history, and so on (Woozley 1959, p. 449). However, with Piaget's work (1972) and with increasing interest on the part of philosophers in naturalizing epistemology (Kornblith 1985; Radnitsky and Bartley 1987), differentiation according to these criteria has become problematic. Just as cosmology, another division of classical metaphysics, has been made a science resting largely on astronomical discoveries, so epistemology is becoming scientific with biological, psychological, and sociological knowledge forming its foundation. It is within this context that the need for interdisciplinarity has been felt. Not only are problems of mind of interest to workers in different fields—philosophy, evolutionary biology, linguistics, psychology, psychiatry, mathematics, neuroscience, physics, computer simulation, and so on—but they also require such varied expertise that it is difficult if not impossible for workers from a single discipline to take them on alone. It is for this reason that many cognitive scientists are involved in interdisciplinary endeavors.

Because psychiatrists often undertake interdisciplinary efforts and because such fields as neuropsychology are in principle interdisciplinary, there is nothing about Gardner's last two key features of cognitive science that would make that science unsuitable for psychiatry. There are, however, interdisciplinary rivalries, disciplinary concerns, and institutional practices that make collaboration difficult. Increasingly, psychoanalysts find it difficult to obtain tenured appointments to psychiatric faculties; departments of psychiatry often offer tenure only to "wet-lab" researchers; psychologists are paid less than physicians; few linguists, sociologists, or anthropologists can hope for positions in departments of psychiatry or neuroscience; and so on. All of this tends to place neuroscientists and biological psychiatrists on top and threatens cooperative collaboration among scientists of equal status (Holzman 1985).

In sum, adopting cognitive science as a psychology for psychiatry leads to certain implications and presents certain problems. On the one hand, cognitive science's contention that mind resides in its formal program regardless of the physical mechanisms that embody it precludes making neuroscience the biomedical basis of psychiatry. While embodying mechanisms may constrain the abstract program in fundamental ways and while they may give rise to specific malfunctions of the system, they cannot, in principle, provide a conceptual basis for a science of the mental. On the other hand, so long as cognitive science models continue to focus on the use of already-constructed knowledge to solve problems and neglect developmental, affective, cultural, motivational, and experiential factors, they will not apply directly to psychiatric problems for the simple reason that, at present, few psychiatric syndromes are conceived or diagnosed in terms of problem-solving deficits. And finally, the conviction held by many biological psychiatrists and neuroscientists that their knowledge is more fundamental, more scientific, and more certain than psychological knowledge must cede to more egalitarian convictions if cognitive science and psychiatry are to be brought together.

In response then, to the third question organizing discussion of Coyle's chapter, I conclude that, as they stand, none of the psychologies Coyle hints at would be adequate to the conceptual problems facing psychiatrists. Enriched, expanded, and integrated into a systematic theory, all of them may contribute, but treated in Coyle's allusive fashion they produce confusion and despair. No wonder psychiatrists toy with the idea of giving up psychology altogether.

Does Narrowing the Cartesian Separation between Mind and Brain Mean Biological Reduction?

The fourth and final question I have posed regarding Coyle's chapter is the question of reductionism. In *The Growth of Biological Thought,* Ernst Mayr (1982) remarked that many physical scientists and philosophers of the physical sciences have held or hold that "all theories of biology can, at least in principle, be reduced to theories of physics" (p. 59) and, therefore, that an autonomous science of life does not exist. But, as Mayr further noted, the term *reduce* has at least three different meanings. One variety, constitutive reductionism, is based on the idea that there are no material constituents of an organism that are not found in the inorganic world and that the events and processes found within living organisms are totally compatible with the physico-chemical laws that rule the universe. A second form, explanatory reductionism, consists of the belief that understanding complex systems is a matter of isolating their components and explaining each down through successive organizational levels to the most elementary.

And finally, theory reductionism, attempts to demonstrate that "theories and laws formulated in one field of science (usually a more complex field of science or one higher in the hierarchy) can be shown to be a special case of theories and laws formulated in some other branch of science" (p. 62). The same three sorts of thinking may, of course, be applied at the mental level, in which case it becomes a matter of reducing mind first to biology and then reducing biology to physics.

As Coyle acknowledges that advances in neurosciences rest on reductionistic approaches and as Gardner (1985) includes a chapter entitled "Neuroscience: The Flirtation with Reductionism" in his history of cognitive science, the question now becomes what sort of reductionism neuroscience has in mind. Because biologists universally accept the idea that organisms are made of ordinary matter and that their processes are composed of ordinary physico-chemical events, and because psychologists admit the same with respect to mental materials and processes, the first variety of reductionism need not be considered.

Explanatory reductionism, however, is another matter. Mayr's exposition begins with the observation that while knowing the structure of DNA made clear the manner in which genes pass on information and while knowledge of the molecular mechanisms within an organ's cells is often necessary to gain full understanding of its function, the generality of the approach is limited. It is possible, for example, to understand the function of a joint without knowing the detailed physiology of the cells and materials that comprise its surfaces. If an orthopedic surgeon wishes to understand why a joint surface has deteriorated, such knowledge is essential; if he wants to construct a prosthesis with which to restore joint function, it is largely unimportant. In fact, observes Mayr, there are numerous instances where false application of explanatory reductionism has done more harm than good, and he cites two examples: early cell theory, which attempted to explain organisms as aggregates of cells, and early population genetics, which considered genotypes to be aggregates of independent genes. According to Mayr (1982), "When a well-known Nobel laureate in biochemistry said, 'There is only one biology, and it is molecular biology,' he simply revealed his ignorance and his lack of understanding" (p. 65).

The problem with explanatory reductionism is that the properties of the components of complex systems are quite different from the properties of the interactions of components with one another. For that reason, the simplification and clarity explanatory reductionism affords come at the price of missing the functioning of the system as a whole; the same is true of the related strategy of reducing complex to simpler systems. Geneticists, for example, first substituted mice, then fruitflies, then yeasts, bacteria, and viruses for the cows and horses with which they began their studies.

Even though this speeded up genetic research without breaking wholes apart, it ended eventually in genetic models that cannot be extrapolated to mammals in important ways. So simplifications of any sort must be undertaken with great care.

As it happens, contemporary psychiatry and neuroscience are much taken with explanatory reductionism of both these sorts: Coyle's neuronal systems constitute examples of the component type; Eric Kandel's work linking reflex withdrawal in aplasia to anxiety in man provides a dramatic example of the "simpler organism" kind. As Coyle's thinking has been discussed already, only the Kandel example needs to be considered in detail.

In a paper entitled "From Metapsychology to Molecular Biology: Explorations into the Nature of Anxiety," Kandel (1983) pursued the argument that recent scientific advances in cognitive psychology and neurobiology make the cell mechanisms of mentation less elusive. To illustrate his thesis, Kandel presented evidence that administering electrical shocks to sea snails renders their defensive reflexes stronger (sensitization) and that such reflexes can also be connected with neutral stimuli by presenting such stimuli before the shock (conditioning). He explained the first finding in terms of altered synaptic transmission due to changes in cyclic AMP and extended that explanation to the second situation, although the cellular mechanisms are not worked out completely. Finally, he interpreted the whole as a model for the development of anxiety states in humans.

There are two great problems with Kandel's thesis. The first has to do with the psychology he invokes. Although Kandel speaks of recent progress in cognitive psychology, the psychology he uses is the reflexology of Ivan Pavlov. It is the psychology from which behaviorism started, and it is a psychology that cognitive science rejected precisely because it could not explain higher mental processes—complexly organized behavior, language, or planning (Gardner 1985, chap. 2; Johnson-Laird 1988, pp. 21–23). So Kandel's psychology is neither cognitive nor recent, and there is no reason to believe that he will be more successful than his predecessors at reducing higher mental processes to simple reflexes.

The second great problem with Kandel's thesis is that it conflates reflex-mediated responsiveness with affect-mediated responsiveness, which are not the same. In effect, both cognitive science and Piagetian developmental psychology hold that the intellectual system evolved because it enables individual organisms to invent adapted behaviors by other than genomic means.[10] Whereas biologically given behaviors (reflexes and instincts) arise through variation and selection in the biological sense, psychologically

[10]See Brown (1990); Brown and Weiss (1987); Cellérier (1979*a,b,* 1987); and Pugh (1977).

created behaviors (habits and intentional behaviors of several levels) are evolved through variation and selection psychologically achieved. For the latter to be possible, both variation and selection have to be accomplished psychologically, and the affective system arose to fulfill the selective function. More specifically, in organic evolution selection is based on thermodynamic stability or "survival" affecting organisms as a whole (Brooks and Wiley 1986; Prigogine and Stengers 1984). If, through homeostatic transformations and reproduction, an organism cannot reverse the disorganizing transformations to which all physical objects are subjected, the organism disappears. In psychological evolution, by contrast, selection is based on evaluation, largely affective, of individual psychological structures. If an act or an idea has negative value overall, it, not the organism, ceases to exist. In this way nature economizes on time and individuals, and behavioral evolution is vastly speeded up.

An important implication of this analysis is that in studies of affectivity, the investigator must take care to distinguish behaviors that are genomically evolved from ones that are psychologically created, and it is precisely by failing to make this distinction that Kandel goes astray. Specifically, Kandel claims that an affect of anxiety mediates between the shocks administered by the experimenter and the sea snail's responses in terms of locomotive escape, siphon retraction, and gill withdrawal. In fact, however, the defensive reflexes of the sea snail are not new behaviors invented by the organism on the spot, and they do not involve affective evaluation of any sort. Rather, they were created by the genomic system during the sea snail's evolution, and their adaptive adequacy was evaluated through thermodynamic processes affecting the organism as a whole. Ironically, Kandel admits as much when he qualifies the behaviors he studies as "pre-wired," thereby indicating their organic origin. In consequence, although it may have some bearing on simple defensive reflexes in humans, as in withdrawing one's hand from hot objects, it is questionable whether Kandel's work is relevant to defensive reactions of more complicated sorts, for example, repression or denial, and it seems unlikely to yield insights into how affective evaluation is accomplished.

The third and final type of reductionism discussed by Mayr is called theory reduction. It consists, or is supposed to consist, in demonstrating that the theories and laws of one science are merely special cases of theories and laws of another, usually simpler, science. According to Mayr, this form of reductionism arises from confusing processes with concepts and, in fact, does not exist. To begin with, the celebrated theory reductions of physics have never been achieved completely. Second, biology has not taken seriously claims to theory reduction. While processes such as meiosis, gastrulation, or predation can be viewed from either biological or physiochemical perspectives, they remain biological concepts and have meaning only in biology. Finally, where psychology is concerned, the idea of theory reduction is even more remote. In the few cases where psychological conceptions have reached scientific status, the process-concept argument applies; in the many cases where folk concepts are at issue, they constitute neither laws nor theories and could not be special cases of another theory. So talk of theory reduction is misleading.

In short, there is no reason to believe that psychology any more than other science will lose its distinctness and autonomy with the advance of neuroscientific knowledge. While much more may be discovered about the neurophysiological mechanisms underlying mental activity, such knowledge will have psychological meaning only insofar as it can be placed within an independent context of a theory of psychology. Neurophysiology itself will never include concepts of motivation, paranoia, consciousness, depression, symbolization, or other psychological categories without which mind and its pathology are inconceivable. Rather than constituting a goal or even a possibility for psychiatry, reduction is a chimera to be avoided.

Conclusion with Respect to Neuroscience

This lengthy examination of Coyle's neuroscience chapter leads to the following conclusions: Psychiatry cannot and should not wish to be biomedical; behavior cannot be analyzed molecularly; mind cannot be adequately dealt with by any of the psychologies Coyle alludes to; and the reduction of psychological to neuroscientific concepts is impossible. At the same time, it would be wrong to deny that neuroscience constitutes an important, albeit partial, basic science of psychiatry that, when wedded to adequate psychological and sociological theories, will lead to psychiatric progress. The question that now needs answering is whether the psychological and sociological theories that psychiatry embraces can do their part in founding psychiatry scientifically.

Psychiatry's Psychology

Not counting the appendixes and index, the *Textbook of Psychiatry* contains 1,178 pages. Of those, 162 (about 14 percent) are devoted to theoretical foundations, and of that portion a little more than half are devoted to topics that one may properly call psychological. Moreover, as noted earlier, the chapter "Epidemiology of Mental Disorders" does not really deal with psychological theory. Rather, it deals with "the quantitative study of the distribution of mental disorders in human populations" and in so doing adopts uncritically the psychology (or psychologies) inherent in DSM-III-R. In a sense, then, it is not about psychology at all but is, rather, about statistical studies applying unexamined psychological concepts of suspect scientific status. As also noted earlier, the "Normal Growth and Development" chapter examines various psychological approaches but exposits no theory in detail and is deeply flawed.[11] And finally, the "Theories of Mind and Psychopathology" chapter focuses almost exclusively on a single psychological theory: Of the chapter's thirty-five pages, seventeen are dedicated to classical analysis, eleven are committed to developments within psychoanalytic theory, four focus on dynamic psychological theories that have split off from the analytic tradition, and three concern cognitive and behavioral approaches lying outside the analytic framework. Nothing is said about why psychiatry has rejected its psychoanalytic basis; the chapter does not address the issue of psychiatry becoming more scientific; none of the issues raised by Coyle is joined; psychopathologic implications are described as "weak"; the concepts presented are not correlated with DSM-III-R's disorders; and the techniques and efficacy of psychoanalytic therapy are left unmentioned.[12]

The result is that the theoretical foundations section leaves the reader with the impression that modern psychiatry—the new scientific psychiatry—has arisen from the illicit union of an exuberant adolescent (neuroscience) and a jaded grande dame (psychoanalysis) with little in common. Brought together by the vagaries of history, these unlikely partners have produced an offspring that is neither handsome nor healthy. One questions, therefore, whether they should have mated or whether cohabitation should continue.

[11]For example, in the discussion of Piaget's developmental theory, the move from sensorimotor to concrete operational stages omits both the notion of the semiotic function and the preoperational part of the concrete operational period (compare Piaget and Inhelder 1969). As a result, not only are internal representations erroneously implied to be sensations split off from motricity, but a gap of approximately five and one-half years is left in the developmental continuum. Errors of this sort along with the failure to deal with conceptual issues nullify the chapter's usefulness.

[12]The situation is made worse by the fact that social and cultural theories are not included. That society and culture are widely held to contribute to our concepts of disease as well as to the etiology and treatment of mental disorders—even to govern the construction of all knowledge—appears to have escaped the attention of the editors. While it is true that one finds references to socioeconomic correlates of disease and family dynamics in other sections of the volume, such passages do not compensate for the conceptual damage that results from excluding the social and the cultural from the discussion of psychiatry's foundations. This issue is, however, too large to be given full discussion.

Less metaphorically, the union of reductionistic neurophysiology with psychoanalysis in a quest for science seems particularly wrong-headed. On the one hand, neuroscience, although espousing scientific methods, remains psychologically naive; on the other, psychoanalysis cannot decide what science is or whether it is itself scientific. Patently, the two disciplines are in very different places. Therefore, I cannot, as I did with regard to neuroscience, ask whether psychoanalysis provides an adequate scientific basis for the diagnosis and treatment of mental disorders. Rather, I must consider whether psychoanalysis is compatible with science. I do so in the context of longstanding polemics that have arisen in relation to analysis.

Is Psychoanalysis Incompatible with Science?

No doubt psychiatry's widely acknowledged shift from psychoanalysis to neuroscience[13] stems from many motives, some less noble than the quest for knowledge. But the fact remains that, alongside manifold ignoble or practical reasons for changing paradigms, uneasiness about psychoanalysis's scientific status is widespread and longstanding. Here are but a few examples: Boring's influential book (1950), *A History of Experimental Psychology,* states, "We can say, without any lack of appreciation for what has been accomplished, that psychoanalysis has been prescientific" (p. 713); Skinner (1953) holds that Freud's theory of mental illness is a modern version of possession by the devil and that his explanations are a set of "fictions" (pp. 374–375); the eminent philosopher of science, Karl Popper (1956), cites Freudian psychology as an instance of "pseudoscience" (p. 163); in his work on empirical studies of psychoanalytical theories, Masling (1983) points out that "despite a vast amount of experimental work, those who write about psychoanalysis present their material, almost without exception, ex cathedra, offering their views with no more substantial base than clinical evidence" (p. ix); and Grünbaum (1984), although not denying the possibility of psychoanalytic science, contends that "the reasoning on which Freud rested the major hypotheses of his edifice was fundamentally flawed" and that "clinical data from the psychoanalytic treatment setting are . . . epistemically quite suspect" (p. 94).

In light of such contentions by so many careful scholars, one wonders what role psychoanalysis could possibly play in a psychiatry that would be science and, conversely, why neuroscience even pays it lip service. Close

[13]See Bailey (1960); Brown (1986); Engle (1977); Frazier (1987); Goode (1988); Grossman (1987); Hart (1988); Holzman (1985); Kandel (1979, 1983); Kelly (1975); Kramer (1988); Meyersburg and Post (1979); Mohl (1987); Mora (1980); Nemiah (1980); Nicholi (1988); Slavney and McHugh (1987); and Snyder (1984).

scrutiny of the literature on this subject identifies two general positions concerning psychoanalysis's scientific status. I shall consider them in turn.

PSYCHOANALYSIS IS NOT A "NATURAL" SCIENCE

The first position holds that psychoanalysis is not a science in the sense that physics, chemistry, and neurophysiology are; that "natural" science of the physical kind is an illegitimate approach to mind; that the human sciences require a mode of explanation other than "causal" attributions of the nomological-deductive or probabilistic sort; and that for all these reasons a wedding of psychoanalysis and neuroscience must needs be grotesque and barren. Grünbaum (1984) identifies this position with the *Geisteswissenschaften* movement of nineteenth-century Germany and with the hermeneutic conceptual framework that certain scholars propose for psychology and the social sciences in general. Wallace (1988) links it to the relativism of Kuhn and Feyerabend. (As mentioned, and significantly, the only epistemological reference in Marmer's chapter in the *Textbook of Psychiatry* is to Kuhn [Marmer 1988, p. 123].) And Eagle (1983) brings out problems inherent in its wish to limit psychoanalysis to motivational explanations only.

Eagle, perhaps, gives the most generous account of how these theorists view science. By "natural science," adherents of this position mean causal explanation "in terms of 'purposeless' physical conditions and processes and factors external to the person as an agent, in contrast to explanation in terms of meaning, purpose, and intention" (Eagle 1983, p. 313). But, he argues, science is defined by its method, not its content. Psychoanalysis has so far failed to become a science not because it includes motivational concepts but for other reasons. First, human conduct cannot be explained in motivational terms alone. When some human action is successfully analyzed in terms of motivations, one then wants to understand why the subject had those motivations. The moment that concepts like temperament, history, or environmental circumstances are invoked, explanation leaves the realm of motives. Second and more simply, psychoanalysis is not science because it does not provide criteria for evaluating the reliability and validity of its explanations. Without that it is impossible to settle disagreements about competing motivational accounts, and science is precluded. To be a science, psychoanalysis must not only include all relevant explanatory factors, but it must also prove what it says.

Grünbaum (1984) makes much the same argument in greater detail. He begins by showing that Freud himself claimed natural science status for his brainchild and argues that hermeneuticists' attempts to split clinical theory from metapsychological theory not only misunderstand natural science but also run afoul of Freud. One by one he takes apart Habermas's ideas that psychoanalytic therapy operates through the "causality of fate" rather than the causality of nature, that psychoanalytic explanations are historical and contextual while physical explanations are not, and that only the patient can decide the truth of psychoanalytic interpretations. He then methodically dismantles Ricoeur's claims that the "facts" of psychoanalysis are not facts of observable behavior, that the "causal" role of fantasies and meanings splits off psychological causation from scientific methods, and that psychoanalytic propositions are true if they are consistent with Freud's theory or lead to therapeutic success. Finally, he condemns Klein's misreading and distortion not only of Freud's epistemic position but also of his clinical theory. Grünbaum's conclusions vis-à-vis hermeneutics are instructive:

> What, then, is the upshot of my scrutiny here of the cardinal tenets of Habermas, Ricoeur, and Klein? First, their proposed philosophical reconstruction of the clinical theory rests on a mythic exegesis of Freud's own perennial notion of scientificity. And, of-a-piece with this contrived reading, their paradigm of the natural sciences is wildly anachronistic. Second, they have traded misleadingly on the "intentionality" appropriate to psychoanalytic motivational explanations by misassimilating it—in one way or another—either to the practical syllogism or to the symbolic functions of a language. Indeed, such Pickwickian intentionality as characterizes human conduct if explained psychoanalytically does not have either the ontological or the epistemic import claimed by their philosophical theses. Thirdly, once the hermeneutic construal is robbed of its scientophobic myths, its sterility for the constructive utilization of the Freudian legacy in psychology and psychiatry becomes apparent. The residue from Dilthey's original version of hermeneutics toward the fruition of research has turned out to be merely a negativistic ideological battle cry. The more recent hermeneutic gloss on psychoanalysis similarly has all the earmarks of an investigative *cul-de-sac,* a blind alley rather than a citadel for psychoanalytic apologetics. (1984, p. 93)

In the same vein, Wallace labels the hermeneutic construal "subjectivist" and includes it in a section entitled "Relativism-Subjectivism." With regard to relativist theses, he quotes Feyerabend to the effect that the choice of scientific theories is not a matter of truth but of taste and that one's scientific beliefs are, therefore, no different from *aesthetic* judgments, religious convictions, or irrational preferences of other sorts. He then links relativist epistemology to psychoanalysis through the work of Schafer and Spence. These theorists argue that clinical empathizing is not right or wrong and its truth cannot be established in the usual way. Spence, says Wallace, reduces such theorizing to an artistic struggle evaluated *aesthetically* in terms of narrative coherence and unproven therapeutic outcome. His conclusions are logically similar to Eagle's and Grünbaum's and his rhetoric as heated as the latter's:

> The relativist-subjectivists inflate partial truths into a thesis as one-sided and erroneous as what they oppose. They alert us to the impact of theoretical presuppositions on the investigator's perceptions, while totally depreciating the contribution of the reality with which he or she interacts. They reason from the fact that perception can be unreliable or illusory to the conclusion that it is always so. That memory can be untrustworthy becomes "it is completely and invariably so." That recollections are subject to reinterpretation over time becomes "we can never approximate to the individual's representation of the event at the time it was experienced." That the clinician brings current interpretive categories to bear upon the patient's history becomes "the clinician is manufacturing that history." That psychical life is ambiguous becomes "the psyche is unknowable." That we must view the world from some perspective and that many vantage points are possible upon the same phenomenon becomes "there is a plurality of imaginatively constructed worlds and no two of us live in the same one." The list of subjectivist misconceptions is endless. . . . Clearly, such doctrines as those of Spence and Feyerabend are convenient for witch doctors, astrologers, chiropractors, and politicians—the notion, to put it bluntly, that no one can call us to account, that we can believe what we want as long as it is pretty and helps somebody. (Wallace 1988, pp. 141–142)

Regarding the proposition that psychoanalysis is not a natural science, I therefore conclude that a convincing case for separate kinds of science has not been made. While it is clear that psychoanalysis deals with a distinct and irreducible set of phenomena, while it must employ special investigative methods, and while it involves a sui generis explanatory logic, it cannot escape the fundamental responsibility of scientific thought—to find ways to produce consensus. Without that it can lay no claim to scientific status. The choice, then, is between developing scientific methods specific to psychology or renouncing all pretense of knowing. It is a choice between justifying one's beliefs in compelling ways or admitting that one does not know.

PSYCHOANALYSIS COULD BE SCIENCE

The second general thesis regarding whether psychoanalysis is incompatible with science holds that science is defined by method and not by content, that motivational explanations are not inherently unscientific, and that nothing in principle precludes psychoanalytic propositions from being studied scientifically. To make psychoanalysis a science, according to adherents of this position, is not so much a matter of splitting off the clinical theory from metapsychology, as many psychoanalytic writers suggest doing, but of providing adequate means of testing the reliability and validity of psychoanalytic theses.

Significantly, neither in the section of his chapter entitled "The Psychoanalytic Tradition: Freud's Theories" nor anywhere else in his chapter does Marmer (1988) mention a single empirical study or raise the possibility of testing psychoanalytic hypotheses empirically. Primary process, secondary process, dreams and dreaming, dream interpretation, instinctual drives, death instinct, narcissism and object relations, anxiety, repression, therapeutic alliance, transference, resistance, and interpretation are presented without the least suggestion that empirical studies have been done (Masling 1983) or the slightest recommendation that they should be. For Marmer (1988) it is enough to say, as he does in the passage quoted earlier, that "such theories represent the ways ingenious investigators have made sense out of human behavior" (p. 123). No matter that the sense they make may be wrong, that apparently coherent accounts may not correspond to mental realities, or that belief and justified belief are distinct categories. It is enough that one's theory be "useful." And usefulness, of course, is an empirical claim. Marmer offers no controlled or systematic evidence that psychoanalysis is therapeutically useful.

By contrast, Grünbaum argues that not only are concepts included in Marmer's list and considered central to psychoanalytic theory based on evidence that is deeply suspect but that, even were that not the case, Freud's logic in relating evidence to theory is faulty. Even if the clinical data of analysis were not irremediably contaminated by suggestion, they would not prove Freud's theses. A concrete example will make this clear.

Marmer (1988) writes that dreams have always had "a special place in psychoanalytic theory," that they constitute the "bedrock" of the theory of the unconscious, and that "Freud discovered the main points of his theory" by interpreting dreams (p. 127). The improbable and temporally disorganized events of the remembered dream represent an amalgam of events of the day, nocturnal stimuli, and unconscious wishes along with their associated childhood memories. Were the wishes—unconscious because repressed for one reason or another—to become conscious in the usual fashion, they would produce anxiety and wake the sleeper. For that reason, primary process and symbolization mechanisms are employed to disguise the content of the dream and prolong sleep. Because the unconscious meaning of the dream rests on the repressed wish, dream interpretation requires that the disguising transformations be reversed. "Through the process of free association, the dreamer will be led back across the associative network to the original repressed memories and drives which stimulated the dream in the first place" (p. 128).

Grünbaum (1984) examines these theses with respect to the Irma dream that Freud (1965, pp. 138–153) offers as paradigmatic of his theory. Irma had anxiety and somatic symptoms that Freud treated psychoanalytically. Although Irma's anxiety lessened, she resisted Freud's interpretation of her somatic problems and her symptoms stayed. The evening before the dream, Freud was frustrated with Irma, angry with a younger colleague's implied criticism of his handling of the case, and desirous of justifying his treatment to his mentor. In the dream, Freud chastises Irma for rejecting his explanation and blames her for the fact that she is not cured. She complains of somatic symptoms. A hurried examination by Freud and his colleagues shows she has diphtheria, leading Freud and his superior to agree tacitly that the younger colleague had injected Irma with a senseless medication and had probably done so with a dirty syringe.

After thinking about it, Freud concludes that the dream was motivated by his desire to make his younger colleague responsible for the persistence of Irma's somatic symptoms. He induces, therefore, that all dreams are motivated unconsciously, that oneiric events consist in acting out one's repressed feelings and wishes, and that the unconscious motives behind a dream can be discovered through free association.

Grünbaum's point is simple. As Freud clearly remembered having felt resentment and frustration toward Irma, anger at his colleague's criticism, and anxiety about his mentor's opinion *consciously* the evening before the dream, one can hardly say that repressed, unconscious memories and drives motivated the dream content. Further, if one examines Freud's associations relative to his colleague, they reveal nothing suggestive of the alleged blaming motive. It is difficult, therefore, to see how free associations played a part in discovering the meaning of the dream.

In fact, Freud's evidence is more consistent with Piaget's theory of how consciousness is taken (Piaget 1974*b,c*). Piaget presents substantial experimental evidence that ideas do not exist unconsciously in their conscious form but that the distortions attributed to the "dream work" by Freud in fact represent unsuccessful attempts to impose that form initially. Even supposing Freud was correct about the motive for the Irma dream, there is no evidence that it existed prior to the dream in the form of his interpretation and was then repressed. On the contrary, it appears that its first conscious structuration occurred at the time of Freud's analysis. Freud's motivational explanation therefore represents the construction of new knowledge and not the laying bare of existing knowledge that has been repressed.

From this and myriad other examples, Grünbaum concludes that Freud's proofs are logically defective and that his evidence does not entail his theory. That, coupled with the fact that Freud's clinical data are contaminated by suggestion, make psychoanalysis, as it stands, an empirically testable but an empirically untested theory.

CONCLUSION

Thus I conclude that the hermeneutic construal of psychoanalysis is incompatible with a discipline that makes psychological and therapeutic claims, that nothing in principle precludes the application of scientific methods to the study of psychoanalytic propositions, that because of contamination by suggestion clinical verification of such propositions is not possible, and that motivational and causal explanations are not fundamentally at odds. At the same time, I recognize that for psychiatry to have a psychology compatible with science, it must seek a tertium quid between a purely motivational mode of explanation and a purely causal one. It is to that intermediary that I now turn.

An Explanatory Tertium Quid

Eagle (1983) discusses current attempts to split off clinical from metapsychological theory in the context of an assumed division between motivational and causal explanations. In the literature he refers to, the first are identified with hermeneutic interpretation and the second with natural science. In an instructive passage, Eagle notes that:

> The history of theories of human behavior are replete with attempts to exclude [either the meaning perspective or the mechanical perspective], and I must confess that in a broad historical context, I view much of the current formulations of the "new teleologists" and much of the insistence on the exclusive legitimacy of the clinical theory [of psychoanalysis] as the most recent expression of the rejection of the organismic. The real challenge, however, has always been over how to integrate these

two perspectives into a unified image of man; or, stated more modestly, over how to enrich one perspective by linking it to the other. (P. 343)

The problem then, if Eagle's formulation is accepted, is to discover how the physical and the mental are articulated. It is to appreciate how clinical theory, motivational explanations, hermeneutics, and teleology relate to rather than oppose metapsychological theory, causal explanations, natural science, and the organismic point of view. To contend that one or the other of these groups of concepts is primary and that the other is subsidiary or irrelevant is profoundly incoherent. Not only does doing so compare phenomena of different logical orders, but it creates confusion by presenting unrelated pieces of what is, in fact, a hierarchy of explanations. To correct the situation, one must clarify the structure of the explanatory accounts used in various domains and integrate that knowledge with what we know about how explanations are constructed. As Piaget is the greatest modern student of causal explanation, it is from the perspective of his epistemology that I continue.

A Theory of Psychological Causation

Piaget considered causal explanation to consist in the establishment of a special sort of coordination between the subject's conceptual structures and the objects or events to be explained. For him, to explain something causally was the acme of biologically adapting to it. In a remarkable series of studies extending over sixty years, he attempted to tease out just what the characteristics of causal explanation are, to understand how explanatory concepts are elaborated by children, to elucidate in several instances how they evolve historically, and to identify the functions that ontogenetic and historical causal constructions share.[14] Broadly speaking, he concluded that causal explanation consists in three interrelated activities that for the sake of clarity may be presented in linear order. First, physical facts are abstracted from experience and may be generalized into laws. Second, these facts or laws are coordinated deductively so that some of them may be deduced from others. And finally, the deductive model is attributed to reality; physical objects are conceived as natural "operators" obeying the rules of the model. Such attribution of deductive models to reality is the source of our feeling that an object's actions are necessary. It is the reason we feel nature must act in the way it does.

Problems arise, however, when this theory of explanation is applied to

[14]See Piaget (1950*b*, 1955, 1960, 1968, 1970, 1974*b*); and Piaget and Garcia (1971, 1983).

people. In his writings on psychological explanation, Piaget (1968) begins his argument in a way uncannily similar to his argument on physical causality: Explanation consists in more than just establishing laws; it requires creating deductive relationships among psychological facts so that some can be deduced from others; and the deductive system is then attributed to something "real." Because psychology's organic substrate is the brain, only deductive models that can be neurophysiologically accomplished will be tenable, but this must not be interpreted to mean that the reality to which the model is attributed—the higher mental processes of another person—are just a matter of neural processes susceptible to biological interpretation. The brain only makes certain functions possible, and it is the exercise of those functions over a greater or lesser history and under myriad circumstances that leads, eventually, to the higher mental structures. The latter remain fundamentally functional and are not contained in or discoverable from the physical structures enabling their realization. "When the neurologist studies the nervous system he, as an active and intelligent subject, uses higher forms of conduct and deductive schemata whose logical necessity is not reducible to material facts" (p. 182).

To escape this paradoxical situation, Piaget looks for a theory that at one and the same time deals with the reality of the feeling of necessity guiding conscious construction and with the organic origins of that feeling. A first solution is that consciousness and brain causally interact. Piaget rejects this notion on the grounds that it requires either that consciousness have force in the physical sense of that term or that neurons move ideas by association, implication, or other "mental" categories. A second solution is that neurophysiological phenomena and consciousness are "parallel," that is, that each state of consciousness corresponds to a concomitant neural state, although the two systems never interact. They simply exist in parallel. Piaget rejects several varieties of this solution on the grounds that they deny consciousness a function. What is needed, in his view, is a theory in which two isomorphic series are envisioned without interaction but with preservation of their functions. The solution that he works out is one in which neurophysiological and psychological realities are formulated using separate sets of concepts. The former are to be conceived using physical and chemical categories including those of energy, matter, and cause; the latter are to be conceived using uniquely psychological concepts including those of meaning, necessity, and truth. Only when this is done does one see, says Piaget, that while neurophysiological mechanisms can lead to consciousness, they cannot themselves produce its products. Only conscious functioning can bring about the construction of logic, mathematics, art, ethics, and the like.

While Piaget's conception has the merit of preserving the uniqueness of psychological functions and at the same time reflecting their organic origins, it contains a glaring contradiction. On the one hand, it is offered as a model of psychological explanation strikingly similar to his account of causal explanation; on the other, it denies the applicability of the causal category to the mind. Like so many others, Piaget seems to have run aground on the problems of coordinating higher mental processes with the physical mechanisms that make them possible. While he sees the problem clearly and refuses to adopt a position prematurely, he does not really solve the problem. For that reason, I turn to the work of one of his most brilliant pupils.

Cellérier's Analysis

Reflecting on *The Historical Genesis of Cybernetics,* Guy Cellérier (1983; Brown 1986) argues that in the history of science, the vitalist-mechanist debate and now the polemic over whether machines can think arise from confusion about what constitutes a causal explanation. The fact is, says Cellérier, inorganic, biological, and psychosociological phenomena can all be analyzed in terms of the mechanisms that *cause* them. It cannot, therefore, be at the causal level that physical, biological, psychological, and sociological phenomena differ, and it is not an opposition between causal and other forms of explanations that is key. The distinctness of scientific domains and the differences in the type of explanations they offer relate to a superordinate level reflecting how the causal mechanisms underlying the phenomena of a given level have been organized. Only when it is decided how a given configuration of interacting causes has been composed is it possible to say whether that configuration is or has been alive or whether it is or has been organized intentionally. In cases where causal events have come together by pure chance (aleatoric morphogenesis), one may speak of "causality" in the Piagetian sense. In cases where they have come together under teleonomical[15] control (teleonomic morphogenesis)—either genomic, psychological, or social—causality loses its Piagetian meaning. Rather, therefore, than distinguishing causal from biological, psychological, or sociological explanations, one must distinguish aleatoric explanations from teleonomic ones, both of which involve causes at a subordinate level. Applied to Piaget's analysis, this means that whatever psychological

[15]Teleonomy is derived from the Aristotelian concepts of teleology and final cause. What differentiates it from Aristotelian doctrine is that it is restricted to certain domains of phenomena involving self-regulation. The teleonomic framework includes notions of function, purpose, goals, and means. At most levels of human action, it involves intentionality.

categories might be chosen, even truth and meaning, one may always wonder what "causal" physical mechanisms are responsible.

Once aleatoric and teleonomic domains have been distinguished, distinctions must be made within the latter due to a multiplicity of regulating systems producing teleonomic compositions of causes. The first such system, the genetic system, produces feedback-corrected organization both in the ontogenetic elaboration of individuals and in the phylogenetic evolution of species. The problem of biological explanation is, therefore, how to account for teleonomic organization without attributing habit formation or intention to the genome. The strategy used by Darwin was to place part of the control structure, that is, evaluation or selection, outside the organism. (This does not mean that there are not internal selective mechanisms. It only means that survival is the final arbiter.) Only in that way can goal-directed composition be acknowledged without lapsing into teleology.

In psychology, the situation is more complex because conduct evolves under four different types of regulation. To begin with, inborn behaviors, such as reflexes and instincts, are formed by genetic regulations, and the explanatory problem remains biological. Second, conduct of the acquired automatic variety, such as habits, represents the product of a new acquisition system made possible by, but outside of, genomic control. In fact, habits are formed by selecting behaviors psychologically, not thermodynamically, and the explanatory problem becomes how to attribute goal-means structure to internalized variation and selection. Usually such explanations are framed in terms of "reinforcements" or other after-the-fact selective principles operating psychologically. Third, intentionally regulated sensorimotor behaviors (Piaget's fourth, fifth, and sixth substages of sensorimotor intelligence) extend the explanatory problems of habits to the internal structure of action sequences. While habits are selected as a piece in terms of global functions, intentional sensorimotor reactions involve independent evaluation of each step in an action sequence in terms of progress toward a goal. Due to the recombinability of means evident at this level, one can legitimately employ concepts of motivation and intention. And finally, at the level of semiotically mediated operations (Piaget's preoperational, concrete operational, and formal operational stages), that framework can be attributed to the subject's symbolic models of the world. Only at the latter level do aleatoric explanations of physical phenomena and teleonomic explanations of biological, psychological, and social phenomena in terms of corresponding internal and external structures become possible. These relationships are summarized in table 10.1.

TABLE 10.1

Aleatoric Versus Teleonomic Explanations of Structure

Aleatoric
Physics and Chemistry
Structures are material and are explained in terms of causal mechanisms that have come together through random interaction and been "selected" by thermodynamic factors (stabilization).
Teleonomic
Biology
Structures are material and are explained in terms of causal mechanisms that have come together through variations of existing autoregulating structure and been selected ultimately by thermodynamic factors.
Psychology
Instincts: Structures are functional and are explained in terms of causal mechanisms that have come together in biological fashion.
Habits: Structures are functional and are explained in terms of causal mechanisms that have come together through variation of instinctual schemes with after-the-fact selection in terms of psychological effects of action as a whole; individual steps are not selected.
Intentional behaviors: Structures are functional and are explained in terms of causal mechanisms that have come together through variation of existing psychological structure with ongoing evaluation and selection of each substep in the series from starting point to goal.

Like the analyses of Eagle, Wallace, and Grünbaum, Cellérier's analysis implies that the opposition between clinical theory, motivation, hermeneutics, and teleology on the one hand and metapsychology, causality, natural science, and biology on the other is incoherent. What makes psychological explanation difficult is the complexity of organizational levels that must be recognized in accounts of human action. At each of those levels, it must be assumed that the subject evolved from inorganic matter and that the phenomena observed rest on physical mechanisms that may be analyzed in terms of causes. What cannot be assumed is the manner in which those causal processes were put together and how they are related to the various functional levels. Cellérier contends that it is this last point that causes all the conflict; unlike the other authors, he offers a solution.

His general thesis is that history, even modern history, is replete with instances where some phenomenon, such as life, is held to be irreducible to causes in the old-fashioned sense (compare Elsasser's "biotonic laws" in Kauffman 1972). In the case of biology's vitalist-mechanist debate, vitalists opposed mechanists' oversimplification while mechanists decried vitalists' vagueness and lack of science. Only with the discovery of precise codes linking the complex functioning recognized by the vitalists to the explicit "causes" required by the mechanists has satisfaction become general. Cellérier offers the discovery of the helical structure of DNA as an example. (Mayr [1982] might disagree. Molecular genetics, in his view, is a genetics of bacteria, not mammals. Although interesting and important, it is incomplete.)

Such codes, according to Cellérier, have to do with machines and programs and with Turing's thesis. Programs, as precise descriptions of an organism's or an artifact's functions, are abstract and susceptible to different physical realizations (for example, calculations may be done by either a biological or an electronic brain). Because of that, full understanding of teleonomically organized phenomena requires not only an exact appreciation of their functional structure but also precise knowledge of the physical mechanisms that make those functions possible. Such explanations Cellérier calls "cybernetic." Anything short of explanation in this form is incomplete and causes tensions of the sort psychiatry struggles with at present; when such understanding is achieved, the tensions disappear. However, there is much controversy currently about whether cybernetic explanations of human conduct are possible in principle (Haugeland 1981; Putnam 1981). I do not believe the question can be settled in advance.

This is not to say that Cellérier accepts Turing's thesis as it stands, that he thinks that current cognitive science captures anything like human knowing whole, or that he believes that Turing's "effective procedures" are the appropriate model for the human mind. What he does believe is that, properly enriched, the ideas that began to emerge with Darwin's functional theory and that have been greatly extended by computer science offer the best hope we have of developing an empirically justified account of human mental functions. (Darwin's theory is framed in terms of the functions of variation and selection; it says nothing about the mechanisms involved. By itself, it would probably not be considered scientific by many present-day mechanists.) But there are limits. At best, properly developed cybernetic models will explain what all people have in common. They will be models only of an epistemic subject, not of individuals rendered unique by their history and their culture. Human experience will always have content that is singular; what is not repeated cannot be studied in any scientific way.

Conclusion

By all appearances, psychiatry's explanatory ideal should be cybernetic. At the same time, adoption of that goal would have wide-reaching implications. To begin with, it would proscribe exclusively psychological or exclusively neurophysiological approaches, it would rule out hermeneutics' misreading of "hard" science, it would dash all hope of biological reduction, and, most important, it would place new conceptual and educational responsibilities upon the discipline. No longer would it be possible for persons trained in anatomy and biochemistry, in neurotransmitters and molecular genetics, in pharmacology and surgery, to approach mental disorders armed only with the psychology of their grandmothers and the social and cultural theories that they have picked up on the street. The cybernetic approach would require basic training in psychological and sociological theory, in anthropology, in computer science and linguistics, and in philosophy of science. After all, it is impossible to model what one knows not of.

The Question of Normality

Before offering some general conclusions, a few more words on normality would seem in order. As stated earlier, any study of normality presupposes conceptualization. As psychiatry, at present, is in the midst of conceptual reformulation, the question of normality, taken in the sense of establishing ideal or average deviations from some norm, is premature. What is needed at this moment and what, therefore, constitutes the first step in studying the normal is a search for conceptualizations that embrace human personality whole, at least in those aspects that are universal. For example, people of every race and culture, of every sex and developmental history, will have thoughts and feelings; every one of them will have a limbic system and dopamine receptors; every one of them will know and act. The first task of a study of normality is, therefore, to identify which list of structures, both physiological and psychological, and which list of functions, both physiological and psychological, specify completely the abstract program we call mind and the causal mechanisms that realize it physically. If such lists seem obvious, why is it that behavioral psychology systematically leaves out feeling and emotion or that neurophysiology has nothing to say about intention? Once acceptable lists are written—and they will be long in coming—the study of normality can be undertaken.

To accept psychiatry's current official formulation and launch into studies of the normal framed within that conceptual system leads to severe problems. For example, the Axis I–Axis II schism is highly arguable. It suggests that syndromes described in terms of dramatic symptoms may occur in normal personalities or that persons with personality disorders may not have dramatic symptoms. Even if the conceptual vagueness (or even degeneracy) of terms such as "personality" and "anxiety" are forgiven, such suggestions glaringly contradict clinical experience. Recall in this regard that anxiety is a mood but that Anxiety Disorders are not Mood Disorders, and so on. If one insists on using language with scientific rigor, discussion becomes impossible: No one knows what anyone else is saying.

My prescription for an ailing psychiatry is, therefore, not a direct attack on the question of what is normal. Rather I advise the thorough examination of psychiatric concepts and metapsychiatric assumptions. Not only must questions such as what is mind, what is mood, or what is thought be asked, but psychiatric ideologies also must be queried. How have we come to hold that mood disorders are chemical imbalances in the brain? Do six-week to three-month studies of changes in an incoherently defined mental entity—mood—really tell us anything profound about a pernicious, recurrent illness such as depression, characterized by exacerbations and remissions? What does it mean that statistical significance between drug effects and placebo disappear when such studies are extended to four months (Elkin et al. 1989)? What will it mean, as preliminary reports suggest, that depressed patients treated with drugs have more frequent recurrences than patients treated psychotherapeutically? And what are the social pressures that have led us to adopt such easy answers? How much do pharmaceutical company research contracts and governmental penny-pinching shape psychiatry's "scientific" conclusions? These are all hurdles that must be vaulted.

I believe the future of psychiatry depends on the extent to which its institutions become equal to the conceptual challenges that confront the discipline. The greatest changes are needed in psychiatric education. At present, psychiatrists as a whole are trained in a narrow biomedical technology. They have no real education in psychology, sociology, or even, most of them, evolutionary biology. They have not considered deeply what a *mental* disorder might be and do not have the conceptual tools to entertain that question seriously. Innocent as they are, they fall easy prey to reductionist zealots encouraged by drug merchants and a selfish society. Only an adequate education can protect them against such enemies and restore them to a position of sapient authority. Only a proper education can justify their studying what is normal.

General Conclusions

From all that I have said so far, I conclude that psychiatry's ambition to become a science that diagnoses, investigates, and treats mental disorders is thwarted by profound incoherences in its thought. On the one hand, its equation of science with neuroscience and its conceit that behavior can be analyzed molecularly disqualify it as a science of the mental. Mind cannot be represented in behavioral terms alone, nor can psychiatrists analyze behaviors of human interest chemically. On the other hand, psychiatry's equation of psychology with psychoanalysis preserves certain aspects of the mental but distances psychiatry from neuroscience and undermines its scientific status. And finally, the supposition that, as they stand, neuroscience and psychoanalysis are compatible makes no sense at all.

While it is easy to understand psychiatry's contradictions in terms of its developmental history, it is more difficult to envision their solution. For psychiatry to be science, it will have to recognize the uniqueness and specificity of psychosocial concepts, renounce its current program of biological reduction in favor of a program of psychological-neurophysiological correlation, and prepare itself to deal with psychology and sociology as sciences. Only then will precise correlation of the functional framework of the mental with the mechanistic framework of biology become feasible. Failing that, psychiatry will continue to lose authority based on knowledge and be forced, as it is now, to struggle in the courts to preserve what privileges remain. Insurance companies will not pay, analysts' offices will stand empty, psychotropic drugs will be the province of nonspecialists, current inroads by "Z"-therapists, scream therapists, sexual surrogates, and other gurus will expand, and "medical coverage" for those psychologically better informed will increasingly become the order of the day.

REFERENCES

American Psychiatric Association. 1980. *Diagnostic and Statistical Manual of Mental Disorders, 3rd ed.* Washington, D. C.: APA.

———. 1987. *Diagnostic and Statistical Manual of Mental Disorders, 3rd ed., rev.* Washington, D. C.: APA.

Bailey, P. 1960. "Modern Attitudes Toward the Relationship of the Brain to Behavior." *Archives of General Psychiatry* 2:361–378.

Black, D. W.; Yates, W. R.; and Andreasen, N. C. 1988. "Schizophrenia, Schizophreniform Disorder, and Delusional (Paranoid) Disorders." In *The American Psychiatric Press Textbook of Psychiatry,* ed. J. A. Talbott, R. E. Hales, and S. C. Yudofsky, pp. 357–402. Washington, D.C.: American Psychiatric Press.

Blanchet, A. 1986. "Rôle des valeurs et des systèmes des valeurs dans la cognition." Archives de Psychologie 54:251–270.

Block, N. 1980. "Introduction: What Is Philosophy of Psychology?" In *Readings in Philosophy of Psychology, vol. 1,* ed. N. Block, pp. 1–10. Cambridge, MA.: Harvard University Press.

Boring, E. G. 1950. *A History of Experimental Psychology.* Englewood Cliffs, NJ: Prentice-Hall.

Brooks, D. R., and Wiley, E. O. 1986. *Evolution as Entropy.* Chicago: University of Chicago Press.

Brown, T. 1986. "Holzman's Fences: Chauvinism or Confusion?" *Archives of General Psychiatry* 43:910–912.

———. 1988. "Ships in the Night: Piaget and American Cognitive Science." *Human Development* 31:60–64.

———. 1990. "The Biological Significance of Affectivity." In *Psychological and Biological Approaches to Emotion,* ed. N. L. Stein, B. L. Leventhal, and T. Trabasso, pp. 405–434. Hillsdale, NJ: Lawrence Erlbaum.

Brown, T., and Weiss, L. 1987. "Structures, Procedures, Heuristics, and Affectivity." *Archives de Psychologie* 55:59–94.

Campbell, R. L., and Bickhard, M. H. 1986. *Knowing Levels and Developmental Stages.* Basel, Switzerland: Karger.

Cellérier, G. 1979*a.* "Structures cognitives et schèmes d'action. I." *Archives de Psychologie* 47:87–106.

———. 1979*b.* "Structures cognitives et schèmes d'action. II." *Archives de Psychologie* 47:107–122.

———. 1983. "The Historical Genesis of Cybernetics: Is Teleonomy a Category of Understanding?" trans. T. A. Brown. *Nature and System* 5:211–225.

———. 1987. "Structures and Functions." In *Piaget Today,* ed. B. Inhelder, D. de Caprona, and A. CornuWells, pp. 15–36. Hillsdale, NJ: Lawrence Erlbaum.

Chomsky, N. 1980. "A Review of B. F. Skinner's *Verbal Behavior.*" In *Readings in the Philosophy of Psychology,* vol. 1, ed. N. Block, pp. 48–63. Cambridge, MA: Harvard University Press.

Coyle, J. T. 1988. "Neuroscience and Psychiatry." In *The American Psychiatric Press Textbook of Psychiatry,* ed., J. A. Talbott, R. E. Hales, and S. C. Yudofsky, pp. 3–32. Washington, D.C.: American Psychiatric Press.

de Koning, A. J. J. 1982. "Phenomenology." In *Phenomenology and Psychiatry,* ed. A. J. J. de Koning and F. A. Jenner, pp. 1–10. New York: Academic Press.

Eagle, M. N. 1983. "A Critical Examination of Motivational Explanation in Psychoanalysis." In *Mind and Medicine,* ed. Larry Laudan, pp. 311–353. Berkeley: University of California.

Elkin, I.; Shea, T.; Watkins, J. T.; Imber, S. D.; Sotsky, S. M.; Collins, J. F.; Glass,

D. R.; Pilkonis, P. A.; Leber, W. R.; Docherty, J. P.; Fiester, S. J.; and Parloff, M. B. 1989. "National Institute of Mental Health Treatment of Depression Collaborative Research Program: General Effectiveness of Treatments." *Archives of General Psychiatry* 46:971–982.

Engel, G. L. 1977. "The Need for a New Medical Model: A Challenge for Biomedicine." *Science* 196:129–136.

Faust, D., and Miner, R. S. 1986. "The Empiricist and His New Clothes: DSM-III in Perspective." *American Journal of Psychiatry* 143:962–967.

Fink, E. 1982. "Psychiatry's Role in the Dehumanization of Health Care." *Journal of Clinical Psychiatry* 43:137–138.

Fodor, J. A. 1980. "Methodological Solipsism Considered as a Research Strategy in Cognitive Psychology." *Behavior and Brain Sciences* 3:63–109.

Fodor, J. A. 1981. *Representations.* Cambridge, MA: MIT Press.

Frazier, S. H. 1987. "Introduction." In *Textbook of Neuropsychiatry,* ed. R. E. Hales and S. C. Yudofsky, pp. xvii–xix. Washington, D.C.: American Psychiatric Press.

Freud, S. 1965. *The Interpretation of Dreams,* trans. J. Strachey. New York: Avon Books.

Gardner, H. 1985. *The Mind's New Science: A History of the Cognitive Revolution.* New York: Basic Books.

Goode, E. E. 1988. "How Psychiatry Forgets the Mind." *U. S. News & World Report,* 21 March, pp. 57–58.

Goodfield, J. 1974. "Changing Strategies: A Comparison of Reductionist Attitudes in Biological and Medical Research in the Nineteenth and Twentieth Centuries." In *Studies in the Philosophy of Biology,* ed. F. J. Ayala and T. Dobzhansky, pp. 65–86. Berkeley: University of California Press.

Grèco, P. 1967. *Épistémologie de la psychologie.* In *Logique et Connaissance Scientifique,* ed. J. Piaget, pp. 927–991. Paris: Encyclopédie de la Pléiade, Éditions Gallimard.

Grossman, R. 1987. "Dialogue vs. Drugs: Psychiatry's Mood Swings Between the Lab and the Couch." *Chicago Tribune,* 10 May, sec. 5, pp. 1, 4.

Grünbaum, A. 1984. *The Foundations of Psychoanalysis: A Philosophical Critique.* Berkeley: University of California Press.

Habermas, J. 1971. *Knowledge and Human Interests,* trans. J. J. Shapiro. Boston: Beacon Press.

Harré, R., and Lamb, R., eds. 1983. *The Encyclopedic Dictionary of Psychology.* Cambridge, MA: MIT Press.

Hart, R. H. 1988. "A Nobel Prize for the Discovery of CPZ?" *Psychiatric Times* 5(7):23.

Haugeland, J. 1981. "The Nature and Plausibility of Cognitivism." In *Mind Design,* ed. J. Haugeland, pp. 243–281. Cambridge, MA: MIT Press.

Heaton, J. M. 1982. "A Discussion on Phenomenology, Psychiatry and Psychotherapy. In *Phenomenology and Psychiatry,* ed. A. J. J. de Koning and F. A. Jenner, pp. 11–33. New York: Academic Press.

Hodges, A. 1983. *Alan Turing: The Enigma.* New York: Simon and Schuster.

Holzman, P. 1985. "The Fences of Psychiatry." *American Journal of Psychiatry* 142:217–218.

Johnson-Laird, P. N. 1988. *The Computer and the Mind: An Introduction to Cognitive Science.* Cambridge, MA: Harvard University Press.

Kandel, E. R. 1979. "Psychotherapy and the Single Synapse: The Impact of Psychiatric Thought on Neurobiologic Research." *New England Journal of Medicine* 301:-1028–1037.

———. 1983. "From Metapsychology to Molecular Biology: Explorations into the Nature of Anxiety." *American Journal of Psychiatry* 140:1277–1293.

Kauffman, S. 1972. "What Can We Know About a Metazoan's Entire Control System?: On Elsasser's, and Other Epistemological Problems in Cell Science." In *Towards a Theoretical Biology: 4. Essays,* ed. C. H. Waddington, pp. 229–247. Chicago: Aldine-Atherton.

Kelly, B. N. 1975. "Significant Trends and Themes in the History of Mental Health." In *Contemporary Issues of Mental Health,* vol. 1, no. 1. Bureau of Research and Training—Mental Health, Commonwealth of Pennsylvania.

Kornblith, H., ed. 1985. *Naturalizing Epistemology.* Cambridge, MA: MIT Press.

Kramer, P. 1988. "Love Feast." *Psychiatric Times* 5(7):3.

Lakatos, I. 1978. *The Methodology of Scientific Research Programmes: Philosophical Papers,* vol. 1, ed. J. Worrall and G. Currie. Cambridge: Cambridge University Press.

Lanteri-Laura, G. 1982. "Phenomenology and a Critique of the Foundations of Psychiatry." In *Phenomenology and Psychiatry,* ed. A. J. J. de Koning and F. A. Jenner, pp. 51–62. New York: Academic Press.

Lyons, J. 1977. "Section 1.6: Theories, Models and Data." In *Semantics,* vol. 1, by J. Lyons, pp. 25–31. Cambridge: Cambridge University Press.

Marmer, S. S. 1988. "Theories of the Mind and Psychopathology." In *The American Psychiatric Press Textbook of Psychiatry,* ed. J. A. Talbott, Robert E. Hales, and Stuart C. Yudofsky, pp. 123–162. Washington, D.C.: American Psychiatric Press.

Masling, J., ed. 1983. *Empirical Studies of Psychoanalytical Theories,* vol. 1. Hillsdale, NJ: Analytic Press.

Mayr, E. 1982. *The Growth of Biological Thought: Diversity, Evolution, and Inheritance.* Cambridge, MA: Belknap Press of the Harvard University Press.

Meyersburg, H. A., and Post, R. M. 1979. "An Holistic Developmental View of Neural and Psychological Processes: A Neurobiologic-psychoanalytic Integration." *British Journal of Psychiatry* 135:139–155.

Mohl, P. C. 1987. "Should Psychotherapy Be Considered a Biological Treatment?" *Psychosomatics* 28:320–326.

Mora, G. 1980. "Historical and Theoretical Trends in Psychiatry." In *Comprehensive Textbook of Psychiatry* III, vol. 1, ed. H. I. Kaplan, A. M. Freedman, and B. J. Sadock, pp. 4–98. Baltimore: Williams & Wilkins.

Nemiah, J. C. 1980. "Psychiatry: The Inexhaustible Science." In *Comprehensive Textbook of Psychiatry* III, vol. 1, ed. H. I. Kaplan, A. M. Freedman, and B. J. Sadock, pp. 1–3. Baltimore: Williams & Wilkins.

Nicholi, A. M., Jr. 1988. "The Therapist-Patient Relationship." In *The New Harvard Guide to Psychiatry,* by A. M. Nicholi, Jr., pp. 7–28. Cambridgde, MA: Harvard University Press.

Piaget, J. 1950*a*. *Introduction à l'Épistémologie Génétique: 1. La Pensée Mathématique.* Paris: Presses Universitaires de France.

———. 1950*b*. "La pensée psychologique, la pensée sociologique, et la logique." In *Introduction à l'Épistémologie Génétique: 3. La Pensée Biologique, la Pensée Psychologique, et la Pensée Sociologique,* by J. Piaget, pp. 133–272. Paris: Presses Universitaires de France.

———. 1955. *The Language and Thought of the Child,* trans. M. Gabain. New York: World.

———. 1960. *The Child's Conception of the World,* trans. J. and A. Tomlinson. Totowa, NJ: Littlefield, Adams.

———. 1967. "Les courants de l'épistémologie scientifique contemporaine." In *Logique et Connaissance Scientifique,* ed. J. Raget, pp. 1225–1271. Paris: Encyclopédie de la Pléiade, Éditions Gallimard.

———. 1968. "Explanation in psychology and psychophysiological parallelism." In *Experimental Psychology: Its Scope and Method. I. History and Method,* ed. P. Fraisse and J. Piaget, trans. J. Chambers, pp. 153–191. New York: Basic Books.

———. 1970. *Structuralism,* trans. C. Maschler. New York: Basic Books.

———. 1971. *Insights and Illusions of Philosophy,* trans. W. Mays. New York: World.

———. 1972. *The Principles of Genetic Epistemology,* trans. W. Mays. New York: Basic Books.

———. 1974*a*. *Recherches sur la Contradiction. I. Les Différentes Formes de la Contradiction.* Paris: Presses Universitaires de France.

———. 1974*b*. *La Prise de Conscience.* Paris: Presses Universitaires de France.

———. 1974*c*. *Réussir et Comprendre.* Paris: Presses Universitaires de France.

Piaget, J., and Garcia, R. 1971. *Les Explications Causales.* Paris: Presses Universitaires de France.

———. 1983. *Psychogenèse et Histoire des Sciences.* Paris: Flammarion.

Piaget, J., and Inhelder, B. 1969. *The Psychology of the Child,* trans. H. Weaver. New York: Basic Books.

Popper, K. R. 1956. *Realism and the Aim of Science.* Totowa, NJ: Rowman and Littlefield.

Prigogine, I., and Stengers, I. 1984. *Order Out of Chaos.* Toronto: Bantam Books.

Pugh, G. E. 1977. *The Biological Origin of Human Values.* New York: Basic Books.

Putnam, H. 1980. "Brains and Behavior." In *Readings in the Philosophy of Psychology,* vol. 1, ed. N. Block, pp. 24–36. Cambridge, MA: Harvard University Press.

———. 1981. "Reductionism and the Nature of Psychology." In *Mind Design,* ed. J. Haugeland, pp. 205–219. Cambridge, MA: MIT Press.

Pylyshyn, Z. W. 1980. "Computation and Cognition: Issues in the Foundation of Cognitive Science." *Behavior and Brain Sciences* 3:111–169.

Quine, W. V. O. 1960. *Word and Object.* Cambridge, MA: MIT Press.

Radnitsky, G., and Bartley, W. W. III. 1987. *Evolutionary Epistemology, Theory of Rationality, and the Sociology of Knowledge.* LaSalle, IL: Open Court.

Sabshin, M. 1988. "Introduction." In *The American Psychiatric Press Textbook of Psychiatry,* ed. J. A. Talbott, R. E. Hales, and S. C. Yudofsky, pp. xix–xx. Washington, D.C.: American Psychiatric Press.

Sarvin, H. 1980. "Introduction: Behaviorism." In *Readings in the Philosophy of Psychology,* vol. 1, ed. N. Block, pp. 11–13. Cambridge, MA: Harvard University Press.

Schmitt, R. 1967. "Edmund Husserl." In *The Encyclopedia of Philosophy,* vol. 3, ed. P. Edwards, pp. 96–99. New York: Macmillan.

Schwartz, M. A., and Wiggins, O. 1985. "Science, Humanism, and the Nature of Medical Practice: A Phenomenological View." *Perspectives in Biology and Medicine* 28:331–361.

Skinner, B. F. 1953. *Science and Human Behavior.* New York: Free Press.

Slavney, P. R., and McHugh, P. R. 1987. *Psychiatric Polarities: Methodology and Practice.* Baltimore: Johns Hopkins University Press.

Smolensky, P. 1988. "On the Proper Treatment of Connectionism." *Behavioral and Brain Sciences* 11: 1–74.

Snyder, S. H. 1984. "Medicated Minds." *Science* 5(9):141–142.

Suppe, F. 1977*a.* "V. Alternatives to the Received View and Their Critics." In *The Structure of Scientific Theories,* ed. F. Suppe, pp. 119–232. Urbana: University of Illinois Press.

———. 1977*b.* "Editorial Interpellation: Shapere on the Instrumentalistic *vs.* Realistic Conception of Theories." In *The Structure of Scientific Theories,* ed. F. Suppe, pp. 566–570. Urbana: University of Illinois Press.

Talbott, J. A.; Hales, R. E.; and Yudofsky, S. C., eds. 1988. *The American Psychiatric Press Textbook of Psychiatry.* Washington, D.C.: American Psychiatric Press.

Timpanaro, S. 1976. *The Freudian Slip,* trans. K. Soper. Atlantic Highlands, NJ: Humanities Press.

Wallace, E. R. IV. 1988. "What Is Truth? Some Philosophical Contributions to Psychiatric Issues." *American Journal of Psychiatry* 145:137–147.

Winokur, G.; Zimmerman, M.; and Cadoret, R. 1988. " 'Cause the Bible Tells Me So." *Archives of General Psychiatry* 45:683–684.

Woozley, A. D. 1959. "Theory of Knowledge." *Encyclopaedia Britannica* vol. 13, pp. 448–461. Chicago: William Benton.

Zelm, G. 1986. "Don't Let Technology Diminish Humanity." *Canadian Medical Association Journal* 135:1186–1189.

CHAPTER 11

Normality: What May We Learn from Evolutionary Theory?

Theodore Millon

This is a time of rapid scientific and clinical advances, a time that seems propitious for ventures designed to bridge new ideas and syntheses. The intersection between the study of "psychopathology" and the study of "normality" is one of these spheres of significant academic activity and clinical responsibility. Theoretical formulations that bridge this intersection would represent a major and valued intellectual step, but to limit our focus to traditional concepts addressing this junction will lead us to overlook the solid footings provided by our more mature sciences (such as physics and evolutionary biology). By failing to coordinate propositions and constructs to principles and laws established in these advanced disciplines, the different facets of our subject will continue to float, so to speak, at their current level, requiring that we return to this task another day.

The goal of this chapter is to connect the conceptual structure of psychological normatology and psychopathology to their foundations in the natural sciences. What will be proposed is akin to Freud's abandoned *Project for a Scientific Psychology* (1895), Wilson's highly controversial *Sociobiology* (1975), and Mandell and Salk's notion of metabiological ontogeny (1984). Each were endeavors to advance our understanding of human nature by exploring interconnections among disciplines that evolved ostensibly unrelated bodies of research and manifestly dissimilar languages.

In what follows, we go beyond current psychologically based conceptual boundaries and propose "intuitive" hypotheses that draw their principles, if not their substance, from our more established, "adjacent" sciences. Not only may such steps bear new conceptual fruits, but they may provide a foundation that can undergird and guide our own discipline's explorations. As noted, much of psychiatry and normatology, no less than psychology as a whole, remains adrift, divorced from broader spheres of scientific knowledge, isolated from firmly grounded if not universal principles. This has led us to continue building the patchwork quilt of concepts and data domains that characterize our field. Preoccupied with but a small part of the larger puzzle, or fearing accusations of reductionism, we have failed to draw on the rich possibilities that may be found in other realms of scholarly pursuit. With few exceptions, cohering concepts that would connect our subject to those of its sister sciences have not been developed. We seem trapped in (obsessed with?) horizontal refinements. A search for integrative schemas and cohesive constructs that will link us to relevant observations and laws in more advanced fields of science is needed. The goal—albeit a rather "grandiose" one—would be to refashion our patchwork quilt into a well-tailored and aesthetic tapestry that interweaves the diverse forms in which nature expresses itself.

There is no better sphere within the psychological sciences to undertake such a synthesis than the subject matter of *personology,* the study of persons. Persons are the only organically integrated system in the psychological and psychiatric domain, evolved through the millennia and inherently created from birth as natural entities, rather than culture-bound and experience-derived gestalts. The intrinsic cohesion of persons is not merely a rhetorical construction but an authentic substantive unity. Personologic features may be differentiated into normal or pathological and may be partitioned conceptually for pragmatic or scientific purposes, but they are segments of an inseparable biopsychosocial entity.

To take this integrative view is not to argue that different spheres of scientific inquiry should be equated, nor is it to insist that there is only one possible conceptual system that may encompass normality and abnormality. Arguing in favor of building explicit links between these domains does not call for a reductionistic philosophy, a belief in substantive identicality, or efforts to so fashion them by formal logic. Rather, we should seek to illustrate their substantive concordance and conceptual interfacing. By tracing their characteristics to the same underlying principles, we may demonstrate that they are merely different expressions of nature's basic evolutionary processes.

Prior volumes in the Offer/Sabshin series (1966, 1984) have provided inquiring readers with comprehensive reviews, incisive analyses, and thoughtful proposals concerning the character of normality. To review the themes and issues covered so well in these earlier texts would be redundant and unproductive. Instead, we set out in a new direction, presenting, albeit briefly, a rationale for conceptualizing the subject of normatology from an explicit theoretical base; further, we propose that the theoretical framework employed be grounded in the principles and concepts of evolution and ecology; and third, we illustrate how these principles can provide a rationale and guide for criteria that define what is meant by normality.

Why Theory?

It was Kurt Lewin (1936) who wrote some fifty years ago that "there is nothing so practical as a good theory" (p. 5). Theory, when properly fashioned, ultimately provides more simplicity and clarity than unintegrated and scattered information. Unrelated knowledge and techniques, especially those based on surface similarities, are a sign of a primitive science, as has been effectively argued by contemporary philosophers of science (Hempel 1965; Quine 1961).

All natural sciences have organizing principles that not only create order but also provide the basis for generating hypotheses and stimulating new knowledge. A good theory not only summarizes and incorporates extant knowledge but is heuristic in that it originates and develops new observations and new methods.

As knowledge advances, overt similarities, whether observed astutely or analyzed quantitatively, have been found to be an insufficient if not often false basis for identifying categories and imbuing them with scientific meaning (Smith and Medin 1981). As Hempel (1965) and Quine (1977) have pointed out, it is theory that provides the glue that holds a subject domain together and gives it its scientific relevance. In his discussion of scientific concepts, Hempel (1965) wrote:

> . . . the development of a scientific discipline may often be said to proceed from an initial "natural history" stage . . . to subsequent more and more "theoretical" stages . . . The vocabulary required in the early stages of this development will be largely observational . . . The shift toward theoretical systematization is marked by the introduction of new, "theoretical" terms . . . more or less removed from the level of directly observable things and events. (P. 139)

Quine (1977) makes a parallel case for the use of theories. Noting the usual progression from what he terms an innate, similarity-based conception of a subject (for example, normality) to a theoretically oriented one, he wrote:

> . . . one's sense of similarity or one's system of kinds develops and changes . . . as one matures . . . And at length standards of similarity set in which are geared to theoretical science. This development is . . . away from the immediate, subjective, animal sense of similarity to the remoter objectivity of a similarity determined by scientific hypotheses . . . and constructs. Things are similar in the later or theoretical sense to the degree that they are . . . revealed by science. (P. 171)

What are the essential elements that distinguish between a true science and a schema that provides a mere explanatory summary of known observations and inferences?

Simply stated, the answer lies in its power to *generate* concepts, propositions, and observations other than those used to construct it. This generative power is what Hempel meant by the "systematic import" of a science. In contrasting what are familiarly known as "natural" (theoretically guided, deductively based) and "artificial" (conceptually barren, similarity based) systems, Hempel (1965) wrote:

> Distinctions between "natural" and "artificial" classifications may well be explicated as referring to the difference between classifications that are scientifically fruitful and those that are not: in a classification of the former kind, those characteristics of the elements which serve as criteria of membership in a given class are associated, universally or with high probability, with more or less extensive clusters of other characteristics.
>
> Classification of this sort should be viewed as somehow having objective existence in nature, as "carving nature at the joints" in contradistinction of "artificial" classifications, in which the defining characteristics have few explanatory or predictive connections with other traits.
>
> In the course of scientific development, classifications defined by reference to manifest, observable characteristics will tend to give way to systems based on theoretical concepts. (Pp. 146–148)

A problem arises when introducing theory into the study of normatology and psychopathology. Given our intuitive ability to "sense" the correctness of a psychological insight or speculation, theoretical efforts that impose structure or formalize these insights into a scientific system are likely to be perceived not only as cumbersome and intrusive but as alien as well. This discomfiture and resistance does not arise in fields such as particle physics, where everyday observations are not readily available and where innovative insights are few and far between. In such subject domains, scientists are not only quite comfortable, but they turn readily to deductive theory as a means of helping them explicate and coordinate knowledge. It is paradoxical but true and unfortunate that psychologists and psychiatrists learn their subject quite well merely by observing the ordinary events of life. As a consequence of this ease, they may shy away from the "obscure and complicating" yet often fertile and systematizing powers inherent in formal theory, especially theories that differ from those learned in their student days.

Adding to these hesitations is the fact that the formal structure of most psychological theories is haphazard and unsystematic; concepts often are vague, and procedures by which empirical consequences may be derived are tenuous. Many theories have generated brilliant deductions and insights, but few of these ideas can be attributed to their structure, the clarity of their central principles, the precision of their concepts, or their formal procedures for hypothesis derivation. It is here, of course, where the concepts and laws of adjacent sciences may come into play, providing substantive laws and data that may undergird and parallel the principles and observations of one's own field.

Despite the shortcomings I see in historic and contemporary theoretical schemas, systematizing principles and abstract concepts can "facilitate a deeper seeing, a more penetrating vision that goes beyond superficial appearances to the order underlying them" (Bowers 1977, p. 130). For example, pre-Darwinian taxonomists such as Linnaeus limited themselves to "apparent" similarities and differences among animals as a means of constructing their categories. Darwin was not "seduced" by appearances. Rather, he sought to understand the principles by which overt features came about. His classifications were based not only on keenly observed descriptive qualities but on genuinely explanatory ones.

Why Evolutionary and Ecological Theory?

What makes evolutionary and ecological theory as meritorious as I propose them to be? Are they truly coextensive with the origins of the universe, the procession of organic life, as well as human modes of adaptation? Is extrapolation to normatology a conjectural fantasy? Is there "justification" for employing them as a basis for understanding "normal" and "pathological" behaviors?

Owing to the mathematical and deductive insights of our colleagues in physics, we have a deeper and clearer sense of the early evolution and structural relations among matter and energy. So too has knowledge progressed in our studies of physical chemistry, microbiology, evolutionary theory, population biology, ecology, and ethology. How odd it is (is it not?) that we have only now again begun to investigate—as we did at the turn of the last century—the interface between the basic building blocks of physical nature and the nature of life as we experience and live it personally. How much more is known today, yet how hesitant are people to undertake a serious rapprochement. As Barash (1982) has commented:

> Like ships passing in the night, evolutionary biology and the social sciences have rarely even taken serious notice of each other, although admittedly, many introductory psychology texts give an obligatory toot of the Darwinian horn somewhere in the first chapter . . . before passing on to discuss human behavior as though it were determined only by environmental factors. (P. 7)

Commenting that serious efforts to undergird the behavioral sciences with the constructs and principles of evolutionary biology is as audacious as it is overdue, Barash (1982) notes further:

> . . . as with any modelling effort, we start with the simple, see how far it takes us, and then either complicate or discard it as it gets tested against reality. The data available thus far are certainly suggestive and lead to the hope that more will shortly be forthcoming, so that tests and possible falsification can be carried out. In the meanwhile, as Darwin said when he first read Malthus, at least we have something to work with! (P. 8)

It is in both the spirit and substance of Darwin's "explanatory principles" that the reader should approach the proposals that follow. The principles employed are essentially the same as those that Darwin developed in seeking to explicate the origins of species. However, they are enlisted here to derive not the origins of species but the structure and style of normal and pathological functioning. Aspects of these formulations have been published in other books (Millon 1969, 1981, 1990), but they are anchored explicitly to normatology for the first time in this work.

The role of evolution is most clearly grasped when it is paired with the principles of ecology. So conceived, the "procession" of evolution represents a series of serendipitous transformations in the structure of a phenomenon (for example, elementary particle, chemical molecule, living organism) that appear to promote survival in both its current and future environments. Such processions usually stem from the consequences of either random fluctuations (such as mutations) or replicative reformations (for example, recombinant mating) among an infinite number of possibilities—some simpler, others more complex, some more and others less organized, some increasingly specialized and others not. Evolution is defined, then, when these restructurings enable a natural entity (for example, species) or its subsequent variants to survive within present and succeeding ecologic milieus. It is the continuity through time of these fluctuations and reformations that comprises the sequence we characterize as evolutionary progression.

To propose that fruitful ideas may be derived by applying evolutionary principles to the development and functions of psychological traits has a long if yet unfulfilled tradition. Spencer (1870) and Huxley (1870) offered suggestions of this nature shortly after Darwin's seminal *Origins* was published. The school of "functionalism," popular in psychology in the early part of this century, likewise drew its impetus from evolutionary concepts as it sought to articulate a basis for individual difference typologies.

In more recent times, we have seen the emergence of sociobiology, a new "science" that explores the interface between human social functioning and evolutionary biology (Wilson 1975, 1978). Contemporary formulations by psychologists have likewise proposed the potentials and analyzed the problems involved in cohering evolutionary notions, individual differences, and personality traits (for example, D. Buss 1984). The common goal among these proposals is not only the desire to apply analogous principles across diverse scientific realms but also to reduce the enormous range of psychological concepts that have proliferated through history; this might be achieved by exploring the power of evolutionary theory to simplify and order previously disparate pathological and normatologic features. For example, all organisms seek to avoid injury, find nourishment, and reproduce their kind if they are to survive and maintain their populations. Each species displays commonalities in its adaptive or survival style. Within each species, however, there are differences in style and differences in the success with which its various members adapt to the diverse and changing environments they face. In these simplest of terms, "personality" would be employed as a term to represent the more or less distinctive style of adaptive functioning that a particular organism of a species exhibits as it relates to its typical range of environments. "Normal personalities," so conceived, would signify the utilization of species-specific modes of adaptation that are effective in "average or expectable" environments. "Disorders" of personality, so formulated, would represent different styles of maladaptive functioning that can be traced to deficiencies, imbalances, or conflicts in a species' capacity to relate to the environments it faces.

A few more words should be said concerning analogies between evolution and ecology, on the one hand, and normal and abnormal personality, on the other.

During its life history an organism develops an assemblage of traits that contribute to its individual survival and reproductive success, the two essential components of "fitness" formulated by Darwin. Such assemblages, termed *complex adaptations* and *strategies* in the literature of evolutionary ecology, are close biological equivalents to what psychologists and psychiatrists have conceptualized as personality styles. In biology, explanations of a life-history strategy of adaptations refer primarily to biogenic variations among constituent traits, their overall covariance structure, and the nature and ratio of favorable to unfavorable ecologic resources that have been available for purposes of extending longevity and optimizing reproduction. Such explanations are not appreciably different from those used to account for the development of normal and pathological personality styles.

Bypassing the usual complications of analogies, a relevant and intriguing parallel may be drawn between the phylogenic evolution of a species' genetic composition and the ontogenic development of an individual organism's adaptive strategies (that is, its "personality style"). At any point in time, a species will possess a limited set of genes that serve as trait potentials. Over succeeding generations the frequency distribution of these genes will likely change in their relative proportions depending on how well the traits they undergird contribute to the species "fittedness" within its varying ecological habitats. In a similar fashion, individual organisms begin life with a limited subset of their species' genes and the trait potentials they subserve. Over time the *salience* of these trait potentials—not the proportion of the genes themselves—will become differentially prominent as the organism interacts with its environments. It "learns" from these experiences which of its traits "fit" best, that is, are optimally suited to its ecosystem. In phylogenesis, then, actual gene *frequencies* change during the generation-to-generation adaptive process, whereas in ontogenesis it is the *salience* or prominence of gene-based traits that changes as adaptive learning takes place. Parallel evolutionary processes occur, one within the life of a species, the other within the life of an organism. What is seen in the individual organism is a shaping of latent potentials into adaptive and manifest styles of perceiving, feeling, thinking, and acting; these distinctive ways of adaptation, engendered by the interaction of biologic endowment and social experience, comprise, in my view, the elements of what is termed *personality styles,* normal or abnormal. It is a formative process in a single lifetime that parallels gene redistributions among species during their evolutionary history.

Two factors beyond the intrinsic genetic trait potentials of advanced social organisms have a special significance in affecting their survival and replicability. First, other members of the species play a critical part in providing postnatal nurturing and complex role models. Second, and no less relevant, is the high level of diversity and unpredictability of their ecological habitats. This requires numerous, multifaceted, and flexible response alternatives, either preprogrammed genetically or acquired subsequently through early learning. Humans are notable for their unusual adaptive pliancy, acquiring a wide repertoire of "styles" or alternate modes of functioning for dealing both with predictable and novel environmental circumstances. Unfortunately, the malleability of early potentials for diverse learnings diminishes as maturation progresses. As a consequence, adaptive styles acquired in childhood, and usually suitable for comparable later environments, become increasingly immutable, resisting modification and relearning. Problems arise in new ecologic settings when these deeply ingrained behavior patterns persist, despite their lessened appropriateness; simply stated, what was learned and was once adaptive may no longer "fit." Perhaps more important than environmental diversity, then, is the divergence between the circumstances of original learning and those of later life, a schism that has become more problematic as humans have progressed from stable and traditional to fluid and inconstant modern societies.

Recent developments bridging ecological and evolutionary theory are well underway, offering some justification for extending their principles to human styles of normal and abnormal adaptation. To provide a conceptual background from these sciences and to furnish a rough model concerning the nature of normal and abnormal personality functioning, three domains or spheres in which evolutionary and ecological principles are demonstrated will be discussed: existence, adaptation, and replication.

Existence relates to the serendipitous transformation of more ephemeral and/or less organized states into those possessing greater stability and/or organization. It pertains to the formation and sustenance of discernible phenomena, to the processes of evolution that enhance and preserve life, and to the psychic polarity of *pleasure and pain.*

Adaptation refers to homeostatic processes employed to foster survival in open ecosystems. It relates to the manner in which extant phenomena adapt to their surrounding ecosystems, to the mechanisms employed in accommodating to or in modifying these environments, and to the psychic polarity of *passivity* and *activity.*

Replication pertains to reproductive styles that maximize the diversification and selection of ecologically effective attributes. It refers to the strategies utilized to replicate ephemeral organisms, to the methods of maximizing reproductive propagation and progeny nurturance, and to the psychic polarity of *self* and *other.*

Although the excursion presented here may in many ways be merely an academic exercise, it will provide the open-minded reader with a contemporary perspective on evolutionary and ecological thought as well as its potential utility in understanding psychological styles of adaptive and maladaptive functioning.

The Three Polarities of Evolution

A few words should be said concerning the bipolar framework used to structure the evolutionary model presented in the following pages.

Bipolar or dimensional schemas are almost universally present in both historic and professional literatures. The earliest may be traced to ancient Eastern religions, most notably the Chinese *I Ching* texts and the Hebrews' Kabala. More modern though equally speculative bipolar systems have been proposed by keen and broadly informed observers, such as Sigmund Freud and Carl Jung. Each of these earlier proposals fascinate either by virtue of their intriguing insights or by the compelling power of their logic. For me, however, all have failed in their quest for the ultimate character of human nature in that their conceptions float, so to speak, above the foundations built by contemporary physical and biological science. Formulas pertaining to psychological processes must not only coordinate with but be anchored firmly to modern principles of physical and biological evolution, the only laws of nature that are universal in that they apply to all spheres of inorganic phenomena and organic life. It is on these universal underpinnings that the polarity model to be presented has been grounded, and from which a deeper and clearer understanding may be obtained concerning the nature of both normal and pathological functioning.

Nevertheless, what follows remains conjectural, if not overly extended in its speculative reach. Some readers will judge these conjectures persuasive; a few will consider them "interesting" but unconfirmable; still others will find little merit in them. Whatever one's appraisal, my theoretical model may best be approached in the spirit in which it was formulated—an effort to bring together observations from different domains of science in the hope that principles derived in adjacent fields can lead to a clearer understanding of their neighbors.

I contend that each of our contemporary sciences share common themes, although their forms and mechanisms differ appreciably. I believe that a careful explication of the structure and functions of each scientific domain will uncover patterns of organization and process that have evolved to counter entropic decomposition and to replicate extant phenomena, be it with mechanisms that serve to bond inorganic matter, or to aggrandize personal territory, or to engage in reproductive mating.

Three major polarities are articulated in this section. Cast here for the first time in evolutionary terms, they have forerunners in psychological theory that may be traced as far back as the early 1900s.

A number of pre–World War I theorists proposed a set of three polarities that were used as the foundation for constructing a variety of psychological processes. Although others formulated parallel schemas earlier than he, I illustrate these conceptions with reference to ideas presented by Sigmund Freud. Freud wrote in 1915 (1925) what many consider to be among his most seminal papers, those on metapsychology and, in particular, the section entitled "The Instincts and Their Vicissitudes." Speculations that foreshadowed several concepts developed more fully later, both by himself and others, were presented in preliminary form in these papers. Particularly notable is a framework that Freud advanced as central to understanding the mind; unfortunately, he never developed his basic system of interlocking polarities as a formal system for conceptualizing psychological patterns of normality and abnormality. He framed these polarities as follows:

> Our mental life as a whole is governed by three polarities, namely, the following antitheses:
> Subject (ego)-Object (external world)
> Pleasure-Pain
> Active-Passive
> The three polarities within the mind are connected with one another in various highly significant ways. (1925, p. 76–77)
>
> We may sum up by saying that the essential feature in the vicissitudes undergone by instincts is their subjection to the influences of the three great polarities that govern mental life. Of these three polarities we

> might describe that of activity-passivity as the biological, that of the ego-external world as the real, and finally that of pleasure-pain as the economic, respectively. (1925, p. 83)

As noted, aspects of these three polarities were "discovered" and employed by theorists earlier than Freud—in France, Germany, Russia, and other European nations as well as in the United States. Variations of the polarities of active-passive, subject-object, and pleasure-pain were identified by Heymans and Wiersma in Holland, McDougall in the United States, Meumann in Germany, Kollarits in Hungary, and others.

Despite the central role Freud assigned these polarities, he failed to capitalize on them as a coordinated system for understanding normal and pathological patterns of human functioning. Although he failed to pursue their potentials, the ingredients he formulated for his tripartite polarity schema were drawn upon by his disciples for many decades to come, seen prominently in the progressive development from instinct or "drive theory," where pleasure and pain were the major forces, to "ego psychology," where the apparatuses of "activity" and "passivity" were central constructs, and, most recently, to "self psychology" and "object relations" theory, where the self-other polarity is the key issue.

Forgotten as a metapsychological speculation by most, the scaffolding comprising these polarities was fashioned anew by this author in the mid-1960s (Millon 1969). Unacquainted with Freud's proposals at the time and employing a biosocial-learning model, I constructed a framework similar to Freud's "great polarities that govern all of mental life." Phrased in the terminology of learning concepts, the model comprised three polar dimensions: *positive vs. negative* reinforcement (pleasure-pain); *self-other* as reinforcement source; and the instrumental styles of *active-passive.* I stated:

> By framing our thinking in terms of *what* reinforcements the individual is seeking, *where* he is looking to find them and *how* he performs we may see more simply and more clearly the essential strategies which guide his coping behaviors.
>
> These reinforcements [relate to] whether he seeks primarily to achieve positive reinforcements (pleasure) or to avoid negative reinforcements (pain) . . .
>
> Some patients turn to others as their source of reinforcement, whereas some turn primarily to themselves. The distinction [is] between *others* and *self* as the primary reinforcement source.
>
> On what basis can a useful distinction be made among instrumental behaviors? A review of the literature suggests that the behavioral di-

> mension of activity-passivity may prove useful. . . . Active patients [are] busily intent on controlling the circumstances of their environment. . . . Passive patients . . . wait for the circumstances of their environment to take their course . . . reacting to them only after they occur. (Millon 1969, pp. 193–195)

Do we find parallels within the disciplines of psychiatry and psychology that correspond to these broad evolutionary polarities?

In addition to the forerunners noted previously, there is a growing group of contemporary scholars whose work relates to these polar dimensions, albeit indirectly and partially. For example, a modern conception anchored to biological foundations has been developed by the distinguished British psychologist Jeffrey Gray (1964, 1973). A three-part model of temperament, matching the three-part polarity model in most regards, has been formulated by the American psychologist Arnold Buss and his associates (Buss and Plomin 1975, 1984). Circumplex formats based on factor analytic studies of mood and arousal that align well with the polarity schema have been published by Russell (1980) and Tellegen (1985). Deriving inspiration from a sophisticated analysis of neuroanatomical substrates, the highly resourceful American psychiatrist Robert Cloninger (1986, 1987) has deduced a threefold schema that is coextensive with major elements of the model's three polarities. Less oriented to biological foundations, recent advances in both interpersonal and psychoanalytic theory have likewise exhibited strong parallels to one or more of the three polar dimensions. A detailed review of these and other parallels has been presented in a recent book by the author (Millon 1990).

The following pages summarize the rationale and characteristics of the three-part polarity model. Later sections draw upon the model as a basis for establishing criteria for "normality" grounded in modern evolutionary and ecological theory.

Aims of Existence

Life Enhancement and Life Preservation: Pleasure-Pain Polarity

The procession of evolution is not limited just to the evolution of life on earth but extends to prelife, to matter, to the primordial elements of our local cosmos, and, in all likelihood, to the elusive properties of a more encompassing universe within which our cosmos is embedded as an incidental part. The demarcations we conceptualize to differentiate states such as nonmatter and matter, or inorganic and organic, are nominal devices that record transitions in this ongoing procession of transformations, an unbroken sequence of re-formed elements that have existed from the very first.

We may speak of the emergence of our local cosmos from some larger universe, or of life from inanimate matter, but if we were to trace the procession of evolution backward all the way we would have difficulty identifying precise markers for each of these transitions. What we define as life would become progressively less clear as we reversed time until we could no longer discern its presence in the matter we were studying. So, too, does it appear to theoretical physicists that if we trace the evolution of our present cosmos back to its ostensive origins, we would lose its existence in the obscurity of an undifferentiated and unrecoverable past. The so-called Big Bang may in fact be merely an evolutionary transformation, one of an ongoing and never-ending series of transitions.

The notion of open systems is of relatively recent origin (Bertalanffy 1945; Lotka 1924; Schrodinger 1944), brought to bear initially to explain how the inevitable consequences of the Second Law of Thermodynamics appear to be circumvented in the biologic realm. By broadening the ecologic field so as to encompass events and properties beyond the local and immediate, it becomes possible to understand how living organisms on earth function and thrive, despite seeming to contradict this immutable physical law (for example, solar radiation, continuously transmitting its ultimately exhaustible supply of energy, temporarily counters the earth's inevitable thermodynamic entropy). The open system concept has been borrowed freely and fruitfully to illuminate processes across a wide range of subjects. In recent decades it has been extended, albeit speculatively, to account for the evolution of cosmic events. These hypotheses suggest that the cosmos as known today may represent a four-dimensional "bubble" or set of "strings" stemming either from the random fluctuations of an open meta-universe characterized primarily by entropic chaos or of transpositions from a larger set of dimensions that comprise the properties of an open mega-universe, that is, dimensions beyond those we apprehend.

These speculations extend the boundaries of the Big Bang theory, which not only fails to account for many of the features of the cosmic firmament but limits expansion and transformations to elements within the confines of our local, closed space-time cosmos. By opening our "cocoon" to phenomena transcending immediate and proximal conditions, extending it to a meta- or to a mega-universe, cosmogony becomes but one phase of a series of evolutionary transformations, another transitional restructuring among infinite possibilities.

Predilections between the meta- versus mega-universe models favor a "nonspace-time" world composed of thermodynamic equilibrium, that is, a perfect entropic state of constant temperature and uniform disorder, from which periodic fluctuations of an entirely random character materialize states of order, most of which collapse, are annihilated, or simply disappear, losing their transitory structure and decomposing back into the vast entropic chaos of nonspace-time equilibrium (nothingness?). The first mathematization of this highly speculative proposal was presented in 1973 by the theoretical physicist Edward Tryon; it has been developed further by the Soviet theorists Alexander Vilenkin and Andrei Linde (Gribbin 1986). They state that our cosmos is but a fluctuation of a vacuum that comprises an infinite meta-universe; the expansion that characterizes our local cosmos stems from a "big whoosh" that blew a tiny speck of a space-time fluctuation into its current enormous and expanding size. By expanding the Big Bang concept to an open system model, it is no longer needed to assume that all matter existing in our present-day cosmos was present within it at the moment of its expansion.

By materializing new matter from fluctuations in a larger and unstable field—that is, by creating existence from nonexistence ("cold dark matter")—any embedded open system might not only expand but form entities displaying "anti-entropic" structure, the future survival of which is determined by the character of parallel materializations and the fortuitous consequences of their interactions (including their ecologic balance, symbiosis, and so on). Beyond fortuitous levels of reciprocal "fitness," some of these anti-entropic structures may possess properties that enable them to facilitate their own self-organization; that is, the forms into which they have been rendered randomly may not only "survive" but be able to amplify themselves and/or to extend their range, sometimes in replicated and sometimes in more comprehensive structures.

Recent mathematical research in both physics and chemistry has begun to elucidate processes that characterize how structures "evolve" from randomness. Whether one evaluates the character of cosmogenesis, the dynamics of open chemical systems, or repetitive patterns exhibited among weather movements, it appears that random fluctuations assume sequences that often become both self-sustaining and recurrent. In chemistry, the theory of dissipative (free energy) structures (Prigogine 1972, 1976) proposes a principle called "order through fluctuation" that relates to self-organizational dynamics; these fluctuations proceed through sequences that not only maintain the integrity of the system but are self-renewing. According to the theory, any open system may evolve when fluctuations exceed a critical threshold, setting in motion a qualitative shift in the nature of the system's structural form. Similar shifts within evolving systems are explained in pure mathematics by what has been termed catastrophic theory (Thom 1972); here sudden "switches" from one dynamic equilibrium state to another occur instantaneously with no intervening bridge. As models portraying how the dynamics of random fluctuation drive prior levels of equilibrium to reconstitute themselves into new structures, both catastrophe and dissipative theories prove fruitful in explicating self-evolving morphogenesis—the emergence of new forms of existence from prior states.

Indirectly related to this are recent mathematical studies into orderly and repetitive patterns that emerge when examining natural phenomena which appear random and unpredictable. Principles of "chaology" (Gleick 1987) pertain both to states of disorder that lie beneath a facade of order as well as to forms of organization that may be deeply hidden within seeming chaos. Random fluctuations and irregularities in ostensibly chaotic states may come to form not only complicated rhythms and patterns, but demonstrate both recurrences and replicated designs, such as seen in geometric "fractal" patterns (Mandelbrot 1977); here the same shapes emerge from fluctuations time and again, taking form sequentially on smaller and smaller scales.

There is a second and equally necessary step to existence, one that maintains "being" by protecting established structures and processes. Here the degrading effects of entropy are counteracted by a diversity of "safeguarding" mechanisms. Among organic substances, such as atoms and molecules, the elements comprising their nuclear structure are tightly bound, held together by the "strong force" that is exceptionally resistant to decomposition (hence the power necessary to "split" the atom). More complicated organic structures, such as plants and animals, also have mechanisms to counter entropic dissolution, that is, to maintain the existence of their "life."

Two intertwined strategies are required, one to achieve existence, the other to preserve it.

The aim of the first is the enhancement of life, that is, creating or strengthening ecologically survivable organisms; the aim of the second is the preservation of life, that is, avoiding events that might terminate it. Although I disagree with Freud's concept of a death instinct (Thanatos), I believe he was essentially correct in recognizing that a balanced yet fundamental biological bipolarity exists in nature, a bipolarity that has its parallel in the physical world. As he wrote in one of his last works, "The analogy of our two basic instincts extends from the sphere of living things to the pair of opposing forces—attraction and repulsion—which rule the inorganic world" (Freud 1940, p. 72). Among humans, the former may be seen in life-enhancing acts that are "attracted" to what we experientially record as "pleasurable" events (positive reinforcers), the latter in life-preserving behaviors oriented to repel events experientially characterized as "painful" (negative reinforcers). More will be said of these fundamental if not universal mechanisms of countering entropic disintegration in the next section.

To summarize, existence reflects a to-be or not-to-be issue. In the inorganic world, "to be" is essentially a matter of possessing qualities that distinguish a phenomenon from its surrounding field, that is, *not* being in a state of entropy. Among organic beings, "to be" is a matter of possessing the properties of life as well as being located in ecosystems that facilitate the enhancement and preservation of that life. In the phenomenological or experiential world of sentient organisms, events that extend life and preserve it correspond largely to metaphorical terms such as pleasure and pain, that is, recognizing and pursuing positive sensations and emotions, on the one hand, and recognizing and eschewing negative sensations and emotions, on the other.

The pleasure-pain bipolarity not only places sensations, motivations, feelings, emotions, moods, and affects on two contrasting dimensions but recognizes that each possess separate and independent quantitative extremes. That is, events such as attractive, gratifying, rewarding, or positively reinforcing may be experienced as weak or strong, as those that are aversive, distressful, sad, or negatively reinforcing can also be experienced as weak or strong.

Efforts to identify specific events or experiences that fit each pole of the pleasure-pain bipolarity are likely to distract from the essential distinction. Thus the particular actions or objects that people find pleasurable (for example, sex, sports, art, or money) are legion, and for every patient who experiences a certain event as rewarding, one can find another who experiences that same event as distasteful or painful; for example, some patients who are driven to seek attention are sexually promiscuous, whereas others are repelled by sexuality in any form. In short, categorizations based on the specific properties of what may be subsumed under the broad constructs of pain or pleasure will prove not only futile and cumbersome but misguiding as well.

Although there are many philosophical and metapsychological issues associated with the "nature" of pain and pleasure as constructs, it is neither our intent nor our task to inquire into them here. That they recur as a polar dimension time and again in diverse psychological domains (for example, learned behaviors, unconscious processes, emotion and motivation as well as their biological substrates) has been elaborated in another publication (Millon 1990). Later I examine their role as constructs for articulating criteria that may usefully define normality.

Modes of Adaptation

Ecologic Accommodation and Ecologic Modification: The Passive-Active Polarity

As noted, to come into existence as an emergent particle, a local cosmos, or a living creature is but an initial phase, the serendipitous presence of a newly formed structure, the chance evolution of a phenomenon distinct from its surroundings. Though extant, such fortuitous transformations may exist only for a fleeting moment. Most emergent phenomena do not survive, that is, possess properties that enable them to retard entropic decomposition. To maintain their unique structure, differentiated from the larger ecosystem of which they are a part, to be sustained as a discrete entity among other phenomena that comprise their environmental field, requires good fortune and the presence of effective modes of adaptation. These modes of basic survival comprise the second essential component of evolution's procession.

The second evolutionary stage relates to what is termed the modes of adaptation; it is also framed as a two-part polarity. The first may best be characterized as the mode of ecologic accommodation, signifying inclinations to passively "fit in," to locate and remain securely anchored in a niche, subject to the vagaries and unpredictabilities of the environment, all acceded to with one crucial proviso: that the elements comprising the surroundings will furnish both the nourishment and the protection needed to sustain existence. Though based on a somewhat simplistic bifurcation among adaptive strategies, this passive and accommodating mode is one of the two fundamental methods that living organisms have evolved as a means of survival. It represents the core process employed in the evolution of what has come to be designated as the plant kingdom, a stationary, rooted, yet essentially pliant and dependent survival mode. By contrast, the second of the two major modes of adaptation is seen in the life-style of the animal kingdom. Here we observe a primary inclination toward ecologic modification, a tendency to change or rearrange the elements comprising the larger milieu, to intrude upon otherwise quiescent settings, a versatility in shifting from one niche to another as unpredictability arises, a mobile and interventional mode that actively stirs, maneuvers, yields, and, at the human level, substantially transforms the environment to meet its own survival aims.

Both modes—passive and active—have proven impressively capable to both nourishing and preserving life. Whether the polarity sketched is phrased in terms of accommodating versus modifying, passive versus active, or plant versus animal, it represents, at the most basic level, the two fundamental modes that organisms have evolved to sustain their existence. This second aspect of evolution differs from the first stage, which is concerned with what may be called existential "becoming," in that it characterizes modes of "being," that is, how what has become endures.

Broadening the model to encompass human experience, the active-passive polarity means that the vast range of behaviors engaged in by humans may fundamentally be grouped in terms of whether initiative is taken in altering and shaping life's events or whether behaviors are reactive to and accommodate those events.

Often reflective and deliberate, those who are passively oriented manifest few overt strategies to gain their ends. They display a seeming inertness, a phlegmatic lack of ambition or persistence, a tendency toward acquiescence, a restrained attitude in which they initiate little to modify events, waiting for the circumstances of their environment to take their course before making accommodations. Some persons may be temperamentally ill-equipped to rouse or assert themselves; perhaps past experience has deprived them of opportunities to acquire a range of competencies or confidence in their ability to master the events of their environment; equally possible is a naive confidence that things will come their way with little or no effort on their part. From a variety of diverse sources, then, those at the passive end of the polarity engage in few direct instrumental activities to intercede in events or generate the effects they desire. They seem suspended, quiescent, placid, immobile, restrained, listless, waiting for things to happen and reacting to them only after they occur.

Descriptively, those who are at the active end of the polarity are best characterized by their alertness, vigilance, liveliness, vigor, forcefulness, stimulus-seeking energy, and drive. Some plan strategies and scan alternatives to circumvent obstacles or avoid the distress of punishment, rejection, and anxiety. Others are impulsive, precipitate, excitable, rash, and hasty, seeking to elicit pleasures and rewards. Although specific goals vary and change from time to time, actively aroused individuals intrude on passing events and energetically and busily modify the circumstances of their environment.

Much can be said for the survival value of fitting a specific niche well, but no less important are flexibilities for adapting to diverse and unpredictable environments. It is here again where a distinction, though not a hard and fast one, may be drawn between the accommodating (plant) and the modifying (animal) mode of adaptation, the former more rigidly fixed and constrained by ecologic conditions, the latter more broad-ranging and more facile in its scope of maneuverability. To proceed in evolved complexity to the human species, we cannot help but recognize the almost endless variety of adaptive possibilities that may (and do) arise as secondary derivatives of a large brain possessing an open network of potential interconnections that permit the functions of self-reflection, reasoning, and abstraction. But this takes us beyond the subject of this chapter. The reader is referred elsewhere (Millon 1990) for a fuller discussion of active-passive parallels in wider domains of psychological thought (for example, the "ego apparatuses" formulated by Hartmann [1939] or the distinction between classical and operant conditioning in the writings of Skinner [1938, 1953]).

"Normal" or optimal functioning, at least among humans, appears to call for a flexible balance that interweaves both polar extremes. In the first evolutionary stage, that relating to existence, behaviors encouraging both life enhancement (pleasure) and life preservation (pain avoidance) are likely to be more successful in achieving survival than actions limited to one or the other alone. Similarly, regarding adaptation, modes of functioning that exhibit both ecologic accommodation and ecologic modification are likely to be more successful than either by itself. Nevertheless, it does appear that the two advanced forms of life on earth—plants and animals—have evolved by giving precedence to one mode rather than both.

In their mature stage organisms possess the requisite competencies to maintain entropic stability. When these competencies can no longer adapt and sustain existence, organisms succumb inexorably to death and decomposition. This fate does not signify finality, however. Prior to their demise, all ephemeral species create duplicates that circumvent their extinction, engaging in acts that enable them to transcend the entropic dissolution of their members' individual existences.

Strategies of Replication

Reproductive Propagation and Reproductive Nurturance: The Self-Other Polarity

If an organism merely duplicates itself prior to death, then its replica is "doomed" to repeat the same fate it suffered. However, if new potentials for extending existence can be fashioned by chance or routine events, then the possibility of achieving a different and conceivably superior outcome may be increased. And it is this co-occurence of random and recombinant processes that does lead to the prolongation of a species' existence. This third hallmark of evolution's procession also undergirds another of nature's fundamental polarities, that between self and other.

At its most basic and universal level, the manifold varieties of organisms living today have evolved, as Mayr (1964) has phrased it, to cope with the challenge of continuously changing and immensely diversified environments, the resources of which are not inexhaustible. The means by which organisms cope with environmental change and diversity are well known. Inorganic structures survive for extended periods of time by virtue of the extraordinary strength of their bonding. This contrasts with the very earliest forerunners of organic life. Until they could replicate themselves, their distinctive assemblages existed precariously, subject to events that could put a swift end to the discrete and unique qualities that characterized their composition, leaving them essentially as transient and ephemeral phenomena. Once replicative procedures were perfected, the chemical machinery for copying organismic life, the DNA double helix, became so precise that it could produce perfect clones, *if* nothing interfered with its structure or its mechanisms of execution. But the patterning and processes of complex molecular change are not immune to accident. High temperatures and radiation dislodge and rearrange atomic structures, producing what are termed mutations, alterations in the controlling and directing DNA configuration that undergirds the replication of organismic morphology.

Despite the deleterious impact of most mutations, it is the genetic variations they give rise to that have served as the primary means by which *simple* organisms acquire traits capable of adapting to diverse and changing environments. But isomorphic replication, aided by an occasional beneficent mutation, is a most inefficient if not hazardous means of surmounting ecologic crises faced by complex and slowly reproducing organisms. Advantageous mutations do not appear in sufficient numbers and with sufficient dependability to generate the novel capabilities required to adapt to frequent or marked shifts in the ecosystem. How then did the more intricate and intermittently reproducing organisms evolve the means to resolve the diverse hazards of unpredictable environments?

The answer to this daunting task was the evolution of a recombinant mechanism, one in which a pair of organisms exchange their genetic resources, that is, develop what we term *sexual mating.* Here, the potentials and traits each partner possesses are sorted into new configurations that differ in their composition from those of their origins, generating thereby new variants and capabilities, of which some may prove more adaptive (and others less so) in changing environments than their antecedents. Great advantages accrue by the occasional favorable combinations that occur through this random shuffling of genes.

Recombinant replication, with its consequential benefits of selective diversification, requires the partnership of two "parents," each contributing its genetic resources in a distinctive and species-characteristic manner. Similarly, the attention and care given the offspring of a species' matings is also distinctive. Worthy of note is the difference between the mating parents in the degree to which they protect and nourish their joint offspring. Although the investment of energy devoted to upbringing is balanced and complementary, rarely is it identical or even comparable in either devotion or determination. This disparity in reproductive "investment" strategies, especially evident among animal species (insects, reptiles, birds, mammals), underlies the evolution of the male and female genders, the foundation for the third cardinal polarity I propose to account for evolution's procession.

Somewhat less profound than that of the first polarity, which represents the line separating the enhancement of order (existence-life) from the prevention of disorder (nonexistence-death), or that of the second polarity, differentiating the adaptive modes of accommodation (passive-plant) from those of modification (active-animal), the third polarity, based on distinctions in replication strategies, is no less fundamental in that it contrasts the maximization of reproductive propagation (self-male) from that of the maximization of reproductive nurturance (other-female).

Evolutionary biologists (Cole 1954; Trivers 1974; Wilson 1975) have recorded marked differences among species in both the cycle and pattern of their reproductive behaviors. Of special interest is the extreme diversity among *and* within species in the number of offspring spawned and the consequent nurturing and protective investment the parents make in the survival of their progeny. Designated the r-strategy and K-strategy in population biology, the former represents a pattern of propagating a vast number of offspring but exhibiting minimal attention to their survival; the latter is typified by the production of few progeny followed by considerable effort to assure their survival. Exemplifying the r-strategy are oysters, which generate some 500 million eggs annually; the K-strategy is found among the great apes, which produce a single offspring every five to six years.

Not only do species differ in where they fall on the r- to K-strategy continuum, but within most animal species an important distinction may be drawn between male and female genders. It is this latter differentiation that undergirds what has been termed the self- versus other-oriented polarity, implications of which will be briefly elaborated.

Human females typically produce about four hundred eggs in a lifetime, of which no more than twenty to twenty-five can mature into healthy infants. The energy investment expended in gestation, nurturing, and caring for each child, both before and during the years following birth, is extraordinary. Not only is the female required to devote much of her energies to bring the fetus to full term, but during this period she cannot be fertilized again; in contrast, the male is free to mate with numerous females. And should her child fail to survive, the waste in physical and emotional exertion is not only enormous, but amounts to a substantial portion of the mother's lifetime reproductive potential. There appears to be good reason, therefore, to encourage a protective and caring inclination on the part of the female, as evident in a sensitivity to cues of distress and a willingness to persist in attending to the needs and nurturing of her offspring.

Although the male discharges tens of millions of sperm on mating, this is but a small investment, given the ease and frequency with which he can repeat the act. On fertilization, his physical and emotional commitment can end with minimal consequences. Although the protective and food-gathering efforts of the male may be lost by an early abandonment of a mother and an offspring or two, much more may be gained by investing energies in pursuits that achieve the wide reproductive spread of his genes. Relative to the female of the species, whose best strategy appears to be the care and comfort of child and kin—that is, the K-strategy—the male is likely to be reproductively more prolific by maximizing self-propagation—that is, adopting the r-strategy. To focus primarily on self-replication may diminish the survival probabilities of a few of a male's progeny, but this occasional reproductive loss may be well compensated for by mating with multiple females and thereby producing multiple offspring.

In sum, males tend to be self-oriented owing to the fact that competitive advantages that inhere within themselves maximize the replication of their genes. Conversely, females tend to be other-oriented owing to the fact that their competence in nurturing and protecting their limited progeny maximizes the replication of their genes.

The consequences of the male's r-strategy are a broad range of what may be seen as self- as opposed to other-oriented behaviors, such as acting in an egotistic, insensitive, inconsiderate, uncaring, and noncommunicative manner. In contrast, females are more disposed to be other-oriented, affiliative, intimate, empathic, protective, and solicitous (Gilligan 1982; Rushton 1985; Wilson 1978).

Polarities and the Criteria of Normality

Important "scientific" advances were introduced in the third edition of the American Psychiatric Association's *Diagnostic and Statistical Manual of Mental Disorders* (DSM-III). Among them was the specification of relatively explicit "diagnostic criteria" for each disorder. Rather than a discursive description, each category was composed of a set of clearly articulated behavior and biographic characteristics. Henceforth, a specified number of these criteria were required for a patient to be assigned a diagnostic label. Despite minor controversies concerning the theoretical and empirical adequacy of the DSM's criteria, there is considerable agreement regarding their ultimate utility (Millon 1986, 1987). This utility should be achieved as well, I believe, if we specify criteria for the "normality" construct. Accordingly, I present a set of "criteria" that reflect the evolutionary polarities described earlier in the chapter. Some limitations and caveats are in order before we proceed.

Owing to the multiple perspectives that can legitimately be brought to bear in defining "normality" (Offer and Sabshin 1966), as well as the many values, functions, and goals the construct may serve, there is little likelihood that any set of criteria would be satisfactory to all. That multiple criteria are needed should be self-evident, although the specifics of which they are composed will remain controversial. Given my belief in the applicability of evolutionary principles to all spheres of nature's expression, I have sought to anchor my criteria as closely as possible to these "universal" principles in the realm of human functioning—that is, in those transactions that relate to existential survival (pain-pleasure), ecological adaptation (passive-active), and species replication (others-self).

A balance among normals must be struck between the two extremes that comprise each polarity; a measure of integration among the three basic polarities themselves is also an index of normality. However, normality does not require precise equidistance between polar extremes. Positions of balance will vary as a function of the overall configuration both within and among polarities, which, in their turn, will depend on the wider ecosystems within which individuals operate. In other words, and as is well recognized, there is no one form or expression of normality. Various polarity positions, and the traits and behaviors they underlie, will permit diverse "styles of normality," just as marked deficits and imbalances among the polarities may manifest themselves in diverse "styles of abnormality" (Millon 1990).

Given the numerous and diverse ecological milieus that humans face in our complex modern environment, there is reason to expect that most "normals" will display multiple adaptive styles, sometimes more active, sometimes less so, occasionally focused on self, occasionally on others, at times oriented to pleasure, at times oriented to the avoidance of pain. Despite the presence of relatively enduring and characteristic styles, adaptive flexibility typifies most normal individuals; that is, they are able to shift from one position on a polar continuum to another as the circumstances of life change.

Let us turn next to the six polarity-based criteria for normality. They are grouped, two each, under the three polarity headings of existence, adaptation, and replication. Each criterion is stated alongside its evolutionary polarity. Elaborated within each section are the data or theory supportive of the criterion—that is, findings, for example, of an ostensive biological substrate for the criterion, formulations by "normality/health" theorists, as well as clinical illustrations that demonstrate some of the pathologic consequences following from failures to meet the criterion.

Existence

An interweaving and shifting balance between the two extremes that comprise the pain-pleasure bipolarity typifies normality. Both of the following criteria should be met in varying degrees as life circumstances require. In essence, a synchronous and coordinated personal style would have developed to answer the question of whether the person should focus on experiencing only the pleasures of life versus concentrating his or her efforts on avoiding its pains.

LIFE PRESERVATION: AVOIDING DANGER AND THREAT

One might assume that a criterion based on the avoidance of psychic or physical pain would be sufficiently self-evident not to require specification. As is well known, debates have arisen in the literature as to whether mental health/normality reflects the absence of mental disorder, being merely the reverse side of the mental illness or abnormality coin. That there is a relationship between health and disease cannot be questioned; the two are intimately connected, conceptually and physically. On the other hand, to define health solely as the absence of disorder will not suffice. As a single criterion among several, however, features of behavior and experience that signify both the lack of (for example, anxiety, depression) and an aversion to (for example, threats to safety and security) pain in its many and diverse forms provide a necessary foundation upon which other, more positively constructed criteria may rest. Substantively, positive normality must comprise elements beyond mere nonnormality or abnormality. And despite the complexities and inconsistencies of personality, from a definitional point of view normality does preclude nonnormality.

Turning to the evolutionary aspect of pain avoidance, that pertaining to a distancing from life-threatening circumstances, psychic and otherwise, we find an early historical reference in the writings of Herbert Spencer, a supportive contemporary of Darwin. In 1870 Spencer averred:

> Pains are the correlative of actions injurious to the organism, while pleasures are the correlatives of actions conducive to its welfare.
>
> Those races of beings only can have survived in which, on the average, agreeable or desired feelings went along with activities conducive to the maintenance of life, while disagreeable and habitually avoided feelings went along with activities directly or indirectly destructive of life.
>
> Every animal habitually persists in each act which gives pleasure, so long as it does so, and desists from each act which gives pain. . . . It is manifest that in proportion as this guidance approaches completeness, the life will be long; and that the life will be short in proportion as it falls short of completeness.
>
> We accept the inevitable corollary from the general doctrine of Evolution, that pleasures are the incentives to life-supporting acts and pains the deterrents from life-destroying acts. (Pp. 279–284)

More recently Freedman and Roe (1958) wrote:

> We . . . hypothesize that psychological warning and warding-off mechanisms, if properly studied, might provide a kind of psychological-evolutionary systematics. Exposure to pain, anxiety, or danger is likely to be followed by efforts to avoid a repetition of the noxious stimulus situation with which the experience is associated. Obviously an animal with a more highly developed system for anticipating and avoiding the threatening circumstance is more efficiently equipped for adaptation and survival. Such unpleasant situations may arise either from within, in its simplest form as tissue deprivation, or from without, by the infliction of pain or injury. Man's psychological superstructure may be viewed, in part, as a system of highly developed warning mechanisms. (P. 458)

As for the biologic substrate of "pain" signals, Gray (1975) suggests two systems, both of which alert the organism to possible dangers in the environment. Those mediating the behavioral effects of unconditioned (instinctive?) aversive events are termed the fight/flight system (FFS). This system elicits defensive aggression and escape and is subserved, according to Gray's pharmacologic inferences, by the amgydala, the ventromedial hypothalamus, and the central gray of the midbrain; neurochemically, evidence suggests a difficult-to-unravel interaction among aminobutyric acids (for example, gamma-ammobutyric acid), serotonin, and endogenous opiates (for example, endorphins). The second major source of sensitivity and action in response to "pain" signals is referred to by Gray as the behavioral inhibition system (BIS), consisting of the interplay of the septal-hippocampal system, its cholinergic projections and monoamine transmissions to the hypothalamus, and then on to the cingulate and prefrontal cortex. Activated by signals of punishment or nonreward, the BIS suppresses associated behaviors, refocuses the organism's attention, and redirects activity toward alternate stimuli.

"Harm avoidance" is a concept proposed recently by Cloninger (1986, 1987). As he conceives the construct, it is a heritable tendency to respond intensely to signals of aversive stimuli (pain) and to learn to inhibit behaviors that might lead to punishment and frustrative nonreward. Those high on this dimension are characterized as cautious, apprehensive, and inhibited; those low on this valence would likely be confident, optimistic, and carefree. Cloninger subscribes essentially to Gray's behavioral inhibition system concept in explicating this polarity, as well as the neuroanatomic and neurochemical hypotheses Gray proposed as the substrates for its "pain-avoidant" mechanisms.

Let us shift from biologic/evolutionary concepts to proposals of a similar cast offered by thinkers of a distinctly psychological turn of mind. Notable here are the contributions of Maslow (1968, 1970), particularly his hierarchic listing of "needs." Best known are the five fundamental needs that lead to self-actualization, the first two of which relate to our evolutionary criterion of life preservation. Included in the first group are the "physiologic" needs such as air, water, food, and sleep, qualities of the ecosystem essential for survival. Next, and equally necessary to avoid danger and threat, are what Maslow terms the *safety needs,* including the freedom from jeopardy, the security of physical protection and psychic stability, as well as the presence of social order and interpersonal predictability.

That pathological consequences can ensue from the failure to attend to the realities that portend danger is obvious; the lack of air, water, and food are not issues of great concern in civilized societies today, although these are matters of considerable import to environmentalists of the future and to contemporary poverty-stricken nations.

It may be of interest next to record some of the psychic pathologies of personality that can be traced to aberrations in meeting this first criterion of normality. For example, among those termed avoidant personalities (Millon 1981), we see an excessive preoccupation with threats to one's psychic security, an expectation of and hyperalertness to the signs of potential rejection that leads these persons to disengage from everyday relationships and pleasures. At the other extreme of the criterion we see a risk-taking attitude, a proclivity to chance hazards and to endanger one's life and liberty, a behavioral pattern characteristic of those we label antisocial personalities. Here there is little of the caution and prudence expected in the normality criterion of avoiding danger and threat; rather, we observe its opposite, a rash willingness to put one's safety in jeopardy, to play with fire and throw caution to the wind. Another pathological style illustrative of a failure to fulfill this evolutionary criterion is seen among those variously designated as masochistic and self-defeating personalities. Rather than avoid circumstances that may prove painful and self-endangering, these nonnormal personality styles set in motion situations in which they will come to suffer physically and/or psychically. Either by virtue of habit or guilt absolution, these individuals induce rather than avoid pain for themselves.

LIFE ENHANCEMENT: SEEKING REWARDING EXPERIENCES

At the other end of the "existence polarity" are attitudes and behaviors designed to foster and enrich life, to generate joy, pleasure, contentment, fulfillment, and thereby strengthen the capacity of the individual to remain vital and competent physically and psychically. This criterion asserts that existence/survival calls for more than life preservation alone; beyond pain avoidance is pleasure enhancement.

This criterion asks us to go at least one step further than Freud's parallel notion that life's motivation is chiefly that of "reducing tensions" (that is, avoiding/minimizing pain), maintaining thereby a steady state, if you will, a homeostatic balance and inner stability. In accord with my view of evolution's polarities, I would assert that normal humans are driven also by the desire to enrich their lives, to seek invigorating sensations and challenges, to venture and explore, all to the end of magnifying if not escalating the probabilities of both individual viability and species replicability.

Regarding the key instrumental role of "the pleasures," Spencer (1870) put it well more than a century ago: "pleasures are the correlatives of actions conducive to [organismic] welfare . . . the incentives to life-supporting acts" (pp. 279, 284). The view that there exists an organismic striving to expand one's inherent potentialties (as well as those of one's kin and species) has been implicit in the literature for ages. That "the pleasures" may be both sign and vehicle for this realization was recorded even in the ancient writings of the Talmud, where it states: "everyone will have to justify himself in the life hereafter for every failure to enjoy a legitimately offered pleasure in this world" (Jahoda 1958, p. 45).

As far as contemporary psychobiological theorists are concerned, brief mention will be made again of the contributions of Gray (1975, 1981) and Cloninger (1986, 1987). Gray's neurobiologic model centers heavily on activation and inhibition (active-passive polarities) as well as on signals of reward and punishment (pleasure-pain polarity). Basing his deductions primarily on pharmacologic investigations of animal behavior, Gray has proposed the existence of several interrelated and neuroanatomically grounded response systems that activate various positive and negative affects. He refers to what he terms the behavioral activation system (BAS) as an "approach system" that is subserved by the reward center uncovered originally by Olds and Milner (1954). Ostensibly mediated at brain stem and cerebellar levels, it is likely to include dopaminergic projections across various striata and is defined as responding to conditioned rewarding and safety stimuli by facilitating behaviors that maximize their future recurrence (Gray 1975). There are intricacies in the manner with which the BAS is linked to external stimuli and its anatomic substrates, but Gray currently views it as a system that subserves signals of reward, punishment relief, and pleasure.

Cloninger (1986, 1987) has generated a theoretical model composed of three dimensions, which he terms "reward dependence," "harm avoidance," to which I referred previously, and "novelty seeking." Proposing that each is a heritable personality disposition, he relates them explicitly to specific monoaminergic pathways; for example, high reward dependence is connected to low noradrenergic activity, harm avoidance to high serotonergic activity, and high novelty seeking to low dopaminergic activity. Cloninger's reward dependence dimension reflects highs and lows on the positive-gratifying-pleasure valence, whereas the harm avoidance dimension represents highs and lows on the negative-pain-displeasure valence. Reward dependence is hypothesized to be a heritable neurobiological tendency to respond to signals of reward (pleasure), particularly verbal signals of social approval, sentiment, and succor, as well as to resist events that might extinguish behaviors previously associated with these rewards. Cloninger portrays those high on reward dependence to be sociable, sympathetic, and pleasant; in contrast, those low on this polarity are characterized as detached, cool, and practical. Describing the undergirding substrate for the reward/pleasure valence as the behavior maintenance system

(BMS), Cloninger speculates that its prime neuromodulator is likely to be norepinephrine, with its major ascending pathways arising in the pons, projecting onward to hypothalamic and limbic structures, and then branching upward to the neocortex.

Turning again to pure psychological formulations, both Rogers (1963) and Maslow (1968) have proposed concepts akin to my criterion of enhancing pleasure. In his notion of "openness to experience," Rogers asserts that the fully functioning person has no aspect of his or her nature closed off. Such individuals are not only receptive to the experiences that life offers but are able also to use them in expanding all of life's emotions, as well as being open to all forms of personal expression. Along a similar vein, Maslow speaks of the ability to maintain a freshness to experience, to keep up one's capacity to appreciate relationships and events. No matter how often events or persons are encountered, one is neither sated nor bored but is disposed to view them with an ongoing sense of "awe and wonder."

Perhaps less dramatic than the conceptions of either Rogers and Maslow, I believe that this openness and freshness to life's transactions is an instrumental means for extending life, for strengthening one's competencies and options, and for maximizing the viability and replicability of one's species. More mundane and pragmatic in orientation than their views, this conception seems both more substantive theoretically and more consonant a rationale for explicating the role the pleasures play in undergirding "reward experience" and "openness to experience."

As before, a note or two should be recorded on the pathological consequences of a failure to meet a criterion. These are seen most clearly in the personality disorders labeled schizoid and avoidant. In the former there is a marked hedonic deficiency, stemming either from an inherent deficit in affective substrates or the failure of stimulative experience to develop either or both attachment behaviors or affective capacity (Millon 1981). Among those designated avoidant personalities, constitutional sensitivities or abusive life experiences have led to an intense attentional sensitivity to psychic pain and a consequent distrust in either the genuineness or durability of the "pleasures," such that these individuals can no longer permit themselves to experience them. Both of these personalities tend to be withdrawn and isolated, joyless and grim, neither seeking nor sharing in the rewards of life.

Adaptation

As with the pair of criteria representing the aims of existence, a balance should be achieved between the two criteria comprising modes of adaptation, those related to ecological accommodation and ecologic modification, or what I have termed the passive-active polarity. Normality calls for a synchronous and coordinated personal style that weaves a balanced answer to the question of whether one should accept what the fates have brought forth or take the initiative in altering the circumstances of one's life.

ECOLOGICAL ACCOMMODATION: ABIDING HOSPITABLE REALITIES

On first reflection, it would seem to be less than optimal to submit meekly to what life presents, to "adjust" obligingly to one's destiny. As described earlier, however, the evolution of plants is essentially grounded (no pun intended) in environmental accommodation, in an adaptive acquiescence to the ecosystem. Crucial to this adaptive course, however, is the capacity of these surroundings to provide the nourishment and protection requisite to the thriving of a species.

Could the same be true for the human species? Are there not circumstances of life that provide significant and assured levels of sustenance and safekeeping (both psychic and physical?) And, if that were the case, would not the acquisition of an accommodating attitude and passive life-style be a logical consequence? The answer, it would seem, is yes. If one's upbringing has been substantially secure and nurturant, would it not be "not normal" to flee or overturn it?

We know that circumstances, other than in infancy and early childhood, rarely persist throughout life. Autonomy and independence is almost inevitable as a stage of maturation, ultimately requiring the adoption of "adult" responsibilities that call for a measure of initiative, decision making, and action. Nevertheless, to the extent that the events of life have been and continue to be caring and giving, is it not perhaps wisest, from an evolutionary perspective, to accept this good fortune and "let matters be"? This accommodating or passive life philosophy has worked extremely well in sustaining and fostering those complex organisms that comprise the plant kingdom. Hence passivity, the yielding to environmental forces, may be in itself not only unproblematic but, where events and circumstances provide the "pleasures" of life and protect against their "pains," positively adaptive and constructive. Accepting rather than overturning a hospitable reality seems a sound course; or as it is said, "If it ain't broke, don't fix it."

Is passivity part of the repertoire of the human species, does it serve useful functions, and where and how is it exhibited? A few words in response to these questions may demonstrate that passivity is not mere inactivity but a stance or process that achieves useful gains.

For example, universal among mammalian species are two basic modes of learning, the respondent or conditioned type and the operant or instrumental type. The former is essentially a *passive* process, the simple pairing of an innate or reflexive response to a stimulus that previously did not elicit that response. In like passive fashion, environmental elements that occur either simultaneously or in close temporal order become connected to each other in the organism's repertoire of learning, such that if one of these elements recurs in the future, the expectation is that the others will follow or be elicited. The organisms do not have to do anything active to achieve these learnings; inborn reflexive responses and/or environmental events are merely associated by contiguity.

Operant or instrumental learnings, in contrast, represent the outcome of an active process on the part of the organism, one that requires an effort and execution on its part that has the effect of altering the environment. Whereas respondent conditioning occurs as a result of the passive observation of a conjoining of events, operant conditioning occurs only as a result of an active modification by the organism of its surroundings, a performance usually followed by a positive reinforcer (pleasure) or the successful avoidance of a negative one (pain). Unconditioned reflexes, such as a leg jerk in reaction to a knee tap, will become a passively acquired conditioned respondent if a bell is regularly sounded prior to the tap, as will the shrinking reflex of an eye pupil passively become conditioned to that bell if it regularly preceded exposure to a shining light.

The passive-active polarity is central to formulations of psychoanalytic theory. Prior to the impressively burgeoning literature on "self" and "object relations" theory of the past two decades, the passive-active antithesis had a major role in both classical "instinct" and post–World War II "ego" schools of analytic thought. The contemporary focus on "self" and "object" is considered in discussions of the third polarity, that of self-other. However, we should not overlook the once key and now less popular constructs of both instinct theory and ego theory. It may be worth noting, as well as of special interest to the evolutionary model presented in this chapter, that the beginnings of psychoanalytic metapsychology were oriented initially to instinctual derivatives (where pleasure and pain were given prominence), and then progressed subsequently to the apparatuses of the ego (Hartmann 1939; Rapaport 1953)—where passivity and activity were centrally involved.

The model of activity, as Rapaport puts it, is a dual one; first, the ego is strong enough to defend against or control the intensity of the id's drive tensions or, second, through the competence and energy of its apparatuses, the ego is successful in uncovering or creating in reality the object of the id's instinctual drives. Rapaport conceives the model of passivity also to be a dual one; first, either the ego gradually modulates or indirectly discharges the instinctual energies of the id or, second, lacking an adequately controlling apparatus, the ego is rendered powerless and subject thereby to instinctual forces. Translating these formulations into evolutionary terms, effective actions by the ego will successfully manage the internal forces of the id, whereas passivity will result either in accommodations or exposure to the internal demands of the id.

Turning to contemporary theorists more directly concerned with normality and health, the humanistic psychologist Maslow (1970) states that "self-actualized" individuals accept their nature as it is, despite personal weaknesses and imperfections. Comfortable with themselves and the world around them, they do not seek to change "the water because it is wet, or the rocks because they are hard" (p. 153). They have learned to accept the natural order of things. Passively accepting nature, they need not hide behind false masks or transform others to fit "distorted needs." Accepting themselves without shame or apology, they are equally at peace with the shortcomings of those with whom they live and relate.

Where do we find clinical nonnormality that reflects failures to meet the accommodating/abiding criterion?

One example of an inability to leave things as they are is seen in what the DSM-III terms the histrionic personality disorder. These individuals achieve their goals of maximizing protection, nurturance, and reproductive success by engaging busily in a series of manipulative, seductive, gregarious, and attention-getting maneuvers. Their persistent and unrelenting manipulation of events is designed to maximize the receipt of attention and favors as well as to avoid social disinterest and disapproval. They show an insatiable if not indiscriminate search for stimulation and approval. Their clever and often artful social behaviors may give the appearance of an inner confidence and self-assurance; but beneath this guise lies a fear that a failure on their part to ensure the receipt of attention will, in short order, result in indifference or rejection, and hence their desperate need for reassurance and repeated signs of approval. Tribute and affection must constantly be replenished and are sought from every interpersonal source. As they are quickly bored and sated, they keep stirring up things, becoming enthusiastic about one activity and then another. There is a restless stimulus-seeking quality in which they cannot leave well enough alone.

At the other end of the polarity are personality disorders that exhibit an excess of passivity, failing thereby to give direction to their own lives. Several Axis II disorders demonstrate this passive style, although their passivity derives from and is expressed in appreciably different ways. Schizoid personalities, for example, are passive owing to their relative incapacity to experience pleasure and pain; without the rewards these emotional valences normally activate, they are devoid of the drive to acquire rewards, leading them to become apathetically passive observers of the ongoing scene. Dependents typically are average on the pleasure/pain polarity, yet they are usually as passive as schizoids. Strongly oriented to "others," they are notably weak with regard to "self." Passivity for them stems from deficits in self-confidence and competence, leading to deficits in initiative and autonomous skills as well as a tendency to wait passively while others assume leadership and guide them. Passivity among obsessive-compulsive personalities stems from their fear of acting independently, owing to intrapsychic resolutions they have made to quell hidden thoughts and emotions generated by their intense self-other ambivalence. Dreading the possibility of making mistakes or engaging in disapproved behaviors, they became indecisive, immobilized, restrained, and passive. High on pain and low on both pleasure and self, self-defeating personalities operate on the assumption that they dare not expect nor deserve to have life go their way; giving up any efforts to achieve a life that accords with their "true" desires, they passively submit to others' wishes, acquiescently accepting their fate. Finally, narcissists, especially high on self and low on others, benignly assume that "good things" will come their way with little or no effort on their part; this passive exploitation of others is a consequence of the unexplored confidence that underlies their self-centered presumptions.

ECOLOGIC MODIFICATION: MASTERING ONE'S ENVIRONMENT

The active end of the bipolarity signifies the taking of initiative in altering and shaping life's events. As stated previously, such persons are best characterized by their alertness, vigilance, liveliness, vigor, and forcefulness, their stimulus-seeking energy and drive. Some plan strategies and scan alternatives to circumvent obstacles or avoid the distress of punishment, rejection, and anxiety. Others are impulsive, precipitate, excitable, rash, and hasty, seeking to elicit pleasures and rewards. Although specific goals vary and change from time to time, actively aroused individuals intrude on passing events and energetically and busily modify the circumstances of their environment.

Neurobiological research has proven to be highly supportive of the activity or arousal construct ever since Papez (1937), Moruzzi and Magoun (1949), and MacLean (1949, 1952) assigned what were to be termed the reticular and limbic systems' both energizing and expressive roles in the central nervous system.

First among historic figures to pursue this theme was Ivan Pavlov. In speaking of the basic properties of the nervous system, Pavlov referred to the strength of the processes of *excitation* and *inhibition,* the equilibrium between their respective strengths, and the mobility of these processes. Although Pavlov's theoretical formulations (1927) dealt with what Donald Hebb (1955) termed a "conceptual nervous system," his experiments and those of his students led to innumerable direct investigations of brain activity. Central to Pavlov's thesis was the distinction between strong and weak types of nervous system.

Closely aligned to Pavlovian theory, Gray (1964) has asserted that those with weak nervous systems are easily aroused, nonsensation-seeking introverts who prefer to experience low stimulation rather than high levels. Conversely, those with strong nervous systems would arouse slowly, be likely to be sensation-seeking extroverts who find low stimulation levels boring and high levels both exciting and pleasant.

Akin also to the active modality are the recent views of Cloninger (1986, 1987). To him, novelty-seeking is a heritable tendency toward excitement in response to novel stimuli or cues for reward (pleasure) or punishment relief (pain) that leads to exploratory activity. Consonant with its correspondence to the activity polarity, individuals who are assumed to be high in novelty-seeking are characterized as impulsive, excitable, and quickly distracted or bored. Conversely, those at the passive polarity or the low end of the novelty-seeking dimension are portrayed as reflective, stoic, slow-tempered, orderly, and only slowly engaged in new interests.

Turning from ostensive biologic substrates to speculative psychological constructs, de Charms (1968) has proposed that "Man's primary motivational propensity is to be effective in producing changes in his environment" (p. 269). A similar view has been conveyed by White (1959) in his concept of effectance, an intrinsic motive, as he views it, that activates persons to impose their desires upon environments. De Charms elaborates his theme with reference to man as "Origin" and as "Pawn," constructs akin to the active polarity, on the one hand, and to the passive polarity, on the other. He states this distinction as follows:

> That man is the origin of his behavior means that he is constantly struggling against being confined and constrained by external forces, against being moved like a pawn into situations not of his own choosing. . . . An Origin is a person who perceives his behavior as determined by his own choosing; a Pawn is a person who perceives his behavior as determined by external forces beyond his control. . . . An Origin has strong feelings of personal causation, a feeling that the locus for causation of effects in his environment lies within himself. The feedback that reinforces this feeling comes from changes in his

> environment that are attributable to personal behavior. This is the crux of personal causation, and it is a powerful motivational force directing future behavior. (1968, pp. 273–274)

Allport (1955) had argued earlier that history records many individuals who were not content with an existence that offered them little variety, a lack of psychic tension, and minimal challenge. Allport considers it normal to be "pulled forward" by a vision of the future that awakened within persons their drive to alter the course of their lives. He suggests that people possess a need to "invent" motives and purposes that would consume their inner energies. In a similar vein, Fromm (1955) proposed a need on the part of man to rise above the roles of passive creatures in an accidental if not random world. To him, humans are driven to transcend the state of merely having been created; instead, humans seek to become the creators, the active shapers of their own destiny. Rising above the passive and accidental nature of existence, humans generate their own purposes and thereby provide themselves with a true basis of freedom.

Replication

As before, I consider both of the following criteria necessary to the definition and determination of normality. I see no necessary antithesis between the two. Humans can be both self-actualizing and other-encouraging, although most persons are likely to lean toward one or the other side. A balance that coordinates the two provides a satisfactory answer to the question of whether one should be devoted to the support and welfare of others or fashion one's life in accord with one's own needs and desires.

REPRODUCTIVE NURTURANCE: CONSTRUCTIVELY LOVING OTHERS

As described earlier, recombinant replication achieved by sexual mating entails a balanced though asymmetric parental investment in both the genesis and nurturance of offspring. By virtue of her small number of eggs and extended pregnancy, the female strategy for replicative success among most mammals is characterized by the intensive care and protection of a limited number of offspring. Oriented to reproductive nurturance rather than reproductive propagation, most adult females, at least until recent decades in Western society, bred close to the limit of their capacity, attaining a reproductive ceiling of approximately twenty viable births. By contrast, not only are males free of the unproductive pregnancy interlude for mating, but they may substantially increase their reproductive output by engaging in repetitive matings with as many available females as possible.

The other versus self antithesis follows from additional aspects of evolution's asymmetric replication strategy. Not only must the female be oriented to and vigilant in identifying the needs of and dangers that may face each of her few offspring, but it is reproductively advantageous for her to be sensitive to and discriminating in her assessment of potential mates. A "bad" mating—one that issues a defective or weak offspring—has graver consequences for the female than for the male. Not only will such an event appreciably reduce her limited reproductive possibilities and cause her to forego a better mate for a period of time, but she may exhaust much of her nurturing and protective energies in attempting to revitalize an inviable or infertile offspring. By contrast, if a male indulges in a "bad" mating, all he has lost are some quickly replaceable sperm, a loss that does little to diminish his future reproductive potentials and activities.

Before we turn to other indices and views of the self-other polarity, let us be mindful that these conceptually derived extremes do not evince themselves in sharp and distinct gender differences. Such proclivities are matters of degree, not absolutes, owing not only to the consequences of recombinant "shuffling" and gene "crossing over" but to the influential effects of cultural values and social learning. Consequently, most "normal" individuals exhibit intermediate characteristics on this as well as on the other two polarity sets.

The reasoning behind different replication strategies derives from the concept of inclusive fitness, the logic of which we owe to the theoretical biologist W. D. Hamilton (1964). The concept's rationale is well articulated in the following quote (Daly and Wilson 1978):

> Suppose a particular gene somehow disposes its bearers to help their siblings. Any child of a parent that has this gene has a one-half of probability of carrying that same gene by virtue of common descent from the same parent bearer. . . . From the gene's point of view, it is as useful to help a brother or sister as it is to help the child.
>
> When we assess the fitness of a . . . bit of behavior, we must consider more than the reproductive consequences for the individual animal. We must also consider whether the reproductive prospects of any kin are in any way altered. *Inclusive fitness is a sum of the consequences for one's own reproduction, plus the consequences for the reproduction of kin multiplied by the degree of relatedness of those kin.*
>
> An animal's behavior can therefore be said to serve a strategy whose goal is the maximization of inclusive fitness. (Pp. 30–31; italics added)

Mutual support and encouragement represents efforts leading to reciprocal fitness, a behavioral pattern consonant with Darwin's fundamental notions. Altruism, however, is a form of behavior in which there is denial of self for the benefit of others, a behavioral pattern acknowledged by Darwin himself as seemingly inconsistent with his theory (1871, p. 130). A simple extrapolation from natural selection suggests that those disposed to engage in self-sacrifice would ultimately leave fewer and fewer descendants; as a consequence, organisms motivated by "self-benefitting" genes would prevail over those motivated by "other-benefitting" genes, a result leading to the eventual extinction of genes oriented to the welfare of others. The distinguished sociobiologist Wilson, states the problem directly: "How then does altruism persist?" (1978, p. 153). An entymologist of note, Wilson had no hesitation in claiming that altruism not only persists but is of paramount significance in the lives of social insects. In accord with his sociobiologic thesis, he illustrates the presence of altruism in animals as diverse as birds, deer, porpoises, and chimpanzees, which share food and provide mutual defense—for example, to protect the colony's hives bees enact behaviors that lead invariably to their death.

Two underlying mechanisms have been proposed to account for cooperative behaviors such as altruism. One derives from the concept of inclusive fitness, briefly described in preceding paragraphs; Wilson (1978) terms this form of cooperative behavior "hard-core" altruism, by which he means that the act is "unilaterally directed" for the benefit of others and that the bestower neither expects nor expresses a desire for a comparable return. Following the line of reasoning originally formulated by Hamilton (1964), J. P. Rushton (1984), a controversial Canadian researcher who has carried out illuminating r/K studies of human behavior, explicates this mechanism as follows:

> Individuals behave so as to maximize their inclusive fitness rather than only their individual fitness; they maximize the production of successful offspring by both themselves and their relatives. . . . Social ants, for example, are one of the most altruistic species so far discovered. The self-sacrificing, sterile worker and soldier ants . . . share 75% of their genes with their sisters and so by devoting their entire existence to the needs of others . . . they help to propagate their own genes. (P. 6)

The second rationale proposed as the mechanism underlying other-oriented and cooperative behaviors Wilson terms "soft-core" altruism to represent his belief that the bestower's actions are ultimately self-serving. The original line of reasoning here stems from Trivers's (1971) notion of reciprocity, a thesis suggesting that genetically based dispositions to cooperative behavior can be explained without requiring the assumption of kinship relatedness. All that is necessary is that the performance of cooperative acts be mutual, that is, result in concurrent or subsequent behaviors that are comparably beneficial in terms of enhancing the original bestower's survivability and/or reproductive fertility.

Wilson's conclusion that the self-other dimension is a bedrock of evolutionary theory is worth quoting:

> In order to understand this idea more clearly, return with me for a moment to the basic theory of evolution. Imagine a spectrum of self-serving behavior. At one extreme only the individual is meant to benefit, then the nuclear family, next the extended family (including cousins, grandparents, and others who might play a role in kin selection), then the band, the tribe, chiefdoms, and finally, at the other extreme, the highest sociopolitical units. (1978, p. 158)

Intriguing data and ideas have been proposed by several researchers seeking to identify specific substrates that may relate to the other-oriented polarities. In what has been termed the affiliation/attachment drive, Everly (1988), for example, provides evidence favoring an anatomic role for the cingulate gyrus. Referring to the work of Henry and Stephens (1977), MacLean (1985), and Steklis and Kling (1985), Everly concludes that the ablation of the cingulate eliminates both affiliative and grooming behaviors. The proximal physiology of this drive has been hypothesized as including serotonergic, noradrenergic, and opoid neurotransmission systems (Everly 1988; Redmond, Maas, and Kling 1971). MacLean (1985) has argued that the affiliative drive may be phylogenically coded in the limbic system and may undergird the "concept of family" in primates. The drive toward other-oriented behaviors, such as attachment, nurturing, affection, reliability, and collaborative play, has been referred to as the "cement of society" by Henry and Stevens (1977).

Let us move now to the realm of psychological and social proposals. Dorothy Conrad (1952) specified a straightforward list of constructive behaviors that manifest "reproductive nurturance" in the interpersonal sphere. She records them as follows:

> *Has positive affective relationship:* The person who is able to relate affectively to even one person demonstrates that he is potentially able to relate to other persons and to society.
>
> *Promotes another's welfare:* Affective relationships make it possible for the person to enlarge his world and to act for the benefit of another, even though that person may profit only remotely.
>
> *Works with another for mutual benefit:* The person is largely formed through

> social interaction. Perhaps he is most completely a person when he participates in a mutually beneficial relationship. (Pp. 456–457)

More eloquent proposals of a similar character have been formulated by the noted psychologists Maslow, Allport, and Fromm.

According to Maslow (1970), once humans' basic safety and security needs are met, they next turn to satisfy the belonging and love needs. Here we establish intimate and caring relationships with significant others in which it is just as important to give love as it is to receive it. Noting the difficulty in satisfying these needs in our unstable and changing modern world, Maslow sees the basis here for the immense popularity of communes and family therapy. These settings are ways to escape the isolation and loneliness that result from our failures to achieve love and belonging.

One of Allport's (1961) criteria of the "mature" personality, which he terms a warm relating of self to others, refers to the capability of displaying intimacy and love for a parent, child, spouse, or close friend. Here the person manifests an authentic oneness with the other and a deep concern for his or her welfare. Beyond one's intimate family and friends, there is an extension of warmth in the mature person to humankind at large, an understanding of the human condition and a kinship with all peoples.

To Fromm (1968), humans are aware of the growing loss of their ties with nature as well as with each other, feeling increasingly separate and alone. Fromm believes humans must pursue new ties with others to replace those that have been lost or can no longer be depended on. To counter the loss of communion with nature, he feels that health requires that we fulfill our need by a brotherliness with mankind, a sense of involvement, concern, and relatedness with the world. And with those with whom ties have been maintained or reestablished, humans must fulfill their other-oriented needs by being vitally concerned with their well-being as well as fostering their growth and productivity.

In a lovely coda to a paper on the role of evolutionary and human behavior, Freedman and Roe (1958) wrote:

> Since his neolithic days, in spite of his murders and wars, his robberies and rapes, man has become a man-binding and a time-binding creature. He has maintained the biological continuity of his family and the social continuity of aggregates of families. He has related his own life experiences with the social traditions of those who have preceded him, and has anticipated those of his progeny. He has accumulated and transmitted his acquired goods and values through his family and through his organizations. He has become bound to other men by feelings of identity and

> by shared emotions, by what clinicians call empathy. His sexual nature may yet lead him to widening ambits of human affection, his acquisitive propensities to an optimum balance of work and leisure, and his aggressive drives to heightened social efficiency through attacks on perils common to all men. (P. 457)

The pathological consequences of a failure to embrace the polarity criterion of "others" are seen most clearly in the personality disorders termed antisocial and narcissistic. Both personalities exhibit an imbalance in their replication strategy; in this case, however, there is a primary reliance on self rather than others. They have learned that reproductive success as well as maximum pleasure and minimum pain is achieved by turning exclusively to themselves. The tendency to focus on self follows two major lines of development.

In the narcissistic personality, development reflects the acquisition of a self-image of superior worth, learned largely in response to admiring and doting parents. Providing self-rewards is highly gratifying if one values oneself or possesses either a "real" or inflated sense of self-worth. Displaying manifest confidence, arrogance, and an exploitative egocentricity in social contexts, this self-orientation has been termed the passive-independent style in the theory, as the individual "already" has all that is important—him- or herself.

Narcissistic individuals are noted for their egotistic self-involvement, experiencing primary pleasure simply by passively being or attending to themselves. Early experience has taught them to overvalue their self-worth; this confidence and superiority may be founded on false premises, however; that is, it may be unsustainable by real or mature achievements. Nevertheless, they blithely assume that others will recognize their specialness. Hence they maintain an air of arrogant self-assurance and, without much thought or even conscious intent, benignly exploit others to their own advantage. Although the tributes of others are both welcome and encouraged, their air of snobbish and pretentious superiority requires little confirmation either through genuine accomplishment or social approval. Their sublime confidence that things will work out well provides them with little incentive to engage in the reciprocal give and take of social life.

Those whom the theory characterizes as exhibiting the active-independent orientation resemble the outlook, temperament, and socially unacceptable behaviors of the DSM-III-R Antisocial personality disorder. They act to counter the expectation of pain at the hand of others; this is done by actively engaging in duplicitous or illegal behaviors in which they seek to exploit others for self-gain. Skeptical regarding the motives of others, they desire autonomy and wish revenge for what are felt as past injustices. Many are irresponsible and impulsive, actions they see as justified because they judge others to be unreliable and disloyal. Insensitivity and ruthlessness with others are the primary means they have learned to head off abuse and victimization.

In contrast to the narcissistic personality, this second pattern of self-orientation develops as a form of protection and counteraction. These types turn to themselves first to avoid the depredation they anticipate and second to compensate by furnishing self-generated rewards in their stead. Learning that they cannot depend on others, these personalities counterbalance this loss not only by trusting themselves alone but by actively seeking retribution for what they see as past humiliations. Turning to self and seeking actively to gain strength, power, and revenge, they act irresponsibly, exploiting and usurping what others possess as sweet reprisal. Their security is never fully "assured," even when they have aggrandized themselves beyond their lesser origins.

In both narcissistic and antisocial persons we see nonnormality arising from an inability to experience a constructive love for others. For the one, there is an excessive self-centeredness, and for the other, there is the acquisition of a compensatory destructiveness driven by social retribution and self-aggrandizement.

REPRODUCTIVE PROPAGATION: ACTUALIZING SELF POTENTIALS

The converse of reproductive nurturance is *not* reproductive propagation but rather the lack of reproductive nuturance. Thus, to fail to love others constructively does not assure the actualization of one's potentials. Both may and should exist in normal/healthy individuals.

Although the dimension of self-other is arranged to highlight its polar extremes, it should be evident that many, if not most, behaviors are employed to achieve the goals of both self and kin reproduction. Both ends are often simultaneously achieved; at other times one may predominate. The behaviors comprising these strategies are "driven," so to speak, by a blend of activation and affect—that is, combinations arising from intermediary positions reflecting both the life enhancement and life preservation polarity of pleasure-pain, interwoven with similar intermediary positions on the ecologic accommodation and ecologic modification polarity of activity-passivity. Phrasing "replication" in terms of the abstruse and metaphorical constructs does not obscure it, I hope, but rather sets this third polarity on the deeper foundations of existence and adaptation, foundations composed of the first two polarities previously described.

Here I provide a few words on certain ostensive biologic substrates associated with a self-orientation, outline the views of several contemporary psychologists and psychiatrists who have assigned the criterion of self-actualization a central role in their formulations, and note an example or two of how the failure to meet this criterion can often result in specific pathologies of personality.

At the self-oriented pole, Everly (1988) proposes an autonomy/aggression substrate that manifests itself in a strong need for control and domination as well as in hierarchic status striving. According to MacLean (1986), it appears that the amygdaloid complex may play a key role in driving organisms into self-oriented behaviors. Early studies of animals with ablated amygdalas showed a notable increase in their docility (Kluver and Bucy 1939), as have nonhuman primates exhibited significant decreases in social hierarchy status (Pribram 1962). Although the evidence remains somewhat equivocal, norepinephrine and dopamine seem to be the prime neurotransmitters of this drive; the testosterone hormone appears similarly implicated (Feldman and Quenzar 1984).

Regarding psychological constructs that parallel the notion of self-actualization, their earliest equivalent was in the writings of Spinoza (1677/1986), who viewed development as that of becoming what one was intended to be, nothing other than that, no matter how exalted the alternative might appear to be.

Carl Jung's (1961) concept of individuation shares important features with that of actualization in that any deterrent to becoming the individual one may have become would be detrimental to life. Any imposed "collective standard is a serious check to individuality," injurious to the vitality of the person, a form of "artificial stunting."

Perhaps it was my own early mentor, Kurt Goldstein (1939, 1940), who first coined the concept under review with the self-actualization designation. As he phrased it, "There is only one motive by which human activity is set going: the tendency to actualize oneself" (1939, p. 196).

The early views of Jung and Goldstein have been enriched by later theorists, notably Fromm, Perls, Rogers, and Maslow.

Focusing on what he terms the sense of identity, Fromm (1955) spoke of the need to establish oneself as a unique individual, a state that places the person apart from others. Further—and it is here where Fromm makes a distinct self-oriented commitment—the extent to which this sense of identity emerges depends on how successful the person is in breaking "incestuous ties" to one's family or clan. Persons with well-developed feelings of identity experience being in control of their lives rather than being controlled by the lives of others.

Perls (1969) enlarged on this theme by contrasting self-regulation versus external regulation. Normal/healthy persons do their own regulating, with no external interference, be it the needs and demands of others or the strictures of a social code. What we must actualize is the "true inner self," not an image we have of what our ideal selves should be. That is the "curse of the ideal." To Perls, each must be what he or she "really is."

Following the views of his forerunners, Maslow (1970) stated that self-actualization is the "supreme development" and use of all our abilities, ultimately becoming what we have the potential to become. Noting that self-actualists often require detachment and solitude, Maslow asserted that such persons are strongly self-centered and self-directed, make up their own mind and reach their own decisions, without the need to gain social approval.

In like manner, Rogers (1963) posited a single, overreaching motive for the normal/healthy person—maintaining, actualizing, and enhancing one's potential. The goal is not that of maintaining a homeostatic balance or a high degree of ease and comfort, but rather to move forward in becoming what is intrinsic to self and to enhance further that which one has already become. Believing that humans have an innate urge to create, Rogers stated that the most creative product of all is one's own self.

Where do we see failures in the achievement of self-actualization, a giving up of self to gain the approbation of others? Two personality disorders can be drawn upon to illustrate forms of self-denial.

Those with dependent personalities have learned that feeling good, secure, confident, and so on—that is, those feelings associated with pleasure or the avoidance of pain—is provided almost exclusively in their relationship with others. Behaviorally, these persons display a strong need for external support and attention; should they be deprived of affection and nurturance, they will experience marked discomfort, if not sadness and anxiety. Any number of early experiences may set the stage for this other-oriented imbalance. Dependent individuals often include those who have been exposed to an overprotective training regimen and who thereby fail to acquire competencies for autonomy and initiative; experiencing peer failures and low self-esteem leads them to forego attempts at self-assertion and self-gratification. They learn early that they themselves do not readily achieve rewarding experiences; the experiences are secured better by leaning on others. They learn not only to turn to others as their source of nurturance and security but to wait passively for others to take the initiative in providing safety and sustenance. Clinically, most are characterized as searching for relationships in which others will reliably furnish affection, protection, and leadership. Lacking both initiative and autonomy, they assume a dependent role in interpersonal relations, accepting what kindness and support they may find and willingly submitting to the wishes of others in order to maintain nurturance and security.

A less benign but equally problematic centering on the wishes of others and the denial of self is seen in the obsessive-compulsive personality. These persons display a picture of distinct other-directedness, a consistency in social compliance and interpersonal respect. Their histories usually indicate having been subjected to constraint and discipline when they transgressed parental strictures and expectations. Beneath the conforming other-oriented veneer they exhibit are intense desires to rebel and assert their own self-oriented feelings and impulses. They are trapped in an ambivalence; to avoid intimidation and punishment they have learned to deny the validity of their own wishes and emotions and, in their stead, have adopted as "true" the values and precepts set forth by others. The disparity they sense between their own urges and the behaviors they must display to avoid condemnation often leads to omnipresent physical tensions and rigid psychological controls.

I hope that readers who have reached this final paragraph have not developed a hardening of the spirit of inquiry, a loss of those imaginative outreachings that open one to fresh albeit conjectural theses. Perhaps this speculative essay will prove to have a modicum of practical and theoretical value. Surely I, and not Darwin, should be faulted if his contributions have unjustly been extended to the subject of normatology.

REFERENCES

Allport, G. 1955. *Becoming: Basic Considerations for a Psychology of Personality.* New Haven: Yale University Press.

———. 1961. *Pattern and Growth in Personality.* New York: Holt, Rinehart & Winston.

American Psychiatric Association. 1980. *Diagnostic and Statistical Manual of Mental Disorders,* 3rd ed. Washington, D.C.: APA.

Barash, D. P. 1982. *Sociobiology and Behavior,* 2nd ed. New York: Elsevier.

Bertalanffy, L. von 1945. *Problems of Life.* New York: John Wiley.

Bowers, K. S. 1977. "There's More to Iago than Meets the Eye: A Clinical Account of Personal Consistency." In *Personality at the Crossroads,* ed. D. Magnusson and N. S. Endler, pp. 63–81. Hillsdale, NJ: Lawrence Erlbaum.

Buss, A. H., and Plomin, R. 1975. *A Temperament Theory of Personality Development.* New York: John Wiley.

———. 1984. *Temperament: Early Developing Personality Traits.* Hillsdale, NJ: Lawrence Erlbaum.

Buss, D. M. 1984. "Evolutionary Biology and Personality Psychology." *American Psychologist* 39:1135–1147.

Cloninger, C. R. 1986. "A Unified Biosocial Theory of Personality and Its Role in the Development of Anxiety States." *Psychiatric Developments* 3:167–226.

———. 1987. "A Systematic Method for Clinical Description and Classification of Personality Variants." *Archives of General Psychiatry* 44:573–588.

Cole, L. C. 1954. "The Population Consequences of Life History Phenomena." *Quarterly Review of Biology* 29:103–137.

Conrad, D. C. 1952. "Toward a More Productive Concept of Mental Health." *Mental Hygiene* 36: 456–466.

Daly, M., and Wilson, M. 1978. *Sex, Evolution and Behavior.* Boston: Grant Press.

Darwin, C. R. 1871. *The Descent of Man and Selection in Relation to Sex.* London: Murray.

de Charms, R. 1968. *Personal Causation: The Internal Affective Determinants of Behavior.* New York: Academic Press.

Everly, G. 1988. "The Biological Basis of Personality: The Contribution of Paleocortical Anatomy and Physiology." Paper presented at the First International Congress on Disorders of Personality, Copenhagen, Denmark, August.

Feldman, R., and Quenzar, L. 1984. *Fundamentals of Neuropharmacology.* Sunderland, MA: Sinauer.

Freedman, L. Z., and Roe, A. 1958. "Evolution and Human Behavior." In *Behavior and Evolution,* ed. A. Roe and G. Simpson, pp. 455–479. New Haven: Yale University Press.

Freud, S. 1895. "Project for a Scientific Psychology." In the *Standard Edition* vol. 1. London: Hogarth Press.

———. [1915] 1925. "The Instincts and Their Vicissitudes." In *The Collected Papers of Sigmund Freud,* ed. E. Jones, vol. 4. London: Hogarth Press.

———. 1940. *An Outline of Psychoanalysis.* New York: Liveright.

Fromm, E. 1955. *The Sane Society.* New York: Holt, Rinehart & Winston.

———. 1968. *The Revolution of Hope: Toward a Humanized Technology.* New York: Harper & Row.

Gilligan, C. 1982. *In a Different Voice.* Cambridge, MA: Harvard University Press.

Gleick, J. 1987. *Chaos: Making a New Science.* New York: Viking.

Goldstein, K. 1939. *The Organism.* New York: American Book.

———. 1940. *Human Nature in the Light of Psychopathology.* Cambridge, MA: Harvard University Press.

Gray, J. A. 1973. "Causal Theories of Personality and How to Test Them." In *Multivariate Analysis and Psychological Theory,* ed. J. R. Royce. New York: Academic Press.

———. 1975. *Elements of a Two-process Theory of Learning.* New York: Academic Press.

———. 1981. "A Critique of Eysenck's Theory of Personality." In *A Model for Personality,* ed. H. J. Eysenck. New York: Springer-Verlag.

Gray, J. A., ed. 1964. *Pavlov's Typology.* New York: Pergamon.

Gribbin, J. 1986. *In Search of the Big Bang.* Toronto: Bantam.

Hamilton, W. D. 1964. "The Genetical Evolution of Social Behavior: I and II." *Journal of Theoretical Biology* 7:1–52.

Hartmann, H. 1939. *Ego Psychology and the Problem of Adaptation.* New York: International Universities Press.

Hebb, D. O. 1955. "Drives and the C.N.S. (Conceptual Nervous System)." *Psychological Review* 62:243–254.

Hempel, C. G. 1965. *Aspects of Scientific Explanation.* New York: Free Press.

Henry, J. P., and Stephens, P. 1977. *Stress, Health, and the Social Environment.* New York: Springer-Verlag.

Huxley, T. H. 1870. "Mr. Darwin's Critics." *Contemporary Review* 18:443–476.

Jahoda, M. 1958. *Current Concepts of Positive Mental Health.* New York: Basic Books.

Jung, C. G. 1961. *Memories, Dreams, Reflections.* New York: Vintage Books.

Kluver, H., and Bucy, P. 1939. "Preliminary Analysis of Functions of the Temporal Lobes in Monkeys." *Archives of Neurology and Psychiatry* 42:979–1000.

Lewin, K. 1936. *Principles of Topological Psychology.* New York: McGraw-Hill.

Lotka, A. J. 1924. *Elements of Mathematical Biology.* New York: Dover.

MacLean, P. 1949. "Psychosomatic Disease and the 'Visceral Brain.' " *Psychosomatic Medicine* 11: 338–353.

———. 1952. "Some Psychiatric Implications of Physiologic Studies on Frontotemporal Portions of the Limbic System." *Electroencephalography and Clinical Neurophysiology* 4:407–418.

———. 1985. "Brain Evolution Relating to Family, Play, and the Separation Call." *Archives of General Psychiatry* 42:405–417.

———. 1986. "Culminating Developments in the Evolution of the Limbic System." In *The Limbic System,* ed. B. Doane and K. Livingston. New York: Raven Press.

Mandelbrot, B. 1977. *The Fractal Geometry of Nature.* New York: Freeman.

Mandell, A. J., and Salk, J. 1984. "Developmental Fusion of Intuition and Reason: A Metabiological Onogeny." In *Normality and the Life Cycle,* ed. D. Offer and M. Sabshin, pp. 302–314. New York: Basic Books.

Maslow, A. H. 1968. *Toward a Psychology of Being,* 2nd ed. New York: Van Nostrand.

———. 1970. *Motivation and Personality,* 2nd ed. New York: Harper & Row.

Mayr, E. 1964. "The Evolution of Living Systems." *Proceedings of the National Academy of Science* 51: 934–941.

Millon, T. 1969. *Modern Psychopathology.* Philadelphia: Saunders (Reprinted 1985. Prospect Heights, IL: Waveland Press).

———. 1981. *Disorders of Personality: DSM-III, Axis II.* New York: Wiley-Interscience.

———. 1986. "Personality Prototypes and Their Diagnostic Criteria." In *Contemporary Directions in Psychopathology,* ed. T. Millon and G. L. Klerman, pp. 671–712. New York: Guilford Press.

———. 1987. "On the Nature of Taxonomy in Psychopathology." In *Issues in Diagnostic Research,* ed. C. Last and M. Hersen, pp. 3–87. New York: Plenum Press.

———. 1990. *Toward a New Personology: An Evolutionary Model.* New York: Wiley-Interscience.

Moruzzi, G., and Magoun, H. 1949. "Brain Stem Reticular Formation and Activation of the EEG." *Electroencephalography and Clinical Neurophysiology* 1:455–473.

Offer, D., and Sabshin, M. 1966. *Normality.* New York: Basic Books.

Offer, D., and Sabshin, M., eds. 1984. *Normality and the Life Cycle.* New York: Basic Books.

Olds, J., and Milner, P. 1954. "Positive Reinforcement Produced by the Electrical Stimulation of Septal Region and Other Regions of Rat Brain." *Journal of Comparative and Physiological Psychology* 47:419–427.

Papez, J. 1937. "A Proposed Mechanism of Emotion." *Archives of Neurology and Psychiatry* 38:725–743.

Pavlov, I. 1927. *Conditioned Reflexes.* Oxford: Oxford University Press.

Perls, F. 1969. *Gestalt Therapy Verbatim.* Lafayette, CA: Real People Press.

Pribram, K. 1962. "Interrelations of Psychology and the Neurological Disciplines." In *Psychology: A Study of a Science,* ed. S. Koch, pp. 119–157. New York: McGraw-Hill.

Prigogine, I. 1972. "Thermodynamics of Evolution." *Physics Today* 25:23–28, 38–44.

———. 1976. "Order Through Fluctuation: Self-organization and Social System." In *Evolution and Consciousness,* ed. E. Jantsch and C. Waddington. Reading, MA: Addison-Wesley.

Quine, W. V. O. 1961. *From a Logical Point of View,* 2nd ed. New York: Harper & Row.

———. 1977. "Natural Kinds." In *Naming, Necessity and Natural Groups,* ed. S. P. Schwartz. Ithaca: Cornell University Press.

Rapaport, D. 1953. "Some Metapsychological Considerations Concerning Activity and Passivity." In *The Collected Papers of David Rapaport* (1967), ed. M. M. Gill, pp. 530–568. New York: Basic Books.

Redmond, D.; Maas, J.; and Kling, A. 1971. "Social Behavior of Monkeys Selectively Depleted of Monoamines." *Science* 174:428–431.

Rogers, C. R. 1963. "Toward a Science of the Person." *Journal of Humanistic Psychology* 3:79–92.

Rushton, J. P. 1984. "Sociobiology: Toward a Theory of Individual and Group Differences in Personality and Social Behavior." In *Annals of Theoretical Psychology,* vol. 2, ed. J. R. Royce and L. P. Moos, pp. 1–48. New York: Plenum Press.

———. 1985. "Differential K Theory: The Sociobiology of Individual and Group Differences." *Personality and Individual Differences* 6:441–452.

Russell, J. A. 1980. "A Circumplex Model of Affect." *Journal of Personality and Social Psychology* 39:1161–1178.

Schrodinger, E. 1944. *What Is Life?* Cambridge: Cambridge University Press.

Skinner, B. F. 1938. *The Behavior of Organisms: An Experimental Analysis.* New York: Appleton.

———. 1953. *Science and Human Behavior.* New York: Macmillan.

Smith, E. E., and Medin, D. L. 1981. *Categories and Concepts.* Cambridge, MA: Harvard University Press.

Spencer, H. 1870. *The Principles of Psychology.* London: Williams and Norgate.

Spinoza, B. de. 1677/1986. *Ethics: On the Correction of Understanding.* London: Dent.

Steklis, H., and Kling, A. 1985. "Neurobiology of Affiliation in Primates." In *The Psychobiology of Attachment and Separation,* ed. M. Reite and T. Fields. Orlando, FL: Academic Press.

Tellegen, A. 1985. "Structure of Mood and Personality and Their Relevance to Assessing Anxiety, with an Emphasis on Self-report." In *Anxiety and the Anxiety Disorders,* ed. A. H. Tuma and J. Maser, pp. 681–706. Hillsdale, NJ: Lawrence Erlbaum.

Thom, R. 1972. *Structural Stability and Morphogenesis.* Reading, MA: Benjamin.

Trivers, R. L. 1971. "The Evolution of Reciprocal Altruism." *Quarterly Review of Biology* 46:35–57.

———. 1974. "Parental Investment and Sexual Selection." In *Sexual Selection and the Descent of Man 1871–1971,* ed. B. Campbell. Chicago: Aldine.

Tryon, E. 1973. "Vacuum Genesis." *Nature* 246: 396–401.

White, R. W. 1959. "Motivation Reconsidered: The Concept of Competence." *Psychological Review* 66: 297–323.

Wilson, E. O. 1975. *Sociobiology: The New Synthesis.* Cambridge, MA: Harvard University Press.

———. 1978. *On Human Nature.* Cambridge, MA: Harvard University Press.

CHAPTER 12

Normatology: The Next Step

Daniel Offer and Melvin Sabshin

Why study normality? Ultimately, we must study normal people, not only disturbed individuals, to know what is normal. After all, to find out more about ancient Egypt, one does not begin with an archaeological dig in Israel!

The field of normatology, the systematized scientific study of normality over the life cycle, is of recent origin. As we pointed out in the introduction, this is the fourth book on normality that we have published over the past twenty-five years. This particular volume is a culmination of our interest in the question "What is normal?" Now the time has come to present a concise statement about why we believe normatology should be an important part of the psychiatry and psychology of the future.

Our first two books on normality (1966, 1974) presented one theoretical position. The books were comprised of scholarly reviews of the field derived from theoretical perspectives of normality and also presented an example of a study of normal adolescents. These studies were used as a model to illustrate the empirical approach to studying normal, or nonpatient, populations (Offer 1969; Offer and Offer 1975). Our third volume on normality (1984) focused on normal development throughout the life cycle and was longitudinal. Our goal was to summarize what is known about normal individuals during different stages of the life cycle, and we emphasized the need for systematized sequential studies of normal individuals throughout the life cycle. In this volume we have focused on diversity rather than on one perspective to emphasize one of our fundamental principles, namely that the study of normal individuals is more complex and variegated than the study of those who are ill.

The excellent overviews on various social contexts presented by the volume contributors are useful in defining parameters of normal behavior. In this chapter we present a brief overview of normatology in the context of present-day psychiatry and psychology. We then outline a normatological model for future studies of nonpatient populations.

Normatology in Context

One hundred years ago the major studies in psychiatry and psychology evolved around psychopathology. Whether the works were on hypnosis (Janet 1903), psychopathology of everyday life (Freud 1901), the severe mental illnesses (Kraeplin 1909–1915), or general subjects (Krafft-Ebing 1894), they all focused on what they conceived of as pathological. True, some behaviorists focused on the universal (for example, Pavlov 1903), or the psychometric (Binet 1905); however, these studies did not represent mainstream clinical psychiatry or psychology. Psychiatrists working with the "insane" were concerned with diagnosis, the natural course of mental illness, and the discovery of cures, or treatments, for the mentally ill. Psychologists by and large were either philosophers who speculated on the nature of man and his soul or scientists who studied the senses, the behavior of animals, and the nature of learning, but who were, for the most part, less interested in the normal psychological development of man as such.

Throughout recorded history humans have been fascinated by the insane and the pathological. Whether the insane were considered possessed by the devil or as close to God, they were often thought to be endowed with special powers that should not be tampered with. To this day some artists believe that neurotic conflicts are necessary for their work, and without them the urge to create will disappear. It is indeed a basic premise of many individuals in today's Western world that psychological conflicts are essential, emotional struggles imperative for anyone who wants to experience life to the fullest. Society is fascinated not only with mental patients. Wars and crime, natural disasters, and, of course, the supernatural are all popular topics. So when we express scientific interest in studying what is normal, it seems to go against a well-established trend in our culture. Many people believe that "normal" means very ordinary. Normal lacks sparkle. It seems unreal, boring, and so uninteresting. Its very existence seems to be counterintuitive. Normal individuals are boring, psychologically unaware, and basically stupid. And this judgment is not confined merely to the nonprofessional segment of our culture. Surprisingly, many colleagues in the mental health professions believe that to be disturbed is to be interesting (see, for example, Offer, Ostrov and Howard [1981] for a study on mental health professionals' understanding of normal adolescents). Many psychotherapists believe that mental suffering often enables people to talk more openly and honestly about their feelings. But does it really? The studies of nonpatient populations definitely contradict this mythology (see, for example, Offer [1969], and Offer and Offer [1975]).

Clinicians' fascination with mental illness in part was due to the fact that they knew much more about abnormality than they did about normality. The assumption has been, to put it simply, that normality was the antonym of abnormality. Whether, as Freud (1937) has put it, "A normal ego is like normality in general, an ideal fiction" or whether it was an obscure phenomenon rarely seen was immaterial. Psychiatrists, clinical psychologists, and other mental health professionals have enough work to do with the mentally ill that they just could not be concerned with those who had no diagnosable mental illness and hence did not need them. Unfortunately, help-seeking behavior is not a valid criterion to distinguish the disordered from the healthy. We know from recent epidemiological studies of mental illness among the general populations that approximately 20 percent of those studied are diagnosed as being psychiatrically disturbed (see, for example, Offer et al. [1991]). Of these 20 percent who are disturbed, in any given year only 25 percent of them (or 5 percent of the total population) receive mental health care. In other words, the majority of individuals in our society who appear to need mental health care do not receive it. It may also be true that some people who receive mental health care should not be considered to be disordered.

In some futuristic, "brave new world," the state may test all citizens to determine whether they are normal or not. Those individuals who are diagnosed accurately by an objective mental health system will be given a number in an agreed-upon international classification system of disease and be told that they have a mental illness. They will be offered some kind of psychiatric therapy or strongly encouraged to seek it. Of course, we are not advocating such a system. We mention it here only to suggest that, in the future, the diagnosis of mental illness and mental health may become more exact. As long as people are given a choice whether to obtain help or not, help-seeking will continue to be a crucial variable. It is not only the mental health professionals' definition of normality and mental illness that is important, it is also the point of view of the person obtaining the help.

As we have stated frequently, many factors other than help-seeking behavior determine the boundaries between disturbance and health. These variables include prevailing definitions of illness, chronicity of behavioral patterns, coping capacities, and comorbid conditions. Unquestionably, the narrower the definition of normality, the more disturbed individuals there will be. We also wish to reemphasize that being psychiatrically disturbed is not a chronically stable state. As Klerman and Weissman (1984) have pointed out, many individuals move in and out of the "patient condition" throughout their lives even without treatment. These variations deserve much more systematic studies. We need to know more about many other variables in order to predict more accurately whether someone will overcome his or her mental illness. A person with good coping abilities has a better chance of overcoming symptoms. Comorbid pathology, subthreshold comorbidity, and the complex interactions between various adaptive and pathological functions can be extremely important but are a relatively unexplored field. As Sabshin (1991) has stated in another context, "Comorbidity is likely to become one of the significant psychiatric code words of the 1990s." We are expanding the usual psychiatric meaning of the term "comorbidity" to include a psychiatric syndrome and its relationship to subthreshold phenomena.

The title of the book, *The Diversity of Normal Behavior,* implies what we strongly postulate: Psychopathology is more rigidly fixed and less varied than is normal behavior.

Normatological Model

Clinical studies of normality have been undertaken with the implicit goal of better understanding mental illness. The clinical contributions in part 1 of this book focus on how to dovetail findings from psychiatric research with the newer concepts of normality. As the chapters in the section indicate, theoretical and practical problems arise when investigators want to go beyond the medical-psychiatric phenomenon. We need newer concepts to describe more accurately the subthreshold of capacities and experiences that help normal growth and development as well as the smaller stresses that may lead to better adjustment, rather than behavioral or psychological problems. The lack of a psychiatric diagnosis has implied, by exclusion, a positive diagnosis of normality. There has not yet been enough scientific interest in normatology for the field to develop a classificatory system for normal conditions.

Before we move on to describe our proposal for the normatological model of classification, we would like briefly to discuss the third revised edition of the *Diagnostic and Statistical Manual of Mental Disorders* (DSM-III-R; American Psychiatric Association 1984; see chapter 1 for an extensive discussion of nosology in psychiatry).

The DSM-III-R is used extensively throughout the world by psychiatrists, psychologists, other mental health professionals, physicians, researchers, mental health professionals, insurance companies, and lawyers. It attempts to distinguish among the main syndromes in psychiatry. Yet it was not until the late 1940s that American psychiatrists decided to classify psychiatric illness in a more systematic way. The first DSM was published in 1948. The theoretical position underlying its use was that behavior, like biological variables, conformed to the Gaussian principle. In other words, most behavior was normal (or average), and both extremes were deviant. Normal behavior, which in statistical terms was one standard deviation of the norm, covered 66.6 percent of the normal range. Both extremes, each covering 16.7 percent of the total range, are, by this type of definition, deviant. Two simple examples will illustrate the widespread use of the statistical approach. One either has too many or too few white blood cells. The statistical average is the normal or healthy. Analogously, activity levels in individuals may vary, with the extremes being indicative of certain psychopathology (for example, mania, depression). Average activity is normal as well as healthy.

The DSM has been revised a number of times and currently is being revised again. Chapter 1 discusses both the DSM-III-R and the upcoming DSM-IV in great detail.

The DSM approach reflects the current culture in which mental health professionals work. The algorithm that defines a particular disturbance or syndrome is a manifestation of clinical experience. Although it is not objective from a purely scientific point of view, it nevertheless is most helpful to clinicians and is also useful as a classification system.

The five axes of the DSM-III-R are very familiar to the mental health professional. They are:

Axis I:	The Clinical Syndromes
Axis II:	Developmental Disorders and Personality Disorders
Axis III:	Physical Disorders and Conditions
Axis IV:	Severity of Psychological Stressors
Axis V:	Global Assessment of Functioning

It is our hope that a parallel system of axes can be developed for the 80 percent of the population who at any time are *not* mentally disturbed. Such an approach to the normatological model would systematize future studies, which we believe should be undertaken on normal populations. Greater precision in the diagnosis of normality would depend on hypotheses evolving from new field studies. As they are undertaken and good data become available, "labeling" theories questioning the validity of mental disorders (see chapter 8) will become less persuasive to studies of mental health and mental illness.

In a multiaxial approach to normatology, a variety of axes will be studied and used to develop new hypotheses about normal behavior. While the DSM axes might be applicable only to a limited degree, here we attempt to draw a parallel where appropriate, consolidate axes where appropriate, and also suggest other axes where indicated.

Axes I and II: Personology[1]

In DSM-III and DSM-III-R there is considerable debate about the utility of subdividing disorders into Axis I and Axis II. In general, the Developmental Disorders and Personality Disorders (Axis II) are conceived to begin in childhood or adolescence and persist in stable form into adult life (see DSM-III-R, p. 16). The Axis I disorders are conceived to be more "florid," which is often interpreted to mean more severe as well as more dramatically disabling. Indeed, there is a significant policy debate in some quarters as to whether or not Axis II disorders fall into a category of subthreshold conditions. This debate has many practical implications.

For normatological classification, the DSM-III-R distinctions between Axis I and Axis II are not possible now. There is no current method to distinguish normal patterns of behavior beginning in childhood or adolescence from normal patterns that "start" in adulthood. It is also not necessarily useful to distinguish "florid" normality from less "florid" normality, even though normal individuals may demonstrate behavior ranging from flamboyant to quiet. While it might be tempting to distinguish normal behavior that is determined strongly by genetic factors (for example, activity patterns in infancy) from normal behavior that is influenced by family interactions and other psychosocial factors, we believe that it is premature to do so at this time. For all these reasons we suggest that normatological multiaxial studies do not use the Axis I–Axis II distinction of DSM-III-R.

The neurobiological bases of behavior are beginning to be understood better, particularly in regard to overt psychiatric illness. The task for deci-

[1]We are using here the term employed by Millon (1990) to describe studies of personality. See also chapter 11 in this volume. It has been first described by Murray and Smith (1990).

phering the neurobiological basis of nonpathological behavior is considerable. As yet, no microanalysis of biological variables is available that can reliably distinguish between different types of normal behavior.

The concept of personality, character, or typology is predominantly defined more around psychosocial variables that appear at birth or soon thereafter. It is believed that phenomena such as temperament, cognition, or arousal form the foundation of personality or character. The special combination of neurobiological substrate with psychosocial typologies has implications far beyond the etiology of the psychopathology; it also forms the basis of normatological variance.

We recognize that the evolution of personological models will take several decades. Millon (1990; see also chapter 11) has made significant contributions to the theoretical foundations of these models.

Daniel and Judith Offer's (1975) work on patterns of behavior is an example of the evaluation of patterns of normal development that has evolved over time. They divided adolescents into three groups that differ according to their growth patterns as well as the presence or absence of symptomatology.

The first of these patterns is the *continuous growth group* (40 percent of the total). These adolescents are favored by circumstances. Their genetic and environmental background is excellent. They are able to cope well with internal and external stimuli. They accept general cultural and societal norms and feel comfortable within this context.

The second group is the *surgent growth group* (40 percent of the total). One of the major differences between subjects in the first two groups is that in group 2 subjects, the genetic or environmental background is not as free of problems and/or traumas as is that of group 1 subjects. Although they cope well with stresses that come their way, their growth is not smooth. They show more anxiety and depression when life does not treat them as well as they expect. It takes them time to readjust.

The third group of adolescents is the *tumultuous growth group* (20 percent of the total). These subjects come from less favorable backgrounds than either of the first two groups. There is significant marital conflict among the parents and there is more of a family history of mental illness than there is in the former two groups. When external trauma occurs, it is seen as a major tragic event. Clinical syndromes often emerge and psychiatric treatment is sought. This group contains the majority of psychiatrically *disturbed adolescents,* those who can be diagnosed by mental health professionals following the criteria set by the DSM-III. The type of disturbance varies from anorexia nervosa, depression, phobias or anxiety, to personality disorders, drug abuse, or schizophrenia.

The majority of psychiatrically disturbed adolescents fall into the tumultuous growth group. In this sense this classification overlaps the psychopathological and normatological systems. Studies of the continuous growth group and the surgent growth group over their life cycles afford an excellent example of normatology per se.

Axis III: Personology and Physical Health

Physical health interacts with mental health in a myriad of ways. These two aspects of a human being are closely interwoven, whether it is through the mind-body dichotomy, psychosomatic medicine, or the psychiatry of the 1990s.

General populations of psychologically normal subjects can be assessed for the presence or absence of physical disorders of a nonmental variety. It could be that many psychologically normal individuals have physical disorders. Their adaptation to the physical disorders may help them cope better psychologically. The study of normatology in the presence of concurrent physical disorders presents many new possibilities. For example, subthreshold physical problems could exist with concurrent physical disorders that involve psychological adaptation or maladaptation. In addition to the study of disorders and subthreshold disorders, there is emerging an entire new field of biological measurements in which the relationship of normal behavior to thousands of biological variables becomes pertinent. We discussed this in our first *Normality* volume (1966).

The next phase in these studies is to determine to what extent varieties of psychological normality affect physical health. Can a certain type of coping style influence biological variables (and hence physical illness)? We believe that it can. It needs to be studied and documented.

Axis IV: Stress and Personality

In the DSM-III-R an effort was made to study the relationship between stress and the onset or worsening of psychopathology. In normatology there are parallel questions, including the relationship between stress and the strengthening of adaptive behavior (that is, the ability to utilize stress constructively as a stimulus for normal growth and development). Because this axis deals specifically with how biological and psychosocial variables interact, its basic structure is consistent across different social, ethnic, and cultural groupings. What is defined as stressful varies considerably across cultures, but stress as a phenomenon is universal and its relationship to the physiological apparatus consistent.

Most individuals who progress from one development stage to another do so successfully. Even when some degree of chronic stress exists, there is no conclusive evidence that physical illness will result. (See, for example, chapter 3.) We believe that this axis, as well as the next one, can be utilized fruitfully in future studies of mental health.

Axis V: Global Well-Being

Global well-being is the assessment of the individual, combining self-esteem, optimal functioning, and the quality of interpersonal relationships. It is, in a way, a summary of the first four axes. Individuals who love, work, and play well are almost always well adjusted. Although they may have psychiatric problems, the likelihood that they do is very low. And if psychiatric problems coexist, they are of low intensity, mild, and last only a short time. In any case, scoring the global well-being remains a fundamental empirical question. Axis V would include the social matrix in which the person lives, which obviously strongly influences his or her adjustment. In chapter 6 Wambolt and Reiss suggest an additional axis (#VI) to include family functioning. In the normatological model, family functioning could be part of this axis. We also think that issues raised by Foulks in chapter 7 on cross-cultural aspects clearly point to the relationship between the individual and his or her social, or cultural, environment. Similarly, in chapter 5 Hales, Cozza, and Plewes point to a specific issue, namely the person in the military. In chapter 9 Morse, Roth, and Wettstein deal with similar issues, but on a more conceptual and philosophical basis, when they discuss the legal system.

The DSM-III-R is used extensively by psychiatric epidemiologists to determine prevalence of mental illness (for example, McGee et al. [1990]; Myers et al. [1984]). Even including the subthreshold diagnoses suggested by Klerman and Weissman (1984), all ranges of psychiatric illnesses would encompass only part of the total sample of a random population. By adding the normatological model, we will also be able to determine the prevalence of normality and mental health in a population. Optimally, this kind of study will complete the cycle—by using both DSM-III-R and normatological methods, we will be able to study a complete population. Why try to develop a new system rather than work with the DSM? The answer is that right now we want to call attention to normatology. Ultimately one system could be used. By being able to make a positive diagnosis of mental health, the whole field will move closer to a scientific discipline based on empirical data from the neurosciences as well as psychosocial sciences.

Our multiaxial studies on normality are not necessarily limited to the axis just outlined. A variety of other axes may prove relevant. While some nosologists question the utility of family system axes in psychopathology, there is no question of the relevance of family system variables in the normatological system (see chapter 6). And while cultural variables are also somewhat underemphasized in the DSM-III system, the normatological axes would pay them very special attention (see chapter 7). The distinction between stable patterns of behavior versus transient coping styles would be important to study. Psychopathology emphasizes investigation of intermittent phases of disorder. Normatology would focus on intermittent phases of adaptation, which may be even more important theoretically and practically. Our aim here is to develop a method whereby a variety of studies can be made on normal populations and the correlations found among them can be used to develop other hypotheses.

Normatology: The Beginning of a New Era

Many scholars believe it is premature to develop a science of normatology, particularly since we seem so far from having conquered the field of mental illness, which is deemed even more important. We believe, however, that the issues of normatology and pathology are closely related. In contrast, Brown (see chapter 10) argues that the "unholy marriage" of neuroscience and psychiatry makes the field conceptually weak and makes it difficult to try to use psychiatry as a base for normatological developments. We have included his chapter not because we agree with its fundamental conclusions but because it highlights major theoretical dilemmas for the study of both psychopathology and normatology. Like Brown, we believe that these theoretical positions deserve thoughtful consideration by the entire behavior and neuroscience fields. We also agree that attention should also be paid to phenomenology, cognitive sciences, and computer systems. In contrast to some of Brown's gloomy conclusions, however, we believe it is possible to work in the field of normatology without waiting for all of the conceptual dilemmas to be resolved. Further, we believe that neuroscience and psychoanalysis can be used to develop normatological hypotheses.

We must acknowledge, however, that in the current phase of developments in psychiatric neuroscience, theory does not appear to be playing a crucial role. Indeed, our efforts to locate a leader in neuroscientific aspects of psychiatry who would attempt a theoretical and empirical chapter on normality were in vain. This is unfortunate, because we believe that it is necessary to understand the neurobiological substrates of normal behavior in order for us to understand the full diversity of normality. Millon's efforts at providing a theoretical overview in chapter 11 reflect the importance of evolutionary neurobiology but do not pretend to be a full discussion of neuroscientific aspects of normality.

We believe that Millon's evolutionary polarities and psychological constructs and his reemphasis of personality afford a significant array of new hypotheses for the field of normatology. His work on nosology helps to bridge the boundaries between normality and psychopathology. The new hypotheses, however, transcend psychopathology in that they emphasize how a variety of polarities may be significant in the full range of normal human behavior.

The next steps in studies in the field of normatology might involve the following areas:

1. *Normatology of Everyday Life.* Just as Freud (1901) launched the interest in studying psychopathology, we suggest that a study of the mosaic of coping strategies used by everyman and everywoman throughout the life cycle would in itself be worthwhile, adding much to our understanding of the diversities of normal behavior.
2. *Prevalence of Mental Health.* To determine prevalence of mental health in various populations, algorithms need to be developed that describe what constitutes normal behavior. These algorithms must include positive behavioral items; they must not be simply an absence of psychopathology. By using the normatological model of classification of mental health (or its equivalent), investigators should be able to make psychologically meaningful hypotheses about mental health and normality.
3. *Mental Health Care.* When the boundaries between mental health and mental illness are better delineated, the outcome of mental health care might be easier to evaluate (Sabshin 1989, 1990). As pointed out by Ursano and Fullerton in chapter 2, the boundaries between psychopathology and normality are not clearly delineated, which makes it difficult to evaluate issues such as when psychotherapy has been successfully terminated. A clearer understanding of when individual patients move from the psychopathological realm to the normatological realm would help mental health care professionals evaluate their work. It will help to determine when care has been sufficient or adequate, if not optimal. It is managed care in the best sense. In the words of Howard (1991), "The long-term goal of this [managed care]

effort is to establish a quality assurance/quality improvement program that will ensure that mental health services are delivered in a timely, cost-effective, satisfying, and quality manner to those who need such services." Howard's mental health services research is not a study on normatology. However, in order to achieve his goal fully, we believe that these studies are essential.

4. *Mental Health Terminology.* Studies of normality and mental health will have to develop new language to encompass phenomena described in the normatological model.

In conclusion, let us say that we are not advocating the formation of a normatological society. However, it is important for workers in the field to be able to identify the commonality of normatological interests and improve communication between normatological investigators from the biological, psychological, and social sciences. As we and the contributors to this book have demonstrated, this is an enormously diverse task.

REFERENCES

Binet, A., and Simon, T. 1905. "Sur la necessite d'etablir un diagnostic scientifique des etats inferieurs de l'intelligence." *L'Ann. Psychol.* 11:162.

Freud, S. [1901] 1961. "Psychopathology of Everyday Life." In *The Standard Edition of the Complete Psychological Works of Sigmund Freud,* ed. James L. Strachey, vol. 6. London: Hogarth Press.

Freud, S. [1937] 1957. "Analysis Terminable and Interminable." *Standard Edition,* ed. James L. Strachey, vol. 23, pp. 209–254. London: Hogarth Press.

Howard K. I. "Assurance/Quality Improvement Program for Managed Care Mental Health Service Delivery." Unpublished manuscript.

Janet, P., and Raymond, F. 1903. *Les Obsessions et la Psychosthenie.* Paris: Felix Alcan.

Klerman, G. L., and Weissman, M. M. 1984. "An Epidemiologic View of Mental Illness, Mental Health, and Normality." In *Normality and the Life Cycle,* ed. D. Offer and M. Sabshin. New York: Basic Books.

Kraeplin, E. 1915. *Psychiatrie: Ein Lehrbuch fur Studierends und Arzte.* Leipzig: Barth.

Krafft-Ebing, R. 1894. *Psychopathia Sexualis.* Philadelphia: F. A. Davis.

McGee, R.; Feehan, M.; Williams, S.; Partridge, F.; Silva, P.; and Kelly, J. 1990. "DSM-III Disorders in a Large Sample of Adolescents." *Journal of the American Academy of Child and Adolescent Psychiatry* 29: 611–619.

Millon, T. 1990. *Toward a New Personology: An Evolutionary Model.* New York: John Wiley & Sons.

Myers, J. K.; Weissman, M. M.; Tischler, G. L.; Holzer, C. E.; Leaf, P. J.; Orbaschel, H.; Anthony, J. C.; Boyd, J. H.; Burke, J. D.; Kramer, M.; and Stoltzman, R. 1984. "Six-month Prevalence of Psychiatric Disturbance in Three Communities in 1980 to 1982." *Archives of General Psychiatry* 41: 959–967.

Offer, D. 1969. *The Psychological World of the Teenager.* New York: Basic Books.

Offer, D.; Howard, K. I.; Schonert, K. A.; and Ostrov, E. "To Whom Do Adolescents Turn for Help?" *Journal of the American Academy of Child and Adolescent Psychiatry* (in press).

Offer, D., and Offer, J. B. 1975. *From Teenage to Young Manhood: A Psychological Study.* New York: Basic Books.

Offer, D.; Ostrov, E.; and Howard, K. I. 1981. *The Adolescent: A Psychological Self-Portrait.* New York: Basic Books.

Offer, D., and Sabshin, M. 1966. *Normality.* New York: Basic Books.

Offer, D., and Sabshin, M. 1974. *Normality* (revised edition). New York: Basic Books.

Offer, D., and Sabshin, M. eds. 1984. *Normality and the Life Cycle.* New York: Basic Books.

Pavlov, I. P. [1903] 1941. *Lectures on Conditioned Reflexes* (two volumes). Translated and edited by W. H. Gautt. New York: International Publishing.

Sabshin, M. 1989. "Normality and the Boundaries of Psychopathology." *Journal of Personality Disorders* 3: 259–273.

Sabshin, M. 1990. "Turning Points in Twentieth-Century American Psychiatry." *American Journal of Psychiatry* 147: 1267–1274.

Sabshin, M. 1991. "Comorbidity: A Central Concern of Psychiatry in the 1990s." *Hospital and Community Psychiatry* 42: 345.

Smith, M. B. 1990. "Personology Launched." *Contemporary Psychology* 35: 537–539.

Index

Index